T0202766

Lecture Notes in Computer Science   14443

The series Lecture Notes in Computer Science (LNCS), including its subseries Lecture Notes in Artificial Intelligence (LNAI) and Lecture Notes in Bioinformatics (LNBI), has established itself as a medium for the publication of new developments in computer science and information technology research, teaching, and education.

LNCS enjoys close cooperation with the computer science R & D community, the series counts many renowned academics among its volume editors and paper authors, and collaborates with prestigious societies. Its mission is to serve this international community by providing an invaluable service, mainly focused on the publication of conference and workshop proceedings and postproceedings. LNCS commenced publication in 1973.

Jian Guo · Ron Steinfeld
Editors

Advances in Cryptology – ASIACRYPT 2023

29th International Conference on the Theory
and Application of Cryptology and Information Security
Guangzhou, China, December 4–8, 2023
Proceedings, Part VI

 Springer

Editors
Jian Guo 🆔
Nanyang Technological University
Singapore, Singapore

Ron Steinfeld 🆔
Monash University
Melbourne, VIC, Australia

ISSN 0302-9743   ISSN 1611-3349 (electronic)
Lecture Notes in Computer Science
ISBN 978-981-99-8735-1   ISBN 978-981-99-8736-8 (eBook)
https://doi.org/10.1007/978-981-99-8736-8

This Springer imprint is published by the registered company Springer Nature Singapore Pte Ltd.
The registered company address is: 152 Beach Road, #21-01/04 Gateway East, Singapore 189721, Singapore

Paper in this product is recyclable.

Preface

The 29th Annual International Conference on the Theory and Application of Cryptology and Information Security (Asiacrypt 2023) was held in Guangzhou, China, on December 4–8, 2023. The conference covered all technical aspects of cryptology, and was sponsored by the International Association for Cryptologic Research (IACR).

We received an Asiacrypt record of 376 paper submissions from all over the world, and the Program Committee (PC) selected 106 papers for publication in the proceedings of the conference. Due to this large number of papers, the Asiacrypt 2023 program had 3 tracks.

The two program chairs were supported by the great help and excellent advice of six area chairs, selected to cover the main topic areas of the conference. The area chairs were Kai-Min Chung for Information-Theoretic and Complexity-Theoretic Cryptography, Tanja Lange for Efficient and Secure Implementations, Shengli Liu for Public-Key Cryptography Algorithms and Protocols, Khoa Nguyen for Multi-Party Computation and Zero-Knowledge, Duong Hieu Phan for Public-Key Primitives with Advanced Functionalities, and Yu Sasaki for Symmetric-Key Cryptology. Each of the area chairs helped to lead discussions together with the PC members assigned as paper discussion lead. Area chairs also helped to decide on the submissions that should be accepted from their respective areas. We are very grateful for the invaluable contribution provided by the area chairs.

To review and evaluate the submissions, while keeping the load per PC member manageable, we selected a record size PC consisting of 105 leading experts from all over the world, in all six topic areas of cryptology. The two program chairs were not allowed to submit a paper, and PC members were limited to submit one single-author paper, or at most two co-authored papers, or at most three co-authored papers all with students. Each non-PC submission was reviewed by at least three reviewers consisting of either PC members or their external sub-reviewers, while each PC member submission received at least four reviews. The strong conflict of interest rules imposed by IACR ensure that papers are not handled by PC members with a close working relationship with the authors. There were approximately 420 external reviewers, whose input was critical to the selection of papers. Submissions were anonymous and their length was limited to 30 pages excluding the bibliography and supplementary materials.

The review process was conducted using double-blind peer review. The conference operated a two-round review system with a rebuttal phase. After the reviews and first round discussions the PC selected 244 submissions to proceed to the second round and the authors were then invited to participate in an interactive rebuttal phase with the reviewers to clarify questions and concerns. The remaining 131 papers were rejected, including one desk reject. The second round involved extensive discussions by the PC members. After several weeks of additional discussions, the committee selected the final 106 papers to appear in these proceedings.

The eight volumes of the conference proceedings contain the revised versions of the 106 papers that were selected. The final revised versions of papers were not reviewed again and the authors are responsible for their contents.

The PC nominated and voted for two papers to receive the Best Paper Awards, and one paper to receive the Best Early Career Paper Award. The Best Paper Awards went to Thomas Espitau, Alexandre Wallet and Yang Yu for their paper "On Gaussian Sampling, Smoothing Parameter and Application to Signatures", and to Kaijie Jiang, Anyu Wang, Hengyi Luo, Guoxiao Liu, Yang Yu, and Xiaoyun Wang for their paper "Exploiting the Symmetry of Z^n: Randomization and the Automorphism Problem". The Best Early Career Paper Award went to Maxime Plancon for the paper "Exploiting Algebraic Structure in Probing Security". The authors of those three papers were invited to submit extended versions of their papers to the Journal of Cryptology. In addition, the program of Asiacrypt 2023 also included two invited plenary talks, also nominated and voted by the PC: one talk was given by Mehdi Tibouchi and the other by Xiaoyun Wang. The conference also featured a rump session chaired by Kang Yang and Yu Yu which contained short presentations on the latest research results of the field.

Numerous people contributed to the success of Asiacrypt 2023. We would like to thank all the authors, including those whose submissions were not accepted, for submitting their research results to the conference. We are very grateful to the area chairs, PC members and external reviewers for contributing their knowledge and expertise, and for the tremendous amount of work that was done with reading papers and contributing to the discussions. We are greatly indebted to Jian Weng and Fangguo Zhang, the General Chairs, for their efforts in organizing the event and to Kevin McCurley and Kay McKelly for their help with the website and review system. We thank the Asiacrypt 2023 advisory committee members Bart Preneel, Huaxiong Wang, Kai-Min Chung, Yu Sasaki, Dongdai Lin, Shweta Agrawal and Michel Abdalla for their valuable suggestions. We are also grateful for the helpful advice and organization material provided to us by the Eurocrypt 2023 PC co-chairs Carmit Hazay and Martijn Stam and Crypto 2023 PC co-chairs Helena Handschuh and Anna Lysyanskaya. We also thank the team at Springer for handling the publication of these conference proceedings.

December 2023   Jian Guo
                                                                   Ron Steinfeld

Organization

General Chairs

Jian Weng   Jinan University, China
Fangguo Zhang   Sun Yat-sen University, China

Program Committee Chairs

Jian Guo   Nanyang Technological University, Singapore
Ron Steinfeld   Monash University, Australia

Program Committee

Behzad Abdolmaleki   University of Sheffield, UK
Masayuki Abe   NTT Social Informatics Laboratories, Japan
Miguel Ambrona   Input Output Global (IOHK), Spain
Daniel Apon   MITRE Labs, USA
Shi Bai   Florida Atlantic University, USA
Gustavo Banegas   Qualcomm, France
Zhenzhen Bao   Tsinghua University, China
Andrea Basso   University of Bristol, UK
Ward Beullens   IBM Research Europe, Switzerland
Katharina Boudgoust   Aarhus University, Denmark
Matteo Campanelli   Protocol Labs, Denmark
Ignacio Cascudo   IMDEA Software Institute, Spain
Wouter Castryck   imec-COSIC, KU Leuven, Belgium
Jie Chen   East China Normal University, China
Yilei Chen   Tsinghua University, China
Jung Hee Cheon   Seoul National University and Cryptolab Inc,
                           South Korea
Sherman S. M. Chow   Chinese University of Hong Kong, China
Kai-Min Chung   Academia Sinica, Taiwan
Michele Ciampi   University of Edinburgh, UK
Bernardo David   IT University of Copenhagen, Denmark
Yi Deng   Institute of Information Engineering, Chinese
                           Academy of Sciences, China

Patrick Derbez	University of Rennes, France
Xiaoyang Dong	Tsinghua University, China
Rafael Dowsley	Monash University, Australia
Nico Döttling	Helmholtz Center for Information Security, Germany
Maria Eichlseder	Graz University of Technology, Austria
Muhammed F. Esgin	Monash University, Australia
Thomas Espitau	PQShield, France
Jun Furukawa	NEC Corporation, Japan
Aron Gohr	Independent Researcher, New Zealand
Junqing Gong	ECNU, China
Lorenzo Grassi	Ruhr University Bochum, Germany
Tim Güneysu	Ruhr University Bochum, Germany
Chun Guo	Shandong University, China
Siyao Guo	NYU Shanghai, China
Fuchun Guo	University of Wollongong, Australia
Mohammad Hajiabadi	University of Waterloo, Canada
Lucjan Hanzlik	CISPA Helmholtz Center for Information Security, Germany
Xiaolu Hou	Slovak University of Technology, Slovakia
Yuncong Hu	Shanghai Jiao Tong University, China
Xinyi Huang	Hong Kong University of Science and Technology (Guangzhou), China
Tibor Jager	University of Wuppertal, Germany
Elena Kirshanova	Technology Innovation Institute, UAE and I. Kant Baltic Federal University, Russia
Eyal Kushilevitz	Technion, Israel
Russell W. F. Lai	Aalto University, Finland
Tanja Lange	Eindhoven University of Technology, Netherlands
Hyung Tae Lee	Chung-Ang University, South Korea
Eik List	Nanyang Technological University, Singapore
Meicheng Liu	Institute of Information Engineering, Chinese Academy of Sciences, China
Guozhen Liu	Nanyang Technological University, Singapore
Fukang Liu	Tokyo Institute of Technology, Japan
Shengli Liu	Shanghai Jiao Tong University, China
Feng-Hao Liu	Florida Atlantic University, USA
Hemanta K. Maji	Purdue University, USA
Takahiro Matsuda	AIST, Japan
Christian Matt	Concordium, Switzerland
Tomoyuki Morimae	Kyoto University, Japan
Pierrick Méaux	University of Luxembourg, Luxembourg

Mridul Nandi	Indian Statistical Institute, Kolkata, India
María Naya-Plasencia	Inria, France
Khoa Nguyen	University of Wollongong, Australia
Ryo Nishimaki	NTT Social Informatics Laboratories, Japan
Anca Nitulescu	Protocol Labs, France
Ariel Nof	Bar Ilan University, Israel
Emmanuela Orsini	Bocconi University, Italy
Adam O'Neill	UMass Amherst, USA
Morten Øygarden	Simula UiB, Norway
Sikhar Patranabis	IBM Research, India
Alice Pellet-Mary	CNRS and University of Bordeaux, France
Edoardo Persichetti	Florida Atlantic University, USA and Sapienza University, Italy
Duong Hieu Phan	Telecom Paris, Institut Polytechnique de Paris, France
Josef Pieprzyk	Data61, CSIRO, Australia and ICS, PAS, Poland
Axel Y. Poschmann	PQShield, UAE
Thomas Prest	PQShield, France
Adeline Roux-Langlois	CNRS, GREYC, France
Amin Sakzad	Monash University, Australia
Yu Sasaki	NTT Social Informatics Laboratories, Japan
Jae Hong Seo	Hanyang University, South Korea
Yaobin Shen	UCLouvain, Belgium
Danping Shi	Institute of Information Engineering, Chinese Academy of Sciences, China
Damien Stehlé	CryptoLab, France
Bing Sun	National University of Defense Technology, China
Shi-Feng Sun	Shanghai Jiao Tong University, China
Keisuke Tanaka	Tokyo Institute of Technology, Japan
Qiang Tang	University of Sydney, Australia
Vanessa Teague	Thinking Cybersecurity Pty Ltd and the Australian National University, Australia
Jean-Pierre Tillich	Inria, Paris, France
Yosuke Todo	NTT Social Informatics Laboratories, Japan
Alexandre Wallet	University of Rennes, Inria, CNRS, IRISA, France
Meiqin Wang	Shandong University, China
Yongge Wang	UNC Charlotte, USA
Yuyu Wang	University of Electronic Science and Technology of China, China
Qingju Wang	Telecom Paris, Institut Polytechnique de Paris, France

Benjamin Wesolowski	CNRS and ENS Lyon, France
Shuang Wu	Huawei International, Singapore, Singapore
Keita Xagawa	Technology Innovation Institute, UAE
Chaoping Xing	Shanghai Jiao Tong University, China
Jun Xu	Institute of Information Engineering, Chinese Academy of Sciences, China
Takashi Yamakawa	NTT Social Informatics Laboratories, Japan
Kang Yang	State Key Laboratory of Cryptology, China
Yu Yu	Shanghai Jiao Tong University, China
Yang Yu	Tsinghua University, Beijing, China
Yupeng Zhang	University of Illinois Urbana-Champaign and Texas A&M University, USA
Liangfeng Zhang	ShanghaiTech University, China
Raymond K. Zhao	CSIRO's Data61, Australia
Hong-Sheng Zhou	Virginia Commonwealth University, USA

Additional Reviewers

Amit Agarwal	Pedro Branco
Jooyoung Lee	Lauren Brandt
Léo Ackermann	Alessandro Budroni
Akshima	Kevin Carrier
Bar Alon	André Chailloux
Ravi Anand	Suvradip Chakraborty
Sarah Arpin	Debasmita Chakraborty
Thomas Attema	Haokai Chang
Nuttapong Attrapadung	Bhuvnesh Chaturvedi
Manuel Barbosa	Caicai Chen
Razvan Barbulescu	Rongmao Chen
James Bartusek	Mingjie Chen
Carsten Baum	Yi Chen
Olivier Bernard	Megan Chen
Tyler Besselman	Yu Long Chen
Ritam Bhaumik	Xin Chen
Jingguo Bi	Shiyao Chen
Loic Bidoux	Long Chen
Maxime Bombar	Wonhee Cho
Xavier Bonnetain	Qiaohan Chu
Joppe Bos	Valerio Cini
Mariana Botelho da Gama	James Clements
Christina Boura	Ran Cohen
Clémence Bouvier	Alexandru Cojocaru
Ross Bowden	Sandro Coretti-Drayton

Anamaria Costache
Alain Couvreur
Daniele Cozzo
Hongrui Cui
Giuseppe D'Alconzo
Zhaopeng Dai
Quang Dao
Nilanjan Datta
Koen de Boer
Luca De Feo
Paola de Perthuis
Thomas Decru
Rafael del Pino
Julien Devevey
Henri Devillez
Siemen Dhooghe
Yaoling Ding
Jack Doerner
Jelle Don
Mark Douglas Schultz
Benjamin Dowling
Minxin Du
Xiaoqi Duan
Jesko Dujmovic
Moumita Dutta
Avijit Dutta
Ehsan Ebrahimi
Felix Engelmann
Reo Eriguchi
Jonathan Komada Eriksen
Andre Esser
Pouria Fallahpour
Zhiyong Fang
Antonio Faonio
Pooya Farshim
Joël Felderhoff
Jakob Feldtkeller
Weiqi Feng
Xiutao Feng
Shuai Feng
Qi Feng
Hanwen Feng
Antonio Flórez-Gutiérrez
Apostolos Fournaris
Paul Frixons

Ximing Fu
Georg Fuchsbauer
Philippe Gaborit
Rachit Garg
Robin Geelen
Riddhi Ghosal
Koustabh Ghosh
Barbara Gigerl
Niv Gilboa
Valerie Gilchrist
Emanuele Giunta
Xinxin Gong
Huijing Gong
Zheng Gong
Robert Granger
Zichen Gui
Anna Guinet
Qian Guo
Xiaojie Guo
Hosein Hadipour
Mathias Hall-Andersen
Mike Hamburg
Shuai Han
Yonglin Hao
Keisuke Hara
Keitaro Hashimoto
Le He
Brett Hemenway Falk
Minki Hhan
Taiga Hiroka
Akinori Hosoyamada
Chengan Hou
Martha Norberg Hovd
Kai Hu
Tao Huang
Zhenyu Huang
Michael Hutter
Jihun Hwang
Akiko Inoue
Tetsu Iwata
Robin Jadoul
Hansraj Jangir
Dirmanto Jap
Stanislaw Jarecki
Santos Jha

Ashwin Jha
Dingding Jia
Yanxue Jia
Lin Jiao
Daniel Jost
Antoine Joux
Jiayi Kang
Gabriel Kaptchuk
Alexander Karenin
Shuichi Katsumata
Pengzhen Ke
Mustafa Khairallah
Shahram Khazaei
Hamidreza Amini Khorasgani
Hamidreza Khoshakhlagh
Ryo Kikuchi
Jiseung Kim
Minkyu Kim
Suhri Kim
Ravi Kishore
Fuyuki Kitagawa
Susumu Kiyoshima
Michael Klooß
Alexander Koch
Sreehari Kollath
Dimitris Kolonelos
Yashvanth Kondi
Anders Konring
Woong Kook
Dimitri Koshelev
Markus Krausz
Toomas Krips
Daniel Kuijsters
Anunay Kulshrestha
Qiqi Lai
Yi-Fu Lai
Georg Land
Nathalie Lang
Mario Larangeira
Joon-Woo Lee
Keewoo Lee
Hyeonbum Lee
Changmin Lee
Charlotte Lefevre
Julia Len

Antonin Leroux
Andrea Lesavourey
Jannis Leuther
Jie Li
Shuaishuai Li
Huina Li
Yu Li
Yanan Li
Jiangtao Li
Song Song Li
Wenjie Li
Shun Li
Zengpeng Li
Xiao Liang
Wei-Kai Lin
Chengjun Lin
Chao Lin
Cong Ling
Yunhao Ling
Hongqing Liu
Jing Liu
Jiahui Liu
Qipeng Liu
Yamin Liu
Weiran Liu
Tianyi Liu
Siqi Liu
Chen-Da Liu-Zhang
Jinyu Lu
Zhenghao Lu
Stefan Lucks
Yiyuan Luo
Lixia Luo
Jack P. K. Ma
Fermi Ma
Gilles Macario-Rat
Luciano Maino
Christian Majenz
Laurane Marco
Lorenzo Martinico
Loïc Masure
John McVey
Willi Meier
Kelsey Melissaris
Bart Mennink

Charles Meyer-Hilfiger
Victor Miller
Chohong Min
Marine Minier
Arash Mirzaei
Pratyush Mishra
Tarik Moataz
Johannes Mono
Fabrice Mouhartem
Alice Murphy
Erik Mårtensson
Anne Müller
Marcel Nageler
Yusuke Naito
Barak Nehoran
Patrick Neumann
Tran Ngo
Phuong Hoa Nguyen
Ngoc Khanh Nguyen
Thi Thu Quyen Nguyen
Hai H. Nguyen
Semyon Novoselov
Julian Nowakowski
Arne Tobias Malkenes Ødegaard
Kazuma Ohara
Miyako Ohkubo
Charles Olivier-Anclin
Eran Omri
Yi Ouyang
Tapas Pal
Ying-yu Pan
Jiaxin Pan
Eugenio Paracucchi
Roberto Parisella
Jeongeun Park
Guillermo Pascual-Perez
Alain Passelègue
Octavio Perez-Kempner
Thomas Peters
Phuong Pham
Cécile Pierrot
Erik Pohle
David Pointcheval
Giacomo Pope
Christopher Portmann

Romain Poussier
Lucas Prabel
Sihang Pu
Chen Qian
Luowen Qian
Tian Qiu
Anaïs Querol
Håvard Raddum
Shahram Rasoolzadeh
Divya Ravi
Prasanna Ravi
Marc Renard
Jan Richter-Brockmann
Lawrence Roy
Paul Rösler
Sayandeep Saha
Yusuke Sakai
Niels Samwel
Paolo Santini
Maria Corte-Real Santos
Sara Sarfaraz
Santanu Sarkar
Or Sattath
Markus Schofnegger
Peter Scholl
Dominique Schröder
André Schrottenloher
Jacob Schuldt
Binanda Sengupta
Srinath Setty
Yantian Shen
Yixin Shen
Ferdinand Sibleyras
Janno Siim
Mark Simkin
Scott Simon
Animesh Singh
Nitin Singh
Sayani Sinha
Daniel Slamanig
Fang Song
Ling Song
Yongsoo Song
Jana Sotakova
Gabriele Spini

Marianna Spyrakou
Lukas Stennes
Marc Stoettinger
Chuanjie Su
Xiangyu Su
Ling Sun
Akira Takahashi
Isobe Takanori
Atsushi Takayasu
Suprita Talnikar
Benjamin Hong Meng Tan
Ertem Nusret Tas
Tadanori Teruya
Masayuki Tezuka
Sri AravindaKrishnan Thyagarajan
Song Tian
Wenlong Tian
Raphael Toledo
Junichi Tomida
Daniel Tschudi
Hikaru Tsuchida
Aleksei Udovenko
Rei Ueno
Barry Van Leeuwen
Wessel van Woerden
Frederik Vercauteren
Sulani Vidhanalage
Benedikt Wagner
Roman Walch
Hendrik Waldner
Han Wang
Luping Wang
Peng Wang
Yuntao Wang
Geng Wang
Shichang Wang
Liping Wang
Jiafan Wang
Zhedong Wang
Kunpeng Wang
Jianfeng Wang
Guilin Wang
Weiqiang Wen
Chenkai Weng
Thom Wiggers

Stella Wohnig
Harry W. H. Wong
Ivy K. Y. Woo
Yu Xia
Zejun Xiang
Yuting Xiao
Zhiye Xie
Yanhong Xu
Jiayu Xu
Lei Xu
Shota Yamada
Kazuki Yamamura
Di Yan
Qianqian Yang
Shaojun Yang
Yanjiang Yang
Li Yao
Yizhou Yao
Kenji Yasunaga
Yuping Ye
Xiuyu Ye
Zeyuan Yin
Kazuki Yoneyama
Yusuke Yoshida
Albert Yu
Quan Yuan
Chen Yuan
Tsz Hon Yuen
Aaram Yun
Riccardo Zanotto
Arantxa Zapico
Shang Zehua
Mark Zhandry
Tianyu Zhang
Zhongyi Zhang
Fan Zhang
Liu Zhang
Yijian Zhang
Shaoxuan Zhang
Zhongliang Zhang
Kai Zhang
Cong Zhang
Jiaheng Zhang
Lulu Zhang
Zhiyu Zhang

Chang-An Zhao
Yongjun Zhao
Chunhuan Zhao
Xiaotong Zhou
Zhelei Zhou

Zijian Zhou
Timo Zijlstra
Jian Zou
Ferdinando Zullo
Cong Zuo

Sponsoring Institutions

- Gold Level Sponsor: Ant Research
- Silver Level Sponsors: Sansec Technology Co., Ltd., Topsec Technologies Group
- Bronze Level Sponsors: IBM, Meta, Sangfor Technologies Inc.

Contents – Part VI

xviii   Contents – Part VI

Security Proofs and Security Models

Homomorphic Encryption

Amortized Bootstrapping Revisited: Simpler, Asymptotically-Faster, Implemented

Antonio Guimarães[1], Hilder V. L. Pereira[1(✉)], and Barry van Leeuwen[2]

[1] Institute of Computing, University of Campinas, Campinas, Brazil
{antonio.guimaraes,hilder}@ic.unicamp.br
[2] imec-COSIC, KU Leuven, Leuven, Belgium
barry.vanleeuwen@kuleuven.be

Abstract. Micciancio and Sorrel (ICALP 2018) proposed a bootstrapping algorithm that can refresh many messages at once with sublinearly many homomorphic operations per message. However, despite the attractive asymptotic cost, it is unclear if their algorithm could ever be practical, which reduces the impact of their results. In this work, we follow their general framework, but propose an amortized bootstrapping procedure that is conceptually simpler and asymptotically cheaper. We reduce the number of homomorphic multiplications per refreshed message from $O(3^\rho \cdot n^{1/\rho} \cdot \log n)$ to $O(\rho \cdot n^{1/\rho})$, and the noise overhead from $\widetilde{O}(n^{2+3\cdot\rho})$ to $\widetilde{O}(n^{1+\rho})$, where n is the security level and $\rho \geq 1$ is a free parameter. We also make it more general, by handling non-binary messages and applying programmable bootstrapping. To obtain a concrete instantiation of our bootstrapping algorithm, we describe a double-CRT (aka RNS) version of the GSW scheme, including a new operation, called *shrinking*, used to speed-up homomorphic operations by reducing the dimension and ciphertext modulus of the ciphertexts. We also provide a C++ implementation of our algorithm, thus showing for the first time the practicability of the amortized bootstrapping. Moreover, it is competitive with existing bootstrapping algorithms, being even around 3.4 times faster than an equivalent non-amortized version of our bootstrapping.

1 Introduction

Since the introduction of the first Fully Homomorphic Encryption (FHE) scheme, by Gentry [15], there has been a quest to improve the efficiency and the security of FHE. The main efficiency bottleneck of any FHE scheme is the *bootstrapping* operation that refreshes the ciphertexts after being involved in a few homomorphic operations, allowing us to perform further operations on them. Hence, most works aiming to make FHE more efficient direct their efforts towards designing faster bootstrapping. For this goal, there are two main strategies:

This paper was mainly written while Hilder V. L. Pereira was in COSIC, KU Leuven.

J. Guo and R. Steinfeld (Eds.): ASIACRYPT 2023, LNCS 14443, pp. 3–35, 2023.
https://doi.org/10.1007/978-981-99-8736-8_1

Heavy-packed bootstrapping tries to pack several messages into a "large" ciphertext. This makes bootstrapping complex and very costly, but refreshes several messages at once, with the aim for the *amortized* cost per message to be low. This type of bootstrapping was proposed for many schemes, [9,10,14,16], obtaining good amortized costs, however these schemes generally were not very efficient regarding noise management, thus, their bootstrapping algorithms often incur quasi-polynomial noise growth. This implies that their security is based on worst-case lattice problems with *superpolynomial approximation factors*. Ideally, we would like to have FHE with assumptions identical to general lattice-based public-key encryption, which assumes worst-case lattice problems with *polynomial approximation factors* only.

On the other front, fast single message bootstrapping encrypts a single message into a "small" ciphertext, hugely simplifying the bootstrapping. The aim here is to execute it much faster, in many cases in a few milliseconds on a common commercial computer [7,11,13,31]. The downside now is the need for one bootstrapping per gate of the circuit being evaluated homomorphically and, since each bootstrapping refreshes a single message, the amortized cost is still high. However, this bootstrapping strategy does attain a polynomial noise overhead, achieving the ideal assumption base: worst-case lattice problems with polynomial approximation factors.

Then, in [28], Micciancio and Sorrell try to obtain the advantages of these two approaches, by proposing a bootstrapping algorithm that follows the blueprint of [13], but packs several messages into a single ciphertext to amortize the cost of the bootstrapping. Therewith, they obtain the first FHE scheme whose security is based on the hardness of worst-case lattice problems with polynomial approximation factors that at the same time is bootstrappable with amortized sublinearly many homomorphic operations. Their main idea is to describe the bootstrapping as a polynomial multiplication, then to evaluate it homomorphically using some fast polynomial multiplication algorithm. Due to the limitations of the functions one can evaluate homomorphically, they cannot simply evaluate a Fast Fourier Transform, thus, they adapt the Nussbaumer Transform [30] to work over power-of-three cyclotomic rings, then use it in their algorithm to bootstrap $O(n)$ messages in time $\tilde{O}(3^\rho \cdot n^{1+1/\rho})$, where ρ is a free parameter. Note that the $\tilde{O}$-notation hides polylogarithmic factors on n. Therefore, their amortized cost is only $\tilde{O}(3^\rho \cdot n^{1/\rho})$ homomorphic operations per message.

Following the blueprint of [28], we propose a simpler and more efficient amortized bootstrapping. Our first contribution is to remove the Nussbaumer Transform, replacing it by a standard (homomorphic) Number Theoretic Transform (NTT). By doing so we make the whole bootstrapping algorithm more straightforward and gain important asymptotic factors decreasing the number of homomorphic operations per message from $O(3^\rho \cdot n^{1/\rho} \cdot \log n)$ to $O(\rho \cdot n^{1/\rho})$, and the noise introduced by the bootstrapping from $\tilde{O}(n^{2+3\rho})$ to $\tilde{O}(n^{1+\rho})$. Moreover, instead of just bits, we can handle n messages in $\mathbb{Z}_t$, for small t. This also means that we support programmable bootstrapping, reducing the noise and simulta-

Table 1. Comparison of number of homomorphic operations and noise growth of bootstrapping algorithms of different schemes based on worst-case lattice problems with polynomial approximation factor. The notation $\tilde{O}$ hides polylogarithmic factors in n.

Scheme	Total cost	Messages	Amortized cost	Noise overhead
[13]	$\tilde{O}(n)$	1	$\tilde{O}(n)$	$\tilde{O}(n^{1.5})$
[11]	$O(n)$	1	$O(n)$	$\tilde{O}(n)$
[28]	$\tilde{O}(3^\rho \cdot n^{1+1/\rho})$	$O(n)$	$\tilde{O}(3^\rho \cdot n^{1/\rho})$	$\tilde{O}(n^{2+3\cdot\rho})$
This work	$O(\rho \cdot n^{1+1/\rho})$	$O(n)$	$O(\rho \cdot n^{1/\rho})$	$\tilde{O}(n^{1+\rho})$

neously applying any function $f : \mathbb{Z}_t \to \mathbb{Z}_t$ to the message. In Table 1, we present a comparison of our work with previous ones.

Although [28] obtains a significant asymptotic improvement over previous works, it is unclear how (in)efficient it would be in practice, since the hidden constants are hard to estimate. Thus, as a second contribution, we present a concrete instantiation of our method. For this, we formalize a double-CRT (RNS) variant of the GSW scheme [17], including a new operation, called *shrinking*, that allows to efficiently reduce the ciphertext size, and thus, the cost of the homomorphic operations, as the noise grows. This also allows us to present a concrete cost analysis, in terms of polynomial multiplications (or NTTs), which gives us a much better idea of the practical cost of the amortized bootstrapping and makes it easier to compare with other works, since the number of times that the NTT is executed is already used to estimate the cost of several previous schemes, such as [7,11,13].

Finally, we also implemented our bootstrapping in C++ and made it publicly available,[1] thus, presenting the first implementation of amortized and providing baseline running times and memory usage for this type of bootstrapping, showing that such a scheme is feasible in practice with running times comparable to some existing schemes.

1.1   Overview of the Amortized Bootstrapping from [28]

The bootstrapping strategy of [3], improved and made practical in [13], works as follows: the whole FHE scheme is organized in two layers, each one composed by one homomorphic scheme. The base scheme is an LWE-based scheme that can perform very limited number of homomorphic operations, then has to be bootstrapped. Then the second scheme, called the accumulator, is used to evaluate the decryption of the base scheme homomorphically, i.e., to bootstrap it. For the accumulator, one uses the GSW scheme [17] instantiated with the RLWE problem, so that it can encrypt polynomials. Because of the slow noise growth of GSW, the noise overhead of the bootstrapping is just polynomial in the security parameter. Essentially, to decrypt an LWE ciphertext $\mathbf{c}$, one has to multiply it by the secret key $\mathbf{s}$. Thus, starting with GSW encryptions of powers of X with

---

[1] GitHub repository: https://github.com/antoniocgj/Amortized-Bootstrapping.

the secret key in the exponent, i.e., X^{s_i}, the GSW homomorphic multiplications are used to compute $\prod_{i=0}^{n} X^{c_i \cdot s_i} = X^{\mathbf{c} \cdot \mathbf{s}}$. Finally, there is an extraction procedure that maps this power of X to the message encrypted by $\mathbf{c}$. Notice that the bootstrapping costs $\tilde{O}(n)$ homomorphic operations, more specifically, GSW multiplications.

The main idea of [28] is to combine $O(n)$ LWE ciphertexts into one single RLWE ciphertext $\mathbf{c} \in \mathcal{R}^2$ encrypting $O(n)$ messages. Then, because the secret is a polynomial s instead of a vector, decrypting $\mathbf{c}$ now boils down to performing a polynomial multiplication on $\mathcal{R}$, which can be done in time $O(n \cdot \log n)$ via standard techniques, such as the Fast Fourier Transform (FFT). Thus, if one could use the accumulator to evaluate an FFT, the amortized cost of such bootstrapping would be only $O(\log n)$ homomorphic operations per message. However, due to limitations in the noise growth of this bootstrapping strategy, it is not possible to evaluate all the $O(\log n)$ recursive levels of the FFT. Thus, [28] sets the recursion level as a parameter ρ.

Moreover, since the GSW scheme is instantiated over the ring $\mathcal{R} := \mathbb{Z}[X]/\langle X^N + 1 \rangle$ and working only with powers of X, whose order is $2N$ in $\mathcal{R}$, there is a limited set linear operations over $\mathbb{Z}_{2N}$ available as homomorphic operations. So, for example, we cannot take an encryption of (X to the power of) m and produce an encryption of $-m$ or of m^{-1}. Therefore, [28] cannot evaluate an FFT. To overcome this limitation, they pack the LWE ciphertexts into an RLWE ciphertext defined over a power-of-three cyclotomic ring, i.e., defined modulo $\Phi_{3^k}(X) = 2 \cdot 3^{k-1} + 3^{k-1} + 1$, and adapt the Nussbaumer transform to replace the FFT and perform polynomial multiplications modulo $\Phi_{3^k}(X)$. The radix-r Nussbaumer transform works as the FFT, by dividing the input by r in each recursive level. However, in their adapted algorithm, there is an expansion by 3, i.e., they obtain r inputs of length $3n/r$ instead of length n/r. Since this expansion happens in all recursive levels, the factor 3 accumulates exponentially and, at the end, their bootstrapping costs $\tilde{O}(3^\rho \cdot n^{1+1/\rho})$ homomorphic operations and the noise introduced by the bootstrapping is $\tilde{O}(n^{2+3\cdot\rho})$.

1.2   Overview of Our Contributions and Techniques

Simpler and More Efficient Amortized Bootstrapping. Micciancio and Sorrell accepted that the accumulator constructed with GSW just provides a limited set of operations over $\mathbb{Z}_{2N}$, where N is a power of two, and tried to adapt the fast polynomial multiplication algorithms to work with that instruction set. We diverge from this by trying to adapt the accumulator to the algorithm we want to evaluate, instead of vice versa. As the Number Theoretic Transform (NTT) is the algorithm of choice to perform multiplications modulo $X^N + 1$ our goal is to obtain an accumulator that can evaluate NTTs.

To obtain that, we use the results from [6] to instantiate the GSW scheme modulo $X^p - 1$, where p is a prime number, but with security based on the RLWE problem. This gives us an equivalent instruction set of [28], but over $\mathbb{Z}_p$. Then, we set $p \equiv 1 \pmod{2N}$, so that we have a $2N$-root of unity in $\mathbb{Z}_p$ and the NTT of dimension N is well-defined. Then, we extend recent results about using automorphisms on bootstrapping algorithms [6,23] to the GSW scheme, which expands the instruction set of our accumulator. In Table 2, we compare both accumulators. Putting it all together we obtain a GSW-based accumulator that allows us to homomorphically evaluate a standard NTT. The only limitation that remains is that the noise overhead of the bootstrapping is still exponential in the number of recursive levels of the NTT, hence restricting to ρ recursive levels as in [28], guarantees that the noise overhead remains polynomial in N.

With a more powerful accumulator, the bootstrapping algorithm becomes much simpler, as its main step is essentially the same as a well-known NTT. Moreover, there is no longer the expansion by 3 within the recursions, which allows us to save a factor of 3^ρ in the time complexity and to reduce the noise overhead from $\tilde{O}(n^{2+3\cdot\rho})$ to $\tilde{O}(n^{1+\rho})$.

Additionally, our accumulator also allows us to replace the algorithm used in [28] to perform the entry-wise vector multiplication in the FFT domain, called SlowMult, by a cheaper and simpler procedure, which yields an additional gain of a $\log n$ factor. Therefore, we reduce the number of homomorphic operations from $O(3^\rho \cdot n^{1+1/\rho} \cdot \log n)$ in [28] to $O(\rho \cdot n^{1+1/\rho})$. In Fig. 1, we present the main steps of our bootstrapping.

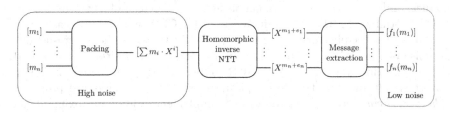

Fig. 1. Main building blocks of our amortized bootstrapping. First we pack high-noise ciphertexts into a single ciphertext encrypting a polynomial with original messages as the coefficients. Then we evaluate the NTT homomorphically, obtaining encryptions of powers of X having the messages plus restricted noise in the exponent. Finally, we execute a message extraction procedure, removing the noise terms and applying any set of desired functions to the messages.

Table 2. Comparison of the accumulator proposed in [28] and ours. The notation [a] means encryption of (X to the power of) a. Negation is not natively supported by [28], thus, for any message m, they actually encrypt (m, −m), which requires two ciphertexts. Negation is then implemented by swapping the ciphertexts so that they encrypt (−m, m). However this doubles the memory and time of all their operations.

	Variable type	Size of enc. message	Available operations				
			$[a], [b] \mapsto [a+b]$	$[a] \mapsto [-a]$	$[a], w \mapsto [a \cdot w]$	Key switching	Shrinking
[28]	$\mathbb{Z}_{2^k}$	2 GSW ciphertexts	✓	*			
Ours	$\mathbb{Z}_p$, prime p	1 GSW ciphertext	✓	✓	✓	✓	✓

Double-CRT Version of GSW. FHE schemes implementing single-message bootstrapping, such as [7,11,13], can use very small parameters when compared to other FHE schemes thanks to the almost linear noise overhead of the bootstrapping. In particular, the ciphertext modulus, Q, is typically an integer between 2^{32} and 2^{64}. Since all homomorphic operations are defined modulo Q, these schemes can be implemented using native integer types of most CPUs.

For other schemes the ciphertext modulus, Q, is much larger, normally with more than one thousand bits. Thus, implementing the operations modulo Q requires more care: one represents Q as a product of small primes q_i's, e.g., with 32 bits, then uses the Chinese Remainder Theorem (CRT) to express operations modulo Q as independent operations modulo each q_i, allowing the use of native integer types again. As all the polynomials composing ciphertexts are stored in the FFT domain and the FFT can be seen as a type of CRT, this representation is often called Double-CRT [20] or, alternatively, RNS representation [19].

Since the amortized bootstrapping has at least quadratic noise overhead, it also typically requires Q with more bits than native types of CPUs. Therefore, to obtain a practical implementation, we formally describe a double-CRT version of the accumulator, i.e. the GSW scheme[2], including all common operations already existing for GSW, such as homomorphic multiplication and external product, and new operations, like Galois automorphisms and key switchings.

One optimization that is commonly used for GSW is to ignore least significant bits of the ciphertexts during the multiplications, as they correspond to the noise of the RLWE samples, i.e., approximate deomposition in the TFHE scheme [11]. However, in the double-CRT representation, as there is no notion of least significant bits, this technique no longer applies. Thus, we propose a *ciphertext shrinking*, which introduces the implementation of approximate gadget decompositions over the double-CRT representation. It takes a GSW ciphertext, which is a $2d \times 2$ matrix where each entry is a polynomial modulo Q, and outputs another GSW ciphertext as a $2d' \times 2$ matrix and defined modulo Q', where $d' < d$ and $Q' < Q$, with basically the same relative noise. Reducing simultaneously d and Q enables a cubic performance improvement in all core homomorphic operations.

We notice that any protocol or scheme that uses GSW can benefit from our new homomorphic operations, thus, this contribution is of independent interest.

Thanks to this low-level description of the GSW scheme, we estimate the cost of our amortized bootstrapping concretely in terms of NTTs and integer (modular) multiplications. This simplifies the comparison with other bootstrapping strategies and also clarifies the practicability of the amortized bootstrapping.

Proof-of-Concept Implementation in C++. We provide the first implementation of a bootstrapping algorithm for FHE based on the worst-case hardness of lattice problems and with polynomial approximation factors with amor-

---

[2] A double-CRT version of GSW is implemented in the Lattigo library, but there is no formal description and analysis of the scheme. Moreover, it only includes external products.

tized sublinearly many homomorphic operations. We show that our construction is practical, being up to 3.4 times faster than the non-packed approach we tested.

Our source code is publicly available, since we believe that this can help the academic community to understand our techniques and also simplify comparisons in future works. We stress that the description of [28] is very high level and also that any implementation of their bootstrapping must be far from practical, even if our double-CRT GSW scheme is used, due to all the hidden constants in the asymptotic costs. Thus, one could reasonably wonder if the amortized bootstrapping would ever be practically feasible, and our algorithms together with our implementation provide a positive answer.

2   Preliminaries

For $a_1, ..., a_k, m_1, ..., m_k \in \mathbb{Z}$, with m_i's being pairwise coprime, let $M = \prod_{i=1}^{k} m_i$ and define $\mathsf{CRT}_{m_1,...,m_k}(a_1, ..., a_k)$ as the unique $a \in \mathbb{Z}_M$ such that $a_i = a \bmod m_i$. Also, for any $a \in \mathbb{Z}_M$, define $\mathsf{CRT}_{m_1,...,m_k}^{-1}(a) = (a \bmod m_1, ..., a \bmod m_k)$. For an element $a(X)$ of any polynomial ring of the form $\mathbb{Z}[X]/\langle f(X) \rangle$, we extend CRT and CRT^{-1} by applying it coefficient wise.

For any vector $\mathbf{u}$, we denote the infinity norm by $\|\mathbf{u}\|$ and the Euclidean norm by $\|\mathbf{u}\|_2$. For any polynomial $a = \sum_{i=0}^{d} a_i \cdot X^i$, we define the norm of a as the norm of the coefficient vector $(a_0, ..., a_d)$. If a is an element of a polynomial ring like $\mathbb{Z}[X]/\langle f(X) \rangle$, we consider $a' \in \mathbb{Z}[X]$ as the unique canonical representation of a, and thus the norm of a is simply the norm of a'.

Rings. We use power-of-two cyclotomic rings of the form $\mathbb{Z}[X]/\langle X^N + 1 \rangle$, where $N = 2^k$ for some $k \in \mathbb{N}$, which we denote by $\hat{\mathcal{R}}$, and circulant rings of the form $\mathbb{Z}[X]/\langle X^p - 1 \rangle$, for some prime number p, which we denote by $\tilde{\mathcal{R}}$. For any positive integer Q, we define $\hat{\mathcal{R}}_Q := \hat{\mathcal{R}}/(Q\hat{\mathcal{R}})$ and $\tilde{\mathcal{R}}_Q := \tilde{\mathcal{R}}/(Q\tilde{\mathcal{R}})$, i.e., the same rings as before but with coefficients of the elements reduced modulo Q.

Plain, Ring and Circulant LWE. In the well-known learning with errors problem (LWE) [32] with parameters n, q, and σ, an attacker has to find a secret vector $\mathbf{s} \in \mathbb{Z}^n$ given many samples of the form $(\mathbf{a}_i, b_i)$, where $\mathbf{a}_i$ is uniformly sampled from $\mathbb{Z}_q^n$ and $b_i := \mathbf{a}_i \cdot \mathbf{s} + e_i \bmod q$, with e_i following a discrete Gaussian distribution with parameter σ.

The ring version of LWE, known as RLWE [26], is used to obtain more efficient cryptographic schemes, since it typically allows us to encrypt larger messages when compared to similar schemes instantiated with LWE. In the RLWE we fix the ring $\mathcal{R} = \mathbb{Z}[X]/\langle \Phi_m(X) \rangle$, where $\Phi_m(X)$ is the m-th cyclotomic ring, and we are given samples of the form (a_i, b_i), where a_i is uniformly sampled from $\mathcal{R}_q$ and $b_i := a_i \cdot s + e_i \bmod q$, for some small noise term e_i, and we have to find the secret polynomial s. Most schemes are constructed on top of the RLWE problem with a power-of-two cyclotomic polynomial, $\Phi_{2N}(X) = X^N + 1$, where $N = 2^k$ for some $k \in \mathbb{N}^*$.

In this work, we also use a variant of the LWE called circulant-LWE (CLWE), which was introduced in [6] and was proved to be as hard as the RLWE on prime-order cyclotomic polynomials. Hence, we restrict ourselves to prime p. Instead of using the ring $\mathcal{R} = \mathbb{Z}[X]/\langle \Phi_p(X) \rangle$ we use the "circulant ring" $\tilde{\mathcal{R}} = \mathbb{Z}[X]/\langle X^p - 1 \rangle$. Then CLWE samples are obtained essentially by projecting RLWE samples from $\mathcal{R}$ to $\tilde{\mathcal{R}}$. This is done by fixing some integer Q prime with p and by defining the map $L_Q : \mathcal{R}_Q \to \tilde{\mathcal{R}}_Q$ as

$$L_Q : \sum_{i=0}^{p-1} a_i \cdot X^i \mapsto \sum_{i=0}^{p-1} a_i \cdot X^i - p^{-1} \cdot \left(\sum_{i=0}^{p-1} a_i \right) \cdot \sum_{i=0}^{p-1} X^i \bmod Q$$

Finally, given an RLWE sample $(a', b' = a' \cdot s' + e') \in \mathcal{R}_Q^2$, we define the corresponding CLWE sample as $(a, b) := (L_Q(a'), L_Q((1-X)\cdot b')) \in \tilde{\mathcal{R}}_Q^2$. Thanks to the homomorphic properties of L_Q, we have $b = a \cdot s + e \bmod Q$, where $e = L_Q((1-X) \cdot e')$ is a small noise term and $s = L_Q((1-X) \cdot s')$ is the CLWE secret. Then, using the CLWE problem, the GSW instantiated over the circulant ring $\tilde{\mathcal{R}}$ is CPA-secure if the message space is restricted to powers of X, that is, if one just encrypts $X^k \in \tilde{\mathcal{R}}$ for $k \in \mathbb{Z}$ [6].

In Sect. 3.5, we extend the results [6] so that we can also encrypt non-powers of X (under some conditions), as this is needed in our bootstrapping algorithm, especially, to use Galois automorphisms on GSW ciphertexts.

Subgaussian Distributions and Independence Heuristic. A random variable X is subgaussian with parameter $\sigma > 0$, in short σ-subgaussian, if for all $t \in \mathbb{R}$ it holds that $\mathbb{E}[\exp(2\pi t X)] \leq \exp(\pi \sigma^2 t^2)$. If X is σ-subgaussian, then $\forall t \in \mathbb{R}$, $\Pr[|X| \geq t] \leq 2\exp(-\pi t^2/\sigma^2)$. This allows one to bound the absolute value of X with overwhelming probability. Namely, by setting $t = \sigma\sqrt{\lambda/\pi}$, we see that $\Pr[|X| \geq \sigma\sqrt{\lambda/\pi}] \leq 2\exp(-\pi(s\sqrt{\lambda/\pi})^2/s^2) = 2\exp(-\lambda) < 2^{-\lambda}$. Linear combinations of independently distributed subgaussians are again subgaussians, i.e., given independent σ_i-subgaussian distributions X_i's, then for any $\mathbf{c} = (c_1, ..., c_n) \in \mathbb{R}^n$, it holds that $Y := \sum_{i=1}^n c_i X_i$ is $\left(\sqrt{\sum_{i=1}^n c_i^2 \sigma_i^2}\right)$-subgaussian. We say that a polynomial a is σ-subgaussian if its coefficients are independent σ_i-subgaussian, with $\sigma_i \leq \sigma$. For any $n \in \mathbb{N}^*$, given f equal to $X^n \pm 1$ and $a, b \in \mathbb{Z}[X]/\langle f \rangle$ following subgaussians with parameters σ_a and σ_b, we assume the independence heuristic, i.e. the coefficients of the noise terms of the LWE, RLWE, and CLWE samples appearing in the linear combinations we consider are independent and concentrated, to say that $a \cdot b$ is $(\sqrt{n} \cdot \sigma_a \cdot \sigma_b)$-subgaussian.

Double-CRT (RNS) Representation for Polynomial Arithmetic. Homomorphic operations of commonly used FHE schemes are composed of some operations over polynomial rings $\mathcal{R}_Q = \mathbb{Z}_Q[X]/\langle f(X) \rangle$, where $f(X)$ is a degree-N polynomial over $\mathbb{Z}_Q[X]$. Here, we suppose that $f(X) = X^N + 1$ or $f(X) = X^N - 1$. Because Q generally has much more than 64 bits, working with elements of $\mathcal{R}_Q$ requires libraries that implement arbitrary precision integers, which is inefficient. To overcome this the residual number system (RNS), aka double-CRT, is typically used. It exploits the decomposition of Q to work with several polynomials modulo each q_i, which then fit in the 32- or 64-bit native integer types of current processors.

In more detail, because $Q = \prod_{i=1}^{\ell} q_i$, by using the Chinese remainder theorem coefficient-wise we have $\mathcal{R}_Q = \mathbb{Z}_Q[X]/\langle f(X) \rangle = \prod_{i=1}^{\ell} \mathbb{Z}_{q_i}[X]/\langle f(X) \rangle$.

Thus, additions and multiplications over $\mathcal{R}_Q$ can be implemented with ℓ independent operations over $\mathcal{R}_{q_i}$. Moreover, since efficiently multiplying polynomials modulo $f(X)$ requires fast Fourier transforms or number-theoretic transforms (NTT), one goes one step forward and represents elements of $\mathcal{R}_{q_i}$ in the "NTT form", i.e., given $a(X) \in \mathcal{R}_Q$, one stores the matrix $\texttt{Mat}(a) \in \mathbb{Z}^{\ell \times N}$ defined as $\texttt{row}_i(\texttt{Mat}(a)) := \texttt{NTT}_{q_i}(a(X))$. Notice that we need to choose q_i such that a suitable primitive root of unity $\omega_i \in \mathbb{Z}_{q_i}$ exists.

Cost of Operations in Double-CRT Representation: We estimate the cost of our algorithms by the number of NTTs and multiplications performed modulo the small primes q_i's. We assume that all those primes have about the same bit length, thus, operations modulo any of them cost essentially the same. Moreover, we assume that a forward and a backward NTT modulo q_i have the same cost, thus, we do not distinguish them in our cost estimations.

Base Extension. In some situations, we may want to operate on polynomials defined modulo different values Q and D. To do this we need to represent both operands on a common modulus with an operation called base extension.

For simplicity, let's assume that $D = \prod_{i=1}^{w} d_i$ divides Q so that we have $Q = P \cdot D$ for some $P = \prod_{i=1}^{v} p_i$. Then, given $a \in \mathcal{R}_Q$ and $b \in \mathcal{R}_D$, both in double-CRT form, we want to lift b to $\mathcal{R}_Q$. This is done by reconstructing each coefficient of b modulo D, then reducing them modulo each p_i. However, to avoid arbitrary precision integers we try to reconstruct $b_i \in \mathbb{Z}_D$ already performing all the operations modulo the p_i's. This means that the conversion is not exact and we obtain $[b_i]_D + u_i \cdot D$ in base P with $|u_i| \leq 1/2$ instead of exactly $[b_i]_D$. So, overall we have the residues of $[b(X)]_D + u(X) \cdot D$ in the basis $P \cdot D$, with $\|u(X)\|_\infty \leq 1/2$ [22].

For completeness, we show this operation in detail in the full version [18]. It costs $v + w$ NTTs and $O(v \cdot w \cdot N)$ modular multiplications, and it is defined as follows:

$$\texttt{FastBaseExtension}(b, D, P) := \left(\sum_{j=1}^{w} \left[b \cdot (D/d_j)^{-1} \right]_{d_j} \cdot (D/d_j) \mod p_i \right)_{i=1}^{v}$$

Gadget Matrix. Consider three positive integers Q, B, and d such that $d \in O(\log Q)$. Let $\mathbf{g}$ be a d-dimensional column vector, $\mathbf{I}_2$ be the 2×2 identity matrix, and $\otimes$ denote the Kronecker tensor product. We say that $\mathbf{G} = \mathbf{I}_2 \otimes \mathbf{g} \in \mathbb{Z}^{2d \times 2}$ is a gadget matrix for the base $\mathbf{g}$ with quality B if there is an efficient decomposition algorithm $G^{-1} : \mathbb{Z}_Q^2 \to \mathbb{Z}^{2 \times 2d}$ such that, if $\mathbf{A} = G^{-1}(a, b)$, then $\|\mathbf{A}\|_\infty \leq B$

and $\mathbf{A} \cdot \mathbf{G} = (a, b) \mod Q$. We naturally extend G^{-1} to a polynomial ring of the form $\mathcal{R}_Q = \mathbb{Z}_Q[X]/\langle f(X) \rangle$ by applying G^{-1} coefficientwise. That is, given $(a, b) \in \mathcal{R}_Q^2$, we define $G^{-1}(a, b) = \sum_{i=0}^{\deg f - 1} G^{-1}(a_i, b_i) \cdot X^i$. We also extend G^{-1} to matrices $\mathbf{C} \in \mathcal{R}_Q^{2d \times 2}$ by applying it to each row. Thus, for $\mathbf{C} \in \mathcal{R}_Q^{2d \times 2}$, we have $G^{-1}(\mathbf{C}) \in \mathcal{R}^{2d \times 2d}$.

The main example of a gadget matrix is the one defined by some base $B \in \mathbb{Z}$, which corresponds to $d = \lceil \log_B(Q) \rceil$, $\mathbf{g} = (B^0, B^1, ..., B^{d-1})^T$, and quality B.

The CRT-gadget decomposition is of central importance in our double-CRT GSW scheme, presented in Sect. 3, and it is defined as follows. Let $q_1, ..., q_\ell$ be prime numbers and $Q := \prod_{i=1}^{\ell} q_i$. Let $d \in \mathbb{N}$ be the "number of digits". For simplicity, assume that $d | \ell$ and define $k := \ell/d \in \mathbb{Z}$. Then, for $1 \le i \le d$, define the i-th "CRT digit" as $D_i := \prod_{j=(i-1) \cdot k+1}^{i \cdot k} q_i$, that is, a product of k consecutive primes. Finally, define $Q_i := Q/D_i$ and $\hat{Q}_i := (Q/D_i)^{-1} \mod D_i$. Then the gadget matrix is $\mathbf{G} = \mathbf{I}_2 \otimes \mathbf{g} \in \mathbb{Z}^{2d \times 2}$ where $\mathbf{g} := (Q_1 \cdot \hat{Q}_1, ..., Q_d \cdot \hat{Q}_d)$. And we define $G^{-1}(a, b) := (\mathsf{CRT}_{D_1, ..., D_d}^{-1}(a), \mathsf{CRT}_{D_1, ..., D_d}^{-1}(b))$. It follows that $G^{-1}(a, b) \cdot \mathbf{G} = (a, b) \mod Q$. Moreover, since each entry of $G^{-1}(a, b)$ is of the form $a \mod D_i$ or $b \mod D_i$, we see that the quality of this gadget matrix is $D := \max(D_1, ..., D_d)$.

Because of the ciphertext shrinking that we present in Sect. 3, we need a more general definition of gadget matrices, which includes an integer scaling factor. Namely, we say that $\mathbf{G}_\alpha$ is a *scaled gadget matrix* with factor α if $G^{-1}(\alpha^{-1} \cdot a, \alpha^{-1} \cdot b) \cdot \mathbf{G}_\alpha = (a, b)$, in other words, we have to multiply the input (a, b) by the inverse of α modulo Q before decomposing it.

Basic Encryption Schemes Based on LWE, RLWE, and CLWE. We define the set of LWE encryptions of a message $m \in \mathbb{Z}_t$, where $t \ge 2$, under a secret key $\mathbf{s} \in \mathbb{Z}^n$, with E-subgaussian noise and scaling factor $\Delta \in \mathbb{Z}$ as

$$\mathsf{LWE}_{\mathbf{s}}^Q(\Delta \cdot m, E) := \{(\mathbf{a}, b) \in \mathbb{Z}_Q^{n+1} : b = [\mathbf{a} \cdot \mathbf{s} + e + \Delta \cdot m]_Q \text{ where } e \text{ is } E\text{-subgaussian }\}.$$

For a power-of-two cyclotomic polynomial $\hat{\mathcal{R}}$, the set of RLWE ciphertexts encrypting a message $m \in \hat{\mathcal{R}}$, with scaling factor $\Delta \in \mathbb{N}$, under a secret key s, and with E-subgaussian noise is

$$\hat{\mathcal{R}}_Q \mathsf{LWE}_s(\Delta \cdot m, E) := \{(a, b) \in \hat{\mathcal{R}}_Q^2 : b = [a \cdot s + e + \Delta \cdot m]_Q \text{ where } e \text{ is } E\text{-subgaussian }\}.$$

Basically the same definition applies to CLWE ciphertexts:

$$\tilde{\mathcal{R}}_Q \mathsf{LWE}_s(\Delta \cdot m, E) := \{(a, b) \in \tilde{\mathcal{R}}_Q^2 : b = [a \cdot s + e + \Delta \cdot m]_Q \text{ where } e \text{ is } E\text{-subgaussian }\}.$$

In any of the three types of ciphertexts, the decryption is done by multiplying the term a (or $\mathbf{a}$) by the secret key and subtracting it from b modulo Q, which produces $e' = e + \Delta \cdot m \mod Q$, then we output $\lfloor e'/\Delta \rceil \mod t$. If $\|e' - \Delta \cdot m\| < Q/(2t)$, then the decryption correctly outputs $m \mod t$.

Common Homomorphic Operations. Generally, FHE schemes allow us to add and multiply ciphertexts homomorphically. In this section we briefly show a list of other common homomorphic operations that apply to RLWE and that will be used here on both RLWE and CLWE ciphertexts. Readers not familiar with them can read the full version [18] for a detailed description.

- *Modulus switching*: takes a ciphertext $\mathbf{c} = (a, b) \in \mathsf{RLWE}_{s,Q}(m, E)$, where $Q = \prod_{i=0}^{\ell-1} q_i$, and prime q diving Q, and outputs $\mathbf{c}' \in \mathsf{RLWE}_{s,Q'}(m, E')$, where $Q' = Q/q$ and $E' \leq \sqrt{(E/q)^2 + \|s\|_2^2/2}$. Moreover, it costs 2ℓ NTTs and $O(k\ell N)$ multiplications on $\mathbb{Z}_{q_i}$.

- *Key Switching*: takes as input a ciphertext $\mathbf{c} = (a, b) \in \tilde{\mathcal{R}}_Q \mathsf{LWE}_z(\Delta \cdot m, E)$ and a key-switching key $\mathbf{K} \in \tilde{\mathcal{R}}_Q \mathsf{KS}_s^d(z, E_k)$, both in double-CRT form. It outputs $\mathbf{c}' \in \tilde{\mathcal{R}}_Q \mathsf{LWE}_s(\Delta \cdot m, E')$, where $E' \leq O(\sqrt{E^2 + dp \cdot D^2 \cdot E_k^2})$, with $D = \max(D_1, ..., D_d)$. Moreover, it costs $d \cdot \ell$ NTTs and $O(\ell^2 \cdot p)$ products on $\mathbb{Z}_{q_i}$.

- *Automorphism*: it takes $\mathbf{c} = (a, b) \in \tilde{\mathcal{R}}_Q \mathsf{LWE}_s(\Delta \cdot m, E)$, $u \in \mathbb{Z}_p$, and $\mathbf{K} \in \tilde{\mathcal{R}}_Q \mathsf{KS}_s^d(s(X^u), E_k)$ as input. It outputs $\mathbf{c}' \in \tilde{\mathcal{R}}_Q \mathsf{LWE}_s(\Delta \cdot m(X^u), E')$. The noise growth and the cost are the same as the ones of the key switching.

Ring Packing. In [28], Micciancio and Sorrell present a ring packing method to transform a set of N LWE samples $(\mathbf{a}_i, b_i := \mathbf{a}_i \cdot \mathbf{s} + e_i + \Delta \mu_i) \in \mathbb{Z}_Q^{n+1}$ into a single RLWE ciphertext encrypting $\mu = \sum_{i=0}^{N-1} \mu_i \cdot X^i$. To do so, they define a "packing key" composed of $n \cdot L$ RLWE ciphertexts as

$$\mathbf{K} := (\mathbf{a}, \mathbf{b} := \mathbf{a} \cdot z + \mathbf{e} + \mathbf{G} \cdot \mathbf{s}) \in \hat{\mathcal{R}}_Q^{n \cdot L \times 2}$$

where $L := \lceil \log_B(Q) \rceil$ and $\mathbf{G} = \mathbf{I}_n \otimes (B^0, ..., B^{\ell-1})^T \in \mathbb{Z}^{n \cdot L \times n}$ is a gadget matrix such that $g^{-1}(\mathbf{u})\mathbf{G} = \mathbf{u}$ for any $\mathbf{u} \in \mathbb{Z}_Q^n$. We show this packing procedure in detail in the full version [18]. Note that it requires $O(n \cdot L)$ multiplications on $\hat{\mathcal{R}}_Q$.

3 Double-CRT GSW Encryption Scheme

In this section, we formalize a double-CRT version of the GSW scheme supporting all the standard operations, like the external product and homomorphic multiplication. We also present two key switching algorithms for GSW, making it possible to evaluate automorphisms on GSW ciphertexts. Moreover, we also include a new operation, which we call *shrinking*.

We present our scheme over the circulant ring $\tilde{\mathcal{R}} := \mathbb{Z}[X]/\langle X^p - 1 \rangle$, where p is prime, and base its security on the circulant-LWE problem. Moreover, since our main goal is to use the GSW scheme to run the amortized bootstrapping, we just define the encryption function to powers of X and do not present the decryption. We stress that is trivial to adapt our scheme to the usual RLWE problem using power-of-two cyclotomic rings and encrypting other types of messages.

We define the GSW ciphertexts in a more general way, by including a correction factor $\alpha \in \mathbb{Z}$, which is introduced by the shrinking operation. In more detail, the set of GSW encryptions m with a scaling factor α is denoted by $\tilde{\mathcal{R}}_Q \mathsf{GSW}_s^d(\alpha \cdot m)$. Any element of this set has the form

$$\mathbf{C} = [\mathbf{a} \mid \mathbf{a} \cdot s + \mathbf{e}] + m \cdot \mathbf{G}_\alpha \in \tilde{\mathcal{R}}_Q^{2d \times 2},$$

where $s \in \tilde{\mathcal{R}}$ is the secret key, $\mathbf{e} \in \tilde{\mathcal{R}}^{2d}$ is the noise term, and $\mathbf{G}_\alpha$ is the scaled gadget matrix, as described in Sect. 2. We can write $\tilde{\mathcal{R}}_Q \mathsf{GSW}_s^d(\alpha \cdot m, E)$ to specify that $\mathbf{e}$ is E-subgaussian.

Saying that $\mathbf{C}$ is in double-CRT form means that each entry $c_{i,j} \in \tilde{\mathcal{R}}_Q$ is stored as $\mathtt{Mat}(c_{i,j})$, as described in Sect. 2.

- GSW.ParamGen(1^λ): Choose a prime number p, standard deviations $\sigma_{\mathsf{err}}, \sigma_{\mathsf{sk}} \in \mathbb{R}$, and an integer $Q := \prod_{i=1}^{\ell} q_i$, where $q_1, ..., q_\ell$ are small primes (say, with 32 bits), such that the $(p, Q, \sigma_{\mathsf{err}}, \sigma_{\mathsf{sk}})$-RLWE problem offers us λ bits of security. Moreover, p and Q must be coprime.
  Let $d \in \mathbb{N}$ be the "number of CRT digits". For simplicity, assume that $d|\ell$ and let $u := \ell/d \in \mathbb{Z}$. Then, for $1 \leq i \leq d$, define each "CRT digit" as $D_i := \prod_{j=(i-1)\cdot u+1}^{i \cdot u} q_i$, that is, a product of u consecutive primes. Output $\mathsf{params} = (p, Q, \sigma_{\mathsf{err}}, \sigma_{\mathsf{sk}}, d, \{q_i\}_{i=1}^{\ell}, \{D_i\}_{i=1}^{d})$.
- GSW.KeyGen(params): Sample $\bar{s}_0, ..., \bar{s}_{p-1}$ following a discrete Gaussian over $\mathbb{Z}$ with parameter σ_{sk}. Let $\bar{s} = \sum_{i=0}^{p-1} \bar{s}_i \cdot X^i$ then project $\bar{s}$ as $s := L((1 - X)\bar{s}) \in \tilde{\mathcal{R}}$. Output $\mathsf{sk} := (s, \bar{s})$.
- GSW.Enc(μ, sk): To encrypt $\mu \in \mathbb{Z}_p$, generate a matrix $\mathbf{V} \in \tilde{\mathcal{R}}_Q^{2d \times 2}$ where each row is a sample from the Circulant-LWE distribution with secret s and noise terms following a discrete Gaussian with parameter σ_{err}. Output $\mathbf{V} + X^\mu \cdot \mathbf{G} \in \tilde{\mathcal{R}}_Q \mathsf{GSW}_s^d(1 \cdot X^\mu)$.

Lemma 1 (Security of GSW). *If the decisional $(p, Q, \sigma_{\mathsf{err}}, \sigma_{\mathsf{sk}})$-RLWE problem is hard, then the GSW scheme over the circulant ring $\tilde{\mathcal{R}}$ is CPA-secure for messages of the form X^k.*

Proof. Lemma 4 of [6]. □

We now present the homomorphic operations that can be performed with GSW.

3.1   Shrinking Gadget Matrices

We begin by defining a new operation called *shrinking*, whose main purpose is to reduce the size of ciphertexts. Let $Q, Q_i, \hat{Q}_i$, and D be as in Sect. 2. Also, let

$\alpha \in \mathbb{Z}_Q$ and $\alpha_i := \alpha \bmod D_i$. Then, the scaled gadget matrix is

$$\mathbf{G}_\alpha = \begin{bmatrix} Q_1 \cdot \hat{Q}_1 \cdot \alpha_1 & 0 \\ \vdots & \\ & 0 \\ Q_d \cdot \hat{Q}_d \cdot \alpha_d & 0 \\ 0 & Q_1 \cdot \hat{Q}_1 \cdot \alpha_1 \\ \vdots & \vdots \\ 0 & Q_d \cdot \hat{Q}_d \cdot \alpha_d \end{bmatrix} \in \mathbb{Z}^{2d \times 2}.$$

Notice that each CRT digit D_i defines two rows of $\mathbf{G}_\alpha$. Ideally, we would choose k digits, say, $D_1, ..., D_k$, remove the two $2k$ rows corresponding to them, and obtain a new gadget matrix with respect to the digits $D_{k+1}, ..., D_d$. However, by doing so, we obtain a scaled gadget matrix $\mathbf{G}_\beta$ with respect to a new scaling factor β.

For this shrinking operation, we define the projection $\pi_k : \mathcal{R}_Q^{2d \times 2} \to \mathcal{R}_Q^{2(d-k) \times 2}$ as the function that takes a matrix $\mathbf{C}$ and outputs $\mathbf{C}'$ such that for $1 \le i \le d - k$, $\mathrm{row}_i(\mathbf{C}') := \mathrm{row}_{i+k}(\mathbf{C})$ and $\mathrm{row}_{d-k+i}(\mathbf{C}') := \mathrm{row}_{i+d+k}(\mathbf{C})$. Then we divide the result by $D^{(k)} := D_1 \cdot ... \cdot D_k$, and compute the new scaling factor β. This procedure is shown in detail in Algorithm 1. In Lemma 2, we prove its correctness.

Algorithm 1: Shrink matrix

    Input: $\mathbf{C} \in \mathcal{R}_Q^{2d \times 2}$, CRT digits $D_1, ..., D_d$, a scaling factor α, and $k \in \mathbb{Z}$ such that $1 \le k < d$.

    Output: $\mathbf{C}' \in \mathcal{R}_{Q'}^{2(d-k) \times 2}$ and $\alpha' \in \mathbb{Z}$.

1 $D^{(k)} := D_1 \cdot ... \cdot D_k$

2 $Q' := Q/D^{(k)}$

3 $\bar{\mathbf{C}} := \pi_k(\mathbf{C})$

4 $\mathbf{C}' := \bar{\mathbf{C}}/D^{(k)} \bmod Q'$

5 $\alpha' := \alpha \cdot \mathrm{CRT}_{D_{k+1}, ..., D_d}(D^{(k)})^{-1} \bmod Q'$.

6 return $\mathbf{C}', \alpha'$

Lemma 2. *Let $Q := \prod_{i=1}^{d} D_i$ for coprime D_i's and k be an integer such that $1 \le k < d$. Define $Q' := Q/(D_1 \cdot ... \cdot D_k)$. Then, given a scaled gadget matrix $\mathbf{G}_\alpha$ with respect to the CRT basis $D_1, ..., D_d$, Algorithm 1 outputs $\mathbf{G}' \in \mathbb{Z}^{2(d-k) \times 2}$ and $\alpha' \in \mathbb{Z}$ such that $\mathrm{CRT}^{-1}(a,b) \cdot \mathbf{G}' = \alpha' \cdot (a,b) \bmod Q'$, for any $(a,b) \in \mathcal{R}_{Q'}^2$, where CRT^{-1} is the decomposition with respect to $D_{k+1}, ..., D_d$.*

Proof. Presented in the full version [18]. □

3.2 Shrinking a Ciphertext

Let $\mathbf{C} = [\mathbf{a} \mid \mathbf{a} \cdot s + \mathbf{e}] + m \cdot \mathbf{G}_\alpha \in \tilde{\mathcal{R}}^{2d \times 2}$ be an encryption of m with scaling factor α. We define the operation GSW.Shrink$(\mathbf{C}, k)$ essentially by applying Algorithm 1 to $\mathbf{C}$, except that dividing $\bar{\mathbf{C}} \in \tilde{\mathcal{R}}_Q^{2(d-k) \times 2}$ by $D^{(k)}$ is done by applying the modulus switching to every row of $\bar{\mathbf{C}}$. This is necessary because we are assuming that $\mathbf{C}$ is stored in double-CRT form. We show this procedure in detail in Algorithm 2 and prove its correctness in Lemma 3.

Algorithm 2: Shrink ciphertext

Input: $\mathbf{C} \in \tilde{\mathcal{R}}_Q^{2d \times 2}$ in double-CRT form, scaling factor α, CRT digits $D_1, ..., D_d$, and $k \in \mathbb{Z}$ such that $1 \leq k < d$.

Output: $\mathbf{C}' \in \tilde{\mathcal{R}}_{Q'}^{2(d-k) \times 2}$ and new correction factor $\alpha' \in \mathbb{Z}$.

Complexity: $4 \cdot (d-k) \cdot \ell$ NTTs and $O(k \cdot \ell^2 \cdot p)$ multiplications on $\mathbb{Z}_{q_i}$.

Noise growth: $E \mapsto O(E/D^{(k)} + \sqrt{p} \cdot S)$

1 $D^{(k)} := D_1 \cdot ... \cdot D_k$

2 $Q' := Q/D^{(k)}$

3 $\bar{\mathbf{C}} := \pi_k(\mathbf{C}) \in \tilde{\mathcal{R}}_{Q'}^{2(d-k) \times 2}$

4 **for** $1 \leq i \leq 2 \cdot (d-k)$ **do**

5 $\quad \lfloor \ \mathbf{c}_i := \mathsf{ModSwt}_{Q \to Q'}(\mathbf{row}_i(\bar{\mathbf{C}}))$

6 Define $\mathbf{C}'$ such that $\mathbf{row}_i(\mathbf{C}') = \mathbf{c}_i$.

7 $\beta := \mathsf{CRT}_{D_{k+1}, ..., D_d}(D^{(k)}, ..., D^{(k)})^{-1} \bmod Q'$.

8 $\alpha' := \alpha \cdot \beta \bmod Q'$

9 **return** $\mathbf{C}', \alpha'$

Lemma 3 (Correctness and Cost of Ciphertext Shrinking). *Let* $\mathbf{C} \in \tilde{\mathcal{R}}_Q \mathsf{GSW}_s^d(\alpha \cdot m, E)$, $k \in \mathbb{N}^*$ *such that* $k < d$, *and* $\mathbf{C}', \alpha'$ *be the output of Algorithm 2. Assume that s is S-subgaussian for some S. Then,* $\mathbf{C}' \in \tilde{\mathcal{R}}_Q \mathsf{GSW}_s^d(\alpha' \cdot m, E')$ *with* $E' \leq O(E/D^{(k)} + \sqrt{p} \cdot S)$.

Moreover, assuming that each CRT digit D_i is a product of ℓ/d primes, the cost of Algorithm 2 is $4 \cdot (d-k) \cdot \ell$ NTTs and $O(k \cdot \ell^2 \cdot p)$ multiplications on $\mathbb{Z}_{q_i}$.

Proof. Presented in the full version [18]. $\qquad \square$

3.3 External Product in RNS Representation

The external product is a homomorphic multiplication between a CLWE ciphertext and a GSW ciphertext. This is a fairly well-known operation, thus we present it in detail and prove its correctness in the full version [18]. It is important to notice that firstly we multiply the CLWE ciphertext by $\alpha^{-1} \bmod Q$ before decomposing it with respect to the scaled gadget matrix $\mathbf{G}_\alpha$, so that the result CLWE ciphertext does not depend on α.

3.4   Homomorphic Multiplication

This operation[3] takes GSW encryptions of two messages and outputs a GSW encryption of their product. This is done by performing one external product for each row of one of the ciphertexts, therefore, the cost is exactly $2 \cdot d$ times the cost of one external product. Since each row is multiplied independently, the noise growth is the same as in the external product. We show this algorithm in detail in the full version [18]. The only caveat is the scaling factor of the output. Both input ciphertexts have scaling factors, say α_0 and α_1, so one could expect that the output would be scaled by $\alpha_0 \cdot \alpha_1$. However, since external products output CLWE encryptions that do not depend on the scaling factor of the GSW ciphertext, the output of the GSW multiplication is scaled only by, say, α_0.

3.5   Key Switching for GSW

If one instantiates the double-CRT GSW scheme over the usual power-of-two cyclotomic ring, i.e. modulo $X^N + 1$, then one can freely choose the keys that will be switched with no issue regarding security. However, we are using the circular ring, $X^p - 1$, and so have to be more careful.

In [6], it is shown that GSW over circulant rings is secure if one just encrypts powers of X. The main problem was that in a circular ring an attacker can interpret an element $a \in \mathcal{R}$ as a polynomial $a' \in \mathbb{Z}[X]$. In this case, it holds that $a' = a + u \cdot (X^p - 1)$ for some $u \in \mathbb{Z}[X]$, and so $a'(1) = a(1) \in \mathbb{Z}$. Thus, a ciphertext evaluated at one would produce the pair $(a(1), b(1) = a(1) \cdot s(1) + \Delta m + e(1)) \in \mathbb{Z}^2$, which could leak information about s or the message.

To solve this Bonnoron, Ducas, and Fillinger [6] apply a function to the RLWE samples that fixes the values of the polynomials when they are evaluated at one, such that $(a(1), b(1)) = (0, \Delta)$, thus are independent of the secret key and leak no information on the message.

However, to key switch from a secret key $s \in \tilde{\mathcal{R}}$ to another secret key $z \in \tilde{\mathcal{R}}$, we have to encrypt z, which is not a power of X. Thus, we extend the results of [6] to show that it is also safe to encrypt z. The crucial property here is: In the case of key-switching keys, we are only encrypting the secret polynomials of the CLWE problem, which are always of the form $s = L((1 - X) \cdot s')$, and so always result in zero when they are evaluated at one. Therefore, as $m(1) = 0$, it is secure to encrypt them under the CLWE problem. We prove this formally for any constant c such that $m(1) = c$ in the full version [18].

GSW Key Switching via Two-Layer Reconstruction. Given $\mathbf{C} \in \tilde{\mathcal{R}}_Q\mathsf{GSW}_z^d(\alpha \cdot m)$, remember that for $1 \leq i \leq d$, $\mathtt{row}_i(\mathbf{C}) \in \tilde{\mathcal{R}}_Q\mathsf{LWE}_z(\Delta_i \cdot m)$, where $\Delta_i := Q_i \cdot \hat{Q}_i \cdot \alpha_i$. Also, for $d+1 \leq i \leq 2 \cdot d$, $\mathtt{row}_i(\mathbf{C}) \in \tilde{\mathcal{R}}_Q\mathsf{LWE}_z(-\Delta_i \cdot m \cdot z)$. Thus, to switch $\mathbf{C}$ to a key s, we just need to use the first d rows. Namely, we use the RLWE/CLWE key switching to obtain CLWE encryptions of $\Delta_i \cdot m$ under

---

[3] In [12], a homomorphic multiplication between two GSW ciphertexts is called *internal product*.

Algorithm 3: GSW key switching

Input: $\mathbf{C} \in \tilde{\mathcal{R}}_Q \mathsf{GSW}_z^d(\alpha \cdot m, E)$, $\mathbf{K} \in \tilde{\mathcal{R}}_Q \mathsf{KS}_s^d(z, E_k)$,
$\quad\quad \mathbf{K}_s \in \tilde{\mathcal{R}}_Q \mathsf{GSW}_s^d(1 \cdot (-s), E_s)$, all in double-CRT form.
Output: $\mathbf{C}' \in \tilde{\mathcal{R}}_Q \mathsf{GSW}_s^d(\alpha \cdot m, E')$,
Complexity: $3 \cdot d^2 \cdot \ell$ NTTs and $O(d \cdot \ell^2 \cdot p)$ products on $\mathbb{Z}_{q_i}$.
Noise growth: $E' \in O(\sqrt{dp} \cdot D \cdot E_s + \sqrt{p} \cdot \|s\| \cdot E + p \cdot \sqrt{d} \cdot D \cdot E_k \cdot \|s\|)$

1 **for** $1 \le i \le d$ **do**
2 $\quad$ $\mathbf{c}_i = \mathsf{KeySwt}(\mathbf{row}_i(\mathbf{C}), \mathbf{K}) \in \tilde{\mathcal{R}}_Q \mathsf{LWE}_s(\Delta_i \cdot m)$
3 $\quad$ $\mathbf{c}_{d+i} = \mathbf{c}_i \boxdot \mathbf{K}_s \in \tilde{\mathcal{R}}_Q \mathsf{LWE}_s(-\Delta_i \cdot m \cdot s)$
4 Let $\mathbf{C}' \in \tilde{\mathcal{R}}_Q^{2d \times 2}$ such that $\mathbf{row}_i(\mathbf{C}') = \mathbf{c}_i$
5 **return** $\mathbf{C}'$

---

s, then we multiply these ciphertexts by $-s$ to construct the last d rows. This procedure is shown in detail in Algorithm 3.

From the costs of the external product and of the key switching, we see that we need $3 \cdot d^2 \cdot \ell$ NTTs and $O(d \cdot \ell^2 \cdot p)$ products on $\mathbb{Z}_{q_i}$. From the noise growth presented in these algorithms, we see that after key switching, the noise is $\hat{E}$-subgaussian, where $\hat{E} \in O(E + \sqrt{dp} \cdot D \cdot E_k)$ and $D = \max(D_1, ..., D_d)$. Thus, after the external products, we have an E'-subgaussian, where $E' \in O(\sqrt{dp} \cdot D \cdot E_s + \sqrt{p} \cdot \hat{E} \cdot \|s\|) = O(\sqrt{dp} \cdot D \cdot E_s + \sqrt{p} \cdot \|s\| \cdot E + p \cdot \sqrt{d} \cdot D \cdot E_k \cdot \|s\|)$

Noise-Reduced GSW Key Switching via Parallel Reconstruction. When we key switching the first d rows from z to s, we generate CLWE samples with a larger noise. Then, when we use these samples to reconstruct the other d rows, we accumulate more noise over them, generating thus samples with even larger noise, proportional to p.

The key switching that we present in this section avoids that "double accumulation" by producing independent CLWE samples that can be subtracted to reconstruct the remaining rows. Because subtraction increases the noise linearly, we accumulate less noise in the last d rows of the GSW ciphertext. In the end, we save a factor $\sqrt{p}$ in the final noise. For this, we need an extra key encrypting the $s \cdot z$ and we replace the GSW encryption of s by a key-switching key from s to s itself. We present this procedure in detail in Algorithm 4, but defer the proof of its correctness to the full version [18].

3.6 GSW Automorphism

Given $\mathbf{C} \in \tilde{\mathcal{R}}_Q \mathsf{GSW}_s^d(\alpha \cdot m, E)$ and $\eta : X \mapsto X^u$, for some $u \in \mathbb{Z}$, we just have to apply η to each row of $\mathbf{C}$, then apply one of the GSW key switching algorithms described in Sect. 3.5.

Notice that the first d rows of $\mathbf{C}$ are regular CLWE encryptions, thus, automorphisms work as usual producing new CLWE encryptions under the key $\eta(s)$. The other d rows can be seen as CLWE encryptions of the $-\Delta_i \cdot m \cdot s$, therefore, the automorphism generates CLWE encryptions of $-\Delta_i \cdot \eta(m) \cdot \eta(s)$, which

---

Algorithm 4: NoiseReducedGSWKeySwt

Input: $\mathbf{C} \in \tilde{\mathcal{R}}_Q \mathsf{GSW}_z^d(\alpha \cdot m, E)$, $\mathbf{K}_z \in \tilde{\mathcal{R}}_Q \mathsf{KS}_s^d(z, E_z)$, $\mathbf{K}_s \in \tilde{\mathcal{R}}_Q \mathsf{KS}_s^d(s, E_s)$, and $\mathbf{K}_{sz} \in \tilde{\mathcal{R}}_Q \mathsf{KS}_s^d(s \cdot z, E_{sz})$, all in double-CRT form.
Output: $\mathbf{C}' \in \tilde{\mathcal{R}}_Q \mathsf{GSW}_s^d(\alpha \cdot m, E')$,
Complexity: $3 \cdot d^2 \cdot \ell$ NTTs and $O(d \cdot \ell^2 \cdot p))$ products on $\mathbb{Z}_{q_i}$.
Noise growth: $E' \in O(\sqrt{dp} \cdot D \cdot E_{sz} + \sqrt{dp} \cdot D \cdot E_s + \sqrt{p} \cdot \|s\| \cdot E)$
▷ Construct the first d rows of the GSW ciphertext
1 **for** $1 \leq i \leq d$ **do**
2      $c_i = \mathsf{KeySwt}(\mathrm{row}_i(\mathbf{C}), \mathbf{K}_z) \in \tilde{\mathcal{R}}_Q \mathsf{LWE}_s(\Delta_i \cdot m)$

    ▷ Now construct the last d rows
3 **for** $1 \leq i \leq d$ **do**
4   Let $(a, b) = \mathrm{row}_i(\mathbf{C}) \in \tilde{\mathcal{R}}_Q \mathsf{LWE}_z(\Delta_i \cdot m)$
5   **for** $1 \leq i \leq d$ **do**
         ▷ Each base extension costs ℓ NTTs and $O(p \cdot \ell^2/d)$
         multiplications on $\mathbb{Z}_{q_i}$
6          $h_i = \mathsf{FastBaseExtension}(a \bmod D_i, D_i, Q/D_i) \in \tilde{\mathcal{R}}_Q$
7          $y_i = \mathsf{FastBaseExtension}(b \bmod D_i, D_i, Q/D_i) \in \tilde{\mathcal{R}}_Q$
8      $\mathbf{h} := (h_1, ..., h_d)$
9      $\mathbf{y} := (y_1, ..., y_d)$
10      $a' := \mathbf{h} \cdot \mathrm{col}_1(\mathbf{K}_{sz}) - \mathbf{y} \cdot \mathrm{col}_1(\mathbf{K}_s)$
11      $b' := \mathbf{h} \cdot \mathrm{col}_2(\mathbf{K}_{sz}) - \mathbf{y} \cdot \mathrm{col}_2(\mathbf{K}_s)$
12      $c_{d+i} := (a', b') \in \tilde{\mathcal{R}}_Q \mathsf{LWE}_s(-\Delta_i \cdot m \cdot s)$
13 Let $\mathbf{C}' \in \tilde{\mathcal{R}}_Q^{2d \times 2}$ such that $\mathrm{row}_i(\mathbf{C}') = c_i$
14 **return** $\mathbf{C}'$

---

correspond to the last d rows of a GSW encryption of $\Delta_i \cdot \eta(m)$ under the key $\eta(s)$. Moreover, η does not change the distribution of the noise. In summary, $\eta(\mathbf{C}) \in \tilde{\mathcal{R}}_Q \mathsf{GSW}_{\eta(s)}^d(\alpha \cdot \eta(m), E)$.

Then, applying GSW key switching on $\eta(\mathbf{C})$ gives us $\mathbf{C}' \in \tilde{\mathcal{R}}_Q \mathsf{GSW}_s^d(\alpha \cdot \eta(m), E')$. Hence, the noise growth and the cost are the same as the ones of the chosen key switching.

3.7 GSW Evaluation of Scalar Products on the Exponent

In this section we consider the problem of evaluating a scalar product between two vectors $\mathbf{u}, \mathbf{v} \in \mathbb{Z}_p^k$, when $\mathbf{u}$ is known in clear and each entry of $\mathbf{v}$ is encrypted as X^{v_i} into a GSW sample. The output is a GSW encryption of $X^{\mathbf{u} \cdot \mathbf{v} \bmod p}$.

The straightforward way of implementing this scalar product is the following: apply the automorphism $X \mapsto X^{u_i}$ to obtain GSW encryptions of $X^{u_i \cdot v_i \bmod p}$, then use the GSW multiplication k times to obtain a GSW encryption of $\prod_{i=1}^k X^{u_i \cdot v_i} = X^{\mathbf{u} \cdot \mathbf{v} \bmod p}$. However, each GSW multiplication costs $2d$ external products, so this naïve implementation needs $2kd$ external products. We want to reduce that to around $k \cdot d$, thus, halving the cost.

Algorithm 5: EvalScalarProd: Evaluate scalar product in the exponent of X

Input: $\mathbf{K}_s \in \tilde{\mathcal{R}}_Q\mathsf{GSW}_s^d(1 \cdot (-s), E_s)$, $\mathbf{K}_v \in \tilde{\mathcal{R}}_Q\mathsf{KS}_s^d(s(X^v), E_k)$ for all $v \in \mathbb{Z}_p$, and for $1 \le i \le k$, $\mathbf{C}_i \in \tilde{\mathcal{R}}_Q\mathsf{GSW}_s^d(\alpha \cdot X^{m_i}, E_i)$ and $u_i \in \mathbb{Z}_p$. All $\mathbf{K}_v$ and $\mathbf{C}_i$ in double-CRT form.

Output: $\mathbf{C}' \in \tilde{\mathcal{R}}_Q\mathsf{GSW}_s^d(\alpha \cdot X^y, E')$ where $y = \sum_{i=1}^k u_i \cdot m_i \bmod p$.

Complexity: $3 \cdot k \cdot d^2 \cdot \ell$ NTTs and $O(k \cdot d \cdot \ell^2 \cdot p)$ products on $\mathbb{Z}_{q_i}$.

Noise growth: $E \mapsto O\left(\sum_{i=1}^k \left(\sqrt{d}Dp \cdot \|s\| \cdot E_i\right) + \sqrt{dp} \cdot D \cdot E_s + \bar{E} + \hat{E}\right)$,

where $\bar{E} = \sqrt{p} \cdot \|s\| \cdot E_1$ and $\hat{E} = \sqrt{p} \cdot \|s\| \cdot \sqrt{k+1} \cdot E_{KS}$ with $E_{KS} \in O(\sqrt{dp} \cdot D \cdot E_k)$.

▷ Consider that $\Delta_i := Q_i \cdot \hat{Q}_i \cdot \alpha_i$, where $\alpha_i = \alpha \bmod D_i$

1 Define $u_{k+1} = 1$
2 **for** $1 \le i \le d$ **do**
3   Let $\mathbf{c}_i := \mathrm{row}_i(\mathbf{C}_1) \in \tilde{\mathcal{R}}_Q\mathsf{LWE}_s(\Delta_i \cdot X^{m_1}, E_1)$
4     $\mathbf{c}_i = \mathsf{Auth}(\mathbf{c}_i, u_1 \cdot u_2^{-1} \bmod p) \in \tilde{\mathcal{R}}_Q\mathsf{LWE}_s(\Delta_i \cdot X^{m_1 \cdot u_1 \cdot u_2^{-1}}, E_1 + E_{KS})$
    ▷ Let $S^{(j)} := u_{j+1}^{-1} \cdot \sum_{i=1}^j m_i \cdot u_i \bmod p$
5   **for** $2 \le j \le k$ **do**
6        $\mathbf{c}_i = \mathbf{c}_i \boxdot \mathbf{C}_j \in$
       $\tilde{\mathcal{R}}_Q\mathsf{LWE}_s(\Delta_i \cdot X^{S^{(j-1)}+m_j}, \sum_{i=2}^j \left(\sqrt{dp} \cdot D \cdot E_i\right) + (E_1 + E_{KS}))$
7        $v = u_j \cdot u_{j+1}^{-1} \bmod p$
8        $\mathbf{c}_i = \mathsf{Auth}(\mathbf{c}_i, v, \mathbf{K}_v) \in$
       $\tilde{\mathcal{R}}_Q\mathsf{LWE}_s(\Delta_i \cdot X^{S^{(j)}}, \sum_{i=1}^j \left(\sqrt{dp} \cdot D \cdot E_i\right) + E_1 + \sqrt{j+1} \cdot E_{KS})$

▷ Now, construct the other d rows of the GSW sample
9 **for** $1 \le i \le d$ **do**
10   Let $\mathbf{c}_{d+i} := \mathbf{c}_i \boxdot \mathbf{K}_s \in \tilde{\mathcal{R}}_Q\mathsf{LWE}_s(-\Delta_i \cdot X^{S^{(k)}} \cdot s, E)$
11 Define $\mathbf{C}' \in \tilde{\mathcal{R}}_Q\mathsf{GSW}_s^d(\alpha \cdot X^{S^{(k)}}, E)$ such that $\mathrm{row}_i(\mathbf{C}') = \mathbf{c}_i$
12 **return** $\mathbf{C}'$

Moreover, instead of using k automorphisms on GSW ciphertexts, which cost essentially $2 \cdot d \cdot k$ CLWE key switchings, we want to use automorphisms on the CLWE samples so that the cost of k automorphisms also drops to $k \cdot d$, that is, halving the cost compared to GSW automorphisms.

Hence, given $\mathbf{C}_i \in \tilde{\mathcal{R}}_Q\mathsf{GSW}_s^d(\alpha \cdot X^{v_i})$, we define $\mathbf{C}_1' = \mathbf{C}_1$, and for $2 \le i \le k$, we want to compute $\mathbf{C}_i' = \mathsf{Auth}(\mathbf{C}_i, u_i) \cdot \mathbf{C}_{i-1}'$.

The main idea is to extract the d rows of $\mathbf{C}_i'$ that correspond to the CLWE samples encrypting X^m for some message m and ignore the other d rows. So, let $\mathbf{c}_j \in \tilde{\mathcal{R}}_Q\mathsf{LWE}_s(\Delta_j \cdot X^m)$ be the j-th row of $\mathbf{C}_i'$. Instead of applying the automorphism u_i to $\mathbf{C}_i'$, we can use a technique from [6] and apply $u_i^{-1} \bmod p$ to $\mathbf{c}_j$, then multiply it with $\mathbf{C}_{i-1}'$ via external product, and apply the automorphism u_i in the end. This gives us

1. $\mathbf{c}_j' = Auth(\mathbf{c}_j, u_i^{-1})$ (encrypts $X^{u_i^{-1} \cdot m}$)
2. $\mathbf{c}_j'' = \mathbf{c}_j' \cdot \mathbf{C}_i$ (encrypts $X^{u_i^{-1} \cdot m + v_i}$)

3. $\mathbf{c}_j''' = Auth(\mathbf{c}_i'', u_i)$ (encrypts $X^{m+u_i \cdot v_i}$)

Repeating this k times, at the end, we have $\mathbf{c}_j''' \in \tilde{\mathcal{R}}_Q\mathsf{LWE}_s(\Delta_j \cdot X^{\sum u_i v_i})$, as desired. Notice that for each i, the first and the third step are automorphisms, so can compose them and run a single key switching instead of two. Finally, repeating this d times, we obtain all the d first rows of the GSW ciphertext encrypting the $X^{\mathbf{u \cdot v}}$, and it remains to construct the other d rows essentially by multiplying by $-s$, as it was done in the GSW key switching in Algorithm 3.

Since the whole algorithm uses $k \cdot d$ external products and $k \cdot d$ CLWE automorphisms, the total cost is $3 \cdot k \cdot d^2 \cdot \ell$ NTTs. Notice that k GSW multiplications plus k GSW automorphisms would cost $7 \cdot k \cdot d^2 \cdot \ell$ NTTs, therefore we are gaining a factor of around 2.33. We show this procedure in detail in Algorithm 5.

4   Bootstrapping

In this section, we show how we can use our circulant GSW scheme to evaluate a bootstrapping algorithm with polynomial noise overhead and sublinear number of homomorphic operations per refreshed message.

4.1   Homomorphic Number Theoretic Transform

With a more expressive accumulator in hand we can finally replace the homomorphic Nussbaumer transform and the SlowMult algorithm used in [28] by the Number Theoretic Transform (NTT) and a simpler point-wise multiplication.

It is well known that over "cyclic polynomial rings" of the form $R_p := \mathbb{Z}_p[X]/\langle X^N - 1 \rangle$, where N is a power of two, we can multiply two elements $a, z \in R_p$ in time $O(N \log N)$ by using the NTT. For this, assume that $p \equiv 1 \pmod{N}$, then there exists a primitive N-root of unity $\omega \in \mathbb{Z}_p$. The NTT is an algorithm that takes $a \in R_p$, interprets it as a polynomial in $\mathbb{Z}_p[X]$, and, in time $O(N \log N)$, outputs the vector $(a(\omega^0), a(\omega^1), ..., a(\omega^{N-1})) \in \mathbb{Z}_p^N$. Now let $\odot : \mathbb{Z}^N \to \mathbb{Z}^N$ be the entrywise multiplication. Then it holds that

$$\mathsf{NTT}^{-1}\left(\mathsf{NTT}(a) \odot \mathsf{NTT}(z)\right) \equiv N \cdot a \cdot z \quad \mathrm{mod} \ \langle X^N - 1, p \rangle.$$

However, over "negacyclic polynomial rings" of the form $\hat{\mathcal{R}}_p := \mathbb{Z}_p[X]/\langle X^N + 1 \rangle$, to perform this multiplication, we first have to multiply the coefficients of a and z by powers of some primitive $2N$-root of unity $\psi \in \mathbb{Z}_p$, then apply the NTT and inverse NTT as usual, and finally multiply by powers of ψ^{-1}. In more detail, let $\boldsymbol{\psi} := (\psi^0, \psi, ..., \psi^{N-1})$ and $\boldsymbol{\psi}^{-1} := (\psi^0, \psi^{-1}, ..., \psi^{-(N-1)})$, where ψ is a $2N$'th root of unity as defined above, then

$$\boldsymbol{\psi}^{-1} \odot \mathsf{NTT}^{-1}(\mathsf{NTT}(\boldsymbol{\psi} \odot \mathbf{a}) \odot \mathsf{NTT}(\boldsymbol{\psi} \odot \mathbf{z})) \equiv N \cdot a \cdot z \quad \mathrm{mod} \ \langle X^N + 1, p \rangle$$

Because we now need a $2N$-root of unity modulo p, we need $p \equiv 1 \pmod{2N}$. Notice that the NTT is of dimension N, not $2N$. Also, given ψ, the N-th root of unity used by the NTT can be defined as $\omega = \psi^2 \bmod p$.

This radix-m version of the NTT algorithm recursively splits the N-dimensional input into m vectors of dimension $\frac{N}{m}$. Then, after ρ recursive levels, we reach the base case of the recursion and we apply a quadratic algorithm to compute the NTT of inputs of size $\frac{N}{m^\rho}$. Typically, one sets $\rho = \log_m(N)$, such that the quadratic step is executed over inputs of size one and are actually void, obtaining the complexity $O(N \cdot \log N)$. However, because the noise overhead of the homomorphic NTT is proportional to N^ρ, we restrict ourselves to instantiating the algorithm with small values of ρ only.

We show the radix-m inverse NTT in detail in Algorithm 6, where the multiplication by ψ^{-1} and also by the inverse of N modulo p is already included in the last step, so that the output already corresponds to the product of the two polynomials. We denote a k-th root of unity in $\mathbb{Z}_p$ by w_k. At the beginning of the algorithm, we start with w_N, then all the others roots of unity that appear in all the recursive calls are just powers of w_N.

Number of Operations of Homomorphic Inverse NTT. The time complexity of a radix-m NTT is standard: the number of operations of lines 7 and 15 can be represented by $T(N) = m \cdot T(N/m) + m \cdot N$. Iterating it ρ times gives us $T(N) = m^\rho \cdot T(N/m^\rho) + \rho \cdot m \cdot N$. Finally, we reach the end of the recursion and use the quadratic algorithm, thus, replacing $T(N/m^\rho)$ by $(N/m^\rho)^2$, we have $T(N) = N^2/m^\rho + \rho \cdot m \cdot N$. By choosing $m = N^{1/\rho}$, we obtain the optimal complexity:

$$O\left(\rho \cdot N \cdot m + \frac{N^2}{m^\rho}\right) = O\left(\rho \cdot N^{1+\frac{1}{\rho}}\right) \tag{1}$$

With this, it is now easy to prove the complexity and noise overhead of the homomorphic evaluations of this algorithm.

Lemma 4 (Time Complexity in Terms of Homomorphic Operations).
The homomorphic evaluation of the inverse NTT, Algorithm 6, of dimension N, can be executed with $O\left(N^{1+\frac{1}{\rho}} \cdot \rho\right)$ homomorphic operations (GSW multiplications and automorphisms).

Proof. The input of the algorithm is a vector of (circulant) GSW ciphertexts encrypting X^{f_i}. To add each term of the sums shown in lines 7, we just have to apply an automorphism, obtaining an encryption of $X^{f_i \cdot u_j \cdot w_n^{-i \cdot j} \bmod p}$, and one homomorphic multiplication, to accumulate the term in the partial sum.

For the sum of line 15, we proceed in the same way, by applying the automorphism $X \mapsto X^w$, where $w = u_j \cdot w_n^{-i \cdot k_1} \cdot w_m^{-i \cdot k_2}$, then one multiplication.

Thus, in total, we have $O\left(N^{1+\frac{1}{\rho}} \cdot \rho\right)$ homomorphic operations. $\square$

Since each GSW multiplication and automorphism can be implemented with $O(d^2 \cdot \ell)$ NTTs and $O(d \cdot \ell^2 \cdot p)$ products on $\mathbb{Z}_{q_i}$ using our double-CRT instantiation of GSW, we have the following result.

Algorithm 6: NTT_m^{-1} - Inverse NTT in time $O\left(\rho \cdot N^{1+\frac{1}{\rho}}\right)$

Input: $(f_0, \ldots, f_{N-1}) \in \mathbb{Z}_p^N, \rho \in \mathbb{Z}^+, \tilde{\rho} \in \mathbb{Z}^+$, where $\tilde{\rho}$ starts at 1, $m \in \mathbb{Z}^+$ s.t. $m \mid N$

Output: $\mathsf{NTT}^{-1}(\mathbf{f})$

1   **if** $\rho = 1$ **then**
2     $u = \psi^{-1} N^{-1} \bmod p$

3   **else**
4     $u = (1, 1, \ldots, 1) \in \mathbb{Z}^N$

5   **if** $\tilde{\rho} = \rho$ **then**
      ▷ **Trivial quadratic algorithm, time** $O\left(N^2\right)$
6   **for** $0 \le j < N$ **do**
7       $a_j = \sum_{i=0}^{n-1} f_i \cdot u_j \cdot w_N^{-i \cdot j} \bmod p$

8   **else**
      ▷ **General case with recursive calls**
9   **for** $0 \le i < m$ **do**
10       $\mathbf{g} = \left(f_i, \, f_{m+i}, \, \ldots, \, f_{m(N/m-1)+i}\right)$
11       $\mathbf{h}^{(i)} = \mathsf{NTT}_m^{-1}(\mathbf{g}, \tilde{\rho} + 1)$
12   **for** $0 \le k_1 < \frac{N}{m}$ **do**
13   **for** $0 \le k_2 < m$ **do**
14         $j = k_1 + \frac{N}{m} \cdot k_2$
15         $a_j = \sum_{i=0}^{m-1} h_{k_1}^{(i)} \cdot u_j \cdot w_N^{-i \cdot k_1} \cdot w_m^{-i \cdot k_2} \bmod p$

16   **return** $(a_0, \ldots, a_{N-1})$

Corollary 1 (Time Complexity in Terms of NTTs and Modular Multiplications).

Let $Q = \prod_{i=1}^{\ell} q_i$ *be the ciphertext modulus. Let d be the number of CRT digits used in the GSW ciphertexts. Then the homomorphic evaluation of the inverse NTT, Algorithm 6, of dimension N, can be executed with* $O\left(N^{1+\frac{1}{\rho}} \cdot \rho \cdot d^2 \cdot \ell\right)$ *NTTs and* $O\left(N^{1+\frac{1}{\rho}} \cdot \rho \cdot d \cdot \ell^2 \cdot p\right)$ *multiplications modulo* q_i.

Finally, by assuming that each sum in lines 7 and 15 is implemented with Algorithm 5, we can have a concrete instead of asymptotic estimation of the number of NTTs.

Lemma 5 (Number of NTTs Used the Homomorphic Inverse NTT).

Let $Q = \prod_{i=1}^{\ell} q_i$ *be the ciphertext modulus. Let d be the number of CRT digits used in the GSW ciphertexts. Consider the Algorithm 6 with recursive level* ρ, *dimension N, and with lines 7 and 15 implemented with the EvalDotProduct, Algorithm 5. If no ciphertext shrinking is used, then the total number of NTTs is*

$$3 \cdot N \cdot d^2 \cdot \ell \cdot \left(\frac{N}{m^\rho} + \rho \cdot m\right). \tag{2}$$

If we use shrinking at the end of each recursive call, then the total number of NTTs is

$$\frac{3 \cdot N^2 \cdot d_\rho^2 \cdot \ell_\rho}{m^\rho} + 3 \cdot N \cdot m \cdot \left(\sum_{i=0}^{\rho-1} d_i^2 \cdot \ell_i\right) + 4 \cdot N \cdot \left(\sum_{i=0}^{\rho-1} d_i \cdot \ell_{i+1}\right) \tag{3}$$

where d_ρ and ℓ_ρ define the dimension of the input ciphertexts (thus, $d = d_\rho > d_{\rho-1} > ... > d_0$ and $\ell = \ell_\rho > \ell_{\rho-1} > ... > \ell_0$).

Proof. The proof follows trivially by defining a recursive formula for the amount of NTTs per recursive call, then applying the number of NTTs already given in Algorithm 5. A detailed proof is provided in the full version [18].   □

Error Growth of the Homomorphic Inverse NTT. Assuming again that the sums in Algorithm 6 are implemented with the EvalScalarProd (Algorithm 5), we have the following result.

Lemma 6. *Consider the homomorphic evaluation of Algorithm 6 on input $\mathbf{C}_i \in \tilde{\mathcal{R}}_Q\mathsf{GSW}_s^d(\alpha \cdot X^{f_i}, E)$, where $0 \leq i < n$. Let $\mathbf{K}_s \in \tilde{\mathcal{R}}_Q\mathsf{GSW}_s^d(1 \cdot (-s), E_s)$ and $\mathbf{K}_v \in \tilde{\mathcal{R}}_Q\mathsf{KS}_s^d(s(X^v), E_k)$ be the keys to compute the sums with Algorithm 5. Moreover, assume that E_s is constant. Then, the noise of the output ciphertexts is bounded by*

$$O\left((\sqrt{d} \cdot D \cdot p \cdot \|s\|)^\rho \cdot \sqrt{N} \cdot (E + E_k)\right)$$

where ρ is the chosen recursive depth.

4.2   Partial Decryption Using NTT_m^{-1}

Remember that to decrypt $(a, b) \in \hat{\mathcal{R}}_p\mathsf{LWE}_z(m, E)$, we have to compute $b^\star := b - a \cdot z \bmod p$, then it holds that $b^\star = e + \Delta \cdot m$, where $\Delta = \lfloor p/t \rceil$. Then we can recover each coefficient m_i by taking the $\log t$ most significant bits. This last step is message extraction and we present it in Sect. 4.3. In this section, we present an algorithm that uses the homomorphic inverse NTT to compute $b^\star$.

The first part of the algorithm computes the forward NTT of a and of b, to obtain $\bar{a} := \mathsf{NTT}(\psi \odot a)$, $\bar{b} := \mathsf{NTT}(\psi \odot b)$, and the bootstrapping key encrypting $\bar{z} := \mathsf{NTT}(-\psi \odot z)$, we use GSW automorphisms to compute the entrywise product $\bar{a} \odot \bar{z} = (\bar{a}_0 \cdot \bar{z}_0, ..., \bar{a}_{N-1} \cdot \bar{z}_{N-1})$. At this point, we also add $\mathsf{NTT}(\psi \odot b)$. Finally, we apply the inverse NTT homomorphically to obtain GSW ciphertexts encrypting $b^\star$.

Lemma 7 (Correctness, Cost, and Noise Overhead of NTTDec). *Given a ciphertext $\mathbf{c} = (a, b) \in \hat{\mathcal{R}}_p\mathsf{LWE}_z(\Delta \cdot m, E^{(in)})$, the bootstrapping keys $\mathbf{K}_i \in \tilde{\mathcal{R}}_Q\mathsf{GSW}_s^d(1 \cdot X^{\bar{z}_i}, E)$, where $(\bar{z}_1, ..., \bar{z}_{N-1}) = \mathsf{NTT}_p(\psi \odot -z)$, and the keys used by Algorithm 5, namely $\mathbf{K}_v \in \tilde{\mathcal{R}}_Q\mathsf{KS}_s^d(s(X^v), E_k)$ for all $v \in \mathbb{Z}_p^*$ and $\mathbf{K}_s \in$*

Algorithm 7: NTTDec, the homomorphic partial decryption

Input: Encryption $\mathbf{c} \in \hat{\mathcal{R}}_p\mathsf{LWE}_z(m, E^{(in)})$. Bootstrapping keys
$\mathbf{K}_i \in \tilde{\mathcal{R}}_Q\mathsf{GSW}_s^d(1 \cdot X^{-\bar{z}_i}, E)$, where $(\bar{z}_0, \dots, \bar{z}_{N-1}) := \mathsf{NTT}(\boldsymbol{\psi} \odot z) \in \mathbb{Z}_p^N$,
and key-switching keys for all the Galois automorphisms $\eta_a : X \mapsto X^a$.
Vectors with powers of $2N$-th root of unity $\boldsymbol{\psi}$ in $\mathbb{Z}_p$, i.e.,
$\boldsymbol{\psi} = (\psi^0, \dots, \psi^{N-1})$ and $\boldsymbol{\psi}^{-1} = (\psi^0, \dots, \psi^{-(N-1)})$
Output: $\bar{\mathbf{C}}_i \in \tilde{\mathcal{R}}_Q\mathsf{GSW}_s^d(\alpha \cdot X^{e_i + \Delta \cdot m_i}, E'')$ for $0 \le i < N$
Complexity: $O\left(N^{1+\frac{1}{\rho}} \cdot \rho \cdot d^2 \cdot \ell\right)$ NTTs and $O\left(N^{1+\frac{1}{\rho}} \cdot \rho \cdot d \cdot \ell^2 \cdot p\right)$ products
over $\mathbb{Z}_{q_i}$
Noise growth: $(E, E_k) \mapsto E'' =$
$$O\left((\sqrt{d} \cdot D \cdot p \cdot \|s\|)^\rho \cdot \sqrt{n \cdot p} \cdot (E \cdot \|s\| + E_k \cdot \sqrt{d} \cdot D)\right)$$

1 Parse $\mathbf{c}$ as $(a,b) \in \hat{\mathcal{R}}_p^2$ where $\hat{\mathcal{R}}_p = \mathbb{Z}_p[X]/\langle X^N+1\rangle$
2 $(\bar{a}_0, \dots, \bar{a}_{N-1}) \leftarrow \boldsymbol{\psi} \odot \mathsf{NTT}(a)$;   ▷ $\mathsf{NTT}(a) \in \mathbb{Z}_p^N$
3 $(\bar{b}_0, \dots, \bar{b}_{N-1}) \leftarrow \boldsymbol{\psi} \odot \mathsf{NTT}(b)$;   ▷ $\mathsf{NTT}(b) \in \mathbb{Z}_p^N$
4 **for** $i \in \{0, \dots, N-1\}$ **do**
5 $\quad \bar{\mathbf{K}}_i = \eta_{\bar{a}_i}(\mathbf{K}_i)$;   ▷ $\bar{\mathbf{K}}_i \in \tilde{\mathcal{R}}_Q\mathsf{GSW}_{\eta_{\bar{a}_i}(s)}^d(1 \cdot X^{-\bar{a}_i \cdot \bar{z}_i}, E)$
6 $\quad \mathsf{KS}_{\eta_{\bar{a}_i}(s) \to s}(\bar{\mathbf{K}}_i)$;   ▷ $\bar{\mathbf{K}}_i \in \tilde{\mathcal{R}}_Q\mathsf{GSW}_s^d(1 \cdot X^{-\bar{a}_i \cdot \bar{z}_i}, E')$
7 $\quad \hat{\mathbf{K}}_i = X^{\bar{b}_i} \cdot \bar{\mathbf{K}}_i$;   ▷ $\hat{\mathbf{K}}_i \in \tilde{\mathcal{R}}_Q\mathsf{GSW}_s^d(1 \cdot X^{\bar{b}_i - \bar{a}_i \cdot \bar{z}_i}, E')$
8 $(\bar{\mathbf{C}}_0, \dots, \bar{\mathbf{C}}_{N-1}) = \mathsf{NTT}^{-1}(\hat{\mathbf{K}}_0, \dots, \hat{\mathbf{K}}_{N-1})$; ▷ $\bar{\mathbf{C}}_i \in \tilde{\mathcal{R}}_Q\mathsf{GSW}_s^d(1 \cdot X^{e_i + \Delta \cdot m_i}, E'')$

$\tilde{\mathcal{R}}_Q\mathsf{GSW}_s^d(1 \cdot (-s), E_s)$, *where E_s is a constant, then Algorithm 7 outputs GSW encryptions of $X^{e_i + \Delta \cdot m_i}$ with E''-subgaussian noise, where*

$$E'' = O\left((\sqrt{d} \cdot D \cdot p \cdot \|s\|)^\rho \cdot \sqrt{N \cdot p} \cdot (E \cdot \|s\| + E_k \cdot \sqrt{d} \cdot D)\right).$$

Moreover, Algorithm 7 costs $O(N^{1+\frac{1}{\rho}} \cdot \rho \cdot d^2 \cdot \ell)$ NTTs and $O(N^{1+\frac{1}{\rho}} \cdot \rho \cdot d \cdot \ell^2 \cdot p)$ multiplication in $\mathbb{Z}_{q_i}$.

Proof. Let $\mathbf{c} = (a,b) \in \hat{\mathcal{R}}_p\mathsf{LWE}_z(m, E^{(in)})$, then $\bar{a}_i$ and $\bar{b}_i$ are computed with a single NTT each, thus $O(N \log N)$ operations over $\mathbb{Z}_p$, in clear. These operations do not contribute to the complexity, since the homomorphic operations dominate them.

In lines 5 and 6, we compute $\bar{\mathbf{K}}_i$ via GSW automorphism. Since this is done for each i, it contributes a total of $3 \cdot N \cdot d^2 \cdot \ell$ NTTs and $O(N \cdot d \cdot \ell^2 \cdot p)$ modular multiplications.

Then, we perform N plaintext-ciphertext multiplications to add $\bar{b}_i$ to the exponent. This costs zero NTTs and $O(N \cdot p \cdot d \cdot \ell)$ modular multiplications, thus, it is already dominated by the cost of the automorphisms.

Finally, we apply the homomorphic inverse NTT, which, by Lemma 4, costs $O\left(N^{1+\frac{1}{\rho}} \cdot \rho \cdot d^2 \cdot \ell\right)$ NTTs and $O\left(N^{1+\frac{1}{\rho}} \cdot \rho \cdot d \cdot \ell^2 \cdot p\right)$ multiplications modulo q_i. Thus, it is clear that this step dominates the total cost.

As for the noise overhead, assuming that the ciphertexts defined in line 6 are obtained by applying the GSW Galois automorphisms defined in Algorithm 4, we have

$$E' = O(\sqrt{dp} \cdot D \cdot E_s + \sqrt{p} \cdot \|s\| \cdot E + \sqrt{dp} \cdot D \cdot E_k).$$

Then, multiplying by $X^{\bar{b}_i}$ modulo $X^p - 1$ only rotates the coefficients of the noise terms, but does not increase them. Thus, the ciphertexts $\tilde{\mathbf{K}}_i$ also have E'-subgaussian noise.

Finally, by Lemma 6, the homomorphic inverse NTT increases the noise from E' to $O\left((\sqrt{d} \cdot D \cdot p \cdot \|s\|)^\rho \cdot \sqrt{N} \cdot (E' + E_k)\right)$. Therefore, using the definition of E' and simplifying the expression by ignoring lower terms, we obtain

$$E'' = O\left((\sqrt{d} \cdot D \cdot p \cdot \|s\|)^\rho \cdot \sqrt{N \cdot p} \cdot (E \cdot \|s\| + E_k \cdot \sqrt{d} \cdot D)\right).$$

$\square$

4.3 Message Extraction

After executing Algorithm 7, we obtain ciphertexts of the form $\tilde{\mathbf{C}} \in \tilde{\mathcal{R}}_Q \mathsf{GSW}_s^d(\alpha \cdot X^{\Delta \cdot m + e})$, and we want to extract the message m from the exponent, $X^{\Delta \cdot m + e} \mapsto m$. This message extraction procedure was introduced in [13] and adapted to different settings in subsequent works [7,11,31]. Usually, it is assumed to work with negacyclic rings, however in Algorithm 8 we provide a version of the message extraction algorithm adapted to the cyclic ring. Here we assume messages in $\mathbb{Z}_t$ instead of in $\{0,1\}$, and apply a programmable bootstrapping, i.e., mapping $X^{\Delta \cdot m + e}$ to $f(m)$ for any given function $f : \mathbb{Z}_t \to \mathbb{Z}_t$. Moreover, our algorithm also takes care of the scaling factor α in the gadget matrix. We prove its correctness and time complexity in the full version [18].

4.4 The Bootstrapping Algorithm

With all the sub-constructions in place, we can now fully define the bootstrapping algorithm and analyze both the complexity and the error growth.

Algorithm 8: MsgExtract

Input: $\mathbf{C} \in \tilde{\mathcal{R}}_Q \mathsf{GSW}_s^d(\alpha \cdot X^{\Delta \cdot m + e}, E)$, where $\Delta = \lfloor p/t \rceil$ and $|e| < \Delta/2$. A
    function $f : \mathbb{Z}_t \to \mathbb{Z}_t$
Output: $\bar{\mathbf{c}} \in \mathsf{LWE}_s^Q(\lfloor Q/t \rceil \cdot f(m), E') \in \mathbb{Z}_Q^{p+1}$
Complexity: $d \cdot \ell$ NTTs and $O(\ell^2 \cdot p)$ products on $\mathbb{Z}_{q_i}$.
Noise growth: $E \mapsto O(\sqrt{dp} \cdot D \cdot E)$
1 Let $t(X) = X^{\Delta/2} \cdot \sum_{i=0}^{t-1} \sum_{j=0}^{\Delta-1} f(i) X^{p-i\Delta-j} \bmod X^p - 1$
2 Let $\bar{\mathbf{c}} = (0, \lfloor Q/t \rceil \cdot t(X)) \in \tilde{\mathcal{R}}_Q^2$ be a trivial and noiseless encryption of $t(X)$
3 $\mathbf{c}' := (a', b') = \mathbf{c} \boxdot \mathbf{C}$; $\triangleright$ $\mathbf{c}' \in \tilde{\mathcal{R}}_Q \mathsf{LWE}_s(\lfloor Q/t \rceil \cdot t(X) \cdot X^{\Delta \cdot m + e}, E')$
4 Let $\mathbf{A} \in \mathbb{Z}^{p \times p}$ be the circulant matrix of a'
5 Let $\mathbf{b} \in \mathbb{Z}^p$ be the coefficient vector of b'
6 Let $\mathbf{u} := (1, 0, ..., 0) \in \{0, 1\}^p$
7 **return** $\bar{\mathbf{c}} = [\mathbf{u} \cdot \mathbf{A}, \mathbf{u} \cdot \mathbf{b}]$; $\triangleright$ $\bar{\mathbf{c}} \in \mathsf{LWE}_s^Q(\lfloor Q/t \rceil \cdot f(m), E')$

The algorithm takes in N LWE samples $\mathbf{c}_i \in \mathsf{LWE}_s^Q(\Delta \cdot m_i) \in \mathbb{Z}^{p+1}$, then packs them into one RLWE ciphertext $\mathbf{c} \in \hat{\mathcal{R}}_Q \mathsf{LWE}_z(\Delta \cdot m(X))$, where $m(X) = \sum m_i X^i$. It proceeds by modulo switching $\mathbf{c}$ from Q to p and running NTTDec, the partial decryption via homomorphic NTT, which generates GSW encryptions of $X^{\Delta' m_i + e_i}$. Finally, the messages m_i are extracted back into LWE ciphertexts. The bootstrapping is shown in detail in Algorithm 9.

Algorithm 9: Bootstrap — for plaintext space $\mathbb{Z}_t$

Input: $\mathbf{c}_i \in \mathsf{LWE}_s^Q(\Delta \cdot m_i, E^{(in)}) \in \mathbb{Z}^{p+1}$ for $0 \le i < N$, where $\Delta = \lfloor Q/t \rceil$. All
    the bootstrapping and key-switching keys used in Algorithm 7.
    Arbitrary functions $f_i : \mathbb{Z}_t \to \mathbb{Z}_t$, for $0 \le i < N$.
Output: $\mathbf{c}_i' \in \mathsf{LWE}_s^Q(\Delta \cdot f_i(m_i)) \in \mathbb{Z}^{p+1}$ for $0 \le i < N$.
Complexity: $O(N^{1+\frac{1}{\rho}} \cdot \rho \cdot d^2 \cdot \ell)$ NTTs and $O(N^{1+\frac{1}{\rho}} \cdot \rho \cdot d \cdot \ell^2 \cdot p)$
    multiplication in $\mathbb{Z}_{q_i}$.
Noise growth: $E^{(in)} \mapsto$
$$O\left((p \cdot \sqrt{d} \cdot D)^{\rho+1} \cdot \|s\|^\rho \cdot \sqrt{N} \cdot (E \cdot \|s\| + E_k \cdot \sqrt{d} \cdot D)\right)$$
1 $(a^{(1)}, b^{(1)}) = \mathsf{PackLWE}(\mathbf{c}_0, ..., \mathbf{c}_{N-1})$; $\triangleright$ $(a^{(1)}, b^{(1)}) \in \hat{\mathcal{R}}_Q \mathsf{LWE}_z(\Delta \cdot m(X), E^{(1)})$
2 $(a^{(2)}, b^{(2)}) = \mathsf{ModSwitch}_{Q \to p}(a^{(1)}, b^{(1)})$;
  $\triangleright$ $(a^{(2)}, b^{(2)}) \in \hat{\mathcal{R}}_p \mathsf{LWE}_z(\Delta' \cdot m(X), E^{(2)})$
3 $(\mathbf{C}_0, ..., \mathbf{C}_{N-1}) = \mathsf{NTTDec}(a^{(2)}, b^{(2)})$; $\triangleright$ $\mathbf{C}_i \in \tilde{\mathcal{R}}_Q \mathsf{GSW}_s^d(\alpha \cdot X^{e_i' + \Delta' \cdot m_i}, \bar{E})$
4 **for** $0 \le i < N$ **do**
5     $\lfloor$ $\mathbf{c}_i' = \mathsf{MsgExtract}(\mathbf{C}_i, f_i)$; $\triangleright$ $\mathbf{c}_i' \in \mathsf{LWE}_s^Q(f_i(m_i), E')$
6 **return** $\mathbf{c}_0', ..., \mathbf{c}_{N-1}'$

Lemma 8. *Given at most N LWE ciphertexts and the keys described in Lemma 7, Algorithm 9 outputs LWE ciphertexts with E'-subgaussian noise,* *where*

$$E' = O\left((p \cdot \sqrt{d} \cdot D)^{\rho+1} \cdot \|s\|^{\rho} \cdot \sqrt{N} \cdot (E \cdot \|s\| + E_k \cdot \sqrt{d} \cdot D)\right).$$

Moreover, it costs $O\left(N^{1+\frac{1}{\rho}} \cdot \rho \cdot d^2 \cdot \ell\right)$ *NTTs and* $O\left(N^{1+\frac{1}{\rho}} \cdot \rho \cdot d \cdot \ell^2 \cdot p\right)$ *multiplication in* $\mathbb{Z}_{q_i}$.

Proof. The cost of Algorithm 9 is asymptotically dominated by the NTTDec, thus, it follows directly from Lemma 7.

Again from Lemma 7, the noise of the GSW ciphertexts $\mathbf{C}_i$ output by NTTDec satisfy $\bar{E} = O\left((\sqrt{d} \cdot D \cdot p \cdot \|s\|)^{\rho} \cdot \sqrt{N \cdot p} \cdot (E \cdot \|s\| + E_k \cdot \sqrt{d} \cdot D)\right)$, where E and E_k are the parameters of the noises from the bootstrapping keys and the key-switching keys, respectively. From Lemma ??, the final noise is then $E' = O(\sqrt{dp} \cdot D \cdot \bar{E})$. Hence, it holds that $E' = O\left((p \cdot \sqrt{d} \cdot D)^{\rho+1} \cdot \|s\|^{\rho} \cdot \sqrt{N} \cdot (E \cdot \|s\| + E_k \cdot \sqrt{d} \cdot D)\right)$ □

Corollary 2. *The bootstrapping algorithm presented in Algorithm 9 has noise overhead of* $\tilde{O}(\lambda^{1.5+\rho})$, *where* λ *is the security parameter.*

Proof. For a security level of λ bits based on the RLWE problem, we can choose $p, N \in \Theta(\lambda)$ and $E, E_k, \|s\| \in O(1)$. Since $d = O(\log Q) = O(\log \lambda)$ and D is constant, we have

$$E' = O\left(\lambda^{\rho+1.5} \cdot (\log \lambda)^{(\rho+2)/2} \cdot D^{\rho+2} \cdot \|s\|^{\rho+1}\right) = \tilde{O}(\lambda^{1.5+\rho}).$$

    □

Theorem 1 (Correctness of Bootstrapping). *For a security parameter λ, let $Q = \tilde{O}(\lambda^{2.5+\rho})$ and consider that the input ciphertexts $\mathbf{c}_i \in \mathsf{LWE}_{\mathbf{s}}^{Q}(\Delta \cdot m_i, E^{(in)}) \in \mathbb{Z}^{p+1}$ satisfy $E^{(in)} = O(Q/\lambda)$. Then, with probability $1 - 2^{-\lambda}$, the output of Algorithm 9 is correct, i.e., it outputs valid LWE encryptions of $f(m_i)$, with E'-subgaussian noise, where $\tilde{O}(\lambda^{1.5+\rho}) = \tilde{O}(Q/\lambda)$, thus, it is composable.*

Proof. From the description of the ring packing algorithm presented in Sect. 2, the parameter $E^{(1)}$ shown in Algorithm 9 satisfy $E^{(1)} = E^{(in)} \cdot \sqrt{N} + \sqrt{nN \log Q} \cdot E_R = O(E^{(in)} \cdot \sqrt{\lambda}) = O(Q/\sqrt{\lambda})$, where we used $n, N, \log Q \in O(\lambda)$ and $E_R = O(1)$. Thus, after modulus switching, by using $p = O(\lambda)$ and $\|s\| = O(1)$, it holds that $E^{(2)} = O(E^{(1)}p/Q + \sqrt{N} \cdot \|s\|) = O(p/\sqrt{\lambda} + \sqrt{N} \cdot \|s\|) = O(p/\sqrt{\lambda})$. Therefore, from the noise bound of the subgaussian distributions, as discussed in Sect. 2, the noise of the packed RLWE ciphertext is $O(E^{(2)}\sqrt{\lambda}) = O(p)$ with probability $1 - 2^{-\lambda}$, which means it is decryptable. In other words, with overwhelming probability, the correctness condition of MsgExtract is satisfied, since there $\Delta = \lfloor p/t \rceil = O(p)$. Hence, the output indeed encrypts $f(m_i)$.

Moreover, by Corollary 2, the final noise is E'-subgaussian with $E' = \tilde{O}(\lambda^{1.5+\rho})$, which is $O(Q/\lambda)$, therefore, satisfies the same bound as the input, and thus, the bootstrapping is composable.   □

Remark 1. One can trivially gain a factor $\sqrt{\lambda}$ in the noise presented in Corollary 2 by partially merging MsgExtract with the homomorphic inverse NTT, Algorithm 6, by starting with encryptions of $\lfloor Q/t \rceil \cdot t(X)$ instead of encryptions of one. This does not change the noise growth of the inverse NTT and we just needs to execute lines 4 to 7 of MsgExtract, which also do not change the noise. With this, the final noise in Corollary 2 is improved to $\tilde{O}(\lambda^{1+\rho})$. This optimization is applied in our implementation.

5 Practical Results

Amortized bootstrapping algorithms introduce significant asymptotic gains compared to non-amortized versions. However, they also introduce some performance overhead by requiring significantly larger parameters. As parameters grow, the asymptotic gains start to materialize, but, at the same time, memory requirements increase sharply to a point in which the implementation might become prohibitive. This is the problem preventing the [28] method from being practical, and, to a lesser extent, is also an issue in our method.

As such, our primary goal when developing a proof-of-concept practical implementation was to find the smallest parameter set in which our amortized bootstrapping starts to present practical gains. We implemented our scheme mostly from scratch using Intel HEXL Library [5] as the arithmetic backend to provide fast polynomial multiplications. We benchmarked our implementation in a m6i.metal instance on AWS (Intel Xeon 8375C at 3.5 GHz with 512 GB of RAM at 3200 MHz). We use Ubuntu 22.04 and G++ 11.3.0. Compiling options and further details are available in our repository. All parameter sets presented in this section consider the 128-bit security level estimated using the Lattice Estimator [2] with the default (MATZOV [27]) cost model.

5.1 Parameter Selection

In general, bootstrapping capabilities are defined by three parameters: The output dimension p, the input error σ_{in}, and the output error σ_{out} of a bootstrapping. Specifically, a k-bit message is correctly bootstrapped with probability $\cdot erf\left(\frac{p/2^{k+1}}{\sigma_{in}\sqrt{2}}\right)$, where erf is the Gauss error function. Let p^* be the modulus of the bootstrapping output, and N be the RLWE input dimension, Eq. 4 estimates the value of σ_{in} for the amortized bootstrapping considering a composed circuit (*i.e.*, when we bootstrap the result of a previous bootstrapping). The first term represents noise introduced by the previous bootstrapping and arithmetic operations. The second term estimates the noise introduced by the key switching from dimensions p to N and the ring packing. These first two terms are scaled down by $\frac{p}{p^*}$ by the modulus switching procedure, which, in turn, introduces some rounding noise, represented by the third term in the equation. Compared to a typical bootstrapping, our amortized method has the additional restriction that there must exist a $2N$-th root of unity modulo p. Therefore, we select $p = 12289$ for bootstrapping RLWE samples of dimension $N = 1024$. As the rounding noise

Table 3. Execution time, in milliseconds, for the INTT for $\ell = 4$ and $\rho = 2$.

p	n	Without shrinking		With shrinking		Shrinking Speedup
		Exec. Time	Amortized Time	Exec. Time	Amortized Time	
12289	512	1,078,033	2,106	695,761	1,359	1.5
12289	1024	3,546,423	3,463	2,132,504	2,083	1.7

is the only one to be introduced directly over modulus p, it is the main limiting factor for our bootstrapping capabilities, and we minimize it by working with sparse ternary keys of Hamming Weight 256.

$$\sigma_{in}^2 \leq \left(\sigma_{out}^2 + (p + N^2)\log_2(p^*)\sigma_{ks}^2\right)\left(\frac{p}{p^*}\right)^2 + \frac{\|s\|_2^2}{12} \tag{4}$$

5.2 Performance of Amortized Bootstrapping

INTT Performance. The homomorphic evaluation of the INTT, Algorithm 6, is the core and most expensive procedure in our amortized bootstrapping. Table 3 shows its execution time for $\ell = d = 4$ and $\rho = 2$, with and without shrinking. We choose these parameters only for benchmarking the INTT implementation and shrinking technique. They are not optimized for message bootstrapping. We note that increasing ρ would multiply the output noise by at least $\sqrt{dpD}\|s\|$ (Lemma 6), which, in turn, would cubically deteriorate performance on the basic arithmetic. While our estimates and experimental data suggest the asymptotic improvements of $\rho = 2$ are greater than the arithmetic overhead, this does not seem to be the case for larger values of ρ.

Bootstrapping Performance. As we move to the complete bootstrapping, we introduce the overhead of calculating several key switchings, but we also can further optimize the INTT evaluation. As we defined, it outputs GSW ciphertexts, from which we extract CLWE samples in the message extraction phase. A more efficient way of implementing it is to run the last recombination step (Lines 12 to 15 in Algorithm 6) already using a CLWE as the accumulator for the summations, replacing GSW multiplications with external products. Further, we can also initialize the accumulator with the test vector at the beginning of this last recombination (similarly as introduced in [11]), which simplifies the message extraction and reduces the output error, as explained in Remark 1. This also allows us to use a smaller modulus, with $\ell = 3$. Table 4 shows the results for complete bootstrapping, including key switchings, with $\rho = 2$ and $p^* = 2^{24}$. The failure probabilities for 7 and 8-bit messages are $2^{-62.4}$ and $2^{-17.2}$, respectively. The parameters $\ell = 4$ and $\ell = 3$ are similar in terms of bootstrapping capabilities, but using $\ell = 4$ reduces σ_{out} significantly (in up 2^{49} times for our parameters), enabling variations of our bootstrapping as we exemplify in Sect. 5.3.

Table 4. Execution time, in milliseconds, for the amortized bootstrapping.

p	n	$\ell = d$	Total Time	Amortized Time
12289	1024	3	871,827	851
		4	1,540,075	1,504

5.3   Comparison with Other Bootstrapping Methods

As the output of the bootstrapping is a set of LWE ciphertexts defined modulo Q, one can classify the bootstrapping algorithms in two categories depending on the size of Q as follows: (1) when Q is small enough to fit into native integer types; (2) when Q is large and double-CRT techniques are needed. The first scenario yields the fastest bootstrapping algorithms known until now, as the ones implemented in TFHE-RS [1], but it is less general, since the output ciphertexts have little noise budget and all the subsequent homomorphic evaluation is done via programmable bootstrapping. The second scenario is more versatile, since we can increase Q to obtain refreshed ciphertexts with more noise budget so that we can compute on them without using programmable bootstrapping. In particular, some constructions require large Q. For example, if one uses scheme switchings, such as Chimera [8], where the slots of a BGV ciphertext are extracted into individual LWE ciphertexts, then functional bootstrapping is applied on each of them, then one needs the output to be defined modulo a large Q so that it is possible to pack the LWE ciphertexts again into a BGV ciphertext. As another example, the high-precision CKKS bootstrapping presented in [21] also requires large Q. Thus, we divide our comparison in those two cases.

Comparison with Small-Q Bootstrapping Algorithms. Our amortized bootstrapping produces ciphertexts with large Q, hence this comparison is complicated, since these two types of bootstrapping offer different capabilities, and unfair, since using small Q allows one to implement the bootstrapping using native integer types, which represents a much faster arithmetic back end compared to double-CRT. Nonetheless, this section contains some discussion about this comparison. The state-of-the art implementation of programmable bootstrapping is TFHE-RS [1]. To achieve their impressive performance, they rely on binary secrets, on an FFT library specially tailored for negacyclic rings used in RLWE, and on small (word-sized) modulus. These are all particularities not shared by our scheme. Furthermore, we must note that the performance of such library is the result of several years of extensive research on techniques, parameters, and implementation optimizations [4]. Whereas, the goal of our implementation is just to provide a the first proof of concept of an entirely novel bootstrapping method, and further research on optimal choice of parameters or implementation optimizations are out of our scope.

All that said, we notice that TFHE-RS bootstraps 8-bit messages in 828.1 ms [1], which is only 3% faster than our amortized time in the same machine.

Comparison with Large-Q Bootstrapping Algorithms. To have a comparable non-amortized version of our bootstrapping, we implemented, using double-CRT, the algorithm defined in [23], which is the latest bootstrapping method for TFHE-like schemes. We start with the implementation of the accumulator using the double-CRT CLWE variant of the GSW scheme described in Sect. 3. We estimate noise using Equation (4), but consider $N = 0$ as we do not have the ring packing in this version. We choose parameters that enable similar bootstrapping capabilities for both methods and optimize performance by minimizing the dimension n. The main restriction for this process is the security level of the input. Specifically, we work with sparse ternary keys to minimize the noise, and we need to perform a key switching from dimensions $p = 12289$ to n, which requires an output modulus of at least $p^* \approx 2^{21}$ to accommodate the noise. Considering this, $n = 896$ is the smallest dimension for which the input ring is secure. We could lower n by using Gaussian keys with a larger distribution σ_s, but it is advantageous to avoid the quadratic impact of σ_s compared to the linear impact of n in the square norm of s (third term of Eq. (4)).

Thus, considering $n = 896$, $\ell = d = 2$, and $p = 12289$, the running time we obtained was around 2.9 s, which is 3.4 times slower than our best amortized running times presented in Table 4. The failure probabilities for 7 and 8-bit messages are $2^{-58.5}$ and $2^{-16.3}$, respectively.

5.4   Comparison to Concurrent Work

Liu and Wang developed two new amortized bootstrapping algorithms that also lead to security based on worst-case lattice problems with polynomial approximation factors. The first paper, [24], proposes a new slot structure for the plaintext space of GSW by computing homomorphic trace functions after each homomorphic multiplication. By using r slots, one can then bootstrap r ciphertexts at once. Thus, they obtain a bootstrapping with an amortized cost of $O(\lambda^{0.75} \cdot \log(\lambda)^k)$ GSW multiplications, for some constant $k \in \mathbb{N}$. Therefore, their bootstrapping is still more expensive than ours in asymptotic terms, since even by just setting $\rho = 2$, we already obtain $O(\lambda^{0.5})$. The second paper, [25], uses the new slot technique from the first to implement a variation of [28] to achieve amortized time complexity $O(\log(\lambda)^k)$ for some integer constant $k \geq 2$. Therefore, their time complexity is better than ours. However, when concretely instantiated, it could be the case that our scheme would still be more efficient, since using $\rho = 2$, our cost is proportional to $2\sqrt{\lambda}$ and this is smaller than $\log(\lambda)^2$ for $\lambda < 6000$. This indicates that for their method to cost less GSW multiplications than ours, they would need to instantiate their scheme with large and unrealistic security level (around 6000) instead of the usual $\lambda = 128$ or $\lambda = 256$.

Recently, Micheli *et al.* [29] proposed a method similar to ours for implementing the amortized bootstrapping of FHEW [13]. As [24,25], however, their work remained purely theoretical, not addressing practical performance or implementation challenges. Key differences in their ideas are the use of prime cyclotomics, which may allow slightly smaller ciphertexts but might introduce additional challenges for implementing the programmable bootstrapping. Moreover, instead of proposing automorphisms for GSW ciphertexts, they work with RLWE automorphisms and convert RLWE ciphertexts to GSW when needed. This approach seems similar to the optimization we introduced in Sect. 3.7).

Ultimately, while these papers provide important theoretical contributions towards efficient amortized bootstrapping, their constructions are still in a very early stage from a practical point of view. On the other hand, our paper is the first one to address the difficulties of instantiating this new bootstrapping framework and, therefore, the first one to present practical results.

5.5   Further Improvements

Since our results are comparable with the state-of-the-art programmable bootstrapping with small ciphertext modulus Q (even though our amortized bootstrapping uses large Q, and thus, needs double-CRT), and faster than non-amortized bootstrapping with large Q, we believe that we achieved the goal of showing that efficient amortized bootstrapping is possible and can be practical. Nonetheless, our implementation is a proof of concept and there are many promising techniques that could be applied to further improve performance. For example, using parameters from Table 4, our implementation requires 76.5 GiB of memory (for $\ell = 3$). However, considering only already existing techniques from the literature (e.g., decomposed automorphisms [23]), we could reduce it to less than 10 GiB of memory.

Acknowledgments. This work has been supported in part by Cyber Security Research Flanders with reference number VR20192203, by the Defence Advanced Research Projects Agency (DARPA) under contract No. HR0011-21-C-0034 DARPA DPRIVE BASALISC, and by the FWO under an Odysseus project GOH9718N. Any opinions, findings and conclusions or recommendations expressed in this material are those of the author(s) and do not necessarily reflect the views of DARPA, the US Government, or Cyber Security Research Flanders. The U.S. Government is authorized to reproduce and distribute reprints for governmental purposes notwithstanding any copyright annotation therein. This work was done while A. Guimarães was visiting the Department of Computer Science of Aarhus University. He is supported by the São Paulo Research Foundation under grants 2013/08293-7, 2019/12783-6, and 2021/09849-5.

References

1. zama-ai/tfhe-rs. (May 2023). https://github.com/zama-ai/tfhe-rs. Accessed 13 Oct 2022
2. Albrecht, M.R., Player, R., Scott, S.: On the concrete hardness of learning with errors. Cryptology ePrint Archive, Report 2015/046 (2015). https://eprint.iacr.org/2015/046
3. Alperin-Sheriff, J., Peikert, C.: Faster bootstrapping with polynomial error. In: Garay, J.A., Gennaro, R. (eds.) CRYPTO 2014, Part I. LNCS, vol. 8616, pp. 297–314. Springer, Heidelberg (Aug 2014). https://doi.org/10.1007/978-3-662-44371-2_17

4. Bergerat, L., et al.: Parameter optimization and larger precision for (T)FHE. Cryptology ePrint Archive, Report 2022/704 (2022). https://eprint.iacr.org/2022/704
5. Boemer, F., Kim, S., Seifu, G., de Souza, F.D., Gopal, V.: Intel HEXL: accelerating homomorphic encryption with intel AVX512-IFMA52. Cryptology ePrint Archive, Report 2021/420 (2021). https://eprint.iacr.org/2021/420
6. Bonnoron, G., Ducas, L., Fillinger, M.: Large FHE gates from tensored homomorphic accumulator. In: Joux, A., Nitaj, A., Rachidi, T. (eds.) AFRICACRYPT 18. LNCS, vol. 10831, pp. 217–251. Springer, Heidelberg (May 2018). https://doi.org/10.1007/978-3-319-89339-6_13
7. Bonte, C., Iliashenko, I., Park, J., Pereira, H.V.L., Smart, N.P.: FINAL: faster FHE instantiated with NTRU and LWE. In: Agrawal, S., Lin, D. (eds.) ASIACRYPT 2022, Part II. LNCS, vol. 13792, pp. 188–215. Springer, Heidelberg (Dec 2022). https://doi.org/10.1007/978-3-031-22966-4_7
8. Boura, C., Gama, N., Georgieva, M., Jetchev, D.: Chimera: Combining ring-IWE-based fully homomorphic encryption schemes. J. Math. Cryptol. 14(1), 316–338 (2020). https://doi.org/10.1515/jmc-2019-0026
9. Brakerski, Z., Gentry, C., Halevi, S.: Packed ciphertexts in LWE-based homomorphic encryption. In: Kurosawa, K., Hanaoka, G. (eds.) PKC 2013. LNCS, vol. 7778, pp. 1–13. Springer, Heidelberg (Feb/Mar 2013). https://doi.org/10.1007/978-3-642-36362-7_1
10. Brakerski, Z., Gentry, C., Vaikuntanathan, V.: (Leveled) fully homomorphic encryption without bootstrapping. In: Goldwasser, S. (ed.) ITCS 2012, pp. 309–325. ACM (Jan 2012). https://doi.org/10.1145/2090236.2090262
11. Chillotti, I., Gama, N., Georgieva, M., Izabachène, M.: Faster fully homomorphic encryption: bootstrapping in less than 0.1 seconds. In: Cheon, J.H., Takagi, T. (eds.) ASIACRYPT 2016, Part I. LNCS, vol. 10031, pp. 3–33. Springer, Heidelberg (Dec 2016). https://doi.org/10.1007/978-3-662-53887-6_1
12. Chillotti, I., Gama, N., Georgieva, M., Izabachène, M.: TFHE: fast fully homomorphic encryption over the torus. J. Cryptol. 33(1), 34–91 (2020). https://doi.org/10.1007/s00145-019-09319-x
13. Ducas, L., Micciancio, D.: FHEW: bootstrapping homomorphic encryption in less than a second. In: Oswald, E., Fischlin, M. (eds.) EUROCRYPT 2015, Part I. LNCS, vol. 9056, pp. 617–640. Springer, Heidelberg (Apr 2015). https://doi.org/10.1007/978-3-662-46800-5_24
14. Fan, J., Vercauteren, F.: Somewhat practical fully homomorphic encryption. Cryptology ePrint Archive, Report 2012/144 (2012). https://eprint.iacr.org/2012/144
15. Gentry, C.: Fully homomorphic encryption using ideal lattices. In: Mitzenmacher, M. (ed.) 41st ACM STOC, pp. 169–178. ACM Press (May/Jun 2009). https://doi.org/10.1145/1536414.1536440
16. Gentry, C., Halevi, S., Smart, N.P.: Fully homomorphic encryption with polylog overhead. In: Pointcheval, D., Johansson, T. (eds.) EUROCRYPT 2012. LNCS, vol. 7237, pp. 465–482. Springer, Heidelberg (Apr 2012). https://doi.org/10.1007/978-3-642-29011-4_28
17. Gentry, C., Sahai, A., Waters, B.: Homomorphic encryption from learning with errors: conceptually-simpler, asymptotically-faster, attribute-based. In: Canetti, R., Garay, J.A. (eds.) CRYPTO 2013, Part I. LNCS, vol. 8042, pp. 75–92. Springer, Heidelberg (Aug 2013). https://doi.org/10.1007/978-3-642-40041-4_5
18. Guimarães, A., Pereira, H.V.L., Leeuwen, B.V.: Amortized Bootstrapping Revisited: Simpler, Asymptotically-Faster, Implemented (2023). https://eprint.iacr.org/2023/014 Report Number: 014

19. Halevi, S., Polyakov, Y., Shoup, V.: An improved RNS variant of the BFV homomorphic encryption scheme. In: Matsui, M. (ed.) CT-RSA 2019. LNCS, vol. 11405, pp. 83–105. Springer, Heidelberg (Mar 2019). https://doi.org/10.1007/978-3-030-12612-4_5

20. Halevi, S., Shoup, V.: Bootstrapping for HElib. In: Oswald, E., Fischlin, M. (eds.) EUROCRYPT 2015, Part I. LNCS, vol. 9056, pp. 641–670. Springer, Heidelberg (Apr 2015). https://doi.org/10.1007/978-3-662-46800-5_25

21. Kim, A., et al.: General bootstrapping approach for RLWE-based homomorphic encryption. Cryptology ePrint Archive, Report 2021/691 (2021). https://eprint.iacr.org/2021/691

22. Kim, A., Polyakov, Y., Zucca, V.: Revisiting homomorphic encryption schemes for finite fields. In: Tibouchi, M., Wang, H. (eds.) ASIACRYPT 2021, Part III. LNCS, vol. 13092, pp. 608–639. Springer, Heidelberg (Dec 2021). https://doi.org/10.1007/978-3-030-92078-4_21

23. Lee, Y., et al.: Efficient FHEW bootstrapping with small evaluation keys, and applications to threshold homomorphic encryption. Cryptology ePrint Archive, Report 2022/198 (2022). https://eprint.iacr.org/2022/198

24. Liu, F.H., Wang, H.: Batch bootstrapping I: a new framework for SIMD bootstrapping in polynomial modulus. In: EUROCRYPT 2023, Part III. LNCS, vol. 14006, pp. 321–352. Springer, Heidelberg (2023). https://doi.org/10.1007/978-3-031-30620-4_11

25. Liu, F.H., Wang, H.: Batch bootstrapping II: bootstrapping polynomial modulus only requires $\tilde{O}(1)$ the multiplications amortization. In: EUROCRYPT 2023, Part III. LNCS, vol. 14006, pp. 353–384. Springer, Heidelberg (2023). https://doi.org/10.1007/978-3-031-30620-4_12

26. Lyubashevsky, V., Peikert, C., Regev, O.: On ideal lattices and learning with errors over rings. In: Gilbert, H. (ed.) EUROCRYPT 2010. LNCS, vol. 6110, pp. 1–23. Springer, Heidelberg (May/Jun 2010). https://doi.org/10.1007/978-3-642-13190-5_1

27. MATZOV: Report on the Security of LWE: Improved Dual Lattice Attack (Apr 2022). https://doi.org/10.5281/zenodo.6412487

28. Micciancio, D., Sorrell, J.: Ring packing and amortized FHEW bootstrapping. In: Chatzigiannakis, I., Kaklamanis, C., Marx, D., Sannella, D. (eds.) ICALP 2018. LIPIcs, vol. 107, pp. 100:1–100:14. Schloss Dagstuhl (Jul 2018).https://doi.org/10.4230/LIPIcs.ICALP.2018.100

29. Micheli, G.D., Kim, D., Micciancio, D., Suhl, A.: Faster Amortized FHEW bootstrapping using Ring Automorphisms (2023). https://eprint.iacr.org/2023/112. Report Number: 112

30. Nussbaumer, H.: Fast polynomial transform algorithms for digital convolution. IEEE Trans. Acoust. Speech Signal Process. **28**(2), 205–215 (1980)

31. Pereira, H.V.L.: Bootstrapping fully homomorphic encryption over the integers in less than one second. In: Garay, J. (ed.) PKC 2021, Part I. LNCS, vol. 12710, pp. 331–359. Springer, Heidelberg (May 2021). https://doi.org/10.1007/978-3-030-75245-3_13

32. Regev, O.: On lattices, learning with errors, random linear codes, and cryptography. In: Gabow, H.N., Fagin, R. (eds.) 37th ACM STOC, pp. 84–93. ACM Press (May 2005). https://doi.org/10.1145/1060590.1060603

Rotation Key Reduction for Client-Server Systems of Deep Neural Network on Fully Homomorphic Encryption

Joon-Woo Lee[1], Eunsang Lee[2(✉)], Young-Sik Kim[3(✉)], and Jong-Seon No[4]

[1] School of Computer Science and Engineering, Chung-Ang University, Seoul, Republic of Korea
`jwlee2815@cau.ac.kr`
[2] Department of Software, Sejong University, Seoul, Republic of Korea
`eslee3209@sejong.ac.kr`
[3] Department of Electrical Engineering and Computer Science, DGIST, Daegu, Republic of Korea
`ysk@dgist.ac.kr`
[4] Department of Electrical and Computer Engineering, INMC, Seoul National University, Seoul, Republic of Korea
`jsno@snu.ac.kr`

Abstract. In this paper, we propose a new concept of *hierarchical rotation key* for homomorphic encryption to reduce the burdens of the clients and the server running on the fully homomorphic encryption schemes such as Cheon-Kim-Kim-Song (CKKS) and Brakerski/Fan-Vercauteran (BFV) schemes. Using this concept, after the client generates and transmits only a small set of rotation keys to the server, the server can generate any required rotation keys from the public key and the smaller set of rotation keys that the client sent. This proposed method significantly reduces the communication cost of the client and the server, and the computation cost of the client. For example, if we implement the standard ResNet-18 network for the ImageNet dataset with the CKKS scheme, the server requires 617 rotation keys. It takes 145.1 s for the client with a personal computer to generate whole rotation keys and the total size is 115.7 GB. If we use the proposed two-level hierarchical rotation key system, the size of the rotation key set generated and transmitted by the client can be reduced from 115.7 GB to 2.91 GB (×1/39.8), and the client-side rotation key generation runtime is reduced from 145.1 s to 3.74 s (×38.8 faster) without any changes in any homomorphic operations to the ciphertexts. If we use the three-level hierarchical rotation key system, the size of the rotation key set generated and transmitted by the client can be further reduced from 1.54 GB (×1/75.1), and the client-side rotation key generation runtime is further reduced to 1.93 s (×75.2 faster) with a slight increase in the key-switching operation to the ciphertexts and further computation in the offline phase.

E. Lee and Y.-S. Kim—Co-corresponding authors.

J. Guo and R. Steinfeld (Eds.): ASIACRYPT 2023, LNCS 14443, pp. 36–68, 2023.
https://doi.org/10.1007/978-981-99-8736-8_2

Keywords: Brakerski/Fan-Vercauteran (BFV) schemes ·
Cheon-Kim-Kim-Song (CKKS) schemes · Fully homomorphic
encryption · Hierarchical rotation key · Privacy-preserving machine
learning

1 Introduction

Fully homomorphic encryption (FHE) is an encryption scheme which supports
the evaluation of arbitrary boolean or arithmetic operations on encrypted data.
It is a primary solution for the privacy issue of outsourcing computation, which
enables the clients to securely entrust enterprises to process their private information while preserving privacy. The main application includes machine learning
[14,25,26], genomic analysis [5,22,23], cloud services [24], and AI-as-a-service
(AIaaS) [31]. Especially, the privacy-preserving AIaaS system is deemed to be
one of the most promising techniques, where the clients provide the encrypted
data on the cloud and the server processes the data by using the deep neural
network, while preserving the privacy of clients' data. Thus, data privacy via
FHE is getting more important.

Among various FHE schemes, Cheon-Kim-Kim-Song (CKKS) [8,10] and
Brakerski/Fan-Vercauteran (BFV) [4,13] schemes are two of the most practical FHE schemes. They can support arithmetic operations for complex numbers
or integers in the single-instruction multiple-data (SIMD) manner. Thus, several
data can be encrypted in one ciphertext, and one homomorphic operation can
simultaneously perform component-wise operations on these multiple message
data. Since the CKKS scheme deals with real or complex number data and supports approximate computation on the encrypted real or complex data, it fits
the situation allowing approximate computation. On the other hand, the BFV
scheme deals with integer data and supports exact computation on the encrypted
integer data, and it fits the situation requiring exact computation. The CKKS
and BFV schemes also support rotation operation, corresponding to a cyclic
shift of message data within a ciphertext. Specifically, it means the cyclic shift
operations for the encrypted message vector in that of the CKKS scheme and for
rows of the encrypted matrix in one ciphertext of the BFV scheme. The homomorphic rotation operation is inevitable if we require operations between data at
different locations in one ciphertext, such as the bootstrapping [2,6,7,28,29], the
matrix multiplication [19], and the convolution in convolutional neural networks
[21,25,26].

In order for the server to perform a rotation operation, an evaluation key for
the operation is required, called a *rotation key*. In the client-server model, the
client owns the data but wants to delegate the data processing operations to the
server, and the server handles the client's data with abundant computational
resources instead of the client. Therefore, a secret key capable of decrypting the
encrypted data is privately owned by the client. The server should ask the client
for a rotation key because the secret key is required to generate these rotation
keys. Then the client generates rotation keys with the secret key and sends them
to the server. It is similar to generating a public key from a private key in a

public key encryption system. (In this paper, the public key only refers to the key used for encryption.) If the rotation of several types of cyclic shifts is required in the homomorphic computation, a distinct rotation key is required for each cyclic shift. Therefore, the server should identify all the cyclic shifts of rotation operation in its computation model in advance and request the corresponding rotation keys to the client. However, this causes several serious problems when trying to use FHE in the industry, as in the following subsection.

1.1   Rotation Key Problems

Communication Costs for Rotation Keys. In the case of complex systems such as machine learning systems, there are many cyclic shifts required for servers to perform the computation model homomorphically. Therefore, the number of the rotation keys that the client has to transmit becomes very large, and the amount of communication that the client and the server should bear dramatically increases. For example, assume that we implement the standard ResNet-20 network for the CIFAR-10 dataset with pre-trained parameters on the CKKS scheme with the polynomial modulus degree $N = 2^{16}$ using the techniques in [25]. Then the size of all 32767 ($= 2^{15} - 1$) rotation keys is about 13 TB, which is an extremely large size to be sent from the client. If the server requests only the required rotation keys for the ResNet-20 network, the server requires 265 rotation keys, corresponding to transmission of 105.6 GB. If we design the ResNet-18 network for the ImageNet dataset using the same techniques, 617 rotation keys are required, and it occupies 197.6 GB of memory in the server.

Computational Costs in the Client. The computational cost for generating whole rotation keys is also a huge burden on the client. Since the client is assumed not to have high-performance computing devices, the runtime for generating these huge amounts of rotation keys can be very large. For example, even if we have a computer with an AMD Ryzen Threadripper PRO 3995WX CPU processor, a high-performance CPU, it takes 13 min to generate whole rotation keys, which is too long to wait for generating keys. Thus, it is desirable to reduce the runtime for rotation key generation in the client.

Lack of Flexibility for Various Services. The server may need to support various services for the client. In this case, the server should request a distinct rotation key set required for each service to the client. Whenever a new computation model is added or an existing model is modified in the server, a new rotation key set should be requested. It is a serious problem for the client because the client has to send a new rotation key set whenever the server's computational model is improved and updated. Someone may think that the server simply needs to receive all kinds of rotation keys in advance because of the uncertainty of the model. However, for CKKS schemes using $N = 2^{16}$, this solution is virtually impossible because generating all kinds of rotation keys requires the transmission and storage of 13 TB of rotation keys.

Information Leakage of Computation Model. The server should find what kind of cyclic shifts is used in the computation model and request the corresponding rotation keys to the client. However, based on the type of cyclic shifts required by the server, the client can reasonably infer some information about the computation model of the server. These computational models are important secret assets of the server, and thus they usually do not want to leak any information about the computational model to the client. To solve this situation, the server may deliberately request additional unnecessary rotation keys to confuse the client so that it does not infer, but it causes additional communication and computation costs by increasing the amount of rotation keys to be requested.

Inefficient Memory Management. Since the server usually handles a large number of clients, a large amount of memory is required to store their rotation keys. For example, if a server handles 10,000 clients and requires 500 GB of memory per client to store rotation keys for several specific services, 5000 TB of memory is required only to store their rotation keys. If each client uses the service infrequently, the server may want to reduce the memory share of the rotation key by temporarily removing the rotation keys that are not currently in use and generating them again when necessary. However, once the rotation keys are removed, the server should request the client to generate and transmit them again.

1.2   Our Contributions

In the conventional rotation key system in CKKS and BFV schemes, all rotation keys should have been generated only through secret keys. However, in the proposed new hierarchical rotation key system, all rotation keys can be generated from public keys or other rotation keys without generating them from secret keys. Specifically, the client creates a small number of so-called "master rotation keys" and sends them to the server with the public key. The server can then generate all required rotation keys from the public key by using the "master rotation keys." That is, the server may convert the public key into a rotation key corresponding to an arbitrary cyclic shift.

We find that the "master rotation key," which allows servers to convert public keys into rotation keys, can be designed by placing a hierarchy on the rotation keys. Therefore, we name the proposed rotation key system the *hierarchical rotation key system*. Rotation keys in the higher level can be used to generate rotation keys in the lower level. The previously mentioned "master rotation key" corresponds to a rotation key in the highest level, and the rotation keys for services are rotation keys in the lowest (level-0) level. These levels are divided according to the size of the total modulus of each rotation key and the special modulus values used.

We propose two fundamental key generation algorithms in the hierarchical rotation key system. The first is a PubToRot algorithm that generates a low-level r-shift rotation key from the public key by using the high-level r-shift rotation key. The second is a RotToRot algorithm that generates a low-level

$r + r'$-shift rotation key from a low-level r'-shift rotation key by using a high-level r-shift rotation key. If the client generates and sends a highest-level rotation key set corresponding to cyclic shift set $S = \{r_0, r_1, \cdots, r_{t-1}\}$ to the server, the server can generate the required lower-level $\sum_{i=0}^{t-1} w_i r_i$-shift rotation keys for some non-negative integers w_i's from the public key by sequentially computing PubToRot operations and RotToRot operations. If the client generates and sends the highest-level rotation keys for cyclic shifts of the powers of some integer p, the server can generate any rotation keys by using p-ary number system. If the server needs to generate a set of many low-level rotation keys simultaneously, it can make the most existing low-level rotation keys to generate each low-level rotation key with minimal operations.

The key idea for the proposed hierarchical rotation key system is that the rotation keys can be generated by using rotation operation to the other rotation keys or the public key. In the proposed hierarchical rotation key system, a public key is treated as a single ciphertext and each rotation key is treated as a set of ciphertexts. If we perform the rotation operation to each ciphertext in a rotation key, a new rotation key for other cyclic shifts can be derived. Since the rotation operation requires a rotation key with a larger modulus than the ciphertext, the rotation key for this rotation key generation should have a higher level than the newly generated rotation key. Thus, we propose to set some hierarchy in the rotation keys by the modulus size. We define the rotation key with a larger modulus as the rotation in 'higher key level'. Thus, each rotation key can generate rotation keys with a lower key level. The client-server system using the hierarchical rotation key system has the following improvements compared to the conventional client-server system using FHE schemes, which solves the above five key problems completely.

i) The communication cost between the client and the server is significantly reduced because the clients only need to transmit a small set of high-level rotation keys.
ii) The computation cost of the client is reduced since the clients can generate only a small set of rotation keys.
iii) Even if multiple services need to be requested by the client or the computation model changes in the middle of the services, the server can create the additional rotation keys without additional requests to the client, making the service more flexible.
iv) Since the server can generate the rotation keys with cyclic shifts required for its computation model, it does not have to disclose this information to the client, preventing information leakage about the computation model.
v) The server can temporarily remove unused rotation keys and regenerate them through high-level rotation keys when needed, thereby significantly lowering the overall memory share of the rotation keys.

Figure 1 shows an example using a hierarchical rotation key system. Figure 1(a) illustrates a case when an FHE-based service is provided with a conventional method. If the server can provide various types of services for each client, the client must generate and transmit all the rotation keys required for

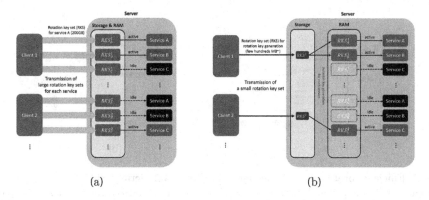

(a)   (b)

Fig. 1. Comparison of conventional rotation key system and hierarchical rotation key system for HE-based services in the client-server model (a) Conventional rotation key system (b) The proposed hierarchical rotation key system.

each service to the server. Therefore, when there are many services that can be provided, the burden on the client increases. Even if the client is currently using only a specific service, there is a burden that the server must store all the rotation keys corresponding to all services that the client is not using. Figure 1(b) shows a case when a hierarchical rotation key system is used. Regardless of how many services are used or how complex the operation is required, the client only needs to send the few high-level rotation keys that the server needs to create rotation keys. In the case of homomorphic encryption parameters that support bootstrapping, communication amount can be reduced from a few hundred GB to several hundred MB. Thereafter, the server can generate rotation keys suitable for the service to be requested by the client and use them for the service. In addition, in the case of a service that the client does not use immediately, the corresponding rotation keys may be removed to use the memory efficiently. If the client wants to resume these services, it can generate and send rotation keys directly with high-level rotation keys to provide the service.

For the contribution 2, some readers may think that the computation amount of the client has simply shifted to the server, and there is no improvement in terms of computation amount. However, due to the nature of the client-server model, which is appropriate for FHE, the server can use high-performance machines and is ready for abundant operations, but the client is not supposed to have high-performance machines and wants to do minimal operations. For this reason, it is a desirable direction in the client-server model that the burden of clients is reduced by transferring a lot of the computational burden of clients to servers, and recent studies related to HE focus on this direction [11,15].

If the hierarchies of rotation keys are further subdivided, various trade-offs can be adjusted. For example, the fewer high-level rotation keys a client creates, the more time the server will need to generate the rotation key. But if there is a hierarchy with three types of key levels, we can mitigate this trade-off. Assume that there is an interval between the time when the rotation keys are transmitted and the time when the service is provided. Then, as in Fig. 2, the

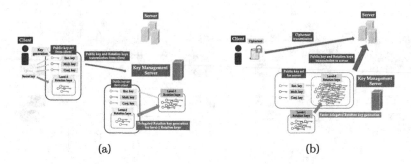

(a)   (b)

Fig. 2. Efficient rotation key management in three-level hierarchical rotation key generation. (a) Public key and level-2 rotation key transmission from the client and preparation for faster level-0 rotation key generation by generating level-1 rotation keys in advance. (b) Faster rotation key generation from public key and level-1 rotation keys.

server can generate a more intermediate level of rotation keys after receiving the highest level of rotation keys. When the server prepares to provide the service (Fig. 2(a)), it is possible to use the highest-level rotation keys and the middle-level rotation keys to generate the required (lowest-level) rotation keys for the service more quickly (Fig. 2(b)). To increase the degree of freedom in rotation key management in this way, we propose a generalized hierarchical rotation key system at multiple key levels.

We further propose several optimization methods for servers to generate keys more efficiently. In most cases, the server must generate a bundle of rotation keys required for a specific service at once. When multiple rotation keys are generated at once, there are many situations in which several types of rotation keys should be generated from one rotation key. In this situation, a *hoisting technique* that can be processed by merging some of the key generation operations is specifically proposed. This reduces the amount of computation by about half. In addition, the amount of computation varies greatly depending on the order of rotation key generation. Finding an efficient generating order for optimization of computation amount can be reduced to a minimum spanning tree problem, which can be solved using Prim's algorithm or Edmonds' algorithm.

We conduct the simulation with the proposed rotation key generation system for the ResNet-20 model with the CIFAR-10 dataset and ResNet-18 model with the ImageNet dataset using an appropriate computing environment for the client-server model. If we implement the standard ResNet-20 network for the CIFAR-10 dataset and the ResNet-18 network for the ImageNet dataset with the CKKS scheme, the server requires 265 and 617 rotation keys. It takes 88.7 s and 145.1 s for the client with a personal computer to generate whole rotation keys and the total size is 38.3 GB and 115.7 GB, respectively.

If we use the proposed two-level hierarchical rotation key system to the ResNet-20 model and the ResNet-18 model, the size of the rotation keys generated and transmitted by the client can be reduced from 38.3 GB to 8.31 GB ($\times 1/4.61$) and from 115.7 GB to 2.91 GB ($\times 1/39.8$), respectively. The client-side rotation key generation runtime is reduced from 88.7 s to 18.9 s (×4.69 faster) and from 145.1 s to 3.74 s (×38.8 faster) without changing any homomorphic operations to the ciphertexts. The server-side rotation key generation requires 16.6 s and 12.5 s. If we may need to make the rotation key generation more efficient at the expense of slightly increasing the key-switching operation time for the ResNet-20 model and the ResNet-18 model, the communication amount for rotation keys significantly reduced to 2.67 GB (×1/14.3) and 1.97 GB (×1/58.7), respectively. The client-side rotation key generation runtime is reduced to 6.30 s (×14.1 faster) and 2.52 s (×57.6 faster), respectively. The server-side rotation key generation requires 10.2 s and 16.1 s. If we use the three-level hierarchical rotation key system for the ResNet-18 model, the size of the rotation key set generated and transmitted by the client can be further reduced to 1.54 GB (×1/75.1), and the client-side rotation key generation runtime is further reduced to 1.93 s (×1/75.2) with a slight increase in the key-switching operation to the ciphertexts and further computation in the offline phase.

Thus, our contribution can be summarized as follows.

- We point out that the rotation key problem of homomorphic ciphers causes many practical problems in the client-server model and propose a concept of a hierarchical rotation key system that can solve these problems.
- To implement a hierarchical rotation key system, fundamental algorithms that can convert the public key into rotation keys were designed to allow the server to generate arbitrary rotation keys from the public key.
- We propose optimization methods that can effectively reduce the computation amount of the server when it needs to generate many kinds of rotation keys.
- We conduct the simulations showing that we can reduce the computational and communication volumes of clients needed for the machine learning services with the ResNet models for the CIFAR-10 or the ImageNet by ×4 ~ ×75.

1.3   Related Works

Benes Network and Composition of Rotation Operations. Halevi and Shoup [16] suggested a method for any permutation on ciphertext with only $\log n$ types of rotation cyclic shift, where n is the number of slots. It uses the fact that all permutations can be represented as a weighted sum of the $\log n$ number of shifted vectors with fixed different cyclic shifts. If the server has only $\log n$ types of rotation keys for different cyclic shifts, all permutations on ciphertext can be performed with the weighted sum of the $\log n$ number of ciphertexts performed by rotation operation with different corresponding cyclic shifts. Thus, if we want to rotate the ciphertext with a specific cyclic shift that is different from the designated cyclic shift from the rotation keys the server has, we can deal with this rotation as a type of permutation so that this can also be performed with the above operation.

However, this simple technique has a crucial drawback in the latency for homomorphic computation. Since the rotation operation is one of the most time-consuming homomorphic operations among the elementary homomorphic operations, the number of rotation operations is very sensitive in that it has a direct effect on the whole latency. If there are many required types of cyclic shift for the rotation operation in the homomorphic computation and the server has whole corresponding types of rotation keys, the server may perform only one rotation operation for each cyclic shift. But if the server has only $\log n$ types of rotation keys with the same situation, the server should perform several rotation operations on average for each cyclic shift. For the simple experiment for the ResNet-20 network model in [25] performed with CPU, the latency of this model becomes 1471.2 s with Benes network while the latency of this model is 646.8 s without Benes, which is a $\times 2.27$ slower result. As the reduction of the long runtime in homomorphic operation is the most sensitive issue in PPML on HE, the simple application of technique in [16] is not desirable. This point is actually the key motivation for this proposal of the hierarchical rotation key concepts.

Our proposed technique solves this issue, in that the clients may generate and send only $\log n$ rotation keys rather than all required rotation keys, and the server can perform only one rotation operation for any cyclic shifts as the server generates any required rotation keys by itself. Since any previous techniques cannot replace this proposed technique for this purpose, the proposed technique is novel in the PPML on HE research area.

Similarly, there are many other techniques in which a slot vector in a ciphertext is rotated or permuted only with a fixed set of rotation keys. Note that the proposed technique does not correspond to this situation but is for the situation that each rotation operation for the ciphertext has to be performed with only one corresponding rotation key because of the efficient latency for ciphertext processing. We perform the key-switching operation with a fixed set of high-level rotation keys to the "rotation keys", not to the "ciphertexts", which are essentially different techniques.

Transciphering Technique. The aim of this work is very similar to the works for the *transciphering technique* [11,15]. These two studies aimed to reduce the computational burden and communication burden of the client by making the server bear the computational load of the client. These studies focused on the client's encryption process and the transmission of ciphertexts. In the case of FHE, it is burdensome for clients to encrypt their data and transmit ciphertexts because the amount of computation used in the encryption process is larger and the size of the ciphertext is larger than that of the symmetric key encryption system. Therefore, these studies proposed algorithms to convert symmetric key ciphertexts into ciphertexts in FHE without a secret key. If the client encrypts data through the encryption process of the symmetric key encryption system and sends it to the server, the server can convert the symmetric key ciphertext into the ciphertext in FHE, reducing the client's computation and communication burden. These studies also mainly mention that the computational power of servers is overwhelmingly stronger than that of clients.

Our paper is the first to note that the same problem is prominent in the rotation keys in homomorphic encryption and to present a solution. In particular, when implementing a privacy-preserving machine learning system using FHE, the size of the encrypted image is hundreds of MB, but the size of the rotation keys required to perform one advanced machine learning system is hundreds of GB. Therefore, in order to apply the machine learning system using FHE to the industry, it is much more important to study the solution to a similar problem as in the transciphering technique. In this respect, our work is consistent with recent research directions in designing FHE systems suitable for client-server systems.

Privacy-Preserving Deep Neural Networks on FHE. CNN models were implemented using only leveled HE that does not use bootstrapping. The types and numbers of operations available on these CNNs were very limited. The operations used in the model were forced to be modified to be easy to compute on FHE, and the number of layers used was also very limited. Recently, the results of successfully implementing the deep neural network on FHE by actively utilizing bootstrapping operations have been presented [25,26]. In these studies, the ResNet model, a renowned CNN model with verified classification performance in plaintext, was performed on FHE using the same pre-trained parameters. In particular, in the study of Lee et al. [25], a ResNet model with 110 layers was also successfully implemented on the CKKS scheme.

We find that the massive size of the rotation key is a major obstacle to making this privacy-preserving machine learning system practical when implementing such a complex advanced machine learning system with FHE. Previously, the size of the rotation keys was not a problem because only simple computation models were used. However, bootstrapping operations and various kinds of convolution operations were used in the advanced computation model, which greatly increased the size of the rotation keys to hundreds of GB. Our work can be seen as the study that solves the most significant problem at this point in time when the study of performing advanced computational models with FHE began.

1.4 Outline

Section 2 formalizes the concept of the hierarchical rotation key system and its application to the specific rotation key management. Section 3 deals with the proposed hierarchical rotation key generation algorithm for CKKS and BFV schemes. Section 4 proposes algorithms for efficiently generating a set of rotation keys with the given set of rotation keys in the higher levels. Section 5 suggests a concrete example of the rotation key management protocol and shows the numerical simulation results with ResNet models. Section 6 concludes the paper and suggests future work.[1]

---

[1] The full version of the paper [27] includes the preliminaries, the proofs of the theorems, and the required cyclic shifts for ResNet models.

2 Concept of Hierarchical Rotation Key System

In this section, we provide an overview of the proposed hierarchical rotation key system. Specific procedures in this system will be described in Sects. 3 and 4.

2.1 Definition of Hierarchical Rotation Key System

We define the hierarchical rotation key system in the cloud computing using FHE. In a k-level hierarchical rotation key system, there are k sets of rotation keys with a hierarchy from a key level $k - 1$ to 0. Each rotation key can be used to generate rotation keys in the lower levels. The additional algorithms for the hierarchical rotation key system are InitRotKeyGen and RotKeyGen. The algorithm InitRotKeyGen generates a set of the highest key-level rotation keys, performed by the client with the secret key. The algorithm RotKeyGen generates a set of intermediate or zero key-level rotation keys using the public key and the set of higher key-level rotation keys. This algorithm is performed by the server or the key management server (KMS) having no secret key. We now assume that the public key and hierarchical rotation keys are managed by the KMS collocated with or separated from the server, and all protocols in the paper also make sense when the KMS and the server are united. These two algorithms are defined as follows, where k denotes the total number of key levels.

- InitRotKeyGen$(s, \mathcal{T}_{k-1}) \rightarrow \{gk_i^{(k-1)}\}_{i \in \mathcal{T}_{k-1}}$: Given a secret key s and a set of cyclic shifts $\mathcal{T}_{k-1}$, generate the rotation keys with cyclic shifts in $\mathcal{T}_{k-1}$ in the highest key level in the client.
- RotKeyGen$(\ell, \mathcal{U}_\ell, \{gk_i^{(\ell_i)}\}_{i \in \mathcal{U}_\ell}, pk, \mathcal{T}_\ell) \rightarrow \{gk_i^{(\ell)}\}_{i \in \mathcal{T}_\ell}$: Given a public key pk, a set of the rotation keys $\{gk_i^{(\ell_i)}\}_{i \in \mathcal{U}_\ell}$ with cyclic shifts in $\mathcal{U}_\ell$ in the key level ℓ_i higher that ℓ, and a set of cyclic shifts $\mathcal{T}_\ell$, generate the rotation keys with cyclic shifts in $\mathcal{T}_\ell$ in key level ℓ in the KMS.

The rotation key $gk_i^{(\ell)}$ denotes the rotation key for the cyclic shift i in the key level ℓ, whose specific definition will be dealt with in Sect. 3. Although the public key pk is represented separately from the rotation keys, the rotation keys are also public in that these keys can be opened to the public. The set of cyclic shifts for each key level, which is an integer set, is denoted by $\mathcal{T}_0, \cdots, \mathcal{T}_{k-1}$, respectively. These sets are pairwisely disjoint. The set of cyclic shifts for each key level higher than ℓ whose rotation keys are generated in advance, is denoted by $\mathcal{U}_\ell$. If all desired rotation keys in the key level higher than ℓ are all generated, $\mathcal{U}_\ell$ is equal to $\bigcup_{i=\ell+1}^{k-1} \mathcal{T}_i$. The conventional rotation key system can be seen as a special case of the proposed hierarchical rotation key system, where there is only the algorithm InitRotKeyGen, and the number of key levels in the hierarchy is one.

2.2 Rotation Key Generation Protocol in Hierarchical Rotation Key System

In our k-level hierarchical rotation key system, we consider both of the following cases: (1) *active* case when a client frequently requests a service and (2) *inactive* case when a service is not used often by a client or what service to be used is not determined. In the active case, since the generation of level-0 rotation keys repetitively for each service is inefficient, it is better to generate level-0 rotation keys in advance to reduce latency. In this case, the server should hold level-0 rotation keys, which takes up some memory. On the other hand, in the case of inactive, it is desirable to generate only rotation keys of level 1 to $k-1$ in advance to remove unnecessary memory usage of level-0 rotation keys. In this way, our system can finely control the trade-off of memory and latency according to the frequency of service. The specific protocols are described in Algorithm 1.

Algorithm 1: Key Management of Hierarchical Rotation Key System with the k Key Levels

---

Input: Encryption parameters *params* for k-level rotation key system (client and server), a set of cyclic shifts for rotation keys in the highest key level $\mathcal{T}_{k-1}$ (client), sets of cyclic shifts for intermediate key-level rotation keys $\mathcal{T}_{k-2}, \cdots, \mathcal{T}_1$ (server), and a homomorphic service $\mathcal{S}$ (server)

Output: A set of rotation keys $\{gk_i^{(0)}\}_{i \in \mathcal{T}_0}$ (server)

Key generation and transmission in client

1. $sk \leftarrow \mathsf{SecGen}(1^\lambda, params)$
2. $pk \leftarrow \mathsf{PubGen}(sk)$
3. $\{gk_i^{(k-1)}\}_{i \in \mathcal{T}_{k-1}} \leftarrow \mathsf{InitRotKeyGen}(s, \mathcal{T}_{k-1})$
4. Transmit $(pk, \{gk_i^{(k-1)}\}_{i \in \mathcal{T}_{k-1}})$ to the server and let $\mathcal{G} = \{gk_i^{(k-1)}\}_{i \in \mathcal{T}_{k-1}}$

Inactive phase: generating rotation keys in the key level $\ell(>1)$

1. $\{gk_i^{(\ell)}\}_{i \in \mathcal{T}_\ell} \leftarrow \mathsf{RotKeyGen}(\ell, \mathcal{U}_\ell, \{gk_i^{(\ell_i)}\}_{i \in \mathcal{U}_\ell}, pk, \mathcal{T}_\ell)$
2. $\mathcal{G} \leftarrow \mathcal{G} \cup \{gk_i^{(\ell)} : i \in \mathcal{T}_\ell\}$

Active phase: generating level-0 rotation keys in server

1. $\mathcal{T}_0 \leftarrow \mathsf{ExtractRotSet}(\mathcal{S})$
2. $\{gk_i^{(0)}\}_{i \in \mathcal{T}_0} \leftarrow \mathsf{RotKeyGen}(0, \mathcal{U}_\ell, \{gk_i^{(1)}\}_{i \in \mathcal{T}_\ell}, pk, \mathcal{T}_0)$

---

3 Proposed Hierarchical Rotation Key System for CKKS and BFV Schemes

In this section, the hierarchical rotation key system for CKKS and BFV schemes is proposed. The CKKS and BFV schemes differ only in the packing structure, the decryption method, and the role of each operation for the encrypted data, but the key-switching operation itself is exactly the same. Thus, we will deal with them at once.

We use the term *ciphertext* as a pair of ring elements $(b, a) \in R_q^2$ for some modulus q. A ciphertext $(b, a) \in R_q^2$ is defined to be a valid ciphertext of m with the secret key s if $b + a \cdot s = m + e \mod q$, where e is a polynomial with small coefficients compared to q.

Let $Q = \prod_{i=0}^{\text{dnum}-1} Q_i$ be a product of several coprime positive integers Q_i's, and P be a positive integer which is coprime to and larger than Q_i's. A *rotation key* $\text{gk}_r = \{\text{gk}_{r,i}\}_{i=0,\cdots,\text{dnum}-1}$ for cyclic shift r with the secret key polynomial $s \in R$ is defined to be valid if each $\text{gk}_{r,i} = (b_{r,i}, a_{r,i}) \in R_{PQ}^2$ is a valid ciphertext of $P \cdot \hat{Q}_i \cdot [\hat{Q}_i^{-1}]_{Q_i} \cdot s(X^{5^r})$ with the secret key s, where $\hat{Q}_i = \prod_{j \neq i} Q_j$. This can be used for the key-switching operation to the ciphertext in the modulus q, where q is a divisor of Q. We call Q the evaluation modulus and P the special modulus.

These rotation keys are used in the rotation operation. The rotation operation of the CKKS scheme is an operation mapping $(v_i) \mapsto (v_{i+r})$ while encrypted, where the addition operation of the subscript is in modulo $N/2$ and N is the polynomial modulus degree. The rotation operation in the BFV scheme is an operation mapping $(v_{i,j}) \mapsto (v_{i,(j+r)})$ while encrypted. In terms of ring elements, these operations can be unified as operations mapping $m(X) \mapsto m(X^{5^r})$. For these operations, we first perform an operation of $(b(X), a(X)) \mapsto (b(X^{5^r}), a(X^{5^r}))$. This processed ciphertext satisfies $b(X^{5^r}) + a(X^{5^r}) \cdot s(X^{5^r}) \approx m(X^{5^r})$, which means that it is a ciphertext of a plaintext polynomial $m(X^{5^r})$ with the secret key $s(X^{5^r})$. We have to convert this ciphertext to a ciphertext of the same plaintext with the original secret key. This is done by taking the key-switching operation from $s(X^{5^r})$ to $s(X)$ using the rotation key for cyclic shift r.

3.1 Generation of Public Key and Rotation Keys in Client

The conventional schemes generate a public key (b, a) with the modulus $Q = \prod_{i=0}^{L} q_i$ because the special modulus is only used in the key-switching operation. In contrast, the proposed hierarchical rotation key generation scheme generates a public key (b, a) with $Q_{k-1} = \prod_{i=0}^{L_{k}-2} q_i$ to prepare to use it to generate rotation keys with key levels smaller than $k - 1$. The highest key-level rotation keys are generated by the client. The set of cyclic shifts $\mathcal{U}_\ell$ of rotation keys in the key level higher than ℓ should be the set that can generate all cyclic shifts $\mathcal{T}_\ell$ of rotation keys with the key level ℓ by the sum allowing repetition. The small size of $\mathcal{T}_{k-1}$ for the highest key level can reduce the computational burden and the communication cost of the client.

In the InitRotKeyGen operation for the proposed scheme, a single highest-level rotation key for cyclic shift r with the secret key polynomial $s \in R$ is the form of $\text{gk}_r^{(k-1)} = \{\text{gk}_{r,i}^{(k-1)}\}_{i=0,\cdots,\text{hdnum}_{k-1}-1}$, where $\text{gk}_{r,i}^{(k-1)} = (b_{r,i}^{(k-1)}, a_{r,i}^{(k-1)}) \in R_{Q_{k-1}P_{k-1}}^2$ such that $a_{r,i}^{(k-1)} \leftarrow R_{Q_{k-1}P_{k-1}}$ and $b_{r,i}^{(k-1)} = -a_{r,i}^{(k-1)} \cdot s + e_{r,i}^{(k-1)} + P_{k-1} \cdot \hat{Q}_{k-1,i} \cdot [\hat{Q}_{k-1,i}^{-1}]_{Q_{k-1,i}} \cdot s(X^{5^r})$ for $e_{r,i}^{(k-1)} \leftarrow \chi$. The RNS bases for $\text{gk}_{r,i}$ are $\mathcal{C} \cup \bigcup_{j=0}^{k-1} \mathcal{B}_j$. Note that the distribution and the form of the rotation keys generated by the client are the same as those in the conventional rotation key generation.

3.2   RotToRot and PubToRot Operations

Two types of operations are required to make the level-ℓ rotation keys for ℓ less than $k-1$. One is the operation PubToRot, which generates a level-ℓ rotation key from the public key, and the other is the operation RotToRot, which generates a level-ℓ rotation key from the existing level-ℓ rotation keys for the other cyclic shifts. The combination of PubToRot operation and RotToRot operation will generate all rotation keys with only the public key and rotation keys in the key level higher than ℓ.

Let the shift-r rotation key be defined as the rotation key for cyclic shift r, and let (r, ℓ) rotation key be defined as the rotation key for cyclic shift r in the key level ℓ. For the convenience of explanation, we will first explain the operation RotToRot. The operation RotToRot is an operation that generates a $(r + r', \ell)$ rotation key from a (r, ℓ) rotation key in the key level ℓ with a shift-r' rotation key in the key level higher than ℓ. To understand this operation, keep in mind that the rotation operation is a map $m(X) \mapsto m(X^{5^r})$ from the perspective of the plaintext polynomial. In other words, the rotation operation can be seen as an operation that generates a ciphertext of $m(X^{5^r})$ from a ciphertext of $m(X)$ [10]. We note that the rotation key for cyclic shift r is a set of ciphertexts $\mathsf{gk}_r^{(\ell)} = \{\mathsf{gk}_{r,i}^{(\ell)}\}_{i=0,\cdots,\text{hdnum}_\ell-1}$, where $\mathsf{gk}_{r,i}^{(\ell)} = (b_{r,i}^{(\ell)}, a_{r,i}^{(\ell)}) \in R_{Q_\ell P_\ell}^2$ and $b_{r,i}^{(\ell)} = -a_{r,i}^{(\ell)} \cdot s + e_{r,i}^{(\ell)} + P_\ell \cdot \hat{Q}_{\ell,i} \cdot [\hat{Q}_{\ell,i}^{-1}]_{Q_{\ell,i}} \cdot s(X^{5^r})$. Each $\mathsf{gk}_{r,i}^{(\ell)}$ is a ciphertext of $P_\ell \cdot \hat{Q}_{\ell,i} \cdot [\hat{Q}_{\ell,i}^{-1}]_{Q_{\ell,i}} \cdot s(X^{5^r})$. If we perform the rotation operation with cyclic shift r' on $\mathsf{gk}_{r,i}^{(\ell)}$, the output is a ciphertext of the following polynomial,

$$P_\ell \cdot \hat{Q}_{\ell,i} \cdot [\hat{Q}_{\ell,i}^{-1}]_{Q_{\ell,i}} \cdot s((X^{5^{r'}})^{5^r})$$

$$= P_\ell \cdot \hat{Q}_{\ell,i} \cdot [\hat{Q}_{\ell,i}^{-1}]_{Q_{\ell,i}} \cdot s(X^{5^{r+r'}}).$$

This rotation operation requires an (r', ℓ') rotation key $\mathsf{gk}_{r'}^{(\ell')}$, where ℓ' is higher than ℓ. If we define this output as $\mathsf{gk}_{r+r',i}^{(\ell)}$, the set $\mathsf{gk}_{r+r'}^{(\ell)} = \{\mathsf{gk}_{r+r',i}^{(\ell)}\}_{i=0,\cdots,\text{hdnum}_\ell-1}$ is a valid $(r + r', \ell)$ rotation key. We will call this operation RotToRot, as shown in Algorithm 2. The following theorem shows the correctness of RotToRot operation.[2]

Theorem 1. *The output of Algorithm 2 is a valid rotation key for the rotation operation for cyclic shift $r + r'$.*

Next, we will describe the operation PubToRot. Note that the above operation is useful only when some rotation keys exist. However, since the server receives no rotation key in the key level lower than $k - 1$ from the client, the rotation key should be generated first with the public key and rotation keys in the higher levels in the server. To this end, we can think of a formal shift-0 rotation key. If a shift-0 rotation key can be generated from a public key, a shift-r' rotation key can be generated by adding a RotToRot operation to the shift-0 rotation

---

[2] The proof can be found in the full version of the paper [27].

key for cyclic shift r'. By definition, the shift-0 rotation key should be the form of $\mathsf{gk}_0^{(\ell)} = \{\mathsf{gk}_{0,i}^{(\ell)}\}_{i=0,\cdots,\mathsf{hdnum}_\ell-1}$, where $\mathsf{gk}_{0,i}^{(\ell)} = (b_{0,i}^{(\ell)}, a_{0,i}^{(\ell)}) \in R_{Q_\ell P_\ell}^2$ and $b_{0,i}^{(\ell)} = -a_{0,i}^{(\ell)} \cdot s + e_{0,i}^{(\ell)} + P_\ell \cdot \hat{Q}_{\ell,i} \cdot [\hat{Q}_{\ell,i}^{-1}]_{Q_{\ell,i}} \cdot s$.

To generate $\mathsf{gk}_{0,i}^{(\ell)}$ from the public key $(b,a) \in R_{Q_{k-1}}^2$, we first reduce the public key to $(b',a') = (b \mod Q_\ell P_\ell, a \mod Q_\ell P_\ell) \in R_{Q_\ell P_\ell}^2$ by simply extracting values for corresponding RNS moduli. Then, we set as $b_{0,i}^{(\ell)} = b'$ and $a_{0,i}^{(\ell)} = a' + P_\ell \cdot \hat{Q}_{\ell,i} \cdot [\hat{Q}_{\ell,i}^{-1}]_{Q_{\ell,i}}$. Then, we can have $b_{0,i}^{(\ell)} = -a_{0,i}^{(\ell)} \cdot s + e_{0,i}^{(\ell)} + P_\ell \cdot \hat{Q}_{\ell,i} \cdot [\hat{Q}_{\ell,i}^{-1}]_{Q_{\ell,i}} \cdot s$. If we define $(b_{0,i}^{(\ell)}, a_{0,i}^{(\ell)})$ as $\mathsf{gk}_{0,i}^{(\ell)}$, the set $\mathsf{gk}_0^{(\ell)} = \{\mathsf{gk}_{0,i}^{(\ell)}\}_{i=0,\cdots,\mathsf{hdnum}_\ell-1}$ is a valid formal $(0,\ell)$ rotation key. Then we can generate a shift-r rotation key by performing a RotToRot operation on it with the (r,ℓ) rotation key.

In addition, we can optimize the operations further by combining the decomposition processes in the key-switching operation. Trivially, the decomposition process is performed hdnum_ℓ times if all the key-switching operations are performed in a black-box manner like RotToRot. Since the decomposition process is the heaviest operation in the key-switching operation [2], reducing the number of these processes is desirable. Rather than performing the decomposition process after adding $P_\ell \cdot \hat{Q}_{\ell,i} \cdot [\hat{Q}_{\ell,i}^{-1}]_{Q_{\ell,i}}$ to a' for each i, we perform the decomposition process to a' only once and add $[P_\ell \cdot \hat{Q}_{\ell,i} \cdot [\hat{Q}_{\ell,i}^{-1}]_{Q_{\ell,i}}]_{Q_{\ell',j}}$ to the j-th decomposed component for each i, where this added value can be pre-computed. Since the number of the decomposition processes is reduced to one, this optimization effectively improves the running time performance. The PubToRot operation is shown in Algorithm 3. The correctness of this optimization is shown in the following theorem,[3] where $P_\ell Q_\ell = Q_{\ell+1} = (\prod_{j=0}^{\mu-2} Q_{\ell',j}) \cdot \bar{Q}_{\ell',\mu-1}$, $\bar{Q}_{\ell',\mu-1}$ is a divisor of $Q_{\ell',\mu-1}$, and $\mu \leq \mathsf{hdnum}_{\ell'}$.

Theorem 2. *The output of Algorithm 3 is a valid rotation key for the rotation operation for cyclic shift r.*

3.3 Rotation Key Generation in the Lower Key Level

We can generate the desired level-ℓ rotation keys with only the public key and the rotation keys in the key level higher than ℓ through RotToRot and PubToRot described in Algorithm 4. It is assumed that a cyclic shift r of a required rotation key can be represented as $r_0 + \cdots + r_{t-1}$, where each r_i is an element in $\mathcal{U}_\ell$, and we deal with the case when only one level-ℓ rotation key is generated. To generate the (r, ℓ) rotation key, we first perform the operation PubToRot with the shift-r_0 rotation key and the public key. Then we perform a RotToRot operation iteratively with the shift-r_i rotation key and the shift-$\sum_{j=0}^{i-1} r_j$ rotation key to generate a shift-$\sum_{j=0}^{i} r_j$ rotation key for $i = 1, \cdots, t-1$, which outputs the (r, ℓ) rotation key at last. The generation algorithm for one rotation key is described in Algorithm 4.

---

[3] The proof can be found in the full version of the paper [27].

Algorithm 2: RotToRot

Input: An (r, ℓ) rotation key, $\mathsf{gk}_r^{(\ell)} = \{(b_{r,i}^{(\ell)}, a_{r,i}^{(\ell)})\}_{i=0,\cdots,\mathrm{hdnum}_\ell - 1} \in (R_{Q_\ell P_\ell}^2)^{\mathrm{hdnum}_\ell}$
and an (r', ℓ') rotation key, where ℓ' is higher than ℓ,
$\mathsf{gk}_{r'}^{(\ell')} = \{(b_{r',i}^{(\ell')}, a_{r',i}^{(\ell')})\}_{i=0,\cdots,\mathrm{hdnum}_{\ell'} - 1} \in (R_{Q_{\ell'} P_{\ell'}}^2)^{\mathrm{hdnum}_{\ell'}}$

Output: An $(r + r', \ell)$ rotation key,
$\mathsf{gk}_{r+r'}^{(\ell)} = \{b_{r+r',i}^{(\ell)}, a_{r+r',i}^{(\ell)}\}_{i=0,\cdots,\mathrm{hdnum}_\ell - 1} \in (R_{Q_\ell P_\ell}^2)^{\mathrm{hdnum}_\ell}$

1 **for** $i = 0$ **to** $\mathrm{hdnum}_\ell - 1$ **do**

2 $\quad (\tilde{b}, \tilde{a}) \leftarrow (b_{r,i}^{(\ell)}(X^{5^{r'}}), a_{r,i}^{(\ell)}(X^{5^{r'}}))$

3 $\quad (b_{r+r',i}^{(\ell)}, a_{r+r',i}^{(\ell)}) \leftarrow$ key-switching operation to $(\tilde{b}, \tilde{a})$ with the rotation key
$\quad\ \mathsf{gk}_{r'}^{(\ell')}$.

4 **return** $\{(b_{r+r',i}^{(\ell)}, a_{r+r',i}^{(\ell)})\}_{i=0,\cdots,\mathrm{hdnum}_\ell - 1}$

Algorithm 3: PubToRot

Input: A public key $(b, a) \in R_{Q_{k-1}}^2$, a (r, ℓ') rotation key,
$\mathsf{gk}_r^{(\ell')} = \{b_{r,j}^{(\ell')}, a_{r,j}^{(\ell')}\}_{j=0,\cdots,\mathrm{hdnum}_{\ell'} - 1} \in (R_{Q_{\ell'} P_{\ell'}}^2)^{\mathrm{hdnum}_{\ell'}}$, and the key level ℓ

Output: A (r, ℓ) rotation key, $\mathsf{gk}_r^{(\ell)} = \{b_{r,i}^{(\ell)}, a_{r,i}^{(\ell)}\}_{i=0,\cdots,\mathrm{hdnum}_\ell - 1} \in (R_{Q_\ell P_\ell}^2)^{\mathrm{hdnum}_\ell}$

1 $(b', a') \leftarrow ([b(X^{5^r})]_{Q_\ell P_\ell}, [a(X^{5^r})]_{Q_\ell P_\ell}) \in R_{Q_\ell P_\ell}^2$

2 Decompose a' into a vector $(a_0, \cdots, a_{\mu-1}) \in R_{P_{\ell'} Q_{\ell+1}}^\mu$, where
$a_j = [a']_{Q_{\ell',j}} + Q_{\ell',j} \cdot \tilde{e}_j$ for small $\tilde{e}_j$'s for $0 \le j \le \mu - 2$ and
$a_{\mu-1} = [a']_{\bar{Q}_{\ell',\mu-1}} + \bar{Q}_{\ell',\mu-1} \cdot \tilde{e}_{\mu-1}$ for small $\tilde{e}_{\mu-1}$.

3 **for** $i = 0$ **to** $\mathrm{hdnum}_\ell - 1$ **do**

4 $\quad (\bar{b}, \bar{a}) \leftarrow (0, 0) \in R_{P_{\ell'} Q_{\ell'}}^2$

5 $\quad$ **for** $j \leftarrow 0$ **to** $\mu - 1$ **do**

6 $\quad\quad$ **if** $j = \mu - 1$ **then**

7 $\quad\quad\quad (\bar{b}, \bar{a}) \leftarrow (\bar{b}, \bar{a}) + (a_{\mu-1} + [P_\ell \cdot \hat{Q}_{\ell,i} \cdot [\hat{Q}_{\ell,i}^{-1}]_{Q_{\ell,i}}]_{\bar{Q}_{\ell',\mu-1}}) \cdot$
$\quad\quad\quad ([b_{r,\mu-1}^{(\ell')}]_{P_{\ell'} Q_{\ell+1}}, [a_{r,\mu-1}^{(\ell')}]_{P_{\ell'} Q_{\ell+1}})$

8 $\quad\quad$ **else**

9 $\quad\quad\quad (\bar{b}, \bar{a}) \leftarrow$
$\quad\quad\quad (\bar{b}, \bar{a}) + (a_j + [P_\ell \cdot \hat{Q}_{\ell,i} \cdot [\hat{Q}_{\ell,i}^{-1}]_{Q_{\ell,i}}]_{Q_{\ell',j}}) \cdot ([b_{r,j}^{(\ell')}]_{P_{\ell'} Q_{\ell+1}}, [a_{r,j}^{(\ell')}]_{P_{\ell'} Q_{\ell+1}})$

10 $\quad (b_{r,i}^{(\ell)}, a_{r,i}^{(\ell)}) \leftarrow (\lfloor P_{\ell'}^{-1} \cdot \bar{b} \rfloor, \lfloor P_{\ell'}^{-1} \cdot \bar{a} \rfloor) \in R_{Q_{\ell+1}}^2 = R_{P_\ell Q_\ell}^2$

11 $\quad b_{r,i}^{(\ell)} \leftarrow b_{r,i}^{(\ell)} + b'$

12 **return** $\{(b_{r,i}^{(\ell)}, a_{r,i}^{(\ell)})\}_{i=0,\cdots,\mathrm{hdnum}_\ell - 1}$

We usually have to generate a bundle of rotation keys rather than only one rotation key for a specific service. We will deal with the more efficient method for the case when we need to make a set of rotation keys at once in Sect. 4.

3.4 Security Aspects

One can be concerned that the server may be able to obtain some information about the secret key using the fact that the rotation keys for any cyclic shifts can be generated by the server indefinitely. However, according to the argument often used in the simulation paradigm in cryptography, if any new information can be efficiently obtained from existing information, this new information is considered to tell us nothing beyond the existing information [30]. Thus, even if new rotation keys are generated indefinitely with the proposed algorithms from the rotation keys sent by the client, these new rotation keys do not give the server any new information beyond the public keys and the rotation keys in the highest key level sent by the client.

Thus, we only need to consider the security of the public key and the rotation keys at the highest key level sent by the client. As mentioned in Sect. 3.1, the generating method for the public key and the highest key-level rotation key by the client is exactly the same as those of the conventional FHE schemes. Just as the conventional FHE schemes are based on the circular security assumption, the proposed hierarchical rotation key generation scheme also requires the circular security assumption. The public key is an element of $R^2_{Q_{k-1}}$, and the highest key-level rotation key is an element of $(R_{Q_{k-1}P_{k-1}})^2)^{\text{hdnum}_{k-1}}$. Since the main factor that affects the security level is the maximum modulus bit-length of rings, the value of $Q_{k-1}P_{k-1}$ is the main factor for security. For a given polynomial modulus degree N and the secret key Hamming weight h, we can be given the maximum modulus bit length to guarantee the security level λ [2,9], and the bit-length of $Q_{k-1}P_{k-1}$ should not exceed this bit length.

Algorithm 4: RotKeyGen for One Rotation Key

Input: A public key $(b, a) \in R^2_{Q_{k-1}}$, a set of rotation keys
$$\mathcal{G}_{\mathcal{U}_\ell} = \{\text{gk}_r^{(\ell_r)} = \{(b_{r,i}^{(\ell_r)}, a_{r,i}^{(\ell_r)})\}_{i=0,\cdots,\text{hdnum}_{\ell_r}-1} \in (R^2_{Q_{\ell_r}P_{\ell_r}})^{\text{hdnum}_{\ell_r}} | r \in \mathcal{U}_\ell\}$$
for cyclic shift generator set $\mathcal{U}_\ell$ in the key level higher than ℓ, and a cyclic shift $r = \sum_{u=0}^{t-1} r_u$ for $r_u \in \mathcal{U}_\ell$

Output: An (r, ℓ) rotation key, $\text{gk}_r^{(\ell)} = \{b_{r,i}^{(\ell)}, a_{r,i}^{(\ell)}\}_{i=0,\cdots,\text{hdnum}_\ell-1} \in (R^2_{Q_\ell P_\ell})^{\text{hdnum}_\ell}$

1   $\{(b_{r_0,i}^{(\ell)}, a_{r_0,i}^{(\ell)})_{i=0,\cdots,\text{hdnum}_\ell}\} \leftarrow$ PubToRot with the public key and the (r_0, ℓ_{r_0}) rotation key

2   **for** $h = 1$ **to** $t - 1$ **do**

3     $\{(b_{\sum_{j=0}^{h} r_j,i}^{(\ell)}, a_{\sum_{j=0}^{h} r_j,i}^{(\ell)})_{i=0,\cdots,\text{hdnum}_\ell}\} \leftarrow$ RotToRot with
    $\{(b_{\sum_{j=0}^{h-1} r_j,i}^{(\ell)}, a_{\sum_{j=0}^{h-1} r_j,i}^{(\ell)})_{i=0,\cdots,\text{hdnum}_\ell}\}$ and the (r_h, ℓ_{r_h}) rotation key

4   **return** $\text{gk}_r^\ell = \{(b_{r,i}^{(\ell)}, a_{r,i}^{(\ell)})_{i=0,\cdots,\text{hdnum}_\ell}\}$

---

4   Efficient Generation Method of Rotation Key Set

In the previous section, we dealt with the specific algorithms needed to make a lower key-level rotation key using the higher key-level rotation keys. However, we often require many rotation keys at once, especially for certain services requested by the client. Thus, it is necessary to efficiently generate a set of rotation keys using the higher key-level rotation keys. We need to reduce the number of these RotToRot operations and PubToRot operations to efficiently generate hierarchical rotation keys. Note that there are many intermediate rotation keys in the hierarchical rotation key system. Given a certain fixed set of higher key-level rotation keys, the key problem is how to minimize the number of operations for generating these intermediate rotation keys by systematically organizing the generating sequence of the rotation keys.

4.1   Reduction to Minimum Spanning Arborescence Problem and Minimum Spanning Tree Problem

Given a set $\mathcal{U}_\ell$ of specific fixed rotation keys in the higher key level than ℓ, generating level-ℓ rotation keys with as few operations as possible is desirable. In other words, it becomes important to use the least amount of operations of RotToRot and PubToRot by arranging the order in which the rotation keys in the set are generated. We propose an algorithm that can determine the order of generating rotation keys in the set in the hierarchical rotation key system to reduce the number of operations.

To this end, we reduce the problem of determining the order of generation of rotation keys to the minimal spanning arborescence problem, a well-known graph-theoretic computational problem. First, set the $|\mathcal{T}_\ell| + 1$ nodes for each element in the $\mathcal{T}_\ell \cup \{0\}$, and then set the directed edge weight between any two nodes a, b as the minimum number of elements in $\mathcal{U}_\ell$ required to add up to $|a - b|$ allowing repetition. The method for setting this edge weight will be given in the next subsection. There are some identical points to the minimum arborescence problem in our ordering of the rotation key generation problem as follows.

- We need to generate each rotation key only once. This fact is related to the property of the arborescence that any node has only one path from the root node.
- Each rotation key can be generated by using a RotToRot or a PubToRot from the public key or existing rotation keys. An edge from the node a to the node b with weight w means that the (b, ℓ) rotation key can be generated from the (a, ℓ) rotation key with w operations of RotToRot and PubToRot.
- All rotation keys should be generated from the public key and the higher level rotation keys. An arborescence has only one root node that is the source of all nodes, and this root node corresponds to the public key.
- We need to minimize the total number of key-switching operations to generate all rotation keys. The minimum spanning arborescence problem is to find the arborescence with the minimum total weight, which corresponds to the total number of PubToRot operations or RotToRot operations.

Therefore, the graph produced in this way can be seen as a directed graph, and our problem is to find a spanning arborescence with a minimum sum of edges, which is the goal of the minimum spanning arborescence problem. If we find a spanning arborescence in the graph, we can view the node with zero as a public key and generate the rotation keys along the obtained tree. The minimum spanning arborescence problem can be solved by Edmonds' algorithm [12], and thus an answer to this problem can be efficiently obtained.

If the rotation keys in the higher key level exist in pairs of different signs of the same absolute value, a faster and more efficient solution for generating the rotation keys in the lower key level can be obtained by reducing to another computation problem. If a shift-r_1 rotation key can be generated with m operations from a shift-r_2 rotation key, we can generate the shift-r_2 rotation key from that of cyclic shift r_1 with the higher-level rotation keys for cyclic shifts having the same absolute value with a different sign. In view of the corresponding graph, any pairs of two edges (r_1, r_2) and (r_2, r_1) exist and have the same edge weight. Thus, we can replace the directed graph with the undirected graph with the same nodes in which each edge has the same weight as the corresponding edge in the directed graph. For the undirected graph, we can reduce this problem to the minimum spanning tree problem, which can be solved by Prim's algorithm [33].

We note that this solution is not exactly the optimal solution since the insertion of additional nodes can reduce the operations further. If we set the nodes for all cyclic shifts (i.e., $\pm 1, \pm 2, \pm 3, \cdots$) in the graph, our problem is to find the minimum Steiner tree for required cyclic shifts. The Steiner tree in a graph is a tree connecting a subset of designated nodes, and the problem of finding the Steiner tree is known as an NP-hard problem. Thus, we choose the near-optimal solution using a more practically feasible algorithm. Designing a fast algorithm to find the solution closer to the optimal solution in the proposed situation is an important future work.

4.2   Edge Weight for p-ary Rotation Keys

We should consider a method to compute the edge of each graph, where we need to find a way to represent the difference between two nodes as a sum of the minimum number of elements in $\mathcal{U}_\ell$, allowing repetition. In general, the server can ask the client for a well-designed set of $\mathcal{U}_\ell$ so that it can be easy to represent any given number as the desired sum in $\mathcal{U}_\ell$. Rather than proposing the general method for unstructured $\mathcal{U}_\ell$, we suggest a specific example of a key management system with $\mathcal{U}_\ell$ with power-of-p integers within the desired interval. We will discuss how to obtain edges for both cases when $\mathcal{U}_\ell$ consists of power-of-p integers with both signs and when it consists of only positive power-of-p integers.

We consider the easier case, a set of positive power-of-p, in which the rotation graph is a directed graph. In this case, each edge can be computed as follows. First, we can find the difference between the end node and the start node of the edge, and then express this difference in the p-ary representation, and then set

---

Algorithm 5: ComputeEdgePos

Input: A power base p for the set $\mathcal{U}_\ell$ with only positive numbers and a number t to be summed

Output: The minimum number of elements in $\mathcal{U}_\ell$ summed to t allowing repetition

1 $(t_0 t_1 \cdots t_{\ell-1})_{(p)} \leftarrow p$-ary representation of t

2 **return** $\sum_{i=0}^{\ell-1} t_i$

---

the sum of the digits as the edge weight. This algorithm is described in Algorithm 5 without proof.

Next, we consider the case of power-of-p integers with both signs in which the rotation graph is an undirected graph, as in Sect. 4.1. In this case, since the power-of-two integers with different signs can add up to the value, expressing them with the p-ary representation is not enough to find the optimal solution. Instead, we propose the following algorithm to obtain the edge weight between any two nodes, which is efficient enough for the input range. Assume that r is the difference between the two given nodes. If r is a multiple of p, then recursively output a value of $\mathsf{Alg}(r/p)$, otherwise find r_1 such that $pr_1 \leq r < p(r_1 + 1)$ and recursively output $\min\{\mathsf{Alg}(r_1) + (r - pr_1), \mathsf{Alg}(r_1 + 1) + (p(r_1 + 1) - r)\}$. This algorithm is described in Algorithm 6. To help understand the reduction to the graph, we depict the corresponding graph and the minimum spanning tree for $\mathcal{T}_\ell = \{1, 13, 16, 17, 19\}$ and $\mathcal{U}_\ell = \{\pm 1, \pm 2, \pm 4, \pm 8, \pm 16\}$ in Fig. 3.

4.3 Hoisted Rotation Key Generation

The previous subsections focus on reducing the number of RotToRot and PubToRot operations. In this subsection, we further reduce the number of the Decompose processes by the hoisting technique. The hoisting technique minimizes the number of operations by interchanging or combining operations without changing functionalities. This technique has been used in the linear trans-

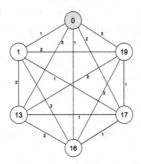

Fig. 3. Rotation key graph for $\mathcal{T}_\ell = \{1, 13, 16, 17, 19\}$ and $\mathcal{U}_\ell = \{\pm 1, \pm 2, \pm 4, \pm 8, \pm 16\}$.

Algorithm 6: ComputeEdgeBoth

Input: A power base p for the set $\mathcal{S}$ with both signs and the number t to be summed

Output: The minimum number of elements in $\mathcal{S}$ summed to t allowing repetition

1   **if** $p|t$ **then**
2 | **return** ComputeEdgeBoth$(p, t/p)$
3   **else**
4 | $r \leftarrow \lfloor |t|/p \rfloor$
5 | **if** $r = 0$ **then**
6 | | **return** $|t|$
7 | **else**
8 | | **return** min$\{$ComputeEdgeBoth$(p, r) + (|t| - pr)$, ComputeEdgeBoth$(p, r + 1) + (p(r + 1) - |t|)\}$

---

formation in the FHE schemes, and optimizing the bootstrapping of the FHE schemes is one of its important applications [2,17]. We propose the hoisting method for generating the rotation key set in the hierarchical rotation key generation systems.

The target situation is when several level-ℓ rotation keys are generated from the public key or one level-ℓ rotation key with rotation keys in the key level ℓ' higher than ℓ. If we want to generate d rotation keys, we can naively perform exactly d PubToRot operations or d RotToRot operations. As stated in Sect. 3.2, the decomposition process is the most time-consuming in the key-switching operation, and thus the decomposition process is desirable to be reduced further. To this end, we postpone the process of automorphism in line 2 of Algorithm 2 or line 1 of Algorithm 3 to the last of the operations to combine the decomposition processes into one process. To maintain the functionality of the operation, we conduct the automorphism inversely to the rotation keys in the key level higher than ℓ before the inner-product with the decomposed components. If the source rotation key is the public key, we reduce the number of decomposition processes from d to one for generating d rotation keys. If the source rotation key is the other rotation key in the same key level, we reduce the number of decomposition processes from $d \cdot \text{hdnum}_\ell$ to hdnum_ℓ. The hoisted version of RotToRot and PubToRot operations are described in Algorithms 7 and 8. The whole generation algorithm is described in Algorithm 9. We use breath-first search when we search each node in the output arborescence. This search method is desirable for the hoisted generation of rotation keys.

5   Simulation Results with ResNet Models

In this section, we numerically verify the validity of the proposed hierarchical rotation key generation method with an appropriate computing environment for the client-server model with the ResNet standard neural network and the CKKS

Algorithm 7: HoistedRotToRot

Input: An (r, ℓ) rotation key, $\text{gk}_r^{(\ell)} = \{(b_{r,i}^{(\ell)}, a_{r,i}^{(\ell)})\}_{i=0,\cdots,\text{hdnum}_\ell - 1} \in (R_{Q_\ell P_\ell}^2)^{\text{hdnum}_\ell}$
and d (r_α', ℓ') rotation keys, where ℓ' is higher than ℓ,
$\text{gk}_{r_\alpha'}^{(\ell')} = \{(b_{r_\alpha',i}^{(\ell')}, a_{r_\alpha',i}^{(\ell')})\}_{i=0,\cdots,\text{hdnum}_\ell - 1} \in (R_{Q_{\ell'} P_{\ell'}}^2)^{\text{hdnum}_{\ell'}}$ for
$\alpha = 0, \cdots, d - 1$

Output: d $(r + r_\alpha', \ell)$ rotation keys,
$\text{gk}_{r+r_\alpha'}^{(\ell)} = \{b_{r+r_\alpha',i}^{(\ell)}, a_{r+r_\alpha',i}^{(\ell)}\}_{i=0,\cdots,\text{hdnum}_\ell - 1} \in (R_{Q_\ell P_\ell}^2)^{\text{hdnum}_\ell}$ for
$\alpha = 0, \cdots, d - 1$

1 for $i = 0$ to $\text{hdnum}_\ell - 1$ **do**

2   Decompose $a_{r,j}^{(\ell)}$ into a vector $(a_0, \cdots, a_{\mu-1}) \in R_{P_{\ell'} Q_{\ell+1}}^\mu$, where
   $a_j = [a]_{Q_{\ell',j}} + Q_{\ell',j} \cdot \tilde{e}_j$ for small $\tilde{e}_j$'s for $0 \le j \le \mu - 2$ and
   $a_{\mu-1} = [a]_{\tilde{Q}_{\ell',\mu-1}} + \tilde{Q}_{\ell',\mu-1} \cdot \tilde{e}_{\mu-1}$ for small $\tilde{e}_{\mu-1}$.

3   **for** $\alpha = 0$ to $d - 1$ **do**

4 $(\bar{b}, \bar{a}) \leftarrow (0,0) \in R_{P_\ell Q_\ell}^2$

5   **for** $j \leftarrow 0$ to $\mu - 1$ **do**

6 $(\bar{b}, \bar{a}) \leftarrow (\bar{b}, \bar{a}) + a_j \cdot ([b_{r_\alpha',j}^{(\ell')}(X^{5^{-r_\alpha'}})]_{P_{\ell'} Q_{\ell+1}}, [a_{r_\alpha',j}^{(\ell')}(X^{5^{-r_\alpha'}})]_{P_{\ell'} Q_{\ell+1}})$

7 $(b_{r+r_\alpha',i}^{(\ell)}, a_{r+r_\alpha',i}^{(\ell)}) \leftarrow (\lfloor P_{\ell'}^{-1} \cdot \bar{b} \rceil, \lfloor P_{\ell'}^{-1} \cdot \bar{a} \rceil) \in R_{Q_{\ell+1}}^2$

8 $b_{r+r_\alpha',i}^{(\ell)} \leftarrow b_{r+r_\alpha',i}^{(\ell)} + b_{r,i}^{(\ell)}$

9 $(b_{r+r_\alpha',i}^{(\ell)}, a_{r+r_\alpha',i}^{(\ell)}) \leftarrow (b_{r+r_\alpha',i}^{(\ell)}(X^{5^{r_\alpha'}}), a_{r+r_\alpha',i}^{(\ell)}(X^{5^{r_\alpha'}}))$

10 return $\{b_{r+r_\alpha',i}^{(\ell)}, a_{r+r_\alpha',i}^{(\ell)}\}_{i=0,\cdots,\text{hdnum}_\ell - 1}$ for $\alpha = 0, \cdots, d - 1$

---

scheme. In the cloud computing model, the server usually has high-performance computing resources, and the client has only a general-purpose personal computer. To simulate this environment, we use a PC with Intel(R) Core(TM) i9-13900K CPU as a client and a high-performance server with NVIDIA GeForce RTX 4090 GPU accelerator as a server.

As a representative example of complex computation models, we assume that the service requested by the client requires the ResNet-20 model for the CIFAR-10 dataset or the ResNet-18 model for the ImageNet dataset. We use the parameters in Lee et al. [25], except that we use the generalized RNS decomposition method [18] in our simulation and the bit lengths of some RNS moduli are reduced with the maintained classification accuracy of the network. The sparse-secret encapsulation method [3] is assumed to be used for the bootstrapping with the dense secret key with more reduced running time and higher precision. The whole rotation steps for each model are computed with the computation method in [25][4].

The CKKS scheme is used for the simulation, and the parameters of the CKKS scheme we use for the simulation are shown in Table 1. The lattigo library [1] is used for the simulation, and the CUDA library by NVIDIA is used for GPU acceleration of the rotation key generation. The rotation key generation

---

[4] The specific rotation steps can be found in the full version of this paper [27].

Algorithm 8: HoistedPubToRot

Input: A public key $(b,a) \in R^2_{Q_{k-1}}$, d (r_α, ℓ') rotation keys, where ℓ' is higher

than ℓ, $\mathsf{gk}^{(\ell')}_{r_\alpha} = \{(b^{(\ell')}_{r_\alpha,i}, a^{(\ell')}_{r_\alpha,i})\}_{i=0,\cdots,\mathrm{hdnum}_{\ell'}-1} \in (R^2_{Q_{\ell'}P_{\ell'}})^{\mathrm{hdnum}_{\ell'}}$ for

$\alpha = 0, \cdots, d-1$, and the key level ℓ

Output: d (r_α, ℓ) rotation keys,

$\mathsf{gk}^{(\ell)}_{r_\alpha} = \{b^{(\ell)}_{r_\alpha,i}, a^{(\ell)}_{r_\alpha,i}\}_{i=0,\cdots,\mathrm{hdnum}_\ell-1} \in (R^2_{Q_\ell P_\ell})^{\mathrm{hdnum}_\ell}$ for $\alpha = 0, \cdots, d-1$

1 Decompose a into a vector $(a_0, \cdots, a_{\mu-1}) \in R^\mu_{P_{\ell'}Q_{\ell+1}}$, where

$a_j = [a]_{Q_{\ell',j}} + Q_{\ell',j} \cdot \tilde{e}_j$ for small $\tilde{e}_j$'s for $0 \le j \le \mu-2$ and

$a_{\mu-1} = [a]_{\bar{Q}_{\ell',\mu-1}} + \bar{Q}_{\ell',\mu-1} \cdot \tilde{e}_{\mu-1}$ for small $\tilde{e}_{\mu-1}$.

2 **for** $i = 0$ **to** $\mathrm{hdnum}_\ell - 1$ **do**

3 $\quad (\bar{b}, \bar{a}) \leftarrow (0,0) \in R^2_{P_\ell Q_\ell}$

4 $\quad$ **for** $\alpha = 0$ **to** $d-1$ **do**

5 $\quad\quad$ **for** $j \leftarrow 0$ **to** $\mu-1$ **do**

6 $\quad\quad\quad$ **if** $j = \mu-1$ **then**

7 $\quad\quad\quad\quad (\bar{b}, \bar{a}) \leftarrow (\bar{b}, \bar{a}) + (a_{\mu-1} + [P_\ell \cdot \hat{Q}_{\ell,i} \cdot [\hat{Q}^{-1}_{\ell,i}]_{Q_{\ell,i}}]_{\bar{Q}_{\ell',\mu-1}}) \cdot$

$\quad\quad\quad\quad ([b^{(\ell')}_{r_\alpha,j}(X^{5^{-r_\alpha}})]_{P_{\ell'}Q_{\ell+1}}, [a^{(\ell')}_{r_\alpha,j}(X^{5^{-r_\alpha}})]_{P_{\ell'}Q_{\ell+1}})$

8 $\quad\quad\quad$ **else**

9 $\quad\quad\quad\quad (\bar{b}, \bar{a}) \leftarrow (\bar{b}, \bar{a}) + (a_j + [P_\ell \cdot \hat{Q}_{\ell,i} \cdot [\hat{Q}^{-1}_{\ell,i}]_{Q_{\ell,i}}]_{Q_{\ell',j}}) \cdot$

$\quad\quad\quad\quad ([b^{(\ell')}_{r_\alpha,j}(X^{5^{-r_\alpha}})]_{P_{\ell'}Q_{\ell+1}}, [a^{(\ell')}_{r_\alpha,j}(X^{5^{-r_\alpha}})]_{P_{\ell'}Q_{\ell+1}})$

10 $\quad\quad (b^{(\ell)}_{r_\alpha,i}, a^{(\ell)}_{r_\alpha,i}) \leftarrow (\lfloor P^{-1}_{\ell'} \cdot \bar{b} \rceil, \lfloor P^{-1}_{\ell'} \cdot \bar{a} \rceil) \in R^2_{Q_{\ell+1}}$

11 $\quad\quad b^{(\ell)}_{r_\alpha,i} \leftarrow b^{(\ell)}_{r_\alpha,i} + [b]_{Q_{\ell+1}}$

12 $\quad\quad (b^{(\ell)}_{r_\alpha,i}, a^{(\ell)}_{r_\alpha,i}) \leftarrow (b^{(\ell)}_{r_\alpha,i}(X^{5^{r_\alpha}}), a^{(\ell)}_{r_\alpha,i}(X^{5^{r_\alpha}}))$

13 **return** $\{b^{(\ell)}_{r_\alpha,i}, a^{(\ell)}_{r_\alpha,i}\}_{i=0,\cdots,\mathrm{hdnum}_\ell-1}$ for $\alpha = 0, \cdots, d-1$

---

with the GPU processor is implemented based on [20]. In the server, algorithms for the preparation of rotation key generation are executed on the CPU processor and all actual rotation key generation is computed by the GPU processor. The running time for rotation key generation by the client, the communication amount between the client and the server, the required storage for rotation keys in the server, and the running time for rotation key generation by the server are measured and presented in this section.

5.1 Parameter and Simulation Setting

We now compare the various performances between the use of the conventional system and a hierarchical rotation key system. To ensure a fair comparison, we have selected parameters based on the following criteria. When determining each special modulus, we first decide the value of dnum to ensure optimal rotation time. Then, we set the special modulus that allows key-switching with that specific dnum. In the case of a two-level hierarchical rotation key system, we assume that the dnum or special modulus of the higher level is not considered when

---

Algorithm 9: RotKeyGen

Input: A cyclic shift set $\mathcal{T}_\ell$ for the key level ℓ, a cyclic shift generator set $\mathcal{U}_\ell$ for the key level higher than ℓ, a set of rotation keys $\mathcal{G}_{\mathcal{U}_\ell}$ for cyclic shifts in $\mathcal{U}_\ell$ in the key level higher than ℓ, and a public key $(b,a) \in R_{Q_{k-1}}$

Output: A set of rotation keys $\mathcal{G}_{\mathcal{T}_\ell}$ for a cyclic shift set $\mathcal{T}_\ell$

1   $V \leftarrow \mathcal{T} \cup \{0\}$

2   $E \leftarrow \{(v,w)|v,w \in V\}$

3   $w(v,w) \leftarrow$ the minimum number of elements in $\mathcal{S}$ summed to $w - v$ allowing repetition

4   $G' = (V, E') \leftarrow$ Edmonds' algorithm with $G = (V, E)$; // It can be replaced with Prim's algorithm when $\mathcal{U}_\ell$ is symmetric around zero.

5   $Q[] \leftarrow$ empty queue for nodes

6   $\mathcal{G}_{\mathcal{T}_\ell} \leftarrow \varnothing$

7   **while** Q is not empty **do**

8      $v \leftarrow$ dequeue from Q

9      $W \leftarrow$ the set of nodes adjacent to v.

10   **if** $v = 0$ **then**

11   Generate the set of rotation keys $\mathcal{G}_W = \{\mathsf{gk}_w^{(\ell)}|w \in W\}$ from (b,a) using PubToRot or HoistedPubToRot

12   **else**

13   Generate the set of rotation keys $\mathcal{G}_W = \{\mathsf{gk}_w^{(\ell)}|w \in W\}$ from $\mathsf{gk}_v^{(\ell)}$ using RotToRot or HoistedRotToRot

14     $\mathcal{G}_{\mathcal{T}_\ell} \leftarrow \mathcal{G}_{\mathcal{T}_\ell} \cup \mathcal{G}_W$

15   Enqueue elements in W to Q.

16 **return** $\mathcal{G}_{\mathcal{T}_\ell}$

---

determining the dnum or special modulus for each level. In other words, the values of dnum and special modulus for ciphertext key-switching are set solely to optimize the key-switching process. For a three-level scheme, we relax these criteria to carefully examine trade-offs, which will be explained in detail when discussing the results for three levels.

The bit length of the special modulus is often approximately the size of $\log Q/\mathtt{dnum}$ when dnum is given, where $\log Q$ is the ciphertext modulus bit length. Therefore, we set the special modulus based on this criterion. If the sum of the ciphertext modulus and special modulus exceeds the maximum modulus bit length, we consider it an unfeasible dnum for the current parameters and only consider larger dnum values for this simulation. Then, the special modulus for each key level is set using the same criteria regarding the product of the ciphertext modulus and all the special modulus for the lower key level as the ciphertext modulus for the corresponding key level.

In the case of the ResNet-20 handling the CIFAR-10 dataset, the ciphertext needs to hold a maximum of 2^{14} data points, and to perform all operations of a single layer with one bootstrapping, it is desirable to use a polynomial modulus degree of $N = 2^{16}$. The maximum modulus bit length for 128-bit security is 1714 bits assuming the secret key distribution is U_3 with the formula in [32]. Thus,

Table 1. Encryption parameters in the CKKS scheme for ResNet models

Parameters	ResNet-20 for CIFAR-10	ResNet-18 for ImageNet
Polynomial modulus degree	2^{16}	2^{17}
Secret key Hamming weight	2^{15}	2^{16}
Gaussian error stand. dev.	3.2	3.2
Minimum security level	128-bit	128-bit
Maximum modulus bit-length	1714	3428

we ensure that the sum of ciphertext modulus bit length and all special modulus bit lengths does not exceed 1714 bits. For ResNet-20 handling the CIFAR-10 dataset, the total ciphertext modulus bit length required is 1321 bits. For all simulations for ResNet-20, we fix the bit length of the maximum modulus and the ciphertext modulus as 1714 and 1321, respectively, independent of the value of dnum and the total number of the key level. Table 2 shows the parameter sets to be compared. In the table, dnum shows the decomposition number for the conventional system and the pair of decomposition numbers ($\text{dnum}_0, \text{dnum}_1$) for a two-level hierarchical system.

There might be questions about whether it is fair to compare the two-level system parameters with the corresponding conventional system parameters using $\log P_0 + \log P_1$ as one special modulus. For instance, in the case of B.i for two-level system parameters ($\log Q, \log P_0, \log P_1$) = (1321, 333, 60), one can argue that the conventional scheme with $\log P_0 + \log P_1 = 393$ as a special modulus needs to be compared. However, we cannot reduce dnum_0 from 4 to 3 by using $\log P_0 + \log P_1$ as a special modulus for a one-level scheme, because a special modulus of approximately 440 bits would be required for $\text{dnum}_0 = 3$, which prevents achieving the 128-bit security. In fact, A.i parameters are more efficient than the claimed parameters for a one-level system because the computation amount with special modulus is reduced. In other words, the A.i parameters are the optimal one-level system parameters in terms of the key-switching operation. Since the A.i and B.i parameters are the optimal parameters in terms of the key-switching operation for one-level system and two-level system, respectively, the comparison between these parameters is valid.

In the case of the ResNet-18 handling the ImageNet dataset, the large image size makes it difficult to accommodate intermediate values in a single ciphertext. Therefore, although it is possible to use a degree of 2^{16}, it is preferable to set the degree to 2^{17} to double the number of slots that can be accommodated in one ciphertext for optimizing bootstrapping time. The maximum modulus bit length for 128-bit security is 3428 bits assuming the secret key distribution is U_3 with the formula in [32]. For the ResNet-18 handling the ImageNet dataset, the total ciphertext modulus bit length required is 1639 bits. For all simulations for the ResNet-18, we fix the bit length of the maximum modulus and the ciphertext modulus as 3428 and 1639, respectively, independent of the value of dnum and the total number of the key level. Table 3 shows the parameter sets to be compared.

In the conventional scheme, the client generates all the required rotation keys and transmits them to the server. In the two-level hierarchical rotation key scheme, the client generates the 16-ary level-1 rotation key sets with both signs and transmits them to the server, where the set of the cyclic shifts is $\{\pm 1, \pm 16, \pm 256, \cdots, \pm 2^{12}\}$. Then, the server generates the required rotation keys for the ResNet models from this 16-ary level-1 rotation key set. In the three-level hierarchical rotation key scheme, the client generates only two level-2 rotation key set, where the set of the cyclic shifts is $\{1, 256\}$. In this system, we assume that there is an inactive phase between key transmissions and an active phase when the service is provided to the client. The server can generate 4-ary level-1 rotation keys using Edmonds' algorithm for faster rotation key generation in the inactive phase before the services so that level-1 rotation keys constitute a 4-ary rotation key set, where the set of the cyclic shifts is $\{\pm 1, \pm 4, \pm 16, \cdots, \pm 2^{12}, 2^{14}\}$. Then, the server generates the required level-0 rotation keys for the ResNet models from this 4-ary level-1 rotation key set just after the services are requested, which is the active phase.

Table 2. Parameter sets with the ResNet-20 for the CIFAR-10 dataset

Rotation Key Generation		dnum	Modulus bit length
Conventional (One-level)	A.i	4	$(\log Q_0, \log P_0) = (1321, 333)$
	A.ii	5	$(\log Q_0, \log P_0) = (1321, 273)$
	A.iii	6	$(\log Q_0, \log P_0) = (1321, 221)$
Two-level	B.i	(4, 28)	$(\log Q_0, \log P_0, \log P_1) = (1321, 333, 60)$
	B.ii	(5, 14)	$(\log Q_0, \log P_0, \log P_1) = (1321, 273, 120)$
	B.iii	(6, 9)	$(\log Q_0, \log P_0, \log P_1) = (1321, 221, 172)$

5.2 Numerical Results

Table 4 shows the number of core operations for each rotation key set generation for ResNet models using a 16-ary rotation key set for the ResNet-20 and a 4-ary

Table 3. Parameter sets with ResNet-18 for ImageNet dataset

Rotation Key Generation		dnum	Modulus bit length
Conventional (One-level)	C.i	1	$(\log Q_0, \log P_0) = (1639, 1639)$
	C.ii	2	$(\log Q_0, \log P_0) = (1639, 820)$
	C.iii	3	$(\log Q_0, \log P_0) = (1639, 547)$
Two-level	D.i	(1, 22)	$(\log Q_0, \log P_0, \log P_1) = (1639, 1639, 150)$
	D.ii	(2, 3)	$(\log Q_0, \log P_0, \log P_1) = (1639, 820, 820)$
	D.iii	(3, 2)	$(\log Q_0, \log P_0, \log P_1) = (1639, 547, 1093)$
Three-level	E.iii	(3, 3, 6)	$(\log Q_0, \log P_0, \log P_1, \log P_2) = (1639, 547, 729, 485)$

Table 4. Number of core operations optimized by hoisted rotation key generation and Prim's algorithm

		ResNet-20 for CIFAR-10	ResNet-18 for ImageNet	
		16-ary	4-ary	16-ary
No. of rotation Keys		265	617	
RotToRot	Total	372	649	721
	Decompose	292	347	529
PubToRot	Total	7	14	8
	Decompose	1	1	1

and a 16-ary rotation key sets for the ResNet-18, and it shows the effectiveness of the hoisted rotation key generation and Prim's algorithm. Note that the total numbers of RotToRot and PubToRot operations are close to the number of rotation keys. Roughly speaking, 1.43 numbers of key-switching operations for a rotation key are needed on average if we use a 16-ary level-1 rotation key set for the ResNet-20, and 1.07 and 1.18 numbers of key-switching operations for a rotation key are needed on average if we use 4-ary and 16-ary level-1 rotation key set for ResNet-18, respectively. It means that most rotation keys can be generated by only one RotToRot or PubToRot operation from other rotation keys, resulting from Prim's algorithm.

Note that the number of the decompose processes is effectively reduced compared to the total numbers of RotToRot and PubToRot operations by the hoisted rotation key generation. The decompose processes are the most time-consuming process in the key-switching operation. If we do not use the hoisted rotation key generation method, the number of the decompose processes is the same as the total number of RotToRot and PubToRot operations. For example, in the A.i parameter, it takes 19.0 s to generate all level-0 rotation keys using 16-ary level-1 rotation keys if we do not use the hoisted method. If we use the hoisted method, it takes 16.6 s to generate all level-0 rotation keys with the same level-1 rotation keys, which is reduced by 12.8%.

Table 5. Simulation results with various parameters with the ResNet-20 for the CIFAR-10 dataset

		CKR(ms)	KGKR(ms)	KGR(C)(s)	CA(GB)	KGR(S)(s)
Conventional	A.i	3.10	N/A	88.7	38.3	N/A
	A.ii	3.38	N/A	109.5	46.6	N/A
	A.iii	3.67	N/A	127.4	54.3	N/A
Two-level	B.i	3.10	12.58	18.9	8.31	16.6
	B.ii	3.38	7.21	9.68	4.16	11.7
	B.iii	3.67	5.18	6.30	2.67	10.2

Table 6. Simulation results with various parameters with the ResNet-18 for the ImageNet dataset

		CKR(ms)	KGKR(ms)	KGKR2(ms)	KGR(C)(s)	CA(GB)	OKGR(S)(s)	KGR(S)(s)
Conventional	C.i	6.50	N/A	N/A	96.1	74.7	N/A	N/A
	C.ii	6.05	N/A	N/A	145.1	115.7	N/A	N/A
	C.iii	6.59	N/A	N/A	207.9	159.1	N/A	N/A
Two-level	D.i	6.50	40.78	N/A	29.1	22.3	N/A	25.0
	D.ii	6.05	9.89	N/A	3.74	2.91	N/A	12.5
	D.iii	6.59	8.30	N/A	2.52	1.97	N/A	16.1
Three-level	E.iii	6.59	9.02	15.62	1.93	1.54	26.9	13.9

Table 5 shows the various performances with the ResNet-20 for the CIFAR-10 dataset when using the parameters in Table 2. Similarly, Table 6 shows the performances with the ResNet-18 for the ImageNet dataset when using the parameters in Table 3. Each column has the following meanings.

- CKR: Ciphertext key-switching runtime
- KGKR: Key generation key-switching runtime (level-1 → level-0)
- KGKR2: Key generation key-switching runtime (level-2 → level-1)
- KGR(C): Key generation runtime (client)
- CA: Communication amount
- OKGR(S): Key generation runtime (server, offline)
- KGR(S): Key generation runtime (server)

We present Tables 7 and 8 for both cases when the rotation keys can be predetermined before the services are provided (Deter.) and when the rotation keys are determined just at the time of the service (Non-Deter.). The term "offline" means when the service is not yet provided, and the term "online" means when the service is being provided. If the types of rotation keys are determined in advance, it is desirable to generate and transmit keys when both the conventional and proposed hierarchical systems are offline. If it is not predetermined, a

Table 7. Simulation results with different situations with the ResNet-20 for the CIFAR-10 dataset. (KU: key-switching unchanged/EG: efficient generation of rotation keys)

		Runtime of client		Comm. amount		Runtime of server	
		Offline	Online	Offline	Online	Offline	Online
Deter.	Conventional	88.7 s	–	38.3 GB	–	–	–
	Two-level (KU)	18.9 s	–	8.31 GB	–	16.6 s	–
	Two-level (EG)	6.30 s	–	2.67 GB	–	10.2 s	–
Non- Deter.	Conventional	–	88.7 s	–	38.3 GB	–	–
	Two-level (KU)	18.9 s	–	8.31 GB	–	–	16.6 s
	Two-level (EG)	6.30 s	–	2.67 GB	–	–	10.2 s

Table 8. Simulation results with different situations with the ResNet-18 for the ImageNet dataset (KU: key-switching unchanged/EG: efficient generation of rotation keys)

		Runtime of client		Comm. amount		Runtime of server	
		Offline	Online	Offline	Online	Offline	Online
Deter.	Conventional	145.1 s	–	115.7 GB	–	–	–
	Two-level (KU)	3.74 s	–	2.91 GB	–	12.5 s	–
	Two-level (EG)	2.52 s	–	1.97 GB	–	16.1 s	–
	Three-level	1.93 s	–	1.54 GB	–	40.8 s	–
Non- Deter.	Conventional	–	145.1 s	–	115.7 GB	–	–
	Two-level (KU)	3.74 s	–	2.91 GB	–	–	12.5 s
	Two-level (EG)	2.52 s	–	1.97 GB	–	–	16.1 s
	Three-level	1.93 s	–	1.54 GB	–	26.9 s	13.9 s

conventional system cannot do anything offline, but it should generate and transmit a large key online, which is a huge burden to the client. On the other hand, in the proposed hierarchical system, if only a few highest-level rotation keys are generated and transmitted offline, communication costs do not occur online, and only a small runtime in the server is required. In other words, it shows that the computational and communication burden of the client is significantly reduced, and a large part of the computations goes to the high-performance server, which balances the computation tasks and the communication amount according to the environment. In Table 7, the parameters of the conventional system, the two-level system with key-switching unchanged, and the two-level system with more efficient rotation key generation are A.i, B.i, and B.iii, respectively. In Table 8, the parameters of the conventional system, the two-level system with key-switching unchanged, the two-level system with more efficient rotation key generation, and the three-level system are C.ii, D.ii, D.iii, and E.iii, respectively.

5.3   Discussion

Discussion of Two-Level System. If optimizing the key-switching operation time for ciphertext is a top priority when setting parameters, firstly, it is desirable to set dnum_0 to optimize the key-switching runtime and then set dnum_1 that is possible with the surplus modulus. For example, in the case of the ResNet-20, the optimal dnum value for key-switching operations is 4 when considering the key-switching operation time. Therefore, irrespective of whether a hierarchical rotation key is used or not, dnum_0 would be chosen as 4. In this setting, we can compare A.i and B.i parameters about the usage of the two-level hierarchical rotation key system. While the ciphertext key-switching runtime remains the same at 3.10 ms, the client-side rotation key generation significantly reduces from 88.7 s to 18.9 s (×4.69 faster), communication amount for rotation keys reduces from 38.3 GB to 8.31 GB (×1/4.61), and server-side rotation key generation takes

16.6 s. In the case of the ResNet-18 parameters, the optimal $\mathbf{dnum}_0$ for key-switching operations is 2. Therefore, we can compare C.ii and D.ii. While the ciphertext key-switching runtime remains the same at 6.05 ms, the client-side rotation key generation significantly reduces from 145.1 s to 3.74 s ($\times 38.8$ faster), the communication amount for rotation keys reduces from 115.7 GB to 2.91 GB ($\times 1/39.8$), and server-side rotation key generation takes 12.5 s.

In some cases, reducing the burden on the client significantly can be more critical than the service delay. Then, we may need to make the rotation key generation more efficient at the expense of slightly increasing the key-switching operation time. For the ResNet-20 model, we can compare A.i and B.iii parameters. In other words, we can slightly increase the value of $\mathbf{dnum}_0$ to set a lower $\log P_0$ and then optimize $\mathbf{dnum}_1$ or $\log P_1$ for more efficient key generation. While the ciphertext key-switching runtime increases from 3.10 ms to 3.67 ms ($\times 1.18$ slower), the client-side rotation key generation more significantly reduces from 88.7 s to 6.30 s ($\times 14.1$ faster), the communication amount for rotation keys reduces from 38.3 GB to 2.67 GB ($\times 1/14.3$), and server-side rotation key generation takes 10.2 s. Therefore, if the actual service execution time is not highly sensitive, using A.ii two-level parameters or A.iii two-level parameters to reduce the client's burden can be advantageous. For the ResNet-18 model, we can compare C.ii and D.iii parameters. While the ciphertext key-switching runtime increases from 6.05 ms to 6.59 ms ($\times 1.08$ slower), the client-side rotation key generation more significantly reduces from 145.1 s to 2.52 s ($\times 57.6$ faster), the communication amount for rotation keys reduces from 115.7 GB to 1.97 GB ($\times 1/58.7$), and server-side rotation key generation takes 16.1 s. Using D.iii parameters to reduce the client's burden can be more advantageous than D.ii.

Discussion of Three-Level System. Three-level usage can be advantageous in scenarios where the client has sent computation keys to the server but the computation model has not yet been agreed upon. In such cases, if there is a waiting time for the computation model to be decided, the runtime required to generate rotation keys for the corresponding model can be included in the online latency. Therefore, reducing the time to generate level-0 rotation keys can be important. However, the D.iii parameters have a larger server-side rotation key generation runtime than the D.ii parameters. Also, in a two-level system, to reduce the time for generating level-0 rotation keys, we may need to send more level-1 rotation keys, increasing the client's burden. For example, we may need to send a 4-ary level-1 rotation key set instead of a 16-ary level-1 rotation key set, which would roughly double the rotation key generation time and communication amount on the client's side. However, by using a three-level rotation key, we can eliminate this trade-off.

For instance, we can compare C.ii parameters with E.iii three-level parameters. While the ciphertext key-switching runtime increases from 6.05 ms to 6.59 ms (x1.08 slower), the client-side rotation key generation more significantly reduces from 145.1 s to 1.93 s (x75.2 faster), the communication amount for rotation keys reduces from 115.7 GB to 1.54 GB (x75.1 less), and server-side rotation key generation takes 13.9 s. In this scenario, the server needs 26.9 s to prepare more level-1 rotation keys while waiting for the computation model to be decided. It allows less client-side rotation key generation and less communication with the similar server-side rotation key generation runtime to the D.ii parameters. Thus, except for the offline server-side rotation key generation, the three-level scheme shows nearly optimal online performance overall in the rotation key generation.

6   Conclusion

We proposed a hierarchical rotation key system for the CKKS and BFV schemes to significantly reduce the computational and communication costs of the client and to make the rotation key management with the reduced memory in the server. It allows the server to generate the rotation keys for the required cyclic shifts using the rotation keys in the higher key level without a secret key or any help from the clients. It can be an important future work that designs a systematic method to perform complex services with limited memory by using the proposed method more efficiently or a fast algorithm for generating a sequence of rotation keys closer to the optimal solution.

Acknowledgements. This work was supported in part by the Institute of Information and Communications Technology Planning and Evaluation (IITP) grant funded by the Korea Government [Ministry of Science and ICT (MSIT)]), Development of Highly Efficient Post-Quantum Cryptography (PQC) Security and Performance Verification for Constrained Devices under Grant 2021-0-00400, and in part by Basic Science Research Program through the National Research Foundation of Korea (NRF) funded by the Ministry of Education (No. 2022R1I1A1A01-06828412), and in part the National Research Foundation of Korea (NRF) grant funded by the Korea government (MSIT) (No. NRF-2021R1A2C2011082).

We would like to express our gratitude to the anonymous reviewers who provided insightful suggestions for effective experiments highlighting the utility of the techniques in this paper.

References

1. Lattigo v3, April 2022. Online: https://github.com/tuneinsight/lattigo, ePFL-LDS, Tune Insight SA
2. Bossuat, J.-P., Mouchet, C., Troncoso-Pastoriza, J., Hubaux, J.-P.: Efficient bootstrapping for approximate homomorphic encryption with non-sparse keys. In: Canteaut, A., Standaert, F.-X. (eds.) EUROCRYPT 2021. LNCS, vol. 12696, pp. 587–617. Springer, Cham (2021). https://doi.org/10.1007/978-3-030-77870-5_21
3. Bossuat, J.P., Troncoso-Pastoriza, J., Hubaux, J.P.: Bootstrapping for approximate homomorphic encryption with negligible failure-probability by using sparse-secret encapsulation. In: Ateniese, G., Venturi, D. (eds.) ACNS 2022, pp. 521–541. Springer, Cham (2022). https://doi.org/10.1007/978-3-031-09234-3_26
4. Brakerski, Z.: Fully homomorphic encryption without modulus switching from classical GapSVP. In: Safavi-Naini, R., Canetti, R. (eds.) CRYPTO 2012. LNCS, vol. 7417, pp. 868–886. Springer, Heidelberg (2012). https://doi.org/10.1007/978-3-642-32009-5_50

5. Çetin, G.S., Chen, H., Laine, K., Lauter, K., Rindal, P., Xia, Y.: Private queries on encrypted genomic data. BMC Med. Genomics **10**(2), 1–14 (2017)
6. Chen, H., Chillotti, I., Song, Y.: Improved bootstrapping for approximate homomorphic encryption. In: Ishai, Y., Rijmen, V. (eds.) EUROCRYPT 2019. LNCS, vol. 11477, pp. 34–54. Springer, Cham (2019). https://doi.org/10.1007/978-3-030-17656-3_2
7. Cheon, J.H., Han, K., Kim, A., Kim, M., Song, Y.: Bootstrapping for approximate homomorphic encryption. In: Nielsen, J.B., Rijmen, V. (eds.) EUROCRYPT 2018. LNCS, vol. 10820, pp. 360–384. Springer, Cham (2018). https://doi.org/10.1007/978-3-319-78381-9_14
8. Cheon, J.H., Han, K., Kim, A., Kim, M., Song, Y.: A full RNS variant of approximate homomorphic encryption. In: Cid, C., Jacobson Jr., M. (eds.) Proceedings of International Conference on Selected Areas in Cryptography (SAC). LNCS, vol. 11349, pp. 347–368. Springer, Cham (2018). https://doi.org/10.1007/978-3-030-10970-7_16
9. Cheon, J.H., Hhan, M., Hong, S., Son, Y.: A hybrid of dual and meet-in-the-middle attack on sparse and ternary secret LWE. IEEE Access **7**, 89497–89506 (2019)
10. Cheon, J.H., Kim, A., Kim, M., Song, Y.: Homomorphic encryption for arithmetic of approximate numbers. In: Takagi, T., Peyrin, T. (eds.) ASIACRYPT 2017. LNCS, vol. 10624, pp. 409–437. Springer, Cham (2017). https://doi.org/10.1007/978-3-319-70694-8_15
11. Cho, J., et al.: Transciphering framework for approximate homomorphic encryption. In: Tibouchi, M., Wang, H. (eds.) ASIACRYPT 2021. LNCS, vol. 13092, pp. 640–669. Springer, Cham (2021). https://doi.org/10.1007/978-3-030-92078-4_22
12. Edmonds, J.: Optimum branchings. J. Res. Natl. Bur. Stan. B **71**(4), 233–240 (1967)
13. Fan, J., Vercauteren, F.: Somewhat practical fully homomorphic encryption. Cryptol. ePrint Arch. Technical report 2012/144 (2012)
14. Gilad-Bachrach, R., Dowlin, N., Laine, K., Lauter, K., Naehrig, M., Wernsing, J.: CryptoNets: applying neural networks to encrypted data with high throughput and accuracy. In: Proceedings of International Conference on Machine Learning (ICML), pp. 201–210. PMLR (2016)
15. Ha, J., Kim, S., Lee, B., Lee, J., Son, M.: Rubato: noisy ciphers for approximate homomorphic encryption. In: Dunkelman, O., Dziembowski, S. (eds.) EUROCRYPT 2022. LNCS, vol. 13275, pp. 581–610. Springer, Cham (2022). https://doi.org/10.1007/978-3-031-06944-4_20
16. Halevi, S., Shoup, V.: Algorithms in HElib. In: Garay, J.A., Gennaro, R. (eds.) CRYPTO 2014. LNCS, vol. 8616, pp. 554–571. Springer, Heidelberg (2014). https://doi.org/10.1007/978-3-662-44371-2_31
17. Halevi, S., Shoup, V.: Faster homomorphic linear transformations in HElib. In: Shacham, H., Boldyreva, A. (eds.) CRYPTO 2018. LNCS, vol. 10991, pp. 93–120. Springer, Cham (2018). https://doi.org/10.1007/978-3-319-96884-1_4
18. Han, K., Ki, D.: Better bootstrapping for approximate homomorphic encryption. In: Jarecki, S. (ed.) CT-RSA 2020. LNCS, vol. 12006, pp. 364–390. Springer, Cham (2020). https://doi.org/10.1007/978-3-030-40186-3_16
19. Jiang, X., Kim, M., Lauter, K., Song, Y.: Secure outsourced matrix computation and application to neural networks. In: Proceedings of the 2018 ACM SIGSAC Conference on Computer and Communications Security (CCS), pp. 1209–1222 (2018)
20. Jung, W., Kim, S., Ahn, J.H., Cheon, J.H., Lee, Y.: Over 100x faster bootstrapping in fully homomorphic encryption through memory-centric optimization with GPUs. IACR Trans. Cryptographic Hardware Embed. Syst. **2021**(4), 114–148 (2021)

21. Juvekar, C., Vaikuntanathan, V., Chandrakasan, A.: GAZELLE: a low latency framework for secure neural network inference. In: Proceedings of the 27th USENIX Security Symposium, pp. 1651–1669 (2018)
22. Kim, M., Lauter, K.: Private genome analysis through homomorphic encryption. In: BMC Medical Informatics and Decision Making, vol. 15, pp. 1–12. BioMed Central (2015)
23. Kim, M., Song, Y., Li, B., Micciancio, D.: Semi-parallel logistic regression for GWAS on encrypted data. BMC Med. Genomics **13**(7), 1–13 (2020)
24. Kocabas, O., Soyata, T.: Towards privacy-preserving medical cloud computing using homomorphic encryption. In: Virtual and Mobile Healthcare: Breakthroughs in Research and Practice, pp. 93–125. IGI Global (2020)
25. Lee, E., et al.: Low-complexity deep convolutional neural networks on fully homomorphic encryption using multiplexed parallel convolutions. In: International Conference on Machine Learning (ICML), pp. 12403–12422. PMLR (2022)
26. Lee, J.W., et al.: Privacy-preserving machine learning with fully homomorphic encryption for deep neural network. IEEE Access **10**, 30039–30054 (2022)
27. Lee, J.W., Lee, E., Kim, Y.S., No, J.S.: Rotation key reduction for client-server systems of deep neural network on fully homomorphic encryption. Cryptol. ePrint Arch., Technical report 2022/532 (2022)
28. Lee, J.-W., Lee, E., Lee, Y., Kim, Y.-S., No, J.-S.: High-precision bootstrapping of RNS-CKKS homomorphic encryption using optimal minimax polynomial approximation and inverse sine function. In: Canteaut, A., Standaert, F.-X. (eds.) EUROCRYPT 2021. LNCS, vol. 12696, pp. 618–647. Springer, Cham (2021). https://doi.org/10.1007/978-3-030-77870-5_22
29. Lee, Y., Lee, J.W., Kim, Y.S., Kang, H., No, J.S.: High-precision and low-complexity approximate homomorphic encryption by error variance minimization. In: EUROCRYPT 2022, pp. 551–580. Springer, Cham (2022)
30. Lindell, Y.: How to simulate it – a tutorial on the simulation proof technique. In: Tutorials on the Foundations of Cryptography. ISC, pp. 277–346. Springer, Cham (2017). https://doi.org/10.1007/978-3-319-57048-8_6
31. Meftah, S., Tan, B.H.M., Aung, K.M.M., Yuxiao, L., Jie, L., Veeravalli, B.: Towards high performance homomorphic encryption for inference tasks on CPU: an MPI approach. Future Gener. Comput. Syst. **134**, 13–21 (2022)
32. Mono, J., Marcolla, C., Land, G., Güneysu, T., Aaraj, N.: Finding and evaluating parameters for BGV. In: El Mrabet, N., De Feo, L., Duquesne, S. (eds.) AFRICACRYPT 2023. LNCS, vol. 14064, pp. 370–394. Springer, Cham (2023). https://doi.org/10.1007/978-3-031-37679-5_16
33. Prim, R.C.: Shortest connection networks and some generalizations. Bell Syst. Tech. J. **36**(6), 1389–1401 (1957)

Homomorphic Polynomial Evaluation Using Galois Structure and Applications to BFV Bootstrapping

Hiroki Okada[2], Rachel Player[1], and Simon Pohmann[1(✉)]

[1] Royal Holloway, University of London, London, UK
`simon@pohmann.de`
[2] KDDI Research, Fujimino, Japan

Abstract. BGV and BFV are among the most widely used fully homomorphic encryption (FHE) schemes. Both schemes have a common plaintext space, with a rich algebraic structure. Our main contribution is to show how this structure can be exploited to more efficiently homomorphically evaluate polynomials. Namely, using Galois automorphisms, we present an algorithm to homomorphically evaluate a polynomial of degree d in only $3\log(d)$ (in some cases only $2\log(d)$) many ciphertext-ciphertext multiplications and automorphism evaluations, where d is bounded by the ring degree. In other words, as long as the degree of the polynomial is bounded, we achieve an exponential speedup compared to the state of the art. In particular, the approach also improves on the theoretical lower bound of $2\sqrt{d}$ many ciphertext-ciphertext multiplications, which would apply if automorphisms were not available.

We investigate how to apply our improved polynomial evaluation to the bootstrapping procedure for BFV, and show that we are able to significantly improve its performance. We demonstrate this by providing an implementation of our improved BFV bootstrapping using the Microsoft SEAL library. More concretely, we obtain a 1.6× speed up compared to the prior implementation given by Chen and Han (Eurocrypt 2018). The techniques are independent of, and can be combined with, the more recent optimisations presented by Geelen *et al.* (Eurocrypt 2023).

As an additional contribution, we show how the bootstrapping approach used in schemes such as FHEW and TFHE can be applied in the BFV context. In particular, we demonstrate that programmable bootstrapping can be achieved for BFV. Moreover, we show how this bootstrapping approach can be improved in the BFV context to make better use of the Galois structure. However, we estimate that its complexity is around three orders of magnitude slower than the classical approach to BFV bootstrapping.

Keywords: homomorphic encryption · bootstrapping · implementation

© International Association for Cryptologic Research 2023
J. Guo and R. Steinfeld (Eds.): ASIACRYPT 2023, LNCS 14443, pp. 69–100, 2023.
https://doi.org/10.1007/978-981-99-8736-8_3

1   Introduction

Fully homomorphic encryption (FHE) allows computations on encrypted data, without decrypting it or having access to the secret key. After the existence of such schemes had been an open problem for many years, Gentry [23] proposed the first FHE scheme based on lattices. Since then, much work has been done to develop more efficient and practical schemes. The BFV scheme [20] and the related BGV scheme [8], which follow from the line of work [7,9], are among the most widely implemented today. Other FHE schemes include the TFHE family of schemes [17,18,27]. Notable also is the CKKS scheme [15], which is technically similar to BFV and BGV, but which differs in that it is an approximate rather than an exact scheme and in that it encrypts real numbers rather than elements in a polynomial ring.

The schemes [8,15,17,18,20,27] all base their security on the Learning with Errors (LWE) problem [48], and hence add some noise when encrypting a message. For the exact schemes, as long as this noise is small enough, it can be removed during decryption and the exact message can be recovered. However, homomorphic operations increase the noise, and after a sufficiently long sequence of operations, the noise will exceed a certain threshold and decryption will fail. The breakthrough of [23] that allows arbitrary computations is the technique called bootstrapping, that provides a mechanism to periodically refresh the noise. The idea is simple: to perform the decryption homomorphically, using an encryption of the secret key. This way, the party performing the bootstrapping does not need the actual secret key in order to evaluate the decryption. However, it does require an additional circular security assumption that, roughly speaking, states that publishing an encryption of the secret key does not help break the scheme.

Bootstrapping for BGV and BFV has traditionally been considered together, due to the technical similarities between the two schemes. Early work approached BGV and BFV bootstrapping via boolean circuits [25]. The main idea was to represent the bootstrapping procedure using bitwise operations, making "simple" operations like multiplication quite expensive.

The algebraic structure of BGV and BFV enables their plaintext spaces to be decomposed into slots, providing single-instruction-multiple-data (SIMD) parallelism [50]. This speed up can be applied to improve bootstrapping [26]. This technique is absolutely vital for performance, and has equally been applied to present batched bootstrapping for the FHEW and TFHE scheme [28,45].

Starting with [2], a line of work [12,22,30] then developed an approach for bootstrapping that avoids using boolean circuits. The main insight is that it is possible to use the algebraic structure of the plaintext space "naturally" during homomorphic decryption. In doing so, algebraic operations can directly be implemented via the corresponding homomorphic operations, vastly decreasing the overhead. However, non-algebraic operations (in particular, rounding) become more expensive, as they have to be implemented with polynomials.

In this paper, we continue the line of work [2,12,22,30], and present new algebraic optimisations that can further improve the bootstrapping procedure for the BFV and BGV scheme. While we will perform our analysis only on BFV, we remark that the same techniques can be applied to BGV in a straightforward way.

1.1 Our Contribution

Many BFV and BGV parameter sets used in practice have the apparent disadvantage of providing few plaintext slots of high algebraic rank, leading to a loss of parallelism. Our first main contribution is to show an advantage of the algebraic structure of these high rank slots. Namely, we show that the algebraic structure can be exploited to evaluate scalar polynomials more efficiently than is possible using generic approaches (e.g. Paterson-Stockmeyer), or with the prior methods of [43,47]. In particular, we show how one can use the Galois structure within these high-rank slots to evaluate polynomials using only $3\log_2(d)$ key-switch operations (or in some cases even only $2\log_2(d)$ key-switch operations). This significantly improves on the previously required number of at least $2\sqrt{d}$ key switches. We apply this technique to the evaluation of the lifting polynomials used during BFV bootstrapping in power-of-two cyclotomic rings.

We remark that our techniques for improved polynomial evaluation are not just applicable to bootstrapping. Intuitively speaking, they can be used for any homomorphic evaluation of a polynomial, where the plaintext space has a high algebraic rank and the polynomial is only evaluated on elements of the prime field (respectively prime ring). As such, our results may be of wider interest.

Our second main contribution is to provide a new implementation of BFV bootstrapping in the Microsoft SEAL [49] library. This incorporates our improved approach to evaluating the lifting polynomials using the Galois structure. A previous implementation of BFV bootstrapping in SEAL has been reported [12], but the source code is not publicly available. Our performance results show that our new techniques give a notable speedup compared to the previous state of the art, being a factor of 1.6 faster than [12].

Our third main contribution is to consider the applicability to BFV of the bootstrapping techniques used in the TFHE family of schemes [17,18,27]. In particular, we demonstrate that so-called programmable bootstrapping, usually considered possible only in the TFHE context (see e.g. [4]), can also be achieved for BFV. Programmable bootstrapping refers to computing an arbitrary, unary function during the bootstrapping process. We propose new optimisations that again make use of the Galois structure to improve the applicability of these techniques in the BFV context. We present a theoretical comparison of a TFHE-style bootstrapping for BFV to the classical approach, which shows that it is expected to be at least three orders of magnitude slower, and so we did not implement it. Nevertheless, we expect this contribution to be of theoretical interest.

1.2 Improved Polynomial Evaluation

Our improvements for polynomial evaluation in BFV rely on the use of Galois theory and the field-theoretic norm $N(\cdot)$ and trace $\mathrm{Tr}(\cdot)$. As observed in previous work (see e.g. [24, 29]), we can compute them in a BFV plaintext slot

$$\mathcal{S} := \mathbb{F}_p[X]/(f), \text{ where } f \in \mathbb{F}_p[X] \text{ is irreducible,}$$

using only $2\log([\mathcal{S} : \mathbb{F}_p])$ operations. We first combine this with the fact that

$$N(\alpha - x) = \text{MiPo}(\alpha)(x)$$

when α generates $\mathcal{S}$ as a ring and $x \in \mathbb{F}_p$, where $\text{MiPo}(\alpha)$ the minimal polynomial of α. This enables us to evaluate irreducible polynomials of degree bounded by $[\mathcal{S} : \mathbb{F}_p]$ using only logarithmically many operations. Furthermore, this naturally extends to plaintext slots of the form $(\mathbb{Z}/p^e\mathbb{Z})[X]/(f)$, and we also study to what extent this can be used to evaluate non-irreducible polynomials.

Additionally, we introduce an alternative to the above norm-based approach, which instead uses the field trace. We discuss how the trace-based approach eliminates the need for heuristic assumptions, and has the advantage of being applicable to a broader range of problems. These include the evaluation of low-degree multivariate polynomials, especially of bilinear forms, and the evaluation of multiple polynomials in the same point. On the other hand, the trace-based approach has slightly worse performance and is more complicated that the norm-based approach.

The trace-based approach to evaluate a polynomial $g \in \mathbb{F}_p[X]$ at $x \in \mathbb{F}_p$ can be summarised as follows. First, we compute the value

$$\beta := \sum_i x^i \zeta^i,$$

where ζ is a generator of $\mathcal{S}$ with certain properties (it turns out that a root of unity works). Then, we multiply β by a constant c_g to get an element β' whose constant coefficient (i.e. coefficient of ζ^0) is $g(x)$. Finally, we use the field trace to extract this constant coefficient, thus finding $f(x)$.

1.3   Programmable Bootstrapping for BFV

Programmable bootstrapping is a feature currently offered by the family of TFHE-type schemes, and refers to computing an arbitrary unary function implicitly during the bootstrapping procedure. In other words, a high-noise encryption of a message m is transformed into a low-noise encryption of $f(m)$. In TFHE-type schemes, the motivation for computing a function during bootstrapping is that the decryption algorithm requires a rounding operation. Since rounding cannot be naturally represented by algebraic operations, it is computed homomorphically using techniques for computing a generic function. Thus, replacing the rounding function by another function that additionally transforms the message does not incur additional overhead.

In BFV, this is not completely true, as an algorithm called digit extraction is known that can compute a rounding operation faster than a generic function (see Sect. 3.2). Nevertheless, in cases where a generic function is required to be computed, it might still be faster to combine evaluation and bootstrapping into one step. To investigate this, we try to modify the TFHE-bootstrapping procedure for BFV.

One of the most surprising ideas in TFHE bootstrapping is that, during the bootstrapping process, messages are stored in the exponent of some basis, usually a root of unity ζ. At first, this seems strange, because now even addition of messages requires an expensive homomorphic multiplication. However, this gives an advantage in the situation that we want to compute an arbitrary unary function. Namely, given an encryption of ζ^μ (where μ is the message) and a sequence a_i of elements, we find that the constant coefficient of

$$\left(\sum a_i \zeta^{-i}\right)\zeta^\mu$$

is a_μ. The use of this phenomena is called blind rotation, since we "rotate" the sequence a_i by the unknown message μ. When this is done, a clever key-switching technique can be used to retrieve the constant coefficient, i.e. a_μ. For details, see e.g. this excellent guide [34]. While this latter part is scheme-specific[1], a similar approach might still have some advantages for BFV. Abstractly, an arbitrary function on the group $\langle \zeta \rangle \subseteq \mathbb{F}_{p^d}^*$ is much cheaper to compute than on $\mathbb{Z}/t\mathbb{Z}$ (assuming $t \approx \mathrm{ord}(\zeta)$), since we can exploit Galois structure.

To be somewhat more concrete, consider the following simplified scenario: Assume we have a generic function $f : \mathbb{Z}/t\mathbb{Z} \to \{0,1\}$ that we want to evaluate on a message $\mu \in \mathbb{Z}/t\mathbb{Z}$. However, now suppose that instead of μ, we are given ζ^μ where $\zeta \in \mathbb{F}_{p^d}$ is a t-th root of unity. Then f can be computed as

$$\zeta^\mu \mapsto \sum_{y \text{ s.t. } f(y)=1} 1 - N(\zeta^\mu - \zeta^y)^{p-1},$$

where $N(\cdot)$ denotes the field-theoretic norm in $\mathbb{F}_{p^d}$. A fundamental optimization in the case of BFV would be to replace the basis (i.e. the root of unity ζ) by a primitive element of $\mathbb{F}_{p^d}$, i.e. a generator α of $\mathbb{F}_{p^d}^*$. Note that this idea does not work in TFHE, since the norm of encrypted messages in TFHE must be small to prevent huge noise growth. For BFV however, we can now choose a very small prime p (e.g. $p = 2$) and $d = \log_p(t) = \log(t)$, which results in a multiplicative depth of only $\log\log(t)$. To compare, if we wanted to compute $f(x)$ directly from x using a circuit over $\mathbb{Z}/t\mathbb{Z}$, this would require multiplicative depth $\log(t)$.

Since the repeated computation of the norm is inefficient, we also investigate other methods with slightly larger multiplicative depth that have better runtime characteristics. However, we find that all these methods for 'programmable bootstrapping' in BFV are slower than the classical approach for BFV bootstrapping by about three orders of magnitude.

---

[1] It relies on the fact that in TFHE, two schemes are used. The bootstrapped scheme is based on LWE, and the "intermediate" scheme uses Ring-LWE.

1.4 Related Work

Bootstrapping for the BFV/BGV family of schemes has been developed in the line of work [12,21,22,30]. We especially want to highlight [21], who also proposed an optimisation for lifting polynomial evaluation during bootstrapping. As we will explain in Sect. 4.2, their techniques are entirely independent of ours and can also be combined, for even better performance.

Concurrent to works on BFV/BGV, there is a lot of work being done on bootstrapping in the TFHE-family. The pioneering works [3,18] form the basis of a bootstrapping procedure that uses completely different techniques than BFV. While these schemes only bootstrap the encryption of a single bit, they are also much faster. The succeeding works [16,17] reduced the required time to lower than 0.1 s. More recent work has focused more on key sizes and formats [35, 39] and decreasing the amortised bootstrapping time when bootstrapping many messages jointly [28,40,41,44,45].

An interesting hybrid in this context is [42], in which it is proposed to use BFV techniques to bootstrap many TFHE-ciphertexts in parallel. To achieve the best amortised timing, the authors of [42] consider a setting with the maximal number of slots, whereas our approach gives a speed up when there are fewer slots of high rank. Combining the two works might thus present an interesting tradeoff for amortised bootstrapping of TFHE-type ciphertexts via BFV.

Finally, there is also a line of work focusing on bootstrapping for CKKS [5,6, 11,14,31,32,36–38]. As an approximate homomorphic scheme that performs non-exact computations on real numbers, the concept of bootstrapping in CKKS is slightly different. A high-level, non-technical comparison of different approaches to bootstrapping is given in [4].

1.5 Organisation of the Paper

The remainder of the paper is organised as follows. In Sect. 2, we provide notation and preliminaries. In Sect. 3, we give an overview of the classical approach to bootstrapping, as developed in [12,30]. In Sect. 4, we present our norm-based and trace-based improvements to polynomial evaluation for BFV, and discuss their application to bootstrapping. In Sect. 5, we report on our new implementation of BFV bootstrapping in SEAL, which includes the norm-based improvements to evaluating the lifting polynomials. In Sect. 6, we study the applicability of programmable bootstrapping techniques in the BFV context.

2 Preliminaries

2.1 Algebraic Background

We denote by $\mathrm{MiPo}(\alpha)$ the minimal polynomial of a field extension element α. For an integer m and a prime p with $p \nmid m$, we consider the m-th cyclotomic polynomial $\Phi_m = \mathrm{MiPo}(\exp(2\pi i/m))$. Mostly, we will assume $m = 2N$ to be a power of two, and consider $\Phi_{2N} = X^N + 1$. We will consider the ring $R = \mathbb{Z}[X]/(X^N + 1)$ and its reduction modulo some prime power $R/p^e R$.

In this work, we will often require the Galois automorphism of the corresponding field extension $(R \otimes \mathbb{Q})/\mathbb{Q}$. It is a result of algebraic number theory that $R = \mathcal{O}_{R \otimes \mathbb{Q}}$ is the ring of integers in $R \otimes \mathbb{Q}$, and so there is no confusion if we denote the Galois group by $\mathrm{Gal}(R/\mathbb{Z})$. Furthermore, each Galois automorphism $\sigma \in \mathrm{Gal}(R/\mathbb{Z})$ also induces a natural automorphism

$$\sigma : R/p^e R \to R/p^e R.$$

Note that the reverse is not true, i.e. there might be automorphisms $R/p^e R \to R/p^e R$ that are not induced by a Galois automorphism of R. Hence, we will sometimes talk about the Galois group $\mathrm{Gal}((R/p^e R)/(\mathbb{Z}/p^e\mathbb{Z}))$ and mean the group of all automorphisms $R/p^e R \to R/p^e R$ that are induced by a Galois automorphism of R.

We note that modulo p, $X^N + 1$ factors into n distinct polynomials[2] of degree d, where $d = \mathrm{ord}_{(\mathbb{Z}/2N\mathbb{Z})^*}(p)$. This factorisation lifts to a factorisation modulo p^e via Hensel's lemma, and so we see that

$$R/p^e R \cong \bigoplus_{i=1}^{n} S,$$

where $S \supseteq \mathbb{Z}/p^e\mathbb{Z}$ is a free ring extension of rank d. We remark that this situation behaves almost the same as the simpler case $e = 1$, in which $S \cong \mathbb{F}_{p^d}$. In particular, there is a subgroup $G \leq \mathrm{Gal}((R/p^e R)/(\mathbb{Z}/p^e\mathbb{Z}))$ of size d that map S to S, if we fix an embedding $S \hookrightarrow R/p^e R$. We denote it by $\mathrm{Gal}(S/(\mathbb{Z}/p^e\mathbb{Z})) := G$. These are exactly the automorphisms induced by the *splitting group*

$$G_{\mathfrak{B}} = \{\sigma \in \mathrm{Gal}(R/\mathbb{Z}) \mid \sigma(\mathfrak{B}) = \mathfrak{B}\},$$

where $\mathfrak{B}$ is any prime ideal of R over p (see e.g. [46, Chapter I.9]).

2.2 The BFV Scheme

The basic parameters for the BFV scheme are the *ciphertext modulus* q, the *plaintext modulus* t and the power-of-two cyclotomic ring R. In this paper, we will always have $t = p^e$, for a prime p. The plaintext space of BFV is then given as $\mathcal{P} := R/tR$ and the ciphertext space is $\mathcal{C} := (R/qR)^2$.

A BFV ciphertext $(c_0, c_1) \in \mathcal{C}$ encrypts a message $\overline{m} \in \mathcal{P}$, if

$$c_0 + c_1 s = \frac{q}{t}\overline{m} + \epsilon,$$

where $s \in R$ is the secret key, and $\epsilon \in (R \otimes \mathbb{R})/qR$ is the noise[3], which has to be small. More precisely, for $\epsilon = \sum \epsilon_i X^i \in (R \otimes \mathbb{R})/qR$, we define the "norm"

---

[2] Since we assume that $p \nmid m$.

[3] A short note on the algebraic structures: Clearly we have a well-defined multiplication $R \times R/qR \to R/qR$, which we can use to define $c_1 s$. Furthermore, while $(R \otimes \mathbb{R})/qR$ is not a ring anymore, it is an additive group, which suffices at this place.

$\|\epsilon\|$ (although it is not a norm) as the ℓ_∞-norm of the smallest representative in $R \otimes \mathbb{R}$. In other words, set

$$\|\epsilon\| := \max_i \|\epsilon_i\| := \max_i \min_{\substack{z \in \mathbb{R} \\ z \equiv \epsilon_i \bmod q\mathbb{Z}}} |z|.$$

This yields the following description of the BFV cryptosystem:

KeyGen: Choose $s \in R$ with coefficients s_i uniformly in $\{-1, 0, 1\}$, i.e. $\|s\| \leq 1$. Then sample $a \in R/qR$ uniformly and $\epsilon \in R/qR$ according to a discrete Gaussian distribution. Output

$$\text{sk} = s, \quad \text{pk} = (as + \epsilon, a).$$

Enc: To encrypt a message $\overline{m} \in R/tR$ with pk $= (b, a)$, sample $\epsilon, \epsilon' \in R/qR$ from the discrete Gaussian distribution and $u \in R$ uniformly in $\{-1, 0, 1\}$ s.t. $\|u\| \leq 1$. Output

$$(c_0, c_1) = \left(bu + \epsilon + \left\lfloor \frac{q}{t}\overline{m} \right\rceil, au + \epsilon'\right).$$

Dec: To decrypt a ciphertext $(c_0, c_1) \in \mathcal{C}$ with secret key s, we compute

$$m = \left\lfloor \frac{t}{q}(c_0 + c_1 s) \right\rceil.$$

Decryption correctly recovers the message, if the noise $c_0 + c_1 s - \frac{q}{t}m$ is smaller than $\frac{q}{2t}$. Homomorphic addition of ciphertexts is achieved by summing the input ciphertexts componentwise. Homomorphic multiplication is more complicated, and we do not present the full details, referring the reader to [20]. We note that homomorphic multiplication relies on a technique called key switching.

Key Switching. Key switching takes an encryption of a message m under a secret key s, and transforms it into an encryption of m under a different secret key s'. For this, a key switching key is needed, which is intuitively an encryption of s under s'.

Apart from supporting multiplication, key switching also allows us to compute the Galois automorphisms $\text{Gal}(R/\mathbb{Z})$ homomorphically, since they preserve the "norm" $\|\cdot\|$. Namely, if (c_0, c_1) encrypts m and $\sigma \in \text{Gal}(R/\mathbb{Z})$, we have

$$\sigma(c_0) + \sigma(c_1)\sigma(s) = \sigma(c_0 + c_1 s) = \sigma(q/t\, m + \epsilon) = \frac{q}{t}\sigma(m) + \sigma(\epsilon).$$

Therefore, $(\sigma(c_0), \sigma(c_1))$ is an encryption of $\sigma(m)$ under $\sigma(s)$. After key-switching, we then obtain an encryption of $\sigma(m)$ under s, since $\|\sigma(\epsilon)\| = \|\epsilon\|$.

Performance and Noise Growth. In terms of performance, key switching is the bottleneck of homomorphic computations (and thus the bottleneck in ciphertext-ciphertext multiplications and evaluation of Galois automorphisms). On the other hand, additions and plaintext-ciphertext multiplications are almost free. Because of this, we will measure the performance of different algorithms by the number of key switches that are required to compute them.

For noise growth, the picture is slightly different. In particular, ciphertext-ciphertext multiplications cause significant noise growth, while Galois automorphisms or additions cause almost negligible noise growth.

Division by p. In BFV bootstrapping, the exact division by p as

$$p(R/p^e R) \to R/p^{e-1}R, \quad x \mapsto x/p$$

is an important operation. Note that here, we change the plaintext modulus from p^e to p^{e-1}. From the definition of a BFV ciphertext, it is immediately obvious that we can implement this operation as the identity without any noise growth, if the value x is exactly divisible by p (i.e. is contained in $p(R/p^e R)$). On the other hand, if x is not exactly divisible by p, it is impossible to naturally perform the operation homomorphically.

Modulus Switching. It is also possible to change the ciphertext modulus q to another ciphertext modulus q', by computing

$$(c_0', c_1') := \left(\left\lfloor \frac{q'}{q} c_0 \right\rceil, \left\lfloor \frac{q'}{q} c_1 \right\rceil \right).$$

The secret key and message remain unchanged, but some additional additive error is introduced. In this work, we only use this technique to switch to the encrypted message to a small ciphertext modulus directly before beginning the bootstrapping procedure.

3 Bootstrapping in BFV

In this section, we recall the classical approach to BFV bootstrapping [12,30]. The BFV bootstrapping procedure is summarised in Fig. 1. Concretely, given a ciphertext $(c_0, c_1) \in \mathcal{C}$ encrypting a message in $R/p^r R$, we proceed as follows. First, we perform a modulus-switch to bring c_0, c_1 into the plaintext space $R/p^e R$ where $e > r$. The space $R/p^e R$ is sometimes called the intermediate plaintext space, as it is only used during bootstrapping. Next, we compute the noisy message $\tilde{m} = c_0 + c_1 s$. Next, we perform a linear transformation to extract the individual coefficients $\tilde{m}_i \in \mathbb{Z}/p^e \mathbb{Z}$ of $\tilde{m}$. Next, we compute the rounded division $m_i = \lfloor \tilde{m}_i/p^{e-r} \rceil \in \mathbb{Z}/p^r \mathbb{Z}$ (this is known as digit extraction). Finally, we perform the inverse linear transformation to combine the rounded coefficients m_i into the result $m \in R/p^r R$.

Slots and the Linear Transform. The digit extraction procedure can only ever compute the rounded quotient $\lfloor \tilde{m}_i/p^{e-r} \rceil$ for a scalar value $\tilde{m}_i \in \mathbb{Z}/p^e \mathbb{Z}$. In bootstrapping, digit extraction must be called for every coefficient of the noisy message, i.e. N times. We can use plaintext *slots* to parallelise this process, noting that if the plaintext space decomposes into a direct sum of rings $S \supseteq \mathbb{Z}/p^e\mathbb{Z}$ as

$$R/p^e R \cong \bigoplus_{i=1}^{n} S,$$

then we can perform n scalar digit extractions at once, as displayed on the left side in Fig. 2. To make use of this, we need to move the coefficients of the noisy message into the slots and back. In [26] it was shown how one can use the Galois automorphisms to do so. Commonly, this step is referred to as the *linear transformation*, even though we are just interested in one specific $\mathbb{Z}/p^e\mathbb{Z}$-linear map $R/p^r R \rightarrow R/p^r R$.

Thin/Slim Bootstrapping. In [12], the authors introduced the notion of "slim bootstrapping", displayed on the right in Fig. 2. This refers to the case that the message to bootstrap contains only one scalar value (i.e. value in $\mathbb{Z}/p^r\mathbb{Z}$) in each slot. In this case, we do not have to perform digit extraction on each of the N coefficients, but we only have to retrieve n scalar values. So, we can interchange the linear transform and the inner product step.

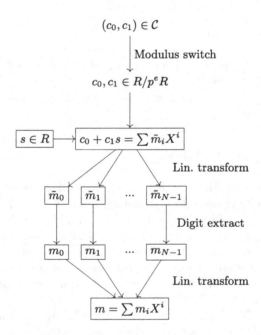

Fig. 1. The abstract bootstrapping procedure for BFV, without using slots. Each rectangle represents one ciphertext.

3.1   The Linear Transform

The basic idea underlying the linear transformation is the fact, established by [30], that any $\mathbb{Z}/p^e\mathbb{Z}$-linear transform can be written as

$$\alpha \mapsto \sum_{\sigma \in G} a_\sigma \sigma(\alpha),$$

where $a_\sigma \in R/p^e R$ and $G = \mathrm{Gal}((R/p^e R)/(\mathbb{Z}/p^e\mathbb{Z}))$. We can evaluate this somewhat efficiently using a baby-step-giant-step approach: First, we choose subsets $G_1, G_2 \subseteq G$ of size approximately $\sqrt{N}$ such that $G_1 \cdot G_2 = G$. Then we can precompute $\sigma(\alpha)$ for all $\sigma \in G_1$ and output

$$\sum_{\tau \in G_2} \tau \left(\sum_{\sigma \in G_1} \tau^{-1}(a_{\tau\sigma})\sigma(\alpha) \right).$$

In our case that $R = \mathbb{Z}[X]/(X^N+1)$ is a power-of-two cyclotomic ring, no better approach is known. However, if $R = \mathbb{Z}[X]/(\Phi_m)$ is the m-th cyclotomic ring such that m has a nontrivial factorization into coprime factors $m_1, \ldots, m_r$, we can do better (see e.g. [22]).

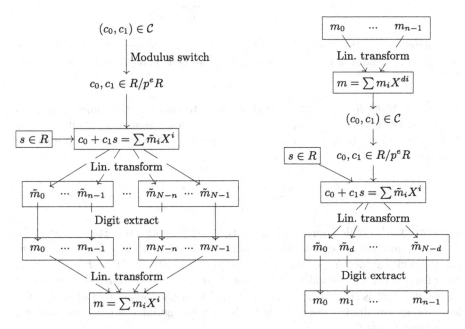

Fig. 2. The abstract bootstrapping procedure for BFV using slots, with "fat" bootstrapping on the left and "thin" bootstrapping on the right. Each rectangle represents one ciphertext.

3.2 Digit Extraction

The idea of digit extraction is to write an input $x \in \mathbb{Z}/p^e\mathbb{Z}$ in base-p representation as

$$x = \sum_{i=0}^{e-1} x_i p^i, \text{ for } x_i \in \{0, ..., p-1\},$$

and give an arithmetic circuit for the "extraction function" $x \mapsto x_0$. This is done by the *lifting polynomials*, defined as follows.

Proposition 3.1 ([30]). *There exists a polynomial $f \in \mathbb{Z}[X]$ of degree at most p such that for all $1 \leq i \leq e$, $z_0 \in \{0, ..., p-1\}$, and $z_1 \in \mathbb{Z}$, have*

$$f(z_0 + p^i z_1) \equiv z_0 \mod p^{i+1}.$$

Proof. Constructed via polynomial interpolation, see Corollary 5.5 in [30]. $\square$

In particular, a repeated application of this polynomial will "extract" the least significant digit (in base-p representation) of an input $x \in \mathbb{Z}/p^e\mathbb{Z}$. Hence, for any $x \in \mathbb{Z}/p^e\mathbb{Z}$, we find that

$$x - f^{\circ(e-1)}(x) = x - \underbrace{f(...f(x))}_{(e-1) \text{ times}}$$

is divisible by p, and quotient $(x - f^{\circ(e-1)}(x))/p$ is the result of the floor division $\lfloor x/p \rfloor$. By adding $p/2$ before doing this, we can then compute the rounded division $\lfloor x/p \rceil$.

Extracting Multiple Digits. Note that we want to compute the rounded division $\lfloor x/p^{e-r} \rceil$, i.e. we want to remove the $v := e - r$ least significant digits from x. Naively, we could do so by removing one digit after another, i.e., we iteratively compute

$$x^{(1)} = \frac{x - f^{\circ(e-1)}(x)}{p}, \quad x^{(2)} = \frac{x^{(1)} - f^{\circ(e-2)}(x^{(1)})}{p}, \ldots, \frac{x^{(v)} - f^{\circ(r)}(x^{(v)})}{p},$$

and output $x^{(v)}$. This approach has multiplicative depth proportional to ev. To do better, note that to extract the second least-significant digit of x, it suffices to run the digit extraction procedure on $(x - f(x))/p$ instead of $(x - f^{\circ(e-1)}(x))/p$. Note that in the expression $x - f(x)$, the digits $2, \ldots, e-1$ may be altered, but the second digit is still the same as the second least-significant digit of x (and the least-significant digit is zero). This leads to a triangular computation pattern, as displayed in [12].

For example, assume $e = 5$ and $r = 2$. Then we compute the values as in Fig. 3 where $x_{ij} = x_i + p^{j+1}z$ for some $z \in \mathbb{Z}$ with the p-adic decomposition $x = \sum x_i p^i$, $x_i \in \{0, ..., p-1\}$.

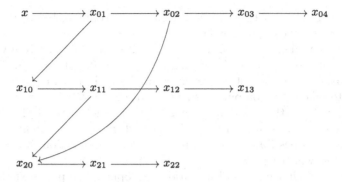

Fig. 3. Multiple digit extraction illustration for $e = 5$ and $r = 2$.

Improvements for Larger r. Chen and Han [12] proposed the use of a second polynomial in addition to the lifting polynomial, which can reduce the multiplicative depth in the case $r > 1$.

Proposition 3.2 (Adapted from [12, Lemma 3]). *There is a polynomial $g \in \mathbb{Z}[X]$ of degree at most $(e-1)(p-1)+1$ such that for $z_0 \in \{-\lfloor \frac{p-1}{2} \rfloor, ..., \lceil \frac{p-1}{2} \rceil\}$ and $z_1 \in \mathbb{Z}$ we have*

$$g(z_0 + pz_1) \equiv z_0 \mod p^e.$$

In other words, this directly extracts the least-significant digit of x. Or, to phrase it in terms of Fig. 3, we directly compute $x_{i0} \mapsto x_{i(e-i-1)}$. Since we require the intermediate values x_{ij} for $i + j \leq v$ to compute $x_{(i+j)0}$, we can only use this to "shorten the tail" in Fig. 3, i.e. to avoid computing x_{ij} for $v - i \leq j < e - i - 1$. However, if $r > 1$, this leads to an improvement in terms of multiplicative depth, which increases as r increases.

The work [21] characterises of all polynomials $g \in \mathbb{Z}[X]$ such that

$$g(z_0 + pz_1) \equiv z_0 \mod p^e$$

for all $z_0 \in \{-\lfloor \frac{p-1}{2} \rfloor, ..., \lceil \frac{p-1}{2} \rceil\}$. In particular, if $e > 1$, the ring $\mathbb{Z}/p^e\mathbb{Z}$ is no longer a field, and there can be many such polynomials, any of which would suffice for bootstrapping. This includes both the lifting polynomials from Proposition 3.1 and the polynomials from Proposition 3.2. Moreover, it is also shown in [21] how to find other polynomials that have lower degree or other favourable properties.

4   Evaluating Polynomials

In this section, we present our improvements to the classical approach to BFV bootstrapping, as described in Sect. 3.

We have seen that for the digit extraction step during BFV bootstrapping, we have to homomorphically evaluate a polynomial $f \in (\mathbb{Z}/p^e\mathbb{Z})[X]$ of degree p (or even of degree $(e-1)(p-1)+1$) at a point in $\mathbb{Z}/p^e\mathbb{Z}$. Since this polynomial is the result of interpolation, there seems to be no special structure that we can exploit for more efficient computation. Hence, we are interested in methods to evaluate a fixed, generic polynomial.

We note that efficient computations of generic polynomials (often viewed as "lookup tables") have already been discussed in the literature (e.g. [33]), and in many cases, the Galois structure is used. We will also use a Galois-based technique to efficiently compute a function $R/pR \to \mathbb{Z}/p\mathbb{Z}$ in Sect. 6.1. This section differs from these examples mainly in the fact that the functions we consider are over the scalar ring $\mathbb{Z}/p^e\mathbb{Z}$. At first glance, one might think that this eliminates all possibilities for using the Galois group action, but this is not the case, as we will see soon.

As ciphertext-ciphertext multiplications (as opposed to plaintext-ciphertext multiplications or additions) require key switches, they are the most expensive operations. Therefore, we seek to minimise this kind of operation. In algebraic complexity theory, this metric is also known as *nonscalar complexity* (since plaintext-ciphertext multiplications are considered scalar operations). In e.g. [10, Prop. 9.2], it is shown that the best way to evaluate a polynomial as an arithmetic circuit is the Paterson-Stockmeyer method, a variant of which was also used by [12,21].

Paterson-Stockmeyer. In spirit, the Paterson-Stockmeyer approach uses a baby-step-giant-step idea. Assume the polynomial f of degree d is given by

$$f = \sum_{i=0}^{d} a_i X^i.$$

On input x, we can now compute the values

$$1, x, x^2, ..., x^m$$

for $m = \lceil \sqrt{d} \rceil$ using $m - 1$ multiplications. Now write f as

$$f = \sum_{i=0}^{\lfloor d/m \rfloor} X^{mi} \underbrace{\sum_{j=0}^{m-1} a_{im+j} X^j}_{=:f_i}.$$

Since we have precomputed x^j for $j \leq m$, we can now evaluate all f_j at x without further ciphertext-ciphertext multiplication. After that, since we also have x^m, we can compute $f(x)$ from the $f_i(x)$ using Horner's method, i.e., as

$$f(x) = f_0(x) + x^m \left(f_1(x) + x^m \left(\cdots \left(f_{\lfloor d/m \rfloor - 1}(x) + x^m f_{\lfloor d/m \rfloor}(x) \right) \cdots \right) \right)$$

using $\lfloor d/m \rfloor \leq m$ further multiplications. This results in nonscalar complexity $2\sqrt{d}$. We remark that this has a low nonscalar complexity, but a (relatively) high multiplicative depth $\geq \sqrt{d}$. For FHE computations, it can thus be better to use variants with slightly higher nonscalar complexity but multiplicative depth logarithmic in d.

The Paterson-Stockmeyer method is optimal for generic (more precisely, Zariski-all) polynomials *in the arithmetic circuit model*. However, in addition to additions and multiplications, we can also homomorphically compute the Galois automorphisms, and thus go beyond that model. In the rest of this section, we show how to exploit this to compute the polynomial evaluation using significantly less than $2\sqrt{d}$ multiplications/key-switches.

4.1 Using the Norm

When the polynomials and the inputs are given in plain, using Galois automorphisms can already lead to small improvements, as shown in [19]. Yet their usefulness is somewhat limited by the fact that arithmetic in algebraic extension fields with nontrivial Galois group is very expensive. If Galois structure is used, it is often to reduce the situation to the scalar case. In contrast, in our situation, since the high ring degree of the plaintext/ciphertext space is necessary for security, we get the extension field arithmetic "for free". This opens up a lot of possibilities, even in the case where all inputs are already in the prime field.

In this subsection we show how to improve polynomial evaluation using the norm in the ring extension $S \supseteq (\mathbb{Z}/p^e\mathbb{Z})$ of rank $d = 2^l$. As in the field case, we define the norm of $\alpha \in S$ as

$$N_{S/(\mathbb{Z}/p^e\mathbb{Z})}(\alpha) := \det(m_\alpha),$$

where $m_\alpha : S \to S$, $x \mapsto \alpha x$ is the multiplication-by-α map. Then, $N_{S/(\mathbb{Z}/p^e\mathbb{Z})}(\alpha)$ is also the constant coefficient in $\mathrm{MiPo}(\alpha)$ and

$$N_{S/(\mathbb{Z}/p^e\mathbb{Z})}(\alpha) = \prod_{\sigma \in \mathrm{Gal}(S/(\mathbb{Z}/p^e\mathbb{Z}))} \sigma(\alpha),$$

given that $S = (\mathbb{Z}/p^e\mathbb{Z})[\alpha]$.

The connection to polynomial evaluation is given by the next standard result of field theory.

Proposition 4.1. *Assume* $S = (\mathbb{Z}/p^e\mathbb{Z})[\alpha]$. *Then for* $x \in \mathbb{Z}/p^e\mathbb{Z}$ *have*

$$N_{S/(\mathbb{Z}/p^e\mathbb{Z})}(\alpha - x) = \mathrm{MiPo}(\alpha)(x).$$

Proof. If $S = (\mathbb{Z}/p^e\mathbb{Z})[\alpha]$ then also $S = (\mathbb{Z}/p^e\mathbb{Z})[\alpha - x]$, and so $\alpha - x$ also has degree d over $\mathbb{Z}/p^e\mathbb{Z}$. Now $\mathrm{MiPo}(\alpha)(T + x)$ has the root $\alpha - x$ and is of degree d, so $\mathrm{MiPo}(\alpha - x) = \mathrm{MiPo}(\alpha)(T + x)$. If we now set $\mathrm{MiPo}(\alpha) = \sum a_i T^i$, we see that

$$\mathrm{MiPo}(\alpha - x) = \sum_{i=0}^{d} a_i (T + x)^i = \sum_{i=0}^{d} \sum_{j=0}^{i} \binom{i}{j} a_i T^j x^{i-j} = \sum_{j=0}^{d} T^j \sum_{i=j}^{d} \binom{i}{j} a_i x^{i-j}$$

has the constant coefficient

$$\sum_{i=0}^{d} \binom{i}{0} a_i x^i = \mathrm{MiPo}(\alpha)(x).$$

The constant coefficient of the minimal polynomial is the norm, and the claim follows.   □

As mentioned before, the norm can also be described as

$$N_{S/(\mathbb{Z}/p^e\mathbb{Z})}(\alpha) = \prod_{\sigma \in \mathrm{Gal}(S/(\mathbb{Z}/p^e\mathbb{Z}))} \sigma(\alpha).$$

As in the case of finite fields, we know that $\mathrm{Gal}(S/(\mathbb{Z}/p^e\mathbb{Z}))$ is cyclic of order d and generated by the Frobenius automorphism[4] $\pi : S \to S$. In the case that we are most interested in, d is a power of two, and so we can factor the norm as

$$N_{S/(\mathbb{Z}/p^e\mathbb{Z})}(\cdot) = (\mathrm{id} \cdot \pi) \circ (\mathrm{id} \cdot \pi^2) \circ (\mathrm{id} \cdot \pi^4) \circ \ldots \circ (\mathrm{id} \cdot \pi^{d/2}).$$

This gives us an algorithm to compute the norm of an arbitrary element in S, using only $\log_2(d)$ ciphertext-ciphertext multiplications and as many Galois automorphisms. To use this for the evaluation of polynomials, we need the following additional assumption.

Heuristic 4.2. *Let $f \in (\mathbb{Z}/p^e\mathbb{Z})[T]$ be a polynomial. Then there is $g = \sum a_i X^{2^i} \in (\mathbb{Z}/p^e\mathbb{Z})[T]$ of degree less than $\deg(f)$ such that $f + g$ is irreducible.*

Note that the fraction of monic irreducible polynomials of degree r in $\mathbb{F}_p[T]$ is about $1/r$, and the corresponding result then also holds for the irreducible polynomials in $(\mathbb{Z}/p^e\mathbb{Z})[X]$. Hence, if we assume the heuristic that any given polynomial of degree r is irreducible with probability $1/r$ (and this is independent for all polynomials), the probability that Heuristic 4.2 holds for $\deg(g) = 1$ (i.e. there is c with $f + c$ is irreducible) is about

$$1 - (1 - 1/r)^p \gtrsim 1 - \exp(-1) > 0.6$$

as wlog $r \leq p$. This probability goes very close to 1 as $\deg(g)$ increases. Thus, we find Heuristic 4.2 a reasonable assumption.

Corollary 4.3. *Let $f \in (\mathbb{Z}/p^e\mathbb{Z})[T]$ with $\deg(f) < 2^l = d$. Assume Heuristic 4.2 for a polynomial depending on f. Then we can evaluate f at $x \in \mathbb{Z}/p^e\mathbb{Z}$ using $3l$ key switches and multiplicative depth l (over S).*

---

[4] This is no longer the map $\alpha \mapsto \alpha^p$, but the unique map π that makes the diagram

$$\begin{array}{ccc} S & \xrightarrow{\;\;\pi\;\;} & S \\ \Big\downarrow{\scriptstyle\mathrm{mod}\ p} & & \Big\downarrow{\scriptstyle\mathrm{mod}\ p} \\ \mathbb{F}_{p^d} & \xrightarrow{\;\alpha \mapsto \alpha^p\;} & \mathbb{F}_{p^d} \end{array}$$

commute. It is induced by a $\sigma \in \mathrm{Gal}(R/\mathbb{Z})$ s.t. $\sigma : R/\mathfrak{B} \to R/\mathfrak{B}$ is the Frobenius, where $\mathfrak{B} \leq R$ is a prime over p.

Proof. Consider $f' = T^d + f(T)$ and $g \in (\mathbb{Z}/p^e\mathbb{Z})[T]$ such that $f' + g$ is irreducible. Then there is $\alpha \in S$ such that $\mathrm{MiPo}(\alpha) = f' + g$. Hence, on input $x \in \mathbb{Z}/p^e\mathbb{Z}$, we first compute the values

$$1, x, x^2, x^4, ..., x^{2^l}$$

using l multiplications. From this, we can then compute $g(x)$ without further multiplications. Finally, we compute

$$N_{S/(\mathbb{Z}/p^e\mathbb{Z})}(\alpha - x)$$

using l multiplications and l automorphisms, and output

$$f(x) = N_{S/(\mathbb{Z}/p^e\mathbb{Z})}(\alpha - x) - x^d - g(x).$$

$\square$

For certain polynomials which wish to evaluate in practice, we can do even better. In particular, we assume the following stronger version of Heuristic 4.2.

Heuristic 4.4. *Let $f \in (\mathbb{Z}/p^e\mathbb{Z})[X]$ be a polynomial. Then it is quite likely that there is $c \in \mathbb{Z}/p^e\mathbb{Z}$ such that $f + c$ is irreducible.*

While Heuristic 4.4 does not hold in many cases, there are still relevant situations in which it does. In particular, bootstrapping for some parameters sets is among them, as we will illustrate in Example 4.6.

Corollary 4.5. *Let $f \in \mathbb{F}_p[T]$ monic of degree $\deg(f) = 2^l + 1$, and have $d = 2^l$. Assume Heuristic 4.4 for a polynomial depending on f. Then we can evaluate f at $x \in \mathbb{Z}/p^e\mathbb{Z}$ using $2l + 1$ key switches and multiplicative depth $l + 1$ (over S).*

Proof. Write $f = \sum_{i=0}^{d+1} a_i T^i$ and consider the polynomial

$$f' = \sum_{i=0}^{d} a_{i+1} T^i.$$

We assume there is $c \in \mathbb{Z}/p^e\mathbb{Z}$ such that $f' + c$ is irreducible, so there is $\alpha \in S$ with $\mathrm{MiPo}(\alpha) = f' + c$. Now we can compute

$$f(x) = (N_{S/(\mathbb{Z}/p^e\mathbb{Z})}(\alpha - x) - c) \cdot x + a_0.$$

$\square$

To summarise, the results of this subsection show how, if a particular heuristic assumption holds, we can evaluate a polynomial f using only $2\log_2(\deg(f))$ key switch operations. This is a significant speedup compared to the $2\sqrt{\deg(f)}$ key switch operations required for the Paterson-Stockmeyer method. In Example 4.6 we show that this can be applied to the lifting polynomials during BFV bootstrapping for certain parameter sets.

Example 4.6 (Applicability of Heuristic 4.4 in the case $p = 257$). A popular parameter choice for bootstrapping is the case $p = 257$ and $e = 3$. In this case, we have $d = 256$ and $n = N/d$ for $N \geq 2^{10}$. Furthermore, the lifting polynomial $f_{\text{lift}} \in (\mathbb{Z}/257^3\mathbb{Z})[x]$ is

$$f_{\text{lift}} = x^{257} + 16941697x^{256} + 12048417x^{257} + \ldots + 11690673x^2 + 12066407x.$$

Since we want to use Corollary 4.5, we want to compute f_{lift}/x fast. Note here that f_{lift} has no constant term, so we can just divide out x.

By Hensel's lemma, irreducibility only depends on the value modulo p, so it suffices to consider $f := f_{\text{lift}}/x \mod 257 \in \mathbb{F}_{257}[x]$. Since irreducibility testing for polynomials over $\mathbb{F}_{257}$ is available in all major algebra packages, it is trivial to check for all $c \in \mathbb{F}_{257}$ whether $f + c$ is irreducible. Using SAGE, we find that $f + 3$ is indeed irreducible. Now we can extract a root $\tilde{\alpha} \in \mathbb{F}_{257^{256}} = S/pS$ of $f + 3$. Using the algorithmic version of Hensel's lemma, we can then lift $\tilde{\alpha} \in \mathbb{F}_{257^{256}}$ to a root $\alpha \in S := (\mathbb{Z}/257^{256}\mathbb{Z})[\zeta]$ of $f_{\text{lift}}/x + 3$. Finally, we compute the evaluation as

$$f_{\text{lift}}(x) = (N_{S/(\mathbb{Z}/257^3\mathbb{Z})}(\alpha - x) - 3) \cdot x.$$

4.2 Using the Trace

In this subsection we show how to improve polynomial evaluation using the trace in the ring extension $S \supseteq (\mathbb{Z}/p^e\mathbb{Z})$ of rank $d = 2^l$. As for the norm, we define the trace as the trace of the multiplication-by-α map $m_\alpha : x \mapsto \alpha x$. As expected, it is equal to

$$\text{Tr}_{S/(\mathbb{Z}/p^e\mathbb{Z})}(\alpha) = \sum_{\sigma \in \text{Gal}(S/(\mathbb{Z}/p^e\mathbb{Z}))} \sigma(\alpha).$$

This avoids the heuristics needed in Sect. 4.1 and may be applicable to improve the evaluation of a broader class of polynomials. The trace approach has further advantages, that we describe in Sect. 4.3. However, to our knowledge, the trace approach cannot match the number of $2\log_2(d)$ key switches, and will thus perform worse than the norm approach described in Sect. 4.1. For this reason, we did not implement the trace approach.

For this subsection, we assume further that S is generated by a primitive $2N$-th root of unity ζ with N a power of two. This is exactly the case that we are typically interested in for FHE.

Lemma 4.7. *Given $x \in S$, we can compute $\alpha_1, \ldots, \alpha_l$ in $2l - 2$ multiplications and multiplicative depth l, where*

$$\alpha_k := \sum_{i=0}^{2^k-1} x^i.$$

Proof. We have the factorisation

$$\alpha_k = \sum_{i=0}^{2^k-1} x^i = \prod_{i=0}^{k-1} (1 + x^{2^i}).$$

Hence, we can first compute the values $x, x^2, x^4, ..., x^{2^{l-1}}$ using $l-1$ multiplications, and then compute the product

$$(1+x)(1+x^2)(1+x^4)...(1+x^{2^{l-1}}).$$

using $l-1$ more multiplications. Note that computing this product from left to right, we achieve multiplicative depth l and produce all the α_i, $i < l$ as intermediate results. □

Lemma 4.7 applied to $x\zeta$ allows us to jointly compute all the powers of x up to a point. This way, we find

$$\sum_{i=0}^{2^l-1} x^i \zeta^i.$$

To deduce the value of any polynomial $f(x)$ with $\deg(f) \leq 2^l - 1$ from this, it is then sufficient to compute a $\mathbb{Z}/p^e\mathbb{Z}$-linear transformation. However, if we want to be able to do this in logarithmically many key switches, we still have to choose a linear transformation that we can compute extraordinarily fast. As it turns out, the trace in the ring extension $S/(\mathbb{Z}/p^e\mathbb{Z})$ is suitable for this.

First, we prove that the minimal polynomial of ζ is sparse in a certain sense.

Lemma 4.8. $\mathrm{MiPo}(\zeta) = T^d + aT^{d/2} + b$ for $a, b \in \mathbb{Z}/p^e\mathbb{Z}$.

Proof. A proof is given in the Supplementary Material of the full version. □

Lemma 4.8 clearly implies that $\mathrm{Tr}(\zeta^k) = 0$ for $k < d$, unless $k \in \{0, d/2\}$. We want to use this to compute the linear transform

$$S \to S, \quad \sum_i a_i \zeta^i \mapsto a_0$$

using only logarithmically many Galois operations.

Lemma 4.9. Let $d = 2^l$ and consider $\alpha = \sum_{i=0}^{d-1} x_i \zeta^i \in S$. We can compute x_0 and $x_{d/2}$ from α using l Galois automorphisms (and no nonscalar multiplications).

Proof. Lemma 4.8 yields that $\mathrm{MiPo}(\zeta) = T^d + aT^{d/2} + b$, and so

$$\mathrm{Tr}(\zeta^k) = \begin{cases} d & \text{if } k = 0, \\ -a & \text{if } k = d/2, \\ 0 & \text{otherwise.} \end{cases}$$

Now note that $\pi(\zeta^{d/2}) = -\zeta^{d/2}$ and $\pi^{2^i}(\zeta^{d/2}) = \zeta^{d/2}$ for any $i > 0$. This means we can compute

$$\beta := \left((\mathrm{id} + \pi^2) \circ (\mathrm{id} + \pi^4) \circ ... \circ (\mathrm{id} + \pi^{d/2}) \right) (\alpha)$$

and it takes us $l-1$ Galois automorphisms to do so. Now we have by the linearity of Tr function,

$$\mathrm{Tr}(\alpha) = (\mathrm{id} + \pi)(\beta) = dx_0 + (-a)x_{d/2}, \text{ and}$$
$$\mathrm{Tr}(\alpha\zeta^{d/2}) = (\mathrm{id} - \pi)(\beta)\zeta^{d/2} = (-a)x_0 + \underbrace{\mathrm{Tr}(\zeta^d)}_{=a^2-bd}x_{d/2}.$$

Finally, we can solve the system for x_0 to find constants c_0, c_1 depending only on a, b, d such that

$$x_0 = c_0(\mathrm{id} + \pi)(\beta) + c_1(\mathrm{id} - \pi)(\beta)\zeta^{d/2}$$

and constants c_0', c_1' such that

$$x_{d/2} = c_0'(\mathrm{id} + \pi)(\beta) + c_1'(\mathrm{id} - \pi)(\beta)\zeta^{d/2}.$$

This only requires computing one more Galois automorphism, namely $\pi(\beta)$. □

Combining Lemma 4.9 with Lemma 4.7 enables us to compute polynomials.

Corollary 4.10. *Let $f \in (\mathbb{Z}/p^e\mathbb{Z})[T]$ with $\deg(f) < 2^l = d$. Assume that $\deg(f) < d/2$ or $\mathrm{MiPo}(\zeta) = T^d + a$. Then we can evaluate f at $x \in \mathbb{Z}/p^e\mathbb{Z}$ using $3l - 2$ key switches and multiplicative depth l (over S).*

Proof. First, compute

$$\alpha = \sum_{i=0}^{D-1} x^i\zeta^i$$

as in Lemma 4.7, where $D = d/2$ if $\deg(f) < d/2$ and $D = d$ otherwise. Let $f = \sum a_i T^i$. Then compute (without any further key switches)

$$\beta = \left(\sum_{i=0}^{\deg(f)} a_i\zeta^{-i}\right)\alpha = \left(\sum_{i=0}^{\deg(f)} a_i\zeta^{-i}\right)\left(\sum_{i=0}^{D-1} x^i\zeta^i\right) = \sum_{i=-\deg(f)}^{D-1} \zeta^i \sum_{j=0}^{D-1} a_{j-i}x^j,$$

where we set $a_i = 0$ if $i > \deg(f)$ or $i < 0$. Now the constant term of β is clearly $f(x) = \sum a_i x^i$, since by assumption no ζ^i for $i \in \{-\deg(f), ..., D-1\} \setminus \{0\}$ has any constant term. Finally, extract that constant term using Lemma 4.9. □

4.3 Advantages of the Trace Approach

Evaluating bivariate polynomials. In contrast to the norm-based methods, we can use the trace-based approach for evaluating a wider class of polynomials. For example, we can evaluate a bivariate polynomial $f \in (\mathbb{Z}/p^e\mathbb{Z})[X, Y]$ with bounded degree in each variable $\deg_X(f), \deg_Y(f) < 2^{\lfloor l/2 \rfloor}$. This is done by first computing

$$\alpha_1 = \sum_{i=0}^{2^{\lfloor l/2 \rfloor}-1} x^i\zeta^i \quad \text{and} \quad \alpha_2 = \sum_{i=0}^{2^{\lfloor l/2 \rfloor}-1} y^i\zeta^{2^{\lfloor l/2 \rfloor}i}$$

and then using Lemma 4.9 to extract the constant term from $c\alpha_1\alpha_2$, where $c \in S$ is an appropriate constant. While this may not be directly applicable to bootstrapping, it might still be valuable for other homomorphic operations.

Table 1. Parameter sets used in our BFV bootstrapping implementation. The set $(p, e) = (257, 2)$ has a small chance of noise-related decryption failure. This can be mitigated either by choosing $e = 3$ and accepting fewer levels, or by using a somewhat sparse secret for reduced noise growth.

p	N	r	e	n	d	Corollary 4.5 usable?	$\log_2(q)$	Estimated levels
127	2^{15}	1	3	64	512	No	881	34/10
257	2^{15}	1	2	128	256	Yes	881	33/19

Evaluating Many Polynomials at One Point. The trace based approach is advantageous in the case that we want to evaluate multiple polynomials $f_1, ..., f_s$ of degree d in the same point x. Using a variant of Paterson-Stockmeyer, we can do this in $2\sqrt{ds}$ multiplications (using $\sqrt{ds}$ baby steps and s times $\sqrt{d/s}$ giant steps). The norm-based method still improves on that, and would give $2s\log(d)$ key switches. However, for the trace method, we only have to compute

$$\alpha = \sum_{i=0}^{d-1} x^i \zeta^i$$

once, using $2\log(d)$ multiplications. Evaluating then every $f_j(x)$ from α then only takes $\log(d)$ further key switches, thus in total $(s+2)\log(d) < 2s\log(d)$ key switches.

This situation is relevant to bootstrapping. For example, it is shown in [21] how to decrease the multiplicative depth in the case $r > 0$ by evaluating multiple digit retain polynomials in the same point x with respect to different e.

Another example of this situation is in [33], where the evaluation requires the output of a scalar function to be put into the exponent, i.e. it is required to compute

$$\tilde{f} : \mathbb{Z}/p\mathbb{Z} \subseteq R/pR \to R/pR, \quad a \mapsto \gamma^{f(a)}$$

for some function $f : \mathbb{Z}/p\mathbb{Z} \to \mathbb{Z}$. This is implemented by decomposing f into its bits, i.e. $f(x) = \sum 2^i f_i(x)$, and then computing

$$\tilde{f}(x) = \prod_i \left(f_i(x)\gamma^{2^i} + (1 - f_i(x)) \right)$$

so that all the functions f_i are evaluated at the same point $x \in \mathbb{Z}/p\mathbb{Z}$.

5 Implementation and Results

We implemented classical BFV bootstrapping with our norm-based improvements from Sect. 4 in the Microsoft SEAL library [49]. We note that the advantages of the trace-based approach discussed in Sect. 4 are not relevant for the application to bootstrapping, and hence we did not implement it.

To our knowledge, this is the second implementation of BFV bootstrapping in SEAL, the first one being [12]. However, their source code does not seem to be publicly available. Some of the parameter choices also differ, as explained below.

Parameters. Our performance results are given for two different parameter sets, which are summarised in Table 1. These parameter sets are similar to the ones used by [12], with the following exceptions. First, we used a uniform ternary secret distribution, instead of a sparse secret. This change affects noise growth and security. To compensate for the increased noise, we choose $e = 3$ for $p = 127$ instead of $e = 2$. Also, since sparse secrets are expected to be less secure, a smaller ciphertext modulus q (with $\log_2(q) = 806$) was used in [12], whereas we are able to use a larger q. In our implementation, the ciphertext modulus q was automatically chosen by SEAL to target a security level of 128 bits for ring dimension N, Gaussian error distribution with standard deviation $\sigma = 3.2$, and uniform ternary secret.

Settings that are Out of Scope. In our implementation, we only consider parameter sets with $r = 1$. In the case $r > 1$, we would also have to implement digit retain polynomials and the techniques of [21] to achieve state-of-the-art performance and noise growth. Note that these techniques can be combined with our trace-based improvements as described in Sect. 4.2. However, choosing the right digit retain polynomial is highly nontrivial, and we decided not to include it in our implementation.

Since our optimizations require high algebraic rank, we also do not consider parameters that provide a high number of low-rank slots, as e.g. used in [13,21,30]. Note that these settings require either very large plaintext moduli or non-power-of-two cyclotomic rings, both of which have significant disadvantages.

Finally, we also do not want to compare with schemes that bootstrap together with every operation. This includes the classical TFHE family of schemes [17,18], their batched variants [28,44,45] and also the BFV-based bootstrapping scheme for TFHE [42]. Such a comparison is difficult, as the number of bootstrapping executions in our case is not necessarily proportional to the number of gates, but depends significantly on the shape of the evaluated circuit.

Performance. The implementation was tested on a system with an Intel i7-7700K 4.20 GHz CPU and 16GB Ram. This system is slightly faster than the one used by [12], with an Intel i7-4770 3.40 GHz CPU and 32 GB Ram. However, the difference in system speed is much smaller than our speedup, demonstrating that the new techniques can indeed improve bootstrapping performance. Both implementations are single-threaded.

The performance for slim bootstrapping with both parameter sets is displayed in Table 2 and Table 3. Note that the performance is expected to be quite sensitive to parameter choices, since the choice of prime p influences the number of slots, the degree of the lifting polynomial, and whether we can use the improved variant of norm-based evaluation given by Corollary 4.5. While [12] does not report timings for the parameter set $(p, e) = (127, 3)$, we do not expect our implementation to yield a significant speedup here. The reason is that we decrease the number of key-switches during digit extraction from about $2\sqrt{p}$ to $3\log_2(p)$, but

$$2\sqrt{127} \approx 23 \quad \text{and} \quad 3\log_2(127) \approx 21.$$

The situation is different for $p = 257$, not only due to the larger difference between $\sqrt{p}$ and $\log_2(p)$ in this case, but also since this parameter set supports the improved version of Corollary 4.5 and so costs only $2\log_2(p)$ key switches. We see from Table 3 that our norm-based improvements result in a speed up of $1.6\times$ compared to the prior reported implementation [12].

Table 2. Performance data for the $(p, e) = (127, 3)$ dataset. Since [12] uses sparse secrets, they do not consider this dataset but instead choose $(p, e) = (127, 2)$.

	Key switches	Time (our impl)
Slots to Coeffs	22	7.5 s
Coeffs to Slots	30	7.8 s
Digit Extract	63	17.0 s
Total	115	32.3 s

Table 3. Performance data for the $(p, e) = (257, 2)$ dataset. Here we also included the timings that were reported by [12].

	Key switches	Time (our impl)	Time [12]
Slots to Coeffs	22	7.9 s	–
Coeffs to Slots	30	8.6 s	–
Digit Extract	17	5.6 s	–
Total	69	22.1 s	36.8 s

Source Code. The source code is available at our github repository[5]. Our implementation provides a convenient interface to compute arbitrary linear transformations efficiently. However, the interface to use the advanced polynomial evaluation techniques currently requires complicated precomputations of the polynomials. To present the implementation results in this paper, these precomputations were done using SAGE and the results were hardcoded.

6 TFHE-Style Programmable Bootstrapping for BFV

In this section, we depart from the classical approach to BFV bootstrapping, as described in Sect. 3, and as improved upon in Sect. 4. Instead, we consider a new approach to bootstrapping BFV using techniques from the literature on TFHE bootstrapping. As a main feature, this enables us to demonstrate programmable bootstrapping for BFV in Algorithm 1. For full details of the TFHE bootstrapping procedure we refer the reader to the excellent guide [34].

---

[5] https://github.com/FeanorTheElf/galois-bootstrapping.

6.1   A TFHE-Style Bootstrapping Approach for BFV

Recall that BFV decryption is given as

$$m = \left\lfloor \frac{t}{q} (c_1 s + c_0) \right\rceil \in R/tR,$$

where the ciphertext ring is R/qR and the plaintext ring is R/tR, where R is generated by a $2N$-th primitive root of unity ζ. Before evaluating decryption homomorphically, we will perform a modulus switch such that $c_0, c_1 \in R/TR$, where $T < q$ is a ciphertext modulus as small as possible, without exceeding the noise threshold. Then, we are left instead with evaluating the expression

$$m = \left\lfloor \frac{t}{T} (c_1 s + c_0) \right\rceil \in R/tR.$$

While we still work in the ring R, assume for now that our message is scalar, i.e. $m \in \mathbb{Z}/t\mathbb{Z}$. Thus, the first step is to compute the noisy message

$$\tilde{m} = c_{00} + c_{10} s_0 - \sum_{i=1}^{N-1} c_{1i} s_{N-i} \in \mathbb{Z}/q\mathbb{Z},$$

the constant coefficient of $c_0 + c_1 s$, where

$$c_i = \sum c_{ij} X^j \quad \text{and} \quad s = \sum s_j X^j.$$

As in TFHE bootstrapping, we do not directly compute $\tilde{m}$ but instead $\alpha^{\tilde{m}}$ where $\alpha \in S = \mathbb{F}_{p^d}$ is a primitive element of one degree-d slot S. In particular, this allows us to take a very small bootstrapping plaintext modulus $p < t$ during bootstrapping, since we only require that $T \leq p^d$. While a small plaintext modulus decreases noise, this now requires a vast number of multiplications. Namely, we have to compute

$$\alpha^{\tilde{m}} = \alpha^{c_0} (\alpha^{s_0})^{c_{10}} \prod_{i=1}^{N-1} (\alpha^{-s_i})^{c_{1(N-i)}}.$$

Usually, we would do this in $N \log(T)$ multiplications, by providing encryptions of $\alpha^{\pm s_i 2^j}$ in the bootstrapping key (for all j). After we homomorphically compute $\alpha^{\tilde{m}}$, we then can proceed to find

$$f(\lfloor t/T \cdot \tilde{m} \rceil) \in \{0, 1, ..., p-1\}.$$

Here, we assume that $f : \mathbb{Z}/t\mathbb{Z} \to \mathbb{Z}/p\mathbb{Z}$ has outputs in $\mathbb{Z}/p\mathbb{Z}$. As in TFHE, we do this by a "homomorphic lookup table", which in our case could correspond to computing

$$f(\lfloor t/T \cdot \tilde{m} \rceil) = \sum_{y \in \mathbb{Z}/p\mathbb{Z}} y \sum_{\substack{x \in \mathbb{Z}/T\mathbb{Z} \text{ s.t.} \\ f(\lfloor t/T \cdot x \rceil) = y}} 1 - N(\alpha^x - \alpha^{\tilde{m}})^{p-1}.$$

Using the fact that $N(x) = \prod_\sigma \sigma(x)$ where σ runs through the Galois automorphisms of $\mathbb{F}_{p^d}$, we can expand this and find

$$\sum_{\substack{y \in \mathbb{Z}/p\mathbb{Z}}} y \sum_{\substack{x \in \mathbb{Z}/T\mathbb{Z} \text{ s.t.} \\ f(\lfloor t/T \cdot x \rceil) = y}} 1 - N(\alpha^x - \alpha^{\tilde{m}})^{p-1} = G(\sigma_0(\alpha^{\tilde{m}}), \sigma_1(\alpha^{\tilde{m}}), ..., \sigma_{d-1}(\alpha^{\tilde{m}}))$$

for some polynomial $G \in \mathbb{F}_{p^d}[X_0, ..., X_{d-1}]$ of degree $p - 1$ in each variable, and $\mathrm{Gal}(\mathbb{F}_{p^d}/\mathbb{F}_p) = \{\sigma_0, ..., \sigma_{d-1}\}$. Naively, we can already use this to compute the result $f(\lfloor t/T \cdot \tilde{m} \rceil)$, but it requires p^d key-switches. To do better, write

$$G = \sum_I X_0^{I_0} ... X_{d/2-1}^{I_{d/2-1}} \cdot G_I(X_{d/2}, ..., X_{d-1}),$$

where I runs over $\{0, ..., p - 1\}^{d/2}$ and the G_I are multivariate polynomials in $d/2$ variables, and degree $p - 1$ in each variable. On input $(x_0, ..., x_{d-1})$, we can now precompute all monomials of the form

$$m_I = x_0^{I_0} ... x_{d/2-1}^{I_{d/2-1}} \quad \text{and} \quad m'_J = x_{d/2}^{J_0} ... x_{d-1}^{J_{d/2-1}}.$$

Now each $G_I(x_{d/2}, ..., x_{d-1})$ is just a linear combination of the m'_J, and so we find

$$G(x) = \sum_I m_I G_I(x_{d/2}, ..., x_{d-1})$$

using just $3p^{d/2}$ key-switches. The multiplicative depth is very low, namely $\log(p - 1) + \log(d)$. The bootstrapping process is summarised in Algorithm 1.

Caveats. While Algorithm 1 can be implemented, we made some assumptions that might be inconvenient in practice. First and foremost, we assumed that our unary function $f : \mathbb{Z}/t\mathbb{Z} \to \mathbb{Z}/p\mathbb{Z}$ has images in $\mathbb{Z}/p\mathbb{Z}$. While we can easily homomorphically compute the map $\mathbb{Z}/p\mathbb{Z} \to \mathbb{Z}/t\mathbb{Z}$ if $p \mid t$, this still limits the amount of possible output values.

Furthermore, we assumed that the message m is scalar, i.e., an element of $\mathbb{Z}/t\mathbb{Z}$. In practice, we are interested in full messages that are any element of R/tR, or at least in messages containing one scalar in each slot. The only way Algorithm 1 can be used to bootstrap many scalars is to use slots for SIMD parallelism. However, this conflicts with the choice of a very small intermediate plaintext modulus p (such as $p = 2$ or $p = 3$). Apart from performance, such a choice can also greatly reduce the noise cause by BFV multiplications, as the growth is proportional to the plaintext modulus.

Complexity. We now give a theoretical analysis of the complexity of TFHE-style BFV bootstrapping. The first step is to homomorphically compute $\alpha^{\tilde{m}}$ using $N \log(T)$ multiplications and multiplicative depth $\log(N) + \log\log(T)$. Then, we perform the "homomorphic lookup table" step to compute $f(\lfloor t/T\tilde{m} \rceil)$, using $3p^{e/2}$ key-switches and multiplicative depth $\log(p - 1) + \log(e)$. Up to now, we

---

Algorithm 1: TFHE-style programmable bootstrapping for BFV.

Input: Ciphertext $(c_0, c_1) \in (R/qR)^2$ encrypting scalar message $m \in \mathbb{Z}/t\mathbb{Z}$;
Bootstrapping keys $(k_0^{(i,j)}, k_1^{(i,j)})$ encrypting $\alpha^{s_0 2^j}$ resp. $\alpha^{-s_i 2^j}$;
Decomposition of $G = \sum_I X_0^{I_0} ... X_{d/2-1}^{I_{d/2-1}} G_I(X_{d/2}, ..., X_{d-1})$

Output: Output $(c_0', c_1') \in (R/qR)^2$ encrypting scalar message $f(m) \in \mathbb{Z}/p\mathbb{Z}$
with low noise

1 Modulus switch (c_0, c_1) to $(\tilde{c}_0, \tilde{c}_1)$ in R/TR
2 Decompose $\tilde{c}_1$ as $\sum_i \sum_j c_{ij} 2^j X^i$ with $c_{ij} \in \{0, 1\}$
3 Compute ciphertext ct as homomorphic evaluation of

$$\tilde{m} := \alpha^{\tilde{c}_0} \prod_j (\alpha^{s_0 2^j})^{c_{0j}} \prod_{i>0,j} (\alpha^{-s_{N-i} 2^j})^{c_{ij}}$$

4 Consider tables $\text{ct}[I]$, $\text{ct}'[I]$ of ciphertexts where $I \in \{0, ..., p-1\}^{d/2}$
5 **for** $i \in \{0, ..., d/2-1\}$ **do**
6 $\quad$ Compute $\text{ct}[e_i]$ as homomorphic evaluation of the Galois conjugate $\sigma_i(\tilde{m})$
$\quad$ $(e_i \in \{0, ..., p-1\}^{d/2}$ is the unit vector)
7 $\quad$ Compute $\text{ct}'[e_i]$ as homomorphic evaluation of $\sigma_{i+d/2}(\tilde{m})$
8 **end**
9 **for** $I \in \{0, ..., p-1\}^{d/2} \setminus \{e_i\}$ *ordered by ascending ℓ_1-norm* **do**
10 $\quad$ Compute $\text{ct}[I]$ as encrypted product of $\text{ct}[\lfloor I/2 \rfloor]$ and $\text{ct}[I - \lfloor I/2 \rfloor]$
11 $\quad$ Compute $\text{ct}'[I]$ as encrypted product of $\text{ct}'[\lfloor I/2 \rfloor]$ and $\text{ct}'[I - \lfloor I/2 \rfloor]$
12 $\quad$ (During rounding in $\lfloor I/2 \rfloor$, assume we round up respectively down
$\quad$ alternately)
13 **end**
14 **for** $I \in \{0, ..., p-1\}^{d/2}$ **do**
15 $\quad$ Compute homomorphic evaluation of $g_I := \sum_J a_J m_J'(\sigma_{d/2}\tilde{m}, ..., \sigma_{d-1}\tilde{m})$
$\quad$ where $G_I = \sum_J a_J m_J'$ as linear combination of the ct'_J
16 $\quad$ Compute ct_I'' as encrypted product of g_I and $m_I(\sigma_0\tilde{m}, ..., \sigma_{d/2-1}\tilde{m})$
17 **end**
18 Output $\sum_I \text{ct}_I''$

---

implicitly assumed $e = d$, but by choosing α to be a generator of a Galois subring of a slot, we can instead work with any $e \mid d$. Hence, the total number of key switches is

$$N \log(T) + 3p^{e/2} = (1 + o(1)) \left(N \log(T) + 3\sqrt{T} \right).$$

Furthermore, the total multiplicative depth is

$$\lceil \log(N) + \log\log(T) \rceil + \lceil \log(p-1) \rceil + \log(e) \leq \log(N \log(T)(p-1)e) + 2.$$

Since the error per multiplication in BFV is $(2 + o(1))(pN^2)$ [20, Lemma 2], this yields a total bootstrapping error of

$$(1 + o(1)) \log(pN^2)(\log(N \log(T)(p-1)e) + 2) = (1 + o(1)) \log(pN^2) \log(Npe \log(T))$$

bits. If we assume that p is a small constant, we find $e = O(\log(T))$ and so the expression of the error simplifies to

$$(2 + o(1)) \log(N) \log(N \log(T)^2) = (1 + o(1))\Big(2 \log(N)^2 + 4 \log(N) \log \log(T)\Big).$$

For parameters used in practice, this is slightly lower than the noise of standard bootstrapping, mainly due to the choice of a very small plaintext modulus.

6.2   Comparison with Classical BFV Bootstrapping

In this subsection, we give a theoretical comparison of the classical approach to BFV bootstrapping with our alternative, TFHE-style approach. The comparison shows that the TFHE-style approach would be significantly slower than the classical approach, and so we did not implement it.

Table 4. Parameter constraints for BFV bootstrapping approaches.

		Classical	TFHE-style (Algo. 1)	Both
e	Exponent		$e \mid d$	
t	Input plaintext modulus	$t = p$		
T	Intermediate plaintext modulus	$T = p^e$	$T = p^e - 1$	$T \geq 4Nt$
d, n	Slot rank, slot count			$N = nd$, $d = \mathrm{ord}(p)$
$\mathcal{P}$	Input plaintext space			$\mathcal{P} = R/tR$
$\mathcal{P}'$	Bootstrapping plaintext space	$\mathcal{P}' = R/TR$	$\mathcal{P}' = R/pR$	

Table 5. An estimate of the performance of classical (slim) bootstrapping (as described in Sect. 3 and Sect. 4, using sparsely packed plaintexts) and TFHE-style programmable bootstrapping (as described in Sect. 6.1). Metrics marked with * are only given up to a factor of $(1 + o(1))$.

	Classical (slim) bootstrapping	TFHE-style bootstrapping (Algorithm 1)
Input scalar message	$m \in \mathcal{P}$, sparsely packed	$m \in \mathbb{Z}/t\mathbb{Z} \subseteq \mathcal{P}$
Total key-switches*	$4\sqrt{n} + \frac{3}{2} \log(p)(e-1)^2$	$N \log(T) + 3p^{e/2}$
if $T \approx p^e$, p, n constant	$\approx \frac{3}{2} \log(T)^2$	$\approx N \log(T) + 3\sqrt{T}$
Multiplicative depth	$\leq (e-1) \log(p) + 2$	$\leq \log(N \log(T)(p-1)e) + 2$
if $T \approx p^e$, p constant	$= (1 + o(1)) \log(T)$	$= (1 + o(1)) \log(N \log(T)^2)$
Bootstrapping noise bits*	$\log(T) \log(N^2 T)$	$\log(Npe \log(T)) \log(N^2 p)$
if $T \approx p^e$, p constant	$= \log(T)^2 + 2 \log(T) \log(N)$	$\approx 2 \log(N)^2 + 4 \log(N) \log \log(T)$

Parameters. In order to compare the both the classical and the TFHE-style bootstrapping approaches, we need to establish a set of shared parameters that we can use in the analysis. We summarise the constraints on the parameters in Table 4.

Table 6. Example concrete parameters for both bootstrapping approaches, with an estimate of their security, and an estimate of their complexity, based on Table 5. The parameters are chosen based on a simple worst-case noise analysis, hence they do not match the parameters used in our implementation in Sect. 5.

	Classical (slim) bootstrapping	TFHE-style bootstrapping (Algorithm 1)
N	2^{16}	2^{15}
p	257	3
T	257^3	$3^{16} - 1$
t	257	257
(n, d)	$(64, 2^{10})$	$(4, 2^{13})$
Key switches	$1.4 \cdot 10^2$	$8.5 \cdot 10^5$
Noise (worst-case, bits)	1345	798
Ciphertext mod q (bits)	1410	840
Security (bits)	128	100
Total complexity	$2^{38} \cdot c$	$2^{48} \cdot c$

Results. In Table 5 we give a performance comparison of both bootstrapping approaches. The asymptotic values for the TFHE-style bootstrapping are as explained in Sect. 6.1. For classical bootstrapping, the asymptotics are obtained by an analogous, straightforward computation, and include the improvements to classical bootstrapping that we have presented in Sect. 4.

In Table 6 we then give an example of concrete parameters for each bootstrapping approach, and corresponding concrete costs according to Table 5. The concrete values are obtained by evaluating the asymptotic expressions, ignoring the $(1 + o(1))$ factor. The security estimates were computed using the Lattice Estimator of [1].

We remark that our estimates of the noise relies on a *worst-case* analysis. An average noise analysis may enable us to choose a smaller ciphertext modulus q. This in turn improves security, which then might allow smaller ring dimension N. However, we believe that the results of the comparison would not look significantly different under an average-case analysis, hence we are satisfied with the simpler, worst-case estimates.

The "total complexity" metric of Table 6 gives a basic approximation of the total number of operations required for the computation. We still only count key switches, but each key switching operation performs

$$c \log(q) N \log(N), \quad c \text{ constant}$$

constant-size arithmetic instructions where $c > 0$ is some constant, using either the base-decomposition method, or an RNS implementation. We expect the time required for each approach to be proportional to the estimate of the total complexity given in Table 6. That is, we estimate that the TFHE-style bootstrapping would be about $2^{10} \approx 1000$ times slower than a classical BFV bootstrapping, and thus entirely impractical.

References

1. Albrecht, M.R., Player, R., Scott, S.: On the concrete hardness of learning with errors. J. Math. Cryptol. **9**(3), 169–203 (2015). https://doi.org/10.1515/jmc-2015-0016

2. Alperin-Sheriff, J., Peikert, C.: Practical bootstrapping in quasilinear time. In: Canetti, R., Garay, J.A. (eds.) CRYPTO 2013. LNCS, vol. 8042, pp. 1–20. Springer, Heidelberg (2013). https://doi.org/10.1007/978-3-642-40041-4_1

3. Alperin-Sheriff, J., Peikert, C.: Faster bootstrapping with polynomial error. In: Garay, J.A., Gennaro, R. (eds.) CRYPTO 2014. LNCS, vol. 8616, pp. 297–314. Springer, Heidelberg (2014). https://doi.org/10.1007/978-3-662-44371-2_17

4. Badawi, A.A., Polyakov, Y.: Demystifying bootstrapping in fully homomorphic encryption. Cryptology ePrint Archive, Paper 2023/149 (2023). https://eprint.iacr.org/2023/149

5. Bossuat, J.-P., Mouchet, C., Troncoso-Pastoriza, J., Hubaux, J.-P.: Efficient bootstrapping for approximate homomorphic encryption with non-sparse keys. In: Canteaut, A., Standaert, F.-X. (eds.) EUROCRYPT 2021, Part I. LNCS, vol. 12696, pp. 587–617. Springer, Cham (2021). https://doi.org/10.1007/978-3-030-77870-5_21

6. Bossuat, J., Troncoso-Pastoriza, J.R., Hubaux, J.: Bootstrapping for approximate homomorphic encryption with negligible failure-probability by using sparse-secret encapsulation. In: Ateniese, G., Venturi, D. (eds.) ACNS 2022. LNCS, vol. 13269, pp. 521–541. Springer, Cham (2022). https://doi.org/10.1007/978-3-031-09234-3_26

7. Brakerski, Z.: Fully homomorphic encryption without modulus switching from classical GapSVP. In: Safavi-Naini, R., Canetti, R. (eds.) CRYPTO 2012. LNCS, vol. 7417, pp. 868–886. Springer, Heidelberg (2012). https://doi.org/10.1007/978-3-642-32009-5_50

8. Brakerski, Z., Gentry, C., Vaikuntanathan, V.: Fully homomorphic encryption without bootstrapping. Cryptology ePrint Archive, Paper 2011/277 (2011). https://eprint.iacr.org/2011/277

9. Brakerski, Z., Vaikuntanathan, V.: Fully homomorphic encryption from ring-LWE and security for key dependent messages. In: Rogaway, P. (ed.) CRYPTO 2011. LNCS, vol. 6841, pp. 505–524. Springer, Heidelberg (2011). https://doi.org/10.1007/978-3-642-22792-9_29

10. Bürgisser, P., Clausen, M., Shokrollahi, M.A.: Algebraic Complexity Theory, vol. 315. Springer, Cham (2013)

11. Chen, H., Chillotti, I., Song, Y.: Improved bootstrapping for approximate homomorphic encryption. In: Ishai, Y., Rijmen, V. (eds.) EUROCRYPT 2019. LNCS, vol. 11477, pp. 34–54. Springer, Cham (2019). https://doi.org/10.1007/978-3-030-17656-3_2

12. Chen, H., Han, K.: Homomorphic lower digits removal and improved FHE bootstrapping. In: Nielsen, J.B., Rijmen, V. (eds.) EUROCRYPT 2018. LNCS, vol. 10820, pp. 315–337. Springer, Cham (2018). https://doi.org/10.1007/978-3-319-78381-9_12

13. Chen, H., Han, K.: Homomorphic lower digits removal and improved FHE bootstrapping. Cryptology ePrint Archive, Paper 2018/067 (2018). https://eprint.iacr.org/2018/067

14. Cheon, J.H., Han, K., Kim, A., Kim, M., Song, Y.: Bootstrapping for approximate homomorphic encryption. In: Nielsen, J.B., Rijmen, V. (eds.) EUROCRYPT 2018.

LNCS, vol. 10820, pp. 360–384. Springer, Cham (2018). https://doi.org/10.1007/978-3-319-78381-9_14

15. Cheon, J.H., Kim, A., Kim, M., Song, Y.: Homomorphic encryption for arithmetic of approximate numbers. In: Takagi, T., Peyrin, T. (eds.) ASIACRYPT 2017. LNCS, vol. 10624, pp. 409–437. Springer, Cham (2017). https://doi.org/10.1007/978-3-319-70694-8_15

16. Chillotti, I., Gama, N., Georgieva, M., Izabachène, M.: Faster fully homomorphic encryption: bootstrapping in less than 0.1 seconds. In: Cheon, J.H., Takagi, T. (eds.) ASIACRYPT 2016. LNCS, vol. 10031, pp. 3–33. Springer, Heidelberg (2016). https://doi.org/10.1007/978-3-662-53887-6_1

17. Chillotti, I., Gama, N., Georgieva, M., Izabachène, M.: TFHE: fast fully homomorphic encryption over the torus. J. Cryptol. **33**(1), 34–91 (2020). https://doi.org/10.1007/s00145-019-09319-x

18. Ducas, L., Micciancio, D.: FHEW: bootstrapping homomorphic encryption in less than a second. In: Oswald, E., Fischlin, M. (eds.) EUROCRYPT 2015. LNCS, vol. 9056, pp. 617–640. Springer, Heidelberg (2015). https://doi.org/10.1007/978-3-662-46800-5_24

19. Elia, M., Rosenthal, J., Schipani, D.: Polynomial evaluation over finite fields: new algorithms and complexity bounds. Appl. Algebra Eng. Commun. Comput. **23**(3–4), 129–141 (2012)

20. Fan, J., Vercauteren, F.: Somewhat practical fully homomorphic encryption. Cryptology ePrint Archive, Paper 2012/144 (2012). https://eprint.iacr.org/2012/144

21. Geelen, R., Iliashenko, I., Kang, J., Vercauteren, F.: On polynomial functions modulo p^e and faster bootstrapping for homomorphic encryption. In: Hazay, C., Stam, M. (eds.) Advances in Cryptology - EUROCRYPT 2023. LNCS, pp. 257–286. Springer, Cham (2023). https://doi.org/10.1007/978-3-031-30620-4_9

22. Geelen, R., Vercauteren, F.: Bootstrapping for BGV and BFV revisited. J. Cryptol. **36**(2), 12 (2023). https://doi.org/10.1007/s00145-023-09454-6

23. Gentry, C.: A fully homomorphic encryption scheme. Stanford university (2009)

24. Gentry, C., Halevi, S., Peikert, C., Smart, N.P.: Ring switching in BGV-style homomorphic encryption. In: Visconti, I., De Prisco, R. (eds.) SCN 2012. LNCS, vol. 7485, pp. 19–37. Springer, Heidelberg (2012). https://doi.org/10.1007/978-3-642-32928-9_2

25. Gentry, C., Halevi, S., Smart, N.P.: Better bootstrapping in fully homomorphic encryption. Cryptology ePrint Archive, Paper 2011/680 (2011). https://eprint.iacr.org/2011/680

26. Gentry, C., Halevi, S., Smart, N.P.: Fully homomorphic encryption with polylog overhead. In: Pointcheval, D., Johansson, T. (eds.) EUROCRYPT 2012. LNCS, vol. 7237, pp. 465–482. Springer, Heidelberg (2012). https://doi.org/10.1007/978-3-642-29011-4_28

27. Gentry, C., Sahai, A., Waters, B.: Homomorphic encryption from learning with errors: conceptually-simpler, asymptotically-faster, attribute-based. In: Canetti, R., Garay, J.A. (eds.) CRYPTO 2013. LNCS, vol. 8042, pp. 75–92. Springer, Heidelberg (2013). https://doi.org/10.1007/978-3-642-40041-4_5

28. Guimarães, A., Pereira, H.V.L., van Leeuwen, B.: Amortized bootstrapping revisited: Simpler, asymptotically-faster, implemented. Cryptology ePrint Archive, Paper 2023/014 (2023). https://eprint.iacr.org/2023/014

29. Halevi, S., Shoup, V.: Algorithms in HElib. In: Garay, J.A., Gennaro, R. (eds.) CRYPTO 2014. LNCS, vol. 8616, pp. 554–571. Springer, Heidelberg (2014). https://doi.org/10.1007/978-3-662-44371-2_31

30. Halevi, S., Shoup, V.: Bootstrapping for HElib. J. Cryptol. **34**(1), 7 (2021)
31. Han, K., Hhan, M., Cheon, J.H.: Improved homomorphic discrete Fourier transforms and FHE bootstrapping. IEEE Access **7**, 57361–57370 (2019)
32. Han, K., Ki, D.: Better bootstrapping for approximate homomorphic encryption. In: Jarecki, S. (ed.) CT-RSA 2020. LNCS, vol. 12006, pp. 364–390. Springer, Cham (2020). https://doi.org/10.1007/978-3-030-40186-3_16
33. Iliashenko, I., Izabachène, M., Mertens, A., Pereira, H.V.: Homomorphically counting elements with the same property. In: Proceedings on Privacy Enhancing Technologies, vol. 4, pp. 670–683 (2022)
34. Joye, M.: Guide to fully homomorphic encryption over the [discretized] torus. Cryptology ePrint Archive, Paper 2021/1402 (2021). https://eprint.iacr.org/2021/1402
35. Joye, M., Paillier, P.: Blind rotation in fully homomorphic encryption with extended keys. In: Dolev, S., Katz, J., Meisels, A. (eds.) Cyber Security, Cryptology, and Machine Learning. LNCS, pp. 1–18. Springer, Cham (2022). https://doi.org/10.1007/978-3-031-07689-3_1
36. Jutla, C.S., Manohar, N.: Sine series approximation of the mod function for bootstrapping of approximate HE. In: Dunkelman, O., Dziembowski, S. (eds.) EUROCRYPT 2022, Part I. LNCS, pp. 491–520. Springer, Cham (2022). https://doi.org/10.1007/978-3-031-06944-4_17
37. Lee, J.-W., Lee, E., Lee, Y., Kim, Y.-S., No, J.-S.: High-precision bootstrapping of RNS-CKKS homomorphic encryption using optimal minimax polynomial approximation and inverse sine function. In: Canteaut, A., Standaert, F.-X. (eds.) EUROCRYPT 2021, Part I. LNCS, vol. 12696, pp. 618–647. Springer, Cham (2021). https://doi.org/10.1007/978-3-030-77870-5_22
38. Lee, Y., Lee, J., Kim, Y., Kim, Y., No, J., Kang, H.: High-precision bootstrapping for approximate homomorphic encryption by error variance minimization. In: Dunkelman, O., Dziembowski, S. (eds.) EUROCRYPT 2022, Part I. LNCS, pp. 551–580. Springer, Cham (2022). https://doi.org/10.1007/978-3-031-06944-4_19
39. Lee, Y., et al.: Efficient FHEW bootstrapping with small evaluation keys, and applications to threshold homomorphic encryption. In: Hazay, C., Stam, M. (eds.) EUROCRYPT 2023, Part III. LNCS, pp. 227–256. Springer, Cham (2023). https://doi.org/10.1007/978-3-031-30620-4_8
40. Liu, F., Wang, H.: Batch bootstrapping I: - a new framework for SIMD bootstrapping in polynomial modulus. In: Hazay, C., Stam, M. (eds.) EUROCRYPT 2023, Part III. LNCS, pp. 321–352. Springe, Cham (2023). https://doi.org/10.1007/978-3-031-30620-4_11
41. Liu, F., Wang, H.: Batch bootstrapping II: - bootstrapping in polynomial modulus only requires $\tilde{o}(1)$ FHE multiplications in amortization. In: Hazay, C., Stam, M. (eds.) EUROCRYPT 2023, Part III. LNCS, pp. 353–384. Springer, Cham (2023). https://doi.org/10.1007/978-3-031-30620-4_12
42. Liu, Z., Wang, Y.: Amortized functional bootstrapping in less than 7ms, with $\tilde{O}(1)$ polynomial multiplications. Cryptology ePrint Archive, Paper 2023/910 (2023). https://eprint.iacr.org/2023/910
43. Maeda, D., Morimura, K., Narisada, S., Fukushima, K., Nishide, T.: Efficient homomorphic evaluation of arbitrary uni/bivariate integer functions and their applications. Cryptology ePrint Archive, Paper 2023/366 (2023). https://doi.org/10.1145/3560827.3563378, https://eprint.iacr.org/2023/366
44. Miccianco, D., Sorrell, J.: Ring packing and amortized FHEW bootstrapping. In: Chatzigiannakis, I., Kaklamanis, C., Marx, D., Sannella, D. (eds.) ICALP 2018, pp. 100:1–100:14 (2018). https://doi.org/10.4230/LIPIcs.ICALP.2018.100

45. Micheli, G.D., Kim, D., Micciancio, D., Suhl, A.: Faster amortized FHEW bootstrapping using ring automorphisms. Cryptology ePrint Archive, Paper 2023/112 (2023). https://eprint.iacr.org/2023/112
46. Neukirch, J.: Algebraic Number Theory, vol. 322. Springer, Cham (2013)
47. Okada, H., Cid, C., Hidano, S., Kiyomoto, S.: Linear depth integer-wise homomorphic division. In: Blazy, O., Yeun, C.Y. (eds.) WISTP 2018. LNCS, vol. 11469, pp. 91–106. Springer, Cham (2019). https://doi.org/10.1007/978-3-030-20074-9_8
48. Regev, O.: On lattices, learning with errors, random linear codes, and cryptography. In: Proceedings of STOC 2005, pp. 84–93. Association for Computing Machinery (2005)
49. Microsoft SEAL (release 4.1). https://github.com/Microsoft/SEAL (2023). microsoft Research, Redmond, WA
50. Smart, N.P., Vercauteren, F.: Fully homomorphic SIMD operations. Des. Codes Crypt. **71**, 57–81 (2014)

Amortized Functional Bootstrapping in Less than 7 ms, with $\tilde{O}(1)$ Polynomial Multiplications

Zeyu Liu$^{(\boxtimes)}$ and Yunhao Wang

Yale University, New Haven, USA
{zeyu.liu,yunhao.wang}@yale.edu

Abstract. Amortized bootstrapping offers a way to refresh multiple ciphertexts of a fully homomorphic encryption scheme in parallel more efficiently than refreshing a single ciphertext at a time. Micciancio and Sorrell (ICALP 2018) first proposed the technique to bootstrap n LWE ciphertexts simultaneously, reducing the total cost from $\tilde{O}(n^2)$ to $\tilde{O}(3^\epsilon n^{1+\frac{1}{\epsilon}})$ for arbitrary $\epsilon > 0$. Several recent works have further improved the asymptotic cost. Despite these amazing progresses in theoretical efficiency, none of them demonstrates the practicality of batched LWE ciphertext bootstrapping. Moreover, most of these works only support limited functional bootstrapping, i.e. only supporting the evaluation of some specific type of function when performing bootstrapping.

In this work, we propose a construction that is not only asymptotically efficient (requiring only $\tilde{O}(n)$ polynomial multiplications for bootstrapping of n LWE ciphertexts) but also concretely efficient. We implement our scheme as a C++ library and show that it takes < 5 ms per LWE ciphertext to bootstrap for a binary gate, which is an order of magnitude faster than the state-of-the-art C++ implementation on LWE ciphertext bootstrapping in OpenFHE. Furthermore, our construction supports batched arbitrary functional bootstrapping. For a 9-bit messages space, our scheme takes ∼6.7 ms per LWE ciphertext to evaluate an arbitrary function with bootstrapping, which is about two to three magnitudes faster than all the existing schemes that achieve a similar functionality and message space.

1 Introduction

Fully homomorphic encryption (FHE) schemes support the evaluation of an arbitrary circuit over the encrypted data without decrypting it. Thus, it is a very powerful tool that can be widely applied in many scenarios, like secure machine learning [30], private information retrieval [32], private set intersection [13], and so on.

There are two major lines of FHE schemes. The first is BGV and its variants [6,7,10,15]. These works encrypt a vector of N messages using an RLWE ciphertext. This line of work allows the "Single Instruction Multiple Data" (SIMD)

Y. Wang—Part of the work was done when the author was at Columbia University.

J. Guo and R. Steinfeld (Eds.): ASIACRYPT 2023, LNCS 14443, pp. 101–132, 2023.
https://doi.org/10.1007/978-981-99-8736-8_4

operations[1]. Thus, they provide an efficient way to evaluate a circuit with a large number of inputs. However, there exist two major limitations of this line of work: (1) they natively only support circuits with some pre-known depth; since each level of circuit evaluation adds extra noise to the RLWE ciphertexts, for deeper circuits, the noise may accumulate to a point that no more operations can be evaluated. Therefore, bootstrapping is needed to reduce the noise inside an RLWE ciphertext. For BGV/BFV, the amortized bootstrapping time for a 16-bit message can be over 300 ms [8, 20]. (2) they only efficiently support addition and multiplication, while non-polynomial evaluation (e.g., comparisons) can be very costly.

The second line of work starts with FHEW [14] and is later improved by TFHE [11] and Lee et al. [25]. These works support bootstrapping in tens of milliseconds. Instead of batching N messages in a single RLWE ciphertext, they encrypt a single bit inside an LWE ciphertext. Bootstrapping is done together with a NAND gate evaluation between two encrypted bits. The output ciphertext maintains the same level of noise as the input ciphertext. Since the NAND gate is a universal gate, these works can be used to evaluate arbitrary circuits. Besides, they provide a more general functionality, called functional bootstrapping: given an LWE ciphertext encrypting a message m, one can obtain an output LWE ciphertext encrypting $f(m)$, while the input ciphertext and output ciphertext have the same level of noise. However, they also have two major limitations: (1) they focus on bootstrapping one message at a time and are not able to take advantage of the SIMD feature as in the other line of work; (2) their functional bootstrapping only supports negacyclic functions (i.e., functions $f : \mathbb{Z}_q \to \mathbb{Z}$ such that $f(x) = -f(x + q/2)$).

[34] first attempts to combine these two lines of work and introduces the batched bootstrapping to support fast bootstrapping over n LWE ciphertexts at the same time. Recently, several works [19, 26, 27, 35] have further greatly improved the asymptotic behavior ([27] gives an algorithm with an amortized cost of $\tilde{O}(1)$ polynomial multiplications per LWE ciphertext bootstrapping). However, whether these works are practical remains an open problem. The only implementation in [19] requires > 1 second to bootstrap a single LWE ciphertext encrypting a 7-bit message (amortized over n ciphertexts).

Therefore, the central question we address is:

Can we construct a batched bootstrapping algorithm for LWE ciphertexts, that is (1) practical, taking only milliseconds per LWE ciphertext bootstrapping; (2) asymptotically efficient, requiring only $\tilde{O}(1)$ polynomial multiplications per LWE ciphertext bootstrapping, and (3) flexible, supporting an arbitrary function evaluation during the bootstrapping procedure?

In this work, we firmly answer *yes* to this question. We design algorithms that are both asymptotically efficient ($\tilde{O}(1)$ polynomial multiplications per LWE ciphertext bootstrapping) and concretely fast (orders of magnitude faster than

---

[1] In other words, they allow evaluating multiplication and additions over two vectors (component-wisely), each with N messages, by evaluating the same operations over the two RLWE ciphertexts encrypting those two vectors.

any existing works), while supporting functional bootstrapping for arbitrary functions.

1.1 Our Contribution

Batched LWE Ciphertext Bootstrapping for NAND. We propose a novel method to perform batched NAND gate evaluation between two LWE ciphertexts without increasing the error. Since the NAND gate is universal and can be used to construct any circuits, this achieves the property of fully homomorphic operation. The asymptotic amortized cost is $\tilde{O}(1)$ homomorphic multiplications per NAND gate, which is almost optimal.

Batched LWE Ciphertext Bootstrapping for General Binary Gates. We extend our scheme to support other types of binary gates without any overhead. Moreover, we support evaluating different gates in parallel (instead of requiring all gates to be the same type) when performing the batched bootstrapping.

Batched Arbitrary Functional Bootstrapping. We further extend our scheme to support arbitrary function evaluation. In more detail, we allow one to evaluate an arbitrary function $f : \mathbb{Z}_p \to \mathbb{Z}_p$ any message $m \in \mathbb{Z}_p$ encrypted in an LWE ciphertext, without increasing the error of the output LWE ciphertexts. The asymptotic amortized cost remains $\tilde{O}(1)$ homomorphic multiplications per LWE ciphertext.

Implementation and Evaluation. We implement our schemes as a C++ library (will be open-sourced) and measure the concrete performance for a variety of parameters to compare with prior works. Salient observations include:

- For arbitrary binary gates, the cost is less than 5 ms per gate, which is *more than an order of magnitude faster* than the state-of-the-art C++ implementation of TFHE bootstrapping (OpenFHE [4]), and more than 3x faster than the state-of-the-art rust implementation (TFHE-rs [40]).
- For arbitrary function evaluation of $m \in \mathbb{Z}_p$, the cost is $\sim$6.7 ms when p is of 9 bits, and $\sim$39 ms when p has 12 bits. Both results are about *two to three orders of magnitude faster* than all the existing arbitrary function evaluation methods providing the same plaintext space.

FHEW/TFHE - BFV/BGV Scheme Switching. Our construction can be adapted to perform scheme switching between FHEW/TFHE-like cryptosystems and BFV/BGV, which is of its own interest. We also benchmark this scheme switching method: $\sim$296 s to switch 32768 LWE ciphertexts into 1 BFV ciphertext, and $\sim$17 s to switch a single BFV ciphertext into 32768 LWE ciphertexts.

1.2 Technical Overview

Main Idea. Our starting point comes from the observation that the BFV/BGV HE schemes operate over a finite field $\mathbb{Z}_t$ for some prime t. Thus, for an LWE ciphertext $(\vec{a}, b) \in \mathbb{Z}_t^{n+1}$, encrypted under secret key $\mathsf{sk} \in \mathbb{Z}_t^n$ (which satisfies $b \equiv \langle \vec{a}, \mathsf{sk} \rangle + \alpha \cdot m + e \bmod t$, for some message m, encoding parameter α and error e), we homomorphically evaluate $b - \langle \vec{a}, \mathsf{sk} \rangle$ resulting in $\alpha \cdot m + e \pmod t \in \mathbb{Z}_t$ instead of $\alpha \cdot m + e + k \cdot t \in \mathbb{Z}$. To recover m, we simply evaluate a polynomial function f over $\mathbb{Z}_t$, where $f : \mathbb{Z}_t \to \mathbb{Z}_t$ is a degree $t - 1$ polynomial function.

Therefore, evaluating $b - \langle \vec{a}, \mathsf{sk} \rangle$ and function f using BFV/BGV homomorphically decrypts an LWE ciphertext into a BFV/BGV ciphertext encrypting m. Due to the SIMD feature of BFV/BGV, the decryption of N LWE ciphertexts can be evaluated at the same time. Then, we just need to switch a BFV/BGV ciphertext with an underlying ring dimension N into N LWE ciphertexts. To achieve this, we adapt the SlotToCoeff algorithm introduced in [9] to the BFV setting followed by the SampleExtract algorithm introduced in [11].

Optimizations. We provide various techniques to further optimize the performance.

- We maximize the number of zero coefficients of the function f to make the evaluation more efficient.
- We minimize the number of rotations and ciphertext multiplications by using the baby-step-giant-step linear transformation [21,30], Paterson-Stockmayer algorithm [37], and generating additional bootstrapping keys.
- To support evaluating different binary gates in parallel when doing bootstrapping, we introduce ways to pre-process and post-process the LWE ciphertexts, so that we can take advantage of the SIMD feature of the underlying BFV scheme even when the gates are distinct.

1.3   Organization

The rest of the paper is organized as follows. Section 2 discusses related works and compares our construction with the existing (batched) LWE ciphertexts bootstrapping methods in terms of asymptotic efficiency and functionality. Section 3 introduces some necessary background on LWE ciphertexts bootstrapping and BFV homomorphic encryption scheme. Section 4 describes our main construction to do batched LWE ciphertexts bootstrapping for NAND gates. Section 5 extends the construction to allow arbitrary binary gates evaluation in parallel. Section 6 further adapts the construction to support batched arbitrary functional bootstrapping. Section 7 discusses our implementation, experimental results, and comparisons with other schemes providing similar or weaker functionalities. Section 8 introduces some extensions of our construction. Section 9 concludes the paper.

2   Related Works

2.1   (Batched) FHEW/TFHE-Like Bootstrapping

We give a comparison between our work and the prior works on FHEW/TFHE-like cryptosystems in Table 1, regarding the asymptotic efficiency and functionalities. For concrete performance comparisons, see Sect. 7.

Non-batched Schemes. FHEW [14] cryptosystem was introduced to focus on evaluating NAND gate between two LWE ciphertexts without increasing the error of the output ciphertext. As NAND gate is universal, such a cryptosystem can be used to homomorphically evaluate any arbitrary binary circuit. It is later improved by TFHE [11] and Lee et al. [25]. However, all of these works primarily focus on evaluating a single NAND gate at a time and are both asymptotically and concretely relatively costly.

Prior Works on Batched Bootstrapping. Batched bootstrapping instead evaluate multiple NAND gates in parallel. [34] was the first to introduce this concept, and was later improved and implemented by [19]. Another work [35] also achieves the same asymptotic efficiency as in [19].

Concurrent and Independent Works on Batched Bootstrapping. Two recent works [26,27] made great progress along this path. [27] improves the asymptotic cost to $\tilde{O}(1)$ homomorphic multiplications per gate bootstrapping, which is asymptotically the same as our construction and is almost optimal. However, to our knowledge, these two works have not yet been implemented, so whether they are concretely efficient remains to be an open problem.

Table 1. Comparisons with prior works. Amortized cost per binary gate bootstrapping counts the number of FHE multiplications per LWE ciphertext bootstrapping (amortized over $N > n$ ciphertexts, where n is the secret key dimension of the LWE ciphertexts). Arbitrary function evaluation is whether the scheme supports arbitrary lookup table evaluation over the plaintext space.

	Ours	Prior works			Concurrent Works	
Scheme(s)	Sect. 4-Sect. 6	[11,14,25]	[34]	[19,35]	[26]	[27]
Amortized Cost per Binary Gate Bootstrapping	$\tilde{O}(1)$	$O(n)$	$\tilde{O}(3^{1/\epsilon} \cdot n^{\epsilon})$	$O(\epsilon \cdot n^{1/\epsilon})$	$\tilde{O}(n^{0.75})$	$\tilde{O}(1)$
Arbitrary Function Evaluation	Yes	No		Yes (by [19])	No	
Implementation	Yes	No		Yes (by [19])	No	

2.2 Arbitrary Function Evaluation

One important feature of FHEW/TFHE-like cryptosystems is that they allow functional bootstrapping: one can evaluate a function over an LWE ciphertext without increasing the error. However, to our knowledge, most of the schemes in Sect. 2.1 (see Table 1) can only be used to evaluate a negacyclic function (i.e., a function $f : \mathbb{Z}_q \to \mathbb{Z}$ satisfying $f(x) = -f(x + q/2)$). Moreover, the input LWE ciphertexts of these works have small precision (normally ≤ 5 bits to remain practical). Thus, the capability is very limited. On the other hand, another line of work constructs arbitrary function evaluation for this kind of cryptosystem, some of which also try to allow larger precision (e.g., 10–20 bits).

Prior Works on Arbitrary Function Evaluation. [12,24,29,41] develop distinct ways to evaluate arbitrary functions (each can be represented as look-up tables (LUT) over the plaintext space). [12,24] rely on homomorphic multiplications ([12] relying on BFV-like multiplications and [24] relying on GSW-based multiplications). [29,41] are instead based on a more lightweight method (only addition between LWE ciphertexts is needed).

Note that the basic methods of all these works only work for small precision. [12,29] provide a way to extend their scheme to allow larger precisions by first dividing a large-precision input ciphertext (e.g., 21-bit precision) into several small-precision ciphertexts (e.g., 7 ciphertexts each with 3-bit precision). Then, these small ciphertexts are fed into the algorithms introduced in [18] to evaluate large-precision functions (large-precision LUTs). A recent concurrent and independent work [31] further improves upon [24,29].

[18] itself provides a way to evaluate a large LUT over a vector of ciphertexts with small plaintext space. [28] (concurrent and independent) further optimize this method. Note that this method assumes the input to be a vector of ciphertexts with small precision, instead of with large precision. Hence, in most applications, the ciphertexts are required to be decomposed first by applying algorithms in [12,29], which introduces an extra overhead.

2.3   Other Related Works

Bootstrapping, first introduced by [16], is greatly explored in many works. Our construction is similar to the bootstrapping procedure introduced in [15] in that we also take advantage of the free modulo t operation when homomorphically evaluating a circuit using BFV, where t is the plaintext space. However, our work is different from [15] in several ways. First, our goal is to support batched functional bootstrapping for LWE ciphertexts, while [15] simply aims to reduce the error for a BFV ciphertext. Thus, our construction not only directly achieves the functionality of FHE, but also provides much more flexibility when evaluating the bootstrapping circuit. Second, [15] discusses t being a power-of-two, which is not very compatible with power-of-two cyclotomics, and thus limits its practicality. Our construction, instead, uses a large prime field t, to guarantee practicality. Third, we introduce additional optimization techniques to make our procedure concretely efficient.

3   Preliminary

Let N be a power of two. Let $\mathcal{R} = \mathbb{Z}[X]/(X^N + 1)$ denote the $2N$-th cyclotomic ring, and $\mathcal{R}_Q = \mathcal{R}/Q\mathcal{R}$ for some $Q \in \mathbb{Z}$. Let $[n]$ denote the set $\{1, \ldots, n\}$. Let $\vec{a}$ denote a vector and $\vec{a}[i]$ denote the i-th element of $\vec{a}$. Similarly, if A is a matrix, let $A[i][j]$ denote the element on the i-th row and j-th column of matrix A. Let $\|\vec{x}\|_\ell$ denote the ℓ-norm for vector $\vec{x}$ (calculated as $(\sum_{i\in|\vec{x}|} \vec{x}[i]^\ell)^{1/\ell}$). If $x \in \mathcal{R}$, let $\|x\|_\ell$ denote the ℓ-norm of the coefficient vector of x, and let $x[i]$ denote the i-th coefficient of x.

When a function needs to take a key but is called without the key (e.g., Dec(ct) where ct is some LWE ciphertext and Dec is the decryption procedure of LWE scheme), it is assumed that the key is taken implicitly and correctly unless otherwise specified.

3.1 Hard Problems

Definition 1 (Decisional learning with error problem). *Let $n, q,$ $\mathcal{D}, \chi$ be parameters dependent on λ. The learning with error (LWE) problem states the following: for $a \leftarrow_\$ \mathbb{Z}_q^n$ sampled uniformly at random, it holds that $(a, \langle a, s \rangle + e) \approx_c (a, b)$, where $s \leftarrow \mathcal{D}, e \leftarrow \chi$ and $b \leftarrow_\$ \mathbb{Z}_q$.*

Let $\mathsf{LWE}_{n,q,\mathcal{D},\chi}$ denote the LWE assumption parameterized by $n, q, \mathcal{D}, \chi$.

Definition 2 (Decisional ring learning with error problem). *Let $N, Q, \mathcal{D}, \chi$ be parameters dependent on λ and N being a power of two. Let $\mathcal{R} = \mathbb{Z}[X]/(X^N + 1)$. The ring learning with error (RLWE) problem states the following: for $a \leftarrow_\$ \mathcal{R}_Q$ sampled uniformly at random, it holds that $(a, a \cdot s + e) \approx_c (a, b)$, where $s \leftarrow \mathcal{D}, e \leftarrow \chi$ and $b \leftarrow_\$ \mathcal{R}_Q$.*

Let $\mathsf{RLWE}_{N,Q,\mathcal{D},\chi}$ denote the RLWE assumption parameterized by $N, Q, \mathcal{D}, \chi$.

3.2 FHEW/TFHE Cryptosystem

FHEW was first introduced in [14], and later improved by TFHE [11]. Recent work [25] also follows this line of work.

All these bootstrapping procedures are based on (CPA secure) LWE encryption parameterized by a secret dimension n, ciphertext modulus q, plaintext modulus p, secret key distribution $\mathcal{D}$, and error distribution χ (such that $\mathsf{LWE}_{n,q,\mathcal{D},\chi}$ holds) defined as follows: under (secret) key $\mathsf{sk} \leftarrow \mathcal{D}$, the LWE encryption of a message $m \in \mathbb{Z}_p$ is a vector $\mathsf{ct} = (\vec{a}, b) \in \mathbb{Z}_q^{n+1}$ such that

$$b = \langle \vec{a}, \mathsf{sk} \rangle + \alpha \cdot m + e \quad (\mathrm{mod}\ q)$$

where $\alpha = \lfloor q/p \rfloor$, and $e \leftarrow \chi$ is a small error term satisfying $|e| < \lfloor q/(2p) \rfloor$. The message m is recovered by computing the LWE decryption function

$$\mathsf{Dec}(\mathsf{sk}, \mathsf{ct}) = \left\lceil \frac{b - \langle \vec{a}, \mathsf{sk} \rangle \quad (\mathrm{mod}\ q)}{\alpha} \right\rfloor$$

Let $\mathsf{err}(\mathsf{ct})$ denote $e \leftarrow \mathsf{Dec}(\mathsf{sk}, \mathsf{ct}) - \alpha \cdot m$, where sk is the corresponding secret key of ct, $m = \mathsf{Dec}(\mathsf{ct})$, and $\alpha = \lfloor q/p \rfloor$.

FHEW/TFHE Functional Bootstrapping. FHEW/TFHE bootstrapping procedure, denoted by $\mathsf{Boot}(\mathsf{btk}, f, \mathsf{ct})$ satisfying the following property:

Given a correct bootstrapping key btk generated from sk, any negacyclic function $f : \mathbb{Z}_q \to \mathbb{Z}$ (i.e., $f(x + q/2) = -f(x)$), and any ciphertext ct with

$\mathsf{err}(\mathsf{ct}) < \beta$ encrypted under sk, let $\mathsf{ct}' \leftarrow \mathsf{Boot}(\mathsf{btk}, f, \mathsf{ct})$, it satisfies that $\mathsf{Dec}(\mathsf{sk}, \mathsf{ct}') \cdot \alpha = f(\mathsf{Dec}(\mathsf{sk}, \mathsf{ct}) \cdot \alpha) \pmod q$ and $\mathsf{err}(\mathsf{ct}') < \beta'$ where $\beta' \leq \beta$.

When we use $\mathsf{Boot}(f, \mathsf{ct})$, we implicitly mean that Boot is called with the correct bootstrapping key btk.

Note that this is the generalized functional bootstrapping achieved by [11,14]. In this paper, we achieve an even stronger functionality than this generalized bootstrapping by removing the requirement that f is negacyclic.

FHEW/TFHE Bootstrapping for the NAND Gate. To evaluate a NAND gate (which is a universal gate) between two LWE ciphertexts without increasing the error, the procedure is as follows (which is a special application of the generalized functional bootstrapping described above):

- Let $p = 4$. Let $\mathsf{ct}_1, \mathsf{ct}_2$ denote the two input LWE ciphertexts, each of which is encrypting either 0 or 1, with error $\mathsf{err}(\mathsf{ct}_b) < q/16$ for $b \in \{1, 2\}$.
- Compute $\mathsf{ct} \leftarrow \mathsf{ct}_1 + \mathsf{ct}_2$, ct encrypting $0, 1$ or 2, with error $< q/16 + q/16 = q/8$.
- Let $f : \mathbb{Z}_q \to \mathbb{Z}$ be defined as follows:

$$f(x) = \begin{cases} q/8 & \text{if } -q/8 \leq x < 3q/8 \\ -q/8 & \text{otherwise} \end{cases}$$

which is a negacyclic function. Compute $(\vec{a}', b') = \mathsf{ct}' \leftarrow \mathsf{Boot}(f, \mathsf{ct})$, and then $b' \leftarrow b' + q/8$, which gives $\mathsf{Dec}(\mathsf{ct}') = 0$ if $\mathsf{Dec}(\mathsf{ct}_1 + \mathsf{ct}_2) = 2$ and $\mathsf{Dec}(\mathsf{ct}') = 1$ otherwise, with $\mathsf{err}(\mathsf{ct}') < q/16$.

FHEW/TFHE bootstrapping uses two additional procedures: modulus switching and key switching, which are also used in our construction, we list those two techniques as follows.

Modulus Switching. Modulus switching procedure is defined as $\mathsf{ModSwitch}(\mathsf{ct}, q') = (q/q')\mathsf{ct} = \lceil (q/q')(\vec{a}, b) \rfloor$ where $\mathsf{ct} = (\vec{a}, b)$ is an LWE ciphertext with ciphertext modulus q. We formalize it using the following lemma, adapted from [14]:

Lemma 1 (Modulus switching). *Let $\mathsf{ct} = (\vec{a}, b) \in \mathbb{Z}_q^{n+1}$ be an LWE encryption of a message $m \in \mathbb{Z}_p$ under secret key $\mathsf{sk} \in \mathbb{Z}^n$, with ciphertext modulus q and noise bound $\mathsf{err}(\mathsf{ct}) < \beta$. Then, for any modulus q', the rounded ciphertext $\mathsf{ct}' = (\vec{a}', b') \leftarrow \mathsf{ModSwitch}(\mathsf{ct}, q')$ is an encryption of the same message m under sk with ciphertext modulus q' and noise bound $|\mathsf{Dec}(\vec{a}', b') - \lfloor q'/p \rfloor m| < (q'/q)\beta + \beta''$, where $\beta'' = \frac{1}{2}(\|\mathsf{sk}\|_1 + 1)$.*

Note that for FHEW/TFHE and other FHE schemes, sk is usually a short vector (i.e., $\|\mathsf{sk}\|_\infty \leq \delta$ for some small δ, e.g., $\delta = 1$ for ternary and binary secret keys).

In practice, when the input ciphertext is sufficiently random, or when modulus switching is performed by *randomized* rounding, it is possible to replace the additive term β'' with a smaller probabilistic bound $O(\|\mathsf{sk}\|_2)$. For uniformly random ternary keys $\mathsf{sk} \in \{0, 1, -1\}^n$, it satisfies $\beta'' \approx \sqrt{n}/3$ as discussed in [14, 29].

Key Switching. Key switching allows converting an LWE encryption under a key $\mathsf{sk} \in \mathbb{Z}_q^n$ into an LWE encryption of the same message with the same ciphertext modulus and plaintext modulus (and slightly larger error) under a different key $\mathsf{sk}' \in \mathbb{Z}_q^{n'}$. The key switching procedure is parameterized by a base B_{ks} (e.g., 2). Let $d_{\mathsf{ks}} = \lceil \log_{B_{\mathsf{ks}}}(q) \rceil$. Let $\mathsf{ksk}_{i,j,v} \in \mathbb{Z}_q^{n'+1} \leftarrow (\vec{\alpha}_{i,j,v}, \langle \vec{\alpha}_{i,j,v}, \mathsf{sk}' \rangle + e + v\mathsf{sk}[i]B_{\mathsf{ks}}^i)$ for $i \in [n], v \in [B_{\mathsf{ks}}], j \in [d_{\mathsf{ks}}]$, where $\vec{\alpha}_{\cdot,\cdot,\cdot}$ is a randomly sampled vector from $\mathbb{Z}_q^{n'}$ and e is some small error sampled from χ_σ (some Gaussian distribution with mean 0 and standard deviation σ). Let $K = \{\mathsf{ksk}_{i,j,v}\}$ denote the key switching key. $\mathsf{KeySwitch}(K, \mathsf{ct})$ is then defined as follows: given $(\vec{a}, b) \in \mathbb{Z}_q^{n+1}$ as the input ciphertext, first compute the base-B_{ks} expansion of $\vec{a}[i] = \sum_{j \in [d_{\mathsf{ks}}]} \vec{a}[i]_j B_{\mathsf{ks}}^j$, for all $i \in [n]$; then, output $\mathsf{ct}' = (\vec{0}, b) - \sum_{i \in [n], j \in [d_{\mathsf{ks}}]} \mathsf{ksk}_{i,j,\vec{a}[i]_j}$. We formalize this property using the following lemma, adapted from [14].

Lemma 2 (Key switching). *Given an LWE ciphertext* $\mathsf{ct} \in \mathbb{Z}_q^{n+1}$ *encrypting message* $m \in \mathbb{Z}_p$ *under secret key* $\mathsf{sk} \in \mathbb{Z}_q^n$, *and a key switching key* K *generated using* sk *and* $\mathsf{sk}' \in \mathbb{Z}_q^{n'}$, *let* $\mathsf{ct}' \in \mathbb{Z}_q^{n'+1} \leftarrow \mathsf{KeySwitch}(K, \mathsf{ct})$, *it holds that* $\mathsf{Dec}(\mathsf{ct}', \mathsf{sk}') = \mathsf{Dec}(\mathsf{ct}, \mathsf{sk})$ *and* $\mathsf{err}(\mathsf{ct}') \leftarrow \chi_{\sigma + n \cdot d_{\mathsf{ks}} \cdot \sigma'}$ *where* σ *is the error standard deviation for* ct *and* σ' *is the error standard deviation for each element in the key switching key.*

The security of key switching is also intuitive. Essentially, key switching is simply summing up key-switching keys, which are all LWE ciphertexts, and since all the information needed is public, the resulting ciphertext is semantically secure.

3.3 B/FV Leveled Homomorphic Encryption

The BFV leveled homomorphic encryption scheme is first introduced in [6] using standard LWE assumption, and later adapted to ring LWE assumption by [15].

Given a polynomial $\in \mathcal{R}_t = \mathbb{Z}_t[X]/(X^N + 1)$, the BFV scheme encrypts it into a ciphertext consisting of two polynomials, where each polynomial is from a larger cyclotomic ring $\mathcal{R}_Q = \mathbb{Z}_Q[X]/(X^N + 1)$ for some $Q > t$. We refer t as the plaintext modulus, Q as the ciphertext modulus, and N as the ring dimension. t satisfies that $t \equiv 1 \mod 2N$, where N is a power of two.

Plaintext Encoding. To encrypt a plaintext $\vec{m} = (m_1, \ldots, m_N) \in \mathbb{Z}_t^N$, BFV creates polynomial $m(X) = \sum_{i \in [N]} m_i X^{i-1}$, and then encodes it by constructing another polynomial $y(X) = \sum_{i \in [N]} y_i X^{i-1}$ where $m_i = y(\eta_j)$, $\eta_j := \eta^{3^j} \mod t$, and η is the $2N$-th primitive root of unity of t. Such encoding can be done using an Inverse Number Theoretic Transformation (INTT), which is a linear transformation (and can be represented as matrix multiplication).

Encryption and Decryption. The BFV ciphertext encrypting $\vec{m}$ under $\mathsf{sk} \leftarrow \mathcal{D}$ has the format $\mathsf{ct} = (a, b) \in \mathcal{R}_Q^2$, satisfying $b - a \cdot \mathsf{sk} = \lfloor Q/t \rfloor \cdot y + e$ where

$\lfloor Q/t \rfloor \cdot y \in \mathcal{R}_Q$ and y is the polynomial encoded in the way above, and e is some small error term sampled from some Gaussian distribution over $\mathcal{R}_Q$. Note that this encryption using $\lfloor Q/t \rfloor \cdot y$ for some message y is exactly the same as the LWE encryption we have above (there we have $\alpha = \lfloor q/p \rfloor$).

Symmetric key encryption can be done by simply sampling a random a and constructing b accordingly using sk. Public key encryption can also be achieved easily but it is not relevant to our paper so we refer the readers to [6,15,23] for details.

Decryption is thus to calculate $y' \leftarrow \lceil (t/Q) \cdot (b - a \cdot \mathsf{sk}) \rfloor \in \mathcal{R}_t$ (note that $(b - a \cdot \mathsf{sk})$ is done over $\mathcal{R}_Q$), and then decodes it by applying a procedure to revert the encoding process (which is also a linear transformation). We assume BFV.Dec outputs plaintext $\in \mathbb{Z}_t^N$, which is the decoded form, for simplicity. Similarly, we assume BFV.Enc contains the encoding process.

BFV Operations. BFV essentially supports addition, multiplication, rotation, and polynomial function evaluation, satisfying the following property:

- (Addition) $\mathsf{BFV.Dec}(\mathsf{ct}_1 + \mathsf{ct}_2) = \mathsf{BFV.Dec}(\mathsf{ct}_1) + \mathsf{BFV.Dec}(\mathsf{ct}_2)$
- (Multiplication) $\mathsf{BFV.Dec}(\mathsf{ct}_1 \times \mathsf{ct}_2) = \mathsf{BFV.Dec}(\mathsf{ct}_1) \times \mathsf{BFV.Dec}(\mathsf{ct}_2)$
- (Rotation) $\mathsf{BFV.Dec}(\mathsf{rot}(\mathsf{ct}, j))[i] = \mathsf{BFV.Dec}(\mathsf{ct})[i + j \pmod{N}]$ for all $i, j \in [N]$
- (Polynomial evaluation) $\mathsf{BFV.Dec}(\mathsf{BFV.Eval}(\mathsf{ct}, f)) = f(\mathsf{BFV.Dec}(\mathsf{ct}))$, where $f : \mathbb{Z}_t \to \mathbb{Z}_t$ is a polynomial function. Note that this is implied by addition and multiplication.

BFV ciphertexts addition is done by adding the two pairs of polynomials accordingly (i.e., $\mathsf{ct}_1 + \mathsf{ct}_2 = (a_1 + a_2, b_1 + b_2)$). Multiplication requires a tensor product between two ciphertexts followed by a relinearization processing (i.e., a way to bring the product result of three ring elements back to two elements), altogether taking $\mathsf{polylog}(Q)$ polynomial multiplications (or equivalently $O(N\mathsf{polylog}(Q)\log(N))$ integer multiplications). Rotation is done via Galois automorphism which also takes $\mathsf{polylog}(Q)$ polynomial multiplications. Multiplication requires a BFV evaluation key for relinearization and rotation requires a BFV rotation key. We assume all keys are correctly and implicitly taken. All operations are operated over the entire plaintext vector $m \in \mathbb{Z}_t^N$. Thus, all messages need to be evaluated using the same polynomial f by default. This is also known as the Single Instruction Multiple Data (SIMD) property of BFV.

Since we use all of these operations as blackboxes, we omit the details and refer the readers to [6,15,23,39].

Short Keys. In practice, $\mathsf{sk} \in \mathcal{R}$ is almost always a short vector (i.e., $\|\mathsf{sk}\|_\infty \leq \delta$ for some small δ, e.g., $\delta = 1$ for ternary and binary secret keys). $\mathsf{sk} \in \mathcal{R}$ can be easily represented in $\mathcal{R}_Q$ (e.g., if $\mathsf{sk}[i] = -1$, it is represented as $Q - 1$). Therefore, we directly view $\mathsf{sk} \in \mathcal{R}_Q$ for simplicity. When sk is transformed to $\mathcal{R}_{Q'}$, the transformation is done in the same way. In this paper, we assume the secret key of BFV is ternary (i.e., $\mathsf{sk}[i] \in \{0, 1, -1\}$ for all $i \in [N]$ for $\mathsf{sk} \in \mathcal{R}$), compliant with FHE standard [1], unless otherwise specified.

BFV Modulus Switching. Similar to the modulus switching procedure described in Sect. 3.2 for FHEW/TFHE, the modulus switching procedure for BFV: BFV.ModSwitch($\mathsf{ct_{BFV}}, Q'$) is as follow: let $\mathsf{ct_{BFV}} = (a, b) \in \mathcal{R}_Q$ be a BFV ciphertext with ring dimension N, ciphertext modulus Q and error e. Then, BFV.ModSwitch($\mathsf{ct_{BFV}}, Q'$) := $(Q'/Q)\mathsf{ct_{BFV}}$ simply takes every coefficient of a, b, divides them by Q, multiplies them by Q', and rounds to the nearest integer.

BFV Key Switching. BFV key switching is much more complicated than the key switching for LWE ciphertexts introduced above, but essentially for the same functionality. We skip the details here and refer the readers to [23].

4 Binary NAND Gate Bootstrapping

In this section, we show in detail how to construct a batched bootstrapping process for NAND gate, i.e., the batch version of the original FHEW/TFHE bootstrapping procedure as introduced in Sect. 3.2.

Given $2N$ LWE ciphertexts $\vec{ct_1} = (\mathsf{ct}_{1,1}, \ldots, \mathsf{ct}_{1,N}), \vec{ct_2} = (\mathsf{ct}_{2,1}, \ldots, \mathsf{ct}_{2,N})$, encrypting either 0 or 1 with ciphertext modulus q, plaintext modulus $p = 3^2$, under the same key sk, with error $< \beta = \lfloor q/12 \rfloor$, we want to construct some procedure Boot($\vec{ct_1}, \vec{ct_2}$, btk) where btk is some bootstrapping key to be discussed later, and output $(\mathsf{ct}'_1, \ldots, \mathsf{ct}'_N)$, all encrypted under sk with error $< \beta$, such that $\mathsf{Dec}(\mathsf{ct}'_i) = \neg(\mathsf{Dec}(\mathsf{ct}_{1,i}) \wedge \mathsf{Dec}(\mathsf{ct}_{2,i}))$ for $i \in [N]$.

We perform the batched bootstrapping using BFV scheme, parametrized by ring dimension N, ciphertext modulus Q, and plaintext modulus t.

4.1 Bootstrapping Key Generation

We start by discussing what bootstrapping keys we need. Since our construction is fully based on BFV HE scheme, we need the public key of BFV BFV.pk, the evaluation key of BFV BFV.evk (for relinearization after multiplications), and the rotation key of BFV BFV.rtk for arbitrary rotations (to perform BFV.Rotate(ct, BFV.rtk, i). For each i, we need to generate a different BFV rotation key. Thus, BFV.rtk essentially includes multiple keys corresponding to multiple rotation step sizes. We will fix the specific number of rotation keys included in BFV.rtk later. Besides, we need $\mathsf{bfvct_{sk}} \leftarrow$ BFV.Enc(sk). Here $\mathsf{sk} \in \mathbb{Z}_q^n$ [3], is the secret key used to encrypt the inputs $\vec{ct_1}, \vec{ct_2}$. Note that the plaintext space of the BFV scheme is $\mathbb{Z}_t^N$, to make it consistent with the modulus of sk, we let $t = q$. Moreover, to make sk a valid input to BFV.Enc, we repeat sk for N/n times and concatenate together[4], i.e. $(\mathsf{sk} || \ldots || \mathsf{sk}) \in \mathbb{Z}_t^N$.

---

[2] Note that prior works use $p = 4$.

[3] Recall that technically $\mathsf{sk} \in \mathbb{Z}^n$. However, it can be transformed to $\mathbb{Z}_q^n$ easily as long as $\|\mathsf{sk}\|_\infty \leq \lfloor q/2 \rfloor$. Thus, for simplicity, we view $\mathsf{sk} \in \mathbb{Z}_q^n$. Similarly for the BFV secret key below.

[4] For simplicity we assume $N/n \in \mathbb{Z}^+$.

All these public keys are generated using a BFV secret key $\mathsf{sk_{BFV}} = \sum_{i \in [N]} s_i X^{i-1} \in \mathcal{R}_Q$, generated independently from the secret key sk (which is used to encrypt the input LWE ciphertexts).

Let $\overrightarrow{\mathsf{sk_{BFV}}} = (s_1, \ldots, s_N)$ denotes the vector of the coefficients of $\mathsf{sk_{BFV}}$. With $\overrightarrow{\mathsf{sk_{BFV}}}$ and sk, we generate the key-switching key K that is used to turn an LWE ciphertext encrypted under $\mathsf{sk_{BFV}}$ to an LWE ciphertext encrypted under sk as introduced in Sect. 3.2.

Based on the CPA security of BFV, all of these keys are not leaking any information about $\mathsf{sk_{BFV}}$ or sk. Thus, our bootstrapping key is $\mathsf{btk} = (\mathsf{BFV.pk}, \mathsf{BFV.evk}, \mathsf{BFV.rtk}, K, \mathsf{bfvct_{sk}})$.

4.2   Pair-Wise Summation

Recall that for an LWE ciphertext $(\vec{a}, b)$ encrypting 1 under sk, we have $b - \langle \mathsf{sk}, \vec{a} \rangle \in (\lfloor q/3 \rfloor - \lfloor q/12 \rfloor, \lfloor q/3 \rfloor + \lfloor q/12 \rfloor)$, as $\mathsf{err}(\mathsf{ct}_{j,i}) < \beta = \lfloor q/12 \rfloor$, and encrypting 0 when $b - \langle \mathsf{sk}, \vec{a} \rangle \in (-\lfloor q/12 \rfloor, \lfloor q/12 \rfloor)$.[5]

Our first step simply adds the two input vectors pair-wisely. For all $i \in [N]$, given $\mathsf{ct}_{1,i} = (\vec{a}_{1,i}, b_{1,i}), \mathsf{ct}_{2,i} = (\vec{a}_{2,i}, b_{2,i})$, compute $\mathsf{ct}_i = (\vec{a}_i, b_i) \leftarrow (\vec{a}_{1,i} + \vec{a}_{2,i}, b_{1,i} + b_{2,i} + \lfloor q/6 \rfloor)$, where the vector addition is done via element-wise addition. (We shift the result by $\lfloor q/6 \rfloor$ to avoid negative numbers for simplicity in the following range analysis.)

Thus, if $\mathsf{Dec}(\mathsf{ct}_{1,i}) = \mathsf{Dec}(\mathsf{ct}_{2,i}) = 1$ we have:

$$
\begin{aligned}
b_i - \langle \mathsf{sk}, \vec{a}_i \rangle &= (b_{1,i} - \langle \mathsf{sk}, \vec{a}_{1,i} \rangle) + (b_{2,i} - \langle \mathsf{sk}, \vec{a}_{2,i} \rangle) + \lfloor q/6 \rfloor \\
&\in (\lfloor q/3 \rfloor + \lfloor q/3 \rfloor - \lfloor q/12 \rfloor - \lfloor q/12 \rfloor + \lfloor q/6 \rfloor, \\
&\qquad \lfloor q/3 \rfloor + \lfloor q/3 \rfloor + \lfloor q/12 \rfloor + \lfloor q/12 \rfloor + \lfloor q/6 \rfloor) \\
&\subseteq (2 \lfloor q/3 \rfloor, q)
\end{aligned}
$$

And similarly, if $\mathsf{Dec}(\mathsf{ct}_{1,i}) = \mathsf{Dec}(\mathsf{ct}_{2,i}) = 0$, we have $b_i - \langle \mathsf{sk}, \vec{a}_i \rangle \in (0, \lfloor q/3 \rfloor)$, otherwise $b_i - \langle \mathsf{sk}, \vec{a}_i \rangle \in (\lfloor q/3 \rfloor, 2 \lfloor q/3 \rfloor)$.

4.3   Homomorphic Decryption Circuit

Our next step is to homomorphically decrypt all the ct_i's. The regular LWE decryption procedure is as follow:

$$
\mathsf{Dec}(\mathsf{sk}, \mathsf{ct} = (\vec{a}, b)) = \left\lceil \frac{b - \langle \vec{a}, \mathsf{sk} \rangle \pmod q}{\alpha} \right\rfloor
$$

which has three steps: (1) *inner product*, (2) *subtraction*, and (3) *division and rounding*. As our goal is to compute a NAND gate and output an LWE ciphertext, during the final step, we also need to map the resulting value in $\mathbb{Z}_3$ into $\{0, \lfloor q/3 \rfloor\}$, which is the encoding of $\{0, 1\}$ correspondingly. Thus, the last step is essentially *division, rounding, and NAND mapping*.

---

[5] Note that $- \lfloor q/12 \rfloor$ is simply $q - \lfloor q/12 \rfloor$.

One *key property* we use is that BFV homomorphically computes over $\mathbb{Z}_t$ where we set t equals q which is the LWE ciphertext modulus. Therefore, the mod operation over t is automatically performed during all computations and we just need to design the circuit over $\mathbb{Z}_t$ with $t = q$.

Inner Product. We start by homomorphically computing the inner product. Let $\mathsf{ct}_i = (\vec{a}_i, b_i)$. To compute $\langle \vec{a}_i, \mathsf{sk} \rangle$ for all $i \in [N]$ is equivalent to compute $A\mathsf{sk}$ where $A = \begin{pmatrix} \vec{a}_1 \\ \vdots \\ \vec{a}_N \end{pmatrix} \in \mathbb{Z}_t^{N \times n}$.

Naively, this matrix multiplication can be computed with N plaintext-by-ciphertext multiplications together with N rotations. However, we improve this by using the baby-step-giant-step technique, which is first introduced in [21] and later improved in [30]. Thus allows us to compute $A\mathsf{sk}$ with N plaintext-by-ciphertext multiplications and just $2\sqrt{N}$ rotations. Note that each rotation requires a specific rotation key generated accordingly. As the BFV key generation is straightforward, we view it as a blackbox and assume all the keys needed are properly included in btk.

We adapt this technique and formally present it in Algorithm 1, which takes a matrix $A \in \mathbb{Z}_t^{N \times n}$, a BFV ciphertext bfvct encrypting a vector $m \in \mathbb{Z}_t^n$, and proper BFV rotation keys, and outputs a BFV ciphertext bfvct' encrypting $(Am)^{\mathsf{T}} \in \mathbb{Z}_t^N$. For the correctness of this algorithm, see [21,30] for details.

Algorithm 1. Homomorhic Linear Transformation

1: **procedure** LT(BFV.rtk, A, bfvct) $\triangleright A \in \mathbb{Z}_t^{N \times n}$
2:    $\triangleright$ bfvct encrypts a vector $\vec{v} \in \mathbb{Z}_t^n$ by repeating v N/n times and encrypting the concatenation of those N/n repetitions.
3:    $\mathsf{rt} \leftarrow \sqrt{n}$
4:    $\triangleright$ We assume $\sqrt{n}$ to be an integer for simplicity. For more general n's, see [30] for details.
5:    **for** $i \in [\mathsf{rt}]$ **do**
6:        $\mathsf{bfvct}_{\mathsf{rot}_i} \leftarrow \mathsf{BFV.Rotate}(\mathsf{bfvct}, \mathsf{BFV.rtk}, i \cdot \mathsf{rt})$
7:    Initialize BFV ciphertexts res_k, for $k \in [\mathsf{rt}]$, each encrypting 0's
8:    **for** $k \in [\mathsf{rt}]$ **do**
9:        **for** $i \in [\mathsf{rt}]$ **do**
10:            Construct $\mathsf{tmp} \in \mathbb{Z}_t^N$, such that $\mathsf{tmp}[j] = A[\mathsf{ind}_{\mathsf{ct}}][\mathsf{ind}_{\mathsf{a}}]$, where $\mathsf{ind}_{\mathsf{ct}} = (j-k) \mod N$, $\mathsf{ind}_{\mathsf{a}} = (j + i \cdot \mathsf{rt}) \mod n$
11:            $\mathsf{c} \leftarrow \mathsf{tmp} \times \mathsf{bfvct}_{\mathsf{rot}_i}$
12:            $\mathsf{res}_k \leftarrow \mathsf{res}_k + \mathsf{c}$
13:    **for** $i \in [\mathsf{rt} - 1]$ **do**
14:        $\mathsf{c} \leftarrow \mathsf{BFV.Rotate}(\mathsf{res}_{\mathsf{rt}-i+1}, \mathsf{BFV.rtk}, 1)$
15:        $\mathsf{res}_{\mathsf{rt}-i} \leftarrow \mathsf{BFV.Add}(\mathsf{res}_{\mathsf{rt}-i}, \mathsf{c})$
16:    **return** $\mathsf{bfvct}' \leftarrow \mathsf{res}_1$

Subtraction. Subtraction can be done by computing $\vec{b} - (A\mathsf{sk})^\mathsf{T}$ where $\vec{b} = (b_1, \ldots, b_N)$. Again, as BFV is computing the circuits over $\mathbb{Z}_t$, "mod t" part comes for free.

Division, Rounding, and NAND Mapping. This step is the most involved component in the decryption procedure. The reason is that BFV only supports multiplication and addition over a finite field , while division and rounding are not supported. Thus, we design a polynomial function over the finite field $\mathbb{Z}_t$ to compute division and rounding.

Recall that if $\mathsf{Dec}(\mathsf{ct}_{1,i}) = \mathsf{Dec}(\mathsf{ct}_{2,i}) = 1$ we have $b_i - \langle \mathsf{sk}, \vec{a}_i \rangle + \lfloor q/6 \rfloor \in (2\lfloor q/3 \rfloor, q)$, where $(\vec{a}_i, b_i) = \mathsf{ct}_i$ computed above in Sect. 4.2. This is the case that should be mapped to 0 for a NANG gate mapping. Otherwise, the result should be mapped to $\lfloor q/3 \rfloor$ (i.e., the encoding of 1).

We first express this division, rounding, and mapping process as a function $\mathsf{DRaM} : \mathbb{Z}_t \to \mathbb{Z}_t$ (recall that $t = q$):

$$\mathsf{DRaM}(x) = \begin{cases} 0 & \text{if } x \geq 2\lfloor t/3 \rfloor \\ \lfloor t/3 \rfloor & \text{otherwise} \end{cases} \tag{1}$$

where DRaM stands for **D**ivision, **R**onding, and **M**apping.

Then, we translate this function into a polynomial function $\mathsf{DRaMpoly} : \mathbb{Z}_t \to \mathbb{Z}_t$ by using the following formula adapted from [22, Equation 2]:

$$\mathsf{DRaMpoly}(x) = \mathsf{DRaM}(0) - \sum_{i=1}^{t-1} x^i \sum_{a=0}^{t-1} \mathsf{DRaM}(a)a^{t-1-i} \ .$$

For any t, DRaMpoly is then equivalent to DRaM and we formalize it by the following lemma.

Lemma 3. *Given any prime p, for any function $f : \mathbb{Z}_p \to \mathbb{Z}_p$, let $f'(x) := f(0) - \sum_{i=1}^{t-1} x^i \sum_{a=0}^{t-1} f(a)a^{t-1-i}$ then it holds that for any $x \in \mathbb{Z}_p$, $f(x) = f'(x)$.*

For correctness proof of the lemma, we refer the readers to [22, Section 3].

Thus, to evaluate the division, rounding, and mapping, we simply need to perform $\mathsf{BFV.Eval}(\mathsf{bfvct}, \mathsf{DRaMpoly})$, where $\mathsf{bfvct} \leftarrow \vec{b} - \mathsf{LT}(\mathsf{BFV.rtk}, A, \mathsf{bfvct_{sk}})$ is the BFV ciphertext resulted by homomorphically computing $\vec{b} - (A\mathsf{sk})^\mathsf{T}$, where $\vec{b} = (b_1, \ldots, b_N), A = \begin{pmatrix} \vec{a}_1 \\ \vdots \\ \vec{a}_N \end{pmatrix}$, and $\mathsf{bfvct_{sk}}$ is the BFV ciphertext encrypting $\mathsf{sk} \in \mathbb{Z}_t^n$ (generated as in Sect. 4.1).

Naively computing the polynomial DRaMpoly requires $O(t)$ ciphertext-by-ciphertext multiplications, which are used to generate x^i for all $i \in [t]$. However, instead, we use the Paterson-Stockmeyer algorithm [37], reducing to $O(\sqrt{t})$ ciphertext-by-ciphertext multiplications.

4.4 BFV Ciphertext to LWE Ciphertexts

After all the processes above, we obtain a BFV ciphertext $\mathsf{bfvct_{res}}$ encrypting the message vector $(m_1, \ldots, m_N)$. Here we have $m_i = 0$ if $\mathsf{Dec}(\mathsf{ct}_{1,i}) = \mathsf{Dec}(\mathsf{ct}_{2,i}) =$

1, and $m_i = \lfloor q/3 \rfloor$ otherwise, where $\mathsf{ct}_{1,i}, \mathsf{ct}_{2,i}$ for $i \in [N]$ are input ciphertexts. Recall that $\mathsf{bfvct}_{\mathsf{res}}$ is in the encoded form introduced in Sect. 3.3.

Our next step is to expand this single BFV ciphertext encrypting N messages into N LWE ciphertexts, each encrypting a single m_i. To do this, we first transform $\mathsf{bfvct}_{\mathsf{res}}$ to a BFV ciphertext encrypting $m(X) = \sum_i m_i X^{i-1}$. In other words, we decode the encoded messages homomorphically. Then, we extract N LWE ciphertexts each encrypting a single coefficient m_i, i.e., switching a Ring-LWE ciphertext into LWE ciphertexts.

Homomorphic Decoding. Recall that in BFV, to encrypt a vector of messages $(m_1, \ldots, m_N) \in \mathbb{Z}_t^N$, we first use canonical embedding to encode them into a polynomial. In more detail, let $m(X) := \sum_{i \in [N]} m_i X^{i-1}$, we construct a polynomial $y(X) = \sum_{i \in [N]} y_i X^{i-1}$, where $y_i = m(\zeta_i)$, where ζ being the $2N$-th primitive root of unity of t, and $\zeta_i := \zeta^{3^i}$. Thus, a ciphertext $\mathsf{bfvct}_{\mathsf{res}}$ encrypting $(m_1, \ldots, m_N)$ encrypts the polynomial $y(X)$.

To revert this process, we can homomorphically compute $\mathsf{bfvct}'_{\mathsf{res}} \leftarrow \mathsf{bfvct}_{\mathsf{res}} U^\top$, where

$$
U := \begin{pmatrix}
1 & \zeta_0 & \zeta_0^2 & \cdots & \zeta_0^{N-1} \\
1 & \zeta_1 & \zeta_1^2 & \cdots & \zeta_1^{N-1} \\
\vdots & \vdots & \vdots & \ddots & \vdots \\
1 & \zeta_{\frac{N}{2}-1} & \zeta_{\frac{N}{2}-1}^2 & \cdots & \zeta_{\frac{N}{2}-1}^{N-1} \\
1 & \bar{\zeta}_0 & \bar{\zeta}_0^2 & \cdots & \bar{\zeta}_0^{N-1} \\
1 & \bar{\zeta}_1 & \bar{\zeta}_1^2 & \cdots & \bar{\zeta}_1^{N-1} \\
\vdots & \vdots & \vdots & \ddots & \vdots \\
1 & \bar{\zeta}_{\frac{N}{2}-1} & \bar{\zeta}_{\frac{N}{2}-1}^2 & \cdots & \bar{\zeta}_{\frac{N}{2}-1}^{N-1}
\end{pmatrix} \in \mathbb{Z}_t^{N \times N}
$$

where $\bar{\zeta}_j := \zeta_j^{-1}$, and the resulting $\mathsf{bfvct}'_{\mathsf{res}}$ is thus encrypting the polynomial $m(X) = \sum_i m_i X^{i-1}$.

This process is first introduced as the SlotToCoeff procedure in [9] for the CKKS HE scheme, and we adapt it to the BFV scheme.

Ring-LWE to LWE. Now $\mathsf{bfvct}'_{\mathsf{res}} = (a_{\mathsf{bfv}}, b_{\mathsf{bfv}}) \in \mathcal{R}_Q^2$ and we have $b_{\mathsf{bfv}} - a_{\mathsf{bfv}} \mathsf{sk}_{\mathsf{BFV}} \approx \lfloor Q/t \rfloor\, m$ where m is the polynomial $m(X)$ defined above with all the coefficients being either 0 or $\lfloor t/3 \rfloor$. Our goal is to obtain N LWE ciphertexts $(\mathsf{ct}_1' = (\vec{a}_1', b_1'), \ldots, \mathsf{ct}_N' = (\vec{a}_N', b_N')) \in \mathbb{Z}_Q^{N \cdot (N+1)}$ such that $b_i' - \langle \vec{a}_i', \vec{s} \rangle \approx \lfloor Q/t \rfloor\, m_i$, where $\vec{s} = (s_1, \ldots, s_N)$ for $\vec{s}$ is the coefficient vector of $\mathsf{sk}_{\mathsf{BFV}}$.

This can be done by using the SampleExtract procedure in [11]. With ciphertext $\mathsf{bfvct}'_{\mathsf{res}} = (a_{\mathsf{bfv}}(X) = \sum_{i \in [N]} a_{\mathsf{bfv}_i} X^{i-1}, b_{\mathsf{bfv}}(X) = \sum_{i \in [N]} b_{\mathsf{bfv}_i} X^{i-1})$, we achieve the extraction from RLWE ciphertext $\mathsf{bfvct}'_{\mathsf{res}}$ to LWE ciphertexts $(\vec{a}_i', b_i')_{i \in [N]}$ by setting $\vec{a}_i' = (\alpha_{i,1}, \ldots, \alpha_{i,N})$ where $\alpha_{i,j} \leftarrow a_{\mathsf{bfv}_{i-j+1}}$ if $j \leq i$ and $\alpha_{i,j} \leftarrow -a_{\mathsf{bfv}_{N-j+i+1}}$ if $j > i$, and $b_i' = b_{\mathsf{bfv}_i}$ for $i \in [N]$.

This procedure is formalized by the following lemma:

Lemma 4. *For any ring elements* $a(X) = \sum_{i \in [N]} a_i X^{i-1}, s(X) = \sum_{i \in [N]} s_i X^{i-1} \in \mathcal{R}_q$, *let* $b(X) = a \cdot s = \sum_{i \in [N]} b_i X^{i-1} \in \mathcal{R}_q$, *it holds that* $b_i = \sum_{j \in [N]} a'_{i,j} \cdot s_j \mod q$ *where* $a'_{i,j} = a_{i-j+1}$ *if* $j \leq i$ *and* $a'_{i,j} = q - a_{N-j+i+1}$ *otherwise.*

The correctness of the lemma is straightforward so we omit the details. The procedure is presented as Extract in Algorithm 2.

Key Switching and Modulus Switching. After all these steps, we now obtain $(\mathsf{ct}'_1 = (\vec{a}'_1, b'_1), \ldots, \mathsf{ct}'_N = (\vec{a}'_N, b'_N)) \in \mathbb{Z}_Q^{N \cdot (n+1)}$ encrypting the NAND results under $\vec{s}$. To obtain N LWE ciphertexts encrypting the NAND results under sk with ciphertext modulus t, two final steps are needed: (1) use key switching KeySwitch introduced in Sect. 3.2 with the key switching key K generated as in Sect. 4.1 to change ct'_i into ciphertexts encrypted under sk instead of $\vec{s}$; (2) use modulus switching to change the ciphertext modulus from Q to t.

We thus complete our algorithm, and formally demonstrate the entire procedure in Algorithm 2.

Theorem 1. *Let* $(\mathsf{pp}_{\mathsf{lwe}} = (n, q, p = 3, \mathcal{D}_1, \chi_\sigma), \mathsf{pp}_{\mathsf{bfv}} = (N, Q, Q', t = q, \mathcal{D}_2, \chi_{\sigma'}), \mathsf{sk}, \mathsf{btk}) \leftarrow \mathsf{Setup}(1^\lambda)$ *in Algorithm 2, for any input LWE ciphertexts* $\vec{\mathsf{ct}}_1 = (\mathsf{ct}_{1,1}, \ldots, \mathsf{ct}_{1,N}), \vec{\mathsf{ct}}_2 = (\mathsf{ct}_{2,1}, \ldots, \mathsf{ct}_{2,N})$ *parameterized by* $\mathsf{pp}_{\mathsf{lwe}}$, *encrypting* $\{0, 1\}$ *under* sk, *and* $\mathsf{err}(\mathsf{ct}_{i,j}) < \lfloor q/12 \rfloor$ *for all* $i \in [2], j \in [N]$; *let* $(\mathsf{ct}_{\mathsf{out}1}, \ldots, \mathsf{ct}_{\mathsf{out}N}) \leftarrow \mathsf{Boot}(\vec{\mathsf{ct}}_1, \vec{\mathsf{ct}}_2, \mathsf{btk})$ *in Algorithm 2, it holds that:* $\mathsf{Dec}(\mathsf{ct}_{\mathsf{out}i}) = NAND(\mathsf{Dec}(\mathsf{ct}_{1,i}), \mathsf{Dec}(\mathsf{ct}_{2,i}))$, $\Pr[\mathsf{err}(\mathsf{ct}_{\mathsf{out}i}) < \lfloor q/12 \rfloor] \geq 1 - \mathsf{negl}(\lambda)$, *and* $\mathsf{ct}_{\mathsf{out}i}$ *is encrypted under secret key* sk, *for all* $i \in [N]$.

Proof (sketch). We show this result from basic correctness (i.e., achieving NAND gate functionality) and noise analysis.

- (Correctness) Correctness (i.e., $\mathsf{Dec}(\mathsf{ct}_{\mathsf{out}i}) = NAND(\mathsf{Dec}(\mathsf{ct}_{1,i}), \mathsf{Dec}(\mathsf{ct}_{2,i}))$) is intuitive. We first homomorphically evaluate a circuit using BFV, which includes the evaluation of Dec function of the LWE ciphertexts and the NAND mapping. Then we extract N LWE ciphertexts out from the resulting BFV ciphertext. The correctness of circuit design is given by Lemma 3, the correctness of the evaluation of the circuit is given by the correctness of BFV (and condition (4) in Setup), and the correctness of extraction (including RLWE to LWE transformation, key switching, and modulus switching) is guaranteed by Lemmas 1, 2 and 4.
- (Noise Analysis) By the correctness of BFV, with bfvct_5 obtained as on line 36 in Algorithm 2, we have $\mathsf{err}(\mathsf{bfvct}_5) \leq (Q'/t)/2$, and this error is from Gaussian distribution χ_{σ_5} with mean 0 and standard deviation σ_5. The key switching procedure introduces an extra noise with a standard deviation of $\sigma_{\mathsf{ks}} = \sigma_{\mathsf{ksk}} N d_{\mathsf{ks}}$ where σ_{ksk} is the error standard deviation of the key switching key and $\sigma_{\mathsf{ksk}} = \sigma'$, where σ' is selected on line 4 in Algorithm 2, and d_{ks} is a key switching parameter, bounded by $\log(N)$ (see details in Sect. 3.2). Thus, after modulus switching, the resulting ciphertexts have error of standard deviation $\sigma = \sqrt{\left(\frac{t}{Q'}(\sigma_5 + \sigma_{\mathsf{ks}})\right)^2 + \sigma_{\mathsf{ms}}^2}$, where $\sigma_{\mathsf{ms}} = \sqrt{\frac{\|\mathsf{sk}\|_2^2 + 1}{3}}$ is the

---

Algorithm 2. Batched FHEW/TFHE bootstrapping for NAND gate

1: **procedure** Setup(1^λ)
2:     Select $(n, q, \mathcal{D}_1, \chi_\sigma, N, Q, \mathcal{D}_2\chi_{\sigma'}, Q')$ minimizing the cost of the entire homomorphic circuit evaluation and also satisfying:
3:       (1) LWE$_{n,q,\mathcal{D}_1,\chi_\sigma}$ holds, and $\Pr[e < \lfloor q/12 \rfloor] \geq 1 - \mathsf{negl}(\lambda)$ where $e \leftarrow \chi_\sigma$.
4:       (2) RLWE$_{N,Q,\mathcal{D}_2,\chi_{\sigma'}}$ hold.
5:       (3) $Q' \leq Q$, LWE$_{n,Q',\mathcal{D}_1,\chi_{\sigma'}}$ holds.
6:       (4) BFV with parameters $N, Q, t = q, \mathcal{D}_2, \chi_{\sigma'}$ is enough to evaluate the circuit in procedure Boot
7:       (5) LWE$_{n,q,\mathcal{D}_1,\chi_{\sigma_{\mathrm{res}}}}$ holds, where $\sigma_{\mathrm{res}} = \sqrt{(\frac{t}{Q'}(\sigma_5 + \sigma_{\mathsf{ks}}))^2 + \sigma_{\mathsf{ms}}{}^2}$, where σ_5 is the noise distribution standard deviation of line 36
8:       (6) $\Pr[e' < \lfloor q/12 \rfloor] \geq 1 - \mathsf{negl}(\lambda)$ where $e' \leftarrow \chi_{\sigma_{\mathrm{res}}}$ ▷ $\sigma_{\mathsf{ks}}, \sigma_{\mathsf{ms}}$ are as introduced in Section 3.2.
9:     sk $\leftarrow \mathcal{D}_1$
10:     Generate BFV secret key sk$_{\mathsf{BFV}} \leftarrow \mathcal{D}_2$.
11:     Generate bootstrapping keys btk = (BFV.pk, BFV.evk, BFV.rtk, K, bfvct$_{\mathsf{sk}}$) as in Section 4.1.
12:   ▷ K generated with sk$_{\mathsf{BFV}}$, sk, $Q', \chi_{\sigma'}$.
13:     **return** (pp $=$ pp$_{\mathsf{lwe}}$ $=$ $(n, q, p$ $=$ $3, \mathcal{D}_1, \chi_\sigma)$, pp$_{\mathsf{bfv}}$ $=$ $(N, Q, Q', t =$ $q, \mathcal{D}_2, \chi_{\sigma'})$, sk, btk)
14: **procedure** Extract(bfvct $= (a_{\mathsf{bfv}}, b_{\mathsf{bfv}})$)
15:   ▷ Extract N LWE ciphertexts from one BFV ciphertext
16:     Initialize ct$_i = (\vec{a}_i, b_i)$ for $i \in [N]$
17:     **for** $i \in [N]$ **do**
18:         **for** $j \in [N]$ **do**
19:             **if** $j \leq i$ **then**
20:                 $\vec{a}_i[j] \leftarrow a_{\mathsf{bfv}}[i - j + 1]$
21:             **else**
22:                 $\vec{a}_i[j] \leftarrow -a_{\mathsf{bfv}}[N - j + i + 1]$
23:                 ▷ Negative number is still in $\mathbb{Z}_q$ where q is the bfvct ciphertext modulus
24:         $b_i = b_{\mathsf{bfv}_i}$
25:     **return** (ct$_1, \ldots,$ ct$_N$)
26: **procedure** Boot($(\mathsf{ct}_{1,1}, \ldots, \mathsf{ct}_{1,N}), (\mathsf{ct}_{2,1}, \ldots, \mathsf{ct}_{2,N}),$ btk)
27:   ▷ ct$_{j,i} = (\vec{a}_{j,i}, b_{j,i})$ for $j \in [2], i \in [N]$
28:     Compute ct$_i = (\vec{a}_i, b_i) \leftarrow (\vec{a}_{1,i} + \vec{a}_{2,i}, b_{1,i} + b_{2,i} + \lfloor q/6 \rfloor), \forall i \in [N]$
29:     $A \leftarrow (\vec{a}_1^\mathsf{T}, \ldots, \vec{a}_N^\mathsf{T})$
30:     bfvct$_1 \leftarrow$ LT(BFV.rtk, A, bfvct$_{\mathsf{sk}}$)
31:     bfvct$_2 \leftarrow (b_1, \ldots, b_N) -$ bfvct$_1$ ▷ Homomorphically computes $\vec{b} - \mathsf{sk}A$
32:     bfvct$_3 \leftarrow$ BFV.Eval(BFV.evk, bfvct$_2$, DRaMpoly)
33:     bfvct$_4 \leftarrow$ LT(BFV.rtk, U^T, bfvct$_3$)
34:   ▷ Recall that U is the matrix defined for packing
35:     bfvct$_5 \leftarrow$ BFV.ModSwitch(bfvct$_4, Q'$)
36:   ▷ BFV.ModSwitch is described in Section 3.3
37:     (ct$_1', \ldots,$ ct$_N'$) $\leftarrow$ Extract(bfvct$_5$)
38:     ct$_i'' \leftarrow$ KeySwitch(K, ct$_i'$), $\forall i \in [N]$
39:             ▷ KeySwitch is defined in Section 3.2, and K is the key switching key
40:     ct$_{\mathsf{out}_i} \leftarrow$ ModSwitch(ct$_i'', q$), $\forall i \in [N]$ ▷ ModSwitch is defined in Section 3.2
41:     **return** (ct$_{\mathsf{out}_1}, \ldots,$ ct$_{\mathsf{out}_N}$)

---

modulus switching error standard deviation, and $\|\mathsf{sk}\|_2$ is the ℓ-2 norm of the secret key of the LWE ciphertexts)

Thus, by condition (6) on line 8 in Algorithm 2, $\mathsf{err}(\mathsf{ct}_{\mathsf{out}i}) < \lfloor q/12 \rfloor, \forall i \in [N]$ with overwhelming probability.

Efficiency Analysis. As explained, the BFV circuit needs $O(\sqrt{n} + \sqrt{N})$ rotations, $O(\sqrt{t})$ ciphertext-by-ciphertext multiplications, and $n + t + N$ plaintext-by-ciphertext multiplications, with multiplicative depth $\ell = \log(t) + 3$ (where we have $\log(t) + 1$ levels for polynomial evaluation, one level for the inner product, and one level for Ring LWE to LWE extraction). Note that all these costs are amortized over N LWE ciphertexts bootstrapping.

All the homomorphic operations take at most $O(\mathsf{poly}(\ell))$ polynomial multiplications (see Sect. 3.3). The only constraint for t is that $t > 2N + 1$ to guarantee that there is a primitive $2N$-th root of unity. Thus, the total cost is $\tilde{O}(N)$ polynomial multiplications per bootstrapping for N LWE ciphertexts. The amortized cost is thus quasi-constant number of polynomial multiplications (which can be done with $O(N \log(N))$ $\mathbb{Z}_Q$ operations using NTT).[6]

Security Analysis. Security analysis, on the other hand, is more involved. By condition (1), the input ciphertexts are semantically secure. To make the whole process secure, we need to make sure that the ciphertexts $\mathsf{bfvct}_1, \mathsf{bfvct}_2, \mathsf{bfvct}_3,$ $\mathsf{bfvct}_4, \mathsf{bfvct}_5, (\mathsf{ct}'_i)_{i \in [N]}$ are all semantically secure. These ciphertexts are secure as long as the keys in $\mathsf{btk} = (\mathsf{BFV.pk}, \mathsf{BFV.evk}, \mathsf{BFV.rtk}, K, \mathsf{bfvct}_{\mathsf{sk}})$ are secure (as all these ciphertexts are obtained by performing operations over the input ciphertexts using these keys). By condition (2) on line 4 in Algorithm 2, together with the semantic security of BFV and the security of key switching process, $\mathsf{bfvct}_1, \mathsf{bfvct}_2, \mathsf{bfvct}_3, \mathsf{bfvct}_4, \mathsf{bfvct}_5, (\mathsf{ct}'_i)_{i \in [N]}$ are semantically secure. Based on the security of BFV, $\mathsf{BFV.pk}, \mathsf{BFV.evk}, \mathsf{BFV.rtk}, \mathsf{bfvct}_{\mathsf{sk}}$ are all secure. By condition (3) on line 5, K is also secure. Thus, the whole process is secure.

4.5   Optimizations

Efficiency of DRaMpoly. For a function

$$f(x) = \begin{cases} 0 \text{ if } x \in (-r, r) \\ y \text{ otherwise} \end{cases}$$

where $r \in [2, \lfloor t/2 \rfloor]$ and $y \in \mathbb{Z}_t$, the function $f'(X) = f(0) - \sum_{i=1}^{t-1} X^i \sum_{a=0}^{t-1} f(a) a^{t-1-i}$ has about half of its coefficients being 0. This

---

[6] LWE ciphertexts addition has the cost of $O(1)$ $\mathbb{Z}_q$ operations per LWE ciphertext. LWE key switching has the cost of $\tilde{O}(N)$ $\mathbb{Z}_{Q'}$ operations per LWE ciphertext. LWE modulus switching has the cost of $O(n)$ $\mathbb{Z}_{Q'}$ operations per LWE ciphertext. Thus, their costs do not affect the asymptotic behavior. Note that the prior works (e.g., [26,34]) use a similar way to compute the asymptotic costs. Concretely, their costs are also much smaller than the BFV circuit evaluation.

means that when homomorphically evaluating f', only half of the plaintext-by-ciphertext multiplications are needed, and only half of the powers are needed, which means fewer ciphertext-by-ciphertext multiplications. Thus, we modify DRaM to be

$$\mathsf{DRaM}(x) = \begin{cases} 0 & \text{if } x \in (\lfloor -t/6 \rfloor, \lfloor t/6 \rfloor) \\ \lfloor t/3 \rfloor & \text{otherwise} \end{cases}$$

and shift the $\mathsf{ct}_i = (\vec{a}_i, b_i)$ (from Sect. 4.2) by $-(2\lfloor t/3 \rfloor + \lfloor t/6 \rfloor)$ (i.e., $b_i \leftarrow b_i - 2\lfloor q/3 \rfloor - \lfloor t/6 \rfloor$). This reduces the complexity of evaluating DRaMpoly while remains everything else the same (recall that $t = q$).

Generating Rotations in Advance. Note that for line 30 in Algorithm 2, we need to rotate $\mathsf{bfvct}_{\mathsf{sk}}$ $\sqrt{n}$ times, as on line 6 in Algorithm 1. However, instead of doing the rotations when evaluating Boot, we can compute those rotations during btk generation and include $\mathsf{bfvct}_{\mathsf{rot}_i}$ in btk for all $i \in [\sqrt{n}]$. This can save $\sqrt{n}$ rotations during bootstrapping.

Level-specific Rotation Keys. With the optimization above, we only need $\sqrt{n}$ rotation keys with full level. After the deep circuit evaluation of DRaMpoly, we also need rotation keys to compute line 32 in Algorithm 2. Instead of generating the rotation keys with modulus Q, we modulus switch bfvct_3 to modulus Q' and generate rotation keys with modulus $Q' \ll Q$ to greatly reduce the bootstrapping key size.

Using BFV Key Switching and Modulus Switching. Note that BFV also supports key switching procedure and modulus switching procedure. Hence, instead of performing these two procedures for each extracted LWE ciphertext, we process directly on the single BFV ciphertext. We first create a polynomial $s'(X) = \sum_{i \in [N]} s'_i X^{i-1} \in \mathcal{R}_Q$ where $s'_i = \mathsf{sk}[i]$ if $i \leq n$ and $s'_i = 0$ if $i > n$, for $i \in [N]$. [7] We use $s'(X)$ as the new key to generate the BFV key switching key K together with $\mathsf{sk}_{\mathsf{BFV}}$. The modulus switching procedure remains the same. The security guarantee of BFV key switching is the same as ring switching introduced in [17] as long as n is a power-of-two. Since the key switching procedure and modulus switching procedure are relatively fast, especially for modulus switching, the runtime may not be majorly affected.

4.6   Additional Discussion

Further tuning n. Note that as on line 5 in Algorithm 2, we need $\mathsf{LWE}_{n,Q',\mathcal{D}_1,\chi_{\sigma'}}$ to hold. However, since Q' is relatively large, although σ' is also huge, n might need to be relatively large (e.g., concretely 1024). While this can be sufficient for many applications, we introduce the following way to even reduce n.

Suppose we choose some n such that $\mathsf{LWE}_{n,Q',\mathcal{D}_1,\chi_{\sigma_5}}$ breaks. To work around this issue, we introduce an intermediate $n' > n$ and first perform a KeySwitch to the intermediate secret key with length n', such that $\mathsf{LWE}_{n',Q',\mathcal{D}_1,\chi_{\sigma_5}}$ holds.

---

[7] Recall that sk is ternary so it can be transformed in $\mathbb{Z}_q$ easily.

Then, we modulus switch the result to $q' < Q'$, with the error standard deviation $\sigma_{\text{tmp}} = \sqrt{(\frac{q'}{Q'}(\sigma_5 + \sigma_{\text{ks}}))^2 + \sigma_{\text{ms}}{}^2}$, such that $\mathsf{LWE}_{n,q',\mathcal{D}_1,\chi_{\sigma_{\text{tmp}}}}$ holds. Finally, we perform another key switching to n and modulus switching to q. The resulted error distribution standard deviation is then $\sqrt{(t/q')(\sigma_{\text{tmp}} + \sigma_{\text{ks}}'^2) + \sigma_{\text{ms}}'^2}$, which can be dominated by σ_{ms}' with careful parameter choosing. One can of course repeat this intermediate step for arbitrary times to find an optimal n.

Use BGV Instead of BFV. Since BGV also evaluates circuits over $\mathbb{Z}_t$, our construction can use BGV instead of BFV. Note that BGV encodes messages using least significant bits (LSBs), and FHEW/TFHE ciphertexts (i.e., LWE ciphertexts) encrypt messages using most significant bits (MSBs). Therefore, can simply use the technique introduced in [3, Appendix A] to convert a BGV ciphertext to a BFV ciphertext before switching back to the LWE ciphertexts. This minor change does not affect the overall functionality or the security analysis.

5   Multi-binary-gate Bootstrapping

NAND gate itself is a universal gate, and thus our bootstrapping for NAND gate evaluation already achieves the functionality requirement of FHE. However, the efficiency is still limited.

To evaluate a circuit, one needs to first translate the circuit to have only NAND gates. This might introduce a lot of overhead on the circuit size. Moreover, it is restrictive that all the N pairs of input LWE ciphertexts are of the same gate.

Thus, in this section, we propose a construction to evaluate an *arbitrary* binary logic gate (including OR, NOR, AND, NAND, XOR, XNOR). Moreover, the batched bootstrapping procedure can take N different gates, and evaluate the N pairs of LWE ciphertexts with respect to these N input gates in parallel, instead of evaluating the same gate for all the N pairs of input ciphertexts. This enhanced flexibility of our scheme does not introduce any overhead [8].

5.1   Construction

Recall that to evaluate the NAND gate, at a high level, we proceed as follows: given two bits $\gamma_1, \gamma_2 \in \{0, 1\}$, step (1): lift them into $\mathbb{Z}_3$, and compute $r \leftarrow \gamma_1 + \gamma_2 \mod 3$; step (2): if $r = 2$, $\gamma' \leftarrow 0$, otherwise $\gamma' \leftarrow 1$. This procedure gives us $\gamma' = \text{NAND}(\gamma_1, \gamma_2)$ as expected.

Recall that step (2) is performed homomorphically using BFV. Since all the slots in a BFV ciphertext need to be evaluated using the same polynomial function by the SIMD nature of BFV, one main challenge is that we cannot

---

[8] For XOR and XNOR, prior constructions have an extra overhead in terms of error, as instead of $\mathsf{ct}_1 + \mathsf{ct}_2$, they need to perform $2(\mathsf{ct}_1 - \mathsf{ct}_2)$ before applying bootstrapping. We refer the readers to [33, Sec 3.2] for details.

modify step (2), i.e., step (2) needs to be shared among all different gates. Hence, our construction focuses on modifying step (1) and adding a step (3).

OR Gate. For the OR gate, we change step (1) to the following: compute $r \leftarrow (\gamma_1 + \gamma_2) - 1 \mod 3$. In this case, if γ_1 and γ_2 are both 0, r is 2, and we get $\gamma' = 0$ in step (2). Otherwise, r is 0 or 1, and we get $\gamma' = 1$.

XNOR Gate. For the XNOR gate, we change step (1) to the following: compute $r \leftarrow (\gamma_1 + \gamma_2) - 2 \mod 3$. In this case, if only one of γ_1 and γ_2 is 1, r is 2, and we get $\gamma' = 0$ as needed. Otherwise, r is 0 or 1, and $\gamma' = 1$.

NOR, AND, XOR Gates. For those three gates, we add a step (3). We first evaluate the result γ' as OR, NAND, and XNOR gate correspondingly using steps (1) and (2). We then perform $\gamma' \leftarrow 1 - \gamma'$, as NOR, AND, and XOR are simply negations of the result of OR, NAND, XNOR.

Translation to LWE Ciphertexts. Recall that our $\mathsf{DRaM}(x)$ function outputs 0 when $x \in (2 \lfloor q/3 \rfloor, q)$ and outputs $\lfloor q/3 \rfloor$ otherwise (see Eq. 1). We show how to evaluate the modification of step (1) described above in $\mathbb{Z}_q$ for different gates, such that this DRaM function in step (2) could be shared.

- (OR gate) Given a pair of ciphertexts $(\mathsf{ct}_1 = (\vec{a}_1, b_1), \mathsf{ct}_2 = (\vec{a}_2, b_2))$, compute $\mathsf{ct} = (\vec{a}, b) \leftarrow (\vec{a}_1 + \vec{a}_2, b_1 + b_2 - \lfloor q/6 \rfloor)$. In this case, iff $\mathsf{Dec}(\mathsf{ct}_1) = 0$ and $\mathsf{Dec}(\mathsf{ct}_2) = 0$, we have $b - \langle \vec{a}, \mathsf{sk} \rangle \in (2 \lfloor q/3 \rfloor, q)$.
- (XNOR gate) Given a pair of ciphertexts $(\mathsf{ct}_1 = (\vec{a}_1, b_1), \mathsf{ct}_2 = (\vec{a}_2, b_2))$, compute $\mathsf{ct} = (\vec{a}, b) \leftarrow (\vec{a}_1 + \vec{a}_2, b_1 + b_2 - \lfloor q/3 \rfloor - \lfloor q/6 \rfloor)$. In this case, iff $\mathsf{Dec}(\mathsf{ct}_1) = 1 \wedge \mathsf{Dec}(\mathsf{ct}_2) = 0$ or $\mathsf{Dec}(\mathsf{ct}_1) = 0 \wedge \mathsf{Dec}(\mathsf{ct}_2) = 1$, we have $b - \langle \vec{a}, \mathsf{sk} \rangle \in (2 \lfloor q/3 \rfloor, q)$.
- (Negation) After obtaining $\mathsf{ct} = (\vec{a}, b)$ encrypting γ', which is either $\lfloor q/3 \rfloor$ or 0, compute $\mathsf{ct} \leftarrow (-\vec{a}, \lfloor q/3 \rfloor - b)$.

Combining all these, we construct a more general binary gate bootstrapping. We formally show the entire procedure in Algorithm 3.

Theorem 2. *Let* $(\mathsf{pp}_{\mathsf{lwe}} = (n, q, p = 3, \mathcal{D}_1, \chi_\sigma), \mathsf{pp}_{\mathsf{bfv}} = (N, Q, Q', t = q, \mathcal{D}_2, \chi_{\sigma'}), \mathsf{sk}, \mathsf{btk}) \leftarrow \mathsf{Setup}(1^\lambda)$ *in Algorithm 3, for any input LWE ciphertexts* $\vec{\mathsf{ct}}_1 = (\mathsf{ct}_{1,1}, \ldots, \mathsf{ct}_{1,N}), \vec{\mathsf{ct}}_2 = (\mathsf{ct}_{2,1}, \ldots, \mathsf{ct}_{2,N})$ *parameterized by* $\mathsf{pp}_{\mathsf{lwe}}$, *encrypting* $\{0, 1\}$ *under* sk, *and* $\mathsf{err}(\mathsf{ct}_{i,j}) < \lfloor q/12 \rfloor$ *for all* $i \in [2], j \in [N]$ *and a vector of gates* $(g_1, \ldots, g_N) \in \{OR, NOR, AND, NAND, XOR, XNOR\}^N$; *let* $(\mathsf{ct}_{\mathsf{out}1}, \ldots, \mathsf{ct}_{\mathsf{out}N}) \leftarrow \mathsf{Boot}(\vec{\mathsf{ct}}_1, \vec{\mathsf{ct}}_2, (g_i)_{i \in [N]}, \mathsf{btk})$ *in Algorithm 3, it holds that:* $\mathsf{Dec}(\mathsf{ct}_{\mathsf{out}i}) = g_i(\mathsf{Dec}(\mathsf{ct}_{1,i}), \mathsf{Dec}(\mathsf{ct}_{2,i})), \Pr[\mathsf{err}(\mathsf{ct}_{\mathsf{out}i}) < \lfloor q/12 \rfloor] \geq 1 - \mathsf{negl}(\lambda)$, *and* $\mathsf{ct}_{\mathsf{out}i}$ *is encrypted under secret key* sk, *for all* $i \in [N]$.

Proof (Proof sketch). Correctness and noise analysis follow similarly as in the proof of Theorem 1.

Efficiency and Security Analysis. This remains exactly the same as the NAND gate analysis in Sect. 4.4. The costs of preprocessing and postprocessing the LWE ciphertexts are only at most $O(n)$ $\mathbb{Z}_q$ operations, and thus do not affect

---

Algorithm 3. Batched FHEW/TFHE bootstrapping for arbitrary binary gates

---

1: **procedure** Setup(1^λ)
2:      Select $(n, q, \mathcal{D}_1, \chi_\sigma, N, Q, \mathcal{D}_2\chi_{\sigma'}, Q')$ minimizing the cost of the entire homomorphic circuit evaluation and also satisfying:
3:      (1) $\mathsf{LWE}_{n,q,\mathcal{D}_1,\chi_\sigma}$ holds, and $\Pr[e < \lfloor q/12 \rfloor] \geq 1 - \mathsf{negl}(\lambda)$ where $e \leftarrow \chi_\sigma$.
4:      (2) $\mathsf{RLWE}_{N,Q,\mathcal{D}_2,\chi_{\sigma'}}$ hold.
5:      (3) $Q' \leq Q, \mathsf{LWE}_{n,Q',\mathcal{D}_1,\chi_{\sigma'}}$ holds.
6:      (4) BFV with parameters $N, Q, \mathcal{D}_2, t = q, \chi_{\sigma'}$ is enough to evaluate the circuit in procedure Boot
7:      (5) $\mathsf{LWE}_{n,q,\mathcal{D}_1,\chi_{\sigma_{\mathrm{res}}}}$ holds, where $\sigma_{\mathrm{res}} = \sqrt{(\frac{t}{Q'}(\sigma_5 + \sigma_{\mathrm{ks}}))^2 + \sigma_{\mathrm{ms}}{}^2}$, where σ_5 is the noise distribution standard deviation of line 37
8:      (6) $\Pr[e' < \lfloor q/12 \rfloor] \geq 1 - \mathsf{negl}(\lambda)$ where $e' \leftarrow \chi_{\sigma_{\mathrm{res}}}$
9:                                      ▷ $\sigma_{\mathrm{ks}}, \sigma_{\mathrm{ms}}$ are as introduced in Section 3.2.
10:      $\mathsf{sk} \leftarrow_\$ \{-1, 0, 1\}^n$
11:      Generate BFV secret key $\mathsf{sk}_{\mathsf{BFV}} \leftarrow \mathcal{D}_2$.
12:      Generate bootstrapping keys $\mathsf{btk} = (\mathsf{BFV.pk}, \mathsf{BFV.evk}, \mathsf{BFV.rtk}, K, \mathsf{bfvct}_{\mathsf{sk}})$ as in Section 4.1.
13:                                 ▷ K generated with $\mathsf{sk}_{\mathsf{BFV}}, \mathsf{sk}, Q', \chi_{\sigma'}$.
14:      **return** ($\mathsf{pp} = \mathsf{pp}_{\mathsf{lwe}} = (n, q, p = 3, \mathcal{D}_1, \chi_\sigma), \mathsf{pp}_{\mathsf{bfv}} = (N, Q, Q', t = q, \mathcal{D}_2, \chi_{\sigma'}), \mathsf{sk}, \mathsf{btk})$
15: **procedure** GateOps($\mathsf{ct}_1 = (\vec{a}_1, b_1), \mathsf{ct}_2 = (\vec{a}_2, b_2), g, q$)
16:      $\mathsf{ct} = (\vec{a}, b) \leftarrow (\vec{a}_1 + \vec{a}_2, b_1 + b_2)$ ▷ Operations in $\mathbb{Z}_q$.
17:      **if** g is AND or NAND **then**
18:          $b \leftarrow b + \lfloor q/6 \rfloor$
19:      **else if** g is OR or NOR **then**
20:          $b \leftarrow b - \lfloor q/6 \rfloor$
21:      **else**   ▷ g is XOR or XNOR
22:          $b \leftarrow b - \lfloor q/3 \rfloor - \lfloor q/6 \rfloor$
23:      **return** ct
24: **procedure** Negation($\mathsf{ct} = (\vec{a}, b), g, q$)
25:      **if** g is NOR or AND or XOR **then**
26:          $\vec{a} \leftarrow -\vec{a}, b \leftarrow \lfloor q/3 \rfloor - b$ ▷ Operations in $\mathbb{Z}_q$.
27:      **return** $\mathsf{ct} = (\vec{a}, b)$
28: **procedure** Boot($(\mathsf{ct}_{1,i})_{i \in [N]}, (\mathsf{ct}_{2,i})_{i \in [N]}, (g_i)_{i \in [N]}, \mathsf{btk}$)
29:      $\mathsf{ct}_i \leftarrow \mathsf{GateOps}(\mathsf{ct}_{1,i}, \mathsf{ct}_{2,i}, g_i, q), \forall i \in [N]$
30:      $A \leftarrow (\vec{a}_1^\intercal, \ldots, \vec{a}_N^\intercal)$
31:      $\mathsf{bfvct}_1 \leftarrow \mathsf{LT}(\mathsf{BFV.rtk}, A, \mathsf{bfvct}_{\mathsf{sk}})$
32:      $\mathsf{bfvct}_2 \leftarrow (b_1, \ldots, b_N) - \mathsf{bfvct}_1$ ▷ Homomorphically computes $\vec{b} - \mathsf{sk}A$
33:      $\mathsf{bfvct}_3 \leftarrow \mathsf{BFV.Eval}(\mathsf{BFV.evk}, \mathsf{bfvct}_2, \mathsf{DRaMpoly})$
34:      $\mathsf{bfvct}_4 \leftarrow \mathsf{LT}(\mathsf{BFV.rtk}, U^\intercal, \mathsf{bfvct}_3)$
35:                         ▷ Recall that U is the matrix defined for packing
36:      $\mathsf{bfvct}_5 \leftarrow \mathsf{BFV.ModSwitch}(\mathsf{bfvct}_4, Q')$
37:                           ▷ BFV.ModSwitch is described in Section 3.3
38:      $(\mathsf{ct}_1', \ldots, \mathsf{ct}_N') \leftarrow \mathsf{Extract}(\mathsf{bfvct}_5)$ ▷ Extract same as in Algorithm 2.
39:      $\mathsf{ct}_i'' \leftarrow \mathsf{KeySwitch}(K, \mathsf{ct}_i'), \forall i \in [N]$
40:             ▷ KeySwitch is defined in Section 3.2, and K is the key switching key
41:      $\mathsf{ct}_{\mathsf{out}_i} \leftarrow \mathsf{ModSwitch}(\mathsf{ct}_i'', q), \forall i \in [N]$ ▷ ModSwitch is defined in Section 3.2
42:      $\mathsf{ct}_{\mathsf{out}_i} \leftarrow \mathsf{Negation}(\mathsf{ct}_{\mathsf{out}_i}, g_i, q), \forall i \in [N]$
43:      **return** $(\mathsf{ct}_{\mathsf{out}_1}, \ldots, \mathsf{ct}_{\mathsf{out}_N})$

---

the asymptotic behavior. Concretely, their costs are also much smaller than the BFV circuit evaluation.

Optimizations. All the optimizations introduced in Sect. 4.5 can still be applied in a similar way.

6   Functional Bootstrapping for Arbitrary Functions

In this section, we discuss an even more general bootstrapping: functional bootstrapping for arbitrary function evaluation. At a high level, functional bootstrapping allows one to evaluate an arbitrary function over an FHE ciphertext without increasing the error of the FHE ciphertext. More formally, the process takes a ciphertext encrypting $m \in \mathbb{Z}_p$ with error $< \left\lfloor \frac{q}{2p} \right\rfloor$, and outputs a ciphertext encrypting $m' \leftarrow f(m)$ for an arbitrary function $f : \mathbb{Z}_p \to \mathbb{Z}_p$, with the error of the output ciphertext also $< \left\lfloor \frac{q}{2p} \right\rfloor$.

In regular FHEW/TFHE bootstrapping, this function f is required to be negacyclic[9]. There have been several recent works trying to allow arbitrary functions [12,24,29]. However, all of them require at least two bootstrapping operations (or equivalent overhead), which is not efficient (not to mention the increasing parameters due to algorithm change, inducing an even larger cost). Moreover, the two works [24,29] with implementation only tolerate small precision ([29] benchmarks for 3 bits, and [24] takes tens seconds for 7 bis of precision, see Sect. 7 for more details).

In this section, we show how to improve our batched multi-binary-gate bootstrapping construction to a bootstrapping construction to evaluate an *arbitrary function*.

6.1   Construction

Recall that for LWE encryption, a message $m \in \mathbb{Z}_p$ is encoded to a message $x \in \mathbb{Z}_q$ by computing $x \leftarrow m \cdot \alpha$, where $\alpha = \lfloor q/p \rfloor$, p is the plaintext modulus of the LWE ciphertext, and q is the ciphertext modulus of the LWE ciphertext. Also recall that we use $t = q$, where t is the plaintext modulus of the BFV scheme.

Our main observation is that given function $f : \mathbb{Z}_p \to \mathbb{Z}_p$, we can create a look-up table $\mathsf{LUT} : \mathbb{Z}_t \to \mathbb{Z}_t$ such that $\mathsf{LUT}(x) = (f(\lfloor x/\alpha \rfloor)) \cdot \alpha$, where $\alpha = \lfloor q/p \rfloor$. Let BFV plaintext space $t = q$, we create the following polynomial function

$$\mathsf{fpoly}(x) = \mathsf{LUT}(0) - \sum_{i=1}^{t-1} x^i \sum_{a=0}^{t-1} \mathsf{LUT}(a) a^{t-1-i} \ . \tag{2}$$

---

[9] More precisely, they require the function to be first transformed into a function $\mathbb{Z}_q \to \mathbb{Z}$ and this transformed function needs to be negacyclic. For details, see [33]. However, either way, this constraint is very strong and makes the functionality much more limited.

Then, we replace DRaMpoly evaluated homomorphically using BFV on line 33 in Algorithm 3 with fpoly, and the other procedures remain exactly the same. This achieves our goal without any cost[10], unlike prior works [12,24,29] (concretely are all at least 5x slower than the binary gate bootstrapping with their implementation, see Sect. 7 for details).

We formalize our constructions in Algorithm 4.

Theorem 3. *For any* $p = \mathrm{poly}(\lambda)$, *let* $(\mathsf{pp}_{\mathsf{lwe}} = (n, q, p, \mathcal{D}_1, \chi_\sigma), \mathsf{pp}_{\mathsf{bfv}} = (N, Q, Q', t = q, \mathcal{D}_2, \chi_{\sigma'}), \mathsf{sk}, \mathsf{btk}) \leftarrow \mathsf{Setup}(1^\lambda, p)$ *in Algorithm 4, for any input LWE ciphertexts* $\vec{\mathsf{ct}}_1 = (\mathsf{ct}_{1,1}, \ldots, \mathsf{ct}_{1,N}), \vec{\mathsf{ct}}_2 = (\mathsf{ct}_{2,1}, \ldots, \mathsf{ct}_{2,N})$ *parameterized by* $\mathsf{pp}_{\mathsf{lwe}}$, $\vec{\mathsf{ct}} = (\mathsf{ct}_1, \ldots, \mathsf{ct}_N)$ *encrypting* $\vec{m} = (m_1, \ldots, m_N)$, *for* $m_{i \in [N]} \in \mathbb{Z}_p$ *under* sk, *and* $\mathsf{err}(\mathsf{ct}_i) < \left\lfloor \frac{q}{2p} \right\rfloor$ *for all* $i \in [N]$ *and a vector of gates* $(g_1, \ldots, g_N) \in \{OR, NOR, AND, NAND, XOR, XNOR\}^N$; *let* $(\mathsf{ct}_{\mathsf{out}_1}, \ldots, \mathsf{ct}_{\mathsf{out}_N}) \leftarrow \mathsf{Boot}(f, \vec{\mathsf{ct}}, \mathsf{btk})$ *in Algorithm 4, it holds that:* $\mathsf{Dec}(\mathsf{ct}_{\mathsf{out}_i}) = f(\mathsf{Dec}(\mathsf{ct}_i))$, $\mathsf{err}(\mathsf{ct}_{\mathsf{out}_i}) < \left\lfloor \frac{q}{2p} \right\rfloor$, *and* $\mathsf{ct}_{\mathsf{out}i}$ *is encrypted under secret key* sk, *for all* $i \in [N]$.

Proof (Proof sketch). We prove from the basic correctness (i.e., evaluating f correctly over the encrypted messages) and noise analysis.

- (Correctness) Correctness (i.e., $\mathsf{Dec}(\mathsf{ct}_{\mathsf{out}_i}) = f(\mathsf{Dec}(\mathsf{ct}_i)))$) is intuitive. Most of the parts remain exactly the same as the proof for Theorem 1. The only thing we need to argue that $\mathsf{LUT} : \mathbb{Z}_t \to \mathbb{Z}_t$ defined as $\mathsf{LUT}(x) = (f(\lfloor x/\alpha \rfloor)) \cdot \alpha$, where $\alpha = \lfloor q/p \rfloor$ and $t = q$, correctly represents an arbitrary function $f : \mathbb{Z}_p \to \mathbb{Z}_p$. This can be demonstrated as follow: given LWE parameters $(n, q, p, \mathcal{D}_1, \chi)$, for all $x \in \mathbb{Z}_q$, let $y \leftarrow \left\lceil \frac{x}{\lfloor q/p \rfloor} \right\rfloor \in \mathbb{Z}_p$, for any LWE secret key $\mathsf{sk} \leftarrow \mathcal{D}_1$, any $\vec{a} \leftarrow_\$ \mathbb{Z}_q^n$, let $\mathsf{ct} \leftarrow (\vec{a} \in \mathbb{Z}_q^n, \langle a, \mathsf{sk} \rangle + \mathsf{LUT}(x) + e)$ where $e \leftarrow \chi$, it holds that $\Pr[\mathsf{Dec}(\mathsf{ct}) = f(y)] \geq 1 - \mathsf{negl}(\lambda)$ (probability over the error sampling), by the correctness of the underlying LWE scheme.
- (Noise Analysis) The noise analysis remains the same as in Theorem 1. Each resulting ciphertext has an error with $\sigma = \sqrt{(\frac{t}{Q'}(\sigma_5 + \sigma_{\mathsf{ks}}))^2 + \sigma_{\mathsf{ms}}^2}$ as the standard deviation. Thus, by condition (6) in Setup, $\mathsf{err}(\mathsf{ct}_{\mathsf{out}_i}) < \left\lfloor \frac{q}{2p} \right\rfloor, \forall i \in [N]$.

Efficiency and Security Analysis. The efficiency and security analysis remain exactly the same as the NAND gate bootstrapping.

6.2   Size of p

Practically, we can achieve p of 9 bits given the parameters we choose (see Sect. 7), without introducing much overhead compared to the binary gate evaluation. This is already an improvement compared to prior state-of-the-art works.

---

[10] Note that concretely, the number of zero coefficients increases as discussed in Sect. 4.5, but this only incurs a small overhead. See Sect. 7 for more details.

Algorithm 4. Batched FHEW/TFHE bootstrapping for arbitrary function over $\mathbb{Z}_p$

1: **procedure** Setup($1^\lambda, p$)
2:   Select $(n, q, \mathcal{D}_1, \chi_\sigma, N, Q, \mathcal{D}_2, \chi_{\sigma'}, Q')$ minimizing the cost of the entire homomorphic circuit evaluation and also satisfying:
3:     (1) LWE$_{n,q,\mathcal{D}_1,\chi_\sigma}$ holds, and $\Pr[e < \lfloor \frac{q}{2p} \rfloor] \geq 1 - \mathsf{negl}(\lambda)$ where $e \leftarrow \chi_\sigma$.
4:     (2) RLWE$_{N,Q,\mathcal{D}_2,\chi_{\sigma'}}$ hold.
5:     (3) $Q' \leq Q$, LWE$_{n,Q',\chi_{\sigma'}}$ holds.
6:     (4) BFV with parameters $N, Q, t = q, \mathcal{D}_2, \chi_{\sigma'}$ is enough to evaluate the circuit in procedure Boot
7:     (5) LWE$_{n,q,\mathcal{D}_1,\chi_{\sigma_{\mathsf{res}}}}$ holds, where $\sigma_{\mathsf{res}} = \sqrt{(\frac{t}{Q'}(\sigma_5 + \sigma_{\mathsf{ks}}))^2 + \sigma_{\mathsf{ms}}{}^2}$, where σ_5 is the noise distribution standard deviation of line 35
8:     (6) $\Pr[e' < \lfloor \frac{q}{2p} \rfloor] \geq 1 - \mathsf{negl}(\lambda)$ where $e' \leftarrow \chi_{\sigma_{\mathsf{res}}}$
9:                                 ▷ $\sigma_{\mathsf{ks}}, \sigma_{\mathsf{ms}}$ are as introduced in Section 3.2.
10:    sk $\leftarrow_\$ \{-1, 0, 1\}^n$
11:    Generate BFV secret key sk$_{\mathsf{BFV}}$.
12:    Generate bootstrapping keys btk $= (\mathsf{BFV.pk}, \mathsf{BFV.evk}, \mathsf{BFV.rtk}, K, \mathsf{bfvct_{sk}})$ as in Section 4.1.
13:                                 ▷ K generated with sk$_{\mathsf{BFV}}$, sk, Q', χ'.
14:    **return** (pp $=$ pp$_{\mathsf{lwe}} = (n, q, p, \mathcal{D}_1, \mathcal{X}_\sigma)$, pp$_{\mathsf{bfv}} = (N, Q, t = q, \mathcal{D}_2, \mathcal{X}_{\sigma'})$, sk, btk)
15: **procedure** Extract(bfvct $= (a_{\mathsf{bfv}}, b_{\mathsf{bfv}})$)   ▷ Extract N LWE ciphertexts from one BFV ciphertext
16:    Initialize ct$_i = (\vec{a}_i, b_i)$ for $i \in [N]$
17:    **for** $i \in [N]$ **do**
18:      **for** $j \in [N]$ **do**
19:        **if** $j \leq i$ **then**
20:          $\vec{a}_i[j] \leftarrow a_{\mathsf{bfv}}[i - j + 1]$
21:        **else**
22:          $\vec{a}_i[j] \leftarrow -a_{\mathsf{bfv}}[N - j + i + 1]$
23:          ▷ Negative number is still in $\mathbb{Z}_q$ where q is the bfvct ciphertext modulus
24:      $b_i = b_{\mathsf{bfv}_i}$
25:    **return** (ct$_1, \ldots,$ ct$_N$)
26: **procedure** Boot($f : \mathbb{Z}_p \to \mathbb{Z}_p, (\mathsf{ct}_1, \ldots, \mathsf{ct}_N)$, btk)
27:    Compute LUT(x) $= (f(\lfloor x/\alpha \rfloor)) \cdot \alpha$, where LUT $: \mathbb{Z}_t \to \mathbb{Z}_t$
28:    Compute fpoly(x) $=$ LUT(0) $- \sum_{i=1}^{t-1} x^i \sum_{a=0}^{t-1} \mathsf{LUT}(a) a^{t-1-i}$
29:    $A \leftarrow (\vec{a}_1^\mathsf{T}, \ldots, \vec{a}_N^\mathsf{T})$
30:    bfvct$_1 \leftarrow$ LT(BFV.rtk, A, bfvct$_{\mathsf{sk}}$)
31:    bfvct$_2 \leftarrow (b_1, \ldots, b_N) -$ bfvct$_1$ ▷ Homomorphically computes $\vec{b} - \mathsf{sk}A$
32:    bfvct$_3 \leftarrow$ BFV.Eval(BFV.evk, bfvct$_2$, fpoly)
33:    bfvct$_4 \leftarrow$ LT(BFV.rtk, U^T, bfvct$_3$)
34:          ▷ Recall that U is the matrix defined for packing
35:    bfvct$_5 \leftarrow$ ModSwitch(bfvct$_4, Q'$)   ▷ ModSwitch is described in Section 3.3
36:    (ct$_1', \ldots,$ ct$_N'$) $\leftarrow$ Extract(bfvct$_5$)
37:    ct$_i'' \leftarrow$ KeySwitch(K, ct$_i'$), $\forall i \in [N]$
38:          ▷ KeySwitch is defined in Section 3.2, and K is the key switching key
39:    ct$_{\mathsf{out}_i} \leftarrow$ ModSwitch(ct$_i'', q$), $\forall i \in [N]$ ▷ ModSwitch is defined in Section 3.2
40:    **return** (ct$_{\mathsf{out}_1}, \ldots,$ ct$_{\mathsf{out}_N}$)

This precision can be useful in many applications like machine learning using FHE [24,30]. However, some other applications might need to further enlarge p. To accommodate a larger p, we need to increase the degree of the underlying polynomial. Note that the number of plaintext-by-ciphertext multiplications grows linearly with p,[11] and the number of ciphertext-by-ciphertext multiplications grows with $\sqrt{p}$. Hence, our scheme still remains practical for some applications for p being 10-15 bits[12].

To more efficiently achieve even larger precision evaluation, one can do a digit decomposition and evaluate the function using additional techniques (e.g., the chain-based or tree-based methods) as explained in more detail in [29, Section 5]. The chain-based and tree-based methods are first introduced in [18] and later optimized by [28]. These techniques can potentially be integrated with our scheme, but we leave this for future works to further explore.

7   Evaluation

We implemented our algorithms proposed in Sects. 4 to 6 in a C++ library. We use Palisade [36] for our LWE ciphertexts implementation, and SEAL [38] for BFV scheme. We benchmark these schemes on several parameter settings on a Google Compute Cloud `e2-standard-4` with 16GB RAM.

Binary Gate Bootstrapping Parameter Selection. We choose LWE parameters as follows: $n = 1024, q = 65537, p = 3, \sigma = 3.2$, and BFV parameters as follows: $N = 32768, \log Q \approx 673, t = 65537, \sigma' = 3.2$. We use Gaussian secret keys with a standard deviation of 3.2 for our LWE ciphertexts. These parameters guarantee > 128-bit security by LWE estimator [2].

Arbitrary Function Evaluation Parameter Selection. n, σ, N, σ' remain unchanged. Set $(t = q = 256^2 + 1, \log Q \approx 673)$ for $p = 2^9$, and $(t = q = 768 \cdot 1024 + 1, \log Q \approx 900)$ for $p = 2^{12}$. We use ternary secret keys for arbitrary function evaluation to reduce the error of modulus switching. These parameters guarantee > 125-bit security by LWE estimator [2].

We choose q, p such that the error of the output ciphertext is larger than $\left\lfloor \frac{q}{2p} \right\rfloor$ with probability $< 2^{-30}$. By performing 1000 trials of bootstrapping, which is of total 32,768,000 LWE ciphertexts, we calculate the standard deviation of the output error to be ~ 10. Thus, we choose q, p accordingly such that $\left\lfloor \frac{q}{2p} \right\rfloor \geq 64$.

Binary Gate Bootstrapping. From Table 2, we can see that our performance is more than 30x faster than the state-of-the-art C++ implementation of the non-batched construction. We are also more than 3x faster compared to the rust

---

[11] Each plaintext-by-ciphertext multiplication only requires N $\mathbb{Z}_Q$ multiplications as the "plaintext" is a scalar.

[12] Asymptotically, the cost of our scheme is dominated by the number of scalar-by-ciphertext multiplications, which grows linear in p. Thus, our scheme becomes impractical when p is too large (e.g., 20 bits or more).

Table 2. Runtime comparison between our construction and state-of-the-art implementation of non-batched FHEW/TFHE-like cryptosystems. Mixed gates means the 32768 input gates contain a mix of AND/NAND/OR/NOR/XOR/XNOR gates ($\sim$32768/6 for each type). For OpenFHE, we benchmark it with Intel HEXL optimizaiton and their own NATIVEOPT. For Concrete, we benchmarked it with AVX512 optimization on.

	TFHE (OpenFHE)	TFHE (TFHE-rs)	Ours (Single Gate)	Ours (Mixed Gates)
Amortized time per LWE ciphertext (ms)	190	17.5	**4.7**	**4.7**
Total time (sec)	0.19	0.0175	**155**	**155**
# of ciphertexts per bootstrapping	1	1	**32768**	**32768**
LWE ciphertexts secret key type	Ternary	Binary	**Gaussian**	**Gaussian**

implementation by TFHE-rs [40]. Moreover, our construction supports Gaussian secret keys without any loss in performance, while the TFHE construction does not. With a secret key generated under a Gaussian distribution (i.e., each secret key element is sampled from a Gaussian distribution $(0, \sigma)$), the scheme is more secure than the one with a ternary or binary secret key.

We only compare with the TFHE construction, not FHEW or Lee et al. [25], as to our knowledge, if simply considering the bootstrapping runtime, TFHE is the most efficient one.

Table 3. Runtime comparison between our work and prior or concurrent works to evaluate an arbitrary function with ≤ 9 bits of precision (i.e., plaintext space ≤ 9 bits). Note that GPL23 [19] and LXDX23 [28] do not have an implementation publicly available so we directly reuse the number from their papers. GBA21 [18] only has the number for 6-bit, so we directly take the numbers reported in [28] for [18]. [19] has environment: Intel Xeon Platinum 8252C CPU at 4.5 GHz with 192 GB of RAM at 2933 MHz, and [28] has environment: i7-10700F at 2.90 GHZ. Both environments are better than our running environment and thus not under-estimating their performance. All other numbers are based on the experiment with the same environment as ours.

Plaintext space	3-bit	7-bit		8-bit			9-bit	
Scheme(s)	LMP22 [29]	GPL23 [19]	FDFB [24]	GBA21 [18]	LXDX23 [28]	LMP22 [29]	PEGASUS [30]	Ours
Amortized time (ms) per LWE ciphertext	1192	1205	35169	2203	409	1793	3476	**6.7**
Total time (sec)	1.192	1234	35.169	2.203	0.409	1.793	3.476	**220**
# of ciphertexts per bootstrapping	1	1024	1	1	1	1	1	**32768**
Input assumption	No	No	No	A vector of LWE ct's with small precision	A vector of LWE ct's with small precision	Only works for sign function and CT decomposition	MSB of the input ciphertext being 0	No

Arbitrary Function Evaluation. Through our experiment, we losslessly support 9 bits of precision with $t = 65537$ for arbitrary function evaluation with bootstrapping. In terms of amortized cost, our construction is about two to three orders of magnitude faster than all the other schemes providing 9-bits or less as

Table 4. Runtime comparison between our work and prior or concurrent works to evaluate an arbitrary function with larger bits of precision (i.e., plaintext space > 9 bits). For experiment environment, same as Table 3, we run the experiments using the code for LMP22 [29] and take the numbers from [28] for [18,28].

Plaintext space	10-bit		12-bit			
Scheme(s)	GBA21 [18]	LXDX23 [28]	LMP22 [29]	GBA21 [18]	LXDX23 [28]	**Ours**
Amortized time (ms) per LWE ciphertext	23667	1779	3998	51085	8092	**39.1**
Total time (sec)	23.667	1.779	3.998	51.085	8.092	**1280**
# of ciphertexts per bootstrapping	1	1	1	1	1	**32768**
Input assumption	A vector of LWE ct's with small precision	A vector of LWE ct's with small precision	Only works for sign function and CT decomposition	A vector of LWE ct's with small precision	A vector of LWE ct's with small precision	**No**

demonstrated in Table 3. For even larger precision, 12-bits, as shown in Table 4, our construction achieves even better results: all more than two orders of magnitude faster than any other existing schemes. All the existing schemes benchmark at most ≤ 12 bits of precision, for an arbitrary function evaluation, so we follow this convention.

Furthermore, we make no assumption on the inputs. On the other hand, PEGAUSUS [30] (implementing TFHE functional bootstrapping) requires the input ciphertexts MSB to be 0; LMP22 [29] can only perform sign function and ciphertext decomposition (i.e., decomposing a large precision ciphertext into a vector of small precision ciphertexts) for larger precision (> 3-bits); LXDX23 [28] follows the route of [18], and thus both [18,28] require the input to be a vector of LWE ciphertexts with small precision, instead of a single LWE ciphertext with large precision[13]. Hence, our scheme is not only much faster, but also much stronger and more flexible in terms of functionality[14].

Bootstrapping Key Size. Our btk size is as follows. The numbers are for $t = 256^2 + 1$ and $t = 768 \cdot 1024 + 1$ for $p = 2^9$ and $p = 2^{12}$ respectively. Our construction requires 32 rotation keys with full-level, $\sim$65 MB and $\sim$107 MB each; 128 rotation keys with 2 levels, both $\sim$1 MB each; 32 BFV ciphertexts with full-level, $\sim$5.2 MB and $\sim$7 MB each; 1 BFV public key, $\sim$5.2 MB and $\sim$7 MB; and 1 BFV relinearization key, $\sim$65 MB and $\sim$107 MB. In total, the btk size is $\sim$2.38 GB for binary gates and 9-bit LUT. For 12-bit LUT, it is $\sim$3.80 GB.

---

[13] To decompose a large precision ciphertext into a vector of small precision ciphertexts, one may use LMP22 [29], which introduces another 5-6 s of overhead for a 12-bit precision LWE ciphertext.

[14] Note that we do not compare with a concurrent and independent work [31], as it focuses on optimizing the schemes in [29] and achieving a 2-3x runtime improvement. We believe that this improvement does not affect our overall comparison, and to our knowledge, there is no open-sourced code available. However, note that this work shows a great improvement over [29] and may be preferred over our result when the number of bootstrapping needed is small.

8   Extension

Scheme Switching. Another important application of our scheme is FHEW/TFHE and BFV/BGV scheme switching (i.e., switching a ciphertext in one scheme to the other). Scheme switching was first introduced by Chimera [5] and later improved by PEGASUS [30]. Our scheme can be used to achieve FHEW/TFHE to BFV switching using ∼296 s (with about 180 bits of noise budget left) and BFV to FHEW/TFHE switching using ∼17 s.

Batched LWE Ciphertext Bootstrapping Based on CKKS. An interesting question is can we use CKKS to do batched LWE ciphertext bootstrapping? To our knowledge, using CKKS for binary gate bootstrapping is easy but arbitrary LUT evaluation is hard. However, this is an interesting direction left for future work to pursue.

In our full version, we have a more detailed discussion of these two extensions.

9   Concluding Remarks

In this work, we show a novel way to do batched bootstrapping for LWE ciphertexts. Based on the benchmark of the implementation, our method is orders of magnitude faster than the prior works when considering the amortized cost, thus adding a strong tool to the FHEW/TFHE line of work. It also opens other new and interesting directions; for example, how to efficiently extend our algorithm to support even larger plaintext space, or how to use CKKS as an alternative for batched functional bootstrapping. These are left for future works to explore.

Acknowledgements. We are grateful to Yuriy Polyakov for his insightful discussions and feedback, and to Wen-jie Lu for answering key-switching implementation questions regarding the SEAL library. We also thank all the reviewers for their insightful comments.

References

1. Albrecht, M., Chase, M., Chen, H., et al.: Homomorphic encryption security standard. Tech. rep., HomomorphicEncryption.org, Toronto, Canada (2018)
2. Albrecht, M.R., Player, R., Scott, S.: On the concrete hardness of learning with errors. J. Math. Cryptol. **9**(3), 169–203 (2015). https://doi.org/10.1515/jmc-2015-0016
3. Alperin-Sheriff, J., Peikert, C.: Practical bootstrapping in quasilinear time, pp. 1–20 (2013)
4. Badawi, A.A., et al.: OpenFHE: open-source fully homomorphic encryption library. Cryptology ePrint Archive, Paper 2022/915 (2022). https://eprint.iacr.org/2022/915. commit: 122f470e0dbf94688051ab852131ccc5d26be934
5. Boura, C., Gama, N., Georgieva, M., Jetchev, D.: CHIMERA: combining ring-LWE-based fully homomorphic encryption schemes. J. Math. Cryptol. **14**(1), 316–338 (2020). https://doi.org/10.1515/jmc-2019-0026

6. Brakerski, Z.: Fully homomorphic encryption without modulus switching from classical GapSVP. In: Safavi-Naini, R., Canetti, R. (eds.) CRYPTO 2012. LNCS, vol. 7417, pp. 868–886. Springer, Heidelberg (2012). https://doi.org/10.1007/978-3-642-32009-5_50

7. Brakerski, Z., Gentry, C., Vaikuntanathan, V.: (leveled) fully homomorphic encryption without bootstrapping. ACM Trans. Comput. Theory (TOCT) **6**(3), 1–36 (2014)

8. Chen, H., Han, K.: Homomorphic lower digits removal and improved FHE bootstrapping (2018)

9. Cheon, J.H., Han, K., Kim, A., Kim, M., Song, Y.: Bootstrapping for approximate homomorphic encryption. In: Nielsen, J.B., Rijmen, V. (eds.) EUROCRYPT 2018. LNCS, vol. 10820, pp. 360–384. Springer, Cham (2018). https://doi.org/10.1007/978-3-319-78381-9_14

10. Cheon, J.H., Kim, A., Kim, M., Song, Y.: Homomorphic encryption for arithmetic of approximate numbers. In: Takagi, T., Peyrin, T. (eds.) ASIACRYPT 2017. LNCS, vol. 10624, pp. 409–437. Springer, Cham (2017). https://doi.org/10.1007/978-3-319-70694-8_15

11. Chillotti, I., Gama, N., Georgieva, M., Izabachène, M.: Faster fully homomorphic encryption: bootstrapping in less than 0.1 seconds. In: Cheon, J.H., Takagi, T. (eds.) ASIACRYPT 2016. LNCS, vol. 10031, pp. 3–33. Springer, Heidelberg (2016). https://doi.org/10.1007/978-3-662-53887-6_1

12. Chillotti, I., Ligier, D., Orfila, J.-B., Tap, S.: Improved programmable bootstrapping with larger precision and efficient arithmetic circuits for TFHE. In: Tibouchi, M., Wang, H. (eds.) ASIACRYPT 2021. LNCS, vol. 13092, pp. 670–699. Springer, Cham (2021). https://doi.org/10.1007/978-3-030-92078-4_23

13. Cong, K., et al.: Labeled PSI from homomorphic encryption with reduced computation and communication. In: Proceedings of the 2021 ACM SIGSAC Conference on Computer and Communications Security. CCS 2021, Association for Computing Machinery (2021)

14. Ducas, L., Micciancio, D.: FHEW: bootstrapping homomorphic encryption in less than a second. In: Oswald, E., Fischlin, M. (eds.) EUROCRYPT 2015. LNCS, vol. 9056, pp. 617–640. Springer, Heidelberg (2015). https://doi.org/10.1007/978-3-662-46800-5_24

15. Fan, J., Vercauteren, F.: Somewhat practical fully homomorphic encryption. IACR Cryptol. ePrint Arch. **2012**, 144 (2012)

16. Gentry, C.: Fully homomorphic encryption using ideal lattices. In: Proceedings of the Forty-First Annual ACM Symposium on Theory of Computing, pp. 169–178 (2009)

17. Gentry, C., Halevi, S., Peikert, C., Smart, N.P.: Ring switching in BGV-Style homomorphic encryption. In: Visconti, I., De Prisco, R. (eds.) SCN 2012. LNCS, vol. 7485, pp. 19–37. Springer, Heidelberg (2012). https://doi.org/10.1007/978-3-642-32928-9_2

18. Guimarães, A., Borin, E., Aranha, D.F.: Revisiting the functional bootstrap in TFHE. IACR Trans. Cryptograph. Hardware Embedded Syst. **2021**, 229–253 (2021). https://doi.org/10.46586/tches.v2021.i2.229-253. https://tches.iacr.org/index.php/TCHES/article/view/8793

19. Guimarães, A., Pereira, H.V.L., van Leeuwen, B.: Amortized bootstrapping revisited: simpler, asymptotically-faster, implemented. Cryptology ePrint Archive, Paper 2023/014 (2023). https://eprint.iacr.org/2023/014

20. Halevi, S., Shoup, V.: Bootstrapping for HElib. Cryptology ePrint Archive, Report 2014/873 (2014). https://eprint.iacr.org/2014/873

21. Halevi, S., Shoup, V.: Design and implementation of HElib: a homomorphic encryption library. Cryptology ePrint Archive, Report 2020/1481 (2020). https://eprint.iacr.org/2020/1481
22. Iliashenko, I., Nègre, C., Zucca, V.: Integer functions suitable for homomorphic encryption over finite fields. Cryptology ePrint Archive, Report 2021/1335 (2021). WAHC 2021
23. Kim, A., Polyakov, Y., Zucca, V.: Revisiting homomorphic encryption schemes for finite fields. In: Tibouchi, M., Wang, H. (eds.) ASIACRYPT 2021. LNCS, vol. 13092, pp. 608–639. Springer, Cham (2021). https://doi.org/10.1007/978-3-030-92078-4_21
24. Kluczniak, K., Schild, L.: FDFB: full domain functional bootstrapping towards practical fully homomorphic encryption. IACR Trans. Cryptograph. Hardware Embedd. Syst. **2023**(1), 501–537 (2022). https://tches.iacr.org/index.php/TCHES/article/view/9960
25. Lee, Y., et al.: Efficient FHEW bootstrapping with small evaluation keys, and applications to threshold homomorphic encryption. In: Hazay, C., Stam, M. (eds.) Advances in Cryptology - EUROCRYPT 2023, pp. 227–256. Springer, Cham (2023). https://doi.org/10.1007/978-3-031-30620-4_8
26. Liu, F.H., Wang, H.: Batch bootstrapping I: A new framework for SIMD bootstrapping in polynomial modulus. In: Hazay, C., Stam, M. (eds.) Advances in Cryptology - EUROCRYPT 2023, pp. 321–352. Springer Nature Switzerland, Cham (2023). https://doi.org/10.1007/978-3-031-30620-4_11
27. Liu, F.H., Wang, H.: Batch bootstrapping I: Bootstrapping in polynomial modulus only requires $\tilde{O}(1)$ FHE multiplications in amortization. In: Hazay, C., Stam, M. (eds.) Advances in Cryptology - EUROCRYPT 2023, pp. 321–352. Springer Nature Switzerland, Cham (2023). https://doi.org/10.1007/978-3-031-30620-4_12
28. Liu, K., Xu, C., Dou, B., Xu, L.: Optimization of functional bootstrap with large LUT and packing key switching. Cryptology ePrint Archive, Paper 2023/631 (2023). https://eprint.iacr.org/2023/631
29. Liu, Z., Micciancio, D., Polyakov, Y.: Large-precision homomorphic sign evaluation using FHEW/TFHE bootstrapping. In: Advances in Cryptology - ASIACRYPT 2022: 28th International Conference on the Theory and Application of Cryptology and Information Security, Taipei, Taiwan, 5–9 December 2022, Proceedings, Part II, pp. 130–160. Springer, Heidelberg (2023). https://doi.org/10.1007/978-3-031-22966-4_5
30. jie Lu, W., Huang, Z., Hong, C., Ma, Y., Qu, H.: PEGASUS: bridging polynomial and non-polynomial evaluations in homomorphic encryption. SP 2021 (2020). https://eprint.iacr.org/2020/1606
31. Ma, S., Huang, T., Wang, A., Wang, X.: Fast and accurate: efficient full-domain functional bootstrap and digit decomposition for homomorphic computation. Cryptology ePrint Archive, Paper 2023/645 (2023). https://eprint.iacr.org/2023/645
32. Menon, S.J., Wu, D.J.: Spiral: Fast, high-rate single-server PIR via FHE composition. In: 2022 IEEE Symposium on Security and Privacy (SP), pp. 930–947 (2022). https://doi.org/10.1109/SP46214.2022.9833700
33. Micciancio, D., Polyakov, Y.: Bootstrapping in FHEW-like Cryptosystems, pp. 17–28. Association for Computing Machinery, New York, NY, USA (2021). https://doi.org/10.1145/3474366.3486924
34. Micciancio, D., Sorrell, J.: Ring packing and amortized FHEW bootstrapping. In: 45th International Colloquium on Automata, Languages, and Programming (ICALP 2018). Leibniz International Proceedings in Informatics (LIPIcs), vol. 107. Schloss Dagstuhl-Leibniz-Zentrum fuer Informatik (2018)

35. Micheli, G.D., Kim, D., Micciancio, D., Suhl, A.: Faster amortized FHEW bootstrapping using ring automorphisms. Cryptology ePrint Archive, Paper 2023/112 (2023). https://eprint.iacr.org/2023/112
36. PALISADE Lattice Cryptography Library (release 1.11.6). https://palisade-crypto.org/ (2022)
37. Paterson, M.S., Stockmeyer, L.J.: On the number of nonscalar multiplications necessary to evaluate polynomials. SIAM J. Comput. **2**(1), 60–66 (1973)
38. Microsoft SEAL (2020). https://github.com/Microsoft/SEAL
39. Smart, N., Vercauteren, F.: Fully homomorphic SIMD operations. Designs, Codes and Cryptography (2011). https://eprint.iacr.org/2011/133
40. Zama-AI, THFE-RS (2023). https://github.com/zama-ai/tfhe-rs. commit: 509bf3e2846bc98dd42d0e8eeb7f27852e5b632a
41. Yang, Z., Xie, X., Shen, H., Chen, S., Zhou, J.: TOTA: fully homomorphic encryption with smaller parameters and stronger security. Cryptology ePrint Archive, Paper 2021/1347 (2021). https://eprint.iacr.org/2021/1347

Encryption with Special Functionalities

Sender-Anamorphic Encryption Reformulated: Achieving Robust and Generic Constructions

Yi Wang[1], Rongmao Chen[1]([✉]), Xinyi Huang[2]([✉]), and Moti Yung[3,4]

[1] School of Computer, National University of Defense Technology, Changsha, China
{wangyi14,chromao}@nudt.edu.cn
[2] The Hong Kong University of Science and Technology (Guangzhou), Guangzhou, China
xinyi@ust.hk
[3] Google LLC, New York, NY, USA
[4] Columbia University, New York, USA
moti@cs.columbia.edu

Abstract. Motivated by the violation of two fundamental assumptions in secure communication - receiver-privacy and sender-freedom - by a certain entity referred to as "the dictator", Persiano et al. introduced the concept of Anamorphic Encryption (AME) for public key cryptosystems (EUROCRYPT 2022). Specifically, they presented receiver/sender-AME, directly tailored to scenarios where receiver privacy and sender freedom assumptions are compromised, respectively. In receiver-AME, entities share a double key to communicate in anamorphic fashion, raising concerns about the online distribution of the double key without detection by the dictator. The sender-AME with no shared secret is a potential candidate for key distribution. However, the only such known schemes (i.e., LWE and Dual LWE encryptions) suffer from an intrinsic limitation and cannot achieve reliable distribution.

Here, we reformulate the sender-AME, present the notion of ℓ-sender-AME and formalize the properties of (strong) security and robustness. Robustness refers to guaranteed delivery of duplicate messages to the intended receiver, ensuring that decrypting normal ciphertexts in an anamorphic way or decrypting anamorphic ciphertexts with an incorrect duplicate secret key results in an explicit abort signal. We first present a simple construction for pseudo-random and robust public key encryption that shares the similar idea of public-key stegosystem by von Ahn and Hopper (EUROCRYPT 2004). Then, inspired by Chen et al.'s malicious algorithm-substitution attack (ASA) on key encapsulation mechanisms (KEM) (ASIACRYPT 2020), we give a generic construction for hybrid PKE with special KEM that encompasses well-known schemes, including ElGamal and Cramer-Shoup cryptosystems.

The constructions of ℓ-sender-AME motivate us to explore the relations between AME, ASA on PKE, and public-key stegosystem. The results show that a strongly secure ℓ-sender-AME is such a strong primitive that implies reformulated receiver-AME, public-key stegosystem, and generalized ASA on PKE. By expanding the scope of sender-

© International Association for Cryptologic Research 2023
J. Guo and R. Steinfeld (Eds.): ASIACRYPT 2023, LNCS 14443, pp. 135–167, 2023.
https://doi.org/10.1007/978-981-99-8736-8_5

anamorphic encryption and establishing its robustness, as well as exploring the connections among existing notions, we advance secure communication protocols under challenging operational conditions.

Keywords: Anamorphic encryption · Public-key stegosystem ·
Algorithm-substitution attack

1   Introduction

In the realm of cryptosystems, there is an implicit assumption that the receiver's secret key remains confidential (referred to as the receiver-privacy assumption), and the sender has the freedom to choose the message to be sent (referred to as the sender-freedom assumption). However, in reality, these fundamental assumptions can be completely violated by a controlling entity known as "the dictator" who possesses the ability to access any individual's secret key and censor the content of messages. Achieving both private and unrestricted communication in such a setting seems futile.

To address this critical issue, Persiano, Phan, and Yung introduced a new concept called "Anamorphic Encryption" [26]. This notion allows a well-established public-key cryptosystem to enable entities to encrypt differently hidden messages in what is called an anamorphic manner, thus evading the censorship imposed by the dictator. Specifically, they defined two variants of anamorphic encryption: receiver-anamorphic encryption and sender-anamorphic encryption, which provide secure communication while eliminating the reliance on the receiver-privacy and sender-freedom assumptions, respectively. Receiver-anamorphic encryption aims to facilitate secure communication in the face of a violating receiver-privacy assumption. By utilizing this technique, entities can engage in anamorphic communication, where the recipient's privacy is protected even in the presence of the dictator. On the other hand, sender-anamorphic encryption focuses on addressing the violation of the sender-freedom assumption. In this case, the sender can encrypt messages in an anamorphic manner, allowing them to transmit information without being constrained or controlled by the dictator.

Obviously, it is impossible to achieve the confidentiality of encrypted message against the dictator when the receiver only holds one secret key and has to reveal this key to the dictator. So, the receiver-anamorphic encryption requires that every pair of sender and receiver must share a double key that is unknown to the dictator. This double key is used to encode/retrieve a secret message into/from an anamorphic ciphertext in symmetric way, which raises a rather important problem: *How to distribute the double key for every entity pair without being detected by the dictator?* A trivial solution is offline key exchange which is extremely inefficient but most unlikely to be caught by the dictator who monitors the online communication constantly. In [26], the authors mentioned that the two-step bootstrap technique [19] of Horel et al. allows two entities to exchange a random string which is used to generate the double key. However, this technique involves the execution of pseudorandom key exchange protocol which is suspicious to the dictator who might ban the usage of such protocol.

The sender-anamorphic encryption formalized in the setting of no-shared secret [26] could be a potential candidate for realizing covert and efficient key distribution (using multiple receiver situations). In particular, when the dictator instructs Alice to send forced message m_0 to Carol, Alice might intend to send duplicate message m_1 (e.g., double key) to Bob. The sender-anamorphic encryption allows Alice to generate randomness via a special coin-toss faking algorithm fRandom that takes as input forced public key fpk (i.e., Carol's public key), duplicate public key dpk (i.e., Bob's public key), forced message m_0 and duplicate message m_1. Then, Alice encrypts forced message m_0 with the selected randomness (produced by fRandom) using forced public key fpk, and obtains an anamorphic ciphertext act which gives duplicate message m_1 when it is decrypted with duplicate secret key dsk (i.e., Bob's secret key). Finally, Alice sends ciphertext act to Carol only via public communication channel such that Bob can observe this ciphertext and retrieve the duplicate message m_1. It is worth noting that the only difference between anamorphic and normal ciphertexts is the distribution of underlying randomness.

Non-Robustness of Sender-Anamorphic Encryption. Persiano et al. [26] pointed out that not every public-key encryption scheme (PKE) can be sender-anamorphic in the setting of no-shared secret, and listed three sufficient conditions, including *common randomness property, message recovery from randomness* and *equal distribution of plaintext*, for a 1-bit PKE to be sender-anamorphic. So far, the only known sender-anamorphic encryptions are the LWE [28] and the Dual LWE [14] encryptions.

One can note that in these two encryptions, decrypting a normal ciphertext with incorrect secret key would return 0 or 1 with equal probability. This feature is undesirable and incurs the following two problems when applying them to distribute the double key (i.e., duplicate message).

- **(Misreading of normal ciphertexts)** Assume that Alice actually does want to send an ℓ-bit message m to Carol, and generates ℓ normal ciphertexts with uniformly sampled randomnesses for message m. In this case, Bob cannot decide whether the observed ciphertexts are normal or anamorphic, and might take the decryption results of normal ciphertexts using his secret key as the duplicate message from Alice.
- **(Misreading of anamorphic ciphertexts)** Assume that Alice sends ℓ anamorphic ciphertexts, which include ℓ-bit duplicate message for Bob, to Carol, and there is a user Dave who also observes these anamorphic ciphertexts. In this case, Dave cannot tell whether these ciphertexts are intended for himself or not, and might take the decryption results of anamorphic ciphertexts using his secret key as the duplicate message from Alice.

To circumvent these problems, it is required that decrypting *normal ciphertext in anamorphic way* or *anamorphic ciphertext with wrong duplicate secret key* should produce an explicit abort signal. However, this demand leads to a contradiction! In particular, the anamorphic ciphertext can be viewed as a normal ciphertext with proper randomness, and the decryption algorithm always returns a bit for normal ciphertext. So, we cannot expect that the decryption algorithm would return an abort for anamorphic ciphertext.

Our observation regarding the non-robust nature of sender-anamorphic encryption was initially inspired by a recent notable work [4], which insightfully identified a similar issue within the context of receiver-anamorphic encryption. Specially, the security definition for receiver-anamorphic encryption in [26] did not consider the case where normal ciphertext is decrypted in an anamorphic way. Consequently, the work [4] defined the property of robustness for receiver-anamorphic encryption, and presented a range of novel constructions applicable to both general PKE schemes and special PKE schemes.

Motivating Question: Sender-Anamorphic Encryption with Robustness? The aforementioned problem seems to be unsolvable under the model of sender-anamorphic encryption with no shared key. That is, it looks impossible to construct "robust" sender-anamorphic encryption. We remark that compared with [4], our definition of robustness for sender-anamorphic encryption also consider an additional case that decrypting anamorphic ciphertexts with wrong duplicate secret key would produce explicit abort signal. Hence, we turn to reformulate the original definition of sender-anamorphic encryption, and try to explore feasible solutions in the tweaked model.

Recall that the sender of the original sender-anamorphic encryption is required to encode both forced and duplicate messages into one ciphertext. Given the fact that every entity in the cryptosystem usually sends more than one ciphertext to the others, we relax this requirement by allowing encoding duplicate message across multiple ciphertexts. In this way, the sender has to collect multiple pairs of forced public key and message to generate randomnesses for anamorphic ciphertexts. Intuitively, it seems that the sender might fail to generate proper randomnesses when the dictator asks the sender to encrypt only one forced message and to send the ciphertext each time. Fortunately, it would not be a problem if the generation of the i-th randomness depends on the first i pairs of forced public key and message only, and it is possible to construct such coin-toss faking algorithm.

On the side of the receiver, the retrieval of duplicate message needs an alternative decryption algorithm that takes as input a set of ciphertexts and duplicate secret key. In particular, this decryption algorithm might provide explicit abort signal when these ciphertexts do not include any duplicate message (i.e., normal ciphertexts) or the duplicate secret key does not match these ciphertexts (i.e., anamorphic ciphertexts). With such an algorithm, it is possible to overcome the problem of misreading, achieving robustness for sender-anamorphic encryption and realize reliable duplicate message distribution. Therefore, a natural question that we mainly consider in this work is:

How to reformulate and construct sender-anamorphic encryption satisfying robustness in the setting of no shared key?

1.1   Our Contributions

In this work, we provide an affirmative answer to the above question. Specifically, we reformulate the syntax of sender-anamorphic encryption by permitting encoding duplicate message across multiple anamorphic ciphertexts (while obviously keeping the cryptosystem building block intact), and then formalize the properties of security and robustness. To show the feasibility of such a primitive, we present a simple construction for pseudo-random and robust PKE. The core idea is similar to the public-key stegosystem by von Ahn and Hopper [32]. Then, inspired by Chen et al.'s asymmetric algorithm-substitution attack (ASA) on key encapsulation mechanism (KEM) [10], we give a generic construction for hybrid PKE with special module-level KEM that encompasses well-known schemes including ElGamal and Cramer-Shoup cryptosystems.

These constructions have enlightened us to investigate whether the reformulated sender-anamorphic encryption might have some relations with existing notions. Indeed, it might be difficult to explore the direct relationship among them individually. So, we present the reformulated version of receiver-anamorphic encryption, and introduce the notion of generalized ASA against PKE as in [8] to facilitate the investigation.

We can now present the summary of main contributions of this work:

- We introduce the notion of ℓ-sender-anamorphic encryption (ℓ-sender-AME), and define the properties of (strong) security and robustness.
- We present two constructions of strongly secure and robust ℓ-sender-AME. One is for pseudo-random and robust PKE and the other is for hybrid PKE with special module-level KEM which can be instantiated with well-known schemes including ElGamal and Cramer-Shoup cryptosystems.
- We explore the relations between ℓ-sender-AME and other related primitives, as shown in Fig. 1, including reformulated receiver-anamorphic encryption (ℓ-receiver-AME), public-key stegosystem, and generalized ASA on PKE.

1.2   Results Overview

A Reformulated Model for Robustness: ℓ-Sender-AME. In sender-AME model, the syntax of PKE is only augmented with a coin-toss faking algorithm that generates randomness according to one pair of forced public key and message, and the duplicate public key and message. In our reformulated model, the coin-toss faking algorithm would take more than one pair of forced public key and message, and there exists an alternative decryption algorithm that retrieves the duplicate message from a set of anamorphic ciphertexts using duplicate secret key. We name the reformulated notion "ℓ-sender-AME," where ℓ denotes the number of anamorphic ciphertexts required for duplicate message embedding. Clearly, this definition includes the original sender-AME ($\ell = 1$ and the alternative decryption algorithm is the decryption algorithm of PKE).

There are two properties defined for ℓ-sender-AME: *security* and *robustness*. The definition of security is extended from that for original sender-AME trivially.

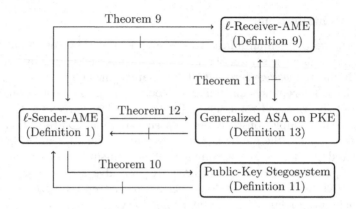

Fig. 1. Relations between ℓ-sender-AME and other related primitives.

Roughly, it indicates that the dictator who knows all the forced public keys cannot distinguish normal and anamorphic ciphertexts outputted by the encryption oracle with overwhelming advantage. Moreover, we consider a strong variant of security by providing the dictator all the forced secret keys and duplicate public key, which also implies the violation of the receiver-privacy assumption to some extent. This strong security permits us to evade the surveillance by the dictator who violates both receiver-privacy and sender-freedom assumptions. As mentioned above, the meaning of robustness is twofold: the alternative decryption algorithm would return abort when 1) the inputted ciphertexts are normal or 2) the inputted anamorphic ciphertexts and duplicate secret key do not match.

Generic Constructions of ℓ-Sender-AME. In this work, we present two generic constructions of ℓ-sender-AME satisfying both strong security and robustness. One is for pseudo-random and robust PKE, and the other is for hybrid PKE with special module-level KEM that encompasses well-known schemes including ElGamal and Cramer-Shoup cryptosystems.

CONSTRUCTION I: *Pseudo-random and Robust PKE.* Pseudo-random PKE produces ciphertext that is indistinguishable from random bits [32]. This feature allows us to embed the ciphertext of duplicate message across multiple ciphertexts without being detected by the dictator. The robustness of PKE [1] ensures that a ciphertext cannot be valid under two different decryption keys, which contributes to the robustness of ℓ-sender-AME.

In more details, we encode the i-th bit of the ciphertext of duplicate message into the i-th anamorphic ciphertext using the rejection sampling technique. That is, repeating randomness sampling until the desired bit can be publicly derived from the i-th anamorphic ciphertext. Even though anyone can retrieve the ciphertext of a duplicate message from multiple anamorphic ciphertexts, the dictator who does not hold the duplicate secret key cannot decide if the obtained string is a ciphertext or a random bit string by the pseudo-randomness of PKE.

So far, there are only a few pseudo-random PKEs [23,32]. Although most well-known public-key cryptosystems do not satisfy pseudo-randomness, it is possible to transform the ciphertext of duplicate message into a pseudo-random string. Here are some optional approaches: removing the distribution bias caused by the algebra [34], applying the covert key exchange technique [36] or encoding elliptic-curve point to be indistinguishable from uniform random string [9,31].

CONSTRUCTION II: *Hybrid PKE with Special KEM.* Hybrid PKE relies on KEM which encapsulates the key for data encapsulation mechanism (DEM) which is used to encrypt the plaintext. Inspired by the generic ASA on KEM of Chen et al. [10], we encode the $(i-1)$-th bit b_{i-1} of duplicate message across the key encapsulation part of the $(i-1)$-th and i-th anamorphic ciphertexts C_{i-1} and C_i. In particular, let r_i denote the underlying randomness of key ciphertext C_i, we generate randomness r_i from r_{i-1} and duplicate public key. If $b_{i-1} = 1$, we add a perturbation to r_i. Otherwise, we do nothing to r_i. In the process of alternative decryption, we first recover randomness r_i' from C_{i-1} and duplicate secret key by the universal decryptability of KEM, and compute the perturbed randomness r_i'' of r_i'. Then, we compare C_i with C_i' and C_i'' derived from r_i' and r_i'' respectively. If $C_i = C_i'$, then $b_{i-1} = 0$. If $C_i = C_i''$, then $b_{i-1} = 1$. Otherwise, the alternative decryption algorithm returns abort. By the key-pseudo-randomness of KEM, it is hard to detect the correlation between C_{i-1} and C_i for the dictator who does not know the duplicate secret key.

We show the robustness of this construction as following: For normal ciphertext, its randomness is uniformly distributed over appropriate space. The probability of the event that r_i is correlated to r_{i-1} and the duplicate public/secret key is negligible. Thus, decrypting normal ciphertexts in anamorphic way would produce explicit abort. For anamorphic ciphertexts, decrypting them with incorrect duplicate secret key does not reveal the correlation between key ciphertexts, and the unintended receiver would receive abort symbol.

We remark that it is possible to encode t-bits string $(t > 1)$ into two successive random fields at the cost of exponential time complexity (in the string length) for alternative decryption algorithm. In particular, the coin-toss faking algorithm converts t-bits string into element in randomness space and then adds it to randomness r_i, while the alternative decryption algorithm has to derive at most 2^t ciphertexts to compare with inputted ciphertext C_i. Thus, such variation is only feasible for short bit string. Another concern with this encoding is that the perturbation over randomnesses disables us from providing a valid explanation on the selection of randomness. (e.g., revealing the pre-image of randomness under one-way hash function specified by the dictator in case it is demanded).

Relations Between Existing Notions. The constructions above suggest that there exist some inner connections among anamorphic encryption, public-key stegosystem, and algorithm-substitution attack.

Relation Between ℓ-Sender-AME and ℓ-Receiver-AME. In receiver-AME, parties share a double key that is used to encode both normal and anamorphic plaintexts into an anamorphic ciphertext or to retrieve anamorphic plaintext from anamorphic ciphertext. Analogous to ℓ-sender-AME, we present the notion of ℓ-receiver-AME where the anamorphic plaintext is encoded across ℓ anamorphic ciphertexts using double key. Once the double key is set as the forced public keys and duplicate public/secret key pair in ℓ-sender-AME, the anamorphic ciphertexts of ℓ-receiver-AME can be generated using the biased randomnesses outputted by the coin-toss faking algorithm in ℓ-sender-AME.

Note that the security model for sender/receiver-AME only captures the violation of sender-freedom or receiver-privacy assumption. It seems hard to reduce one security notion to another. We overcome this problem by strengthening the ability of the adversary in the security game for ℓ-sender-AME. In the game of strong security, the adversary knows all the forced secret keys and the duplicate public key. Now, we get the following result.

Theorem 1. (Informal). *For any strongly secure ℓ-sender-AME PKE, it is also a secure ℓ-receiver-AME.*

It is obvious that not any ℓ-receiver-AME is an ℓ-sender-AME, as the double key in ℓ-receiver-AME may not be parsed as a public/secret key pair.

Relation between ℓ-Sender-AME and Public-Key Stegosystem. Parties in public-key stegosystem with no shared secret key are able to communicate in steganographic way over a public channel such that no eavesdropper of the channel can detect the existence of hidden messages. The notion of ℓ-sender-AME is similar to the public-key stegosystem in the sense of, both, setting and target. Note that the pseudo-random PKE was first proposed to construct public-key stegosystem, and our first ℓ-sender-AME construction is designed for pseudo-random PKE. It is naturally leading us to the following result.

Theorem 2. (Informal). *For any strongly secure ℓ-sender-AME PKE, there exists a public-key stegosystem PKS built over PKE.*

Conversely, it seems that every public-key stegosystem should imply an ℓ-sender-AME. However, constructing public-key stegosystem is more diverse than that of ℓ-sender-AME. For instance, the chosen-stegotext secure stegosystem in [32] uses a sender's secret key to generate stegotexts, while the input of coin-toss faking algorithm in ℓ-sender-AME does not involve any secret keys.

Relations Between AME and Generalized ASA on PKE. The attacker in ASA on PKE substitutes the encryption algorithm in PKE with subverted version so as to recover the underlying plaintext from subverted ciphertext using subversion key, which is rather different from the goal of anamorphic encryption. Instead, we present the notion of generalized ASA on PKE as in [8] where the subverted encryption algorithm also encodes a subliminal message into the ciphertext and the attacker's goal is extracting this subliminal message from subverted ciphertext. The original ASA on PKE is a special case of generalized ASA on PKE where the subliminal message equals to the plaintext for encryption.

Depending on how the subversion key is generated and used, the generalized ASA on PKE can be classified into two types: symmetric and asymmetric. In symmetric ASA, there is only one subversion key used by both subverted encryption and extraction algorithms. Recall that, in ℓ-receiver-AME, the same double key is used to encode and extract anamorphic plaintext. In this case, the subversion key corresponds to the double key. Furthermore, we shows that a symmetric ASA on PKE implies the underlying PKE is an ℓ-receiver-AME.

Theorem 3. (Informal). *Let* PKE *be a CPA secure PKE. If there exists a symmetric and generalized ASA on* PKE, *then* PKE *is also a secure ℓ-receiver-AME.*

In ASA on PKE, the subversion key is independent of the public and secret key for subverted encryption algorithm. Once the generation of double key in ℓ-receiver-AME relies on the secret key, it might be impossible to construct subversion key generation algorithm with anamorphic key generation algorithm. Thus, not every ℓ-receiver-AME implies a symmetric ASA on PKE.

In asymmetric ASA, the subversion key is a pair of public/secret key, where the public subversion key is hardwired into the subverted encryption algorithm and the extraction of subliminal message requires secret subversion key. Note that if the duplicate public/secret key pair in ℓ-sender-AME is also a subversion key pair for ASA, we can built an ASA on PKE from ℓ-sender-AME.

Theorem 4. (Informal). *Let* PKE *be a strongly secure ℓ-sender-AME. Then there exists an asymmetric and generalized ASA on* PKE.

Conversely, not every asymmetric ASA on PKE directly implies that the underlying PKE is an ℓ-sender-AME. In particular, when the subversion key generation of ASA is different from the key generation of PKE, it is unlikely to build the coin-toss faking algorithm following the core idea of ASA, as this algorithm only takes normal public keys and messages as input.

1.3 Related Work

Anamorphic Cryptography. Since the notion of anamorphic encryption was first proposed in 2022, several works [4,21,22] have been presented to expand the scope of anamorphic cryptography. In particular, Banfi et al. [4] and Kutylowski et al. [22] both refined the definition of original receiver-AME but for different purposes. In [4], the generation of anamorphic key pair and double key is decoupled, and the authors aims to build receiver-AME satisfying robustness. In [22], both anamorphic public key and double key, instead of double key only, are used to encode normal and anamorphic plaintexts into an anamorphic ciphertext. This refinement permits some wide range of cryptosystems, including RSA-OAEP [7], Goldwasser-Micali [15], Paillier [25], ElGamal [13] and Cramer-Shoup [11], to be receiver-anamorphic. Kutylowski et al. [21] introduced the notion of anamorphic signature scheme where a signature is embedded with an anamorphic message, which is only readable to the one owning the double key.

Steganography. The work of Simmons [30] initiated the study of steganography forty years ago. In 2002, the first complexity-theoretic model of provably secure steganography was present by Hopper et al. [18]. Further, von Ahn and Hopper [32] explored the public-key variant of steganography and proposed the notion of public-key stegosystem and steganographic key exchange protocol. Backes and Cachin [3] enhanced the security model of public-key stegosystem to defend against active attacks. Note that our results in this work might provide a new way to build public-key stegosystem from ℓ-sender-AME.

Algorithm-Substitution Attack. At Crypto 2014, Bellare et al. introduced the notion of algorithm-substitution attack [6], which considers the ability of attackers to subvert the implementation of cryptographic algorithms in reality. This concept dates back to the notion of kleptography [34] by Young and Yung. In a series of works [34–36] on kleptography, the subversion of the key generation algorithm enables attacker to recover the secret information exclusively. The Snowden revelations in 2013 reignited the enthusiasm of the academic community about this topic [2,5,6,8,10,12,29]. Although the ASA on encryption scheme helps the dictator to conduct mass-surveillance without being detected, our work shows that the ordinary users can also take advantage of the rationale behind ASA to communicate in a covert way against the dictator. Namely, the users employ malicious cryptography against the malice of the dictator!

2 Preliminaries

NOTATIONS. For any $n \in \mathbb{N}^+$, we denote the negligible function over n as $\mathsf{negl}(n)$. For any $i \in \mathbb{N}^+$, $[i]$ denotes integer set $\{1, 2, \cdots, i\}$. For any $i, j \in \mathbb{N}$ with $i < j$, $[i, j]$ denotes integer set $\{i, i+1, \cdots, j\}$. For any non-empty set $\mathcal{X}$, $x \leftarrow_{\$} \mathcal{X}$ denotes sampling x from $\mathcal{X}$ uniformly at random. For any randomized algorithm $\mathsf{Alg}(x)$, $y \leftarrow_{\$} \mathsf{Alg}(x)$ denotes the random output of $\mathsf{Alg}(x)$. For any deterministic algorithm $\mathsf{Alg}(x)$, $y := \mathsf{Alg}(x)$ denotes the deterministic output of $\mathsf{Alg}(x)$. For n elements $\mathsf{a}_1, \mathsf{a}_2, \cdots, \mathsf{a}_n$, we denote the set $\{\mathsf{a}_i\}_{i \in [n]}$ as A.

2.1 Public-Key Encryption (PKE)

A public-key encryption scheme PKE consists of following algorithms:

- $\mathsf{Setup}(1^n)$ takes as input 1^n, and returns the public parameter pp which is an implicit input of encryption and decryption algorithms.
- $\mathsf{Gen}(\mathsf{pp})$ takes as input pp and returns a public/secret key pair $(\mathsf{pk}, \mathsf{sk})$.
- $\mathsf{Enc}(\mathsf{pk}, \mathsf{m})$ takes as input pk and a plaintext m, and returns a ciphertext ct.
- $\mathsf{Dec}(\mathsf{sk}, \mathsf{ct})$ take as input sk and ct, and returns m' or an abort symbol $\bot$.

Correctness. PKE is correct if, let $\mathcal{M}$ be the plaintext space, for any $\mathsf{m} \in \mathcal{M}$,

$$\Pr\left[\mathsf{Dec}(\mathsf{sk}, \mathsf{ct}) \neq \mathsf{m} : \begin{array}{l} \mathsf{pp} \leftarrow_{\$} \mathsf{Setup}(1^n) \\ (\mathsf{pk}, \mathsf{sk}) \leftarrow_{\$} \mathsf{Gen}(\mathsf{pp}) \\ \mathsf{ct} \leftarrow_{\$} \mathsf{Enc}(\mathsf{pk}, \mathsf{m}) \end{array}\right] \leq \mathsf{negl}(n).$$

Security. PKE is CPA secure if for any PPT adversary $\mathcal{A}_1$ and $\mathcal{A}_2$,

$$\left| \Pr \left[b = b' : \begin{array}{l} \mathsf{pp} \leftarrow_s \mathsf{Setup}(1^n) \\ (\mathsf{pk}, \mathsf{sk}) \leftarrow_s \mathsf{Gen}(\mathsf{pp}) \\ (\mathtt{m}_0, \mathtt{m}_1, \mathtt{st}) \leftarrow \mathcal{A}_1(\mathsf{pp}, \mathsf{pk}) \\ b \leftarrow_s \{0,1\} \\ \mathtt{ct}^* \leftarrow_s \mathsf{Enc}(\mathsf{pk}, \mathtt{m}_b) \\ b' \leftarrow \mathcal{A}_2(\mathtt{st}, \mathtt{ct}^*) \end{array} \right] - \frac{1}{2} \right| \leq \mathsf{negl}(n).$$

The notion of anamorphic encryption is defined over public-key encryption. We present the definitions of anamorphic encryption [26] in the full version.

2.2 Entropy Smoothing Hash Functions

Let $\mathcal{H} = \{H_{\hat{k}}\}_{\hat{k} \in \hat{\mathcal{K}}}$ be a keyed hash function family associated with key space $\hat{\mathcal{K}}$, groups X, Y and hash function $H_{\hat{k}} : X \to Y$. We say $\mathcal{H}$ is entropy smoothing if for any PPT adversary $\mathcal{A}$ and $\hat{k} \leftarrow_s \hat{\mathcal{K}}$,

$$\left| \Pr \left[\mathcal{A}(\hat{k}, H_{\hat{k}}(x)) = 1 \Big| x \leftarrow_s X \right] - \Pr \left[\mathcal{A}(\hat{k}, y) = 1 \Big| y \leftarrow_s Y \right] \right| \leq \mathsf{negl}(n).$$

3 Reformulating Sender-Anamorphic Encryption

In this section, we first present the reformulated version of sender-AME in the setting of no shared secret key, and then define the properties of (strong) security and robustness for this new primitive.

3.1 ℓ-Sender-Anamorphic Encryption (ℓ-Sender-AME)

Definition 1 (ℓ-Sender-Anamorphic Encryption). *Let* PKE *be a public key encryption scheme. For* $\ell \in \mathbb{N}^+$, *we say* PKE *is* ℓ*-sender-anamorphic if 1) there exists a sender-anamorphic extension* (fRandom, dDec):

- fRandom(FPK, FM, dpk, dm) *takes a forced public key set* FPK $= \{\mathtt{fpk}_i\}_{i \in [\ell]}$, *a forced plaintext set* FM $= \{\mathtt{fm}_i\}_{i \in [\ell]}$, *a duplicate public key* dpk *and a duplicate plaintext* dm, *and returns a randomness set* $R = \{r_i\}_{i \in [\ell]}$;
- dDec(dsk, CT) *takes as input a duplicate secret key* dsk *and a ciphertext set* CT, *and returns the duplicate plaintext* dm,

and 2) let $\mathcal{M}$ *and* $\overline{\mathcal{M}}$ *be the forced and duplicate plaintext space respectively, for any* FM $\in \mathcal{M}^\ell$, *any* dm $\in \overline{\mathcal{M}}$,

$$\Pr \left[\mathsf{dDec}(\mathsf{dsk}, \mathtt{CT}) \neq \mathtt{dm} : \begin{array}{l} \mathsf{pp} \leftarrow_s \mathsf{Setup}(1^n) \\ (\mathtt{fpk}_i, \mathtt{fsk}_i)_{i \in [\ell]}, (\mathsf{dpk}, \mathsf{dsk}) \leftarrow_s \mathsf{Gen}(\mathsf{pp}) \\ R \leftarrow_s \mathsf{fRandom}(\mathtt{FPK}, \mathtt{FM}, \mathsf{dpk}, \mathtt{dm}) \\ \mathtt{CT} := \{\mathsf{Enc}(\mathtt{fpk}_i, \mathtt{fm}_i; r_i)\}_{i \in [\ell]} \end{array} \right] \leq \mathsf{negl}(n)$$

When $\ell = 1$ and algorithm dDec is the decryption algorithm Dec of PKE, the definition above is the original sender-AME in [26].

$\mathsf{Ideal}_{\ell,\mathsf{PKE},\mathcal{A}}(n)$	$\mathsf{Real}_{\ell,\mathsf{PKE},\mathcal{A}}^{\mathsf{fRandom}}(n)$
$\mathsf{pp} \leftarrow_\$ \mathsf{Setup}(1^n)$	$\mathsf{pp} \leftarrow_\$ \mathsf{Setup}(1^n)$
$(\mathtt{fpk}_i, \mathtt{fsk}_i)_{i\in[\ell]}, (\mathtt{dpk}, \mathtt{dsk}) \leftarrow_\$ \mathsf{Gen}(\mathsf{pp})$	$(\mathtt{fpk}_i, \mathtt{fsk}_i)_{i\in[\ell]}, (\mathtt{dpk}, \mathtt{dsk}) \leftarrow_\$ \mathsf{Gen}(\mathsf{pp})$
$b \leftarrow \mathcal{A}^{\mathrm{ENC}(\cdot,\cdot)}(\mathsf{pp}, \mathsf{FPK})$	$b \leftarrow \mathcal{A}^{\mathrm{ENC}'(\cdot,\cdot)}(\mathsf{pp}, \mathsf{FPK})$
return b	**return** b
$\mathrm{ENC}(\mathtt{FM}, \mathtt{dm})$	$\mathrm{ENC}'(\mathtt{FM}, \mathtt{dm})$
$(r_i)_{i\in[\ell]} \leftarrow_\$ \mathcal{R}$	$R^* \leftarrow_\$ \mathsf{fRandom}(\mathsf{FPK}, \mathtt{FM}, \mathtt{dpk}, \mathtt{dm})$
return $\{\mathsf{Enc}(\mathtt{fpk}_i, \mathtt{fm}_i; r_i)\}_{i\in[\ell]}$	**return** $\{\mathsf{Enc}(\mathtt{fpk}_i, \mathtt{fm}_i; r_i^*)\}_{i\in[\ell]}$

Fig. 2. Definition of game $\mathsf{Ideal}_{\ell,\mathsf{PKE},\mathcal{A}}(n)$ and $\mathsf{Real}_{\ell,\mathsf{PKE},\mathcal{A}}^{\mathsf{fRandom}}(n)$.

3.2 Security

The property of security means that it is hard for anyone who does not possess the duplicate secret key to distinguish a set of ciphertexts generated with uniformly sampled randomnesses from the output of coin-toss faking algorithm with overwhelming advantage.

Definition 2 (Secure ℓ-Sender-AME). *Let* $\mathsf{PKE} = (\mathsf{Setup}, \mathsf{Gen}, \mathsf{Enc}, \mathsf{Dec})$ *be an ℓ-sender-AME associated with extension* $(\mathsf{fRandom}, \mathsf{dDec})$. *We say* PKE *is a secure ℓ-sender-AME if 1)* PKE *is CPA secure, and 2) for any PPT adversary $\mathcal{A}$ in Fig. 2,*

$$\left| \Pr[\mathsf{Ideal}_{\ell,\mathsf{PKE},\mathcal{A}}(n) = 1] - \Pr[\mathsf{Real}_{\ell,\mathsf{PKE},\mathcal{A}}^{\mathsf{fRandom}}(n) = 1] \right| \leq \mathsf{negl}(n).$$

If condition 2) still holds when $\mathcal{A}$ also owns $\mathsf{FSK} := \{\mathtt{fsk}_i\}_{i\in[\ell]}$ *and* $\mathtt{dpk}$, *we say* PKE *is a strongly secure ℓ-sender-AME.*

In fact, the definition of strongly secure ℓ-sender-AME also captures the violation of receiver-privacy assumption. Specifically, the adversary $\mathcal{A}$ owns the forced secret keys of receivers, and can decrypt ciphertexts to obtain the forced plaintexts. As will be shown later, this strong security for sender-AME implies the security for receiver-AME. Hence, we are interested in constructing strongly secure ℓ-sender-AME.

3.3 Robustness

Roughly, the property of robustness indicates that both decrypting normal ciphertexts in the anamorphic way and decrypting anamorphic ciphertexts with incorrect duplicate secret key would return abort signaling explicitly.

Definition 3 (Robust ℓ-Sender-AME). *Let* $\mathsf{PKE} = (\mathsf{Setup}, \mathsf{Gen}, \mathsf{Enc}, \mathsf{Dec})$ *be an ℓ-sender-AME associated with extension* $(\mathsf{fRandom}, \mathsf{dDec})$. *We say* PKE *is a robust ℓ-sender-AME if for any PPT adversary* $\mathcal{A}$,

$$
\Pr \left[\mathsf{dDec}(\mathsf{dsk}, \mathsf{CT}) \neq \perp :
\begin{array}{l}
\mathsf{pp} \leftarrow_s \mathsf{Setup}(1^n) \\
(\mathsf{fpk}_i, \mathsf{fsk}_i)_{i \in [\ell]}, (\mathsf{dpk}, \mathsf{dsk}) \leftarrow_s \mathsf{Gen}(\mathsf{pp}) \\
\mathsf{FM} \leftarrow \mathcal{A}(\mathsf{pp}, \mathsf{FPK}); \ (r_i)_{i \in [\ell]} \leftarrow_s \mathcal{R} \\
\mathsf{CT} := \{\mathsf{Enc}(\mathsf{fpk}_i, \mathsf{fm}_i; r_i)\}_{i \in [\ell]}
\end{array}
\right] \leq \mathsf{negl}(n),
$$

where $\mathsf{FM} \in \mathcal{M}^\ell$, *and*

$$
\Pr \left[\mathsf{dDec}(\mathsf{dsk}', \mathsf{CT}) \neq \perp :
\begin{array}{l}
\mathsf{pp} \leftarrow_s \mathsf{Setup}(1^n) \\
(\mathsf{fpk}_i, \mathsf{fsk}_i)_{i \in [\ell]}, (\mathsf{dpk}, \mathsf{dsk}) \leftarrow_s \mathsf{Gen}(\mathsf{pp}) \\
(\mathsf{dpk}', \mathsf{dsk}') \leftarrow_s \mathsf{Gen}(\mathsf{pp}) \\
(\mathsf{FM}, \mathsf{dm}) \leftarrow \mathcal{A}(\mathsf{pp}, \mathsf{FPK}, \mathsf{dpk}) \\
R \leftarrow_s \mathsf{fRandom}(\mathsf{FPK}, \mathsf{FM}, \mathsf{dpk}, \mathsf{dm}) \\
\mathsf{CT} := \{\mathsf{Enc}(\mathsf{fpk}_i, \mathsf{fm}_i; r_i)\}_{i \in [\ell]}
\end{array}
\right] \leq \mathsf{negl}(n),
$$

where $\mathsf{FM} \in \mathcal{M}^\ell$ *and* $\mathsf{dm} \in \overline{\mathcal{M}}$.

4   Construction I: Pseudo-random and Robust PKE

In this section, we show that any pseudo-random and robust PKE is ℓ_{ct}-sender-anamorphic, where ℓ_{ct} is the bit length of ciphertext. The core idea is embedding the ciphertext of duplicate message into multiple normal ciphertexts bit-by-bit using the rejection sampling technique, which is inspired by the construction of public-key stegosystem in [32]. By pseudo-randomness, the dictator cannot distinguish whether observed ciphertexts carry the ciphertext of duplicate message or not. By robustness, decrypting the ciphertext of duplicate message with incorrect duplicate secret key would return an abort symbol.

4.1   Pseudo-random and Robust PKE

We recall the definition of pseudo-randomness for PKE in [32] as below.

Definition 4 (Pseudo-randomness [32]). *Let* $\mathsf{PKE} = (\mathsf{Setup}, \mathsf{Gen}, \mathsf{Enc}, \mathsf{Dec})$ *be a PKE scheme. We say* PKE *is indistinguishable from random bits under chosen plaintext attack (pseudo-random) if for any PPT adversary* $\mathcal{A}_1, \mathcal{A}_2$,

$$
\left| \Pr \left[b = b' :
\begin{array}{l}
\mathsf{pp} \leftarrow_s \mathsf{Setup}(1^n) \\
(\mathsf{pk}, \mathsf{sk}) \leftarrow_s \mathsf{Gen}(\mathsf{pp}) \\
(\mathsf{m}^*, \mathsf{st}) \leftarrow \mathcal{A}_1(\mathsf{pp}, \mathsf{pk}) \\
\mathsf{ct}_0 \leftarrow_s \mathsf{Enc}(\mathsf{pk}, \mathsf{m}^*) \\
\mathsf{ct}_1 \leftarrow_s \{0, 1\}^{|\mathsf{ct}_0|} \\
b \leftarrow_s \{0, 1\} \\
b' \leftarrow \mathcal{A}_2(\mathsf{st}, \mathsf{ct}_b)
\end{array}
\right] - \frac{1}{2} \right| \leq \mathsf{negl}(n).
$$

$\text{Rob}_{\text{PKE},\mathcal{A}}(n)$	$\text{TEST}(\mathtt{m}, i, j)$
$\mathtt{pp} \leftarrow_{\$} \text{Setup}(1^n)$	**if** $(i \notin [id]) \lor (j \notin [id])$:
$id := 0$	**return** false
$(\mathtt{m}, i, j) \leftarrow \mathcal{A}^{\text{GEN}()}(\mathtt{pp})$	**if** $i = j$:
return $\text{TEST}(\mathtt{m}, i, j)$	**return** false
	$\mathtt{m}_1 := \mathtt{m}$
$\text{GEN}()$	$\mathtt{ct} \leftarrow_{\$} \text{Enc}(\mathtt{pk}_i, \mathtt{m}_1)$
$id := id + 1$	$\mathtt{m}_2 := \text{Dec}(\mathtt{sk}_j, \mathtt{ct})$
$(\mathtt{pk}_{id}, \mathtt{sk}_{id}) \leftarrow_{\$} \text{Gen}(\mathtt{pp})$	**return** $(\mathtt{m}_1 \neq \bot) \land (\mathtt{m}_2 \neq \bot)$
return $(id, \mathtt{pk}_{id})$	

Fig. 3. Definition of game $\text{Rob}_{\text{PKE},\mathcal{A}}(n)$.

The robustness presented by Abdalla et al. [1] for PKE captures the difficulty of generating a ciphertext which is valid under two different decryption keys. Specifically, they formalized four definitions for robustness including weak and strong robustness in the setting of CPA and CCA security respectively (i.e., WROB-CPA, WROB-CCA, SROB-CPA, SROB-CCA). Here we require the PKE to satisfy the WROB-CPA property and recall its definition below.

Definition 5 (Robustness [1]). *Let* PKE = (Setup, Gen, Enc, Dec) *be a PKE scheme. We say* PKE *is robust if for any PPT adversary* $\mathcal{A}$ *in Fig. 3,*

$$\Pr\left[\text{Rob}_{\text{PKE},\mathcal{A}}(n) = \text{true}\right] \leq \text{negl}(n).$$

So far, there are only a few pseudo-random PKE [23,32], where Möller's scheme [23] also satisfies robustness. It seems that the coverage of this construction is rather limited. The following description of sender-anamorphic extension indicates that we only need the ciphertext (of duplicate message) can be encoded into a string which is indistinguishable from a uniform random, and here are several approaches [9,31,34,36] to achieve such an encoding.

4.2   Sender-Anamorphic Extension

Let PKE be a pseudo-random and robust PKE with plaintext space $\mathcal{M}$, randomness space $\mathcal{R}$ and ciphertext space $\mathcal{C}$. The length of ciphertext in PKE is denoted by ℓ_{ct}. Figure 4 depicts the details of sender-anamorphic extension for PKE, and PKE is an ℓ_{ct}-sender-AME with duplicate plaintext space $\mathcal{M}$. We point out that the keyed hash function $H_{\hat{k}} : \mathcal{C} \rightarrow \{0, 1\}$ used in algorithm fRandom and dDec is entropy smoothing and accessible to the public including the dictator.

4.3   Security Analysis

Theorem 5 (Robustness). *Let* PKE *be a pseudo-random and robust PKE.* PKE *is a robust* ℓ_{ct}*-sender-AME with extension algorithms (in Fig. 4).*

PKE.fRandom$(\mathsf{FPK}, \mathsf{FM}, \mathsf{dpk}, \mathsf{dm})$	PKE.dDec$(\mathsf{dsk}, \mathsf{CT})$
$\mathsf{ct} \leftarrow_\$ \mathsf{Enc}(\mathsf{dpk}, \mathsf{dm})$	$\mathsf{CT} := \{\mathsf{ct}_i\}_{i \in [\ell_{\mathsf{ct}}]}$
for $i \in [\ell_{\mathsf{ct}}]$ **do** :	**for** $i \in [\ell_{\mathsf{ct}}]$ **do** :
do :	$b_i' := H_{\hat{k}}(\mathsf{ct}_i)$
$r^* \leftarrow_\$ \mathcal{R}$	$\mathsf{ct}' := b_1' \Vert b_2' \Vert \cdots \Vert b_{\ell_{\mathsf{ct}}}'$
$\mathsf{ct}^* \leftarrow \mathsf{Enc}(\mathsf{fpk}_i, \mathsf{fm}_i; r^*)$	$\mathsf{dm}' := \mathsf{Dec}(\mathsf{dsk}, \mathsf{ct}')$
$b_i := H_{\hat{k}}(\mathsf{ct}^*)$	**return** dm'
while $b_i \neq \mathsf{ct}[i]$	
$r_i := r^*$	
return $R := \{r_i\}_{i \in [\ell_{\mathsf{ct}}]}$	

Fig. 4. Sender-anamorphic extension for pseudo-random and robust PKE.

Proof. The algorithm dDec returns $\perp$ when algorithm Dec decrypting ct' with dsk returns $\perp$.

If CT is a set of normal ciphertexts, by the pseudo-randomness of PKE and the entropy smoothness of $\{H_{\hat{k}}\}_{\hat{k} \in \hat{\mathcal{K}}}$, every bit b_i' is uniformly distributed over $\{0,1\}$ and ct' is uniformly distributed over $\{0,1\}^{\ell_{\mathsf{ct}}}$ in adversary $\mathcal{A}$'s view. Let $|\mathcal{K}|$ denote the size of secret key space, the pseudo-randomness of PKE indicates that $1/|\mathcal{K}|$ is a negligible function over n. Otherwise, adversary might guess the secret key, decrypt ct_b and output correct b with non-negligible advantage. Thus, the probability of event that ct' is a valid ciphertext under dsk is negligible, and the algorithm Dec returns $\perp$ with overwhelming probability.

If CT is a set of anamorphic ciphertexts under duplicate public key dpk^*, then dsk is the incorrect duplicate secret key for CT. Clearly, ct' is a valid ciphertext under dpk^*. By the robustness of PKE, the probability of $\mathsf{Dec}(\mathsf{dsk}, \mathsf{ct}') \neq \perp$ is negligible. □

Theorem 6 (Security). *Let* PKE *be a pseudo-random and robust PKE. Then,* PKE *is a strongly secure ℓ_{ct}-sender-AME with extension algorithms in Fig. 4*

Proof. By the correctness of PKE, one can easily verify that PKE is ℓ_{ct}-sender-anamorphic with extension algorithms in Fig. 4. The pseudo-randomness of PKE implies CPA security.

We now prove that for any PPT adversary $\mathcal{A}$, the advantage of $\mathcal{A}$ distinguishing games $\mathsf{Ideal}_{\ell_{\mathsf{ct}}, \mathsf{PKE}, \mathcal{A}}(n)$ and $\mathsf{Real}^{\mathsf{fRandom}}_{\ell_{\mathsf{ct}}, \mathsf{PKE}, \mathcal{A}}(n)$ is negligible. Assume that $\mathcal{A}$ makes at most q encryption queries (providing a forced plaintext set FM and a duplicate plaintext dm each time).

Let $\mathbf{H}_0 = \mathsf{Real}^{\mathsf{fRandom}}_{\ell_{\mathsf{ct}}, \mathsf{PKE}, \mathcal{A}}(n)$, and $\mathbf{H}_i$ is the same as $\mathbf{H}_{i-1}$ except that challenger samples $(r_j)_{j \in [\ell_{\mathsf{ct}}]} \leftarrow_\$ \mathcal{R}$ to encrypt $\{\mathsf{fm}_j\}_{j \in [\ell_{\mathsf{ct}}]}$ in the i-th encryption query for $i \in [q]$. We have $\mathbf{H}_q = \mathsf{Ideal}_{\ell_{\mathsf{ct}}, \mathsf{PKE}, \mathcal{A}}(n)$.

Lemma 1. *By the pseudo-randomness of* PKE, $\mathbf{H}_{i-1} \approx_c \mathbf{H}_i$ *for $i \in [q]$.*

Proof. We build adversary $\mathcal{B}_1^i$ and $\mathcal{B}_2^i$ to break the pseudo-randomness of PKE. In specific, $\mathcal{B}_1^i$ receives $(\mathrm{pp}, \mathrm{pk})$ and returns challenge plaintext m^* and state st. $\mathcal{B}_2^i$ receives $(\mathrm{st}, \mathrm{ct}_b)$ and has to guess the bit b.

Adversary $\mathcal{B}_1^i$ and $\mathcal{B}_2^i$ simulate $\mathbf{H}_{i-1}$ or $\mathbf{H}_i$ for $\mathcal{A}$ as follows.

- $\mathcal{B}_1^i$ runs Gen(pp) to generate ℓ_{ct} pairs of forced public/secret key $(\mathrm{fpk}_j, \mathrm{fsk}_j)$, and sets pk as the duplicate public key dpk;
- $\mathcal{B}_1^i$ provides $(\mathrm{pp}, \mathrm{FPK} := \{\mathrm{fpk}_j\}_{j\in[\ell_{\mathrm{ct}}]}, \mathrm{FSK} := \{\mathrm{fsk}_j\}_{j\in[\ell_{\mathrm{ct}}]}, \mathrm{dpk} := \mathrm{pk})$ to $\mathcal{A}$;
- Let $(\mathrm{FM}, \mathrm{dm})$ be the i-th encryption query by $\mathcal{A}$. $\mathcal{B}_1^i$ returns dm and $\mathrm{st} = (\mathrm{pp}, \mathrm{dpk}, \mathrm{FPK}, \mathrm{FSK})$;
- $\mathcal{B}_2^i$ answers the first $(i-1)$ encryption queries by encrypting FM with randomnesses generated by fRandom(FPK, FM, dpk, dm) in Fig. 4, and the last $(q-i)$ queries with randomnesses uniformly sampled from $\mathcal{R}$;
- $\mathcal{B}_2^i$ answers the i-th query by encrypting FM with randomnesses generated by fRandom$'$(FPK, FM, ct_b) which is the same as fRandom(FPK, FM, dpk, dm) except that ct is replaced by ct_b.

If ct_b is an encryption of dm under pk, then fRandom$'$(FPK, FM, ct_b) is actually the same as fRandom(FPK, FM, dpk, dm), and $\mathcal{B}_1^i, \mathcal{B}_2^i$ simulate $\mathbf{H}_{i-1}$ for $\mathcal{A}$.

If ct_b is uniformly sampled from $\{0,1\}^{\ell_{\mathrm{ct}}}$, then each randomness generated by fRandom$'$(FPK, FM, ct_b) is uniformly distributed over $\mathcal{R}$, and $\mathcal{B}_1^i, \mathcal{B}_2^i$ simulate $\mathbf{H}_i$ for $\mathcal{A}$. □

By Lemma 1, we have $\mathbf{H}_0 \approx_c \mathbf{H}_q$, from which this theorem follows. □

5 Construction II: Hybrid PKE with Special KEM

In this section, we demonstrate that a wide range of hybrid PKE schemes are strongly secure and robust $(\ell+1)$-sender-AME for duplicate plaintext with ℓ bits. We first depict such PKE schemes with a generic framework, then provide the details of their sender-anamorphic extension, and finally prove the properties of strong security and robustness rigorously.

5.1 Hybrid PKE with Special KEM

To better describe the proposed sender-anamorphic extension for hybrid PKE, we recall the module-level syntax of KEM and related properties (i.e., universal decryptability and key-pseudo-randomness) by Chen et al. [10] as below. In fact, these two properties are the "perfect correctness" and "CPA security" for typical KEM respectively.

- KEM.Setup(1^n) returns the public parameter pp including the key space $\mathcal{K}_{\mathsf{KEM}}$ and randomness space $\mathcal{R}_{\mathsf{KEM}}$.
- KEM.Gen(pp) returns a key pair $(\mathrm{pk} = (\mathrm{ek}, \mathrm{tk}), \mathrm{sk} = (\mathrm{dk}, \mathrm{vk}))$ by running following sub-algorithms.
  - KEM.Ek(pp) produces an en/decapsulation key pair $(\mathrm{ek}, \mathrm{dk})$.

- KEM.Tk(pp) produces a tag generation/verification key pair (tk, vk).
- KEM.Enc(pk) returns key K and ciphertext $\psi = (C, \pi)$ by running following sub-algorithms.
  - KEM.Rg(pp) picks a randomness r from $\mathcal{R}_{\mathsf{KEM}}$.
  - KEM.Kg(ek, r) produces a key $K \in \mathcal{K}_{\mathsf{KEM}}$.
  - KEM.Cg(r) produces a ciphertext C of key K.
  - KEM.Tg(tk, r) produces the ciphertext tag π of C.
- KEM.Dec(sk, $\psi = (C, \pi)$) returns the key K or $\bot$ by running following sub-algorithms.
  - KEM.Kd(dk, C) produces a key K.
  - KEM.Vf(vk, C) produces a ciphertext tag π'.
  If $\pi' = \pi$, KEM.Dec returns K. Otherwise, it returns $\bot$.

We remark that algorithms related to the ciphertext tag (including KEM.Tk, KEM.Tg and KEM.Vf) are optional and do not appear in certain KEMs.

Definition 6 (Universal Decryptability [10]). *Let* KEM *be a module-level KEM. We say* KEM *satisfies universal decryptability if for any* $n \in \mathbb{N}$,

$$\Pr\left[\mathsf{KEM.Kg(ek}, r) \neq \mathsf{KEM.Kd(dk}, C) : \begin{array}{l} \mathsf{pp} \leftarrow_s \mathsf{KEM.Setup}(1^n) \\ (\mathsf{ek}, \mathsf{dk}) \leftarrow_s \mathsf{KEM.Ek(pp)} \\ r \leftarrow_s \mathsf{KEM.Rg(pp)} \\ C := \mathsf{KEM.Cg}(r) \end{array}\right] \leq \mathsf{negl}(n).$$

Definition 7 (Key-Pseudo-Randomness [10]). *Let* KEM *be a module-level KEM. We say* KEM *is key-pseudo-random if for any PPT adversary* $\mathcal{A}$,

$$\left| \Pr\left[b = b' : \begin{array}{l} \mathsf{pp} \leftarrow_s \mathsf{KEM.Setup}(1^n) \\ (\mathsf{ek}, \mathsf{dk}) \leftarrow_s \mathsf{KEM.Ek(pp)} \\ r \leftarrow_s \mathsf{KEM.Rg(pp)} \\ C := \mathsf{KEM.Cg}(r) \\ b \leftarrow_s \{0, 1\}; K_0 \leftarrow_s \mathcal{K}_{\mathsf{KEM}} \\ K_1 := \mathsf{KEM.Kg(ek}, r) \\ b' \leftarrow \mathcal{A}(\mathsf{pp}, \mathsf{ek}, K_b, C) \end{array}\right] - \frac{1}{2} \right| \leq \mathsf{negl}(n).$$

Here we introduce the homomorphic property for module-level KEM.

Definition 8 (Homomorphic Property). *Let* KEM *be a module-level KEM with key space* $\mathcal{K}_{\mathsf{KEM}}$ *and randomness space* $\mathcal{R}_{\mathsf{KEM}}$. *We say* KEM *is homomorphic if for any* $n \in \mathbb{N}^+$, $\mathsf{pp} \leftarrow_s \mathsf{KEM.Setup}(1^n)$, $(\mathsf{ek}, \mathsf{dk}) \leftarrow_s \mathsf{KEM.Ek(pp)}$, *any* $r_1, r_2 \in \mathcal{R}_{\mathsf{KEM}}$,

1) KEM.Kg(ek, $r_1 \oplus r_2$) = KEM.Kg(ek, r_1) $\odot$ KEM.Kg(ek, r_2) *where* $\oplus$ *and* $\odot$ *are operations defined over* $\mathcal{R}_{\mathsf{KEM}}$ *and* $\mathcal{K}_{\mathsf{KEM}}$ *respectively, and*
2) KEM.Cg($r_1 \oplus r_2$) = KEM.Cg(r_1) $\otimes$ KEM.Cg(r_2) *where* $\otimes$ *is an operation defined over the support of* KEM.Cg(r).

PKE.Setup(1^n)	PKE.Enc(pk, m; r)	PKE.Dec(sk, ct)
pp $\leftarrow_\$$ KEM.Setup(1^n)	/*$r \leftarrow_\$$ KEM.Rg(pp)*/	$K' :=$ KEM.Kd(dk, C)
return pp	$K :=$ KEM.Kg(ek, r)	m$' :=$ DEM.Dec(K', D)
	$C :=$ KEM.Cg(r)	$\pi' :=$ KEM.Vf(vk, C)
PKE.Gen(pp)	$\pi :=$ KEM.Tg(tk, r)	if $\pi' = \pi$ then m $:=$ m$'$
(ek, dk) $\leftarrow_\$$ KEM.Ek(pp)	$D :=$ DEM.Enc(K, m)	else m $:= \perp$
(tk, vk) $\leftarrow_\$$ KEM.Tk(pp)	ct $:= (C, \pi, D)$	return m
pk $:=$ (ek, tk)	return ct	
sk $:=$ (dk, vk)		
return (pk, sk)		

Fig. 5. Hybrid PKE built on module-level KEM and DEM.

Let KEM be a module-level KEM satisfying universal decryptability, key-pseudo-randomness and homomorphic property, and DEM = (Enc, Dec) be the data encapsulation mechanism (DEM) that is a symmetric encryption scheme that has indistinguishable encryptions in the presence of an eavesdropper (please refer to the full version for formal definition). Figure 5 shows the hybrid PKE PKE built on KEM and DEM.

Some KEMs including Cramer-Shoup KEMs under DDH, DCR and QR assumptions [11], Kurosawa-Desmedt KEM [20] and Hofheinz-Kiltz KEM [17] have been demonstrated to be universally decryptable and key-pseudo-random in [10]. One can refer to the details of these KEMs in [10] and verify that all these KEMs also satisfy the homomorphic property. Analogous to the DDH-based Cramer-Shoup KEM, the ElGamal KEM also meets the requirement.

5.2 Sender-Anamorphic Extension

Figure 6 depicts the details of sender-anamorphic extension for the above hybrid PKE. Also, this extension requires an entropy smoothing keyed hash function $H_{\hat{k}}$ that maps the key of KEM into the randomness space $\mathcal{R}_{\mathsf{KEM}}$. We assume $\mathcal{R}_{\mathsf{KEM}}$ is an additive and cyclic group and $1_{\mathcal{R}_{\mathsf{KEM}}}$ denotes a generator of $\mathcal{R}_{\mathsf{KEM}}$.

We note that some cryptosystems are built over such hybrid PKE (e.g., Naor-Yung paradigm [24], double-strand paradigm [16,27,33]) are strongly secure and robust 1-sender-AMEs for 1-bit duplicate message. More details are provided in the full version.

5.3 Security Analysis

Let PKE be a hybrid PKE in Fig. 5 with KEM satisfying universal decryptability, key-pseudo-randomness and homomorphic property and DEM that has indistinguishable encryptions in the presence of an eavesdropper.

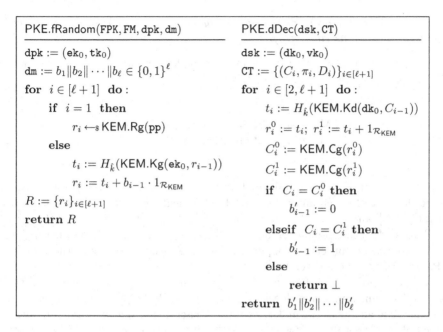

Fig. 6. Sender-anamorphic extension for hybrid PKE with special KEM.

Theorem 7 (Robustness). PKE *is a robust* $(\ell+1)$-*sender-AME with extension algorithms in Fig. 6.*

Proof. Given inputs $\mathtt{dsk} = (\mathtt{dk}_0, \mathtt{vk}_0)$ and $\mathtt{CT} = \{(C_i, \pi_i, D_i)\}_{i \in [\ell+1]}$, algorithm dDec returns $\perp$ when $C_i \neq C_i^0$ and $C_i \neq C_i^1$ for $i \in [2, \ell+1]$. In particular, we have $C_i = \mathsf{KEM.Cg}(r_i)$ and

$$C_i^b = \mathsf{KEM.Cg}(H_{\hat{k}}(\mathsf{KEM.Kd}(\mathtt{dk}_0, C_{i-1})) + b_{i-1} \cdot 1_{\mathcal{R}_{\mathsf{KEM}}})$$
$$= \mathsf{KEM.Cg}(H_{\hat{k}}(\mathsf{KEM.Kd}(\mathtt{ek}_0, r_{i-1})) + b_{i-1} \cdot 1_{\mathcal{R}_{\mathsf{KEM}}})$$

for $b_{i-1} \in \{0, 1\}$ by the universal decryptability of KEM. Let $\mathcal{E}_i$ denote the event that $C_i = C_i^0$ or $C_i = C_i^1$ for $i \in [2, \ell+1]$.

If CT is a set of normal ciphertexts, then r_i is uniformly sampled from $\mathcal{R}$ for all $i \in [\ell+1]$. By the key-pseudo-randomness of KEM and entropy smoothness of $\mathcal{H}$, the probability of event that $r_i = H_{\hat{k}}(\mathsf{KEM.Kd}(\mathtt{ek}_0, r_{i-1})) + b_{i-1} \cdot 1_{\mathcal{R}_{\mathsf{KEM}}}$ is negligible. By the homomorphic property of KEM, the probability of event $\mathcal{E}_i$ is negligible for $i \in [2, \ell+1]$.

If CT is a set of anamorphic ciphertexts under duplicate public key $\mathtt{dpk}^* = (\mathtt{ek}^*, \mathtt{tk}^*)$, then dsk is the incorrect duplicate secret key for CT. In this case, r_1 is uniformly sampled from $\mathcal{R}$ and $r_i = H_{\hat{k}}(\mathsf{KEM.Kg}(\mathtt{ek}^*, r_{i-1})) + b_{i-1} \cdot 1_{\mathcal{R}_{\mathsf{KEM}}}$. Since $\mathtt{ek}^* \neq \mathtt{ek}_0$, by the entropy smoothness of $\mathcal{H}$, the probability of event that $r_i = H_{\hat{k}}(\mathsf{KEM.Kd}(\mathtt{ek}_0, r_{i-1})) + b_{i-1} \cdot 1_{\mathcal{R}_{\mathsf{KEM}}}$ is negligible, and the probability of event $\mathcal{E}_i$ is negligible for $i \in [2, \ell+1]$. $\square$

Theorem 8 (Security). PKE *is a strongly secure* $(\ell + 1)$*-sender-AME with extension algorithms (in Fig. 6).*

Proof. We first prove that PKE is $(\ell + 1)$-sender-anamorphic and claim that $b'_i = b_i$ for $i \in [\ell]$. In $\mathtt{ct}_i := (C_i, \pi_i, D_i)$,

$$
\begin{aligned}
C_i &= \mathsf{KEM.Cg}(r_i) \\
&= \mathsf{KEM.Cg}(H_{\hat{k}}(\mathsf{KEM.Kg}(\mathsf{ek}_0, r_{i-1})) + b_{i-1} \cdot 1_{\mathcal{R}_{\mathsf{KEM}}}) \\
&= \mathsf{KEM.Cg}(H_{\hat{k}}(\mathsf{KEM.Kd}(\mathsf{dk}_0, C_{i-1})) + b_{i-1} \cdot 1_{\mathcal{R}_{\mathsf{KEM}}}) \\
&= \mathsf{KEM.Cg}(r_i^{b_{i-1}}) = C_i^{b_{i-1}},
\end{aligned}
$$

where $i \in [2, \ell + 1]$. By the universal decryptability of KEM, the probability of event that the third equality does not hold is negligible. Note that if $b_{i-1} = 0$ then $C_i = C_i^0$ and $b'_{i-1} = 0$. Otherwise, we have $b_{i-1} = 1$, $C_i = C_i^1$ and $b'_{i-1} = 1$.

Since KEM is key-pseudo-random and DEM has indistinguishable encryptions in the presence of an eavesdropper, PKE is CPA secure. We defer the proof of CPA security to the full version.

We now prove that for any PPT adversary $\mathcal{A}$, the advantage of adversary $\mathcal{A}$ distinguishing games $\mathsf{Ideal}_{\ell+1,\mathsf{PKE},\mathcal{A}}(n)$ and $\mathsf{Real}^{\mathsf{fRandom}}_{\ell+1,\mathsf{PKE},\mathcal{A}}(n)$ is negligible. Assume that adversary $\mathcal{A}$ makes at most q encryption queries, and provides a forced plaintext set $\mathsf{FM} := \{\mathsf{fm}_i\}_{i \in [\ell+1]}$ and a duplicate plaintext dm in each query.

Let $\mathbf{H}_0 = \mathsf{Real}^{\mathsf{fRandom}}_{\ell+1,\mathsf{PKE},\mathcal{A}}(n)$, and $\mathbf{H}_i$ is the same as $\mathbf{H}_{i-1}$ except that challenger samples $(r_i)_{i \in [\ell+1]} \leftarrow_\$ \mathcal{R}_{\mathsf{KEM}}$ to encrypt forced messages $\{\mathsf{fm}_j\}_{j \in [\ell+1]}$ in the i-th encryption query for $i \in [q]$. Obviously, $\mathbf{H}_q = \mathsf{Ideal}_{\ell+1,\mathsf{PKE},\mathcal{A}}(n)$.

Let $\mathbf{H}_{i-1,0} = \mathbf{H}_{i-1}$ for $i \in [q]$, and $\mathbf{H}_{i-1,j}$ is the same as $\mathbf{H}_{i-1,j-1}$ except that the challenger samples $r_j \leftarrow_\$ \mathcal{R}_{\mathsf{KEM}}$ to encrypt fm_j in the i-th encryption query for $j \in [\ell + 1]$. Obviously, $\mathbf{H}_{i-1,\ell+1} = \mathbf{H}_i$. Note that $r_1^* \leftarrow_\$ \mathsf{KEM.Rg}(\mathsf{pp})$, namely, $r_1^* \leftarrow_\$ \mathcal{R}_{\mathsf{KEM}}$, in algorithm fRandom, we have $\mathbf{H}_{i-1,0} = \mathbf{H}_{i-1,1}$ for $i \in [q]$.

Let $\mathbf{H}'_{i-1,j-1}$ be the same as $\mathbf{H}_{i-1,j-1}$ except that the challenger computes $r_j := H_{\hat{k}}(K) + b_{j-1} \cdot 1_{\mathcal{R}_{\mathsf{KEM}}}$, where $K \leftarrow_\$ \mathcal{K}_{\mathsf{KEM}}$ and b_{j-1} is the $(j-1)$-th bit of dm, to encrypt fm_j in the i-th encryption query for $j \in [2, \ell + 1]$.

Now, there is a series of games between $\mathbf{H}_0$ and $\mathbf{H}_q$ as below.

$$
\begin{aligned}
\{\ &\mathbf{H}_0(\mathbf{H}_{0,0}), &&\mathbf{H}_{0,1}, &&\mathbf{H}'_{0,1}, &&\cdots, &&\mathbf{H}_{0,\ell}, &&\mathbf{H}'_{0,\ell}, \\
&\mathbf{H}_1(\mathbf{H}_{0,\ell+1}, \mathbf{H}_{1,0}), &&\mathbf{H}_{1,1}, &&\mathbf{H}'_{1,1}, &&\cdots, &&\mathbf{H}_{1,\ell}, &&\mathbf{H}'_{1,\ell}, \\
&\cdots, \\
&\mathbf{H}_{q-1}(\mathbf{H}_{q-2,\ell+1}, \mathbf{H}_{q-1,0}), &&\mathbf{H}_{q-1,1}, &&\mathbf{H}'_{q-1,1}, &&\cdots, &&\mathbf{H}_{q-1,\ell}, &&\mathbf{H}'_{q-1,\ell}, \\
&\mathbf{H}_q(\mathbf{H}_{q-1,\ell+1})\}
\end{aligned}
$$

Lemma 2. *By the key-pseudo-randomness of* KEM, $\mathbf{H}'_{i-1,j-1} \approx_c \mathbf{H}_{i-1,j-1}$ *for* $i \in [q]$ *and* $j \in [2, \ell + 1]$.

Proof. We show how to build an adversary $\mathcal{D}_{i-1,j-1}$ breaking the key-pseudo-randomness of module-level KEM. Specifically, $\mathcal{D}_{i-1,j-1}$ receives $(\mathsf{pp}, \mathsf{ek}^*, K^*, C^*)$ and has to guess the bit b. If $b = 0$, K^* is uniformly sampled from $\mathcal{K}_{\mathsf{KEM}}$. Otherwise, $K^* = \mathsf{KEM.Kg}(\mathsf{ek}^*, r)$ with $r \leftarrow_\$ \mathsf{KEM.Rg}(\mathsf{pp})$ and $C^* = \mathsf{KEM.Cg}(r)$.

$\mathcal{D}_{i-1,j-1}(\mathbf{pp}, \mathbf{ek}^*, K^*, C^*)$	$\mathsf{dEnc}(\mathbf{FPK}, \mathbf{FM}, \mathbf{dpk}^*, \mathbf{dm})$
$(\mathbf{fpk}_i, \mathbf{fsk}_i)_{i \in [\ell+1]} \leftarrow_\$ \mathsf{Gen}(\mathbf{pp})$	$\mathbf{dm} := b_1 b_2 \cdots b_\ell \in \{0,1\}^\ell;\ b_0 := 0$
$((\mathbf{ek}_0, \mathbf{tk}_0), \mathbf{dsk}) \leftarrow_\$ \mathsf{Gen}(\mathbf{pp})$	for $i \in [\ell+1]$ do :
$\mathbf{dpk}^* := (\mathbf{ek}^*, \mathbf{tk}_0)$	$\quad$ if $i < j-1$ then
$b \leftarrow \mathcal{A}^{\mathrm{ENC}(\cdot,\cdot)}(\mathbf{pp}, \mathbf{FPK}, \mathbf{FSK}, \mathbf{dpk}^*)$	$\quad\quad r_i \leftarrow_\$ \mathcal{R}_{\mathsf{KEM}}$
return b	$\quad\quad \mathbf{ct}_i := \mathsf{Enc}(\mathbf{fpk}_i, \mathbf{fm}_i; r_i)$
	$\quad$ elseif $i = j-1$ then
$\underline{\mathrm{ENC}(\mathbf{FM}, \mathbf{dm})}$	$\quad\quad C_i := C^* + b_{i-1} \cdot \mathsf{KEM.Cg}(1_{\mathcal{R}_{\mathsf{KEM}}})$
/*the k-th encryption query*/	$\quad\quad \pi_i := \mathsf{KEM.Vf}(\mathbf{vk}_i, C_i)$
if $k = i$ then	$\quad\quad K_i := \mathsf{KEM.Kd}(\mathbf{dk}_i, C_i)$
$\quad$ return $\mathsf{dEnc}(\mathbf{FPK}, \mathbf{FM}, \mathbf{dpk}^*, \mathbf{dm})$	$\quad\quad D_i := \mathsf{DEM.Enc}(K_i, \mathbf{fm}_i)$
if $k \le i-1$ then	$\quad\quad \mathbf{ct}_i := (C_i, \pi_i, D_i)$
$\quad (r_i)_{i \in [\ell+1]} \leftarrow_\$ \mathcal{R}_{\mathsf{KEM}}$	$\quad$ elseif $i = j$ then
else $\cdots\cdots$ /*$k > i$*/	$\quad\quad s_i := b_{i-2} \cdot \mathsf{KEM.Kg}(\mathbf{ek}^*, 1_{\mathcal{R}_{\mathsf{KEM}}})$
$\quad R \leftarrow_\$ \mathsf{fRandom}(\mathbf{FPK}, \mathbf{FM}, \mathbf{dpk}^*, \mathbf{dm})$	$\quad\quad t_i := H_{\hat{k}}(K^* + s_i)$
return $\{\mathsf{Enc}(\mathbf{fpk}_i, \mathbf{fm}_i; r_i)\}_{i \in [\ell+1]}$	$\quad\quad r_i := t_i + b_{i-1} \cdot 1_{\mathcal{R}_{\mathsf{KEM}}}$
	$\quad\quad \mathbf{ct}_i := \mathsf{Enc}(\mathbf{fpk}_i, \mathbf{fm}_i; r_i)$
	$\quad$ else $\cdots\cdots$ /*$i > j$*/
	$\quad\quad t_i := H_{\hat{k}}(\mathsf{KEM.Kg}(\mathbf{ek}^*, r_{i-1}))$
	$\quad\quad r_i := t_i + b_{i-1} \cdot 1_{\mathcal{R}_{\mathsf{KEM}}}$
	$\quad\quad \mathbf{ct}_i := \mathsf{Enc}(\mathbf{fpk}_i, \mathbf{fm}_i; r_i)$
	return $\mathbf{CT} := \{\mathbf{ct}_i\}_{i \in [\ell+1]}$

Fig. 7. Adversary $\mathcal{D}_{i-1,j-1}$ breaking the key-pseudo-randomness of KEM in the proof of Lemma 2.

Adversary $\mathcal{D}_{i-1,j-1}$ simulates $\mathbf{H}_{i-1,j-1}$ or $\mathbf{H}'_{i-1,j-1}$ for $\mathcal{A}$ as shown in Fig. 7. In particular, the duplicate public key $\mathbf{dpk}^*$ is a valid public key, as the generation of encapsulation key $\mathbf{ek}$ and tag generation key $\mathbf{tk}$ in PKE is independent.

$\mathcal{D}_{i-1,j-1}$ runs algorithm dEnc to generate ciphertexts $\{\mathbf{ct}_i\}_{i \in [\ell+1]}$ for the i-th encryption query. In $\mathbf{ct}_{j-1}$, $C_{j-1} = C^* + b_{j-2} \cdot \mathsf{KEM.Cg}(1_{\mathcal{R}_{\mathsf{KEM}}})$, $D_{j-1} = \mathsf{DEM.Enc}(K_{j-1}, \mathbf{fm}_{j-1})$, π_{j-1} and K_{j-1} are derived from C_{j-1} using $\mathbf{fsk}_{j-1} = (\mathbf{dk}_{j-1}, \mathbf{vk}_{j-1})$. Note that $C^* = \mathsf{KEM.Cg}(r)$, we have $C_{j-1} = \mathsf{KEM.Cg}(r_{j-1}) = \mathsf{KEM.Cg}(r + b_{j-2} \cdot 1_{\mathcal{R}_{\mathsf{KEM}}})$ by the homomorphic property of $\mathsf{KEM.Cg}$, and $\mathbf{ct}_{j-1} = \mathsf{Enc}(\mathbf{fpk}_{j-1}, \mathbf{fm}_{j-1}; r_{j-1})$. In $\mathbf{ct}_j$, the underlying randomness $r_j = H_{\hat{k}}(K^* + b_{j-2} \cdot \mathsf{KEM.Kg}(\mathbf{ek}^*, 1_{\mathcal{R}_{\mathsf{KEM}}})) + b_{j-1} \cdot 1_{\mathcal{R}_{\mathsf{KEM}}}$.

If $K^* = \mathsf{KEM.Kg}(\mathbf{ek}^*, r)$, by the homomorphic property of $\mathsf{KEM.Kg}$,

$$r_j = H_{\hat{k}}(\mathsf{KEM.Kg}(\mathbf{ek}^*, r + b_{j-2} \cdot 1_{\mathcal{R}_{\mathsf{KEM}}})) + b_{j-1} \cdot 1_{\mathcal{R}_{\mathsf{KEM}}}$$
$$= H_{\hat{k}}(\mathsf{KEM.Kg}(\mathbf{ek}^*, r_{j-1})) + b_{j-1} \cdot 1_{\mathcal{R}_{\mathsf{KEM}}}.$$

$$
\begin{array}{|ll|}
\hline
\end{array}
$$

$\mathcal{B}_{i-1,j-1}(\hat{k}, y)$	$\widetilde{\mathsf{fRandom}}(\mathsf{dpk}, \mathsf{dm})$
$\mathsf{pp} \leftarrow_{\$} \mathsf{Setup}(1^n)$	$\mathsf{dpk} := (\mathsf{ek}_0, \mathsf{tk}_0)$
$(\mathsf{fpk}_i, \mathsf{fsk}_i)_{i \in [\ell+1]} \leftarrow_{\$} \mathsf{Gen}(\mathsf{pp})$	$\mathsf{dm} := b_1 b_2 \cdots b_\ell \in \{0,1\}^\ell$
$(\mathsf{dpk}, \mathsf{dsk}) \leftarrow_{\$} \mathsf{Gen}(\mathsf{pp})$	$\text{for } i \in [\ell+1] \text{ do}:$
$b \leftarrow \mathcal{A}^{\mathrm{ENC}(\cdot,\cdot)}(\mathsf{pp}, \mathrm{FPK}, \mathrm{FSK}, \mathsf{dpk})$	$\quad \text{if } i < j \text{ then}$
$\textbf{return } b$	$\quad\quad r_i \leftarrow_{\$} \mathcal{R}_{\mathsf{KEM}}$
	$\quad \textbf{else}$
$\underline{\mathrm{ENC}(\mathrm{FM}, \mathsf{dm})}$	$\quad\quad \text{if } i > j \text{ then}$
$/^*\text{the } k\text{-th encryption query}^*/$	$\quad\quad\quad t_i := H_{\hat{k}}(\mathsf{KEM}.\mathsf{Kg}(\mathsf{ek}_0, r_{i-1}))$
$\textbf{if } k \leq i-1 \textbf{ then}$	$\quad\quad \textbf{else} \cdots\cdots /^* i = j^*/$
$\quad (r_i)_{i \in [\ell+1]} \leftarrow_{\$} \mathcal{R}_{\mathsf{KEM}}$	$\quad\quad\quad t_i := y$
$\textbf{elseif } k > i \textbf{ then}$	$\quad\quad r_i := t_i + b_{i-1} \cdot 1_{\mathcal{R}_{\mathsf{KEM}}}$
$\quad R \leftarrow_{\$} \mathsf{fRandom}(\mathrm{FPK}, \mathrm{FM}, \mathsf{dpk}, \mathsf{dm})$	$R := \{r_i\}_{i \in [\ell+1]}$
$\textbf{else} \cdots\cdots /^* k = i^*/$	$\textbf{return } R$
$\quad R \leftarrow_{\$} \widetilde{\mathsf{fRandom}}(\mathsf{dpk}, \mathsf{dm})$	
$\textbf{return } \{\mathsf{Enc}(\mathsf{fpk}_i, \mathsf{fm}_i; r_i)\}_{i \in [\ell+1]}$	

Fig. 8. Adversary $\mathcal{B}_{i-1,j-1}$ breaking the entropy smoothness of hash function family $\mathcal{H}$ in the proof of Lemma 3.

ct_j is computed in the same way as in fRandom, and $\mathcal{D}_{i-1,j-1}$ simulates $\mathbf{H}_{i-1,j-1}$ for $\mathcal{A}$. Otherwise, $K^* \leftarrow_{\$} \mathcal{K}_{\mathsf{KEM}}$, $K^* + b_{j-2} \cdot \mathsf{KEM}.\mathsf{Kg}(\mathsf{ek}^*, 1_{\mathcal{R}_{\mathsf{KEM}}})$ is uniformly distributed over $\mathcal{K}_{\mathsf{KEM}}$ and $\mathcal{D}_{i-1,j-1}$ simulates $\mathbf{H}'_{i-1,j-1}$ for $\mathcal{A}$. $\square$

Lemma 3. *By the entropy smoothness of hash function family* $\mathcal{H} = \{H_{\hat{k}}\}_{\hat{k} \in \hat{\mathcal{K}}}$ *with* $H_{\hat{k}} : \mathcal{K}_{\mathsf{KEM}} \to \mathcal{R}_{\mathsf{KEM}}$, $\mathbf{H}_{i-1,j} \approx_c \mathbf{H}'_{i-1,j-1}$ *for* $i \in [q]$ *and* $j \in [2, \ell+1]$.

Proof. We show how to build an adversary $\mathcal{B}_{i-1,j-1}$ breaking the entropy smoothness of hash function family $\mathcal{H}$ with $H_{\hat{k}} : \mathcal{K}_{\mathsf{KEM}} \to \mathcal{R}_{\mathsf{KEM}}$. Specifically, $\mathcal{B}_{i-1,j-1}$ receives $(\hat{k}, y)$ and has to decide whether $y = H_{\hat{k}}(x)$ with $x \leftarrow_{\$} \mathcal{K}_{\mathsf{KEM}}$ or $y \leftarrow_{\$} \mathcal{R}_{\mathsf{KEM}}$.

Adversary $\mathcal{B}_{i-1,j-1}$ simulates $\mathbf{H}_{i-1,j-1}$ or $\mathbf{H}'_{i-1,j-1}$ for $\mathcal{A}$ as shown in Fig. 8. In particular, $\mathcal{B}_{i-1,j-1}$ runs algorithm $\widetilde{\mathsf{fRandom}}$ to generate R for the i-th encryption query. In algorithm $\widetilde{\mathsf{fRandom}}$, the value of t_j is set as y.

If y is uniformly sampled from $\mathcal{R}_{\mathsf{KEM}}$, then randomness r_j is also uniformly sampled from $\mathcal{R}_{\mathsf{KEM}}$, and $\mathcal{B}_{i-1,j-1}$ simulates $\mathbf{H}_{i-1,j}$ for $\mathcal{A}$. If $y = H_{\hat{k}}(x)$ with $x \leftarrow_{\$} \mathcal{K}_{\mathsf{KEM}}$, then $\mathcal{B}_{i-1,j-1}$ simulates $\mathbf{H}'_{i-1,j-1}$ for $\mathcal{A}$. $\square$

By Lemma 2, Lemma 3 and $\mathbf{H}_{i-1,0} = \mathbf{H}_{i-1,1}$ for $i \in [q]$, we have $\mathbf{H}_0 \approx_c \mathbf{H}_q$. That is, for any PPT adversary $\mathcal{A}$, the advantage of adversary $\mathcal{A}$ distinguishing games $\mathsf{Ideal}_{\ell+1,\mathsf{PKE},\mathcal{A}}(n)$ and $\mathsf{Real}^{\mathsf{fRandom}}_{\ell+1,\mathsf{PKE},\mathcal{A}}(n)$ is negligible. $\square$

$\mathsf{nGame}_{\ell,\mathsf{PKE},\mathcal{D}}(n)$	$\mathsf{faGame}_{\ell,\mathsf{PKE},\mathcal{D}}(n)$
$\mathrm{pp} \leftarrow_\$ \mathsf{Setup}(1^n)$	$\mathrm{pp} \leftarrow_\$ \mathsf{aSetup}(1^n)$
$(\mathrm{pk}_i,\mathrm{sk}_i)_{i\in[\ell]} \leftarrow_\$ \mathsf{Gen}(\mathrm{pp})$	$((\mathrm{apk}_i,\mathrm{ask}_i)_{i\in[\ell]},\mathrm{dkey}) \leftarrow_\$ \mathsf{aGen}(\mathrm{pp})$
$b \leftarrow \mathcal{D}^{\mathrm{ENC}(\cdot,\cdot)}(\mathrm{pp},(\mathrm{pk}_i,\mathrm{sk}_i)_{i\in[\ell]})$	$b \leftarrow \mathcal{D}^{\mathrm{AENC}(\cdot,\cdot)}(\mathrm{pp},(\mathrm{apk}_i,\mathrm{ask}_i)_{i\in[\ell]})$
return b	return b
$\mathrm{ENC}(\mathtt{M},\bar{\mathtt{m}})$	$\mathrm{AENC}(\mathtt{M},\bar{\mathtt{m}})$
return $\{\mathsf{Enc}(\mathrm{pk}_i,\mathtt{m}_i)\}_{i\in[\ell]}$	return $\mathsf{aEnc}(\mathrm{dkey},\mathtt{M},\bar{\mathtt{m}})$

Fig. 9. Definitions of game $\mathsf{nGame}_{\ell,\mathsf{PKE},\mathcal{D}}(n)$ and $\mathsf{faGame}_{\ell,\mathsf{PKE},\mathcal{D}}(n)$.

6 Relation Between ℓ-Receiver/Sender-AME

6.1 ℓ-Receiver-Anamorphic Encryption (ℓ-Receiver-AME)

Definition 9 (ℓ-Receiver-Anamorphic Encryption). *Let* PKE *be a public key encryption scheme. We say* PKE *is ℓ-receiver-anamorphic if 1) there exists a receiver-anamorphic extension* (aSetup, aGen, aEnc, aDec)

- aSetup(1^n) *takes as input* 1^n, *and produces the public parameter* pp;
- aGen(pp) *takes as input* pp, *and produces ℓ anamorphic public/secret key pairs* $(\mathrm{apk}_i,\mathrm{ask}_i)_{i\in[\ell]}$, *and a double key* dkey;
- aEnc(dkey, M, $\bar{\mathtt{m}}$) *takes as input the double key* dkey, *a normal plaintext set* $\mathtt{M} = \{\mathtt{m}_i\}_{i\in[\ell]}$ *and an anamorphic plaintext* $\bar{\mathtt{m}}$, *and produces an anamorphic ciphertext set* $\mathtt{ACT} = \{\mathtt{act}_i\}_{i\in[\ell]}$;
- aDec(dkey, ACT) *takes as input the double key* dkey *and the ciphertext set* ACT, *and returns the anamorphic plaintext* $\bar{\mathtt{m}}$,

and for any $\mathtt{M} \in \mathcal{M}^\ell$, *any* $\bar{\mathtt{m}} \in \overline{\mathcal{M}}$,

$$\Pr\left[\mathsf{aDec}(\mathrm{dkey},\mathtt{ACT}) \neq \bar{\mathtt{m}} : \begin{array}{c} \mathrm{pp} \leftarrow_\$ \mathsf{aSetup}(1^n) \\ ((\mathrm{apk}_i,\mathrm{ask}_i)_{i\in[\ell]},\mathrm{dkey}) \leftarrow_\$ \mathsf{aGen}(\mathrm{pp}) \\ \mathtt{ACT} \leftarrow_\$ \mathsf{aEnc}(\mathrm{dkey},\mathtt{M},\bar{\mathtt{m}}) \end{array}\right] \leq \mathsf{negl}(n).$$

Definition 10 (Secure ℓ-Receiver-AME). *Let* PKE *be an ℓ-receiver-AME with extension* (aSetup, aGen, aEnc, aDec). *We say* PKE *is a secure ℓ-receiver-AME if following conditions hold,*

- PKE *is CPA secure;*
- *For any plaintext set* $\widehat{M} \in \mathcal{M}^\ell$, $\mathsf{fAME}_{\widehat{M}} = (\mathsf{aSetup}, \mathsf{aGen}_{2\ell+1}, \mathsf{aEnc}_{1,\widehat{M}}, \mathsf{aDec})$ *is a symmetric encryption scheme, where* aGen_i *denotes selecting the ith component of the triplet generated by* aGen *as the output,* $\mathsf{aEnc}_{1,\widehat{M}}$ *denotes running* aEnc *with the normal plaintext set* $\mathtt{M} = \widehat{M}$;
- *For any PPT adversary* $\mathcal{D}$,

$$|\Pr[\mathsf{nGame}_{\ell,\mathsf{PKE},\mathcal{D}}(n) = 1] - \Pr[\mathsf{faGame}_{\ell,\mathsf{PKE},\mathcal{D}}(n) = 1]| \leq \mathsf{negl}(n).$$

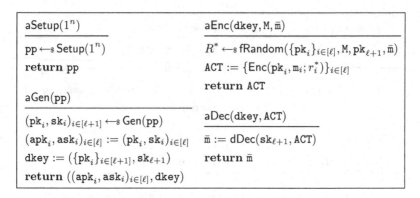

Fig. 10. Receiver-anamorphic extension built on sender-anamorphic extension.

6.2 ℓ-Sender-AME $\Rightarrow$ ℓ-Receiver-AME

Theorem 9. *Let* PKE *be a strongly secure ℓ-sender-AME with anamorphic extension* (fRandom, dDec) *and duplicate plaintext space* $\overline{\mathcal{M}}$. PKE *is also a secure ℓ-receiver-AME with extension in Fig. 10 and anamorphic plaintext space* $\overline{\mathcal{M}}$.

Proof. One can easily verify that the correctness of ℓ-sender-AME implies the correctness of ℓ-receiver-AME, and, for any plaintext set $\widehat{M} \in \mathcal{M}^\ell$, $\mathsf{fAME}_{\widehat{M}} =$ (aSetup, aGen$_{2\ell+1}$, aEnc$_{1,\widehat{M}}$, aDec) is a symmetric encryption scheme.

Next, we prove that for any PPT adversary $\mathcal{D}$, the advantage of distinguishing games nGame$_{\ell,\mathsf{PKE},\mathcal{D}}(n)$ and faGame$_{\ell,\mathsf{PKE},\mathcal{D}}(n)$ in Fig. 9 is negligible.

We show how to build an adversary $\mathcal{B}$ distinguishing with games Ideal$_{\ell,\mathsf{PKE},\mathcal{B}}(n)$ and Real$^{\mathsf{fRandom}}_{\ell,\mathsf{PKE},\mathcal{B}}(n)$. In specific, $\mathcal{B}$ receives (pp, FPK, FSK, dpk) and can makes encryption queries with (FM, dm). The encryption oracle encrypts FM with $(r_i)_{i\in[\ell]} \leftarrow_\$ \mathcal{R}$ in Ideal$_{\ell,\mathsf{PKE},\mathcal{B}}(n)$, and $R^* \leftarrow_\$ \mathsf{fRandom}$(FPK, FM, dpk, dm) in Real$^{\mathsf{fRandom}}_{\ell,\mathsf{PKE},\mathcal{B}}(n)$.

$\mathcal{B}$ forwards (pp, FPK, FSK) to $\mathcal{D}$. To answer the encryption query (M, $\bar{\mathsf{m}}$) from $\mathcal{D}$, $\mathcal{B}$ queries its encryption oracle with (M, $\bar{\mathsf{m}}$) and returns the ciphertexts to $\mathcal{D}$. The simulation is perfect. If the encryption oracle encrypts M with $(r_i)_{i\in[\ell]} \leftarrow_\$ \mathcal{R}$, $\mathcal{B}$ simulates nGame$_{\ell,\mathsf{PKE},\mathcal{D}}(n)$ for $\mathcal{D}$. Otherwise, the encryption oracle encrypts M with $R^* \leftarrow_\$ \mathsf{fRandom}$(FPK, M, dpk, $\bar{\mathsf{m}}$), $\mathcal{B}$ simulates faGame$_{\ell,\mathsf{PKE},\mathcal{D}}(n)$ for $\mathcal{D}$. $\square$

Obviously, not every ℓ-receiver-AME is also ℓ-sender-anamorphic. In particular, the construction of ℓ-receiver-AME might rely on the anamorphic setup and key generation algorithms, or the double key for anamorphic encryption and decryption algorithms might cannot be parsed as a public/secret key pair.

7 Relation Between ℓ-Sender-AME and Public-Key Stegosystem

In this section, we recall the definition of public-key stegosystem and its security in [32], and rigorously prove that a strongly secure ℓ-sender-AME implies a secure public-key stegosystem.

7.1 Public-Key Stegosystem

Definition 11 (Public-Key Stegosystem [32]). *A public-key stegosystem* PKS *consists of four algorithms* $(\mathsf{sSetup}, \mathsf{sGen}, \mathsf{sEnc}, \mathsf{sDec})$

- $\mathsf{sSetup}(1^n)$ *takes as input* 1^n, *and returns the public parameter* pp;
- $\mathsf{sGen}(\mathsf{pp})$ *takes as input* pp, *and returns a public/secret key pair* $(\mathsf{pk}, \mathsf{sk})$;
- $\mathsf{sEnc}(\mathsf{pk}, \mathsf{m}, \mathsf{h})$ *takes* pk, *a string* $\mathsf{m} \in \{0, 1\}^*$ *(i.e., the hiddentext) and a history* h, *and returns a list of documents* $\mathsf{ST} = (\mathsf{st}_1, \mathsf{st}_2, \cdots, \mathsf{st}_\ell)$ *(i.e., the stegotext). Also, it can access a oracle* $M(\mathsf{h})$ *that samples a document according to a channel distribution* $\mathcal{C}_\mathsf{h}$;
- $\mathsf{sDec}(\mathsf{sk}, \mathsf{ST}, \mathsf{h})$ *takes* sk, $\mathsf{ST} = (\mathsf{st}_1, \mathsf{st}_2, \cdots, \mathsf{st}_\ell)$ *and a history* h, *and returns the string* m.

and for any polynomial $\ell(n)$, *any* $\mathsf{m} \in \{0, 1\}^{\ell(n)}$,

$$\Pr\left[\mathsf{sDec}(\mathsf{sk}, \mathsf{ST}, \mathsf{h}) \neq \mathsf{m} : \begin{array}{l} \mathsf{pp} \leftarrow_s \mathsf{sSetup}(1^n) \\ (\mathsf{pk}, \mathsf{sk}) \leftarrow_s \mathsf{sGen}(\mathsf{pp}) \\ \mathsf{ST} \leftarrow_s \mathsf{sEnc}(\mathsf{pk}, \mathsf{m}, \mathsf{h}) \end{array}\right] \leq \mathsf{negl}(n).$$

Definition 12 (CHA Security [32]). *Let* PKS $= (\mathsf{sSetup}, \mathsf{sGen}, \mathsf{sEnc}, \mathsf{sDec})$ *be a public-key stegosystem. We say* PKS *is secure against chosen hiddentext attacks (CHA secure) over channel* $\mathcal{C}$ *if for any PPT warden* $\mathcal{W}_1, \mathcal{W}_2$,

$$\left| \Pr\left[b = b' : \begin{array}{l} \mathsf{pp} \leftarrow_s \mathsf{sSetup}(1^n) \\ (\mathsf{pk}, \mathsf{sk}) \leftarrow_s \mathsf{sGen}(\mathsf{pp}) \\ (\mathsf{m}^*, \mathsf{h}^*, \mathsf{st}) \leftarrow \mathcal{W}_1^{M(\mathsf{h})}(\mathsf{pp}, \mathsf{pk}) \\ \mathsf{ST}_0 \leftarrow_s \mathsf{sEnc}(\mathsf{pk}, \mathsf{m}^*, \mathsf{h}^*) \\ \mathsf{ST}_1 \leftarrow_s \mathcal{C}_{\mathsf{h}^*}^{|\mathsf{ST}_0|} \\ b \leftarrow_s \{0, 1\} \\ b' \leftarrow \mathcal{W}_2^{M(\mathsf{h})}(\mathsf{st}, \mathsf{ST}_b) \end{array}\right] - \frac{1}{2} \right| \leq \mathsf{negl}(n).$$

7.2 ℓ-Sender-AME $\Rightarrow$ Public-Key Stegosystem

Let PKE $= (\mathsf{Setup}, \mathsf{Gen}, \mathsf{Enc}, \mathsf{Dec})$ be a PKE scheme. We define a channel $\mathcal{C}_{\mathsf{PKE},n}(\ell)$ for PKE with security parameter $n \in \mathbb{N}^+$ and $\ell = \mathsf{poly}(n)$, and specify the distributions for any history h as below.

- CASE 1: $(\mathsf{h} = \emptyset)$. $\mathcal{C}_{\mathsf{PKE},n,\mathsf{h}}(\ell)$ is the distribution of all the public parameters generated by $\mathsf{Setup}(1^n)$;
- CASE 2: $(\mathsf{h} = \mathsf{pp} \| (\mathsf{pk}_1, \mathsf{sk}_1) \| \cdots \| (\mathsf{pk}_r, \mathsf{sk}_r)$ with $r \in [0, \ell-1])$. $\mathcal{C}_{\mathsf{PKE},n,\mathsf{h}}(\ell)$ is the distribution of all the key pairs generated by $\mathsf{Gen}(\mathsf{pp})$;
- CASE 3: $(\mathsf{h} = \mathsf{pp} \| (\mathsf{pk}_1, \mathsf{sk}_1) \| \cdots \| (\mathsf{pk}_\ell, \mathsf{sk}_\ell) \| \mathsf{m}_1 \| \cdots \| \mathsf{m}_r$ with $\mathsf{m}_i \in \mathcal{M}$, $r \in [0, \ell-1])$. $\mathcal{C}_{\mathsf{PKE},n,\mathsf{h}}(\ell)$ is the uniform distribution over message space $\mathcal{M}$;
- CASE 4: $(\mathsf{h} = \mathsf{pp} \| (\mathsf{pk}_1, \mathsf{sk}_1) \| \cdots \| (\mathsf{pk}_\ell, \mathsf{sk}_\ell) \| \mathsf{m}_1 \| \cdots \| \mathsf{m}_\ell \| \mathsf{ct}_1 \| \cdots \| \mathsf{ct}_r$ with $\mathsf{m}_i \in \mathcal{M}$, $\mathsf{ct}_i \leftarrow_s \mathsf{Enc}(\mathsf{pk}_{i'}, \mathsf{m}_{i'})$, $i' = ((i-1) \bmod \ell) + 1)$. $\mathcal{C}_{\mathsf{PKE},n,\mathsf{h}}(\ell)$ is the distribution of $\mathsf{Enc}(\mathsf{pk}_{r'}, \mathsf{m}_{r'})$ where $r' = (r \bmod \ell) + 1$.

$\mathsf{sSetup}(1^n)$	$\mathsf{sEnc}(\mathbf{pk}^*, \mathbf{m}^*, \mathbf{h})$
$\mathbf{pp} \leftarrow_\$ \mathsf{PKE.Setup}(1^n)$	$\mathbf{if}\ \mathbf{h} = \emptyset :$
$\mathbf{return}\ \mathbf{pp}$	$\quad \mathbf{return}\ \mathbf{pp} \leftarrow_\$ \mathsf{PKE.Setup}(1^n)$
	$\mathbf{elseif}\ \mathbf{h} = \mathbf{pp}\|(\mathbf{pk}_1, \mathbf{sk}_1)\| \cdots \|(\mathbf{pk}_j, \mathbf{sk}_j) :$
$\mathsf{sGen}(\mathbf{pp})$	$\quad \mathbf{return}\ (\mathbf{pk}_{j+1}, \mathbf{sk}_{j+1}) \leftarrow_\$ \mathsf{PKE.Gen}(\mathbf{pp})$
$(\mathbf{pk}^*, \mathbf{sk}^*) \leftarrow_\$ \mathsf{PKE.Gen}(\mathbf{pp})$	$\mathbf{elseif}\ \mathbf{h} = \mathbf{pp}\|(\mathbf{pk}_1, \mathbf{sk}_1)\| \cdots \|(\mathbf{pk}_\ell, \mathbf{sk}_\ell)\|\mathbf{m}_1\| \cdots \|\mathbf{m}_j :$
$\mathbf{return}\ (\mathbf{pk}^*, \mathbf{sk}^*)$	$\quad \mathbf{return}\ \mathbf{m}_{j+1} \leftarrow_\$ \mathcal{M}$
	$\mathbf{elseif}\ \mathbf{h} = \mathbf{pp}\|(\mathbf{pk}_1, \mathbf{sk}_1)\| \cdots \|(\mathbf{pk}_\ell, \mathbf{sk}_\ell)\|\mathbf{m}_1\| \cdots \|\mathbf{m}_\ell\|$
$\mathsf{sDec}(\mathbf{sk}^*, \mathbf{ST}, \mathbf{h})$	$\qquad\qquad \mathbf{ct}_1\| \cdots \|\mathbf{ct}_j :$
$\mathbf{st}_1\|\mathbf{st}_2\| \cdots \|\mathbf{st}_{3\ell+1} := \mathbf{ST}$	$\quad \mathbf{if}\ j = 0 :$
$\mathbf{CT} := \{\mathbf{st}_i\}_{i \in [2\ell+2, 3\ell+1]}$	$\qquad R^* \leftarrow_\$ \mathsf{PKE.fRandom}(\mathbf{PK}, \mathbf{M}, \mathbf{pk}^*, \mathbf{m}^*)$
$\mathbf{m}^* := \mathsf{PKE.dDec}(\mathbf{sk}^*, \mathbf{CT})$	$\quad j' := (j \bmod \ell) + 1$
$\mathbf{return}\ \mathbf{m}^*$	$\quad \mathbf{return}\ \mathsf{PKE.Enc}(\mathbf{pk}_{j'}, \mathbf{m}_{j'}; r_{j'}^*)$
	$\mathbf{return}\ \bot$

Fig. 11. Generic public-key stegosystem built on ℓ-sender-AME.

Theorem 10. *Let* $\mathsf{PKE} = (\mathsf{Setup}, \mathsf{Gen}, \mathsf{Enc}, \mathsf{Dec})$ *be a strongly secure ℓ-sender-AME. The public-key stegosystem* $\mathsf{PKS} = (\mathsf{sSetup}, \mathsf{sGen}, \mathsf{sEnc}, \mathsf{sDec})$ *in Fig. 11 over channel* $\mathcal{C}_{\mathsf{PKE},n}(\ell)$ *is CHA secure.*

Proof. We demonstrate how adversary $\mathcal{A}$ distinguishes game $\mathsf{Ideal}_{\ell, \mathsf{PKE}, \mathcal{A}}(n)$ and $\mathsf{Real}_{\ell, \mathsf{PKE}, \mathcal{A}}^{\mathsf{fRandom}}(n)$ by leveraging the warden $\mathcal{W}_1$ and $\mathcal{W}_2$ in CHA security game. $\mathcal{A}$ simulates the game for $\mathcal{W}_1$ and $\mathcal{W}_2$ as follows.

$\mathcal{A}$ receives $\mathbf{pp}$, ℓ forced key pairs $\{(\mathbf{fpk}_i, \mathbf{fsk}_i)\}_{i \in [\ell]}$ and $\mathbf{dpk}$, and can make encryption queries on $(\mathbf{FM}, \mathbf{dm})$. $\mathcal{A}$ forwards $(\mathbf{pp}, \mathbf{pk})$ to $\mathcal{W}_1$ and simulates the oracle $M(\mathbf{h})$ as follows.

- If $\mathbf{h} = \emptyset$, $\mathcal{A}$ returns $\mathbf{pp}$ to $\mathcal{W}_1$;
- If $\mathbf{h} = \mathbf{pp}\|(\mathbf{pk}_1, \mathbf{sk}_1)\| \cdots \|(\mathbf{pk}_r, \mathbf{sk}_r)$ with $r \in [0, \ell-1]$, $\mathcal{A}$ returns the $(r+1)$-th forced key pair $(\mathbf{fpk}_{r+1}, \mathbf{fsk}_{r+1})$ to $\mathcal{W}_1$;
- If $\mathbf{h} = \mathbf{pp}\|(\mathbf{pk}_1, \mathbf{sk}_1)\| \cdots \|(\mathbf{pk}_\ell, \mathbf{sk}_\ell)\|\mathbf{m}_1\| \cdots \|\mathbf{m}_r$ with $r \in [0, \ell-1]$, $\mathcal{A}$ samples $\mathbf{m}_{r+1}$ uniformly from $\mathcal{M}$, and outputs $\mathbf{m}_{r+1}$;
- If $\mathbf{h} = \mathbf{pp}\|(\mathbf{pk}_1, \mathbf{sk}_1)\| \cdots \|(\mathbf{pk}_\ell, \mathbf{sk}_\ell)\|\mathbf{m}_1\| \cdots \|\mathbf{m}_\ell\|\mathbf{ct}_1\| \cdots \|\mathbf{ct}_r$ with $r \geq 0$, $\mathcal{A}$ computes $\mathbf{ct}_{r+1} \leftarrow_\$ \mathsf{PKE.Enc}(\mathbf{pk}_{r'}, \mathbf{m}_{r'})$, where $r' = (r \bmod \ell) + 1$, and outputs $\mathbf{ct}_{r+1}$.

One can note that $\mathcal{A}$ simulates the channel $\mathcal{C}_{\mathsf{PKE},n}(\ell)$ perfectly. After receiving $(\mathbf{m}^*, \mathbf{h}^*)$ from $\mathcal{W}_1$, $\mathcal{A}$ simulates the challenge stegotext $\mathbf{ST}_b$ as follows.

- If $\mathbf{h}^* = \emptyset$, $\mathcal{A}$ outputs $\mathbf{pp}$;
- If $\mathbf{h}^* = \mathbf{pp}\|(\mathbf{pk}_1, \mathbf{sk}_1)\| \cdots \|(\mathbf{pk}_r, \mathbf{sk}_r)$ with $r \in [0, \ell-1]$, $\mathcal{A}$ outputs the $(r+1)$-th forced key pair $(\mathbf{fpk}_{r+1}, \mathbf{fsk}_{r+1})$;

– If $h^* = pp\|(pk_1, sk_1)\| \cdots \|(pk_\ell, sk_\ell)\|m_1\| \cdots \|m_r$ with $r \in [0, \ell-1]$, $\mathcal{A}$ samples m_{r+1} uniformly from $\mathcal{M}$, and outputs m_{r+1};

– If $h^* = pp\|(pk_1, sk_1)\| \cdots \|(pk_\ell, sk_\ell)\|m_1\| \cdots \|m_\ell\|ct_1\| \cdots \|ct_r$ with $r \geq 0$: If $(r \bmod \ell) = 0$, $\mathcal{A}$ queries the encryption oracle on $M := \{m_i\}_{i \in [\ell]}$ and m^*, saves the ciphertext set CT and outputs the first ciphertext ct_1. Otherwise, $\mathcal{A}$ only needs to output the r'-th ciphertext $ct_{r'}$ where $r' = (r \bmod \ell) + 1$.

If $\mathcal{A}$ is in game $\mathsf{Ideal}_{\ell, \mathsf{PKE}, \mathcal{A}}(n)$, then ST_b is sampled from $\mathcal{C}_{\mathsf{PKE}, n, h^*}(\ell)$. If $\mathcal{A}$ is in game $\mathsf{Real}^{\mathsf{fRandom}}_{\ell, \mathsf{PKE}, \mathcal{A}}(n)$, then ST_b is the output of $\mathsf{sEnc}(pk, m^*, h^*)$. $\qquad\square$

We remark that not every public-key stegosystem implies an ℓ-sender-AME. In particular, the chosen-stegotext secure construction in [32] also uses the secret key of sender (i.e., Alice) to generate the stegotexts, while the input of algorithm fRandom in ℓ-sender-AME only involves public keys and plaintexts.

8   Relation Between AME and Generalized ASA on PKE

8.1   ASA Model for PKE

In this section, we extend the generalized ASA model in [8] for PKE. Unlike symmetric encryption, PKE uses *public key* to encrypt messages, and it is impossible to extract the corresponding secret key from the ciphertext. Hence, one natural goal of ASA against PKE is recovering underlying plaintext or other subliminal messages from the ciphertext.

Definition 13 (Generalized ASA on PKE). *Let* $\mathsf{PKE} = (\mathsf{Setup}, \mathsf{Gen}, \mathsf{Enc}, \mathsf{Dec})$ *be a PKE. For* $pp \leftarrow_s \mathsf{PKE.Setup}(1^n)$ *and* $(pk, sk) \leftarrow_s \mathsf{PKE.Gen}(pp)$*, an ASA on* PKE *is* $\mathsf{ASA} = (\mathsf{Gen}, \mathsf{Enc}, \mathsf{Ext})$.

– $\mathsf{ASA.Gen}(pp)$ *returns a subversion key* skey.
– $\mathsf{ASA.Enc}(\mathsf{skey}, \mathsf{sm}, \mathsf{pk}, \mathsf{m}, \tau)$ *takes as input* skey, *a subliminal message* $\mathsf{sm} \in \overline{\mathcal{M}}$*, a public key* pk, *an encryption message* $\mathsf{m} \in \mathcal{M}$ *and a (possible) state* τ*, returns a ciphertext* ct *and updates the state* τ.
– $\mathsf{ASA.Ext}(\mathsf{skey}, \{ct_i\}_{i \in [\ell]})$ *takes as input* skey *and a ciphertext set* $\{ct_i\}_{i \in [\ell]}$ *with* $\ell = \mathsf{poly}(n)$*, and returns the subliminal message* sm.

We remark that when message sm is set as plaintext m, the goal of ASA is recovering the plaintext from ciphertext. In some cases, it is unlikely to encode all the bits of message sm into one ciphertext ct. Instead, adversary takes advantage of the fact that the user would invoke algorithm ASA.Enc multiple times to embed the message sm into a bunch of ciphertexts $\{ct_i\}_{i \in [\ell]}$, and the subverted encryption algorithm can be denoted as below.

$$\mathsf{ASA.Enc}^\ell(\mathsf{skey}, \mathsf{sm}, \mathsf{PK} := \{pk_i\}_{i \in [\ell]}, \mathsf{M} := \{m_i\}_{i \in [\ell]})$$

1 : $\tau := \varepsilon$
2 : **for** $i \in [\ell]$ **do** :
3 : $\qquad ct_i \leftarrow_s \mathsf{ASA.Enc}(\mathsf{skey}, \mathsf{sm}, pk_i, m_i, \tau)$
4 : **return** $\mathsf{CT} := \{ct_i\}_{i \in [\ell]}$

$\text{Undet}_{\text{ASA},\mathcal{D}}(n)$	$\text{ENC}(\text{M}, \text{sm})$
$\text{pp} \leftarrow_s \text{PKE.Setup}(1^n)$	**if** $b = 0$:
$(\text{pk}_i, \text{sk}_i)_{i \in [\ell]} \leftarrow_s \text{PKE.Gen}(\text{pp})$	**for** $i \in [\ell]$ **do** :
$\text{skey} \leftarrow_s \text{ASA.Gen}(\text{pp})$	$\text{ct}_i \leftarrow_s \text{PKE.Enc}(\text{pk}_i, \text{m}_i)$
$\overline{(\text{psk}, \text{ssk}) \leftarrow_s \text{ASA.Gen}(\text{pp})}$	$\text{CT} := \{\text{ct}_i\}_{i \in [\ell]}$
$b \leftarrow_s \{0,1\}$	**else**
$b' \leftarrow \mathcal{D}^{\text{ENC}(\cdot,\cdot)}(\text{pp}, \text{PK}, \text{SK})$	$\text{CT} \leftarrow_s \text{ASA.Enc}^\ell(\text{skey}, \text{sm}, \text{PK}, \text{M})$
$\overline{b' \leftarrow \mathcal{D}^{\text{ENC}(\cdot,\cdot,\cdot)}(\text{pp}, \text{PK}, \text{SK}, \text{psk})}$	$\overline{\text{CT} \leftarrow_s \text{ASA.Enc}^\ell(\text{psk}, \text{sm}, \text{PK}, \text{M})}$
return $[b = b']$	**return** CT

Fig. 12. Definition of game $\text{Undet}_{\text{ASA},\mathcal{D}}(n)$.

We say ASA is *asymmetric* if 1) subversion key skey can be parsed as a subversion key pair (psk, ssk), 2) ASA.Enc takes public subversion key psk as input instead of skey and 3) ASA.Ext takes secret subversion key ssk as input instead of skey. The generalized ASA in Definition 13 can be regarded as *symmetric*. Clearly, asymmetric ASA is a special case of symmetric ASA. The definitions of properties for these two types of ASAs are slightly different.

To capture the recovery of subliminal message, we present the definition of recoverability as follows. In particular, for asymmetric ASA, only public subversion key psk is hardwired into the subverted encryption algorithm ASA.Enc, and extracting subliminal message requires secret subversion key ssk.

Definition 14 (Recoverability). *Let* ASA = (Gen, Enc, Ext) *be an ASA on* PKE = (Setup, Gen, Enc, Dec). *We say* ASA *satisfies recoverability if for any* $\text{M} \in \mathcal{M}^\ell$ *and any* $\text{sm} \in \overline{\mathcal{M}}$,

$$\Pr\left[\begin{array}{c|c} \begin{array}{c} \text{ASA.Ext}(\text{skey}, \text{CT}) \neq \text{sm} \\ \overline{\text{ASA.Ext}(\text{ssk}, \text{CT}) \neq \text{sm}} \end{array} & \begin{array}{c} \text{pp} \leftarrow_s \text{PKE.Setup}(1^n) \\ \text{skey} \leftarrow_s \text{ASA.Gen}(\text{pp}) \\ \overline{(\text{psk}, \text{ssk}) \leftarrow_s \text{ASA.Gen}(\text{pp})} \\ (\text{pk}_i, \text{sk}_i)_{i \in [\ell]} \leftarrow_s \text{PKE.Gen}(\text{pp}) \\ \text{CT} \leftarrow_s \text{ASA.Enc}^\ell(\text{skey}, \text{sm}, \text{PK}, \text{M}) \\ \overline{\text{CT} \leftarrow_s \text{ASA.Enc}^\ell(\text{psk}, \text{sm}, \text{PK}, \text{M})} \end{array} \end{array}\right] \leq \text{negl}(n).$$

For clarity, the differences of recoverability for asymmetric ASA are marked with dashed boxes.

The stealthy feature of ASA on PKE requires that the ordinary users cannot distinguish the honest or subverted implementation of underlying encryption algorithm with overwhelming advantage (Fig. 12).

Definition 15 (Undetectability). *Let* ASA = (Gen, Enc, Ext) *be an ASA on* PKE = (Setup, Gen, Enc, Dec). *We say* ASA *satisfies secret undetectability if for any PPT detector* $\mathcal{D}$, *the advantage of* $\mathcal{D}$ *in game* $\text{Undet}_{\text{ASA},\mathcal{D}}(n)$ *is negligible.*

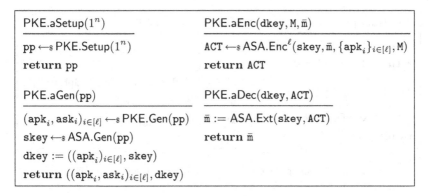

Fig. 13. Generic ℓ-receiver-AME built on ASA against PKE.

If detector $\mathcal{D}$ in game $\mathsf{Undet}_{\mathsf{ASA},\mathcal{D}}(n)$ is not provided with $\mathsf{SK} = \{\mathsf{sk}_i\}_{i \in [\ell]}$, we say ASA satisfies public undetectability.

8.2 Symmetric ASA on PKE $\Rightarrow$ ℓ-Receiver-AME

Theorem 11. Let $\mathsf{ASA} = (\mathsf{Gen}, \mathsf{Enc}, \mathsf{Ext})$ be an ASA on CPA-secure $\mathsf{PKE} = (\mathsf{Setup}, \mathsf{Gen}, \mathsf{Enc}, \mathsf{Dec})$ with subliminal message space $\overline{\mathcal{M}}$. Then, PKE is a secure ℓ-receiver-AME with extension in Fig. 13 and anamorphic plaintext space $\overline{\mathcal{M}}$.

Proof. By the recoverability of ASA, PKE with extension in Fig. 13 is an ℓ-receiver-AME with anamorphic plaintext space $\overline{\mathcal{M}}$.

One can note that for every plaintext set $\widehat{M} \in \mathcal{M}^\ell$, $\mathsf{fAME}_{\widehat{M}}$ is a symmetric encryption scheme.

Next we prove that if ASA satisfies indistinguishability, then PKE with algorithms in Fig. 13 satisfies the third condition of secure ℓ-receiver-AME. In particular, we show how to break the indistinguishability of ASA using the adversary $\mathcal{D}$ in game $\mathsf{nGame}_{\mathsf{PKE},\mathcal{D}}(n)$ or $\mathsf{faGame}_{\mathsf{PKE},\mathcal{D}}(n)$.

Simulator $\mathcal{B}$ plays the role of detector in game $\mathsf{Undet}_{\mathsf{ASA},\mathcal{B}}(n)$ and simulates the game $\mathsf{nGame}_{\mathsf{PKE},\mathcal{D}}(n)$ or $\mathsf{faGame}_{\mathsf{PKE},\mathcal{D}}(n)$ for $\mathcal{D}$ as follows. $\mathcal{B}$ receives $(\mathsf{pp}, \mathsf{PK}, \mathsf{SK})$ and forwards them to $\mathcal{D}$. To answer the encryption query $(\mathtt{M}, \bar{\mathtt{m}})$ from $\mathcal{D}$, $\mathcal{B}$ queries its own encryption oracle on $(\mathtt{M}, \bar{\mathtt{m}})$ and returns the results to $\mathcal{D}$.

The simulation above is perfect. If $b = 0$ in game $\mathsf{Undet}_{\mathsf{ASA},\mathcal{B}}(n)$, $\mathcal{B}$ simulates $\mathsf{nGame}_{\mathsf{PKE},\mathcal{D}}(n)$ for $\mathcal{D}$; Otherwise, it simulates $\mathsf{faGame}_{\mathsf{PKE},\mathcal{D}}(n)$. $\square$

We remark that not every ℓ-receiver-AME implies an ASA on PKE. In particular, the subversion key in ASA is independent of public and secret keys, while the double key in ℓ-receiver-AME might include the secret key. Thus, it might be impossible to build algorithm Gen for ASA with algorithm aGen in ℓ-receiver-AME. A concrete example is provided in the full version.

ASA.Gen(pp)	ASA.Enc$^\ell$(skey, sm, PK, M)
(dpk, dsk) $\leftarrow_\$$ PKE.Gen(pp)	$\tau := \varepsilon$
return skey $:=$ (dpk, dsk)	**for** $i \in [\ell]$:
	$\quad r_i^* \leftarrow_\$$ PKE.fRandom$_{\mathsf{sub}}$(pk$_i$, m$_i$, dpk, sm, τ)
ASA.Ext(skey, CT)	$\quad$ ct$_i$:= PKE.Enc(pk$_i$, m$_i$; r_i^*)
sm$'$:= PKE.dDec(dsk, CT)	**return** CT := $\{$ct$_i\}_{i \in [\ell]}$
return sm$'$	

Fig. 14. Generalized ASA on PKE from ℓ-sender-AME.

8.3 ℓ-Sender-AME $\Rightarrow$ Asymmetric ASA on PKE

Note that the algorithm ASA.Enc$^\ell$ runs the subverted encryption ASA.Enc for ℓ times sequentially. To achieve this, it is required that the algorithm PKE.fRandom could be rewrote as the iteration of running (possibly stateful) sub-algorithm PKE.fRandom$_{\mathsf{sub}}$ that take as input a forced public key, a forced plaintext, a duplicate public key, a duplicate plaintext and a state (if exists), and outputs a randomness. In this case, the subverted encryption ASA.Enc runs PKE.fRandom$_{\mathsf{sub}}$ to generate randomness r_i^* and PKE.Enc to encrypt the forced plaintext m$_i$ with forced public key pk$_i$ and randomness r_i^*.

Theorem 12. *Let* PKE *be a strongly secure ℓ-sender-AME associated with algorithm* fRandom *and* dDec. *Then, there exists an asymmetric ASA on* PKE, *as shown in Fig. 14, satisfying both recoverability and secret undetectability.*

Proof. By the definition of ℓ-sender-AME, for any FM $\in \mathcal{M}^\ell$, any dm $\in \overline{\mathcal{M}}$,

$$
\Pr\left[
\begin{array}{c}
\text{PKE.dDec(dsk, CT)} \\
\neq \text{dm}
\end{array}
:
\begin{array}{l}
\text{pp} \leftarrow_\$ \text{PKE.Setup}(1^n) \\
(\text{fpk}_i, \text{fsk}_i)_{i \in [\ell]} \leftarrow_\$ \text{PKE.Gen(pp)} \\
(\text{dpk, dsk}) \leftarrow_\$ \text{PKE.Gen(pp)} \\
R^* \leftarrow_\$ \text{PKE.fRandom(FPK, FM, dpk, dm)} \\
\text{CT} := \{\text{PKE.Enc(fpk}_i, \text{fm}_i; r_i^*)\}_{i \in [\ell]}
\end{array}
\right] \leq \mathsf{negl}(n)
$$

According to the description of ASA in Fig. 14, one can note that the following inequality also holds for any M $\in \mathcal{M}^\ell$ and any sm $\in \overline{\mathcal{M}}$.

$$
\Pr\left[
\text{ASA.Ext(skey, CT)} \neq \text{sm}
:
\begin{array}{l}
\text{pp} \leftarrow_\$ \text{PKE.Setup}(1^n) \\
(\text{pk}_i, \text{sk}_i)_{i \in [\ell]} \leftarrow_\$ \text{PKE.Gen(pp)} \\
\text{skey} \leftarrow_\$ \text{ASA.Gen(pp)} \\
\text{CT} \leftarrow_\$ \text{ASA.Enc}^\ell(\text{skey, sm, PK, M})
\end{array}
\right] \leq \mathsf{negl}(n).
$$

To prove the secret undetectability of ASA, we demonstrate how adversary $\mathcal{A}$ distinguishes game $\mathsf{Ideal}_{\ell, \mathsf{PKE}, \mathcal{A}}(n)$ and $\mathsf{Real}^{\mathsf{fRandom}}_{\ell, \mathsf{PKE}, \mathcal{A}}(n)$ in Fig. 2 by leveraging the detector $\mathcal{D}$ in game $\mathsf{Undet}_{\mathsf{ASA}, \mathcal{D}}(n)$. Adversary $\mathcal{A}$ plays the role of challenger for $\mathcal{D}$ as follows.

$\mathcal{A}$ receives pp, ℓ forced public/secret key pairs $\{(\mathbf{fpk}_i, \mathbf{fsk}_i)\}_{i\in[\ell]}$ and duplicate public key $\mathbf{dpk}$, and can make encryption query for normal plaintext set $\mathtt{M} = \{\mathtt{m}_i\}_{i\in[\ell]}$ and anamorphic plaintext $\bar{\mathtt{m}}$. $\mathcal{A}$ forwards $(\mathsf{pp}, \mathsf{FPK} := \{\mathbf{fpk}_i\}_{i\in[\ell]}, \mathsf{FSK} := \{\mathbf{fsk}_i\}_{i\in[\ell]}, \mathbf{dpk})$ to $\mathcal{D}$ and answers the encryption query from $\mathcal{D}$ with the ciphertexts generated by the oracle. If $\mathcal{A}$ is in game $\mathsf{Ideal}_{\ell,\mathsf{PKE},\mathcal{A}}(n)$, then $\mathcal{A}$ simulates the game $\mathsf{Undet}_{\mathsf{ASA},\mathcal{D}}(n)$ with $b = 0$. Otherwise, $\mathcal{A}$ is in game $\mathsf{Real}_{\ell,\mathsf{PKE},\mathcal{A}}^{\mathsf{fRandom}}(n)$ and simulates the game $\mathsf{Undet}_{\mathsf{ASA},\mathcal{D}}(n)$ with $b = 1$. $\qquad\square$

Finally, we remark that not every asymmetric ASA on PKE directly implies that the underlying PKE is an ℓ-sender-AME. In particular, when the generation of subversion key pair in asymmetric ASA is different from the key generation of PKE, we might be unable to construct coin-toss faking algorithm fRandom using the idea of this ASA. A concrete example is provided in the full version.

Acknowledgements. We would like to thank all anonymous reviewers for their valuable comments. This work is supported in part by the National Natural Science Foundation of China (Grant No. 62122092, No. 62202485, No. 62032005).

References

1. Abdalla, M., Bellare, M., Neven, G.: Robust encryption. In: Micciancio, D. (ed.) TCC 2010. LNCS, vol. 5978, pp. 480–497. Springer, Heidelberg (2010). https://doi.org/10.1007/978-3-642-11799-2_28
2. Ateniese, G., Magri, B., Venturi, D.: Subversion-resilient signature schemes. In: Proceedings of the 22nd ACM SIGSAC Conference on Computer and Communications Security, pp. 364–375 (2015)
3. Backes, M., Cachin, C.: Public-key steganography with active attacks. In: Kilian, J. (ed.) TCC 2005. LNCS, vol. 3378, pp. 210–226. Springer, Heidelberg (2005). https://doi.org/10.1007/978-3-540-30576-7_12
4. Banfi, F., Gegier, K., Hirt, M., Maurer, U.: Anamorphic encryption, revisited. Cryptology ePrint Archive, Paper 2023/249 (2023)
5. Bellare, M., Jaeger, J., Kane, D.: Mass-surveillance without the state: strongly undetectable algorithm-substitution attacks. In: Proceedings of the 22nd ACM SIGSAC Conference on Computer and Communications Security, pp. 1431–1440 (2015)
6. Bellare, M., Paterson, K.G., Rogaway, P.: Security of symmetric encryption against mass surveillance. In: Garay, J.A., Gennaro, R. (eds.) CRYPTO 2014. LNCS, vol. 8616, pp. 1–19. Springer, Heidelberg (2014). https://doi.org/10.1007/978-3-662-44371-2_1
7. Bellare, M., Rogaway, P.: Optimal asymmetric encryption. In: De Santis, A. (ed.) EUROCRYPT 1994. LNCS, vol. 950, pp. 92–111. Springer, Heidelberg (1995). https://doi.org/10.1007/BFb0053428
8. Berndt, S., Liśkiewicz, M.: Algorithm substitution attacks from a steganographic perspective. In: Proceedings of the 2017 ACM SIGSAC Conference on Computer and Communications Security, pp. 1649–1660 (2017)
9. Bernstein, D.J., Hamburg, M., Krasnova, A., Lange, T.: Elligator: elliptic-curve points indistinguishable from uniform random strings. In: Proceedings of the 2013 ACM SIGSAC Conference on Computer & Communications Security, pp. 967–980 (2013)

10. Chen, R., Huang, X., Yung, M.: Subvert KEM to break DEM: practical algorithm-substitution attacks on public-key encryption. In: Moriai, S., Wang, H. (eds.) ASIACRYPT 2020. LNCS, vol. 12492, pp. 98–128. Springer, Cham (2020). https://doi.org/10.1007/978-3-030-64834-3_4

11. Cramer, R., Shoup, V.: Universal hash proofs and a paradigm for adaptive chosen ciphertext secure public-key encryption. In: Knudsen, L.R. (ed.) EUROCRYPT 2002. LNCS, vol. 2332, pp. 45–64. Springer, Heidelberg (2002). https://doi.org/10.1007/3-540-46035-7_4

12. Degabriele, J.P., Farshim, P., Poettering, B.: A more cautious approach to security against mass surveillance. In: Leander, G. (ed.) FSE 2015. LNCS, vol. 9054, pp. 579–598. Springer, Heidelberg (2015). https://doi.org/10.1007/978-3-662-48116-5_28

13. ElGamal, T.: A public key cryptosystem and a signature scheme based on discrete logarithms. IEEE Trans. Inf. Theory **31**(4), 469–472 (1985)

14. Gentry, C., Peikert, C., Vaikuntanathan, V.: Trapdoors for hard lattices and new cryptographic constructions. In: Proceedings of the Fortieth Annual ACM Symposium on Theory of Computing, pp. 197–206 (2008)

15. Goldwasser, S., Micali, S.: Probabilistic encryption. J. Comput. Syst. Sci. **28**(2), 270–299 (1984)

16. Golle, P., Jakobsson, M., Juels, A., Syverson, P.: Universal re-encryption for mixnets. In: Okamoto, T. (ed.) CT-RSA 2004. LNCS, vol. 2964, pp. 163–178. Springer, Cham (2004). https://doi.org/10.1007/978-3-540-24660-2_14

17. Hofheinz, D., Kiltz, E.: Secure hybrid encryption from weakened key encapsulation. In: Menezes, A. (ed.) CRYPTO 2007. LNCS, vol. 4622, pp. 553–571. Springer, Heidelberg (2007). https://doi.org/10.1007/978-3-540-74143-5_31

18. Hopper, N.J., Langford, J., von Ahn, L.: Provably secure steganography. In: Yung, M. (ed.) CRYPTO 2002. LNCS, vol. 2442, pp. 77–92. Springer, Heidelberg (2002). https://doi.org/10.1007/3-540-45708-9_6

19. Horel, T., Park, S., Richelson, S., Vaikuntanathan, V.: How to subvert backdoored encryption: Security against adversaries that decrypt all ciphertexts. In: 10th Innovations in Theoretical Computer Science Conference (ITCS 2019). Schloss Dagstuhl-Leibniz-Zentrum fuer Informatik (2018)

20. Kurosawa, K., Desmedt, Y.: A new paradigm of hybrid encryption scheme. In: Franklin, M. (ed.) CRYPTO 2004. LNCS, vol. 3152, pp. 426–442. Springer, Heidelberg (2004). https://doi.org/10.1007/978-3-540-28628-8_26

21. Kutylowski, M., Persiano, G., Phan, D.H., Yung, M., Zawada, M.: Anamorphic signatures: Secrecy from a dictator who only permits authentication! Cryptology ePrint Archive, Paper 2023/356 (2023)

22. Kutylowski, M., Persiano, G., Phan, D.H., Yung, M., Zawada, M.: The self-anticensorship nature of encryption: On the prevalence of anamorphic cryptography. Cryptology ePrint Archive, Paper 2023/434 (2023)

23. Möller, B.: A public-key encryption scheme with pseudo-random ciphertexts. In: Samarati, P., Ryan, P., Gollmann, D., Molva, R. (eds.) ESORICS 2004. LNCS, vol. 3193, pp. 335–351. Springer, Heidelberg (2004). https://doi.org/10.1007/978-3-540-30108-0_21

24. Naor, M., Yung, M.: Public-key cryptosystems provably secure against chosen ciphertext attacks. In: Proceedings of the Twenty-Second Annual ACM Symposium on Theory of Computing, pp. 427–437 (1990)

25. Paillier, P.: Public-key cryptosystems based on composite degree residuosity classes. In: Stern, J. (ed.) EUROCRYPT 1999. LNCS, vol. 1592, pp. 223–238. Springer, Heidelberg (1999). https://doi.org/10.1007/3-540-48910-X_16

26. Persiano, G., Phan, D.H., Yung, M.: Anamorphic encryption: private communication against a dictator. In: Advances in Cryptology-EUROCRYPT 2022: 41st Annual International Conference on the Theory and Applications of Cryptographic Techniques, Proceedings, Part II, pp. 34–63. Springer, Cham (2022). https://doi.org/10.1007/978-3-031-07085-3_2

27. Prabhakaran, M., Rosulek, M.: Rerandomizable RCCA encryption. In: Menezes, A. (ed.) CRYPTO 2007. LNCS, vol. 4622, pp. 517–534. Springer, Heidelberg (2007). https://doi.org/10.1007/978-3-540-74143-5_29

28. Regev, O.: On lattices, learning with errors, random linear codes, and cryptography. J. ACM (JACM) 56(6), 1–40 (2009)

29. Russell, A., Tang, Q., Yung, M., Zhou, H.S.: Generic semantic security against a kleptographic adversary. In: Proceedings of the 2017 ACM SIGSAC Conference on Computer and Communications Security, pp. 907–922 (2017)

30. Simmons, G.J.: The prisoners' problem and the subliminal channel. In: Advances in Cryptology: Proceedings of Crypto 83, pp. 51–67. Springer (1984)

31. Tibouchi, M.: Elligator squared: uniform points on elliptic curves of prime order as uniform random strings. In: Christin, N., Safavi-Naini, R. (eds.) FC 2014. LNCS, vol. 8437, pp. 139–156. Springer, Heidelberg (2014). https://doi.org/10.1007/978-3-662-45472-5_10

32. von Ahn, L., Hopper, N.J.: Public-key steganography. In: Cachin, C., Camenisch, J.L. (eds.) EUROCRYPT 2004. LNCS, vol. 3027, pp. 323–341. Springer, Heidelberg (2004). https://doi.org/10.1007/978-3-540-24676-3_20

33. Wang, Y., Chen, R., Yang, G., Huang, X., Wang, B., Yung, M.: Receiver-anonymity in rerandomizable RCCA-secure cryptosystems resolved. In: Malkin, T., Peikert, C. (eds.) CRYPTO 2021. LNCS, vol. 12828, pp. 270–300. Springer, Cham (2021). https://doi.org/10.1007/978-3-030-84259-8_10

34. Young, A., Yung, M.: Kleptography: using cryptography against cryptography. In: Fumy, W. (ed.) EUROCRYPT 1997. LNCS, vol. 1233, pp. 62–74. Springer, Heidelberg (1997). https://doi.org/10.1007/3-540-69053-0_6

35. Young, A., Yung, M.: The prevalence of kleptographic attacks on discrete-log based cryptosystems. In: Kaliski, B.S. (ed.) CRYPTO 1997. LNCS, vol. 1294, pp. 264–276. Springer, Heidelberg (1997). https://doi.org/10.1007/BFb0052241

36. Young, A., Yung, M.: Kleptography from standard assumptions and applications. In: Garay, J.A., De Prisco, R. (eds.) SCN 2010. LNCS, vol. 6280, pp. 271–290. Springer, Heidelberg (2010). https://doi.org/10.1007/978-3-642-15317-4_18

Efficient Secure Storage with Version Control and Key Rotation

Long Chen[1], Hui Guo[2], Ya-Nan Li[3(✉)], and Qiang Tang[3]

[1] Institute of Software Chinese Academy of Sciences, Beijing, China
chenlong@iscas.ac.cn
[2] The State Key Laboratory of Cryptology, Beijing, China
[3] The University of Sydney, Sydney, Australia
{yanan.li,qiang.tang}@sydney.edu.au

Abstract. Periodic key rotation is a widely used technique to enhance key compromise resilience. Updatable encryption (UE) schemes provide an efficient approach to key rotation, ensuring post-compromise security for both confidentiality and integrity. However, these UE techniques cannot be directly applied to frequently updated databases due to the risk of a malicious server inducing the client to accept an outdated version of a file instead of the latest one.

To address this issue, we propose a scheme called Updatable Secure Storage (USS), which provides a secure and key updatable solution for dynamic databases. USS ensures both data confidentiality and integrity, even in the presence of key compromises. By using efficient key rotation and file update procedures, the communication costs of these operations are independent of the size of the database. This makes USS particularly well-suited for managing large and frequently updated databases with secure version control. Unlike existing UE schemes, the integrity provided by USS holds even when the server learns the current secret key and intentionally violates the key update protocol.

Keywords: Vector commitment · Updatable encryption · Cloud storage

1 Introduction

An increasing number of companies, government bodies, and personal users are choosing to store their data on the cloud instead of local devices. However, as a public infrastructure, frequent data breaches from the cloud have been reported. One potential mitigation strategy is to allow users to upload encrypted data and keep the decryption key locally. However, even with encryption mechanisms in place, there is still a risk that users' decryption keys may become compromised over time.

To address this issue, it is widely acknowledged and implemented in the industry to periodically refresh the secret key used to protect the data and

J. Guo and R. Steinfeld (Eds.): ASIACRYPT 2023, LNCS 14443, pp. 168–198, 2023.
https://doi.org/10.1007/978-981-99-8736-8_6

to update the corresponding ciphertext in the cloud. For example, the Payment Card Industry Data Security Standard (PCI DSS) [6, 13] requires credit card data to be stored in encrypted form and mandates key rotation, whereby encrypted data is regularly refreshed from an old to a newly generated key. This strategy has also been adopted by many cloud storage providers, such as Google and Amazon [12]. By regularly refreshing encryption keys, the risk of data compromise can be significantly reduced. This approach ensures that even if a decryption key is compromised, it will only affect a limited amount of data that was encrypted with that key. Furthermore, this strategy is relatively easy to implement and can be automated, making it an effective way to improve cloud security.

While standardized encryption tools are available, facilitating key rotation requires careful consideration. A naive solution is to have the client download all encrypted data, decrypt it, choose a new key, encrypt the data, and upload the new ciphertext to the cloud server. However, this approach is inefficient, especially for large amounts of data. To address this issue, Boneh et al. [4] proposed a new primitive called updatable encryption (UE) for efficiently updating ciphertexts with a new key. Everspaugh et al. [12] gave a systematic study of Updatable Authenticated Encryption (UAE), especially on the key rotation on *authenticated encryption*, which is the standard practice for encryption. Standard UAE constructions can guarantee the confidentiality and integrity of the plaintext. With UAE, a client only needs to retrieve at most a short piece of information (known as the header) and generate a short update token that enables the server to re-encrypt the data from the existing ciphertext while preserving encryption security.

UAE constructions [3, 5, 9, 14, 16] are particularly appealing due to their ability to provide post-compromise security. This ensures that outsourced storage can regain its security, even in the event of a temporary client hack, as long as the system executes the update process by updating both the secret key and ciphertext. Notably, after re-encryption, adversaries cannot determine whether the data has been modified, even if they have seen both the old key and the previous version of the ciphertext.

Integrity vs. Frequent Data Update. In numerous real-world applications, such as E-commerce websites, social media platforms, financial institutions, and logistics companies, users require dynamic databases that can accommodate real-time changes in data. For instance, E-commerce websites need to manage inventory in real-time as products are added, sold, or restocked. Social media platforms must store and update user-generated content, such as posts, comments, and likes, in real-time. Financial institutions require the processing and storage of large volumes of transactional data in real-time, such as stock trades or credit card transactions. Logistics companies need to track and manage shipments in real-time as they move through the supply chain. These databases must be capable of handling continuous updates and modifications. To handle large volumes of data with varying attributes, such databases must be designed to facilitate fast data retrieval and frequent data updates.

However, despite the existence of several proposed constructions for Updatable Encryption (UE) in the literature [3,5,9,12,14], these schemes mainly focus on ensuring the confidentiality and integrity of static databases and cannot be applied directly to dynamic databases. If the client encrypts each file using traditional UE before uploading it to the server, this approach fails to ensure data integrity if the client performs data updates on the database. The main issue with this approach is that the client needs a mechanism to revoke the previous UE ciphertexts associated with outdated data stored by the untrusted server. Otherwise, the server may provide the client with an obsolete version of the file instead of the latest one. Although the client could keep track of every change locally, this contradicts the primary objective of utilizing fewer resources compared to storing the entire database locally.

A promising approach for tracking changes of all files in a database is to use vector commitment (VC), a powerful primitive proposed by Catalano and Fiore [8]. VCs enable the commitment of an ordered sequence of n values $(m_1, \ldots, m_n)$ into a concise commitment while allowing for later opening of the commitment at specific positions with a membership proof to prove that m_i is the i-th committed message. To ensure security, VCs must satisfy the position-binding property, which requires that an adversary cannot open a commitment to two different values at the same position. The size of the commitment and each opening must be independent of the vector degree. To guarantee the integrity of a dynamic database, each file could be treated as an element of the vector.

The vector commitment property, especially its support for element updates, plays a crucial role in ensuring the integrity of a dynamic database. VC has two algorithms to update the commitment and corresponding openings. The first algorithm updates a commitment Com by changing the i-th message from m_i to m_i', and results in a modified Com' containing the updated message. The second algorithm updates an opening for a message at position j with respect to Com to a new opening with respect to the new Com'. Indeed, Catalano and Fiore [8] have shown that the verifiable database with efficient updates (VDB) [1] can be constructed from the VC scheme.

Key Rotation for a Verifiable Database. Although VC can address the integrity problem of dynamic databases, its compatibility with encryption schemes featuring key rotation is not straightforward. Specifically, applying VC to commit UE ciphertexts as vector elements may result in linear communication costs with the entire storage during each key update. This is because updating the VC content requires linear communication with the updated ciphertext, which constitutes the entire content of the user's encrypted storage.

An alternative approach to reducing communication costs is to apply VC and UE directly to the plaintext, similar to the Enc-and-Mac combination of AE. In this approach, users store the UE ciphertext and VC membership proof of each file on the server while keeping the commitment locally as metadata for integrity checks. However, this construction fails to satisfy the confidentiality requirement if using a general VC without position hiding property, as the vector commitment and membership proofs could potentially leak information about the plaintexts.

Although this information leakage can be avoided by committing each file first and running VC on those commitments, it is not sufficient to achieve post-compromise security. Since the membership proofs are not updated during key rotation, an adversary may be able to learn the updated pattern of the files in each vector element. This information leakage can further reveal whether each file has been updated after the epoch has evolved, which is a critical concern for post-compromise security. Therefore, it is important to hide the information of the membership proofs, as well as the plaintext, when considering post-compromise security.

To address the information leakage of VC proofs, one possible suggestion is to encrypt the VC proofs using UE schemes as well. However, this means that updating one file would require updating all other VC proofs in the UE construction. One straightforward solution would be to retrieve all ciphertexts, decrypt them, update their contents, re-encrypt them, and then upload them. However, this approach incurs linear communication costs for each file update in relation to the entire storage. To mitigate the information leakage of the vector commitment, a desirable solution would be to have re-randomizable vector commitment that supports periodic re-randomization.

To tackle these challenges, new encryption with key rotation and vector commitment techniques are needed that can adapt to the evolving needs of dynamic databases. In a nutshell, the following question arises:

Is there an efficient method that enables the highest levels of confidentiality and integrity in a frequently updated database, while minimizing communication overhead?

1.1 Our Contributions

This paper introduces a novel primitive called updatable secure storage (short for USS), which provides a secure solution for dynamic databases with version control. The USS scheme ensures both data confidentiality and integrity, even in the event of key compromises. By using efficient key rotation and file update procedures, the communication costs of these operations are independent of the size of the database. This makes the USS scheme particularly well-suited for managing large and frequently updated databases in a secure and efficient manner. The USS scheme is built on the KEM + DEM paradigm, where the DEM part can be any UE ciphertext with IND-CPA security. This allows the USS scheme to benefit from the efficiency of existing UE schemes while also providing strong security guarantees against attacks on data confidentiality and integrity. Overall, the USS scheme provides an effective solution for secure database management in dynamic environments, where frequent data updates are necessary.

Confidentiality in the Event of Key Leakage. The USS scheme is designed to ensure basic content confidentiality even in the event of temporary key leakage or storage breach, as long as the server conducts the key rotation process in an honest manner. This process of key rotation is an essential aspect of the storage system, serving to limit the amount of data that could be compromised in the event of a key breach. More precisely, USS can guarantee the confidentiality of the data unless the attacker can learn the key and the ciphertexts in the same epoch. In more precise terms, the USS scheme can guarantee data confidentiality, unless the attacker can learn both the key and the ciphertexts within the same epoch. Hence USS scheme can effectively mitigate the impact of key breaches, as it reduces the window of opportunity for attackers to gain access to both pieces of information simultaneously.

Integrity for Dynamic Databases. The USS scheme provides strong integrity guarantees in dynamic databases, where a malicious server may attempt to deceive the client by providing an outdated version of data. More precisely, the strong integrity allows the server to be fully malicious and may not follow the protocol to behave most of the time. In contrast, existing UE schemes, such as those proposed in [3,5,9,12,14,16], assume that the server will honestly proceed with the key rotation procedure. However, this assumption is unrealistic in many scenarios, and it limits the ability of UE schemes to provide comprehensive protection against attacks on data integrity. Furthermore, while UE schemes exclude the case where an adversary forges ciphertexts after learning the current secret key, the USS scheme can guarantee data integrity even if the secret key is leaked. This is a significant advantage of the USS scheme, which offers stronger protection against a wider range of attacks.

Post-Compromise Security. The USS scheme offers post-compromise security for confidentiality. Specifically, if an adversary compromises both the secret key and storage in some epoch, they cannot gain any advantage in decrypting ciphertexts obtained in epochs after the compromisation. To capture the notion of post-compromise security, we introduce a security game called key update unlinkability. This game requires that attackers cannot distinguish whether an updated ciphertext is key updated from a previously corrupted ciphertext. Additionally, the USS scheme provides file update unlinkability, which guarantees that attackers who corrupt storage before and after a file update operation learn nothing about the update itself, such as whether the file content has changed and what the current content is. These security notions are essential for protecting sensitive data in scenarios where confidentiality is of utmost importance, such as in healthcare, finance, and government applications.

1.2   Technique Overview

Intuitively, USS can be regarded as a secure version of Github that provides secure outsourced storage and version control services even when the server is not fully trusted. USS enables users to create remote repositories on the server while keeping a secret key and a public stub on the client side. Its primary goal is to provide the best possible security under the key compromise. To this end, USS employs a periodic key rotation mechanism similar to UE schemes, which prevents an adversary from learning stored data even with a leaked key.

Unlike UE schemes, the integrity of USS relies on the public stub of the repository rather than the secret key. As long as the stub is correctly kept by the user, the server cannot deceive the user. Keeping a public stub is much easier than secretly keeping a key on the client side. Furthermore, the stub changes if any file in the repository gets updated, which makes it convenient for users to track the versions of the entire repository. Even if the server is malicious, it cannot force the client to accept an old version of a file instead of the latest one.

One possible solution is to use a vector commitment to commit to all files in the repository. The commitment value, which is the stub stored on the client side, can be updated efficiently using the vector commitment whenever there are changes to the files [8]. However, this approach raises the concern that the commitment value itself may reveal information about the repository. Another approach is to encrypt the files during updates and use a vector commitment to commit to the resulting ciphertexts. However, this approach faces the challenge that the ciphertexts may change during key updates, causing the commitment value to update accordingly. Since the new ciphertexts are computed on the server side, the client cannot update the stub locally.

An alternative solution is to use a classic commitment to commit to each file and then use a vector commitment to commit to each classic commitment value. The content of each file can then be encrypted using the updated encryption. However, this approach may raise concerns about post-compromise security. Specifically, an attacker who gains access to the server can track the membership proofs and the vector commitment value stored on the server. These values will not change if the files remain unchanged, allowing the attacker to easily determine whether any files have been modified.

Homomorphic Vector Commitment. To address this dilemma, we introduce the concept of homomorphic vector commitment (HVC), which extends the classical additive homomorphic commitment (e.g., Pedersen commitment [17]). Besides the position-binding property, HVC offers a significant advantage over existing VC constructions [2,7,8,15] by satisfying both the position hiding and homomorphic properties simultaneously. The *position hiding* property states that one cannot distinguish whether a commitment was created to a vector $(m_1, \ldots, m_n)$ or $(m'_1, \ldots, m'_n)$, even after seeing the openings of some same elements. Although many existing vector commitment constructions already satisfy the homomorphic property, we observe that augmenting them with position hiding using the hybrid methodology would destroy the homomorphic property. By contrast, HVC provides a more elegant solution that preserves both properties. Specifically, HVC allows a user to commit to a vector of values and later reveal the value at a certain position of the committed vector without revealing any information about other vector elements. Moreover, HVC supports efficient homomorphic operations on both the commitment and the openings. The detailed construction of HVC is in Sect. 4.

In our proposed USS construction, each file in the repository is represented as an entry in a vector. The commitment to this vector serves as a concise stub representing the entire repository. The binding property of HVC ensures that any changes to the files will be detected by the client, even if the stub is public and the key is leaked. The homomorphic property of HVC allows the client to efficiently update the stub by homomorphically adding a new commitment to the vector of changes whenever any file in the repository changes. Finally, the hiding property of HVC ensures that an adversary cannot learn any information about individual files from the public stub and other files' membership proofs. When entering a new epoch, the client can re-randomize the stub by homomorphically adding a commitment to the zero vector. This approach is effective because an attacker cannot distinguish between the commitment to the zero vector and to the difference vector of the new and old files, and thus cannot track whether files have been changed or not.

Homomorphic Updatable Encryption. However, the above approach alone is insufficient to guarantee post-compromise security. If an attacker gains access to the membership proof of the vector commitment, they could determine whether a file has changed over two epochs. One possible way is to wrap the vector commitment membership proofs with UE, but this approach may present additional challenges for proof updates, particularly when updating a single file. In VC, changes to one element require updates to membership proofs of all elements [10]. Therefore, all UE ciphertexts of the membership proofs must be updated with the plaintext. To ensure efficient database management, the updatable encryption scheme must enable the server to compute the membership proof update in a homomorphic manner without requiring the retrieval of the ciphertexts of the membership proof.

Thus, homomorphic updatable encryption is a critical feature for efficient database management, as it enables updates to be performed on the server side on the ciphertexts of the membership proofs without decryption. This reduces communication costs and enhances the scalability of the system. To the best of our knowledge, only one existing updatable encryption scheme, RISE [16], has homomorphic properties for plaintexts. RISE only supports the homomorphic operation by multiplying a new element. Fortunately, we discovered that the opening update of the bilinear pairing-based VC [8] also involves the multiplication of group elements. As a result, VC membership proofs could be encrypted via RISE [16] and we can leverage RISE's homomorphic property to update the encryption of the VC membership proofs.

2   Preliminary

Here we describe the hardness assumption and several primitives that will be used in our constructions.

2.1   Square-CDH Assumption

Recall the definition of bilinear groups. Let $\mathbb{G}$, $\mathbb{G}_T$ be bilinear groups of prime order p equipped with a bilinear map $e : \mathbb{G} \times \mathbb{G} \to \mathbb{G}_T$. Let $g \in \mathbb{G}$ be random generators. For an algorithm $\mathcal{B}$, define its advantage as

$$\mathrm{Adv}_{\mathcal{B}}^{\mathrm{Square\text{-}CDH}}(\lambda) = |\Pr[\mathcal{B}(g, g^a) = g^{a^2}]$$

where $a \leftarrow_{\$} \mathbb{Z}_p$ are randomly chosen. We say that the Square-CDH (Square Computational Diffie-Hellman) assumption holds, if for any probabilistic polynomial time (PPT) algorithm $\mathcal{B}$, its advantage $\mathrm{Adv}_{\mathcal{B}}^{\mathrm{Square\text{-}CDH}}(\lambda)$ is negligible in λ, where λ is the security parameter.

2.2 Updatable Encryption

Updatable encryption (UE) is a cryptographic technique that allows periodic updates of the secret key of encrypted outsourced data. The syntax of UE is defined as follows:

Definition 1 (Updatable Encryption). *The updatable encryption (UE) consists of the following six algorithms*

$$UE = (Setup, Keygen, Enc, Dec, Next, Upd).$$

- *UE.Setup(1^{λ}) is a randomized algorithm run by the client. It takes the security parameter λ as input and outputs the public parameter pp which will be shared with the server. Later all algorithms take pp as input implicitly.*
- *UE.Keygen(e) is a client-run randomized algorithm. It takes the epoch index e as input and outputs a secret key k_e for the epoch e.*
- *UE.Enc(k_e, m) is a client-run randomized algorithm. It takes the secret key k_e and the message m as inputs, and outputs the ciphertext C_e.*
- *UE.Dec(k_e, C_e) is a deterministic algorithm run by the client. It takes the secret key k_e and the ciphertext C_e as inputs, and outputs the message m or the symbol $\perp$.*
- *UE.Next(k_e, k_{e+1}) is a randomized algorithm run by the client. It takes the old secret key k_e of the last epoch and the new secret key k_{e+1} of the current epoch as inputs and outputs a re-encrypt token Δ_e or the symbol $\perp$.*
- *UE.Upd(Δ_e, C_e) is a deterministic algorithm run by the server. It takes the re-encrypt token Δ_e and the ciphertext C_e as inputs, and outputs a new ciphertext C_{e+1} under the secret key k_{e+1} or the symbol $\perp$.*

The correctness of an updatable encryption scheme ensures that an update of a valid ciphertext C_e from epoch e to $e+1$ leads to a valid ciphertext C_{e+1} that can be decrypted under the new epoch key k_{e+1}. The UE security definitions of IND-ENC and IND-UPD can be found in [16].

RISE. In this paper, we leverage the homomorphic updatable encryption-RISE [16]. Recall the RISE construction as follows:

- RISE.Setup(1^{λ}): return pp as public parameter, also an implicit input of the following algorithms.
- RISE.Keygen(e): $k_e \leftarrow_{\$} \mathbb{Z}_p^{*}$.

- RISE.Enc(k_e, m): $y = g^{k_e}$, $r \leftarrow\!\!\$\ \mathbb{Z}_q$, return $C_e \leftarrow (y^r, g^r m)$.
- RISE.Dec(k_e, C_e): parse $C_e = (C_1, C_2)$, return $m \leftarrow C_2 \cdot C_1^{-1/k_{e+1}}$.
- RISE.Next(k_e, k_{e+1}): $\Delta_{e+1} \leftarrow (k_{e+1}/k_e, g^{k_{e+1}})$, return Δ_{e+1}.
- RISE.Upd(Δ_{e+1}, C_e): parse $\Delta_{e+1} = (\Delta, y')$ and $C_e = (C_1, C_2)$, $r' \leftarrow\!\!\$\ \mathbb{Z}_q$, $C_1' \leftarrow C_1^\Delta \cdot y'^{r'}$, $C_2' \leftarrow C_2 \cdot g^{r'}$, return $C_{e+1} \leftarrow (C_1', C_2')$.

The updatable RISE encryption scheme has been proven to be IND-ENC and IND-UPD secure under the decisional Diffie-Hellman (DDH) assumption [16]. Furthermore, it has been observed that RISE is homomorphic under its encryption algorithm Enc and decryption algorithm Dec. Specifically, given two plaintexts m and m', their respective RISE ciphertexts are RISE.Enc$(k_e, m) = (C_1, C_2)$ and RISE.Enc$(k_e, m') = (C_1', C_2')$. Then, their product is computed as RISE.Enc$(k_e, m) \cdot$ RISE.Enc$(k_e, m') = (C_1 \cdot C_1', C_2 \cdot C_2')$. The decryption algorithm of RISE satisfies RISE.Dec(RISE.Enc$(k_e, m) \cdot$ RISE.Enc$(k_e, m')) = m \cdot m'$.

3   Updatable Secure Storage

As previously introduced, an updatable secure storage (USS) system can be considered a secure version of GitHub that offers secure outsourced storage and version control services, even in scenarios where the trustworthiness of the server is not fully assured. USS provides users with the capability to create and update remote encrypted repositories on the server while maintaining a secret key and a public stub on the client side. The stored data and its updated version remain confidential and can only be accessed by authorized parties with the secret key. Additionally, USS ensures that a malicious server is unable to manipulate the client into accepting a tampered database or an outdated file, even if it gains access to the client's secret key and violates the protocol during each interactive procedure including file updates, key updates, and data retrieval.

Moreover, the USS system supports *key rotation*, a feature that is similar to updatable encryption schemes [12]. Key rotation is a critical security mechanism that ensures the confidentiality of the database, even if either the key or the storage is compromised, but not both simultaneously. By periodically rotating the secret key, the USS system can prevent an attacker who has gained access to an old key from knowing the current plain version of the database. This is particularly important in scenarios where the key may have been compromised, as it ensures that any data stored on the server remains secure.

Furthermore, we consider the possibility of external attackers gaining access to the repository stored on the server temporarily and occasionally, mirroring frequently reported data breaches. Despite the repository being encrypted, monitoring the alterations in the encrypted repository could unveil its update history, which has the potential to expose users' activities and preferences, thus compromising the privacy of the individual. For instance, if the user updates a file related to their medical records, an attacker who gains access to the update history can infer that the user has medical issues, even if they cannot access the actual contents of the file. To mitigate this issue, we propose a *file update unlinkability* mechanism in USS during key rotation. This mechanism utilizes a re-randomization algorithm to conceal the update history of the database if the attacker has only intermittent access to the stored encrypted repository.

To ensure system efficiency, USS uses efficient data update techniques and secret key refresh/rotation mechanisms. These mechanisms guarantee that communication costs and client workloads remain independent of the number and size of files stored in the system.

3.1 Syntax of USS

To ensure the security of remotely stored data, the USS creates a unique secret key for each encrypted repository. The user will possess the secret key and a unique stub associated with the respective repository on the client side. Each repository can store a predetermined number of encrypted files. When a specific file is required, the user can retrieve it from the remote repository, decrypt its content using the secret key, and verify its integrity. If a file needs to be updated, the client will interactively communicate with the server to modify the file within the repository. Additionally, the client will periodically generate new keys and update the encrypted files in the repository to maintain security.

Accordingly, the syntax of USS should be as follows.

- USS.ParGen($1^\lambda, \mathcal{M}, n$) $\rightarrow$ pp: Given the security parameter λ, the description of message space $\mathcal{M}$, and the size of vector degree n, the **parameter generation** algorithm generates the public parameter pp.
- USS.KeyGen($1^\lambda, pp$) $\rightarrow$ sk: Given the security parameter λ and the public parameter pp, the **key generation** algorithm generates the secret key sk.
- USS.Store(db, sk, pp) $\rightarrow$ (rep, sb): Given a database db that contains n independent files $m_1, \ldots, m_n$, and the public parameter pp, the client executes the **data storing** algorithm. The output of this algorithm is a repository $rep = (c_1, \ldots, c_n)$, which will be stored on the server side, along with a stub sb that will be accessible to both the server and the client. Each c_i is the ciphertext corresponding to the file m_i.
- USS.Rev$_{client}$(i, sk, sb, pp) $\leftrightarrows$ USS.Rev$_{server}$(rep, sb, pp) $\rightarrow$ $\langle m_i/\bot; \cdot \rangle$: The **data retrieval** algorithm is an interactive procedure that enables the client to retrieve file i from the server. The client provides the index i, secret key sk, stub sb, and public parameter pp. The server holds the repository rep and public parameter pp. If the data retrieval procedure succeeds, the client will output m_i; otherwise, it will output $\bot$.
- USS.FileUp$_{client}$(i, m_i', sk, sb, pp) $\leftrightarrows$ USS.FileUp$_{server}$(rep, sb, pp) $\rightarrow$ $\langle sb'; sb', rep' \rangle$: The **file update** is an interactive procedure that allows the client to update the i-th file to m_i'. Specifically, the client holds the index i, the new i-th file m_i', the secret key sk, the stub sb and the public parameter pp, and the server has the storing repository rep together with the public parameter pp. After the interaction, the client will have a new stub sb', and the server will store a new repository rep'.

- USS.KeyUp$_{client}$(sk, sk', sb, pp) $\leftrightarrows$ USS.KeyUp$_{server}$(sb, rep, pp) $\rightarrow$ $\langle sb'; rep' \rangle$:
  The **key update** is an interactive procedure that makes the server to update
  the storing ciphertexts to encryptions under a new key sk'. After the interaction, the client will have a new stub sb', and the server will store a new
  repository rep'.

Basically, the USS scheme should satisfy the following properties for correctness and efficiency.

Correctness. The correctness guarantees that when the client invokes the **data
retrieval** procedure to fetch the i-th file if the server is honest, the client
always successfully gets m_i no matter how many times the key has been
updated and m_i is the latest updated version of the i-th file deposited by the
client.

Client storage efficiency. The client storage efficiency requires that the size
of the information stored on the client side, including the secret key sk and
the stub sb, should be independent of the size of database db and even the
number of the files n.[1]

Retrieve efficiency. To ensure efficient retrieval, the communication cost for
the interactive procedure **data retrieval** should be independent of the size
of other plaintext files m_j for $j \neq i$ and the number of files n in the entire
repository when retrieving the i-th file. However, it may depend on the size
of the retrieved file m_i.

File update efficiency. For efficient file updates, the communication cost for
the **file update** procedure should be independent of the size of other plaintext
files m_j for $j \neq i$ and the number of files n in the entire repository when
updating the i-th file. However, it may depend on the size of the updating
file m_i.

Key update efficiency. In order to ensure efficient key updates, it is desirable that the communication cost associated with the key update procedure
remains independent of the size of all files m_i for $i = 1, \ldots, n$. If the communication cost is also independent of the number of files n in the repository, we
classify these schemes as ciphertext-independent. Conversely, if the communication cost depends on the number of files, we refer to them as ciphertext-
dependent schemes.[2]

3.2 Security Models

The security threats associated with USS arise from three main sources. Firstly,
the system must safeguard the confidentiality of the stored database against
the honest but curious server and external attackers who have temporary and

---

[1] The size of public parameter stored on both client and server should be independent
of the size of database db, although it may be related to the number of files n.

[2] This notion is directly borrowed from the updatable encryption framework, which
distinguishes between ciphertext-dependent and ciphertext-independent versions.

intermittent access to server storage and user secrets with no time overlap. Secondly, the system must retain the integrity of the stored database against the malicious server. Thirdly, given the possibility of the encrypted repository being compromised by external attackers multiple times, and potentially exposing the update history of the repository, the system must offer security guarantees that prevent update history leakage, even if the user's secret is ever revealed once simultaneously.

We present three models aimed at addressing confidentiality security challenges: IND-DD-CPA (indistinguishability of dynamic databases under chosen plaintext attacks), IND-REENC-CPA (indistinguishability of re-encryption ciphertext under chosen plaintext attacks), and ciphertext indistinguishability for file update (IND-FileUp-CPA for short). The IND-DD-CPA and IND-FileUp-CPA models ensure the fundamental confidentiality of the original database and updated files respectively, while the IND-REENC-CPA model provides post-compromise security and the ability to conceal the update history of the repository. Intuitively, the IND-DD-CPA model stipulates that an adversary cannot distinguish between two vectors of messages once they are encrypted. This holds even if the adversary has the ability to corrupt keys, trigger file updates, or initiate key rotations. The IND-FileUp-CPA model ensures that an adversary cannot distinguish between two files used to replace the current file in the repository, even if the attacker knows the previously stored data. On the other hand, the IND-REENC-CPA model ensures that an adversary cannot distinguish whether the ciphertexts have been updated after a key rotation. This is also true even if the adversary has the ability to corrupt keys, trigger file updates, or initiate key rotations. Our proposed models are similar to the IND-ENC and IND-UPD models presented in [16], respectively.

To address the security challenges related to message integrity, we propose a model called ordered full plaintext integrity (OF-PTXT for short). Intuitively, OF-PTXT imposes stricter requirements than the INT-PTXT game for the updatable encryption proposed in [14], as it guarantees message integrity even in the presence of a leaked secret key and non-compliant servers that do not rotate keys as required by the protocol.

Confidentiality. Our confidentiality-related models consider three critical security properties: message confidentiality (IND-DD-CPA), file update unlinkability (IND-FileUp-CPA), and re-encryption indistinguishability (IND-REENC-CPA). In these models, the adversary may attempt to compromise the confidentiality of any files in a target repository. The encryption of the target file is referred to as challenge ciphertext. Furthermore, the repository that contains the target files is called the challenge repository. However, since the key is rotated when the epoch evolves, the key-updated version of the challenge ciphertext is referred to as challenge-equal ciphertext. For simplicity, we also use the term "challenge-equal ciphertext" to represent both original and key-updated versions of the challenge ciphertext. Consequently, the repository containing the challenge-equal ciphertexts is called the challenge-equal repository.

More precisely, the challenger maintains the following internal states.

e: The current epoch number. It is initialized as 1.

e^*: The epoch number from which the challenge begins. It is initialized as $\bot$.

sb^*: The current stub of a repository including challenge-equal ciphertexts, which is initialized as $\bot$.

$\mathcal{K}$: The set of epochs in which the adversary has corrupted the epoch key by querying the key corruption oracle.

$\mathcal{C}$: The set of epochs in which the adversary corrupts a challenge-equal ciphertext by querying the challenge-equal ciphertext corruption oracle.

$\mathcal{I}$: The set of indices of challenge-equal ciphertexts in the repository. Before the adversary submits the challenge, the set is empty $\mathcal{I} = \emptyset$.

$\mathcal{L}$: The collection consists of tuples (t, sb, rep, db) which will be used to track all the repositories on the server, where t represents the epoch number, sb represents the corresponding stub, and rep and db represent the corresponding encrypted repository and plaintext database, respectively.

$\mathcal{S}$: The collection contains tuples (t, Trans), where t represents the epoch number and Trans represents all the corresponding key update transcripts from epoch $t - 1$ to epoch t.

$\mathcal{F}$: The collection of challenge-equal ciphertexts' file update transcripts contains tuples (sb, t, i, ft_i), where ft_i represents the file update transcript generated in the file update query $\mathcal{O}.\mathsf{FileUp}(sb, m_i', i)$ at epoch t, and the index i is the index of a challenge-equal ciphertext.

$\mathcal{T}$: The set of epochs in which the adversary queries the key update transcript oracle. If the transcript of the key update procedure from sk_t to sk_{t+1} is corrupted, it is represented as $t \in \mathcal{T}$. The set $\mathcal{T}$ is initially empty, indicating that the adversary has not yet queried the key update transcript oracle.

The adversary is given the following oracles.

- $\mathcal{O}.\mathsf{Store}(db)$: The purpose of this oracle is to enable the adversary to deposit a database on the server. To this end, the challenge invokes the storing algorithm $\mathsf{Store}(sk, db, pp)$ to generate the stored file rep and the stub sb, which are then given to the adversary. Furthermore, the challenger adds the tuple (e, sb, rep, db) to the set $\mathcal{L}$.

- $\mathcal{O}.\mathsf{Next}$: The adversary uses this oracle to initiate the update of all repositories on the server. The adversary will automatically gain access to their updated versions, except for the challenge-equal ciphertexts.

  Specifically, the challenger retrieves all entries (e, sb, rep, db) from the database $\mathcal{L}$ having the current epoch number e. Subsequently, the challenger generates a new epoch key sk' and executes the key update procedure to produce new stubs sb' and new repository rep' for each retrieved entry. The transcripts of the generated key updates are denoted as Trans. The current epoch number is then incremented to $e+1$, and new entries (e, sb', rep', db) are appended to the database $\mathcal{L}$. Additionally, a new entry (e, Trans) is added to the list $\mathcal{S}$. Furthermore, if there exists an entry $(e, sb, *, *) \in \mathcal{L}$ with $sb = sb^*$, then sb^* is also updated accordingly. The challenger provides the adversary with the stub and ciphertext elements having non-challenge indices $\{j\}_{j \notin \mathcal{I}}$ for the current epoch. For all other entries $(e, sb, *, *) \in \mathcal{L}$ such that $sb \neq sb^*$, the adversary is furnished with the updated versions of (sb, rep).

- $\mathcal{O}.\mathsf{KeyCorr}(t)$: The purpose of this oracle is to facilitate the adversary in retrieving the secret key. If the epoch number t is not greater than the current epoch number e, the oracle will provide the adversary with the secret key sk_t corresponding to epoch t. Additionally, epoch t will be included in the set of key corruptions $\mathcal{K}$.

- $\mathcal{O}.\mathsf{KeyUpTrans}(t)$: The purpose of this oracle is to facilitate the adversary in retrieving the key update transcript. If epoch number t is no more than the current epoch number e, retrieve the entry (t, Trans), and return the key update transcript Trans of all ciphertexts from epoch $t - 1$ to epoch t to the adversary. Add epoch t to the set of key corruptions $\mathcal{T}$.

- $\mathcal{O}.\mathsf{FileUp}(sb, m_i', i)$: This oracle enables the adversary to modify the i-th file of the current epoch to be the encryption of m_i'. The input includes the stub sb, the new file m_i', and its index i, where $i \in [1, n]$. The challenger first retrieves the entry (t, sb, rep, db) in $\mathcal{L}$ with the current epoch number $t = e$ and the same stub sb. If the entry is empty, the oracle outputs $\bot$. Otherwise, the challenger executes $\mathsf{FileUp}_{client}(i, m_i', sk_e, sb, pp) \leftrightarrows \mathsf{FileUp}_{server}(rep, sb, pp)$ and updates the entry with (e, sb', rep', db).

  If $sb \neq sb^*$, then the challenger returns (sb', rep') and the file update transcript ft_i to the adversary. If $sb = sb^*$, which means that the queried stub sb is the stub of a challenge-equal ciphertext in the current epoch, then the challenger updates $sb^* \leftarrow sb'$ and checks whether index i belongs to a challenge-equal ciphertext. If $i \in \mathcal{I}$, remove i from $\mathcal{I}$, add a tuple (sb, e, i, ft_i) to collection $\mathcal{F}$. The challenger returns the updated stub sb' and each updated ciphertext f_j' with index $j \notin \mathcal{I}$ to the adversary. If $i \notin \mathcal{I}$, the challenger returns the updated stub sb', the file update transcript ft_i, and each updated ciphertext f_j' with index $j \notin \mathcal{I}$ to the adversary.

- $\mathcal{O}.\mathsf{ChaCTCorr}(j)$: This oracle helps the adversary to learn the jth ciphertext of the challenge-equal ciphertext vector in the current epoch. If $j \in \mathcal{I}$, the jth element is a challenge-equal ciphertext for the current epoch. Then the challenger finds the entry (t, sb, rep, db) of $\mathcal{L}$ with the current epoch number $t = e$ and the stub sb is equal to $sb^* \neq \bot$, and add the current epoch e to the challenge-equal ciphertext corruption set $\mathcal{C}$ and give the adversary the jth ciphertext f_j where $rep = (f_1, \ldots, f_n)$. If $j \notin \mathcal{I}$, return $\bot$.

- $\mathcal{O}.\mathsf{ChaFTCorr}(sb, t, i)$: This oracle helps the adversary to learn the file update transcripts of challenge-equal ciphertexts. The challenger finds the entry (sb, t, i, ft_i) of F with the same stub sb, epoch t, and index i, and returns the transcript ft_i to the adversary

Trivial Win Condition. Adversaries could trivially win the confidentiality game if they corrupt both the epoch key and the challenge ciphertext or the updated version at that epoch. Since adversaries are given access to multiple oracles, where key update transcripts could help to update ciphertexts to the new key due to USS's function and even downgrade ciphertexts to the previous key if

USS's update function is bi-directional. To exclude the trivial win conditions, we define an extended ciphertext corruption set $\tilde{\mathcal{C}}$ to record the epochs at which adversaries corrupt the challenge ciphertext via directly querying the challenge ciphertext oracle $\mathcal{O}$.ChaCTCorr or indirectly referring to the challenge ciphertext based on queries of $\mathcal{O}$.KeyUpTrans and $\mathcal{O}$.ChaCTCorr. Here we assume the key update transcripts could update/downgrade ciphertexts in bi-direction since the scheme we use to construct USS supports it. Then we have $i \in \tilde{\mathcal{C}}$ if $i \in \mathcal{C}$, or $i-1 \in \mathcal{C}$ & $i \in \mathcal{T}$, or $i+1 \in \mathcal{C}$ and $i+1 \in \mathcal{T}$. The trivial win condition is $\mathcal{K} \cap \tilde{\mathcal{C}} \neq \emptyset$.

Message Confidentiality. Here we defined IND-DD-CPA security which aims to capture CPA style message confidentiality in the key updatable and file updatable setting. Concretely, the adversary can query $\mathcal{O}$.Store oracle for repository encryption in the storage. The adversary is allowed to engage the key rotation and get the update of non-challenge-equal files via the $\mathcal{O}$.Next oracle. The adversary can also corrupt some epoch key and challenge-equal file via the $\mathcal{O}$.KeyCorr, $\mathcal{O}$.ChaCTCorr oracles. Furthermore, the adversary is allowed to query file update of each repository via $\mathcal{O}$.FileUp oracle. To exclude the trivial win of the security game, the adversary is not allowed to see the key and the challenge-equal file encryption simultaneously. Such requirements are similar to the restrictions in the security models of the updatable encryptions [14]. Formally, we have the IND-DD-CPA game as Fig. 1.

$\mathsf{Exp}_{\mathsf{USS},\mathcal{A}}^{\mathsf{ind\text{-}dd\text{-}cpa}}(1^{\lambda}, \mathcal{M}, n, b)$

$pp \leftarrow \mathsf{ParGen}(1^{\lambda}, \mathcal{M}, n)$, Initialize $e = 1, e^* = \perp, sb^* = \perp$,   Set $\mathcal{K}, \mathcal{C}, \mathcal{I}, \mathcal{L}, \mathcal{S}, \mathcal{T}, \mathcal{F}$ as $\emptyset$

$sk_1 \leftarrow \mathsf{KeyGen}(pp)$

$(db_0, db_1, state) \leftarrow \mathcal{A}_1^{\mathcal{O}.\mathsf{Store}, \mathcal{O}.\mathsf{Next}, \mathcal{O}.\mathsf{FileUp}, \mathcal{O}.\mathsf{KeyCorr}, \mathcal{O}.\mathsf{KeyUpTrans}}(pp)$

Parse $db_0 = (m_{0,1}, \ldots, m_{0,n}), db_1 = (m_{1,1}, \ldots, m_{1,n})$

$(sb^*, rep^*) \leftarrow \mathsf{Store}(db_b, sk_e, pp)$

$e^* = e, \quad \mathcal{L} = \mathcal{L} \cup (e, sb^*, rep^*, db_b)$

for $i = 0$ *to* n

  if $m_{0,i} \neq m_{1,i}$, **then** $\mathcal{I} = \mathcal{I} \cup \{i\}$

$b' \leftarrow \mathcal{A}_2^{\mathcal{O}.\mathsf{Store}, \mathcal{O}.\mathsf{Next}, \mathcal{O}.\mathsf{FileUp}, \mathcal{O}.\mathsf{KeyCorr}, \mathcal{O}.\mathsf{KeyUpTrans}, \mathcal{O}.\mathsf{ChaFTCorr}, \mathcal{O}.\mathsf{ChaCTCorr}}(state, rep^*)$

return b' **if** $\mathcal{K} \cap \tilde{\mathcal{C}} = \emptyset$

Fig. 1. The game of IND-DD-CPA.

Definition 2 (IND-DD-CPA). *An updatable secure storage scheme USS is called IND-DD-CPA secure if for any* PPT *adversary $\mathcal{A}$ the following advantage* *is negligible in the security parameter λ:*

$$\mathsf{Adv}_{USS,\mathcal{A}}^{ind\text{-}dd\text{-}cpa}(1^\lambda, \mathcal{M}, n) :=$$

$$\left| \Pr[\mathsf{Exp}_{USS,\mathcal{A}}^{ind\text{-}dd\text{-}cpa}(1^\lambda, \mathcal{M}, n, 0) = 1] - \Pr[\mathsf{Exp}_{USS,\mathcal{A}}^{ind\text{-}dd\text{-}cpa}(1^\lambda, \mathcal{M}, n, 1) = 1] \right|$$

File Update Unlinkability. To capture the security that the file update operation does not leak the confidentiality of the updated file, we define the file update unlinkability via the following experiment with the adversary. Intuitively, it ensures that attackers corrupting the storage before and after a file update operation learn nothing about file updates, such as whether the file content has changed, and what the current file content is.

We describe the file update security experiment $\mathsf{Exp}_{USS,\mathcal{A}}^{ind\text{-}fileup\text{-}cpa}$ for the key updatable dynamic secure storage scheme USS and adversary $\mathcal{A}$. In $\mathsf{Exp}_{USS,\mathcal{A}}^{ind\text{-}fileup\text{-}cpa}$ experiment, $\mathcal{A}$ submits two possible file $(m_{0,i}, m_{1,i})$ for challenge, where $i \in \{1, \ldots, n\}$. The challenger updates the i-th file of the stored storage with one of the two submissions selected randomly and gives the updated ciphertext to the adversary as the challenge ciphertext. $\mathcal{A}$'s goal is to give a correct guess on which file is chosen to update. The trivial win situation is that the adversary corrupts both the epoch key and the challenge-equal ciphertext at the same epoch, i.e., $\mathcal{K} \cap \mathcal{C} \neq \emptyset$ (Fig. 2).

$\mathsf{Exp}_{USS,\mathcal{A}}^{ind\text{-}fileup\text{-}cpa}(1^\lambda, \mathcal{M}, n, b)$

$pp \leftarrow \mathsf{ParGen}(1^\lambda, \mathcal{M}, n)$, Initialize $e = 1, e^* = \bot, sb^* = \bot$, Set $\mathcal{K}, \mathcal{C}, \mathcal{I}, \mathcal{L}, \mathcal{S}, \mathcal{T}, \mathcal{F}$ as $\emptyset$

$sk_1 \leftarrow \mathsf{KeyGen}(pp)$

$(sb, i, m_{0,i}, m_{1,i}, state_1) \leftarrow \mathcal{A}_1^{\mathcal{O}.\mathsf{Store}, \mathcal{O}.\mathsf{Next}, \mathcal{O}.\mathsf{FileUp}, \mathcal{O}.\mathsf{KeyCorr}, \mathcal{O}.\mathsf{KeyUpTrans}}(pp)$

if $(e, sb, *, *) \notin \mathcal{L}$, or $i \notin \{1, \ldots, n\}$, or $|m_{0,i}| \neq |m_{1,i}|$, **then return** $\bot$

Retrieve $(e, sb, rep, db = (m_1, \ldots, m_n))$,   Set $e^* = e$, $\mathcal{I} = \mathcal{I} \cup \{i\}$, $\mathcal{C} = \mathcal{C} \cup \{e\}$

Run $\mathsf{FileUp}_{token}(sk_e, sb, m_{b,i}, i, pp) \leftrightarrows \mathsf{FileUp}_{server}(sb, rep, pp) \rightarrow \langle sb^*; rep^* \rangle$

$\mathcal{L} = \mathcal{L} \cup (e, sb^*, rep^*, db_b = (m_1, \ldots, m_{b,i}, \ldots, m_n))$

Record the file update transcript as fpt

$b' \leftarrow \mathcal{A}_2^{\mathcal{O}.\mathsf{Store}, \mathcal{O}.\mathsf{Next}, \mathcal{O}.\mathsf{FileUp}, \mathcal{O}.\mathsf{KeyCorr}, \mathcal{O}.\mathsf{KeyUpTrans}, \mathcal{O}.\mathsf{ChaFTCorr}, \mathcal{O}.\mathsf{ChaCTCorr}}(state_1, sb^*, rep^*, fpt)$

return b' if $\mathcal{K} \cap \tilde{\mathcal{C}} = \emptyset$

Fig. 2. The game of IND-FileUp-CPA

Definition 3 (IND-FileUp-CPA). *An updatable secure storage scheme USS is called IND-FileUp-CPA secure if for any PPT adversary $\mathcal{A}$ the following advantage is negligible in the security parameter λ:*

$$\mathsf{Adv}_{USS,\mathcal{A}}^{ind\text{-}fileup\text{-}cpa}(1^\lambda, \mathcal{M}, n) :=$$

$$\left| \Pr[\mathsf{Exp}_{USS,\mathcal{A}}^{ind\text{-}fileup\text{-}cpa}(1^\lambda, \mathcal{M}, n, 0) = 1] - \Pr[\mathsf{Exp}_{USS,\mathcal{A}}^{ind\text{-}fileup\text{-}cpa}(1^\lambda, \mathcal{M}, n, 1) = 1] \right|$$

Key Update Unlinkablity. Intuitively, key update unlinkability is aimed to capture the security for key updates after both corruptions. More concretely, attackers may corrupt both the client and the server at the same epoch. After the key rotation, attackers corrupt the server and obtain the updated ciphertext. Key update unlinkability ensures that attackers cannot detect whether the updated ciphertext contains the same plaintext as the previous corrupted ciphertext. The security is similar to the IND-UPD security of UE [16] since we provide the adversary with all the oracles IND-UPD security provides. In addition, our key update unlinkability allows the adversary to have additional access to the file update oracle.

We define the following security experiment $\text{Exp}_{\text{USS},\mathcal{A}}^{\text{ind-reenc-cpa}}$ for updatable secure cloud storage scheme USS and adversary $\mathcal{A}$, who has access to the oracle tuple $(\mathcal{O}.\text{Store}, \mathcal{O}.\text{Next}, \mathcal{O}.\text{KeyCorr}, \mathcal{O}.\text{FileUp}, \mathcal{O}.\text{KeyUpTrans}, \mathcal{O}.\text{ChaCTCorr})$ like in the above confidentiality games. So, the trivial win condition is triggered in the same case (Fig. 3).

$\text{Exp}_{\text{USS},\mathcal{A}}^{\text{ind-reenc-cpa}}(1^\lambda, \mathcal{M}, n, b)$

$pp \leftarrow \text{ParGen}(1^\lambda, \mathcal{M}, n)$, Initialize e, e^*, sb^*, Set $\mathcal{K}, \mathcal{C}, \mathcal{I}, \mathcal{L}, \mathcal{S}, \mathcal{T}, \mathcal{F}$ as $\emptyset$

$sk_1 \leftarrow \text{KeyGen}(pp)$

$(sb_0, sb_1, state_1) \leftarrow \mathcal{A}_1^{\mathcal{O}.\text{Store}, \mathcal{O}.\text{Next}, \mathcal{O}.\text{FileUp}, \mathcal{O}.\text{KeyCorr}, \mathcal{O}.\text{KeyUpTrans}}(pp)$

Retrieve $(e, sb_0, rep_0 = (c_{0,1} \ldots, c_{0,n}), db_0), (e, sb_1, rep_1 = (c_{1,1}, \ldots, c_{1,n}), db_1)$ from $\mathcal{L}$

Set $\mathcal{I} = \{i\}_{i \in \{1,\ldots,n\}, c_{0,i} \neq c_{1,i}}$, $e = e + 1$, $e^* = e$, $\mathcal{C} = \mathcal{C} \cup \{e\}$

$sk_e \leftarrow \text{KeyGen}(pp)$

Run $\text{KeyUp}_{client}(sk_{e-1}, sk_e, sb_b, pp) \leftrightarrows \text{KeyUp}_{server}(rep_b, pp)$ to output $\langle sb^*; rep^* \rangle$

for each $(e-1, sb, rep, db) \in \mathcal{L}$, where $sb \notin \{sb_0, sb_1\}$

    Run $\text{KeyUp}_{client}(sk_{e-1}, sk_e, sb, pp) \leftrightarrows \text{KeyUp}_{server}(rep, pp)$ to output $\langle sb'; rep' \rangle$

    Set $\mathcal{L} = \mathcal{L} \cup (e, sb', rep', db)$

$b' \leftarrow \mathcal{A}_2^{\mathcal{O}.\text{Store}, \mathcal{O}.\text{Next}, \mathcal{O}.\text{FileUp}, \mathcal{O}.\text{KeyCorr}, \mathcal{O}.\text{KeyUpTrans}, \mathcal{O}.\text{ChaCTCorr}}(state_1, sb^*, rep^*, \text{all } (sb', rep'))$

return b' if $\mathcal{K} \cap \tilde{\mathcal{C}} = \emptyset$

Fig. 3. The game of IND-REENC-CPA

Definition 4 (IND-REENC-CPA). *An updatable secure storage scheme USS is called IND-REENC-CPA secure if for any* PPT *adversary $\mathcal{A}$ the following advantage is negligible in the security parameter λ:*

$$\text{Adv}_{\text{USS},\mathcal{A}}^{\text{ind-reenc-cpa}}(1^\lambda, \mathcal{M}, n) :=$$

$$\left| \Pr[\text{Exp}_{\text{USS},\mathcal{A}}^{\text{ind-reenc-cpa}}(1^\lambda, \mathcal{M}, n, 0) = 1] - \Pr[\text{Exp}_{\text{USS},\mathcal{A}}^{\text{ind-reenc-cpa}}(1^\lambda, \mathcal{M}, n, 1) = 1] \right|$$

Integrity. We define a kind of strong plaintext integrity notion called *ordered full plaintext integrity* (OF-PTXT for short). For the classic authenticated encryption schemes, plaintext integrity ensures that attackers cannot make any forgery for new plaintext except the queried ones, which work for static storage with appending function. But for dynamic storage, where some storage may be changed or even deleted, the old or deleted messages could be leveraged by dishonest storage providers to cheat users, which is not covered by classic integrity. Here OF-PTXT provides stronger integrity in the dynamic storage setting, where data could be updated dynamically. OF-PTXT ensures attackers cannot forge for a plaintext that does not belong to the current storage. To be formal, we show a security experiment between the adversary who acts as the malicious storage server, and the challenger who acts as the honest user. More precisely, the challenger will maintain the following list to record the latest version of databases.

$\mathcal{R}$: The list recording the latest stub and the message vector pair (sb, db) generated during the integrity game. $\mathcal{R}$ is initialized as empty and will be updated for each file update and key update. $\mathcal{R}$ has only entries for the latest epoch.

We use the stub to track the target stored database. For a certain pair (sb, db) of $\mathcal{R}$ and a certain index i, the adversary aims to make the client accept m_i' as the i-th element of the database but $m_i' \neq db[i]$.

Moreover, we allow the adversary to launch active attacks in the integrity game. The server which may be corrupted by the adversary may manipulate the storage and even to not follow the protocol during the file update or key update procedures. To capture adversary's above capability, three special oracles, including the database storing oracle $\mathcal{O}.\mathsf{StoreINT}$, the next oracle $\mathcal{O}.\mathsf{NextINT}$ and the file update token oracle $\mathcal{O}.\mathsf{FileUpINT}$ are provided for the adversary in integrity game. Besides, the adversary in the integrity game can also learn the security key via the key corruption oracle $\mathcal{O}.\mathsf{KeyCorr}$, which means USS can guarantee the integrity even when the key is leaked.

We will elaborate the special oracles for the integrity game in the following. For brevity, please refer to our previous descriptions about the similar oracles in the confidentiality Sect. 3.2.

- $\mathcal{O}.\mathsf{StoreINT}(db)$: This oracle is to let the adversary learn the stored file generated by the storing algorithm. The challenge will invoke the storing algorithm $\mathsf{Store}(sk_e, db, pp)$ to generate the stored file rep and the stub sb, and give rep and sb to the adversary. And add the pair (sb, db) to $\mathcal{R}$.
- $\mathcal{O}.\mathsf{NextINT}$: This oracle is to let the adversary to invoke the client to launch the key update procedure. The challenger updates the epoch number $e = e+1$, runs the KeyGen algorithm to generate the new epoch key $sk_e = sk'$, and runs the key update client-side algorithm to update all stubs sbs into the corresponding $sb's$ and to generate client-side key update transcripts Trans_c for the server. Then the challenger returns all the new stubs $sb's$ and transcripts Trans_c to the adversary, and updates each entry (sb, db) in $\mathcal{R}$ with the corresponding (sb', db).

– $\mathcal{O}.\mathsf{FileUpINT}(m'_i, i, sb)$: The adversary uses this oracle to invoke the client to launch the file update procedure and replace the i-th element of the database to m'_i. More precisely, the input of this oracle contains the new file m'_i, its index i, and the corresponding stub sb. The challenger will first check whether the stub is contained in the list $\mathcal{R}$. During this interaction, the client will communicate with the corrupted server according to the specification of the designed scheme, while the adversary could respond to the client with an arbitrary message and violate the protocol design. If the client finally accepts the update results, the challenger will update the entry (sb, db) of $\mathcal{R}$ with (sb', db').

We describe the integrity experiment $\mathsf{Exp}^{\text{of-ptxt}}_{\mathsf{USS},\mathcal{A}}$ for key updatable dynamic secure storage scheme USS and adversary $\mathcal{A}$, who has access to the oracle tuple $(\mathcal{O}.\mathsf{StoreINT}, \mathcal{O}.\mathsf{NextINT}, \mathcal{O}.\mathsf{FileUpINT}, \mathcal{O}.\mathsf{KeyCorr})$ (Fig. 4).

$$
\begin{array}{|l|}
\hline
\mathsf{Exp}^{\text{of-ptxt}}_{\mathsf{USS},\mathcal{A}}(1^\lambda, \mathcal{M}, n) \\
\hline
pp \leftarrow \mathsf{ParGen}(1^\lambda, \mathcal{M}, n), \text{Initialize } \mathcal{R}, e \\
sk_e \leftarrow \mathsf{KeyGen}(pp) \\
(sb, i, state_1) \leftarrow \mathcal{A}_1^{\mathcal{O}.\mathsf{StoreINT}, \mathcal{O}.\mathsf{NextINT}, \mathcal{O}.\mathsf{FileUpINT}, \mathcal{O}.\mathsf{KeyCorr}}(pp) \\
\textbf{if } (sb, *) \notin \mathcal{R} \text{ or } i \notin [1, n] \quad \textbf{return } 0 \\
\textbf{else Run } \mathsf{Rev}_{client}(i, sk_e, sb, pp) \leftrightarrows \mathcal{A} \text{ to output } \langle m_i^*; \cdot \rangle \\
\quad \textbf{for } \forall \mathbf{m} \text{ s.t. } (sb, \mathbf{m}) \in \mathcal{R} \\
\quad\quad \textbf{if } m_i^* \neq \mathbf{m}[i] \quad \textbf{return } 1 \\
\quad \textbf{endfor} \\
\textbf{return } 0 \\
\hline
\end{array}
$$

Fig. 4. The game of OF-PTXT

Definition 5 (OF-PTXT). *An updatable secure storage scheme USS is called OF-PTXT secure if for any* PPT *adversary $\mathcal{A}$ the following advantage is negligible in the security parameter λ:*

$$
\mathsf{Adv}^{\text{of-ptxt}}_{\mathsf{USS},\mathcal{A}}(1^\lambda, \mathcal{M}, n) := \Pr[\mathsf{Exp}^{\text{of-ptxt}}_{\mathsf{USS},\mathcal{A}}(1^\lambda, \mathcal{M}, n) = 1]
$$

4   Homomorphic Vector Commitment

This section presents an introduction to Homomorphic Vector Commitment (HVC) and explores the difficulties involved in constructing an HVC that can simultaneously satisfy both the position hiding and homomorphic properties.

4.1 Syntax and Notions

HVC is defined with the following algorithms:

HVC = (HVC.Setup, HVC.Com, HVC.Open, HVC.Ver, HVC.ComHom, HVC.OpenHom)

that works as following:

- HVC.Setup($1^\lambda, \mathcal{M}, n$) → crs_n: Given the security parameter λ, the description of committed message space $\mathcal{M}$, and the size of committed vector n, the probabilistic setup algorithm outputs a common reference string crs_n.
- HVC.Com$_{crs_n}$(**m**) → (C, aux): On input an ordered sequence of n messages **m** = $(m_1, \ldots, m_n)$ and the common reference string crs_n, the commitment algorithm outputs a commitment string C and the auxiliary information aux. We denote the commitment space as $\mathcal{C}$. The auxiliary information aux is succinct, say independent of the vector degree n.
- HVC.Open$_{crs_n}$(i, **m**, aux) → Λ_i: This algorithm is run by the committer to produce a proof (also known as opening) Λ_i that the i-th element **m**$[i]$ is the committed message. We denote the proof space as $\mathcal{P}$.
- HVC.Ver$_{crs_n}$(C, m, i, Λ_i) → $1/0$: The verification algorithm outputs 1 only if Λ_i is a valid proof that m is the i-th committed message to the C.
- HVC.ComHom$_{crs_n}$($C, C' \in \mathcal{C}$) → C'': This algorithm can be run by any user who holds two commitment belonging to the commitment space $\mathcal{C}$, and it allows the user to compute another commitment $C'' = C \oplus C' \in \mathcal{C}$, where $\oplus$ denotes the homomorphic operation for the commitment.
- HVC.OpenHom$_{crs_n}$($\Lambda_j, \Lambda_j' \in \mathcal{P}$) → Λ_j'': This algorithm can be run by any user who holds two membership proofs Λ_j and Λ_j' for some message on position j w.r.t. to some C and C'' (which contains m and m' as the message at position j), and it allows the user to compute another proof $\Lambda_j'' = \Lambda_j \otimes \Lambda_j' \in \mathcal{P}$ (w.r.t. some C'' which contains m'' as the new message at position j), where $\otimes$ denotes the homomorphic operation for the proof.

Basically, a HVC scheme should satisfy correctness, conciseness and homomorphic property.

Correctness. A vector commitment is correct if for all honestly generated crs_n ← HVC.Setup($1^\lambda, \mathcal{M}, n$), $\forall i \in [n]$, if C is a commitment on a vector $(m_1, \cdots, m_n) \in \mathcal{M}^n$, Λ_i is a proof for position i generated by HVC.Open$_{crs_n}$, then HVC.Ver$_{crs_n}$(C, m_i, i, Λ_i) outputs 1 with overwhelming probability.

Conciseness. A vector commitment is concise if the size of the commitment C and the outputs of HVC.Open are both independent of the size n of the vector.

Homomorphic Property. Formally, $\forall i \in [n]$, for all honestly generated crs_n ← HVC.Setup($1^\lambda, \mathcal{M}, n$), for all honestly generated

$$(C, aux) \leftarrow \text{HVC.ComHom}_{crs_n}(\mathbf{m}), \ (C', aux') \leftarrow \text{HVC.ComHom}_{crs_n}(\mathbf{m}'),$$

$$\Lambda_i \leftarrow \text{HVC.Open}_{crs_n}(i, \mathbf{m}, aux), \ \Lambda_i' \leftarrow \text{HVC.Open}_{crs_n}(i, \mathbf{m}', aux'),$$

where $\mathbf{m} = (m_1, \ldots, m_n), \mathbf{m}' = (m'_1, \ldots, m'_n)$, if

$$C'' \leftarrow \mathsf{HVC.ComHom}_{crs_n}(C, C'), \quad \Lambda''_i \leftarrow \mathsf{HVC.OpenHom}_{crs_n}(\Lambda_i, \Lambda'_i)$$

then we have $\mathsf{HVC.Ver}_{crs_n}(C'', m_i + m'_i, i, \Lambda''_i) = 1$.

4.2   Security Models

In this section, we formally define the security models for binding and hiding on the situation that the corresponding membership proofs are leaked.

Position-Binding: It requires that for any well-formed commitment, the *PPT* adversary cannot find two different messages on the same position that the verification algorithm accepts both. Formally, we have the HVC Position-Binding game as Fig. 5.

$\mathsf{Exp}^{\mathsf{position\text{-}binding}}_{\mathsf{HVC},\mathcal{A}}(1^\lambda, \mathcal{M}, n)$

$crs_n \leftarrow \mathsf{HVC.Setup}(1^\lambda, \mathcal{M}, n)$

$(C, i, m_i, m'_i, \Lambda_i, \Lambda'_i) \leftarrow \mathcal{A}_1(crs_n)$

if $m_i \neq m'_i \ \wedge \ \mathsf{HVC.Ver}_{crs_n}(C, m, i, \Lambda_i) = 1 \ \wedge \ \mathsf{HVC.Ver}_{crs_n}(C, m', i, \Lambda'_i) = 1$

return 1,   **else return** 0

Fig. 5. The game of HVC Position-Binding

The advantage of $\mathcal{A}$ is defined as

$$\mathsf{Adv}^{\mathsf{position\text{-}binding}}_{\mathsf{HVC},\mathcal{A}}(1^\lambda, \mathcal{M}, n) = \Pr[\mathsf{Exp}^{\mathsf{position\text{-}binding}}_{\mathsf{HVC},\mathcal{A}}(1^\lambda, \mathcal{M}, n) = 1].$$

Definition 6. *A HVC scheme satisfies HVC Position-Binding if for every PPT adversary $\mathcal{A}$ the advantage function $\mathsf{Adv}^{\mathsf{position\text{-}binding}}_{\mathsf{HVC},\mathcal{A}}(1^\lambda, \mathcal{M}, n)$ is negligible in λ.*

Position-Hiding: The position hiding property not only requires that the adversary cannot distinguish whether a commitment is for a vector $(m_1, \ldots, m_n)$ or $(m'_1, \ldots, m'_n)$, but also guarantees that the adversary cannot learn any information about m_i from the opening of m_j where $i \neq j$. Formally, we have the HVC Position-Hiding game as Fig. 6.

The advantage of $\mathcal{A}$ is defined as

$$\mathsf{Adv}^{\mathsf{position\text{-}hiding}}_{\mathsf{HVC},\mathcal{A}}(1^\lambda, \mathcal{M}, n) =$$
$$\left| \Pr[\mathsf{Exp}^{\mathsf{position\text{-}hiding}}_{\mathsf{HVC},\mathcal{A}}(1^\lambda, \mathcal{M}, n, 0) = 1] - \Pr[\mathsf{Exp}^{\mathsf{position\text{-}hiding}}_{\mathsf{HVC},\mathcal{A}}(1^\lambda, \mathcal{M}, n, 1) = 1] \right|$$

Definition 7. *A HVC scheme satisfies HVC Position-Hiding if for every PPT adversary $\mathcal{A}$ the advantage function $\mathsf{Adv}^{\mathsf{position\text{-}hiding}}_{\mathsf{HVC},\mathcal{A}}(1^\lambda, \mathcal{M}, n)$ is negligible in λ.*

$$\mathsf{Exp}^{\text{position-hiding}}_{\mathsf{HVC},\mathcal{A}}(1^\lambda, \mathcal{M}, n, b)$$

$crs_n \leftarrow \mathsf{HVC.Setup}(1^\lambda, \mathcal{M}, n)$

$(i, m_1, \cdots, m_{i-1}, m_{i,0}, m_{i,1}, m_{i+1}, \cdots m_n, state) \leftarrow \mathcal{A}_1(crs_n)$

$\mathbf{m}_b = (m_1, \ldots, m_{i-1}, m_{i,b}, m_{i+1}, \ldots, m_n)$

$(C, aux) \leftarrow \mathsf{HVC.com}(\mathbf{m}_b)$

$\Lambda_j \leftarrow \mathsf{HVC.open}(j, \mathbf{m}_b, aux), \forall j \in [n]/\{i\}$

$\forall j \in [n]/\{i\}, \Lambda_i \leftarrow VC.open(i, m_{i,b}, aux)$

$b' \leftarrow \mathcal{A}_2(crs_n, C, \{\Lambda_j\}_{j \in [n] \setminus \{i\}}, state),$

return b'

Fig. 6. The game of HVC Position-Hiding

4.3 Construction

Although there are several vector commitment (VC) constructions [2,7,8,15] that satisfy the homomorphic property, none of them can directly satisfy both the position hiding and homomorphic properties simultaneously. Furthermore, they cannot be made position hiding through the composition approach. For example, if one first commits to each message using a standard commitment scheme and then applies a VC to the resulting sequence of commitments, the resulting hybrid scheme will not satisfy the homomorphic property.

Even if one first commits to each message separately using a homomorphic commitment scheme (such as Pedersen commitment) and then applies a VC construction to the obtained sequence of commitments, the compatibility of the algebraic structures of these two underlying primitives is still unclear.[3] Some existing VC schemes are based on bilinear maps [8,15], or RSA groups [2,7,8,15], or lattice assumptions [18]. However, for pairing-based or RSA-based VC constructions, the messages (commitment values themselves in the above composition construction) are encoded into the exponents of group elements, which restricts the operation on messages to addition. This means that we require a homomorphic commitment scheme where the committed values lie in an additive group. Unfortunately, the existence of such a commitment scheme is elusive as most of the well-known computational assumptions do not hold, making it unclear how to construct such a scheme. For example, the homomorphic operation for Peterson commitment is multiplication, making it incompatible with pairing-based or RSA-based VC constructions for obtaining an HVC. Similarly, the message space of lattice-based VC consists of short vectors, while the standard lattice commitment consists of pseudorandom ring elements. It is also challenging to

---

[3] Some recently proposed functional commitment schemes [11,19] may also satisfy similar security requirements of HVC. However, it is unclear how to make these schemes compatible with UE schemes and thus integrate them into our proposed USS construction.

directly combine a lattice-based VC with a lattice-based commitment scheme to obtain an HVC.

Our proposed HVC construction is based on the pairing-based VC scheme introduced by Catalano et al. [8], which already possesses homomorphic properties and position binding. To achieve position hiding without compromising the homomorphic property, we add a dummy position at the end of the vector, which is used to store a random value. The random value is then used to mask the information about the membership proof, thus achieving position hiding. Since the dummy position is not used for any actual file, it does not affect the integrity of the VC scheme. With this approach, we can achieve both homomorphic properties and position hiding in our HVC scheme, which is essential for our proposed construction in a USS system.

Let $\mathbb{G}, \mathbb{G}_T$ be bilinear groups of prime order p equipped with a bilinear map $e : \mathbb{G} \times \mathbb{G} \to \mathbb{G}_T$. Let $g \in \mathbb{G}$ be random generators.

- HVC.Setup$(1^\lambda, \mathcal{M}, n) \to crs_n$: Randomly choose $z_1, \ldots, z_n, z_{n+1} \xleftarrow{\$} \mathbb{Z}_p$. For all $i = 1, \ldots, n+1$, set $h_i = g^{z_i}$, For all $i, j = 1, \ldots, n+1, i \neq j$ set $h_{i,j} = g^{z_i z_j}$. Output $crs_n = (g, \{h_i\}_{i \in [n+1]}, \{h_{i,j}\}_{i,j \in [n+1], i \neq j})$.
- HVC.Com$_{crs_n}(\mathbf{m} = (m_1, \ldots, m_n)) \to (C, aux)$: Randomly select $r \xleftarrow{\$} \mathbb{Z}_p$, Compute $C = h_1^{m_1} h_2^{m_2} \cdots h_n^{m_n} \cdot h_{n+1}^r$ and output C and the auxiliary information $aux = r$
- HVC.Open$_{crs_n}(\mathbf{m}, i, aux) \to \Lambda_i$: Compute

$$\Lambda_i = \prod_{j=1, j \neq i}^{n} h_{i,j}^{m_j} \cdot h_{i,n+1}^r = \left(\prod_{j=1, j \neq i}^{n} h_j^{m_j} \cdot h_{n+1}^r \right)^{z_i}$$

- HVC.Ver$_{crs_n}(C, m, i, \Lambda_i) \to 1/0$: Check $e(C/h_i^m, h_i) = e(\Lambda_i, g)$.
- HVC.ComHom$_{crs_n}(C, C' \in \mathcal{C}) \to C''$: Compute $C'' = C \cdot C'$.
- HVC.OpenHom$_{crs_n}(\Lambda_j, \Lambda_j' \in \mathcal{P}) \to \Lambda_j''$:Compute $\Lambda_j'' = \Lambda_j \cdot \Lambda_j'$.

The correctness and homomorpihc property of the scheme can be easily verified by inspection. We prove its security via the following theorem.

Theorem 1. *If the Square-CDH Assumption holds, then the scheme defined above satisfies the Position-Binding property.*

Proof. We prove the theorem by showing that the scheme satisfies the Position-Binding property. For sake of contradiction assume that there exists an efficient adversary $\mathcal{A}$ who produces two valid openings to two different messages at the same position, then we show how to build an efficient algorithm $\mathcal{B}$ that uses $\mathcal{A}$ to break the Square-CDH Assumption.

To break the Square-CDH Assumption, $\mathcal{B}$ takes as input $g, g^a \in \mathbb{G}$ and its goal is to compute g^{a^2}.

First, $\mathcal{B}$ selects a random $i \xleftarrow{\$} [n]$ as a guess for the index i on which $\mathcal{A}$ will break the position binding. And set $h_i = g^a$ Next, $\mathcal{B}$ chooses $z_j \xleftarrow{\$} \mathbb{Z}_p$, $\forall j \in [n+1] \backslash \{i\}$ and it computes:

$$\forall j \in [n+1] \backslash \{i\} : h_j = g^{z_j}, h_{i,j} = h_i^{z_j} = g^{a z_j}$$

$$\forall k, j \in [n+1]\backslash\{i\}, k \neq j : h_{k,j} = g^{z_k z_j}$$

and outputs $crs_n = (g, \{h_j\}_{j \in [n+1]}, \{h_{j,k}\}_{j,k \in [n+1], j \neq k})$. Notice that the public parameters are perfectly distributed as the real ones. The adversary is supposed to output a tuple $(C, m, m', \Lambda, \Lambda')$ such that: $m \neq m'$ and both Λ and Λ' correctly verify at position i. If the position is not i, then $\mathcal{B}$ aborts the simulation. Otherwise, it computes $g^{a^2} = (\Lambda/\Lambda')^{(m'-m)^{-1}}$.

To see that the output is correct, observe that since the two openings verify correctly, then it holds: $e(C, h_i) = e(h_i^{m'}, h_i)e(\Lambda', g) = e(h_i^m, h_i)e(\Lambda, g)$. Notice that if $\mathcal{A}$ succeeds with probability ϵ, then $\mathcal{B}$ has probability ϵ/n of breaking the Square-CDH assumption. □

Theorem 2. *The scheme defined above is perfectly position hiding.*

Proof. We prove the theorem by showing that for two given vectors of messages $\mathbf{m}_0 = \{m_1, \ldots, m_{i-1}, m_{i,0}, m_{i+1}, \ldots, m_n\}$ and $\mathbf{m}_1 = \{m_1, \ldots, m_{i-1}, m_{i,1}, m_{i+1}, \ldots, m_n\}$, we can find two random values r_0 and r_1 such that $(\mathbf{m}_0, r_0)$ and $(\mathbf{m}_1, r_1)$ map to the same commitment value C and same proofs $\{\Lambda_j\}_{j \in [n]\backslash\{i\}}$ except Λ_{ib}. Since r_0, r_1 are chosen with equal probabilities according to the commitment algorithm HVC.Com, any adversary $\mathcal{A}$ has a success to win the Position-Hiding game with a probability of exactly $1/2$.

Concretely, the challenger $\mathcal{C}$ sets the public parameters as the real environment: randomly choose $z_1, \ldots, z_n, z_{n+1} \xleftarrow{\$} \mathbb{Z}_p$. For all $i = 1, \ldots, n+1$, set $h_i = g^{z_i}$. For all $i, j = 1, \ldots, n+1$, $i \neq j$ set $h_{i,j} = g^{z_i z_j}$.

Upon receiving $\{m_1, \ldots, m_{i-1}, m_{i,0}, m_{i,1}, m_{i+1}, \ldots, m_n\}$ from $\mathcal{A}$, $\mathcal{C}$ randomly chooses r_0, computes commitment $C = h_1^{m_1} \cdot h_{i-1}^{m_{i-1}} \cdot h_i^{m_{i,0}} \cdot h_{i+1}^{m_{i+1}} \cdots h_n^{m_n} \cdots h_{n+1}^{r_0}$, and proofs $\Lambda_j = (C/h_j^{m_j})^{z_j}, j \in [n]\backslash\{i\}$. Obviously, $(C, \{\Lambda_j\}_{j \in [n]\backslash\{i\}})$ is the corresponding commitment and openings to $(\mathbf{m}_0, r_0)$. $\mathcal{C}$ outputs $(C, \{\Lambda_j\}_{j \in [n]\backslash\{i\}})$. Note that if we set $r_1 = r_0 + (m_{i,0} - m_{i,1})z_i/z_{n+1}$, then the tuple $(C, \{\Lambda_j\}_{j \in [n]\backslash\{i\}})$ mentioned above can also serve as a commitment and openings for $(\mathbf{m}_1, r_1)$.

Since r_0 is randomly chosen, both r_0 and r_1 occur with equal probability. Therefore, the probability for $\mathcal{A}$ to win the Hiding game is exactly $1/2$. □

5 Construction of USS

In this section, we present our construction for achieving both confidentiality and integrity in a USS system. Our approach combines UE for confidentiality and VC for integrity. Specifically, we follow the VC-then-UE paradigm, where each file is treated as an element of VC, and its membership proof is appended at the end of the file. The file and its membership proof are then encrypted using UE schemes.

The main challenge in this approach is that updating one file changes all other membership proofs, which are encrypted together with the files using UE. However, general UE does not support file updates, which means that all storage must be retrieved, decrypted, and re-encrypted after each update. To reduce communication and user computation costs, we require a UE with homomorphic properties. To our knowledge, only the scheme RISE [16] satisfies this requirement and is compatible with the update operation of the membership proofs of our HVC scheme in Sect. 4.

More precisely, let UE be any IND-ENC and IND-UPD secure updatable encryption scheme. RISE [16] is an IND-ENC and IND-UPD secure updatable encryption with homomorphic property described in Subsect. 2.2. Let COM be a standard commitment scheme with the hiding and binding property, and HVC be a homomorphic vector commitment with the position hiding and position binding property.

- USS.ParGen($1^\lambda, \mathcal{M}, n$): λ is the security parameter. $\mathcal{M}$ denotes the message space. n specifies the vector degree and the total number of stored files.
  - Run the setup of UE and RISE to generate public parameter $ue.pp, rise.pp$.
  - Let $hvc.crs_n$ be the public parameter of HVC.
  - Let $com.pp$ be the public parameter of COM.

  Then the public parameter $pp = (hvc.crs_n, ue.pp, rise.pp, com.pp)$ will be taken as the implicit input of the following algorithm.
- USS.KeyGen(pp): take the public parameter pp as input, run the key generation algorithm of UE and RISE to generate the secret key $ue.sk, rise.sk$, and output the secret key $sk = (ue.sk, rise.sk)$.
- USS.Store($\mathbf{m}, sk, pp$): $\mathbf{m} = \{m_1, \ldots, m_n\}$, where each m_i denotes one file. The algorithm proceeds as follows:
  1. For each $i \in [n]$, randomly sample $r_i \leftarrow_\$ \{0,1\}^\lambda$, run $\mathsf{COM}(m_i; r_i) \to h_i$.
  2. For each $i \in [n]$, run $\mathsf{UE.Enc}(ue.sk, i\|m_i\|h_i\|r_i) \to \bar{f}_i$, where $\|$ denotes concatenation in this paper. Run $\mathsf{HVC.Com}(\mathbf{h})$ to get the vector commitment C and the auxiliary input aux, where the message vector is $\mathbf{h} = (h_1, \ldots, h_n)$.
  3. For each $i \in [n]$, compute the proof Λ_i via running $\mathsf{HVC.Open}(i, \mathbf{h}, aux)$.
  4. For each $i \in [n]$, run $\mathsf{RISE.Enc}(rise.sk, \Lambda_i) \to \hat{f}_i$.
  5. Let $f_i = (\bar{f}_i, \hat{f}_i)$. Upload the total ciphertexts $\mathbf{f} = (f_1, \ldots, f_n)$ to the cloud storage service. Client stores the stub $sb = C$ and the secret key sk for the current epoch in the local storage.
- USS.Rev$_{client}(i, sk, sb, pp) \leftrightarrows$ USS.Rev$_{server}(\mathbf{f}, sb, pp)$: The client interacts with the server to retrieve the i-th file through the following procedure.
  - Rev$_{request}(i, sk, sb, pp) \to (q_{rev}, st_{rev})$: The client sends $q_{rev} = i$ to the server, where $i \in [n]$ and keeps a state $st_{rev} = ($ "retrieve", $i)$.
  - The server holds the public parameter pp, and the storing file $\mathbf{f}$. When given the retrieve request q_{rev}, the server returns the q_{rev}-th file $f_{q_{rev}}$ as the response r_{rev}.
  - Rev$_{decrypt}(sk, sb, pp, st_{rev}, r_{rev}) \to m_i/\perp$: When given the server's response r_{rev}, the client parses the $sk = (ue.sk, rise.sk)$ and $f_i = (\bar{f}_i, \hat{f}_i)$. Run UEdecryption algorithm $\mathsf{UE.Dec}(ue.sk, \bar{f}_i) \to i\|m_i\|h_i\|r_i$. Run RISE decryption algorithm $\mathsf{RISE.Dec}(rise.sk, \hat{f}_i) \to \Lambda_i$.
  - If the commitment verification $\mathsf{Com.Open}(com_i, m_i, r_i) \to 1$ and the homomorphic vector commitment verification $\mathsf{HVC.Ver}(C, h_i, i, \Lambda_i) \to 1$, then the client will output m_i, otherwise output $\perp$.

- USS.FileUp$_{client}(m_i', i, sk, sb, pp) \leftrightarrows$ USS.FileUp$_{server}(\mathbf{f}, pp)$: is an interactive procedure that allows the client to update the i-th file m_i to m_i' with the collaboration of the server. More precisely, the interaction procedure is as follows.

  1. FileUp$_{request}(m_i', i, sk, sb, pp) \rightarrow q_{fup}, st_{fup}$: The client sends the file update request $q_{fup} = ($ "$FileUpdate$", $i) = st_{fup}$ to the server to request the i-th encrypted file and keep a state st_{fup}.

  2. FileUp$_{response}(\mathbf{f}, pp, q_{fup}) \rightarrow (f_i, sr_{fup})$: The server returns the i-th encrypted file f_i to the client as the response r_{fup} and keep the internal state $sr_{fup} = ($ "$FileUpdate$", $i)$.

  3. FileUp$_{token}(sk, sb, pp, m_i', f_i, st_{fup}) \rightarrow (sb', tk_{fup})$: The client first parses $sk = (ue.sk, rise.sk)$ and $f_i = (\bar{f}_i, \hat{f}_i)$. Then run UE decryption algorithm UE.Dec$(ue.sk, \bar{f}_i) \rightarrow i\|m_i\|h_i\|r_i/\perp$, and RISE decryption algorithm RISE.Dec$\left(rise.sk, \hat{f}_i\right) = \Lambda_i/\perp$. If both decryptions are not $\perp$, then run the following verification algorithms. If the commitment opens to the different file COM.open$(h_i; r_i) \neq m_i$, or the homomorphic vector commitment verification HVC.Ver$(sb, h_i, i, \Lambda_i) \neq 1$, then output $\perp$, otherwise compute the following procedures.

     The client replaces the plaintext file with m_i', samples a randomness $r_i' \leftarrow\$ \{0,1\}^\lambda$, and commits it by running COM$(m_i'; r_i') \rightarrow h_i'$. Encrypt the new file with UE.Enc$(ue.sk, i\|m_i'\|h_i'\|r_i') \rightarrow \bar{f}_i'$. Set the change of message vector $\mathbf{m}_\delta = (0, \ldots, \delta_i = h_i' - h_i, \ldots, 0)$, and get homomorphic vector commitment $C_{\mathbf{m}_\delta}$ via running HVC.Com$(\mathbf{m}_\delta) = (C_{\mathbf{m}_\delta}, aux)$. Then update the stub sb by running the vector commitment homomorphic algorithm HVC.ComHom$(sb, C_{\mathbf{m}_\delta}) = sb'$.

     The client keeps the new stub sb' and sends the file update token $tk_{fup} = (\bar{f}_i', \mathbf{m}_\delta, aux, y = g^{rise.sk})$ to the server. Please note that the change of message vector $\mathbf{m}_\delta$ could be compressed to a constant size independent of the vector degree since it contains redundant 0 with $n-1$ degrees.

  4. FileUp$_{update}(\mathbf{f}, pp, sr_{fup}, tk_{fup}) \rightarrow \mathbf{f}'$: On receiving $tk_{fup} = (\bar{f}_i', \mathbf{m}_\delta, aux, y)$ from the client, parse $\mathbf{f} = \left((\bar{f}_1, \hat{f}_1), \ldots, (\bar{f}_n, \hat{f}_n)\right)$. For all $j \in [n]$, the server will run HVC.Open$(j, \mathbf{m}_\delta, aux) = \Lambda_{\delta_j}$, get RISE ciphertext $rise.C_{\delta_j} = (y^r, g^r \cdot \Lambda_{\delta_j})$, and get updated proof encryption

$$\hat{f}_j' = \hat{f}_j \cdot rise.C_{\delta_j} = \text{RISE.Enc}(rise.sk, \Lambda_j) \cdot rise.C_{\delta_j} = \text{RISE.Enc}(rise.sk, \Lambda_j \cdot \Lambda_{\delta_j})$$

  (The last equation is a result of the homomorphic property of RISE). Then the updated ciphertexts are $\mathbf{f}' = (f_1', \ldots, f_n')$, where $f_j' = (\bar{f}_j, \hat{f}_j')$ for $j \in [n] \setminus i$ and $f_i' = (\bar{f}_i', \hat{f}_i')$.

- USS.KeyUp$_{client}(sk, sk', sb, pp) \leftrightarrows$ USS.KeyUp$_{server}(\mathbf{f}, pp)$: The interactive procedure between the client and the server updates the stored ciphertexts to the encryption under a new key sk'. The details are as follows.

  1. KeyUp$_{token}(sk, sk', sb, pp) \rightarrow (tk, sb')$: The client first parses $sk = (ue.sk, rise.sk)$, $sk' = (ue.sk', rise.sk')$. Then get a homomorphic commitment

on $\mathbf{0}$ via HVC.Com$(\mathbf{0}) = (C_0, aux)$, and re-randomize the stub via running HVC.ComHom$(sb, C_0) \to sb'$. Run UEtoken generation algorithm UE.Next$(ue.sk, ue.sk') \to \Delta$ to generate the UE key update token Δ. Run RISE token generation algorithm RISE.Next$(rise.sk, rise.sk') \to rise.\Delta$ to generate the RISE key update token $rise.\Delta = (rise.\Delta_1, y)$. Send $tk = (\Delta, rise.\Delta, \mathbf{0}, aux)$ as the key update token for the repository. The stub is updated as sb'. Please note that $\mathbf{0}$ could be compressed into constant size, so tk is still succinct.

2. KeyUp$_{update}(\mathbf{f}, pp, tk) \to (\mathbf{f'})$: Server parses $tk = (\Delta, rise.\Delta, \mathbf{0}, aux)$, $rise.\Delta = (rise.\Delta_1, y)$, and $\mathbf{f} = (f_1, \ldots, f_n)$, where $f_i = (\bar{f}_i, \hat{f}_i)$ for $i \in [n]$. For each $i \in [n]$, run UE re-encryption algorithm UE.Upd$(\Delta, \bar{f}_i) \to \bar{f}'_i$ to update the data part. For each $i \in [n]$, run RISE re-encryption algorithm RISE.Upd$(rise.\Delta_1, \hat{f}_i) \to \hat{f}'_i$ to re-encrypt the proof part. Then for $i \in [n]$, the server runs HVC.Open$(i, \mathbf{0}, aux) = \Lambda_{\mathbf{0}_i}$, get RISE its encryption $rise.C_i = (y^r, g^r \cdot \Lambda_{\mathbf{0}_i})$ and to re-randomize the updated proof encryption

$$\hat{f}''_i = \hat{f}'_i \cdot rise.C_i = \mathsf{RISE.Enc}(rise.sk', \Lambda_i \cdot \Lambda_{\mathbf{0}_i}).$$

(The last equation is because of the homomorphic property of RISE) Finally, the updated ciphertexts are $\mathbf{f'} = (f''_1, \ldots, f''_{n-1})$, where $f''_i = \left(\bar{f}'_i, \hat{f}''_i\right)$ for $i \in [n]$.

Instantiation. In the USS construction, the HVC is instantiated in Sect. 4, the COM scheme could be instantiated with any secure commitment scheme with hiding and binding property, and the UE could be instantiated with any IND-ENC and IND-UPD secure UE schemes [16]. We know that in USS, the membership proof of HVC is encrypted by the RISE encryption algorithm. We require that the homomorphism of HVC and RISE is compatible.

5.1 Security Analysis

We formally state the security properties of the construction USS in the following theorems and prove our theorems.

Theorem 3. *If UE is an IND-ENC secure updatable encryption scheme, COM is a secure commitment scheme with hiding property, then our USS is IND-DD-CPA secure.*

Proof. We establish the IND-DD-CPA security of our scheme through a sequence of games. Initially, we consider the game $\mathsf{Exp}_{\mathsf{USS},\mathcal{A}}^{\mathsf{ind\text{-}dd\text{-}cpa}}(1^\lambda, \mathcal{M}, n, 0)$ as the starting point. In the first game, we replace the updatable encryption ciphertexts $\bar{f}_i$ with ciphertexts of random strings. The IND-ENC security of UE ensures indistinguishability. In the second game, we replace the commitment of message $m_{0,i}$ with the commitment values of message $m_{1,i}$. In the third game, we replace the updatable encryption ciphertexts $\bar{f}_i$ with ciphertexts of $i\|m_{1,i}\|h_{1,i}\|r_{1,i}$. The final game is $\mathsf{Exp}_{\mathsf{USS},\mathcal{A}}^{\mathsf{ind\text{-}dd\text{-}cpa}}(1^\lambda, \mathcal{M}, n, 1)$. A detailed proof can be found in the full version of our paper. $\square$

Theorem 4. *If UE is an IND-ENC secure updatable encryption scheme, COM is a secure commitment scheme with hiding property, then our USS is IND-FileUp-CPA secure.*

Proof. We establish the IND-FileUp-CPA security of our scheme through a sequence of games. Specifically, we start from the original game $\mathsf{Exp}_{\mathsf{USS},\mathcal{A}}^{\mathsf{ind\text{-}fileup\text{-}cpa}}(1^\lambda, \mathcal{M}, n, 0)$. In the first game, we replace the updatable encryption ciphertexts $\bar{f}_i$ with ciphertexts generated during the execution of $\mathsf{FileUp}_{token}(sk_e, sb, m_{0,i}, i, pp) \leftrightarrows \mathsf{FileUp}_{server}(sb, rep, pp) \rightarrow \langle sb^*; rep^* \rangle$. The IND-ENC security of UE ensures indistinguishability. In the second game, we replace the commitment of message $m_{0,i}$ with the commitment values of message $m_{1,i}$. In the third game, we replace the updatable encryption ciphertexts $\bar{f}_i$ with ciphertexts of $i\|m_{1,i}, \|h_{1,i}\|r_{1,i}$ generated during the execution of

$$\mathsf{FileUp}_{token}(sk_e, sb, m_{0,i}, i, pp) \leftrightarrows \mathsf{FileUp}_{server}(sb, rep, pp) \rightarrow \langle sb^*; rep^* \rangle.$$

The final game is $\mathsf{Exp}_{\mathsf{USS},\mathcal{A}}^{\mathsf{ind\text{-}fileup\text{-}cpa}}(1^\lambda, \mathcal{M}, n, 1)$. A detailed proof can be found in the full version of our paper.

$\square$

Theorem 5. *If UE is an IND-UPD secure updatable encryption scheme, RISE is an IND-ENC and IND-UPD secure updatable encryption scheme with homomorphic property, and HVC is a secure vector commitment with homomorphic property and position hiding, then our USS is IND-REENC-CPA secure.*

Proof. We prove the IND-REENC-CPA security via a sequence of games. On the high level, we start from $\mathsf{Exp}_{\mathsf{USS},\mathcal{A}}^{\mathsf{ind\text{-}reenc\text{-}cpa}}(1^\lambda, \mathcal{M}, n, 0)$ as the original game. In the first game, replaces $c_{0,i} = (\bar{f}_{0,i}, \hat{f}_{0,i})$ in rep_0 with $c_{r,i} = (\bar{f}_{r,i}, \hat{f}_{0,i})$ for a random message, commitment and its randomness as input to run the KeyUp procedure. In the second game, the encryption of the membership proof is replaced with the encryption of random elements due to the security of RISE scheme. Next, the homomorphic vector commitment of zero vectors introduced during the key update can be replaced by the homomorphic vector commitment of a random vector due to the hiding property of HVC. After that, the view of the adversary is completely independent to the starting database, hence the IND-REENC-CPA is obvious. The detailed proof can be found in the full version.

$\square$

Theorem 6. *Let USS denote an updatable secure storage scheme. COM is secure commitment with binding property, and HVC is a secure vector commitment with position binding, then USS is OF-PTXT secure.*

Proof. Intuitively, we first assume that USS is not OF-PTXT secure, and then construct contradictions with the existing properties of building blocks to prove the theorem. In the $\mathsf{Exp}_{\mathsf{USS},\mathcal{A}}^{\mathsf{of\text{-}ptxt}}(1^\lambda, \mathcal{M}, n)$ experiment, given the stub sb_e and the epoch key sk_e, to win the game, $\mathcal{A}$ needs to provide a ciphertext f_i and interact with challenger running USS.Rev procedure and enable the challenger to retrieve a file m_i' which is different from the i-th element m_i of the latest message vector **m** corresponding to the stub sb_e.

Since we assume the USS is not OF-PTXT secure, then there exists $\mathcal{A}$ winning the experiment $\mathsf{Exp}_{\mathsf{USS},\mathcal{A}}^{\mathsf{of\text{-}ptxt}}(1^\lambda, \mathcal{M}, n)$ by enabling the file $m_i' \neq m_i$ retrieval. That means the commitment of m_i' passes the verification algorithm of HVC. So $\mathcal{A}$ could win in two cases: one case is $\mathcal{A}$ finds a collision for the commitment h_i, i.e., $\mathsf{COM}(m_i'; r_i') = \mathsf{COM}(m_i; r_i) = h_i$, which is contradictory with the binding property of COM; the other case is that $\mathcal{A}$ finds the collision for the HVC, i.e., two different elements $h_i \neq h_i'$ pass the i-th vector commitment verification for the same stub sb_e, which is contradictory with HVC's position-binding property. So we can reduce USS's OF-PTXT property to COM's binding property and HVC's position binding.

$\square$

6   Future Works

Although Updatable Encryption (UE) is a promising approach for secure storage of data, it cannot be directly applied to frequently updated databases due to the risk of a malicious server inducing the client to accept an outdated version of a file instead of the latest one. To address this issue, we propose a scheme called Updatable Secure Storage (USS) that provides a secure and key-rotatable solution for dynamic databases. However, we acknowledge that the USS scheme presented in this paper is still far from practical due to its high computational and communication overheads. Therefore, we suggest several directions for future work to improve the efficiency and usability of the USS scheme.

General Construction for General UE. In this paper, we present a construction based on ciphertext-independent UE (CIUE) schemes, which we describe using the UE syntax introduced in this work. Our construction can be extended to more general ciphertext-dependent UE (CDUE) schemes. From a construction perspective, this extension is straightforward. However, ensuring security in the presence of both CIUE and CDUE requires a careful consideration of the security model. CDUE models offer more fine-grained control over token corruption, which requires a more nuanced modeling and analysis approach. We show that existing CDUE schemes are secure under some applicable security models and can be used as black-box components in the proof of USS security. This result has not been formalized or proven before.

Enhancing Performance for Files of Significant Size. Our USS scheme has the potential to offer practical efficiency, even when encrypting large files, thanks to its adherence to the KEM + DEM paradigm. Specifically, the DEM component of our scheme can be any UE ciphertext with IND-CPA security, allowing for the construction of an efficient DEM component directly from existing UE schemes. A black-box approach, such as the one proposed in [3], can be used to achieve this goal, thereby leveraging the efficiency of UE schemes. Meanwhile, the KEM component operates on a constant amount of data, ensuring strong security guarantees against attacks on data confidentiality and integrity without sacrificing efficiency. The ability to efficiently encrypt large files is particularly important in scenarios where substantial volumes of data are outsourced.

Towards Full-Fledged Version Control. In this paper, we focus on achieving the first step of version control, which involves ensuring the integrity of the latest version of a database. However, we do not currently support a fall-back function that would allow users to revert to any prior version of the database. Enabling this feature would require the database to store all historical versions or changes. One approach to implementing a limited fall-back function involves pre-configuring a set of versions for a file with empty or meaningless data and updating the corresponding version when the user makes changes. The stub would contain information on all versions to prevent malicious servers from manipulating any version to deceive users. During each key update, all versions of ciphertext undergo key rotation to hide the update history from external attackers.

Acknowlegements. We thank anonymous reviewers from ASIACRYPT'23 for their valuable comments. Long Chen was supported by the National Key R&D Program of China 2022YFB3102500 and the CAS Project for Young Scientists in Basic Research Grant YSBR-035. Hui Guo was supported by the National Natural Science Foundation of China (Grant Nos. 61802021, 62022018, 61932019).

References

1. Benabbas, S., Gennaro, R., Vahlis, Y.: Verifiable delegation of computation over large datasets. In: Rogaway, P. (ed.) CRYPTO 2011. LNCS, vol. 6841, pp. 111–131. Springer, Heidelberg (2011). https://doi.org/10.1007/978-3-642-22792-9_7
2. Boneh, D., Bünz, B., Fisch, B.: Batching techniques for accumulators with applications to IOPs and stateless blockchains. In: Boldyreva, A., Micciancio, D. (eds.) CRYPTO 2019. LNCS, vol. 11692, pp. 561–586. Springer, Cham (2019). https://doi.org/10.1007/978-3-030-26948-7_20
3. Boneh, D., Eskandarian, S., Kim, S., Shih, M.: Improving speed and security in updatable encryption schemes. In: Moriai, S., Wang, H. (eds.) ASIACRYPT 2020. LNCS, vol. 12493, pp. 559–589. Springer, Cham (2020). https://doi.org/10.1007/978-3-030-64840-4_19
4. Boneh, D., Lewi, K., Montgomery, H., Raghunathan, A.: Key homomorphic PRFs and their applications. In: Canetti, R., Garay, J.A. (eds.) CRYPTO 2013, Part I. LNCS, vol. 8042, pp. 410–428. Springer, Heidelberg (2013). https://doi.org/10.1007/978-3-642-40041-4_23
5. Boyd, C., Davies, G.T., Gjøsteen, K., Jiang, Y.: Fast and secure updatable encryption. In: Micciancio, D., Ristenpart, T. (eds.) CRYPTO 2020. LNCS, vol. 12170, pp. 464–493. Springer, Cham (2020). https://doi.org/10.1007/978-3-030-56784-2_16
6. Bradley, M., Dent, A.: Payment card industry data security standard (2010)
7. Campanelli, M., Fiore, D., Greco, N., Kolonelos, D., Nizzardo, L.: Vector commitment techniques and applications to verifiable decentralized storage. IACR Cryptology ePrint Archive 2020:149 (2020)
8. Catalano, D., Fiore, D.: Vector commitments and their applications. In: Kurosawa, K., Hanaoka, G. (eds.) PKC 2013. LNCS, vol. 7778, pp. 55–72. Springer, Heidelberg (2013). https://doi.org/10.1007/978-3-642-36362-7_5

9. Chen, L., Li, Y., Tang, Q.: CCA updatable encryption against malicious re-encryption attacks. In: Moriai, S., Wang, H. (eds.) ASIACRYPT 2020. LNCS, vol. 12493, pp. 590–620. Springer, Cham (2020). https://doi.org/10.1007/978-3-030-64840-4_20

10. Christ, M., Bonneau, J.: Limits on revocable proof systems, with applications to stateless blockchains. IACR Cryptology ePrint Archive, p. 1478 (2022)

11. de Castro, L., Peikert, C.: Functional commitments for all functions, with transparent setup and from sis. In: Hazay, C., Stam, M. (eds.) EUROCRYPT 2023, Part III. LNCS, vol. 14006, pp. 287–320. Springer, Cham (2023). https://doi.org/10.1007/978-3-031-30620-4_10

12. Everspaugh, A., Paterson, K., Ristenpart, T., Scott, S.: Key rotation for authenticated encryption. In: Katz, J., Shacham, H. (eds.) CRYPTO 2017, Part III. LNCS, vol. 10403, pp. 98–129. Springer, Cham (2017). https://doi.org/10.1007/978-3-319-63697-9_4

13. Payment Card Industry. Data Security Standard. Requirements and Security Assessment Procedures. Version 3.2 PCI Security Standards Council (2016)

14. Klooß, M., Lehmann, A., Rupp, A.: (R)CCA secure updatable encryption with integrity protection. In: Ishai, Y., Rijmen, V. (eds.) EUROCRYPT 2019, Part I. LNCS, vol. 11476, pp. 68–99. Springer, Cham (2019). https://doi.org/10.1007/978-3-030-17653-2_3

15. Lai, R.W.F., Malavolta, G.: Subvector commitments with application to succinct arguments. In: Boldyreva, A., Micciancio, D. (eds.) CRYPTO 2019. LNCS, vol. 11692, pp. 530–560. Springer, Cham (2019). https://doi.org/10.1007/978-3-030-26948-7_19

16. Lehmann, A., Tackmann, B.: Updatable encryption with post-compromise security. In: Nielsen, J.B., Rijmen, V. (eds.) EUROCRYPT 2018, Part III. LNCS, vol. 10822, pp. 685–716. Springer, Cham (2018). https://doi.org/10.1007/978-3-319-78372-7_22

17. Pedersen, T.P.: Non-interactive and information-theoretic secure verifiable secret sharing. In: Feigenbaum, J. (ed.) CRYPTO 1991. LNCS, vol. 576, pp. 129–140. Springer, Heidelberg (1992). https://doi.org/10.1007/3-540-46766-1_9

18. Peikert, C., Pepin, Z., Sharp, C.: Vector and functional commitments from lattices. In: Nissim, K., Waters, B. (eds.) TCC 2021. LNCS, vol. 13044, pp. 480–511. Springer, Cham (2021). https://doi.org/10.1007/978-3-030-90456-2_16

19. Wee, H., Wu, D.J.: Succinct vector, polynomial, and functional commitments from lattices. In: Hazay, C., Stam, M. (eds.) EUROCRYPT 2023, Part III. LNCS, vol. 14006, pp. 385–416. Springer, Cham (2023). https://doi.org/10.1007/978-3-031-30620-4_13

Fine-Grained Proxy Re-encryption: Definitions and Constructions from LWE

Yunxiao Zhou[1,2], Shengli Liu[2,3]($\boxtimes$) ![ID], Shuai Han[1,2]($\boxtimes$) ![ID], and Haibin Zhang[4] ![ID]

[1] School of Cyber Science and Engineering, Shanghai Jiao Tong University, Shanghai 200240, China
{cloudzhou,dalen17}@sjtu.edu.cn
[2] State Key Laboratory of Cryptology, P.O. Box 5159, Beijing 100878, China
[3] Department of Computer Science and Engineering, Shanghai Jiao Tong University, Shanghai 200240, China
slliu@sjtu.edu.cn
[4] Beijing Institute of Technology, Beijing 100081, China
bchainzhang@aliyun.com

Abstract. Proxy re-encryption (PRE) allows a proxy with a re-encryption key to translate a ciphertext intended for Alice (delegator) to another ciphertext intended for Bob (delegatee) without revealing the underlying message. However, with PRE, Bob can obtain the whole message from the re-encrypted ciphertext, and Alice cannot take flexible control of the extent of the message transmitted to Bob.

In this paper, we propose a new variant of PRE, called Fine-Grained PRE (FPRE), to support fine-grained re-encryptions. An FPRE is associated with a function family $\mathcal{F}$, and each re-encryption key $rk_{A \to B}^f$ is associated with a function $f \in \mathcal{F}$. With FPRE, Alice now can authorize re-encryption power to proxy by issuing $rk_{A \to B}^f$ to it, with f chosen by herself. Then the proxy can translate ciphertext encrypting m to Bob's ciphertext encrypting $f(m)$ with such a fine-grained re-encryption key, and Bob only obtains a function of message m. In this way, Alice can take flexible control of the message spread by specifying functions.

For FPRE, we formally define its syntax and formalize security notions including CPA security, ciphertext pseudo-randomness, unidirectionality, non-transitivity, collusion-safety under adaptive corruptions in the multi-user setting. Moreover, we propose a new security notion named *ciphertext unlinkability*, which blurs the link between a ciphertext and its re-encrypted ciphertext to hide the proxy connections between users. We establish the relations between those security notions.

As for constructions, we propose two FPRE schemes, one for bounded linear functions and the other for deletion functions, based on the learning-with-errors (LWE) assumption. Our FPRE schemes achieve all the aforementioned desirable securities under adaptive corruptions in the standard model. As far as we know, our schemes provide the *first* solution to PRE with security under adaptive corruptions in the standard model.

© International Association for Cryptologic Research 2023
J. Guo and R. Steinfeld (Eds.): ASIACRYPT 2023, LNCS 14443, pp. 199–231, 2023.
https://doi.org/10.1007/978-981-99-8736-8_7

1   Introduction

A proxy re-encryption (PRE) scheme is a public-key encryption (PKE) scheme augmented with two functionalities. One is the generation of re-encryption key $rk_{i\to j}$ for user i and user j. The other is ciphertext re-encryption which translates a ciphertext $ct^{(i)}$ encrypting message m under user i's public key $pk^{(i)}$ to a ciphertext $ct^{(j)}$ encrypting the same message m under user j's public key $pk^{(j)}$. With PRE, user i (delegator) can authorize re-encryption power to a proxy by issuing a re-encryption key $rk_{i\to j}$. Then the proxy can use $rk_{i\to j}$ to accomplish the ciphertext translation from $ct^{(i)}$ to $ct^{(j)}$, which further enables user j (delegatee) to recover the message. Beyond the traditional semantic security of PKE, PRE also requires that the knowledge of $rk_{i\to j}$ does not help any proxy to gain (in a computational sense) any information on the message encrypted in ciphertexts $ct^{(i)}$ and $ct^{(j)}$.

PRE has found lots of applications since introduced by Blaze et al. [3]. For example, a patient i may issue a re-encryption key $rk_{i\to j}$ to a hospital. When he receives his own medical testing report $ct^{(i)}$ encrypted under his public key $pk^{(i)}$ and would like to see a doctor for diagnosis, he can forward $ct^{(i)}$ to the hospital. Then the hospital converts $ct^{(i)}$ to $ct^{(j)}$ under doctor j's public key, and the doctor can use his/her own secret key $sk^{(j)}$ to decrypt $ct^{(j)}$ to recover the patient's original medical testing report, which helps him for disease diagnosis.

- **Unidirectional vs. Bidirectional.** A PRE scheme is *unidirectional* if $rk_{i\to j}$ only allows re-encryption from $pk^{(i)}$ to $pk^{(j)}$ but *not vice versa*. In contrast, a *bidirectional* PRE scheme allows bidirectional ciphertext translations between $pk^{(i)}$ and $pk^{(j)}$ with a single $rk_{i\leftrightarrow j}$. Compared to unidirectional PRE, the proxies in a bidirectional PRE scheme are authorized more re-encryption power, and this is not welcomed especially when the other direction is not permitted by user j. Therefore, unidirectional PRE is preferable to its bidirectional counterpart. Moreover, as shown by [5], a unidirectional PRE implies a bidirectional one.
- **Single-hop vs. Multi-hop.** A PRE scheme is *single-hop* if a re-encrypted ciphertext cannot be further re-encrypted by any re-encryption key. In contrast, with a *multi-hop* PRE, a ciphertext $ct^{(i)}$ is translated to $ct^{(j)}$ by $rk_{i\to j}$, and $ct^{(j)}$ can be further translated to $ct^{(k)}$ by $rk_{j\to k}$. With the multi-hop property, a malicious proxy may lead to lost of control of authorization. For example, a proxy with $rk_{i\to j}, rk_{j\to k}$ can easily obtains re-encryption power from i to k which may be undesirable for user i.
- **Non-Interactive vs. Interactive.** A PRE scheme is *non-interactive* if the generation of re-encryption key $rk_{i\to j}$ does not need user j's secret key $sk^{(j)}$. In contrast, an *interactive* PRE needs $sk^{(j)}$, and hence user j must be on-line and involved in the generation of $rk_{i\to j}$. Clearly the non-interactive property is preferable to the interactive one.

In this paper, we focus on *unidirectional*, *single-hop* and *non-interactive* PRE.

Security of PRE. PRE is usually deployed in multi-user settings, where the adversary is able to corrupt some users by obtaining their secret keys, and it is also able to obtain re-encryption keys between some users. The main security notion for a PRE scheme is indistinguishability under chosen-plaintext attacks (CPA) or chosen-ciphertext attacks (CCA) for some challenge ciphertext ct^* under some target user i^*, against probabilistic polynomial-time (PPT) adversaries who corrupt users and obtain re-encryption keys of its own choices. Of course, the knowledge of corrupted secret keys and re-encryption keys should not lead to trivial decryption of ct^*. According to the way that the adversary corrupts the users, there are two types of security notions.

- **Security under selective corruptions.** At the beginning of the security game, the adversary submits a set of users that it wants to corrupt, and the challenger returns all the secret keys of users in the corruption set.
- **Security under adaptive corruptions.** Throughout the security game, the adversary issues corruption queries adaptively.

Obviously, CPA/CCA security under adaptive corruptions is stronger than that under selective corruptions. In [11], Fuchsbauer et al. proposed a security reduction from selective corruptions to adaptive corruptions for PRE, but it suffers from a super-polynomial security loss $n^{O(\log n)}$ with n the number of users. To the best of our knowledge, all existing PRE schemes with adaptive corruptions are based on the Random Oracle (RO) model, and there is no PRE scheme achieving even CPA security under adaptive corruptions in the standard model.

Similarly, the rest of security notions including CPR, UNID, NTR, CUL, CS can be defined either under selective corruptions or under adaptive corruptions.

- **Ciphertext Pseudo-Randomness** (CPR). CPR is similar to but stronger than CPA security. It requires that the challenge ciphertext is computationally indistinguishable to an element randomly chosen from the ciphertext space.
- **Unidirectionality** (UNID). Roughly speaking, unidirectionality requires that it is hard for adversaries to compute $rk_{i \to j}$ with the knowledge of $rk_{j \to i}$.
- **Non-Transitivity** (NTR). For a single-hop unidirectional PRE scheme, non-transitivity requires that it is hard for adversaries to compute $rk_{i \to k}$ even with the knowledge of $rk_{i \to j}$ and $rk_{j \to k}$. It is easy to see that NTR, as well as UNID, captures the precise authorization of re-encryption power.
- **Ciphertext Unlinkability** (CUL). For a single-hop unidirectional PRE scheme, if $ct^{(j)}$ is encrypted from $ct^{(i)}$ with re-encryption key $rk_{i \to j}$, then $ct^{(j)}$ is linked to $ct^{(i)}$. Ciphertext unlinkability requires that the linked ciphertext pair $(ct^{(i)}, ct^{(j)})$ is computationally indistinguishable from independently generated ciphertexts $ct'^{(i)}$ and $ct'^{(j)}$. The indistinguishability should also be considered in the corruption scenario in the multi-user settings. As far as we know, there is no formal security definition for ciphertext-unlinkability yet.
- **Collusion-Safety** (CS). For a single-hop unidirectional PRE scheme, collusion-safety requires that it is hard for adversaries to compute secret key $sk^{(i)}$ even with the knowledge of $rk_{i \to j}$ and $sk^{(j)}$. This notion is also called *master secret security* in [2,8,15,19–21]. Note that secret key $sk^{(i)}$ may not be unique w.r.t. $pk^{(i)}$. Therefore, in this paper, we consider a stronger notion

of Collusion-Safety (CS), which requires the CPA security of the ciphertext under public key $pk^{(i)}$ against adversaries who obtains $rk_{i \to j}, sk^{(j)}$ and can also corrupt users and issue re-encryption queries. Clearly, CS implies the master secret security.

Related Works. Let us recall existing works on single-hop unidirectional PRE. In [21], Shao et al. designed the first CCA-secure unidirectional single-hop PRE scheme from the DDH assumption under adaptive corruptions in the RO model. However, Chow et al. [8] showed an attack on the scheme of [21], and presented a fixed PRE scheme, which achieves CCA-security but only under selective corruptions in the RO model. Moreover, Selvi et al. [19] pointed out a weakness in the proof in [8] and presented a PRE scheme achieving CCA security under selective corruptions, also in the RO model. Later, Canard et al. [4] proposed a CCA-secure PRE scheme under adaptive corruptions again in the RO model.

As for standard model, Ateniese et al. [2] designed the first unidirectional single-hop PRE scheme from the DBDH assumption, achieving weak-CPA security. Later, Libert et al. [15] designed the first CCA-secure scheme from 3-QDBDH assumption. In [13], Kirshanova proposed the first lattice-based weak CCA1-secure scheme. However, Fan et al. [10] pointed out a mistake of the proof in [13] and presented a new latticed-based scheme, achieving tag-based CCA (tbCCA) security, with a security level between weak-CCA1 in [13] and CCA security in [15]. Unfortunately, these schemes only achieve selective security in the standard model.

There are also a variety of PRE with extended functionalities. Shao [20] proposed the notion of anonymous identity-based PRE and presented a scheme achieving CCA security under adaptive corruptions in the RO model. Chandran et al. [6,7] generalized PRE to functional re-encryption scheme and constructed functional PRE schemes from obfuscations, which are secure under selective corruption. In their schemes, the policy function F defines the access policy. Only the policy is satisfied, can a user decrypt the re-encrypted ciphertext to recover the original message successfully. Similarly, Weng et al. [23] and Liang et al. [14] proposed attribute-based conditional PRE schemes to achieve attribute-based policy control, and their schemes are CPA secure under selective corruptions. Recently, Miao et al. [16] proposed a unidirectional multi-hop updatable PRE from DDH with security under selective corruptions in the standard model.

The related works on PRE shows that there is no PRE or its variant schemes achieving CPA or CCA security under adaptive corruptions in the standard model.[1] It is natural to ask:

Q1: *Can we construct a PRE scheme meeting the* CPA *security under adaptive corruptions in the standard model, possibly also achieving ciphertext unlinkability, unidirectionality, non-transitivity and collusion-safety?*

---

[1] In fact, to the best of our knowledge, there is no PRE with security under adaptive corruptions in the standard model, no matter single-hop or multi-hop, unidirectional or bidirectional, interactive or non-interactive PREs.

Fine-Grained PRE. Up to now, the re-encryption of $ct^{(i)}$ under $pk^{(i)}$ only generates $ct^{(j)}$ under $pk^{(j)}$ encrypting the same message as $ct^{(i)}$. This is an *all-or-nothing* style of re-encryption.

Let us take the patient-hospital-doctor example again. With PRE, either a doctor sees all the medical testing data, say (m_1, m_2, m_3), in the reports or nothing at all. In fact, the patient may only want to reveal a part of the data, like $(m_1, *, m_3)$, to the doctor and hide some sensitive data m_2 from the doctor. Even more generally, the patient may only allow revealing a function of his data, say $f(m_1, m_2, m_3)$, to another party. If we resort to PRE, then the PRE must be able to do a fine-grained re-encryption authorization to proxies. More precisely, re-encryption key $rk^f_{i \to j}$ for user i and user j must be associated with a function f. With $rk^f_{i \to j}$, the proxy is authorized with re-encryption power, but limited by function f. Accordingly, the proxy is only able to translate a ciphertext $ct^{(i)}$ encrypting message m under user i's public key $pk^{(i)}$ to a ciphertext $ct^{(j)}$ encrypting $f(m)$ under $pk^{(j)}$ of user j. Such a fine-grained single-hop unidirectional PRE is able to accurately control message spread to other parties by means of functions $\{f\}$. Up to now, there is no work on this topic. Thus, question Q1 is now upgraded to another interesting question:

Q2: *Can we construct a* <u>*Fine-Grained*</u> *PRE scheme achieving the* CPA *security under adaptive corruptions in the standard model, possibly also achieving ciphertext unlinkability, unidirectionality, non-transitivity and collusion-safety?*

Our Contributions. In this work, we answer the above question in the affirmative. Our contributions are three-fold.

– *Formal Definitions for Fine-Grained PRE and Its Securities.* We present the formal definitions for the new concept Fine-Grained PRE (FPRE), which generalizes PRE by enabling fine-grained re-encryption power.

  Moreover, we present the formal definitions for a set of security notions for FPRE, including CPA security, ciphertext pseudorandomness (CPR), unidirectionality (UNID), non-transitivity (NTR) and collusion-safety (CS). We also propose a new security notion named ciphertext unlinkability (CUL), which blurs the link between a ciphertext and its re-encrypted ciphertext. All the security notions are formalized in a multi-user setting where the adversary is able to corrupt users and obtain re-encryption keys *adaptively*.

  We establish the relations between these security notions: CPA implies both UNID and NTR, CUL implies CPA, and CPR (trivially) implies CPA. See Fig. 1 for an overview.

– *Construction of FPRE for Bounded Linear Functions from LWE.* We propose a unidirectional, single-hop, non-interactive FPRE scheme $\mathsf{FPRE}^{\mathsf{lin}}_{\mathsf{LWE}}$, and the fine-grained function family consists of bounded linear functions $\mathcal{F}_{\mathsf{lin}}$ (with coefficients of bounded norm). Our $\mathsf{FPRE}^{\mathsf{lin}}_{\mathsf{LWE}}$ achieves CPA, UNID, NTR, CS and CUL security *under adaptive corruptions in the standard model*, based on the learning-with-errors (LWE) assumption. The LWE assumption makes our scheme quantum-safe. In addition, our scheme is *key-optimal* (in the sense of [2]), where the delegatee's secret storage remains constant regardless of the number of delegations it accepts.

When setting the linear function to be the identity function, we immediately get a single-hop unidirectional (traditional) PRE scheme, which contributes as the *first* PRE scheme with security under adaptive corruptions in the standard model.

- *Construction of FPRE for Deletion Functions from LWE.* As a by-product, our $\mathsf{FPRE}_{\mathsf{LWE}}^{\mathsf{lin}}$ for bounded linear functions can be easily adapted to a scheme $\mathsf{FPRE}_{\mathsf{LWE}}^{\mathsf{del}}$ for deletion functions $\mathcal{F}_{\mathsf{del}}$, which can be applied in various realistic scenarios.

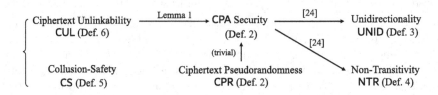

Fig. 1. Security notions of FPRE under adaptive corruptions and their relations.

We refer to Table 1 for a comparison of our scheme with known single-hop unidirectional PRE schemes.[2]

Technical Overview of Our LWE-Based FPRE Scheme. Below we give a high-level overview of our FPRE scheme $\mathsf{FPRE}_{\mathsf{LWE}}^{\mathsf{lin}}$ for the bounded linear function family based on LWE, and in particular, explain how we realize fine-grained re-encryptions. For simplicity, we do not specify the dimensions of matrices/vectors.

We start with the dual Regev PKE scheme [18] encrypting a multiple-bit message $\mathbf{m} \in \{0,1\}^{\ell}$. The ciphertext under user i's public key $\mathbf{A}^{(i)} = \binom{\overline{\mathbf{A}}^{(i)}}{\underline{\mathbf{A}}^{(i)}}$ is

$$ct^{(i)} = \mathbf{A}^{(i)}\mathbf{s} + \mathbf{e} + \begin{pmatrix} \mathbf{0} \\ \lfloor q/2 \rfloor \mathbf{m} \end{pmatrix} = \begin{pmatrix} \overline{\mathbf{A}}^{(i)}\mathbf{s} + \mathbf{e}_1 \\ \underline{\mathbf{A}}^{(i)}\mathbf{s} + \mathbf{e}_2 + \lfloor q/2 \rfloor \cdot \mathbf{m} \end{pmatrix}, \qquad (1)$$

where $\mathbf{e} = \binom{\mathbf{e}_1}{\mathbf{e}_2}$ is an error vector.

---

[2] We explain the security notions in Table 1: "weak-CPA/CCA1" does not allow the adversary to issue any re-encryption key query from an honest user to a corrupted user, while "CPA/CCA" allows such queries (except for trivial attacks). "tbCCA" refers to tag-based CCA and was first introduced in [10], with a security level between weak-CCA1 and CCA. "HRA" refers to security against honest re-encryption attacks), proposed in [9], and its does not allow such re-encryption key query, but provides re-encryption oracle to answer re-encryptions of honestly generated ciphertexts for corrupted users. On the one hand, HRA does not allow the adversary to obtain any re-encryption key from the honest user to the corrupted user, which is weaker than our CPA; on the other hand, the adversary in the HRA model can obtain re-encryptions of the honestly-generated ciphertexts from the challenge user to the corrupted user, which is not allowed in our CPA model.

Table 1. Comparison of single-hop unidirectional PRE schemes. The column **Standard Model?** asks whether the security is proved in the standard model. The column **Adaptive Corruptions?** asks whether all the security notions support adaptive corruptions. The column **Security** shows the type of security that the scheme achieves, where "HRA" refers to security against honest re-encryption attack [9] and "tbCCA" refers to tag-based CCA [10]. The column **UNID** shows whether the scheme has unidirectionality. The column **CUL** shows whether the scheme has ciphertext unlinkability. The column **NTR** shows whether the scheme has non-transitivity. The column **CS** shows whether the scheme is collusion-safe. The column **Assumption** shows the assumptions that the security of the scheme is based on, where DBDH refers to the Decision Bilinear Diffie-Hellman assumption, DCDH refers to the Divisible CDH assumption and 3-QDBDH refers to the 3-Quotient DBDH assumption. The column **Post Quantum?** asks whether the scheme is based on a post quantum assumption like LWE. The column **Fine-Grained?** asks whether the scheme supports fine-grained re-encryptions. "–" means that no proof is provided.

PRE Scheme	Standard Model?	Adaptive Corruptions?	Security	UNID	NTR	CUL	CS	Assumption	Post Quantum?	Fine–Grained?
SC09 [21]	×	✓	CCA	✓	✓	–	✓	DDH	×	×
CWYD10 [8]	×	×	CCA	✓	✓	–	✓	CDH	×	×
CDL11 [4]	×	✓	CCA	✓	✓	–	✓	CDH	×	×
Shao12 [20]	×	✓	CCA	✓	✓	–	✓	DBDH	×	×
SPR17 [19]	×	×	CCA	✓	✓	–	✓	DCDH	×	×
AFGH05 [2]	✓	×	weak-CPA	✓	–	–	✓	DBDH	×	×
LV08 [15]	✓	×	CCA	✓	✓	–	✓	3-QDBDH	×	×
Kirshanova14 [13]	✓	×	weak-CCA1	✓	–	–	–	LWE	✓	×
FL19 [10]	✓	×	tbCCA	✓	✓	–	–	LWE	✓	×
SDDR21 [22]	✓	×	HRA	✓	✓	–	–	LWE	✓	×
LWYYJW21 [14]	✓	×	CPA	✓	–	–	–	LWE	✓	×
This work	✓	✓	CPA	✓	✓	✓	✓	LWE	✓	✓

(a) The generation of re-encryption key. Let $\mathbf{I}$ be the identity matrix. Multiplying a small-norm matrix $\left(\mathbf{R} \mid \begin{matrix} \mathbf{0} \\ \mathbf{I} \end{matrix} \right)$ to $ct^{(i)}$ yields

$$\left(\mathbf{R} \,\Big|\, \begin{matrix} \mathbf{0} \\ \mathbf{I} \end{matrix} \right) \cdot ct^{(i)} = \underbrace{\left(\mathbf{R}\overline{\mathbf{A}}^{(i)} + \begin{pmatrix} \mathbf{0} \\ \mathbf{I} \end{pmatrix} \underline{\mathbf{A}}^{(i)} \right)}_{(*)} \cdot \mathbf{s} + \underbrace{\mathbf{Re}_1 + \begin{pmatrix} \mathbf{0} \\ \mathbf{I} \cdot \mathbf{e}_2 \end{pmatrix}}_{\mathbf{e}'} + \begin{pmatrix} \mathbf{0} \\ \lfloor q/2 \rfloor \cdot \mathbf{I} \cdot \mathbf{m} \end{pmatrix}.$$

With the help of the trapdoor $\mathbf{T}^{(i)}$ of $\overline{\mathbf{A}}^{(i)}$, a small-norm $\mathbf{R}$ can be found with the pre-image sampling algorithm [12] so that $\mathbf{R}\overline{\mathbf{A}}^{(i)} = \mathbf{A}^{(j)} - \binom{\mathbf{0}}{\mathbf{I}}\underline{\mathbf{A}}^{(i)}$. Consequently, $\mathbf{A}^{(j)} = (*)$ and $ct^{(j)} := \left(\mathbf{R} \,\Big|\, \begin{matrix} \mathbf{0} \\ \mathbf{I} \end{matrix} \right) \cdot ct^{(i)} = \mathbf{A}^{(j)} \cdot \mathbf{s} + \mathbf{e}' + \binom{\mathbf{0}}{\lfloor q/2 \rfloor \cdot \mathbf{m}}$, which can be decrypted to recover message $\mathbf{m}$ by user j. Taking $\mathbf{R}$ as the re-generation key $rk_{i \to j}$, then we can translate $ct^{(i)}$ to $ct^{(j)}$ successfully.

(b) The CPA security of $ct^{(i)}$. There is a dilemma to prove the CPA security of $ct^{(i)}$: applying the LWE assumption to $ct^{(i)}$ requires $\mathbf{A}^{(i)}$ be a uniformly distributed matrix with trapdoor unknown; but the generation of $rk_{i \to j} = \mathbf{R}$ needs a trapdoor $\mathbf{T}^{(i)}$. Moreover, we can hardly change the generation of $\mathbf{R}$ to avoid using $\mathbf{T}^{(i)}$ since the relation between public keys $pk^{(i)} = \mathbf{A}^{(i)}, pk^{(j)} = \mathbf{A}^{(j)}$ and the re-generation key $\mathbf{R}$ can be easily checked by $\mathbf{R}\overline{\mathbf{A}}^{(i)} = \mathbf{A}^{(j)} - \binom{\mathbf{0}}{\mathbf{I}}\underline{\mathbf{A}}^{(i)}$.

To solve the problem, we change the way of generating $rk_{i \to j} = \mathbf{R}$: now $\mathbf{R}$ is sampled with the pre-image sampling algorithm so that $\mathbf{R}\overline{\mathbf{A}}^{(i)} = \mathbf{A}^{(j)} \cdot \mathbf{S} + \mathbf{E} - \binom{\mathbf{0}}{\mathbf{I}}\underline{\mathbf{A}}^{(i)}$, instead of $\mathbf{R}\overline{\mathbf{A}}^{(i)} = \mathbf{A}^{(j)} - \binom{\mathbf{0}}{\mathbf{I}}\underline{\mathbf{A}}^{(i)}$, where $\mathbf{S}$ and $\mathbf{E}$ are small-norm matrices following discrete Gaussian distribution. Thus, $\mathbf{A}^{(j)} \cdot \mathbf{S} + \mathbf{E} = (*)$ and

$$ct^{(j)} := \left(\mathbf{R} \ \Big| \ \begin{matrix} \mathbf{0} \\ \mathbf{I} \end{matrix} \right) \cdot ct^{(i)} = \mathbf{A}^{(j)} \cdot \mathbf{S} \cdot \mathbf{s} + \underbrace{\mathbf{E} \cdot \mathbf{s} + \mathbf{e}'}_{\mathbf{e}''} + \left(\begin{matrix} \mathbf{0} \\ \lfloor q/2 \rfloor \cdot \mathbf{I} \cdot \mathbf{m} \end{matrix} \right). \qquad (2)$$

When $\mathbf{s}$ is a small-norm vector, $\mathbf{e}''$ is small enough so that $ct^{(j)}$ can also be successfully decrypted by user j's secret key.

When targeting on the CPA security of $ct^{(i)}$, the adversary must not corrupt j if it has already obtained $rk_{i \to j} = \mathbf{R}$ (to avoid trivial attacks). According to the LWE assumption, $\mathbf{A}^{(j)} \cdot \mathbf{S} + \mathbf{E}$ is computationally indistinguishable to a uniform distribution, and so is $\mathbf{R}\overline{\mathbf{A}}^{(i)} \left(= \mathbf{A}^{(j)} \cdot \mathbf{S} + \mathbf{E} - \binom{\mathbf{0}}{\mathbf{I}}\underline{\mathbf{A}}^{(i)} \right)$. Then we can modify the generation of $rk_{i \to j} = \mathbf{R}$ by sampling from a discrete Gaussian distribution independently. According to [12], such a $\mathbf{R}$ makes $\mathbf{R}\overline{\mathbf{A}}^{(i)}$ uniformly distributed. Therefore, the adversary hardly realizes this modification of $\mathbf{R}$. Now the generation of $\mathbf{R}$ is free of trapdoor $\mathbf{T}^{(i)}$, and the LWE assumption assures the pseudo-randomness of $ct^{(i)}$.

Up to now, we obtain a multi-hop PRE since $ct^{(j)}$ can be similarly re-encrypted to $ct^{(k)}$ with $rk_{j \to k}$ generated in a similar way.

(c) Achieving single-hop with ciphertexts of two levels. We resort to two level ciphertexts to achieve single-hop for PRE, inspired by [2,15]. The first-level ciphertext $ct_1^{(i)}$ is defined as in (1). The second-level ciphertext $ct_2^{(i)} = \mathbf{A}'^{(i)}\mathbf{s} + \mathbf{e} + \binom{\mathbf{0}}{\lfloor q/2 \rfloor \mathbf{m}}$ is also a dual Regev ciphertext. Then user i's public key is $pk^{(i)} = (\mathbf{A}^{(i)}, \mathbf{A}'^{(i)})$ and secret key is $sk^{(i)} = (\mathbf{T}^{(i)}, \mathbf{K}^{(i)})$ with $\underline{\mathbf{A}}'^{(i)} = \mathbf{K}^{(i)}\overline{\mathbf{A}}'^{(i)}$. Now the re-encryption key $rk_{i \to j}$ translates the first-level ciphertext $ct_1^{(i)}$ under i to the second-level ciphertext $ct_2^{(j)}$ under j. If user j has no trapdoor for $\overline{\mathbf{A}}'^{(j)}$, then he cannot generate re-encryption key $rk_{j \to k}$ for further hops. This can be accomplished by putting $\overline{\mathbf{A}}'(= \overline{\mathbf{A}}'^{(j)})$ in public parameter and shared by all users. In this way, we obtain a single-hop PRE.

(d) Achieving fine-grained re-encryption for deletion functions and bounded linear functions. According to (2), the re-encrypted ciphertext $ct_2^{(j)}$ is in fact an encryption of $\mathbf{I} \cdot \mathbf{m}$. If $\mathbf{I}$ is replaced by a binary matrix $\mathbf{M}$ (of bounded norm), then $rk_{i \to j} := \left(\mathbf{R} \ | \ \begin{smallmatrix} \mathbf{0} \\ \mathbf{M} \end{smallmatrix} \right)$ and $ct_2^{(j)}$ becomes an encryption of $\mathbf{M} \cdot \mathbf{m}$, which is a bounded linear function of $\mathbf{m}$. For example, setting $\mathbf{M} := \mathbf{I}'$ with $\mathbf{I}'$ is almost equal to $\mathbf{I}$ except that its v-th row is a zero-row, then the v-th entry in $\mathbf{I} \cdot \mathbf{m}$ is erased to 0. This highlights the idea of designing fine-grained PRE with deletion functions (see Sect. 5 for details.) To support larger message space and more linear functions, we set $q = p^2$ and replace $\lfloor q/2 \rfloor$ with p in ciphertexts. In this way, the message space and (small-norm) $\mathbf{M}$ can be defined over $\mathbb{Z}_p$.

(e) Achieving adaptive security for fine-grained PRE. The CPA security of fine-grained PRE focuses on the first-level ciphertext $ct_1^{(i)}$ for the target user i, even if the adversary obtains re-encryption keys and corrupts users adaptively. We allow the adversary obtains $rk_{i' \to j'}$ and corrupts j' to obtain $sk^{(j')}$, as long as $i' \neq i$ ($i' = i$ will lead to a trivial attack). Therefore, our CPA security is actually stronger than the CPA notion defined in [2,9,11], where $rk_{i' \to j'}$ is invisible to the adversary when i' is uncorrupted and j' is corrupted.

To prove adaptive CPA security, we first use the guessing strategy for the target user i, and this only leads to a security loss of $\mathfrak{n}$, the number of users. Note that if j is corrupted, then the adversary cannot see $rk_{i \to j}$ (to avoid trivial attacks). But the adversary is able to obtain $rk_{i \to j}$ for all uncorrupted j. For those $rk_{i \to j}$, the generation of $\mathbf{R}$ can be indistinguishably changed to independently sampling $\mathbf{R}$ with some discrete Gaussian distribution, thanks to the LWE assumption which makes $\mathbf{R}\overline{\mathbf{A}}^{(i)} (= \mathbf{A}'^{(j)} \cdot \mathbf{S} + \mathbf{E} - \binom{0}{1}\underline{\mathbf{A}}^{(i)})$ pseudo-random. As a result, all $rk_{i \to j}$ w.r.t. uncorrupted j are independent of the challenge ciphertext $ct_1^{(i)}$. Meanwhile, the generations of $rk_{i' \to j'}$ and $sk^{(i')}$ with $i' \neq i$ are only related to $\mathbf{A}^{(i')}$, and hence are also independent of $ct_1^{(i)}$. Then we can use the LWE assumption to prove the pseudo-randomness of the challenge ciphertext $ct_1^{(i)}$, and CPA security follows.

Moreover, the sampling of $\mathbf{R}$ retains enough entropy, and a uniform $ct_1^{(i)}$ can act as an extractor on $\mathbf{R}$ so that $ct_2^{(j)} := \left(\mathbf{R} \mid \begin{matrix} \mathbf{0} \\ \mathbf{I} \end{matrix}\right) \cdot ct_1^{(i)}$ is statistically close to a uniform distribution. Hence it is hard for an adversary to realize the link between $ct_1^{(i)}$ and its re-encrypted ciphertext $ct_2^{(j)}$, thus CUL security is achieved.

It is easy to check that CPA security implies unidirectionality (UNID) and non-transitivity (NTR). In the CPA security, adversary is able to see $rk_{i' \to i}$ and a corrupted secret key $sk^{(i')}$. If UNID does not hold, then the adversary can recover $rk_{i \to i'}$ from $rk_{i' \to i}$ and obtain the ability to decrypt the challenge ciphertext of i from $rk_{i \to i'}$ and $sk^{(i')}$, thus breaking the CPA security. Similarly, in the CPA security, adversary is able to see $rk_{i \to j}$, $rk_{j \to k}$ and a corrupted secret key $sk^{(k)}$. If NTR does not hold, the adversary can recover $rk_{i \to k}$ from $rk_{i \to j}$ and $rk_{j \to k}$. Then it obtains the ability to decrypt the challenge ciphertext of i from $rk_{i \to k}$ and $sk^{(k)}$, thus breaking the CPA security.

2 Preliminaries

Notations. Let $\lambda \in \mathbb{N}$ denote the security parameter throughout the paper, and all algorithms, distributions, functions and adversaries take 1^λ as an implicit input. If x is defined by y or the value of y is assigned to x, we write $x := y$. For $i, j \in \mathbb{N}$ with $i < j$, define $[i, j] := \{i, i+1, ..., j\}$ and $[j] := \{1, 2, ..., j\}$. For a set $\mathcal{X}$, denote by $x \leftarrow_\$ \mathcal{X}$ the procedure of sampling x from $\mathcal{X}$ uniformly at random. If $\mathcal{D}$ is distribution, $x \leftarrow_\$ \mathcal{D}$ means that x is sampled according to $\mathcal{D}$. All our algorithms are probabilistic unless stated otherwise. We use $y \leftarrow_\$ \mathcal{A}(x)$ to define the random variable y obtained by executing algorithm $\mathcal{A}$ on input

x. If $\mathcal{A}$ is deterministic we write $y \leftarrow \mathcal{A}(x)$. "PPT" abbreviates probabilistic polynomial-time. Denote by negl some negligible function. By $\mathrm{Pr}_i[\cdot]$ we denote the probability of a particular event occurring in game G_i.

For random variables X and Y, the min-entropy of X is defined as $\mathbf{H}_\infty(X) := -\log(\max_x \Pr[X = x])$, and the statistical distance between X and Y is defined as $\Delta(X, Y) := \frac{1}{2} \cdot \sum_x |\Pr[X = x] - \Pr[Y = x]|$. If $\Delta(X, Y) = \mathsf{negl}(\lambda)$, we say that X and Y are statistically indistinguishable (close), and denote it by $X \approx_s Y$.

Let $n, m, m', q \in \mathbb{N}$, and let $\mathbf{A} \in \mathbb{Z}_q^{m \times n}$, $\mathbf{v} \in \mathbb{Z}_q^n$, $\mathbf{B} \in \mathbb{Z}_q^{m' \times n}$. Define the lattice $\Lambda(\mathbf{A}) := \{\mathbf{Ax} \mid \mathbf{x} \in \mathbb{Z}^n\}$, the q-ary lattice $\Lambda_q(\mathbf{A}) := \{\mathbf{Ax} \mid \mathbf{x} \in \mathbb{Z}_q^n\} + q\mathbb{Z}^m$, its "orthogonal" lattice $\Lambda_q^\perp(\mathbf{A}) := \{\mathbf{x} \in \mathbb{Z}^m \mid \mathbf{x}^\top \mathbf{A} = \mathbf{0} \mod q\}$, and the "shifted" lattice $\Lambda_q^{\mathbf{v}}(\mathbf{A}) := \{\mathbf{r} \in \mathbb{Z}^m \mid \mathbf{r}^\top \mathbf{A} = \mathbf{v}^\top \mod q\}$, which can be further extended to $\Lambda_q^{\mathbf{B}}(\mathbf{A}) := \{\mathbf{R} \in \mathbb{Z}^{m' \times m} \mid \mathbf{RA} = \mathbf{B} \mod q\}$. Let $\|\mathbf{v}\|$ (resp., $\|\mathbf{v}\|_\infty$) denote its ℓ_2 (resp., infinity) norm. For a matrix $\mathbf{A}$, we define $\|\mathbf{A}\|$ (resp., $\|\mathbf{A}\|_\infty$) as the largest ℓ_2 (resp., infinity) norm of $\mathbf{A}$'s rows. A distribution χ is B-bounded if its support is limited to $[-B, B]$. Let $\mathbb{Z}_q$ be the ring of integers modulo q, and its elements are represented by the integers in $(-q/2, q/2]$.

Due to space limitations, we present lattice backgrounds in the full version [24], where we recall the definitions of discrete Gaussian, LWE assumption, and the TrapGen, Invert, SamplePre algorithms introduced in [1,12,17].

3   Fine-Grained PRE

In this section, we propose a new primitive called *Fine-Grained PRE* (FPRE), by extending the concept of proxy re-encryption (PRE) to fine-grained settings. Moreover, we formalize a set of security notions for FPRE, including CPA security, ciphertext pseudorandomness (CPR), unidirectionality (UNID), non-transitivity (NTR), collusion safety (CS), and ciphertext unlinkability (CUL), all of which are under *adaptive corruptions*. We refer to Fig. 1 in the introduction for an overview of the relations between these security notions.

Single-hop PRE can prevent the proxies from spreading ciphertexts without permission, and it is usually achieved by ciphertexts of two levels. Only the first level ciphertexts can be re-encrypted (to second level ciphertexts) and the second level ciphertexts can not be re-encrypted anymore. Accordingly, we define FPRE with two encryption and two decryption algorithms.

Now we present the syntax of fine-grained PRE.

Definition 1 (Fine-Grained PRE). *Let $\mathcal{F}$ be a family of functions from $\mathcal{M}$ to $\mathcal{M}$, where $\mathcal{M}$ is a message space. A fine-grained proxy re-encryption (FPRE) scheme for function family $\mathcal{F}$ is defined with a tuple of PPT algorithms* FPRE = (Setup, KGen, FReKGen, Enc₁, Enc₂, FReEnc, Dec₁, Dec₂).

- pp ←s Setup: *The setup algorithm outputs a public parameter* pp, *which serves as an implicit input of other algorithms.*
- $(pk, sk) \leftarrow_s$ KGen(pp): *Taking* pp *as input, the key generation algorithm outputs a pair of public key and secret key* (pk, sk).

- $rk_{i \to j}^{f} \leftarrow_\$ \mathsf{FReKGen}(pk^{(i)}, sk^{(i)}, pk^{(j)}, f)$: *Taking as input a public-secret key pair $(pk^{(i)}, sk^{(i)})$, another public key $pk^{(j)}$ and a function $f \in \mathcal{F}$, the fine-grained re-encryption key generation algorithm outputs a fine-grained re-encryption key $rk_{i \to j}^{f}$ that allows re-encrypting ciphertexts intended to i into ciphertexts encrypted for j.*
- $ct_1 \leftarrow_\$ \mathsf{Enc}_1(pk, m)$: *Taking as input a public key pk and a message $m \in \mathcal{M}$, this algorithm outputs a first-level ciphertext ct_1 that can be further re-encrypted into a second-level ciphertext.*
- $ct_2 \leftarrow_\$ \mathsf{Enc}_2(pk, m)$: *Taking as input a public key pk and a message $m \in \mathcal{M}$, this algorithm outputs a second-level ciphertext ct_2 that cannot be re-encrypted anymore.*
- $ct_2^{(j)} \leftarrow_\$ \mathsf{FReEnc}(rk_{i \to j}^{f}, ct_1^{(i)})$: *Taking as input a re-encryption key $rk_{i \to j}$ and a first-level ciphertext intended for i, the fine-grained re-encryption algorithm outputs a second-level ciphertext re-encrypted for user j.*
- $m \leftarrow \mathsf{Dec}_1(sk, ct_1)$: *Taking as input a secret key sk and a first-level ciphertext ct_1, the deterministic decryption algorithm outputs a message m.*
- $m \leftarrow \mathsf{Dec}_2(sk, ct_2)$: *Taking as input a secret key sk and a second-level ciphertext ct_2, the deterministic decryption algorithm outputs a message m.*

Correctness. For all $m \in \mathcal{M}$, $\mathsf{pp} \leftarrow_\$ \mathsf{Setup}$, $(pk, sk) \leftarrow_\$ \mathsf{KGen}(\mathsf{pp})$, $ct_1 \leftarrow_\$ \mathsf{Enc}_1$ (pk, m) and $ct_2 \leftarrow_\$ \mathsf{Enc}_2(pk, m)$, it holds that $\mathsf{Dec}_1(sk, ct_1) = m = \mathsf{Dec}_2(sk, ct_2)$.

Fine-Grained One-Hop Correctness. For all $m \in \mathcal{M}, f \in \mathcal{F}$, $\mathsf{pp} \leftarrow_\$ \mathsf{Setup}$, $(pk^{(i)}, sk^{(i)}) \leftarrow_\$ \mathsf{KGen}(\mathsf{pp})$, $(pk^{(j)}, sk^{(j)}) \leftarrow_\$ \mathsf{KGen}(\mathsf{pp})$, $rk_{i \to j}^{f} \leftarrow_\$ \mathsf{FReKGen}$ $(pk^{(i)}, sk^{(i)}, pk^{(j)}, f)$, $ct_1^{(i)} \leftarrow_\$ \mathsf{Enc}_1(pk^{(i)}, m)$ and $ct_2^{(j)} \leftarrow \mathsf{FReEnc}(rk_{i \to j}^{f}, ct_1^{(i)})$, it holds

$$\mathsf{Dec}_2(sk^{(j)}, ct_2^{(j)}) = f(m).$$

The notion of FPRE generalizes PRE by enabling fine-grained re-encryption, which is captured by the two fine-grained algorithms $\mathsf{FReKGen}$ and FReEnc. With a fine-grained re-encryption key $rk_{i \to j}^{f}$ generated by $\mathsf{FReKGen}$, one can convert a first-level ciphertext $ct_1^{(i)}$ encrypting message m for user i into a second-level ciphertext $ct_2^{(j)}$ encrypting a function $f(m)$ of m for another user j by invoking FReEnc, where $f \in \mathcal{F}$. If the function family $\mathcal{F}$ consists of only the identity function, i.e., $f(m) = m$, then we recover the (traditional) PRE.

Next, we formalize the indistinguishability of ciphertexts under chosen-plaintext attacks (CPA) and Ciphertext Pseudorandomness (CPR) for FPRE.

Definition 2 (CPA Security & Ciphertext Pseudorandomness for FPRE). *An FPRE scheme FPRE is CPA secure, if for any PPT adversary $\mathcal{A}$ and any polynomial $\mathfrak{n}$, it holds that $\mathsf{Adv}_{\mathsf{FPRE}, \mathcal{A}, \mathfrak{n}}^{\mathsf{CPA}}(\lambda) := \big| \Pr[\mathsf{Exp}_{\mathsf{FPRE}, \mathcal{A}, \mathfrak{n}}^{\mathsf{CPA}} \Rightarrow 1] - \frac{1}{2} \big| \leq \mathsf{negl}(\lambda)$, where the experiment $\mathsf{Exp}_{\mathsf{FPRE}, \mathcal{A}, \mathfrak{n}}^{\mathsf{CPA}}$ is defined in Fig. 2.*

An FPRE scheme FPRE has ciphertext pseudorandomness (CPR), if for any PPT $\mathcal{A}$ and any polynomial $\mathfrak{n}$, it holds that $\mathsf{Adv}_{\mathsf{FPRE}, \mathcal{A}, \mathfrak{n}}^{\mathsf{CPR}}(\lambda) :=$

$\left| \Pr[\mathsf{Exp}_{\mathsf{FPRE},\mathcal{A},n}^{\mathsf{CPR}}(\lambda) \Rightarrow 1] - \frac{1}{2} \right| \leq \mathsf{negl}(\lambda)$, *where* $\mathsf{Exp}_{\mathsf{FPRE},\mathcal{A},n}^{\mathsf{CPR}}$ *is also defined in Fig. 2.*

$\boxed{\mathsf{Exp}_{\mathsf{FPRE},\mathcal{A},n}^{\mathsf{CPA}}} \,/\, \mathsf{Exp}_{\mathsf{FPRE},\mathcal{A},n}^{\mathsf{CPR}}$:

$pp \leftarrow_\$ \mathsf{Setup}$. For $i \in [n]$: $(pk^{(i)}, sk^{(i)}) \leftarrow_\$ \mathsf{KGen}(pp)$

$\mathcal{Q}_{rk} := \emptyset$ // record re-encryption key queries

$\mathcal{Q}_c := \emptyset$ // record corruption queries

$i^* := \perp$ // record challenge user

$\boxed{(i^*, m_0, m_1, st) \leftarrow_\$ \mathcal{A}^{\mathcal{O}_{\mathrm{ReKey}}(\cdot,\cdot,\cdot), \mathcal{O}_{\mathrm{Cor}}(\cdot)}(pp, \{pk^{(i)}\}_{i\in[n]})}$

$(i^*, m, st) \leftarrow_\$ \mathcal{A}^{\mathcal{O}_{\mathrm{ReKey}}(\cdot,\cdot,\cdot), \mathcal{O}_{\mathrm{Cor}}(\cdot)}(pp, \{pk^{(i)}\}_{i\in[n]})$

If $(i^* \in \mathcal{Q}_c)$ or $(\exists j \in \mathcal{Q}_c \text{ s.t. } (i^*, j) \in \mathcal{Q}_{rk})$:

    Return $b \leftarrow_\$ \{0,1\}$ // avoid **TA1, TA2**

$\beta \leftarrow_\$ \{0,1\}$

$\boxed{ct_1^* \leftarrow_\$ \mathsf{Enc}_1(pk^{(i^*)}, m_\beta)}$

If $\beta = 0$: $ct_1^* \leftarrow_\$ \mathsf{Enc}_1(pk^{(i^*)}, m)$; Else: $ct_1^* \leftarrow_\$ \mathcal{C}$

$\beta' \leftarrow_\$ \mathcal{A}^{\mathcal{O}_{\mathrm{ReKey}}(\cdot,\cdot,\cdot), \mathcal{O}_{\mathrm{Cor}}(\cdot)}(st, ct_1^*)$

If $\beta' = \beta$: Return 1; Else Return 0.

$\mathcal{O}_{\mathrm{ReKey}}(i, j, f)$:

    If $(i = i^*)$ and $(j \in \mathcal{Q}_c)$:

        Return $\perp$ // avoid **TA2**

    $\mathcal{Q}_{rk} := \mathcal{Q}_{rk} \cup \{(i,j)\}$

    $rk_{i \rightarrow j}^f \leftarrow_\$ \mathsf{FReKGen}(pk^{(i)}, sk^{(i)}, pk^{(j)}, f)$

    Return $rk_{i \rightarrow j}^f$

$\mathcal{O}_{\mathrm{Cor}}(i)$:

    If $(i = i^*)$ or $(i^*, i) \in \mathcal{Q}_{rk}$:

        Return $\perp$ // avoid **TA1, TA2**

    $\mathcal{Q}_c := \mathcal{Q}_c \cup \{i\}$

    Return $sk^{(i)}$

Fig. 2. The CPA security experiment $\mathsf{Exp}_{\mathsf{FPRE},\mathcal{A},n}^{\mathsf{CPA}}$ (with $\boxed{\text{framed boxes}}$) & the Ciphertext Pseudorandomness (CPR) security experiment $\mathsf{Exp}_{\mathsf{FPRE},\mathcal{A},n}^{\mathsf{CPR}}$ (with gray boxes) for FPRE, where $\mathcal{C}$ denotes the ciphertext space.

Remark 1 (On the formalization of CPA *and* CPR *securities and discussion on trivial attacks).* We formalize the CPA and CPR security notions by defining the experiments $\mathsf{Exp}_{\mathsf{FPRE},\mathcal{A},n}^{\mathsf{CPA}}$ and $\mathsf{Exp}_{\mathsf{FPRE},\mathcal{A},n}^{\mathsf{CPR}}$, respectively, in Fig. 2. More precisely, we consider a multi-user setting, and the adversary $\mathcal{A}$ is allowed to make two kinds of oracle queries *adaptively*:

– through $\mathcal{O}_{\mathrm{ReKey}}(i, j, f)$ query, $\mathcal{A}$ can get re-encryption keys $rk_{i \rightarrow j}^f$, and
– through $\mathcal{O}_{\mathrm{Cor}}(i)$ query, $\mathcal{A}$ can corrupt user i and obtain its secret key $sk^{(i)}$.

We stress that the adversary can issue multiple $\mathcal{O}_{\mathrm{ReKey}}(i, j, f)$ queries, even for the same delegator i and same delegatee j, thus achieving *multiple delegations*. At some point, $\mathcal{A}$ generates an output and receives a challenge ciphertext ct_1^*, which are the only different places in the two experiments. In $\mathsf{Exp}_{\mathsf{FPRE},\mathcal{A},n}^{\mathsf{CPA}}$, $\mathcal{A}$ outputs a challenge user index i^* as well as a pair of messages (m_0, m_1), and receives a challenge ciphertext ct_1^* which encrypts m_β under $pk^{(i^*)}$, where β is the challenge bit that $\mathcal{A}$ aims to guess. This captures the *indistinguishability* of ciphertexts. In $\mathsf{Exp}_{\mathsf{FPRE},\mathcal{A},n}^{\mathsf{CPR}}$, $\mathcal{A}$ outputs a challenge user index i^* and a single message m, and receives a challenge ciphertext ct_1^* which either encrypts m under $pk^{(i^*)}$ or is uniformly chosen from the ciphertext space $\mathcal{C}$, depending on the challenge bit β. This captures the *pseudorandomness* of ciphertexts. Clearly, CPR is stronger than CPA.

Note that CPA (and CPR) only consider the security of the *first-level* ciphertexts. In fact, the CPA security for the *second-level* ciphertexts can be similarly defined: $\mathcal{A}$ outputs a challenge (j^*, m_0, m_1), receives a challenge ciphertext

$ct_2^* \leftarrow_\$ \mathsf{Enc}_2(pk^{(j^*)}, m_\beta)$, and aims to guess the challenge bit β. Here we do not capture the CPA security for the second-level ciphertexts in the CPA security definition, but instead, we will formalize it in the security definition of collusion safety (CS) later (cf. Definition 5).

To prevent trivial attacks from $\mathcal{A}$, we keep track of two sets: $\mathcal{Q}_c$ records the corrupted users, and $\mathcal{Q}_{rk}$ records the tuples (i, j) that $\mathcal{A}$ obtains a re-encryption key $rk_{i \to j}^f$. Based on that, there are two trivial attacks **TA1-TA2** to obtain information about the plaintext underlying the challenge ciphertext ct_1^*.

TA1: $i^* \in \mathcal{Q}_c$, i.e., $\mathcal{A}$ ever corrupts user i^* and obtains its secret key $sk^{(i^*)}$. In this case, $\mathcal{A}$ can decrypt ct_1^* directly by invoking $\mathsf{Dec}_1(sk^{(i^*)}, ct_1^*)$.

TA2: $\exists j \in \mathcal{Q}_c$, s.t. $(i^*, j) \in \mathcal{Q}_{rk}$, i.e., $\mathcal{A}$ gets a re-encryption key $rk_{i^* \to j}^f$ starting from the challenge user i^* to some corrupted user j that $\mathcal{A}$ ever obtains its secret key $sk^{(j)}$. In this case, $\mathcal{A}$ can re-encrypt ct_1^* to a ciphertext $ct_2^{(j)}$ encrypted for j via $ct_2^{(j)} \leftarrow_\$ \mathsf{FReEnc}(rk_{i^* \to j}^f, ct_1^*)$, then simply decrypt $ct_2^{(j)}$ with $sk^{(j)}$ to obtain a function of the plaintext underlying ct_1^*, which is $f(m_\beta)$ in $\mathsf{Exp}_{\mathsf{FPRE}, \mathcal{A}, \mathfrak{n}}^{\mathsf{CPA}}$, and is $f(m)$ in the case of $\beta = 0$ in $\mathsf{Exp}_{\mathsf{FPRE}, \mathcal{A}, \mathfrak{n}}^{\mathsf{CPR}}$.

As such, we exclude the above trivial attacks in both CPA and CPR experiments.

Below, we formalize the property of Unidirectionality (UNID), which basically means that the proxy ability in one direction shouldn't imply the proxy ability in the other direction. Roughly speaking, it requires that given a fine-grained re-encryption key $rk_{j^* \to i^*}^f$, it is hard for an adversary to come up with a fine-grained re-encryption key $rk_{i^* \to j^*}^{f'}$ of the other direction.

Definition 3 (Unidirectionality for FPRE). *An FPRE scheme* FPRE *is unidirectional (*UNID*), if for any PPT adversary $\mathcal{A}$ and any polynomial $\mathfrak{n}$, it holds that* $\mathsf{Adv}_{\mathsf{FPRE}, \mathcal{A}, \mathfrak{n}}^{\mathsf{UNID}}(\lambda) := \Pr[\mathsf{Exp}_{\mathsf{FPRE}, \mathcal{A}, \mathfrak{n}}^{\mathsf{UNID}} \Rightarrow 1] \leq \mathsf{negl}(\lambda)$, *where the experiment* $\mathsf{Exp}_{\mathsf{FPRE}, \mathcal{A}, \mathfrak{n}}^{\mathsf{UNID}}$ *is defined in Fig. 3.*

$\mathsf{Exp}_{\mathsf{FPRE}, \mathcal{A}, \mathfrak{n}}^{\mathsf{UNID}}$:

$pp \leftarrow_\$ \mathsf{Setup}$. For $i \in [\mathfrak{n}]$: $(pk^{(i)}, sk^{(i)}) \leftarrow_\$ \mathsf{KGen}(pp)$

$\mathcal{Q}_{rk} := \emptyset$ //record re-encryption key queries

$\mathcal{Q}_c := \emptyset$ //record corruption queries

$i^* := \perp, j^* := \perp$ //record challenge users

$(i^*, j^*, f, st) \leftarrow_\$ \mathcal{A}^{\mathcal{O}_{\mathsf{ReKey}}(\cdot, \cdot, \cdot), \mathcal{O}_{\mathsf{Cor}}(\cdot)}(pp, \{pk^{(i)}\}_{i \in [\mathfrak{n}]})$

If $(i^* = j^*)$ or $(i^* \in \mathcal{Q}_c)$ or $((i^*, j^*) \in \mathcal{Q}_{rk})$ or $(\exists j \in \mathcal{Q}_c$ s.t. $(i^*, j) \in \mathcal{Q}_{rk})$:

    Return $\perp$ //avoid **TA1'**, **TA2'**, **TA3'**, **TA4'**

$rk_{j^* \to i^*}^f \leftarrow_\$ \mathsf{FReKGen}(pk^{(j^*)}, sk^{(j^*)}, pk^{(i^*)}, f)$

$\mathcal{Q}_{rk} := \mathcal{Q}_{rk} \cup \{(j^*, i^*)\}$

$(rk_{i^* \to j^*}^{f'}, f') \leftarrow_\$ \mathcal{A}^{\mathcal{O}_{\mathsf{ReKey}}(\cdot, \cdot, \cdot), \mathcal{O}_{\mathsf{Cor}}(\cdot)}(st, rk_{j^* \to i^*}^f)$

If f' does not have output diversity: Return $\perp$ //avoid **TA5'**

//check the functionality of $rk_{i^* \to j^*}^{f'}$ in the following way

$m \leftarrow_\$ \mathcal{M}$, $ct_1^{(i^*)} \leftarrow_\$ \mathsf{Enc}_1(pk^{(i^*)}, m)$, $ct_2^{(j^*)} \leftarrow_\$ \mathsf{FReEnc}(rk_{i^* \to j^*}^{f'}, ct_1^{(i^*)})$

If $\mathsf{Dec}_2(sk^{(j^*)}, ct_2^{(j^*)}) = f'(m)$: Return 1; Else: Return 0

$\mathcal{O}_{\mathsf{ReKey}}(i, j, f)$:

If $(i = i^*)$ and $(j = j^*$ or $j \in \mathcal{Q}_c)$:

    Return $\perp$ //avoid **TA3'**, **TA4'**

$\mathcal{Q}_{rk} := \mathcal{Q}_{rk} \cup \{(i, j)\}$

$rk_{i \to j}^f \leftarrow_\$ \mathsf{FReKGen}(pk^{(i)}, sk^{(i)}, pk^{(j)}, f)$

Return $rk_{i \to j}^f$

$\mathcal{O}_{\mathsf{Cor}}(i)$:

If $(i = i^*)$ or $(i^*, i) \in \mathcal{Q}_{rk}$:

    Return $\perp$ //avoid **TA2'**, **TA4'**

$\mathcal{Q}_c = \mathcal{Q}_c \cup \{i\}$

Return $sk^{(i)}$

Fig. 3. The Unidirectionality (UNID) security experiment $\mathsf{Exp}_{\mathsf{FPRE}, \mathcal{A}, \mathfrak{n}}^{\mathsf{UNID}}$ for FPRE, where "output diversity" is defined as $\Pr[m_0, m_1 \leftarrow_\$ \mathcal{M} : f'(m_0) \neq f'(m_1)] \geq 1/\mathsf{poly}(\lambda)$ (see the full version [24] for more details).

In the full version [24], we give some explanations of the UNID security definition, discuss the trivial attacks **TA1′-TA5′**, and show that the UNID security is implied by the CPA security.

Next, we formalize the property of Non-Transitivity (NTR), which essentially requires that given two fine-grained re-encryption keys $rk_{i^*\to k^*}^{f_1}$ and $rk_{k^*\to j^*}^{f_2}$ from i^* to k^* and from k^* to j^*, respectively, it is hard for an adversary to compute a fine-grained re-encryption key $rk_{i^*\to j^*}^{f'}$ from i^* directly to j^*. Below we present the formal definition of NTR security.

Definition 4 (Non-Transitivity for FPRE). *An FPRE scheme* FPRE *is non-transitive (*NTR*), if for any PPT adversary $\mathcal{A}$ and any polynomial $\mathfrak{n}$, it holds that* $\mathsf{Adv}_{\mathsf{FPRE},\mathcal{A},\mathfrak{n}}^{\mathsf{NTR}}(\lambda) := \Pr[\mathsf{Exp}_{\mathsf{FPRE},\mathcal{A},\mathfrak{n}}^{\mathsf{NTR}} \Rightarrow 1] \le \mathsf{negl}(\lambda)$, *where the experiment* $\mathsf{Exp}_{\mathsf{FPRE},\mathcal{A},\mathfrak{n}}^{\mathsf{NTR}}$ *is defined in Fig. 4.*

$\mathsf{Exp}_{\mathsf{FPRE},\mathcal{A},\mathfrak{n}}^{\mathsf{NTR}}$:

$pp \leftarrow_{\$} \mathsf{Setup}$. For $i \in [\mathfrak{n}]$: $(pk^{(i)}, sk^{(i)}) \leftarrow_{\$} \mathsf{KGen}(pp)$

$\mathcal{Q}_{rk} := \emptyset$ // record re-encryption key queries

$\mathcal{Q}_c := \emptyset$ // record corruption queries

$i^*, k^*, j^* := \perp$ // record challenge users

$(i^*, k^*, j^*, f_1, f_2, st) \leftarrow_{\$} \mathcal{A}^{\mathcal{O}_{\mathrm{ReKey}}(\cdot,\cdot,\cdot), \mathcal{O}_{\mathrm{Cor}}(\cdot)}(pp, \{pk^{(i)}\}_{i \in [\mathfrak{n}]})$

If $(i^* = k^*$ or $k^* = j^*$ or $j^* = i^*)$ or $(i^* \in \mathcal{Q}_c)$ or $((i^*, j^*) \in \mathcal{Q}_{rk})$

     or $(\exists j \in \mathcal{Q}_c$ s.t. $(i^*, j) \in \mathcal{Q}_{rk})$:

     Return $\perp$ // avoid **TA1′, TA2′, TA3′, TA4′**

$rk_{i^*\to k^*}^{f_1} \leftarrow_{\$} \mathsf{FReKGen}(pk^{(i^*)}, sk^{(i^*)}, pk^{(k^*)}, f_1)$

$rk_{k^*\to j^*}^{f_2} \leftarrow_{\$} \mathsf{FReKGen}(pk^{(k^*)}, sk^{(k^*)}, pk^{(j^*)}, f_2)$

$\mathcal{Q}_{rk} = \mathcal{Q}_{rk} \cup \{(i^*, k^*)\} \cup \{(k^*, j^*)\}$

$(rk_{i^*\to j^*}^{f'}, f') \leftarrow \mathcal{A}^{\mathcal{O}_{\mathrm{ReKey}}(\cdot,\cdot,\cdot), \mathcal{O}_{\mathrm{Cor}}(\cdot)}(st, rk_{i^*\to k^*}^{f_1}, rk_{k^*\to j^*}^{f_2})$

If f' does not have output diversity: Return $\perp$ // avoid **TA5′**

// check the functionality of $rk_{i^*\to j^*}^{f'}$ in the following way

$m \leftarrow_{\$} \mathcal{M}$, $ct_1^{(i^*)} \leftarrow_{\$} \mathsf{Enc}_1(pk^{(i^*)}, m)$, $ct_2^{(j^*)} \leftarrow \mathsf{FReEnc}(rk_{i^*\to j^*}^{f'}, ct_1^{(i^*)})$

If $\mathsf{Dec}_2(sk^{(j^*)}, ct_2^{(j^*)}) = f'(m)$: Return 1;   Else: Return 0

$\mathcal{O}_{\mathrm{ReKey}}(i, j, f)$:

   If $(i = i^*) \wedge (j = j^*$ or $j \in \mathcal{Q}_c)$:

     Return $\perp$ // avoid **TA3′, TA4′**

     $\mathcal{Q}_{rk} := \mathcal{Q}_{rk} \cup \{(i, j)\}$

     $rk_{i\to j}^{f} \leftarrow_{\$} \mathsf{FReKGen}(pk^{(i)}, sk^{(i)}, pk^{(j)}, f)$

     Return $rk_{i\to j}^{f}$

$\mathcal{O}_{\mathrm{Cor}}(i)$:

   If $(i = i^*)$ or $(i^*, i) \in \mathcal{Q}_{rk}$:

     Return $\perp$ // avoid **TA2′, TA4′**

     $\mathcal{Q}_c = \mathcal{Q}_c \cup \{i\}$

     Return $sk^{(i)}$

Fig. 4. The Non-Transitivity (NTR) security experiment $\mathsf{Exp}_{\mathsf{FPRE},\mathcal{A},\mathfrak{n}}^{\mathsf{NTR}}$ for FPRE, where "output diversity" is defined as $\Pr[m_0, m_1 \leftarrow_{\$} \mathcal{M} : f'(m_0) \neq f'(m_1)] \ge 1/\mathsf{poly}(\lambda)$.

In the full version [24], we give some explanations of the NTR security definition, discuss the trivial attacks **TA1′-TA4′**, and show that the NTR security is implied by the CPA security.

Now, we formalize the Collusion-Safety (CS) for FPRE. Our CS security definition captures the *CPA security for the second-level ciphertexts*, instead of the master secret security as defined in [2,15]. Nevertheless, we note that our CS security is at least as strong as theirs. See the full version [24] for more discussions. Below we present the formal definition of our CS security.

Definition 5 (Collusion-Safety for FPRE). *An FPRE scheme* FPRE *is collusion-safe (*CS*), if for any PPT adversary $\mathcal{A}$ and any polynomial $\mathfrak{n}$, it holds that* $\mathsf{Adv}_{\mathsf{FPRE},\mathcal{A},\mathfrak{n}}^{\mathsf{CS}}(\lambda) := \big| \Pr[\mathsf{Exp}_{\mathsf{FPRE},\mathcal{A},\mathfrak{n}}^{\mathsf{CS}} \Rightarrow 1] - \frac{1}{2} \big| \le \mathsf{negl}(\lambda)$, *where the experiment* $\mathsf{Exp}_{\mathsf{FPRE},\mathcal{A},\mathfrak{n}}^{\mathsf{CS}}$ *is defined in Fig. 5.*

$\mathsf{Exp}^{\mathsf{CS}}_{\mathsf{FPRE},\mathcal{A},\mathsf{n}}$:	$\mathcal{O}_{\mathrm{ReKey}}(i,j,f)$:
$\mathsf{pp} \leftarrow_\$ \mathsf{Setup}$. For $i \in [\mathsf{n}]$: $(pk^{(i)}, sk^{(i)}) \leftarrow_\$ \mathsf{KGen}(\mathsf{pp})$	$rk^f_{i \to j} \leftarrow_\$ \mathsf{FReKGen}(pk^{(i)}, sk^{(i)}, pk^{(j)}, f)$
$\mathcal{Q}_c := \emptyset$ //record corruption queries	Return $rk^f_{i \to j}$
$i^* := \bot$ //record challenge user	
$(i^*, m_0, m_1, st) \leftarrow_\$ \mathcal{A}^{\mathcal{O}_{\mathrm{ReKey}}(\cdot,\cdot,\cdot),\mathcal{O}_{\mathrm{Cor}}(\cdot)}(\mathsf{pp}, \{pk^{(i)}\}_{i\in[\mathsf{n}]})$	$\mathcal{O}_{\mathrm{Cor}}(i)$:
If $i^* \in \mathcal{Q}_c$: Return $\bot$ //avoid trivial attacks	If $i = i^*$:
$\beta \leftarrow_\$ \{0,1\}$	Return $\bot$ //avoid trivial attacks
$ct_2^* \leftarrow_\$ \mathsf{Enc}_2(pk^{(i^*)}, m_\beta)$	$\mathcal{Q}_c = \mathcal{Q}_c \cup \{i\}$
$\beta' \leftarrow_\$ \mathcal{A}^{\mathcal{O}_{\mathrm{ReKey}}(\cdot,\cdot,\cdot),\mathcal{O}_{\mathrm{Cor}}(\cdot)}(st, ct_2^*)$	Return $sk^{(i)}$
If $\beta' = \beta$: Return 1; Else Return 0.	

Fig. 5. The Collusion-Safety (CS) security experiment $\mathsf{Exp}^{\mathsf{CS}}_{\mathsf{FPRE},\mathcal{A},\mathsf{n}}$ for FPRE.

Remark 2 (On the formalization of CS security). We formalize the CS security by defining the experiment $\mathsf{Exp}^{\mathsf{CS}}_{\mathsf{FPRE},\mathcal{A},\mathsf{n}}$ in Fig. 5. Similar to previous security notions, we consider a multi-user setting, and the adversary $\mathcal{A}$ is allowed to make $\mathcal{O}_{\mathrm{ReKey}}$ and $\mathcal{O}_{\mathrm{Cor}}$ queries *adaptively*. At some point, $\mathcal{A}$ outputs a challenge user index i^* as well as a pair of messages (m_0, m_1), and receives a challenge second-level ciphertext ct_2^* which encrypts m_β under $pk^{(i^*)}$, where β is the challenge bit that $\mathcal{A}$ aims to guess. This captures the *indistinguishability* of second-level ciphertexts. Clearly, to avoid trivial attack, $\mathcal{A}$ cannot obtain the secret key $sk^{(i^*)}$.

In real world, re-encryption relations between ciphertexts often imply the proxy connections between users, therefore it is desirable to hide the relations/connections. We formalize this as the property of *Ciphertext Unlinkability* (CUL), which basically requires that given two ciphertexts (ct_1^*, ct_2^*), it is hard for an adversary to tell whether ct_2^* is a re-encryption of ct_1^*, or the two ciphertexts are independently and freshly generated. Below we present the formal definition.

Definition 6 (Ciphertext Unlinkability for FPRE). *An FPRE scheme* FPRE *has ciphertext unlinkability (CUL), if for any PPT adversary $\mathcal{A}$ and any polynomial n, it holds that* $\mathsf{Adv}^{\mathsf{CUL}}_{\mathsf{FPRE},\mathcal{A},\mathsf{n}}(\lambda) := \left| \Pr[\mathsf{Exp}^{\mathsf{CUL}}_{\mathsf{FPRE},\mathcal{A},\mathsf{n}} \Rightarrow 1] - \frac{1}{2} \right| \leq \mathsf{negl}(\lambda)$, *where the experiment* $\mathsf{Exp}^{\mathsf{CUL}}_{\mathsf{FPRE},\mathcal{A},\mathsf{n}}$ *is defined in Fig. 6.*

$\mathsf{Exp}^{\mathsf{CUL}}_{\mathsf{FPRE},\mathcal{A},\mathsf{n}}$:	$\mathcal{O}_{\mathrm{ReKey}}(i,j,f)$:
$\mathsf{pp} \leftarrow_\$ \mathsf{Setup}$. For $i \in [\mathsf{n}]$: $(pk^{(i)}, sk^{(i)}) \leftarrow_\$ \mathsf{KGen}(\mathsf{pp})$	If $(i = i^*)$ and $(j \in \mathcal{Q}_c)$:
$\mathcal{Q}_{rk} := \emptyset$ //record re-encryption key queries	Return $\bot$ //avoid **TA2''**
$\mathcal{Q}_c := \emptyset$ //record corruption queries	$\mathcal{Q}_{rk} := \mathcal{Q}_{rk} \cup \{(i,j)\}$
$i^* := \bot, j^* := \bot$ //record challenge users	$rk^f_{i \to j} \leftarrow_\$ \mathsf{FReKGen}(pk^{(i)}, sk^{(i)}, pk^{(j)}, f)$
$(i^*, j^*, (f, m), (m_1, m_2), st) \leftarrow_\$ \mathcal{A}^{\mathcal{O}_{\mathrm{ReKey}}(\cdot,\cdot,\cdot),\mathcal{O}_{\mathrm{Cor}}(\cdot)}(\mathsf{pp}, \{pk^{(i)}\}_{i\in[\mathsf{n}]})$	Return $rk^f_{i \to j}$
If $(i^* \in \mathcal{Q}_c)$ or $(j^* \in \mathcal{Q}_c)$ or $(\exists j \in \mathcal{Q}_c \text{ s.t. } (i^*, j) \in \mathcal{Q}_{rk})$:	
Return $b \leftarrow_\$ \{0,1\}$ //avoid **TA1''**, **TA2''**	$\mathcal{O}_{\mathrm{Cor}}(i)$:
$\beta \leftarrow_\$ \{0,1\}$	If $(i = i^*)$ or $(i = j^*)$ or $(i^*, i) \in \mathcal{Q}_{rk}$:
If $\beta = 0$: //ciphertexts generated with re-encryption relation	Return $\bot$ //avoid **TA1''**, **TA2''**
$ct_1^* \leftarrow_\$ \mathsf{Enc}_1(pk^{(i^*)}, m)$	$\mathcal{Q}_c = \mathcal{Q}_c \cup \{i\}$
$rk^f_{i^* \to j^*} \leftarrow_\$ \mathsf{FReKGen}(pk^{(i^*)}, sk^{(i^*)}, pk^{(j^*)}, f)$, $ct_2^* \leftarrow_\$ \mathsf{FReEnc}(rk^f_{i^* \to j^*}, ct_1^*)$	Return $sk^{(i)}$
If $\beta = 1$: //ciphertexts generated independently	
$ct_1^* \leftarrow_\$ \mathsf{Enc}_1(pk^{(i^*)}, m_1)$, $ct_2^* \leftarrow_\$ \mathsf{Enc}_2(pk^{(j^*)}, m_2)$	
$\beta' \leftarrow_\$ \mathcal{A}^{\mathcal{O}_{\mathrm{ReKey}}(\cdot,\cdot,\cdot),\mathcal{O}_{\mathrm{Cor}}(\cdot)}(st, ct_1^*, ct_2^*)$	
If $\beta' = \beta$: Return 1; Else Return 0.	

Fig. 6. The Ciphertext Unlinkability (CUL) security experiment $\mathsf{Exp}^{\mathsf{CUL}}_{\mathsf{FPRE},\mathcal{A},\mathsf{n}}$ for FPRE.

Remark 3 (On the formalization of CUL security and discussion on trivial attacks). We formalize the CUL security by defining the experiment $\mathsf{Exp}^{\mathsf{CUL}}_{\mathsf{FPRE},\mathcal{A},\mathfrak{n}}$ in Fig. 6. Similar to previous security notions, we consider a multi-user setting, and the adversary $\mathcal{A}$ is allowed to make $\mathcal{O}_{\mathrm{REKEY}}$ and $\mathcal{O}_{\mathrm{COR}}$ queries *adaptively*. At some point, $\mathcal{A}$ outputs a pair of challenge users (i^*, j^*), a pair of function and message (f, m) as well as a pair of messages (m_1, m_2), and receives two challenge ciphertexts (ct_1^*, ct_2^*) which are

- (Case $\beta = 0$) *either* two ciphertexts generated with re-encryption relation, namely $ct_1^* \leftarrow_\$ \mathsf{Enc}_1(pk^{(i^*)}, m)$, $rk^f_{i^* \to j^*} \leftarrow_\$ \mathsf{FReKGen}(pk^{(i^*)}, sk^{(i^*)}, pk^{(j^*)}, f)$ and $ct_2^* \leftarrow_\$ \mathsf{FReEnc}(rk^f_{i^* \to j^*}, ct_1^*)$,
- (Case $\beta = 1$) *or* two ciphertexts that are generated independently, namely $ct_1^* \leftarrow_\$ \mathsf{Enc}_1(pk^{(i^*)}, m_1)$ and $ct_2^* \leftarrow_\$ \mathsf{Enc}_2(pk^{(j^*)}, m_2)$.

$\mathcal{A}$ aims to guess which case it is.

Actually, there are two trivial attacks **TA1″-TA2″** to obtain information about the plaintexts underlying the challenge ciphertexts (ct_1^*, ct_2^*).

TA1″: $i^* \in \mathcal{Q}_c$ or $j^* \in \mathcal{Q}_c$, i.e., $\mathcal{A}$ ever obtains $sk^{(i^*)}$ or $sk^{(j^*)}$. In this case, $\mathcal{A}$ can decrypt the challenger ciphertext ct_1^* or ct_2^* itself and trivially win.

TA2″: $\exists\, j \in \mathcal{Q}_c$, s.t. $(i^*, j) \in \mathcal{Q}_{rk}$, i.e., $\mathcal{A}$ gets $sk^{(j)}$ and $rk^f_{i^* \to j}$ for some user j. In this case, $\mathcal{A}$ can re-encrypt ct_1^* to a ciphertext $ct_2^{(j)}$ encrypted for j via $ct_2^{(j)} \leftarrow_\$ \mathsf{FReEnc}(rk^f_{i^* \to j}, ct_1^*)$, then simply decrypt $ct_2^{(j)}$ with $sk^{(j)}$ to obtain a function of the plaintext underlying ct_1^*, which is $f(m)$ in the case of $\beta = 0$ and is $f(m_1)$ in the case of $\beta = 1$.

As such, we exclude the above trivial attacks in the CUL experiment.

Below we show that the CUL security is stronger than the CPA security via Lemma 1, with proof postponed to the full version [24] due to space limitations.

Lemma 1 (CUL $\Rightarrow$ CPA). *For any PPT adversary $\mathcal{A}$ breaking the CPA security of FPRE and any polynomial $\mathfrak{n}$, there exists a PPT adversary $\mathcal{B}$ breaking the CUL security of FPRE with $\mathsf{Adv}^{\mathsf{CUL}}_{\mathsf{FPRE},\mathcal{B},\mathfrak{n}+1}(\lambda) = \frac{1}{2} \cdot \mathsf{Adv}^{\mathsf{CPA}}_{\mathsf{FPRE},\mathcal{A},\mathfrak{n}}(\lambda)$.*

4   Fine-Grained PRE for Bounded Linear Functions from LWE

In this section, we present a construction of fine-grained PRE (FPRE) scheme $\mathsf{FPRE}^{\mathsf{lin}}_{\mathsf{LWE}}$ for the family of bounded linear functions $\mathcal{F}_{\mathrm{lin}}$ (with coefficient of bounded norm). Then based on the LWE assumption, we prove the security of our $\mathsf{FPRE}^{\mathsf{lin}}_{\mathsf{LWE}}$, including CPA security in Theorem 1, ciphertext pseudorandomness (CPR) in Corollary 1, ciphertext unlinkability (CUL) in Theorem 2, and collusion-safety (CS) in Theorem 3. Since the CPA security implies UNID and NTR as shown in the full version [24], our $\mathsf{FPRE}^{\mathsf{lin}}_{\mathsf{LWE}}$ also achieves unidirectionality (UNID) and non-transitivity (NTR).

Parameters. Let $\mathsf{pp}_{\mathsf{LWE}} = (p, q, n, N, \ell, \gamma, \Delta, \chi)$ be LWE-related parameters that meet the following conditions:

- $p, q, n, N, \ell, \gamma, \Delta \in \mathbb{N}$ are integers, where $q := p^2$, $N \geq 2n \log q + 2\omega(\log \lambda)$ and $\gamma \geq O(\sqrt{n \log q}) \cdot \omega(\sqrt{\log n})$;
- χ is a B-bounded distribution, where B satisfies $\gamma \cdot \omega(\log n) \leq B < \min\{p/2, q/(10N)\}$ and $(N+1)(nB + NB + \ell\Delta)B < p/2$.

More precisely, see Table 2 for a concrete parameter choice. For simplicity, we assume that all algorithms of our FPRE scheme take $\mathsf{pp}_{\mathsf{LWE}}$ as an implicit input.

Table 2. Concrete parameters setting, where λ denotes the security parameter.

Parameters	p	q	n	N	ℓ	γ	Δ	B
Settings	λ^5	λ^{10}	λ	$21\lambda \log \lambda$	λ	$\sqrt{\lambda}(\log \lambda)^2$	λ	$\sqrt{\lambda}(\log \lambda)^4$

Bounded Linear Function family. The message space is $\mathcal{M} := \mathbb{Z}_p^\ell$. Define the family of bounded linear functions $\mathcal{F}_{\mathrm{lin}}$ from $\mathcal{M}$ to $\mathcal{M}$ over $\mathbb{Z}_p$ as follows:

$$\mathcal{F}_{\mathrm{lin}} = \left\{ \begin{array}{c} f_{\mathbf{M}} : \mathbb{Z}_p^\ell \to \mathbb{Z}_p^\ell \\ \mathbf{m} \mapsto \mathbf{M} \cdot \mathbf{m} \bmod p \end{array} \;\middle|\; \mathbf{M} \in \mathbb{Z}_p^{\ell \times \ell}, \|\mathbf{M}\|_\infty \leq \Delta \right\}. \tag{3}$$

LWE-Based FPRE Scheme for $\mathcal{F}_{\mathrm{lin}}$. Let $\mathsf{TrapGen}, \mathsf{SamplePre}, \mathsf{Invert}$ be the PPT algorithms introduced in [1,12,17]. Our LWE-based FPRE scheme $\mathsf{FPRE}_{\mathsf{LWE}}^{\mathrm{lin}} = (\mathsf{Setup}, \mathsf{KGen}, \mathsf{FReKGen}, \mathsf{Enc}_1, \mathsf{Enc}_2, \mathsf{FReEnc}, \mathsf{Dec}_1, \mathsf{Dec}_2)$ for the bounded linear function family $\mathcal{F}_{\mathrm{lin}}$ defined in (3) is shown in Fig. 7.

$\underline{\mathsf{pp} \leftarrow_{\$} \mathsf{Setup}:}$
$\overline{\mathbf{A}'} \leftarrow_{\$} \mathbb{Z}_q^{N \times n}$
Return $\mathsf{pp} := \overline{\mathbf{A}'}$

$\underline{(pk, sk) \leftarrow_{\$} \mathsf{KGen}(\mathsf{pp}):}$
$(\overline{\mathbf{A}} \in \mathbb{Z}_q^{N \times n}, \mathbf{T}) \leftarrow \mathsf{TrapGen}(1^n, 1^N), \quad \underline{\mathbf{A}} \leftarrow_{\$} \mathbb{Z}_q^{\ell \times n}$
$\mathbf{A} := \binom{\overline{\mathbf{A}}}{\underline{\mathbf{A}}} \in \mathbb{Z}_q^{(N+\ell) \times n}$
$\mathbf{K} \leftarrow_{\$} \{0,1\}^{\ell \times N}, \quad \underline{\mathbf{A}'} := -\mathbf{K}\overline{\mathbf{A}'}$
$pk := (\mathbf{A}, \underline{\mathbf{A}'}), sk := (\mathbf{T}, \mathbf{K})$
Return (pk, sk)

$\underline{rk_{i \to j}^{f_{\mathbf{M}}} \leftarrow_{\$} \mathsf{FReKGen}(pk^{(i)} = (\mathbf{A}^{(i)}, \underline{\mathbf{A}'}^{(i)}), sk^{(i)} = (\mathbf{T}^{(i)}, \mathbf{K}^{(i)}),}$
$\qquad\qquad pk^{(j)} = (\mathbf{A}^{(j)}, \underline{\mathbf{A}'}^{(j)}), f_{\mathbf{M}} \in \mathcal{F}_{\mathrm{lin}}):$
$\mathbf{S} \leftarrow_{\$} \chi^{n \times n}, \mathbf{E} \leftarrow_{\$} \chi^{(N+\ell) \times n}$
$\mathbf{A}'^{(j)} := \binom{\overline{\mathbf{A}'}}{\underline{\mathbf{A}'}^{(j)}}$
$\mathbf{R} \in \mathbb{Z}^{(N+\ell) \times N} \leftarrow_{\$} \mathsf{SamplePre}\left(\mathbf{T}^{(i)}, \overline{\mathbf{A}}^{(i)}, \mathbf{A}'^{(j)}\mathbf{S} + \mathbf{E} - \binom{\mathbf{0}}{\mathbf{M}}\mathbf{A}^{(i)}, \gamma\right)$
$rk_{i \to j}^{f_{\mathbf{M}}} := \begin{pmatrix} \mathbf{R} & \mathbf{0} \\ & \mathbf{M} \end{pmatrix} \in \mathbb{Z}_p^{(N+\ell) \times (N+\ell)}$ //M is the description of $f_{\mathbf{M}}$
Return $rk_{i \to j}^{f_{\mathbf{M}}}$

$\underline{ct_1 \leftarrow_{\$} \mathsf{Enc}_1(pk = (\mathbf{A}, \underline{\mathbf{A}'}), \mathbf{m} \in \mathcal{M}):}$
$\mathbf{s} \leftarrow_{\$} \chi^n, \mathbf{e} \leftarrow_{\$} \chi^{N+\ell}$
$ct_1 := \mathbf{A}\mathbf{s} + \mathbf{e} + \binom{\mathbf{0}}{\mathbf{pm}} \in \mathbb{Z}_q^{N+\ell}$
Return ct_1

$\underline{ct_2 \leftarrow_{\$} \mathsf{Enc}_2(pk = (\mathbf{A}, \underline{\mathbf{A}'}), \mathbf{m} \in \mathcal{M}):}$
$\mathbf{s} \leftarrow_{\$} \chi^n, \mathbf{e} \leftarrow_{\$} \chi^{N+\ell}$
$\mathbf{A}' := \binom{\overline{\mathbf{A}'}}{\underline{\mathbf{A}'}}$
$ct_2 := \mathbf{A}'\mathbf{s} + \mathbf{e} + \binom{\mathbf{0}}{\mathbf{pm}} \in \mathbb{Z}_q^{N+\ell}$
Return ct_2

$\underline{ct_2^{(j)} \leftarrow \mathsf{FReEnc}(rk_{i \to j}^{f_{\mathbf{M}}} \in \mathbb{Z}_p^{(N+\ell) \times (N+\ell)},}$
$\qquad\qquad ct_1^{(i)} \in \mathbb{Z}_q^{N+\ell}):$
$ct_2^{(j)} := rk_{i \to j}^{f_{\mathbf{M}}} \cdot ct_1^{(i)} \in \mathbb{Z}_q^{N+\ell}$
Return $ct_2^{(j)}$

$\underline{\mathbf{m} \leftarrow \mathsf{Dec}_1(sk = (\mathbf{T}, \mathbf{K}), ct_1 \in \mathbb{Z}_q^{N+\ell}):}$
Parse $ct_1 = \binom{\overline{ct_1} \in \mathbb{Z}_q^N}{\underline{ct_1} \in \mathbb{Z}_q^\ell}$
$(\mathbf{s}, \mathbf{e}_1) \leftarrow \mathsf{Invert}(\mathbf{T}, \overline{ct_1})$
$\tilde{\mathbf{m}} = (\tilde{m}_1, \ldots, \tilde{m}_\ell) := \underline{ct_1} - \underline{\mathbf{A}}\mathbf{s}$
For all $i \in [\ell]$:
$\quad m_i := \lceil \tilde{m}_i / p \rfloor$
Return $\mathbf{m} = (m_1, \ldots, m_\ell)$

$\underline{\mathbf{m} \leftarrow \mathsf{Dec}_2(sk = (\mathbf{T}, \mathbf{K}), ct_2 \in \mathbb{Z}_q^{N+\ell}):}$
$\tilde{\mathbf{m}} = (\tilde{m}_1, \ldots, \tilde{m}_\ell) := (\mathbf{K} \mid \mathbf{I}_{\ell \times \ell}) \cdot ct_2$
For all $i \in [\ell]$:
$\quad m_i := \lceil \tilde{m}_i / p \rfloor$
Return $\mathbf{m} = (m_1, \ldots, m_\ell)$

Fig. 7. The LWE-based FPRE scheme $\mathsf{FPRE}_{\mathsf{LWE}}^{\mathrm{lin}}$ for the linear function family $\mathcal{F}_{\mathrm{lin}}$.

Correctness. Let $pp = \overline{\mathbf{A}'}$, $pk = (\mathbf{A}, \underline{\mathbf{A}'})$ and $sk = (\mathbf{T}, \mathbf{K})$. For a first-level ciphertext ct_1 generated by $\mathsf{Enc}_1(pk, \mathbf{m})$, we have $ct_1 = \begin{pmatrix} \overline{ct_1} \\ \underline{ct_1} \end{pmatrix} = \begin{pmatrix} \overline{\mathbf{A}}\mathbf{s} + \mathbf{e}_1 \\ \underline{\mathbf{A}}\mathbf{s} + \mathbf{e}_2 + p\mathbf{m} \end{pmatrix}$, where $\mathbf{e}_1 \leftarrow_\$ \chi^N$, $\mathbf{e}_2 \leftarrow_\$ \chi^\ell$, and the upper part is an LWE instance of $\overline{\mathbf{A}}$. Since $\mathbf{e}_1$ is B-bounded with $B < q/(10N)$, $\|\mathbf{e}_1\| \le \sqrt{N}\|\mathbf{e}_1\|_\infty \le \sqrt{N}B < q/(10 \cdot \sqrt{N})$. Then by the property of Invert (cf. the full version [24]), $(\mathbf{s}, \mathbf{e}_1)$ can be correctly recovered via $(\mathbf{s}, \mathbf{e}_1) \leftarrow \mathsf{Invert}(\mathbf{T}, \overline{ct_1})$. Thus according to the decryption algorithm $\mathsf{Dec}_1(sk, ct_1)$, we get $\tilde{\mathbf{m}} = \underline{ct_1} - \underline{\mathbf{A}}\mathbf{s} = \mathbf{e}_2 + p\mathbf{m}$, and by parsing $\mathbf{e}_2 = (e_{21}, \ldots, e_{2\ell})^\top$, we have that $\tilde{m}_i = e_{2i} + pm_i$ for all $i \in [\ell]$. Moreover, since $\mathbf{e}_2$ is B-bounded with $B < p/2$, each $|e_{2i}| \le B < p/2$. Consequently, $\lceil \tilde{m}_i/p \rfloor = m_i$ and Dec_1 can recover $\mathbf{m}$ correctly from ct_1.

For a second-level ciphertext ct_2 generated by $\mathsf{Enc}_2(pk, \mathbf{m})$, we have

$$ct_2 = \begin{pmatrix} \overline{\mathbf{A}'}\mathbf{s} + \mathbf{e}_1 \\ \underline{\mathbf{A}'}\mathbf{s} + \mathbf{e}_2 + p\mathbf{m} \end{pmatrix} = \begin{pmatrix} \overline{\mathbf{A}'}\mathbf{s} + \mathbf{e}_1 \\ -\mathbf{K}\overline{\mathbf{A}'}\mathbf{s} + \mathbf{e}_2 + p\mathbf{m} \end{pmatrix},$$

where $\mathbf{e}_1 \leftarrow_\$ \chi^N$, $\mathbf{e}_2 \leftarrow_\$ \chi^\ell$. According to the decryption algorithm $\mathsf{Dec}_2(sk, ct_2)$, we get $\tilde{\mathbf{m}} = (\mathbf{K} \mid \mathbf{I}) \cdot ct_2 = \mathbf{K}\mathbf{e}_1 + \mathbf{e}_2 + p\mathbf{m}$, and by defining $\mathbf{e}' = (e_1', \ldots, e_\ell') := \mathbf{K}\mathbf{e}_1 + \mathbf{e}_2$, we have that $\tilde{\mathbf{m}} = \mathbf{e}' + p\mathbf{m}$ and $\tilde{m}_i = e_{2i}' + pm_i$ for all $i \in [\ell]$. Since $\mathbf{e}_1, \mathbf{e}_2$ are B-bounded with B satisfying $(N+1)(nB + NB + \ell\Delta)B < p/2$ and $\mathbf{K} \in \{0,1\}^{\ell \times N}$, we have $\|\mathbf{e}'\|_\infty \le (N+1)B < p/2$ and each $|e_{2i}'| \le B < p/2$. Consequently, $\lceil \tilde{m}_i/p \rfloor = m_i$ and Dec_2 can recover $\mathbf{m}$ correctly from ct_2.

Fine-Grained One-Hop Correctness. Let $ct_1^{(i)} \leftarrow_\$ \mathsf{Enc}_1(pk^{(i)}, \mathbf{m})$ and $rk_{i \to j}^{f_\mathsf{M}} \leftarrow_\$ \mathsf{FReKGen}(pk^{(i)}, sk^{(i)}, pk^{(j)}, f_\mathsf{M})$. For a fine-grained re-encrypted ciphertext $ct_2^{(j)} \leftarrow_\$ \mathsf{FReEnc}(rk_{i \to j}^{f_\mathsf{M}}, ct_1^{(i)})$, we have

$$ct_2^{(j)} := \left(\mathbf{R} \,\middle|\, \begin{matrix} \mathbf{0} \\ \mathbf{M} \end{matrix} \right) \cdot ct_1^{(i)} = \left(\mathbf{R} \,\middle|\, \begin{matrix} \mathbf{0} \\ \mathbf{M} \end{matrix} \right) \cdot \left(\begin{pmatrix} \overline{\mathbf{A}}^{(i)} \\ \underline{\mathbf{A}}^{(i)} \end{pmatrix}\mathbf{s} + \begin{pmatrix} \mathbf{e}_1 \\ \mathbf{e}_2 \end{pmatrix} + \begin{pmatrix} \mathbf{0} \\ p\mathbf{m} \end{pmatrix} \right)$$

$$= \left(\mathbf{R}\overline{\mathbf{A}}^{(i)} + \begin{pmatrix} \mathbf{0} \\ \mathbf{M} \end{pmatrix}\underline{\mathbf{A}}^{(i)} \right) \cdot \mathbf{s} + \mathbf{R}\mathbf{e}_1 + \begin{pmatrix} \mathbf{0} \\ \mathbf{M}\mathbf{e}_2 \end{pmatrix} + \begin{pmatrix} \mathbf{0} \\ p\mathbf{M}\mathbf{m} \end{pmatrix}.$$

Since $\mathbf{R}$ is generated by $\mathbf{R} \leftarrow_\$ \mathsf{SamplePre}(\mathbf{T}^{(i)}, \overline{\mathbf{A}}^{(i)}, \mathbf{A}'^{(j)}\mathbf{S} + \mathbf{E} - \begin{pmatrix} \mathbf{0} \\ \mathbf{M} \end{pmatrix}\underline{\mathbf{A}}^{(i)}, \gamma)$, by the property of $\mathsf{SamplePre}$ (cf. the full version [24]), we have $\mathbf{R}\overline{\mathbf{A}}^{(i)} = \mathbf{A}'^{(j)}\mathbf{S} + \mathbf{E} - \begin{pmatrix} \mathbf{0} \\ \mathbf{M} \end{pmatrix}\underline{\mathbf{A}}^{(i)}$. Consequently, we get

$$ct_2^{(j)} = \mathbf{A}'^{(j)}\underbrace{\mathbf{S}\mathbf{s}}_{:=\tilde{\mathbf{s}}} + \underbrace{\mathbf{E}\mathbf{s} + \mathbf{R}\mathbf{e}_1 + \begin{pmatrix} \mathbf{0} \\ \mathbf{M}\mathbf{e}_2 \end{pmatrix}}_{:=\tilde{\mathbf{e}}} + \Big(p \cdot \underbrace{\begin{matrix} \mathbf{0} \\ \mathbf{M}\mathbf{m} \end{matrix}}_{=f_\mathsf{M}(\mathbf{m})} \Big).$$

Moreover, by the property of $\mathsf{SamplePre}$, we know that $\|\mathbf{R}\|_\infty \le \gamma \cdot \omega(\log n)$, which further yields $\|\mathbf{R}\|_\infty \le B$ due to $\gamma \cdot \omega(\log n) \le B$. Now that $\mathbf{E}, \mathbf{s}, \mathbf{R}, \mathbf{e}_1, \mathbf{e}_2$ are all B-bounded and $\mathbf{M}$ is Δ-bounded, so we have $\|\tilde{\mathbf{e}}\|_\infty \le (nB + NB + \ell\Delta)B$. By a similar argument like the correctness of second-level ciphertexts, since $(N+1)\|\tilde{\mathbf{e}}\|_\infty \le (N+1)(nB + NB + \ell\Delta)B < p/2$, the decryption algorithm Dec_2 can recover the function value $f_{\mathbf{M}}(\mathbf{m}) = \mathbf{M} \cdot \mathbf{m}$ correctly from the re-encrypted ciphertext $ct_2^{(j)}$.

Next, we show the CPA security of our $\mathsf{FPRE}_{\mathsf{LWE}}^{\mathsf{lin}}$ scheme.

Theorem 1 (CPA Security of $\mathsf{FPRE}_{\mathsf{LWE}}^{\mathsf{lin}}$). *Assume that the $\mathsf{LWE}_{n,q,\chi,N+\ell}$-assumption holds, then the scheme $\mathsf{FPRE}_{\mathsf{LWE}}^{\mathsf{lin}}$ proposed in Fig. 7 is CPA secure. More precisely, for any PPT adversary $\mathcal{A}$ that makes at most Q times of $\mathcal{O}_{\mathrm{REKEY}}$ queries and for any polynomial $\mathfrak{n}$, there exists a PPT algorithm $\mathcal{B}$ against the LWE assumption s.t. $\mathsf{Adv}_{\mathsf{FPRE},\mathcal{A},\mathfrak{n}}^{\mathsf{CPA}}(\lambda) \leq (\mathfrak{n}^2 nQ + \mathfrak{n}) \cdot \mathsf{Adv}_{[n,q,\chi,N+\ell],\mathcal{B}}^{\mathsf{LWE}}(\lambda) + \mathsf{negl}(\lambda).$*

Proof of Theorem 1. We prove the theorem via a sequence of games $\mathsf{G}_0 - \mathsf{G}_5$, where G_0 is the CPA experiment, and in G_5, $\mathcal{A}$ has a negligible advantage.

Game G_0: This is the CPA experiment $\mathsf{Exp}_{\mathsf{FPRE},\mathcal{A},\mathfrak{n}}^{\mathsf{CPA}}$ (cf. Fig. 2). Let Win denote the event that $\beta' = \beta$. By definition, $\mathsf{Adv}_{\mathsf{FPRE},\mathcal{A},\mathfrak{n}}^{\mathsf{CPA}}(\lambda) = |\operatorname{Pr}_0[\mathsf{Win}] - \frac{1}{2}|$.

Let $pp = \overline{\mathbf{A}'}$ and let $pk^{(i)} = (\mathbf{A}^{(i)}, \underline{\mathbf{A}}'^{(i)})$, $sk^{(i)} = (\mathbf{T}^{(i)}, \mathbf{K}^{(i)})$ denote the public key and secret key of user $i \in [\mathfrak{n}]$. In this game, the challenger answers $\mathcal{A}$'s $\mathcal{O}_{\mathrm{REKEY}}$, $\mathcal{O}_{\mathrm{COR}}$ queries and generates the challenge ciphertext ct_1^* as follows.

- On receiving a re-encryption key query $\mathcal{O}_{\mathrm{REKEY}}(i,j,f_{\mathbf{M}})$ from $\mathcal{A}$, the challenger returns $\perp$ to $\mathcal{A}$ directly if trivial attacks ($i = i^*$) and ($j \in \mathcal{Q}_c$) occur. Otherwise, the challenger adds (i,j) to $\mathcal{Q}_{rk}$, samples $\mathbf{S} \leftarrow_\$ \chi^{n \times n}$, $\mathbf{E} \leftarrow_\$ \chi^{(N+\ell) \times n}$, invokes $\mathbf{R} \leftarrow_\$ \mathsf{SamplePre}\left(\mathbf{T}^{(i)}, \overline{\mathbf{A}}^{(i)}, \mathbf{A}'^{(j)}\mathbf{S} + \mathbf{E} - \binom{\mathbf{0}}{\mathbf{M}}\underline{\mathbf{A}}^{(i)}, \gamma\right)$, where $\mathbf{A}'^{(j)} = \binom{\overline{\mathbf{A}'}}{\mathbf{A}'^{(j)}}$, and returns $rk_{i \to j}^{f_{\mathbf{M}}} := (\mathbf{R} \mid \begin{smallmatrix} 0 \\ \mathsf{M} \end{smallmatrix})$ to $\mathcal{A}$.
- On receiving a corruption query $\mathcal{O}_{\mathrm{COR}}(i)$ from $\mathcal{A}$, the challenger returns $\perp$ to $\mathcal{A}$ directly if trivial attacks ($i = i^*$) or $(i^*, i) \in \mathcal{Q}_{rk}$ occur. Otherwise, the challenger adds i to $\mathcal{Q}_c$ and returns $sk^{(i)}$ to $\mathcal{A}$.
- On receiving the challenge tuple $(i^*, \mathbf{m}_0, \mathbf{m}_1)$ from $\mathcal{A}$, the challenger first checks if trivial attacks ($i^* \in \mathcal{Q}_c$) or ($\exists j \in \mathcal{Q}_c$ s.t. $(i^*,j) \in \mathcal{Q}_{rk}$) occur. If yes, the challenger aborts the game with $\mathcal{A}$ by returning a random bit. Otherwise, the challenger chooses a random bit $\beta \leftarrow_\$ \{0,1\}$, samples $\mathbf{s} \leftarrow_\$ \chi^n$, $\mathbf{e} \leftarrow_\$ \chi^{N+\ell}$, and sends $ct_1^* := \mathbf{A}^{(i^*)}\mathbf{s} + \mathbf{e} + \binom{\mathbf{0}}{p\mathbf{m}_\beta}$ to $\mathcal{A}$.

Game G_1: It is the same as G_0, except that, at the beginning of the game, the challenger chooses a random user index $i' \leftarrow_\$ [\mathfrak{n}]$ uniformly as the guess of the challenge user i^*, and will abort the game and return a random bit in the following cases.

- **Case 1.** $\mathcal{A}$ issues the challenge tuple $(i^*, \mathbf{m}_0, \mathbf{m}_1)$ but $i' \neq i^*$.
- **Case 2.** $\mathcal{A}$ issues a re-encryption key query $\mathcal{O}_{\mathrm{REKEY}}(i,j,f_{\mathbf{M}})$ such that $(i = i')$ and $(j \in \mathcal{Q}_c)$ before issuing its challenge.
- **Case 3.** $\mathcal{A}$ issues a corruption query $\mathcal{O}_{\mathrm{COR}}(i)$ such that $(i = i')$ or $(i', i) \in \mathcal{Q}_{rk}$ before issuing its challenge.

Case 1 suggests that the challenger's guess is wrong. Now in G_1, the challenger will abort the game if the guess is wrong. If the guess is correct, i.e., $i' = i^*$, Case 2 and Case 3 are in fact trivial attacks, so they will lead to abort anyway in G_0 and do not contribute to $\mathcal{A}$'s advantage. Since the challenger will guess i^* correctly with probability $1/\mathsf{n}$, we have $\left| \Pr_0[\mathsf{Win}] - \frac{1}{2} \right| = \frac{1}{\mathsf{n}} \left| \Pr_1[\mathsf{Win}] - \frac{1}{2} \right|$.

Game $\mathsf{G}_{1.v}, v \in [0, \mathsf{n}]$: It is the same as G_1, except for the reply to $\mathcal{A}$'s re-encryption key query $\mathcal{O}_{\text{REKEY}}(i, j, f_M)$ which does not lead to any trivial attack.

- If $i = i'$ and $j \le v$, the challenger uniformly samples $\mathbf{U} \leftarrow_{\$} \mathbb{Z}_q^{(N+\ell) \times n}$ and invokes $\mathbf{R} \leftarrow_{\$} \mathsf{SamplePre}\left(\mathbf{T}^{(i)}, \overline{\mathbf{A}}^{(i)}, \mathbf{U}, \gamma \right)$ to get $rk_{i' \to j}^{f_M} := \left(\mathbf{R} \mid {}^{\mathbf{0}}_{\mathbf{M}} \right)$, rather than using $\mathbf{A}'^{(j)} \mathbf{S} + \mathbf{E} - \left({}^{\mathbf{0}}_{\mathbf{M}} \right) \mathbf{A}^{(i)}$ with $\mathbf{S} \leftarrow_{\$} \chi^{n \times n}, \mathbf{E} \leftarrow_{\$} \chi^{(N+\ell) \times n}$ as in G_1.
- Otherwise, the challenger answers the query just like G_1, that is, $\mathbf{R} \leftarrow_{\$}$ $\mathsf{SamplePre}\left(\mathbf{T}^{(i)}, \overline{\mathbf{A}}^{(i)}, \mathbf{A}'^{(j)} \mathbf{S} + \mathbf{E} - \left({}^{\mathbf{0}}_{\mathbf{M}} \right) \underline{\mathbf{A}}^{(i)}, \gamma \right)$ with $\mathbf{S} \leftarrow_{\$} \chi^{n \times n}, \mathbf{E} \leftarrow_{\$}$ $\chi^{(N+\ell) \times n}$.

Clearly, $\mathsf{G}_{1.0}$ is identical to G_1. Thus, we have $\Pr_1[\mathsf{Win}] = \Pr_{1.0}[\mathsf{Win}]$

For $v \in [\mathsf{n}]$, let Corr_v denote the event that $\mathcal{A}$ queries v to the corruption oracle $\mathcal{O}_{\text{COR}}$. If Corr_v occurs, $\mathcal{A}$ is not allowed to issue any re-encryption key query of the form $\mathcal{O}_{\text{REKEY}}(i', v, f_M)$ to avoid trivial attacks. Therefore, $\mathsf{G}_{1.v-1}$ is identical to $\mathsf{G}_{1.v}$ in the case Corr_v occurs, i.e., $\Pr_{1.v-1}[\mathsf{Win} \wedge \mathsf{Corr}_v] = \Pr_{1.v}[\mathsf{Win} \wedge \mathsf{Corr}_v]$. Consequently, we have

$$\left| \Pr_{1.v-1}[\mathsf{Win}] - \Pr_{1.v}[\mathsf{Win}] \right| = \left| \Pr_{1.v-1}[\mathsf{Win} \wedge \neg \mathsf{Corr}_v] - \Pr_{1.v}[\mathsf{Win} \wedge \neg \mathsf{Corr}_v] \right|. \quad (4)$$

Claim 1. For each $v \in [\mathsf{n}]$, $\left| \Pr_{1.v-1}[\mathsf{Win}] - \Pr_{1.v}[\mathsf{Win}] \right| \le \mathsf{Adv}_{[n,q,\chi,N+\ell],\mathcal{B}}^{nQ\text{-LWE}}(\lambda)$.

Proof. We construct a PPT algorithm $\mathcal{B}$ to break the $nQ\text{-LWE}_{n,q,\chi,N+\ell}$ assumption by simulating $\mathsf{G}_{1.v-1}/\mathsf{G}_{1.v}$ for $\mathcal{A}$ as follows.

Algorithm $\mathcal{B}$. Given $(\mathbf{B} \in \mathbb{Z}_q^{(N+\ell) \times n}, \mathbf{Z} \in \mathbb{Z}_q^{(N+\ell) \times nQ})$, $\mathcal{B}$ wants to distinguish $\mathbf{Z} = \mathbf{BS} + \mathbf{E}$ from $\mathbf{Z} \leftarrow_{\$} \mathbb{Z}_q^{(N+\ell) \times nQ}$, where $\mathbf{B} \leftarrow_{\$} \mathbb{Z}_q^{(N+\ell) \times n}, \mathbf{S} \leftarrow_{\$} \chi^{n \times nQ}$, $\mathbf{E} \leftarrow_{\$} \chi^{(N+\ell) \times nQ}$. $\mathcal{B}$ parses $\mathbf{B} = \left({}^{\overline{\mathbf{B}}}_{\underline{\mathbf{B}}} \right)$ with $\overline{\mathbf{B}} \in \mathbb{Z}_q^{N \times n}, \underline{\mathbf{B}} \in \mathbb{Z}_q^{\ell \times n}$, and parses $\mathbf{Z} = (\mathbf{Z}_1 \mid \cdots \mid \mathbf{Z}_Q)$ with each $\mathbf{Z}_k \in \mathbb{Z}_q^{(N+\ell) \times n}$. In the case of $\mathbf{Z} = \mathbf{BS} + \mathbf{E}$, if we parse $\mathbf{S} = (\mathbf{S}_1 \mid \cdots \mid \mathbf{S}_Q)$ with each $\mathbf{S}_k \in \mathbb{Z}_q^{n \times n}$ and parse $\mathbf{E} = (\mathbf{E}_1 \mid \cdots \mid \mathbf{E}_Q)$ with each $\mathbf{E}_k \in \mathbb{Z}_q^{(N+\ell) \times n}$, then we have $\mathbf{Z}_k = \mathbf{BS}_k + \mathbf{E}_k$. In the case of $\mathbf{Z} \leftarrow_{\$} \mathbb{Z}_q^{(N+\ell) \times nQ}$, we have that $\mathbf{Z}_k$ is uniformly distributed over $\mathbb{Z}_q^{(N+\ell) \times n}$.

$\mathcal{B}$ simulates $\mathsf{G}_{1.v-1}/\mathsf{G}_{1.v}$ for $\mathcal{A}$ as follows. $\mathcal{B}$ sets $\mathsf{pp} = \overline{\mathbf{A}'} := \overline{\mathbf{B}}$. For the user v, $\mathcal{B}$ invokes $(\overline{\mathbf{A}}^{(v)}, \mathbf{T}^{(v)}) \leftarrow_{\$} \mathsf{TrapGen}(1^n, 1^N)$, samples $\underline{\mathbf{A}}^{(v)} \leftarrow_{\$} \mathbb{Z}_q^{\ell \times n}$, and sets $pk^{(v)} := (\mathbf{A}^{(v)} := \left({}^{\overline{\mathbf{A}}^{(v)}}_{\underline{\mathbf{A}}^{(v)}} \right), \mathbf{A}'^{(v)} := \underline{\mathbf{B}})$. It is clearly that $\mathbf{A}'^{(v)} = \left({}^{\overline{\mathbf{A}'}}_{\underline{\mathbf{A}'^{(v)}}} \right) = \left({}^{\overline{\mathbf{B}}}_{\underline{\mathbf{B}}} \right) = \mathbf{B}$. For all other users $i \in [\mathsf{n}] \setminus \{v\}$, $\mathcal{B}$ invokes $\mathsf{KGen}(\mathsf{pp})$ honestly to generate $(pk^{(i)}, sk^{(i)})$. $\mathcal{B}$ sends $(\mathsf{pp}, \{pk^{(i)}\}_{i \in [\mathsf{n}]})$ to $\mathcal{A}$. $\mathcal{B}$ also chooses a random user index $i' \leftarrow_{\$} [\mathsf{n}]$ uniformly as the guess of the challenge user i^*.

- On receiving a re-encryption key query $\mathcal{O}_{\text{REKEY}}(i, j, f_{\mathbf{M}})$ from $\mathcal{A}$, if $(i = i')$ and $(j \in \mathcal{Q}_c)$, $\mathcal{B}$ aborts the game, just like $\mathsf{G}_{1.v-1}$ and $\mathsf{G}_{1.v}$. Otherwise, $\mathcal{B}$ replies the query as follows:
  - If $i = i'$ and $j \leq v - 1$, $\mathcal{B}$ samples $\mathbf{U} \leftarrow_\$ \mathbb{Z}_q^{(N+\ell) \times n}$ and invokes $\mathbf{R} \leftarrow_\$ \mathsf{SamplePre}\left(\mathbf{T}^{(i)}, \overline{\mathbf{A}}^{(i)}, \mathbf{U}, \gamma\right)$ to get $rk_{i' \to j}^{f_{\mathbf{M}}} := \left(\mathbf{R} \mid {}^0_{\mathbf{M}}\right)$, the same as $\mathsf{G}_{1.v-1}$ and $\mathsf{G}_{1.v}$.
  - If $i = i'$ and $j = v$, suppose that this is the k-th $\mathcal{O}_{\text{REKEY}}$ query with $k \in [Q]$, $\mathcal{B}$ makes use of $\mathbf{Z}_k$ to invoke $\mathbf{R} \leftarrow_\$ \mathsf{SamplePre}\left(\mathbf{T}^{(i')}, \overline{\mathbf{A}}^{(i')}, \mathbf{Z}_k - \left({}^0_{\mathbf{M}}\right)\mathbf{A}^{(v)}, \gamma\right)$ to get $rk_{i' \to v}^{f_{\mathbf{M}}} := \left(\mathbf{R} \mid {}^0_{\mathbf{M}}\right)$.
    In the case of $\mathbf{Z} = \mathbf{BS} + \mathbf{E}$, we have $\mathbf{Z}_k = \mathbf{BS}_k + \mathbf{E}_k = \mathbf{A}'^{(v)}\mathbf{S}_k + \mathbf{E}_k$ for $\mathbf{S}_k \leftarrow_\$ \chi^{n \times n}$ and $\mathbf{E} \leftarrow_\$ \chi^{(N+\ell) \times n}$, so $\mathcal{B}$'s simulation is identical to $\mathsf{G}_{1.v-1}$. In the case of $\mathbf{Z} \leftarrow_\$ \mathbb{Z}_q^{(N+\ell) \times nQ}$, we have that $\mathbf{Z}_k$ is uniformly distributed over $\mathbb{Z}_q^{(N+\ell) \times n}$, so $\mathcal{B}$'s simulation is identical to $\mathsf{G}_{1.v}$.
  - Otherwise, $\mathcal{B}$ samples $\mathbf{S} \leftarrow_\$ \chi^{n \times n}, \mathbf{E} \leftarrow_\$ \chi^{(N+\ell) \times n}$ and invokes $\mathbf{R} \leftarrow_\$ \mathsf{SamplePre}\left(\mathbf{T}^{(i)}, \overline{\mathbf{A}}^{(i)}, \mathbf{A}'^{(j)}\mathbf{S} + \mathbf{E} - \left({}^0_{\mathbf{M}}\right)\mathbf{A}^{(i)}, \gamma\right)$ to get $rk_{i' \to j}^{f_{\mathbf{M}}} := \left(\mathbf{R} \mid {}^0_{\mathbf{M}}\right)$, the same as $\mathsf{G}_{1.v-1}$ and $\mathsf{G}_{1.v}$.
- On receiving a corruption query $\mathcal{O}_{\text{COR}}(i)$ from $\mathcal{A}$, if $(i = i')$ or $(i', i) \in \mathcal{Q}_{rk}$, $\mathcal{B}$ aborts the game, just like $\mathsf{G}_{1.v-1}$ and $\mathsf{G}_{1.v}$. If $i = v$ (which means that Corr_v occurs), $\mathcal{B}$ also aborts the game. Otherwise, $\mathcal{B}$ returns $sk^{(i)}$ to $\mathcal{A}$.
- On receiving the challenge tuple $(i^*, \mathbf{m}_0, \mathbf{m}_1)$ from $\mathcal{A}$, if $i' \neq i^*$, $\mathcal{B}$ aborts the game. Otherwise, $\mathcal{B}$ chooses a random bit $\beta \leftarrow_\$ \{0, 1\}$ and generates the challenge ciphertext ct_1^* which encrypts $\mathbf{m}_\beta$, just like $\mathsf{G}_{1.v-1}$ and $\mathsf{G}_{1.v}$.
- Finally, $\mathcal{B}$ receives a bit β' from $\mathcal{A}$, and $\mathcal{B}$ outputs 1 to its own challenger if and only if $\beta' = \beta$ and $\mathcal{A}$ never corrupts v (i.e., $\neg\mathsf{Corr}_v$).

Now we analyze the advantage of $\mathcal{B}$. Overall, if $\mathbf{Z} = \mathbf{BS} + \mathbf{E}$, $\mathcal{B}$ simulates $\mathsf{G}_{1.v-1}$ perfectly for $\mathcal{A}$ in the case $\neg\mathsf{Corr}_v$, and if $\mathbf{Z} \leftarrow_\$ \mathbb{Z}_q^{(N+\ell) \times nQ}$, $\mathcal{B}$ simulates $\mathsf{G}_{1.v}$ perfectly for $\mathcal{A}$ in the case $\neg\mathsf{Corr}_v$. Thus, we have

$$\mathsf{Adv}_{[n,q,\chi,N+\ell],\mathcal{B}}^{nQ\text{-LWE}}(\lambda) = \left| \Pr[\mathcal{B}(\mathbf{B}, \mathbf{Z} = \mathbf{BS} + \mathbf{E}) = 1] - \Pr[\mathcal{B}(\mathbf{B}, \mathbf{Z} \leftarrow_\$ \mathbb{Z}_q^{(N+\ell) \times nQ}) = 1] \right|$$
$$= \left| \Pr_{1.v-1}[\mathsf{Win} \wedge \neg\mathsf{Corr}_v] - \Pr_{1.v}[\mathsf{Win} \wedge \neg\mathsf{Corr}_v] \right|. \tag{5}$$

Taking (4) and (5) together, Claim 1 follows. ∎

Game G_2: It's the same as G_1, except for the reply to $\mathcal{A}$'s re-encryption query $\mathcal{O}_{\text{REKEY}}(i', j, f_{\mathbf{M}})$ when the query leads to no trivial attacks.

- If $i = i'$ (and $j \in [\mathfrak{n}]$), the challenger uniformly samples $\mathbf{U} \leftarrow_\$ \mathbb{Z}_q^{(N+\ell) \times n}$ and uses $\mathbf{U}$ to invoke $\mathbf{R} \leftarrow_\$ \mathsf{SamplePre}\left(\mathbf{T}^{(i')}, \overline{\mathbf{A}}^{(i')}, \mathbf{U}, \gamma\right)$ to obtain $rk_{i' \to j}^{f_{\mathbf{M}}} := \left(\mathbf{R} \mid {}^0_{\mathbf{M}}\right)$, and return $rk_{i' \to j}^{f_{\mathbf{M}}}$ to $\mathcal{A}$.

Clearly, $\mathsf{G}_2 = \mathsf{G}_{1.\mathfrak{n}}$ and $\Pr_2[\mathsf{Win}] = \Pr_{1.\mathfrak{n}}[\mathsf{Win}]$. Thus by Claim 1, we have

$$\left| \Pr_1[\mathsf{Win}] - \Pr_2[\mathsf{Win}] \right| \leq \mathfrak{n} \cdot \mathsf{Adv}_{[n,q,\chi,N+\ell],\mathcal{B}}^{nQ\text{-LWE}}(\lambda). \tag{6}$$

Game G_3: It is the same as G_2, except for the reply to $\mathcal{A}$'s re-encryption query $\mathcal{O}_{\text{ReKey}}(i = i', j, f_M)$. If the query does not lead to any trivial attack, then the challenger samples $\mathbf{R}$ by $\mathbf{R} \leftarrow_\$ D_{\mathbb{Z}^{(N+\ell) \times N}, \gamma}$, instead of invoking $\mathbf{R} \leftarrow_\$ \text{SamplePre}\left(\mathbf{T}^{(i')}, \overline{\mathbf{A}}^{(i')}, \mathbf{U} \leftarrow_\$ \mathbb{Z}_q^{(N+\ell) \times n}, \gamma\right)$ as in G_2.

Since $\gamma \geq O(\sqrt{n \log q}) \cdot \omega(\sqrt{\log n})$, according to the indistinguishability of preimage-sampling SamplePre (as recalled in the full version [24]), G_3 is statistically close to G_2. Thus, $|\text{Pr}_2[\text{Win}] - \text{Pr}_3[\text{Win}]| \leq \text{negl}(\lambda)$.

Note that in G_3, the trapdoor $\mathbf{T}^{(i')}$ is not needed any more.

Game G_4: It is the same as G_3, except for the generation of $pk^{(i')} = (\mathbf{A}^{(i')}, \mathbf{A}'^{(i')})$. In this game, the challenger samples $\mathbf{A}^{(i')} \leftarrow_\$ \mathbb{Z}_q^{(N+\ell) \times n}$ uniformly, rather than using the algorithm TrapGen as in G_3. According to the property of TrapGen (cf. the full version [24]), G_4 is statistically close to G_3. Thus, $|\text{Pr}_3[\text{Win}] - \text{Pr}_4[\text{Win}]| \leq \text{negl}(\lambda)$.

Game G_5: It is the same as G_4, except for the generation of the challenge ciphertext ct_1^*. Now the challenger picks $ct_1^* \leftarrow_\$ \mathbb{Z}_q^{N+\ell}$ uniformly, rather than generating it by $ct_1^* := \mathbf{A}^{(i^*)}\mathbf{s} + \mathbf{e} + \binom{\mathbf{0}}{pm_\beta}$ with $\mathbf{s} \leftarrow_\$ \chi^n, \mathbf{e} \leftarrow_\$ \chi^{N+\ell}$ as in G_4.

Clearly, the challenge bit β is completely hidden to $\mathcal{A}$, thus $\text{Pr}_5[\text{Win}] = \frac{1}{2}$. Next we show that G_4 and G_5 are computationally indistinguishable.

Claim 2. $|\text{Pr}_4[\text{Win}] - \text{Pr}_5[\text{Win}]| \leq \text{Adv}_{[n,q,\chi,N+\ell],\mathcal{B}'}^{\text{LWE}}(\lambda)$.

Proof. We construct a PPT algorithm $\mathcal{B}'$ to break the $\text{LWE}_{n,q,\chi,N+\ell}$ assumption by simulating G_4/G_5 for $\mathcal{A}$ as follows.

Algorithm $\mathcal{B}'$. Given $(\mathbf{B} \in \mathbb{Z}_q^{(N+\ell) \times n}, \mathbf{z} \in \mathbb{Z}_q^{N+\ell})$, $\mathcal{B}'$ wants to distinguish $\mathbf{z} = \mathbf{B}\mathbf{s} + \mathbf{e}$ from $\mathbf{z} \leftarrow_\$ \mathbb{Z}_q^{N+\ell}$, where $\mathbf{B} \leftarrow_\$ \in \mathbb{Z}_q^{(N+\ell) \times n}$, $\mathbf{s} \leftarrow_\$ \chi^n$ and $\mathbf{e} \leftarrow_\$ \chi^{N+\ell}$.

$\mathcal{B}'$ simulates G_4/G_5 for $\mathcal{A}$ as follows. $\mathcal{B}'$ invokes Setup honestly to generate $pp = \overline{\mathbf{A}'}$, and chooses a random user index $i' \leftarrow_\$ [n]$ uniformly as the guess of the challenge user i^*. For the user i', $\mathcal{B}'$ samples $\mathbf{K}^{(i')} \leftarrow_\$ \{0,1\}^{\ell \times N}$, and sets $pk^{(i')} = (\mathbf{A}^{(i')} := \mathbf{B}, \mathbf{A}'^{(i')} := -\mathbf{K}^{(i')}\overline{\mathbf{A}'})$ and $sk^{(i')} = \perp$. For all other users $i \in [n] \setminus \{i'\}$, $\mathcal{B}'$ invokes $\text{KGen}(pp)$ honestly to generate $(pk^{(i)}, sk^{(i)})$. $\mathcal{B}'$ sends $(pp, \{pk^{(i)}\}_{i \in [n]})$ to $\mathcal{A}$.

- On receiving a re-encryption key query $\mathcal{O}_{\text{ReKey}}(i, j, f_M)$ from $\mathcal{A}$, $\mathcal{B}'$ replies $\mathcal{A}$ just like G_4 and G_5. More precisely, if $(i = i')$ and $(j \in \mathcal{Q}_c)$, $\mathcal{B}$ aborts the game; otherwise, $\mathcal{B}'$ replies the query as follows:
  - If $i = i'$, $\mathcal{B}'$ samples $\mathbf{R} \leftarrow_\$ D_{\mathbb{Z}^{(N+\ell) \times N}, \gamma}$ to get $rk_{i' \to j}^{f_M} := (\mathbf{R} \mid \begin{smallmatrix} \mathbf{0} \\ \mathbf{M} \end{smallmatrix})$.
  - If $i \neq i'$, $\mathcal{B}'$ invokes $\mathbf{R} \leftarrow_\$ \text{SamplePre}\left(\mathbf{T}^{(i)}, \overline{\mathbf{A}}^{(i)}, \mathbf{A}'^{(j)}\mathbf{S} + \mathbf{E}, \gamma\right)$ to get $rk_{i' \to j}^{f_M} := (\mathbf{R} \mid \begin{smallmatrix} \mathbf{0} \\ \mathbf{M} \end{smallmatrix})$ using the secret key $sk^{(i)} = (\mathbf{T}^{(i)}, \mathbf{K}^{(i)})$ of user i.
- On receiving a corruption query $\mathcal{O}_{\text{Cor}}(i)$ from $\mathcal{A}$, $\mathcal{B}'$ replies $\mathcal{A}$ just like G_4 and G_5. More precisely, if $(i = i')$ or $(i', i) \in \mathcal{Q}_{rk}$, $\mathcal{B}'$ aborts the game; otherwise, $\mathcal{B}'$ returns $sk^{(i)}$ to $\mathcal{A}$.

- On receiving the challenge tuple $(i^*, \mathbf{m}_0, \mathbf{m}_1)$ from $\mathcal{A}$, if $i' \neq i^*$, $\mathcal{B}'$ aborts the game. Otherwise, $\mathcal{B}'$ chooses a random bit $\beta \leftarrow_{\$} \{0, 1\}$ and computes $ct_1^* := \mathbf{z} + \binom{\mathbf{0}}{\mathbf{pm}_\beta}$. Then $\mathcal{B}'$ sends ct_1^* to $\mathcal{A}$.

  In the case of $\mathbf{z} = \mathbf{Bs} + \mathbf{e}$, $ct_1^* = \mathbf{Bs} + \mathbf{e} + \binom{\mathbf{0}}{\mathbf{pm}_\beta} = \mathbf{A}^{(i^*)}\mathbf{s} + \mathbf{e} + \binom{\mathbf{0}}{\mathbf{pm}_\beta}$, so $\mathcal{B}'$'s simulation is identical to G_4. In the case of $\mathbf{z} \leftarrow_{\$} \mathbb{Z}_q^{N+\ell}$, $ct_1^* = \mathbf{z} + \binom{\mathbf{0}}{\mathbf{pm}_\beta}$ is uniformly distributed, so $\mathcal{B}'$'s simulation is identical to G_5.

- Finally, $\mathcal{B}'$ receives a bit β' from $\mathcal{A}$, and $\mathcal{B}'$ outputs 1 to its own challenger if and only if $\beta' = \beta$.

Now we analyze the advantage of $\mathcal{B}'$. Overall, if $\mathbf{z} = \mathbf{Bs} + \mathbf{e}$, $\mathcal{B}'$ simulates G_4 perfectly for $\mathcal{A}$, and if $\mathbf{z} \leftarrow_{\$} \mathbb{Z}_q^{N+\ell}$, $\mathcal{B}'$ simulates G_5 perfectly for $\mathcal{A}$. Thus,

$$\mathsf{Adv}^{\mathsf{LWE}}_{[n,q,\chi,N+\ell],\mathcal{B}'}(\lambda) = \big| \Pr[\mathcal{B}'(\mathbf{B}, \mathbf{z} = \mathbf{Bs} + \mathbf{e}) = 1] - \Pr[\mathcal{B}'(\mathbf{B}, \mathbf{z} \leftarrow_{\$} \mathbb{Z}_q^{N+\ell}) = 1] \big|$$
$$= \big| \Pr_4[\mathsf{Win}] - \Pr_5[\mathsf{Win}] \big|. \qquad \blacksquare$$

Finally, taking all things together, Theorem 1 follows.   □

Note that in the proof of Theorem 1, in G_5, the challenge ciphertext ct_1^* has been replaced by a random vector in $\mathbb{Z}_q^{N+\ell}$, thus, we have the following corollary.

Corollary 1 (Ciphertext Pseudorandomness of $\mathsf{FPRE}^{\mathsf{lin}}_{\mathsf{LWE}}$). *Assume that the $\mathsf{LWE}_{n,q,\chi,N+\ell}$-assumption holds, then the scheme $\mathsf{FPRE}^{\mathsf{lin}}_{\mathsf{LWE}}$ proposed in Fig. 7 has ciphertext pseudorandomness (CPR). More precisely, for any PPT adversary $\mathcal{A}$ that makes at most Q times of $\mathcal{O}_{\mathrm{REKEY}}$ queries and for any polynomial $\mathfrak{n}$, there exists a PPT algorithm $\mathcal{B}$ against the LWE assumption such that $\mathsf{Adv}^{\mathsf{CPR}}_{\mathsf{FPRE},\mathcal{A},\mathfrak{n}}(\lambda) \leq (2\mathfrak{n}^2 nQ + \mathfrak{n}) \cdot \mathsf{Adv}^{\mathsf{LWE}}_{[n,q,\chi,N+\ell],\mathcal{B}}(\lambda) + \mathsf{negl}(\lambda)$.*

Proof Sketch. We can prove the corollary via a sequence of games $\mathsf{G}_0 - \mathsf{G}_9$. Here G_0-G_5 are similar to those in the proof of Theorem 1, and in particular, in G_5, the challenge ciphertext ct_1^* is already pseudorandom. The only thing we need to do is to reverse the changes introduced in $\mathsf{G}_1 - \mathsf{G}_4$, and this can be done by the additional games $\mathsf{G}_6 - \mathsf{G}_9$ which are symmetric to $\mathsf{G}_4 - \mathsf{G}_0$.   □

Theorem 2 (Ciphertext Unlinkability of $\mathsf{FPRE}^{\mathsf{lin}}_{\mathsf{LWE}}$). *Assume that the $\mathsf{LWE}_{n,q,\chi,N+\ell}$-assumption holds, then the scheme $\mathsf{FPRE}^{\mathsf{lin}}_{\mathsf{LWE}}$ proposed in Fig. 7 has ciphertext unlinkability (CUL). More precisely, for any PPT adversary $\mathcal{A}$ that makes at most Q times of $\mathcal{O}_{\mathrm{REKEY}}$ queries and for any polynomial $\mathfrak{n}$, there exists a PPT algorithm $\mathcal{B}$ against the LWE assumption such that*

$$\mathsf{Adv}^{\mathsf{CUL}}_{\mathsf{FPRE},\mathcal{A},\mathfrak{n}}(\lambda) \leq (3\mathfrak{n}^2 nQ + \mathfrak{n}^2 + 2\mathfrak{n}) \cdot \mathsf{Adv}^{\mathsf{LWE}}_{[n,q,\chi,N+\ell],\mathcal{B}}(\lambda) + \mathsf{negl}(\lambda).$$

Proof of Theorem 2. We prove the theorem via a sequence of games G_0'-G_9', where G_0' is the CUL experiment, and in G_9', $\mathcal{A}$ has a negligible advantage.

Game $\underline{\mathsf{G}_0'}$: This is the CUL experiment $\mathsf{Exp}^{\mathsf{CUL}}_{\mathsf{FPRE},\mathcal{A},\mathfrak{n}}$ (cf. Fig. 6). Let Win denote the event that $\beta' = \beta$. By definition, $\mathsf{Adv}^{\mathsf{CUL}}_{\mathsf{FPRE},\mathcal{A},\mathfrak{n}}(\lambda) = | \Pr_0'[\mathsf{Win}] - \frac{1}{2}|$.

Let $pp = \overline{\mathbf{A}'}$ and $pk^{(i)} = (\mathbf{A}^{(i)}, \underline{\mathbf{A}}'^{(i)})$, $sk^{(i)} = (\mathbf{T}^{(i)}, \mathbf{K}^{(i)})$ the public key and secret key of user $i \in [\mathfrak{n}]$. In this game, the challenger answers $\mathcal{A}$'s $\mathcal{O}_{\text{ReKey}}$, $\mathcal{O}_{\text{COR}}$ queries and generates the challenge ciphertexts (ct_1^*, ct_2^*) as follows.

- On receiving a re-encryption key query $\mathcal{O}_{\text{ReKey}}(i, j, f_{\mathbf{M}})$ from $\mathcal{A}$, the challenger returns $\bot$ to $\mathcal{A}$ directly if trivial attacks $(i = i^*)$ and $(j \in \mathcal{Q}_c)$ occur. Otherwise, the challenger adds (i, j) to $\mathcal{Q}_{rk}$, samples $\mathbf{S} \leftarrow_{\$} \chi^{n \times n}$, $\mathbf{E} \leftarrow_{\$} \chi^{(N+\ell) \times n}$, invokes $\mathbf{R} \leftarrow_{\$} \text{SamplePre}\left(\mathbf{T}^{(i)}, \overline{\mathbf{A}}^{(i)}, \mathbf{A}'^{(j)}\mathbf{S} + \mathbf{E}\right.$
$\left. - \binom{0}{\mathbf{M}}\underline{\mathbf{A}}^{(i)}, \gamma\right)$, where $\mathbf{A}'^{(j)} = \left(\begin{smallmatrix}\overline{\mathbf{A}'}\\ \underline{\mathbf{A}}'^{(j)}\end{smallmatrix}\right)$, and returns $rk_{i \to j}^{f_{\mathbf{M}}} := (\mathbf{R} \mid {}^{0}_{\mathbf{M}})$ to $\mathcal{A}$.
- On receiving a corruption query $\mathcal{O}_{\text{COR}}(i)$ from $\mathcal{A}$, the challenger returns $\bot$ to $\mathcal{A}$ directly if trivial attacks $(i = i^*)$ or $(i = j^*)$ or $(i^*, i) \in \mathcal{Q}_{rk}$ occur. Otherwise, the challenger adds i to $\mathcal{Q}_c$ and returns $sk^{(i)}$ to $\mathcal{A}$.
- On receiving the challenge tuple $(i^*, j^*, (f_{\mathbf{M}}, \mathbf{m}), (\mathbf{m}_1, \mathbf{m}_2))$ from $\mathcal{A}$, the challenger first checks if trivial attacks $(i^* \in \mathcal{Q}_c)$ or $(j^* \in \mathcal{Q}_c)$ or $(\exists j \in \mathcal{Q}_c \text{ s.t. } (i^*, j) \in \mathcal{Q}_{rk})$ occur. If yes, the challenger aborts the game with $\mathcal{A}$ by returning a random bit. Otherwise, the challenger chooses a random bit $\beta \leftarrow_{\$} \{0, 1\}$. In the case $\beta = 0$, the challenger generates ct_1^* by invoking $ct_1^* \leftarrow_{\$} \text{Enc}_1(pk^{(i^*)}, \mathbf{m})$ and generates ct_2^* by invoking $ct_2^* \leftarrow_{\$} \text{FReEnc}(rk_{i^* \to j^*}^{f_{\mathbf{M}}}, ct_1^*)$ where $rk_{i^* \to j^*}^{f_{\mathbf{M}}} \leftarrow_{\$} \text{FReKGen}(pk^{(i^*)}, sk^{(i^*)}, pk^{(j^*)}, f_{\mathbf{M}})$. In the case $\beta = 1$, the challenger generates ct_1^* by invoking $ct_1^* \leftarrow_{\$} \text{Enc}_1(pk^{(i^*)}, \mathbf{m}_1)$ and generates ct_2^* by invoking $ct_2^* \leftarrow_{\$} \text{Enc}_2(pk^{(j^*)}, \mathbf{m}_2)$. The challenger sends the challenge ciphertexts (ct_1^*, ct_2^*) to $\mathcal{A}$.

Game G_1': This game is similar to G_0', except that, in the case of $\beta = 0$, the challenger picks the first-level challenge ciphertext $ct_1^* \leftarrow_{\$} \mathbb{Z}_q^{N+\ell}$ uniformly at random, rather than generating it by $ct_1^* \leftarrow_{\$} \text{Enc}_1(pk^{(i^*)}, \mathbf{m})$ as in G_0'.

Claim 3. $\left| \text{Pr}_0'[\text{Win}] - \text{Pr}_1'[\text{Win}] \right| \leq \text{Adv}_{\text{FPRE}, \mathcal{B}, \mathfrak{n}}^{\text{CPR}}(\lambda)$.

Proof. We construct a PPT algorithm $\mathcal{B}$ to break the ciphertext pseudorandomness (CPR) of $\text{FPRE}_{\text{LWE}}^{\text{lin}}$ by simulating $\mathsf{G}_0'/\mathsf{G}_1'$ for $\mathcal{A}$ as follows.

Algorithm $\mathcal{B}$. Algorithm $\mathcal{B}$ is given the public parameter pp, $\{pk^{(i)}\}_{i \in [\mathfrak{n}]}$ from its own challenger and has access to its own oracles $\mathcal{O}_{\text{ReKey}}$, $\mathcal{O}_{\text{COR}}$. $\mathcal{B}$ initializes $\mathcal{Q}_{rk} = \emptyset, \mathcal{Q}_c = \emptyset, i^* = \bot, j^* = \bot$ and sends pp, $\{pk^{(i)}\}_{i \in [\mathfrak{n}]}$ to $\mathcal{A}$.

- On receiving a re-encryption key query $(i, j, f_{\mathbf{M}})$ from $\mathcal{A}$, $\mathcal{B}$ checks $\mathcal{A}$'s trivial attack by checking if $(i = i^*)$ and $(j \in \mathcal{Q}_c)$, just like G_0' and G_1'. If trivial attacks occur, $\mathcal{B}$ returns $\bot$ to $\mathcal{A}$, otherwise $\mathcal{B}$ adds (i, j) to $\mathcal{Q}_{rk}$ and queries $(i, j, f_{\mathbf{M}})$ to its own oracle $\mathcal{O}_{\text{ReKey}}$. On receiving $rk_{i \to j}^{f_{\mathbf{M}}}$ from $\mathcal{O}_{\text{ReKey}}(i, j, f_{\mathbf{M}})$, $\mathcal{B}$ returns $rk_{i \to j}^{f_{\mathbf{M}}}$ to $\mathcal{A}$.
- On receiving a corruption query i from $\mathcal{A}$, $\mathcal{B}$ checks $\mathcal{A}$'s trivial attack by checking if $(i = i^*)$ or $(i = j^*)$ or $(i^*, i) \in \mathcal{Q}_{rk}$, just like G_0' and G_1'. If trivial attacks occur, $\mathcal{B}$ returns $\bot$ to $\mathcal{A}$, otherwise $\mathcal{B}$ adds i to $\mathcal{Q}_c$ and queries i to its own oracle $\mathcal{O}_{\text{COR}}$. On receiving $sk^{(i)}$ from $\mathcal{O}_{\text{COR}}(i)$, $\mathcal{B}$ returns $sk^{(i)}$ to $\mathcal{A}$.

- On receiving the challenge tuple $(i^*, j^*, (f_M, \mathbf{m}), (\mathbf{m}_1, \mathbf{m}_2))$ from $\mathcal{A}$, $\mathcal{B}$ first checks if $(i^* \in \mathcal{Q}_c)$ or $(j^* \in \mathcal{Q}_c)$ or $(\exists j \in \mathcal{Q}_c$ s.t. $(i^*, j) \in \mathcal{Q}_{rk})$ to identify trivial attacks, just like G_0' and G_1'. If yes, trivial attacks happen, and $\mathcal{B}$ aborts the game with $\mathcal{A}$ and returns a random bit $b' \leftarrow_\$ \{0,1\}$ to its own challenger. Otherwise, $\mathcal{B}$ queries (i^*, j^*, f_M) to its own oracle $\mathcal{O}_{\mathrm{REKEY}}$ to obtain $rk_{i^* \to j^*}^{f_M}$. Moreover, $\mathcal{B}$ sends a challenge tuple $(i^*, \mathbf{m})$ to its own challenger, and receives a challenge ciphertext $\widetilde{ct}_1^*$ from its own challenger, which either encrypts $\mathbf{m}$ under $pk^{(i^*)}$, i.e., $\widetilde{ct}_1^* \leftarrow_\$ \mathsf{Enc}_1(pk^{(i^*)}, \mathbf{m})$, or is uniformly chosen from $\mathbb{Z}_q^{N+\ell}$, i.e., $\widetilde{ct}_1^* \leftarrow_\$ \mathsf{Enc}_1(pk^{(i^*)}, \mathbf{m})$, depending on the challenge bit b that $\mathcal{B}$'s challenge picks. Then $\mathcal{B}$ chooses a random bit $\beta \leftarrow_\$ \{0,1\}$. In the case $\beta = 0$, $\mathcal{B}$ sets $ct_1^* := \widetilde{ct}_1^*$ and generates ct_2^* by invoking $ct_2^* \leftarrow_\$ \mathsf{FReEnc}(rk_{i^* \to j^*}^{f_M}, ct_1^*)$. In the case $\beta = 1$, $\mathcal{B}$ generates ct_1^* by invoking $ct_1^* \leftarrow_\$ \mathsf{Enc}_1(pk^{(i^*)}, \mathbf{m}_1)$ and generates ct_2^* by invoking $ct_2^* \leftarrow_\$ \mathsf{Enc}_2(pk^{(j^*)}, \mathbf{m}_2)$, just like G_0' and G_1'.
- Finally, $\mathcal{B}$ receives a bit β' from $\mathcal{A}$, and $\mathcal{B}$ outputs 1 if and only if $\beta' = \beta$.

In the simulation, as long as $\mathcal{A}$ implements trivial attacks $i^* \in \mathcal{Q}_c$ or $j^* \in \mathcal{Q}_c$ or $(\exists j \in \mathcal{Q}_c$ s.t. $(i^*, j) \in \mathcal{Q}_{rk})$, $\mathcal{B}$ will abort the experiment, just like G_0' and G_1'. Otherwise, no trivial attacks from $\mathcal{A}$ implies that $i^* \notin \mathcal{Q}_c$ and there doesn't exist any re-encryption key query $(i^*, j) \in \mathcal{Q}_{rk} \cup \{(i^*, j^*)\}$ from i^* to $j \in \mathcal{Q}_c$, where $\mathcal{Q}_{rk} \cup \{(i^*, j^*)\}$ is exactly the re-encryption key query set for $\mathcal{B}$'s challenger. Therefore, $\mathcal{B}$'s query (i^*, j^*, f_M) to its own oracle $\mathcal{O}_{\mathrm{REKEY}}$ does not lead to any trivial attacks in the ciphertext pesudorandomness (CPR) experiment (cf. Fig. 2), and $\mathcal{B}$'s challenger will answer this query and return $rk_{i^* \to j^*}^{f_M}$ to $\mathcal{B}$. So $\mathcal{B}$'s simulation of $rk_{i^* \to j^*}^{f_M}$ for $\mathcal{A}$ is perfect.

Now we analyze the advantage of $\mathcal{B}$. Overall, if the challenge ciphertext $\widetilde{ct}_1^*$ that $\mathcal{B}$ received from its own challenger is generated by $\widetilde{ct}_1^* \leftarrow_\$ \mathsf{Enc}_1(pk^{(i^*)}, \mathbf{m})$, $\mathcal{B}$ simulates G_0' perfectly for $\mathcal{A}$, and if $\widetilde{ct}_1^*$ is uniformly chosen from $\mathbb{Z}_q^{N+\ell}$ by $\mathcal{B}$'s challenger, $\mathcal{B}$ simulates G_1' perfectly for $\mathcal{A}$. Therefore, $\mathcal{B}$ will successfully distinguish $\widetilde{ct}_1^* \leftarrow_\$ \mathsf{Enc}_1(pk^{(i^*)}, \mathbf{m})$ from $\widetilde{ct}_1^* \leftarrow_\$ \mathbb{Z}_q^{N+\ell}$ and break the ciphertext pesudorandomness (CPR) of $\mathsf{FPRE}_{\mathsf{LWE}}^{\mathrm{lin}}$ as long as the probability that Win occurs in G_0' differs non-negligibly from that in G_1', and we have $\left| \Pr_0'[\mathsf{Win}] - \Pr_1'[\mathsf{Win}] \right| \leq \mathsf{Adv}_{\mathsf{FPRE},\mathcal{B},n}^{\mathrm{CPR}}(\lambda)$. ∎

Game G_2': It is the same as G_1', except that, at the beginning of the game, the challenger chooses $i' \leftarrow_\$ [n]$ uniformly as the guess of the challenge user i^*, and will abort the game and return a random bit in the following cases.

- **Case 1.** $\mathcal{A}$ issues the challenge tuple $(i^*, j^*, (f_M, \mathbf{m}), (\mathbf{m}_1, \mathbf{m}_2))$ but $i' \neq i^*$.
- **Case 2.** $\mathcal{A}$ issues a re-encryption key query $\mathcal{O}_{\mathrm{REKEY}}(i, j, f_M)$ such that $(i = i')$ and $(j \in \mathcal{Q}_c)$ before issuing its challenge.
- **Case 3.** $\mathcal{A}$ issues a corruption query $\mathcal{O}_{\mathrm{COR}}(i)$ such that $(i = i')$ or $(i = j^*)$ or $(i', i) \in \mathcal{Q}_{rk}$ before issuing its challenge.

Case 1 suggests that the challenger's guess is wrong. Now in G_2', the challenger will abort the game if the guess is wrong. If the guess is correct, i.e., $i' = i^*$,

Case 2 and Case 3 are in fact trivial attacks, so they will lead to abort anyway in G_1' and do not contribute to $\mathcal{A}$'s advantage. Since the challenger will guess i^* correctly with probability $1/n$, we have $\left|\Pr_1'[\mathsf{Win}] - \frac{1}{2}\right| = \frac{1}{n}\left|\Pr_2'[\mathsf{Win}] - \frac{1}{2}\right|$.

Game G_3': It is the same as G_2', except for the reply to $\mathcal{A}$'s re-encryption query $\mathcal{O}_{\mathrm{ReKey}}(i', j, f_{\mathbf{M}})$ which does not lead to any trivial attack.

- If $i = i'$ (and $j \in [n]$), the challenger uniformly samples $\mathbf{U} \leftarrow_\$ \mathbb{Z}_q^{(N+\ell)\times n}$ and uses $\mathbf{U}$ to invoke $\mathbf{R} \leftarrow_\$ \mathsf{SamplePre}\left(\mathbf{T}^{(i')}, \overline{\mathbf{A}}^{(i')}, \mathbf{U}, \gamma\right)$ to obtain $rk_{i'\to j}^{f_{\mathbf{M}}} := \left(\mathbf{R} \mid {}^0_{\mathbf{M}}\right)$, and return $rk_{i'\to j}^{f_{\mathbf{M}}}$ to $\mathcal{A}$.

Moreover, G_3' also differs from G_2' in the generation of the second-level challenge ciphertext ct_2^* in the case of $\beta = 0$. Recall that in G_2', in the case of $\beta = 0$, the challenger invokes $rk_{i^*\to j^*}^{f_{\mathbf{M}}} \leftarrow_\$ \mathsf{FReKGen}(pk^{(i^*)}, sk^{(i^*)}, pk^{(j^*)}, f_{\mathbf{M}})$ to compute $ct_2^* \leftarrow_\$ \mathsf{FReEnc}(rk_{i^*\to j^*}^{f_{\mathbf{M}}}, ct_1^*)$. Now in this game, the challenger also uniformly samples $\mathbf{U} \leftarrow_\$ \mathbb{Z}_q^{(N+\ell)\times n}$, uses $\mathbf{U}$ to invoke $\mathbf{R} \leftarrow_\$ \mathsf{SamplePre}\left(\mathbf{T}^{(i^*)}, \overline{\mathbf{A}}^{(i^*)}, \mathbf{U}, \gamma\right)$ to obtain $rk_{i^*\to j^*}^{f_{\mathbf{M}}} := \left(\mathbf{R} \mid {}^0_{\mathbf{M}}\right)$, then uses $rk_{i^*\to j^*}^{f_{\mathbf{M}}}$ to compute $ct_2^* \leftarrow_\$ \mathsf{FReEnc}(rk_{i^*\to j^*}^{f_{\mathbf{M}}}, ct_1^*)$.

With a similar argument like G_1-$G_2(= G_{1.0}$-$G_{1.n})$ in the proof of Theorem 1, cf. (6), we have $\left|\Pr_2'[\mathsf{Win}] - \Pr_3'[\mathsf{Win}]\right| \le n \cdot \mathsf{Adv}_{[n,q,\chi,N+\ell],\mathcal{B}_1}^{nQ\text{-LWE}}(\lambda)$.

Game G_4': It is the same as G_3', except for the reply to $\mathcal{A}$'s re-encryption query $\mathcal{O}_{\mathrm{ReKey}}(i = i', j, f_{\mathbf{M}})$. If the query does not lead to any trivial attack, then the challenger samples $\mathbf{R}$ by $\mathbf{R} \leftarrow_\$ D_{\mathbb{Z}^{(N+\ell)\times N},\gamma}$, instead of invoking $\mathbf{R} \leftarrow_\$ \mathsf{SamplePre}\left(\mathbf{T}^{(i')}, \overline{\mathbf{A}}^{(i')}, \mathbf{U} \leftarrow_\$ \mathbb{Z}_q^{(N+\ell)\times n}, \gamma\right)$ as in G_3'.

Moreover, G_4' also differs from G_3' in the generation of ct_2^* in the case of $\beta = 0$. Now in this game, in the case of $\beta = 0$, the challenger also samples $\mathbf{R}$ by $\mathbf{R} \leftarrow_\$ D_{\mathbb{Z}^{(N+\ell)\times N},\gamma}$, instead of invoking $\mathbf{R} \leftarrow_\$ \mathsf{SamplePre}\left(\mathbf{T}^{(i^*)}, \overline{\mathbf{A}}^{(i^*)}, \mathbf{U} \leftarrow_\$ \mathbb{Z}_q^{(N+\ell)\times n}, \gamma\right)$ to obtain $rk_{i^*\to j^*}^{f_{\mathbf{M}}} := \left(\mathbf{R} \mid {}^0_{\mathbf{M}}\right)$, and uses $rk_{i^*\to j^*}^{f_{\mathbf{M}}}$ to compute $ct_2^* \leftarrow_\$ \mathsf{FReEnc}(rk_{i^*\to j^*}^{f_{\mathbf{M}}}, ct_1^*)$.

With a similar argument like G_2-G_3 in the proof of Theorem 1, we know that G_4' is statistically close to G_3'. Thus, $\left|\Pr_3'[\mathsf{Win}] - \Pr_4'[\mathsf{Win}]\right| \le \mathsf{negl}(\lambda)$.

Note that in G_4', the trapdoor $\mathbf{T}^{(i')}$ is not needed any more.

Game G_5': It is the same as G_4', except for the generation of ct_2^* in the case of $\beta = 0$. In this game, in the case of $\beta = 0$, the challenger picks the second-level challenge ciphertext $ct_2^* \leftarrow_\$ \mathbb{Z}_q^{N+\ell}$ uniformly at random.

Recall that in G_4', ct_2^* is generated by invoking $ct_2^* \leftarrow_\$ \mathsf{FReEnc}(rk_{i^*\to j^*}^{f_{\mathbf{M}}}, ct_1^*)$, where $ct_1^* \leftarrow_\$ \mathbb{Z}_q^{N+\ell}$ and $rk_{i^*\to j^*}^{f_{\mathbf{M}}} := \left(\mathbf{R} \mid {}^0_{\mathbf{M}}\right)$ with $\mathbf{R} \leftarrow_\$ D_{\mathbb{Z}^{(N+\ell)\times N},\gamma}$, thus

$$ct_2^* := rk_{i^*\to j^*}^{f_{\mathbf{M}}} \cdot ct_1^* = \left(\mathbf{R} \;\middle|\; \begin{matrix}\mathbf{0}\\\mathbf{M}\end{matrix}\right) \cdot ct_1^* = \mathbf{R}\cdot \overline{ct_1^*} + \begin{pmatrix}\mathbf{0}\\\mathbf{M}\end{pmatrix}\cdot \underline{ct_1^*}.$$

Since $\mathbf{R} \leftarrow_\$ D_{\mathbb{Z},\gamma}^{(N+\ell)\times N}$ with $\gamma \ge O(\sqrt{n\log q})\cdot \omega(\sqrt{\log n})$ and $\overline{ct_1^*}$ is uniformly distributed over $\mathbb{Z}_q^N$, according to the indistinguishability of preimage-sampling

SamplePre (cf. the full version [24]), we have that $\mathbf{R} \cdot \overline{ct_1^*}$ is statistically close to the uniform distribution over $\mathbb{Z}_q^{N+\ell}$. Due to the independence between $\mathbf{R} \cdot \overline{ct_1^*}$ and $\binom{0}{\mathbf{M}} \cdot ct_1^*$, we know that the second-level challenge ciphertext $ct_2^* = \mathbf{R} \cdot \overline{ct_1^*} + \binom{0}{\mathbf{M}} \cdot \underline{ct_1^*}$ generated in G_4' is statistically indistinguishable from the uniformly chosen $ct_2^* \leftarrow_\$ \mathbb{Z}_q^{N+\ell}$ in G_5'. Thus we have $\left| \Pr_4'[\mathsf{Win}] - \Pr_5'[\mathsf{Win}] \right| \leq \mathsf{negl}(\lambda)$.

Game G_6': It is the same as G_5', except for the generation of $pk^{(i')} = (\mathbf{A}^{(i')}, \mathbf{A}'^{(i')})$. Recall that from G_4' on, the trapdoor $\mathbf{T}^{(i')}$ of $\overline{\mathbf{A}}^{(i')}$ is not needed any more. In G_6', the challenger samples $\mathbf{A}^{(i')} \leftarrow_\$ \mathbb{Z}_q^{(N+\ell)\times n}$ uniformly, rather than using algorithm TrapGen as in G_5'. According to the property of TrapGen (cf. the full version [24]), G_6' is statistically close to G_5'. Thus, $\left| \Pr_5'[\mathsf{Win}] - \Pr_6'[\mathsf{Win}] \right| \leq \mathsf{negl}(\lambda)$.

Game G_7': It is the same as G_6', except that, in the case of $\beta = 1$, the challenger also picks the first-level challenge ciphertext $ct_1^* \leftarrow_\$ \mathbb{Z}_q^{N+\ell}$ uniformly at random, rather than generating it by $ct_1^* \leftarrow_\$ \mathsf{Enc}_1(pk^{(i^*)}, \mathbf{m}_1)$ as in G_6', i.e., $ct_1^* := \mathbf{A}^{(i^*)}\mathbf{s} + \mathbf{e} + \binom{0}{p\mathbf{m}_1}$ with $\mathbf{s} \leftarrow_\$ \chi^n, \mathbf{e} \leftarrow_\$ \chi^{N+\ell}$ in G_6'.

Due to the game changes introduced in G_2' and G_6', we have that $i' = i^*$ and $\mathbf{A}^{(i^*)} = \mathbf{A}^{(i')}$ is uniformly sampled from $\mathbb{Z}_q^{(N+\ell)\times n}$. Then according to the LWE assumption, $\mathbf{A}^{(i^*)}\mathbf{s} + \mathbf{e}$ is computationally indistinguishable from the uniform distribution over $\mathbb{Z}_q^{N+\ell}$. Thus the challenge ciphertext $ct_1^* := \mathbf{A}^{(i^*)}\mathbf{s} + \mathbf{e} + \binom{0}{p\mathbf{m}_1}$ generated in G_6' in the case of $\beta = 1$ is also computationally indistinguishable from the uniformly chosen $ct_1^* \leftarrow_\$ \mathbb{Z}_q^{N+\ell}$ in G_7' in the case of $\beta = 1$. Thus we have $\left| \Pr_6'[\mathsf{Win}] - \Pr_7'[\mathsf{Win}] \right| \leq \mathsf{Adv}_{[n,q,\chi,N+\ell],\mathcal{B}_2}^{\mathsf{LWE}}(\lambda)$.

Game G_8': It is the same as G_7', except for the following differences. Firstly, at the beginning of the game, the challenger also chooses a random user index $j' \leftarrow_\$ [\mathfrak{n}]$ uniformly as the guess of the challenge user j^*, and will abort the game and return a random bit in the following cases.

- **Case 1.** $\mathcal{A}$ issues the challenge tuple $(i^*, j^*, (f, \mathbf{m}), (\mathbf{m}_1, \mathbf{m}_2))$ but $j' \neq j^*$.
- **Case 2.** $\mathcal{A}$ issues a corruption query $\mathcal{O}_{\mathrm{COR}}(i)$ s.t. $i = j'$ before challenge.

Case 1 suggests that the challenger's guess is wrong. Case 2 will lead to abort anyway and does not contribute to $\mathcal{A}$'s advantage, just like G_7'.

Secondly, for the generation of $pk^{(j')} = (\mathbf{A}^{(j')}, \mathbf{A}'^{(j')})$, now the challenger generates $\mathbf{A}'^{(j')}$ by sampling $\mathbf{A}'^{(j')} \leftarrow_\$ \mathbb{Z}_q^{\ell\times n}$, instead of computing $\mathbf{A}'^{(j')} := \mathbf{K}^{(j')}\overline{\mathbf{A}'}$ with $\mathbf{K}^{(j')} \leftarrow_\$ \{0,1\}^{\ell\times N}$ as in G_7'. Note that for each row of $\mathbf{K}^{(j')} \leftarrow_\$ \{0,1\}^{\ell\times N}$ and for any q's prime factor p', we have that $\mathbf{H}_\infty(\text{each row of } \mathbf{K}^{(j')} \bmod p') = N$. Given $N \geq 2n\log q + 2\omega(\log \lambda)$, we know that $\mathbf{H}_\infty(\text{each row of } \mathbf{K}^{(j')} \bmod p') \geq 2n\log q + 2\omega(\log \lambda)$. Then according to the leftover hash lemma (as recalled in the full version [24]), $\mathbf{A}'^{(j')} := \mathbf{K}^{(j')}\overline{\mathbf{A}'}$ generated in G_7' is statistically close to the uniform distribution $\mathbf{A}'^{(j')} \leftarrow_\$ \mathbb{Z}_q^{\ell\times n}$ as in G_8'. Moreover, since j^* is not allowed to be corrupted by $\mathcal{A}$, it is needless to keep $\mathbf{K}^{(j')}$ as long as $j' = j^*$.

Since the challenger will guess j^* correctly with probability $1/\mathfrak{n}$, we have $\left| \Pr_7'[\mathsf{Win}] - \frac{1}{2} \right| = \frac{1}{\mathfrak{n}} \left| \Pr_8'[\mathsf{Win}] - \frac{1}{2} \right|$.

Game G_9': It is the same as G_8', except for the generation of ct_2^* in the case of $\beta = 1$. In this game, in the case of $\beta = 1$, the challenger also picks the second-level challenge ciphertext $ct_2^* \leftarrow_\$ \mathbb{Z}_q^{N+\ell}$ uniformly at random.

Now in G_9', both ct_1^* and ct_2^* are independently and uniformly chosen from $\mathbb{Z}_q^{N+\ell}$, regardless of the value of β. Thus, the challenge bit β is completely hidden to $\mathcal{A}$, and we have $\Pr_9'[\mathsf{Win}] = \frac{1}{2}$. Next we show that G_8' and G_9' are computationally indistinguishable.

Recall that in G_8', ct_2^* is generated by invoking $ct_2^* \leftarrow_\$ \mathsf{Enc}_1(pk^{(j^*)}, \mathbf{m}_2)$, i.e., $ct_2^* := \mathbf{A}'^{(j^*)} \mathbf{s} + \mathbf{e} + \binom{\mathbf{0}}{p\mathbf{m}_2}$ with $\mathbf{s} \leftarrow_\$ \chi^n$ and $\mathbf{e} \leftarrow_\$ \chi^{N+\ell}$. Due to the game change introduced in G_8', we have that $j' = j^*$ and $\mathbf{A}'^{(j^*)} = \left(\frac{\overline{\mathbf{A}'}}{\underline{\mathbf{A}'^{(j^*)}}} \right) = \left(\frac{\overline{\mathbf{A}'}}{\underline{\mathbf{A}'^{(j')}}} \right)$ is uniformly sampled from $\mathbb{Z}_q^{(N+\ell) \times n}$. Then according to the LWE assumption, $\mathbf{A}'^{(j^*)} \mathbf{s} + \mathbf{e}$ is computationally indistinguishable from the uniform distribution over $\mathbb{Z}_q^{N+\ell}$. Thus the challenge ciphertext $ct_2^* := \mathbf{A}'^{(j^*)} \mathbf{s} + \mathbf{e} + \binom{\mathbf{0}}{p\mathbf{m}_2}$ generated in G_8' in the case of $\beta = 1$ is also computationally indistinguishable from the uniformly chosen $ct_2^* \leftarrow_\$ \mathbb{Z}_q^{N+\ell}$ in G_9' in the case of $\beta = 1$. Thus we have $\left| \Pr_8'[\mathsf{Win}] - \Pr_9'[\mathsf{Win}] \right| \le \mathsf{Adv}_{[n,q,\chi,N+\ell],\mathcal{B}_3}^{\mathsf{LWE}}(\lambda)$.

Finally, taking all things together, Theorem 2 follows. $\qquad\square$

Theorem 3 (Collusion-Safety of $\mathsf{FPRE}_{\mathsf{LWE}}^{\mathsf{lin}}$). *Assume that the $\mathsf{LWE}_{n,q,\chi,N+\ell}$-assumption holds, then the scheme $\mathsf{FPRE}_{\mathsf{LWE}}^{\mathsf{lin}}$ proposed in Fig. 7 is collusion-safe (CS). More precisely, for any PPT adversary $\mathcal{A}$ and any polynomial $\mathfrak{n}$, there exists a PPT algorithm $\mathcal{B}$ against the LWE assumption such that* $\mathsf{Adv}_{\mathsf{FPRE},\mathcal{A},\mathfrak{n}}^{\mathsf{CS}}(\lambda) \le \mathfrak{n} \cdot \mathsf{Adv}_{[n,q,\chi,N+\ell],\mathcal{B}}^{\mathsf{LWE}}(\lambda) + \mathsf{negl}(\lambda)$.

Due to space limitations, we postpone the proof of Theorem 3 to the full version [24].

5   Fine-Grained PRE for Deletion Functions for LWE

In this section, we construct an FPRE scheme $\mathsf{FPRE}_{\mathsf{LWE}}^{\mathsf{del}}$ for deletion function family $\mathcal{F}_{\mathsf{del}}$ based on the scheme $\mathsf{FPRE}_{\mathsf{LWE}}^{\mathsf{lin}}$ proposed in Sect. 4 for the bounded linear function family $\mathcal{F}_{\mathsf{lin}}$.

Deletion Function Family. Let $\ell \in \mathbb{N}$ and $\mathcal{M} := \{0, 1, *\}^\ell$ be the message space, where "$*$" is a special symbol indicating that this bit is invalid or deleted. Given a subset $\mathcal{P} \subseteq [\ell]$, the *deletion function* $f_{\mathcal{P}} : \mathcal{M} \to \mathcal{M}$ indexed by $\mathcal{P}$ is

$$f_{\mathcal{P}}(m_1, \ldots, m_\ell) := (m_1', \ldots, m_\ell'), \text{ where } m_i' := \begin{cases} *, & \text{if } i \in \mathcal{P}; \\ m_i, & \text{if } i \notin \mathcal{P}. \end{cases}$$

That is, $f_{\mathcal{P}}$ will delete the message bits whose indices are contained in the set $\mathcal{P}$ by setting them as the invalid symbol $*$.

Then we define the family of deletion functions $\mathcal{F}_{\text{del}}$ from $\mathcal{M}$ to $\mathcal{M}$ as

$$\mathcal{F}_{\text{del}} = \left\{ f_{\mathcal{P}} : \{0,1,*\}^{\ell} \to \{0,1,*\}^{\ell} \mid \mathcal{P} \subseteq [\ell] \right\}.$$

Message Encoding and Expressing Deletion Functions in $\mathcal{F}_{\text{del}}$ as Bounded Linear Functions in $\mathcal{F}_{\text{lin}}$. In order to construct an FPRE scheme $\mathsf{FPRE}_{\mathsf{LWE}}^{\text{del}}$ with message space $\mathcal{M} = \{0,1,*\}^{\ell}$ for deletion function family $\mathcal{F}_{\text{del}}$ based on the scheme $\mathsf{FPRE}_{\mathsf{LWE}}^{\text{lin}}$ in Fig. 7 for the bounded linear function family $\mathcal{F}_{\text{lin}}$, we will show

- how to encode a message $\mathbf{m} \in \mathcal{M} = \{0,1,*\}^{\ell}$ to a message $\tilde{\mathbf{m}} \in \tilde{\mathcal{M}} = \{0,1\}^{2\ell} \subseteq \mathbb{Z}_p^{2\ell}$ with an encoding algorithm Encode (and also how to decode with an decoding algorithm Decode) so that the symbol "$*$" of erasure can be encoded by binary bits and later be correctly decoded, and
- how to express a deletion function $f_{\mathcal{P}} \in \mathcal{F}_{\text{del}}$ as a bounded linear function $f_{\mathbf{M}} \in \mathcal{F}_{\text{lin}}$ with a converting function $\Psi : \mathcal{F}_{\text{del}} \to \mathcal{F}_{\text{lin}}$.

The algorithms Encode and Decode and the converting function Ψ should be *compatible* in the sense that for any $\mathbf{m} \in \mathcal{M} = \{0,1,*\}^{\ell}$ and any $f_{\mathcal{P}} \in \mathcal{F}_{\text{del}}$, by setting $f_{\mathbf{M}} := \Psi(f_{\mathcal{P}})$, we have

$$f_{\mathcal{P}}(\mathbf{m}) = \mathsf{Decode}(f_{\mathbf{M}}(\mathsf{Encode}(\mathbf{m}))). \tag{7}$$

The encoding algorithm $\mathsf{Encode} : \{0,1,*\}^{\ell} \to \{0,1\}^{2\ell}$ and the corresponding decoding algorithm $\mathsf{Decode} : \{0,1\}^{2\ell} \to \{0,1,*\}^{\ell}$ are defined as follows.

- $\tilde{\mathbf{m}} \in \{0,1\}^{2\ell} \leftarrow \mathsf{Encode}(\mathbf{m} \in \{0,1,*\}^{\ell})$: Parse $\mathbf{m} = (m_1, \ldots, m_{\ell})$. For $i \in [\ell]$, set $\tilde{m}_{2i-1}\tilde{m}_{2i} = 00$ if $m_i = *$, set $\tilde{m}_{2i-1}\tilde{m}_{2i} = 01$ if $m_i = 0$, and set $\tilde{m}_{2i-1}\tilde{m}_{2i} = 10$ if $m_i = 1$. Return $\mathbf{m} := (\tilde{m}_1, \ldots, \tilde{m}_{2\ell})$.
- $\mathbf{m} \in \{0,1,*\}^{\ell} \leftarrow \mathsf{Decode}(\tilde{\mathbf{m}} \in \{0,1\}^{2\ell})$: Parse $\tilde{\mathbf{m}} = (\tilde{m}_1, \ldots, \tilde{m}_{2\ell})$. For $i \in [\ell]$, set $m_i := *$ if $\tilde{m}_{2i-1}\tilde{m}_{2i} = 00$, set $m_i := 0$ if $\tilde{m}_{2i-1}\tilde{m}_{2i} = 01$, and set $m_i := 1$ if $\tilde{m}_{2i-1}\tilde{m}_{2i} = 10$. Return $\mathbf{m} := (m_1, \ldots, m_{\ell})$.

The converting function $\Psi : \mathcal{F}_{\text{del}} \to \mathcal{F}_{\text{lin}}$ is defined as follows. On input a deletion function $f_{\mathcal{P}}$ with $\mathcal{P} \subseteq \{0,1\}^{\ell}$, $\Psi(f_{\mathcal{P}}) := f_{\mathbf{M}}$, where $\mathbf{M} = (M_{i,j}) \in \{0,1\}^{2\ell \times 2\ell}$

$$\text{with} \begin{cases} M_{2i-1,2i-1} = M_{2i,2i} = 0 & \text{if } i \in \mathcal{P}, i \in [\ell]; \\ M_{2i-1,2i-1} = M_{2i,2i} = 1 & \text{if } i \notin \mathcal{P}, i \in [\ell]; \\ M_{i,j} = 0 & \text{if } i \neq j, \ i,j \in [2\ell]. \end{cases}$$

It is routine to check that the $(\mathsf{Encode}, \mathsf{Decode}, \Psi)$ defined above are compatible, i.e., satisfying (7). More precisely, for any $\mathbf{m} = (m_1, \ldots, m_{\ell}) \in \{0,1,*\}^{\ell}$ and any $f_{\mathcal{P}} \in \mathcal{F}_{\text{del}}$, let $\tilde{\mathbf{m}} = (\tilde{m}_1, \ldots, \tilde{m}_{2\ell}) := \mathsf{Encode}(\mathbf{m})$ and $f_{\mathbf{M}} := \Phi(f_{\mathcal{P}})$, we have $f_{\mathbf{M}}(\mathsf{Encode}(\mathbf{m})) = \mathbf{M}\tilde{\mathbf{m}}$. Let $\tilde{\mathbf{m}}' = (\tilde{m}_1', \tilde{m}_2', \ldots, \tilde{m}_{2\ell}') := \mathbf{M}\tilde{\mathbf{m}}$. We will show that $\mathsf{Decode}(\tilde{\mathbf{m}}')$ successfully recovers $f_{\mathcal{P}}(\mathbf{m})$, i.e., $\mathsf{Decode}(\tilde{m}_{2i-1}'\tilde{m}_{2i}') = *$ for all $i \in \mathcal{P}$ and $\mathsf{Decode}(\tilde{m}_{2i-1}'\tilde{m}_{2i}') = m_i$ for all $i \in [\ell] \setminus \mathcal{P}$.

- If $i \in \mathcal{P}$, we have $\tilde{m}'_{2i-1}\tilde{m}'_{2i} = 00$, since $M_{2i-1,j} = M_{2i,j} = 0$ for all $j \in [2\ell]$. Then Decode will result in $m_i = *$, and thus the i-th bit of $\mathbf{m}$ is deleted.
- If $i \in [\ell] \setminus \mathcal{P}$, we have $\tilde{m}'_{2i-1}\tilde{m}'_{2i} = \tilde{m}_{2i-1}\tilde{m}_{2i}$, since $M_{2i-1,2i-1} = M_{2i,2i} = 1$, $M_{2i-1,j} = 0$ for all $j \in [2\ell] \setminus \{2i-1\}$ and $M_{2i,j} = 0$ for all $j \in [2\ell] \setminus \{2i\}$. Then Decode keeps m_i unchanged.

Therefore, we have $\mathsf{Decode}(\tilde{\mathbf{m}}') = f_{\mathcal{P}}(\mathbf{m})$ and (7) follows.

Constructing FPRE Scheme $\mathsf{FPRE}^{\mathsf{del}}_{\mathsf{LWE}}$ for $\mathcal{F}_{\mathsf{del}}$ from $\mathsf{FPRE}^{\mathsf{lin}}_{\mathsf{LWE}}$ for $\mathcal{F}_{\mathsf{lin}}$. Let $\mathsf{FPRE}^{\mathsf{lin}}_{\mathsf{LWE}} = (\mathsf{Setup}, \mathsf{KGen}, \mathsf{FReKGen}, \mathsf{Enc}_1, \mathsf{Enc}_2, \mathsf{FReEnc}, \mathsf{Dec}_1, \mathsf{Dec}_2)$ be the FPRE scheme for the bounded linear function family $\mathcal{F}_{\mathsf{lin}}$ as described in Fig. 7 in Sect. 4 with message space $\tilde{\mathbf{m}} \in \tilde{\mathcal{M}} = \{0,1\}^{2\ell}$, and let $(\mathsf{Encode}, \mathsf{Decode}, \Psi)$ be the encoding algorithm, decoding algorithms and the converting function defined above. We are ready to present the FPRE scheme $\mathsf{FPRE}^{\mathsf{del}}_{\mathsf{LWE}}$ for the deletion function family $\mathcal{F}_{\mathsf{del}} := \{f_{\mathcal{P}} : \{0,1,*\}^{\ell} \to \{0,1,*\}^{\ell} \mid \mathcal{P} \subseteq \{0,1\}^{\ell}\}$ with message space $\mathcal{M} = \{0,1\}^{\ell}$. The scheme $\mathsf{FPRE}^{\mathsf{del}}_{\mathsf{LWE}} = (\mathsf{Setup}', \mathsf{KGen}', \mathsf{FReKGen}', \mathsf{Enc}'_1, \mathsf{Enc}'_2, \mathsf{FReEnc}', \mathsf{Dec}'_1, \mathsf{Dec}'_2)$ is described as follows. For the ease of reading, we emphasize the parts related to $(\mathsf{Encode}, \mathsf{Decode}, \Psi)$ in gray boxes.

- $\mathsf{pp} \leftarrow_{\$} \mathsf{Setup}'$: It invokes $\mathsf{pp} \leftarrow_{\$} \mathsf{Setup}$ and returns pp.
- $(pk, sk) \leftarrow_{\$} \mathsf{KGen}'(\mathsf{pp})$: It invokes $(pk, sk) \leftarrow_{\$} \mathsf{KGen}(\mathsf{pp})$ and returns (pk, sk).
- $rk^{f_{\mathcal{P}}}_{i \to j} \leftarrow_{\$} \mathsf{FReKGen}'(pk^{(i)}, sk^{(i)}, pk^{(j)}, f_{\mathcal{P}})$: It first computes $f_{\mathbf{M}} := \Psi(f_{\mathcal{P}})$, invokes $rk^{f_{\mathbf{M}}}_{i \to j} \leftarrow_{\$} \mathsf{FReKGen}(pk^{(i)}, sk^{(i)}, pk^{(j)}, f_{\mathbf{M}})$, and returns $rk^{f_{\mathcal{P}}}_{i \to j} := rk^{f_{\mathbf{M}}}_{i \to j}$.
- $ct_1 \leftarrow_{\$} \mathsf{Enc}'_1(pk, \mathbf{m} \in \{0,1,*\}^{\ell})$: It first encodes $\tilde{\mathbf{m}} \leftarrow \mathsf{Encode}(\mathbf{m})$, then invokes $ct_1 \leftarrow_{\$} \mathsf{Enc}_1(pk, \tilde{\mathbf{m}})$, and returns ct_1.
- $ct_2 \leftarrow_{\$} \mathsf{Enc}'_2(pk, \mathbf{m} \in \{0,1,*\}^{\ell})$: It first encodes $\tilde{\mathbf{m}} \leftarrow \mathsf{Encode}(\mathbf{m})$, then invokes $ct_2 \leftarrow_{\$} \mathsf{Enc}_2(pk, \tilde{\mathbf{m}})$, and returns ct_2.
- $ct^{(j)}_2 \leftarrow_{\$} \mathsf{FReEnc}'(rk^{f_{\mathcal{P}}}_{i \to j}, ct^{(i)}_1)$: It invokes $ct^{(j)}_2 \leftarrow_{\$} \mathsf{FReEnc}(rk^{f_{\mathcal{P}}}_{i \to j}, ct^{(i)}_1)$ and returns $ct^{(j)}_2$.
- $\mathbf{m} \leftarrow \mathsf{Dec}'_1(sk, ct_1)$: It invokes $\tilde{\mathbf{m}} \leftarrow \mathsf{Dec}_1(sk, ct_1)$, then decodes $\mathbf{m} \leftarrow \mathsf{Decode}(\tilde{\mathbf{m}})$, and returns $\mathbf{m}$.
- $\mathbf{m} \leftarrow \mathsf{Dec}'_2(sk, ct_2)$: It invokes $\tilde{\mathbf{m}} \leftarrow \mathsf{Dec}_2(sk, ct_2)$, then decodes $\mathbf{m} \leftarrow \mathsf{Decode}(\tilde{\mathbf{m}})$, and returns $\mathbf{m}$.

We also present a full description of $\mathsf{FPRE}^{\mathsf{del}}_{\mathsf{LWE}}$ in the full version [24] for completeness.

Correctness and fine-grained one-hop correctness of $\mathsf{FPRE}^{\mathsf{del}}_{\mathsf{LWE}}$ follow from those of $\mathsf{FPRE}^{\mathsf{lin}}_{\mathsf{LWE}}$ and the compatibility of $(\mathsf{Encode}, \mathsf{Decode}, \Psi)$, i.e., (7).

Remark 4 (Further optimization of $\mathsf{FPRE}_{\mathsf{LWE}}^{\mathsf{del}}$ *).* Note that in our construction of $\mathsf{FPRE}_{\mathsf{LWE}}^{\mathsf{del}}$, we only require the underlying $\mathsf{FPRE}_{\mathsf{LWE}}^{\mathsf{lin}}$ to work with a message space of $\tilde{\mathcal{M}} = \{0, 1\}^{2\ell}$ (rather than $\mathbb{Z}_p^{2\ell}$). This enables us to optimize the $\mathsf{Enc}_1, \mathsf{Enc}_2$ and $\mathsf{Dec}_1, \mathsf{Dec}_2$ algorithms as follows. In $ct_1 := \mathbf{As} + \mathbf{e} + \binom{\mathbf{0}}{p\mathbf{m}}$ and $ct_2 := \mathbf{A}'\mathbf{s} + \mathbf{e} + \binom{\mathbf{0}}{p\mathbf{m}}$, the multiplication factor p can be replaced by $\lfloor q/2 \rfloor$, i.e., $ct_1 := \mathbf{As} + \mathbf{e} + \binom{\mathbf{0}}{\lfloor q/2 \rfloor \mathbf{m}}$ and $ct_2 := \mathbf{A}'\mathbf{s} + \mathbf{e} + \binom{\mathbf{0}}{\lfloor q/2 \rfloor \mathbf{m}}$. Correspondingly, the decryption algorithms output 0 or 1 depending on the intermediate result is close to 0 or $q/2$. In this way, the parameters q can be much smaller. For example, in the parameter setting in Table 2, q can be set as $q = 2\lambda^5$ instead of $q = \lambda^{10}$.

Acknowledgments. We would like to thank the reviewers for their valuable comments. Yunxiao Zhou, Shengli Liu and Shuai Han were partially supported by the National Key R&D Program of China under Grant 2022YFB2701500, National Natural Science Foundation of China (Grant Nos. 61925207, 62372292, 62002223), Guangdong Major Project of Basic and Applied Basic Research (2019B030302008), and Young Elite Scientists Sponsorship Program by China Association for Science and Technology (YESS20200185). Haibin Zhang was partially supported by the National Key R&D Program of China under Grant 2022YFB2701500, the National Natural Science Foundation of China under 62272043, Major Program of Shandong Provincial Natural Science Foundation for the Fundamental Research under ZR2022ZD03.

References

1. Ajtai, M.: Generating hard instances of lattice problems (extended abstract). In: 28th ACM STOC, pp. 99–108. ACM Press (1996)
2. Ateniese, G., Fu, K., Green, M., Hohenberger, S.: Improved proxy re-encryption schemes with applications to secure distributed storage. In: NDSS 2005. The Internet Society (2005)
3. Blaze, M., Bleumer, G., Strauss, M.: Divertible protocols and atomic proxy cryptography. In: Nyberg, K. (ed.) EUROCRYPT 1998. LNCS, vol. 1403, pp. 127–144. Springer, Heidelberg (1998). https://doi.org/10.1007/bfb0054122
4. Canard, S., Devigne, J., Laguillaumie, F.: Improving the security of an efficient unidirectional proxy re-encryption scheme. J. Internet Serv. Inf. Secur. **1**(2/3), 140–160 (2011). https://doi.org/10.22667/JISIS.2011.08.31.140
5. Canetti, R., Hohenberger, S.: Chosen-ciphertext secure proxy re-encryption. In: Ning, P., De Capitani di Vimercati, S., Syverson, P.F. (eds.) ACM CCS 2007, pp. 185–194. ACM Press (2007)
6. Chandran, N., Chase, M., Liu, F.H., Nishimaki, R., Xagawa, K.: Re-encryption, functional re-encryption, and multi-hop re-encryption: a framework for achieving obfuscation-based security and instantiations from lattices. In: Krawczyk, H. (ed.) PKC 2014. LNCS, vol. 8383, pp. 95–112. Springer, Heidelberg (2014). https://doi. org/10.1007/978-3-642-54631-0_6
7. Chandran, N., Chase, M., Vaikuntanathan, V.: Functional re-encryption and collusion-resistant obfuscation. In: Cramer, R. (ed.) TCC 2012. LNCS, vol. 7194, pp. 404–421. Springer, Heidelberg (2012). https://doi.org/10.1007/978-3-642-28914-9_23

8. Chow, S.S.M., Weng, J., Yang, Y., Deng, R.H.: Efficient unidirectional proxy re-encryption. In: Bernstein, D.J., Lange, T. (eds.) AFRICACRYPT 2010. LNCS, vol. 6055, pp. 316–332. Springer, Heidelberg (2010). https://doi.org/10.1007/978-3-642-12678-9_19

9. Cohen, A.: What about bob? The inadequacy of CPA security for proxy reencryption. In: Lin, D., Sako, K. (eds.) PKC 2019. LNCS, vol. 11443, pp. 287–316. Springer, Cham (2019). https://doi.org/10.1007/978-3-030-17259-6_10

10. Fan, X., Liu, F.-H.: Proxy re-encryption and re-signatures from lattices. In: Deng, R.H., Gauthier-Umaña, V., Ochoa, M., Yung, M. (eds.) ACNS 2019. LNCS, vol. 11464, pp. 363–382. Springer, Cham (2019). https://doi.org/10.1007/978-3-030-21568-2_18

11. Fuchsbauer, G., Kamath, C., Klein, K., Pietrzak, K.: Adaptively secure proxy re-encryption. In: Lin, D., Sako, K. (eds.) PKC 2019. LNCS, vol. 11443, pp. 317–346. Springer, Cham (2019). https://doi.org/10.1007/978-3-030-17259-6_11

12. Gentry, C., Peikert, C., Vaikuntanathan, V.: Trapdoors for hard lattices and new cryptographic constructions. In: Ladner, R.E., Dwork, C. (eds.) 40th ACM STOC, pp. 197–206. ACM Press (2008)

13. Kirshanova, E.: Proxy re-encryption from lattices. In: Krawczyk, H. (ed.) PKC 2014. LNCS, vol. 8383, pp. 77–94. Springer, Heidelberg (2014). https://doi.org/10.1007/978-3-642-54631-0_5

14. Liang, X., Weng, J., Yang, A., Yao, L., Jiang, Z., Wu, Z.: Attribute-based conditional proxy re-encryption in the standard model under LWE. In: Bertino, E., Shulman, H., Waidner, M. (eds.) ESORICS 2021. LNCS, vol. 12973, pp. 147–168. Springer, Cham (2021). https://doi.org/10.1007/978-3-030-88428-4_8

15. Libert, B., Vergnaud, D.: Unidirectional chosen-ciphertext secure proxy re-encryption. In: Cramer, R. (ed.) PKC 2008. LNCS, vol. 4939, pp. 360–379. Springer, Heidelberg (2008). https://doi.org/10.1007/978-3-540-78440-1_21

16. Miao, P., Patranabis, S., Watson, G.J.: Unidirectional updatable encryption and proxy re-encryption from DDH. In: Boldyreva, A., Kolesnikov, V. (eds.) PKC 2023, Part II. LNCS, vol. 13941, pp. 368–398. Springer, Cham (2023). https://doi.org/10.1007/978-3-031-31371-4_13

17. Micciancio, D., Peikert, C.: Trapdoors for lattices: simpler, tighter, faster, smaller. In: Pointcheval, D., Johansson, T. (eds.) EUROCRYPT 2012. LNCS, vol. 7237, pp. 700–718. Springer, Heidelberg (2012). https://doi.org/10.1007/978-3-642-29011-4_41

18. Regev, O.: On lattices, learning with errors, random linear codes, and cryptography. In: Gabow, H.N., Fagin, R. (eds.) 37th ACM STOC, pp. 84–93. ACM Press (2005)

19. Sharmila Deva Selvi, S., Paul, A., Pandurangan, C.: A provably-secure unidirectional proxy re-encryption scheme without pairing in the random oracle model. In: Capkun, S., Chow, S.S.M. (eds.) CANS 2017. LNCS, vol. 11261, pp. 459–469. Springer, Cham (2018). https://doi.org/10.1007/978-3-030-02641-7_21

20. Shao, J.: Anonymous ID-based proxy re-encryption. In: Susilo, W., Mu, Y., Seberry, J. (eds.) ACISP 2012. LNCS, vol. 7372, pp. 364–375. Springer, Heidelberg (2012). https://doi.org/10.1007/978-3-642-31448-3_27

21. Shao, J., Cao, Z.: CCA-secure proxy re-encryption without pairings. In: Jarecki, S., Tsudik, G. (eds.) PKC 2009. LNCS, vol. 5443, pp. 357–376. Springer, Heidelberg (2009). https://doi.org/10.1007/978-3-642-00468-1_20

22. Susilo, W., Dutta, P., Duong, D.H., Roy, P.S.: Lattice-based HRA-secure attribute-based proxy re-encryption in standard model. In: Bertino, E., Shulman, H., Waidner, M. (eds.) ESORICS 2021. LNCS, vol. 12973, pp. 169–191. Springer, Cham (2021). https://doi.org/10.1007/978-3-030-88428-4_9
23. Weng, J., Deng, R.H., Ding, X., Chu, C.K., Lai, J.: Conditional proxy re-encryption secure against chosen-ciphertext attack. In: Li, W., Susilo, W., Tupakula, U.K., Safavi-Naini, R., Varadharajan, V. (eds.) ASIACCS 2009, pp. 322–332. ACM Press (2009)
24. Zhou, Y., Liu, S., Han, S., Zhang, H.: Fine-grained proxy re-encryption: Definitions & constructions from LWE. Cryptology ePrint Archive, 2023/1324 (2023). https://eprint.iacr.org/2023/1324

Injection-Secure Structured and Searchable Symmetric Encryption

Ghous Amjad[1]([✉]), Seny Kamara[2,3], and Tarik Moataz[2]

[1] Google, Menlo Park, USA
gamjad@google.com
[2] MongoDB, New York, USA
{seny.kamara,tarik.moataz}@mongodb.com
[3] Brown University, Providence, USA

Abstract. Recent work on dynamic structured and searchable symmetric encryption has focused on achieving the notion of forward-privacy. This is mainly motivated by the claim that forward privacy protects against adaptive file injection attacks (Zhang, Katz, Papamanthou, *Usenix Security, 2016*). In this work, we revisit the notion of forward-privacy in several respects. First, we observe that forward-privacy does not necessarily guarantee security against adaptive file injection attacks if a scheme reveals other leakage patterns like the query equality. We then propose a notion of security called *correlation security* which generalizes forward privacy. We then show how correlation security can be used to formally define security against different kinds of injection attacks. We then propose the first injection-secure multi-map encryption scheme and use it as a building block to design the first injection-secure searchable symmetric encryption (SSE) scheme. Towards achieving this, we also propose a new fully-dynamic volume-hiding multi-map encryption scheme which may be of independent interest.

1 Introduction

Structured encryption (STE) schemes encrypt data structures in such a way that they can be privately queried. Roughly speaking, STE schemes are secure if they leak nothing about the structure and queries beyond a well-specified and "reasonable" leakage function. Encrypted data structures are one of the main building blocks in the design of *sub-linear* algorithms on encrypted data,[1] for example, sub-linear encrypted search, graph and database algorithms [16, 17,36]. Many aspects of STE have been studied and improved over the years including its expressiveness [13,25,32,34,42], its locality [4,5,15,19,22] and its leakage profiles [35,36,43]. A special case of STE is multi-map encryption which

---

[1] Another approach relies on property-preserving encryption (PPE) which also achieves sub-linear efficiency but with qualitatively different leakage profiles.

G. Amjad—Work done while at Brown University.

S. Kamara and T. Moataz—Work done while at Brown University and Aroki Systems.

J. Guo and R. Steinfeld (Eds.): ASIACRYPT 2023, LNCS 14443, pp. 232–262, 2023.
https://doi.org/10.1007/978-981-99-8736-8_8

is a fundamental building block in the design of almost all sub-linear encrypted algorithms. Roughly speaking, encrypted multi-maps store label/tuple pairs and support get operations which, given a label, return the associated tuple.

Dynamism. An STE scheme is *static* if it supports queries over an encrypted data structure that never changes and it is *dynamic* if it supports queries over an encrypted structure that can be modified using, e.g., add, delete, or edit operations. Sub-linear dynamic EMMs were first achieved in [38] but in such a way that update operations could be correlated with search operations. In other words, while the adversary could not tell which label was being updated or queried, it could tell that a particular update was for a label that was queried in the past. This motivated Stefanov, Papamanthou and Shi to propose the notion of *forward-privacy* which, intuitively, guarantees that update operations cannot be linked to previous search operations [47]. Stefanov et al. also described the first forward-private EMM; achieving sub-linear query complexity with sub-linear client storage. A few years later, Bost proposed a formal definition of forward-privacy and the first forward-private EMM with optimal query complexity and client storage linear in the number of labels [8]. In [34], however, Kamara and Moataz pointed out that Bost's definition does not necessarily capture the notion of forward-privacy and suggested a different formalization.

Searchable Symmetric Encryption from EMMs. As mentioned above, EMMs are main building block needed to achieve sub-linear and optimal searchable symmetric encryption (SSE) [17].[2] Given a document collection, the client builds a multi-map that indexes the document collection, i.e., its labels are keywords and the tuples are the identifiers of the documents that contain that keyword. It then encrypts the multi-map and the documents with a multi-map encryption scheme and a standard symmetric encryption scheme, respectively, and sends the EMM and encrypted documents to the server. To search for a keyword w, the client privately queries the EMM on w which reveals to the server the identifiers of the (encrypted) documents that need to be returned. EMMs that reveal the response to a query are called *response-revealing* and ones that do not are called response-hiding.[3]

Injection Attacks. Injection attacks were introduced by Zhang, Katz and Papamanthou [50] and one of the main motivations to achieve forward-privacy (besides simply minimizing leakage) is that it prevents *adaptive* injection attacks. In a standard/non-adaptive injection attack the adversary inserts files into the client's document collection and combines the EMM' s leakage with knowledge of its chosen files to recover the client's queries. More precisely, in the first phase of the attack, the server finds a way to insert documents with carefully-chosen

---

[2] Note that there exist several ways to build an SSE scheme from an EMM and each approach leads to a different efficiency vs. security tradeoff. For simplicity, we only describe the most natural approach to do so.

[3] Response-hiding EMMs can also be used but at the cost of an extra communication round.

subsets of the keyword space.[4] This results in the new documents being indexed and encrypted, and the EMM being updated to account for the new keywords. Later, when the client searches for a keyword w the server will learn the identifiers of the documents that contain w. If some of those documents are injected documents then it has learned some information about the client's query.

In an adaptive injection attack, the server injects files *after* the client makes its queries and uses the leakage of the EMM's update operation to correlate the update (and its contents) to previous queries. Forward privacy prevents such attacks because it guarantees that the updates caused by the adversary's adaptive file injections cannot be linked to previous queries.

The cost of injection attacks is measured in the number of documents that need to be injected and their size. Zhang et al. describe a non-adaptive attack that can recover all of a client's queries at the cost of injecting $\log \#\mathbb{W}$ files each of size $\#\mathbb{W}/2$, where $\mathbb{W}$ is the keyword space. Note that this attack—and others given in [50]—crucially rely on response identity leakage which can be hidden using, e.g., response-hiding EMMs or ORAM-based solutions. However, Blackstone, Kamara and Moataz [7] described file injection attacks that rely only on volume leakage which makes them applicable to almost all constructions including ORAM-based solutions.

Limitations of Forward-Privacy. While forward privacy is an important notion it has limitations. For conceptual clarity, we propose an alternative view on forward privacy and the security guarantees it provides against injection attacks. Instead of considering adaptive vs. non-adaptive injection attacks we will say that an injection attack is one where the adversary injects a file (and therefore causes an update) at any time during a sequence of client operations. We then ask whether the scheme reveals *correlations* between the update and the queries, where a correlation is leakage that reveals whether two operations are for the same label. Injection attacks essentially cause an update with an adversarially-known label and then use correlations between that update and adversarially-unknown queries to learn the unknown query labels.

The first limitation of forward privacy is that it only prevents correlations between updates and pre-injection queries. This was already pointed out in [50] as the authors explained that forward privacy only prevents adaptive injection attacks. To see why, consider the following sequence of operations on an EMM:

$$\mathbf{op} = (\mathsf{op}_1, \mathsf{op}_2, \mathsf{op}_3, \mathsf{op}_4) = \big((\mathsf{qry}, \ell_5), (\mathsf{qry}, \ell_2), (\mathsf{app}, \ell_5, \mathbf{v}), (\mathsf{qry}, \ell_5)\big),$$

where $\mathsf{op}_i = (\mathsf{qry}, \ell_i)$ is a query operation on label ℓ_i and $\mathsf{op}_3 = (\mathsf{app}, \ell_5, \mathbf{v})$ is an adversarially-chosen append operation on ℓ_5 (i.e., append the tuple $\mathbf{v}$ to ℓ_5's pre-existing tuple) that results from a file injection. If the EMM is not forward-private, then its leakage on the append reveals that op_3 and op_1 are for the same label. If, on the other hand, the EMM is forward-private this correlation is not revealed when the op_3 occurs. Note, however, that the correlation between op_3 and op_4 could be revealed when op_4 occurs. Forward-privacy does not explicitly

---

[4] This can be achieved in various ways depending on the application scenario.

prevent this and, indeed, most forward-private constructions [1,8,10,24,47] leak this information and provide no guarantees for post-injection queries.

The second limitation is that forward privacy only provides a relatively weak form of security in the sense that it only prevents *direct* correlations between updates and pre-injection queries but not *indirect* correlations which could occur if additional patterns are leaked. This means that forward privacy doesn't *necessarily* protect pre-injection queries. To see why, consider a setting where the sequence of operations above is executed with a scheme that is forward private but leaks the query equality. In this case, forward privacy guarantees that op_3 cannot be directly correlated with op_1. But an adversary can still learn op_1's label by observing that op_4 is correlated with op_3 (which is not prevented by forward privacy) and then using the query equality to learn that op_4 is correlated with op_1. The combination of these two correlations mean that op_1's label is ℓ_5.

1.1 Our Contributions

In this work, we focus on the security of dynamic structured encryption schemes. We make several contributions including new security definitions and constructions.

Correlation Attacks. As illustrated by the discussion above, forward-privacy has several limitations including that it provides no guarantees for post-injection queries and that it does not necessarily protect pre-injection queries against injection attacks because it does not prevent indirect correlations. We also observe that the attacks considered in [50] capture only a fraction of how injections can be used to attack STE schemes. This motivates us to consider a broader class of attacks we call *correlation attacks* that work as follows. First, the adversary learns the labels/keywords associated to a subset of *operations*. Note that as opposed to injection attacks where the adversary chooses the label/keyword for an update operation, in a correlation attack the adversary could learn the label/keyword of any operation, e.g., queries, inserts, deletes etc. Furthermore, this can be achieved using injections but not necessarily; it could also be achieved using inference attacks or a known-data attack [7,11,31].[5] In the second phase, the adversary uses the leakage to correlate known operations to to unknown operations. Note that here we are concerned with correlations to *any* operation not just queries. In other words, the adversary's goal is not necessarily to learn the labels/keywords of unknown queries but could be to learn the labels/keywords of unknown updates, deletes etc.

Equality Patterns and Correlation Graphs. Correlation attacks exploit leakage patterns that reveal correlations between operations; the most immediate examples of such patterns are *equality patterns* like the *query equality* which reveals if and when queries are for the same label/keyword, the *operation equality* which reveals if and when operations are for the same label/keyword or the

---

[5] When a correlation attack is used after an inference or known-data attack it is effectively "boosting" that attack.

backward query equality which reveals only if and when past queries are for the same label/keyword. Equality patterns can be defined in various ways but in this work we introduce a simple and useful representation we call *correlation graphs*. The correlation graph of a given equality pattern on a sequence of operations is a graph with operations as vertices and edges between equal operations. Correlation graphs can be composed to describe the correlations that result from leaking multiple equality patterns. Specifically, given two (or more) equality patterns patt_1 and patt_2 with correlation graphs $\mathcal{G}_1$ and $\mathcal{G}_2$, their union $\mathcal{G}_1 \cup \mathcal{G}_2$ captures all the correlations revealed by the two patterns.

Correlation and Injection Security. We introduce and formalize the notion of *correlation security* which, intuitively, guarantees that a leakage profile does not reveal certain correlations between operations. In the context of correlation graphs we ask that no path exist between certain types of operations. We formalize this intuition using a game-based definition that guarantees that operations are indistinguishable given the correlation graph of the leakage on an adversarially-chosen sequence of operations. By constraining exactly how the adversary can choose the sequence, we can capture security against various kinds of correlation attacks. In particular, we show how to define security against injection attacks by which we mean protection of both pre- and post-injection queries. We also prove that if a scheme leaks *only* the query equality then it is injection-secure. While this might seem counter-intuitive given the example above, note that in the example pre-injection queries were correlated with updates by exploiting both the query equality between op_4 and op_1 and the correlation between op_4 and op_3 together.

An Injection-Secure EMM. We describe a dynamic multi-map encryption scheme called FIX that only leaks the query equality. What this means intuitively is that, given a sequence of queries and updates, the only thing leaked is the correlation between queries. Note that achieving this leakage profile is quite surprising considering the scheme is dynamic. In fact, most dynamic constructions—even forward-private ones—leak more; including correlations between queries and past updates.

At a very high level, the scheme works by handling update operations (appends and deletes) on a fixed but random schedule. This is accomplished by storing update operations in a stash at the client and "pushing" them to the remotely-stored EMM only according to the schedule. If a query occurs for a label whose updates have not been pushed yet, the information in the stash is combined with the "stale" results from the remote EMM to provide a correct answer. Because the schedule is fixed and independent of the update operations, the leakage is as well. We stress that this is a very high level description of our approach and that it does not capture many of the subtleties and challenges involved.

FIX is the first injection-secure multi-map; i.e., the first to protect both pre- and post-injection queries which solves an important problem left open since [50]. It has query complexity $O(\log \#\mathbb{L})$ and append and delete complexity

$O(\log^2 \#\mathbb{L})$, where $\#\mathbb{L}$ is the size of the label space, under some assumptions and parameterization which we detail in Sect. 4.

A Dynamic Volume-Hiding EMM. Our construction makes black-box use of a static volume-hiding multi-map encryption scheme and of a dynamic volume-hiding multi-map encryption scheme. The former can be instantiated using many well-known constructions [35, 44]. To instantiate the latter, we design a new fully-dynamic volume-hiding multi-map encryption scheme we call DVLH (Sect. 5.1). DVLH is a dynamic variant of the static volume-hiding encrypted multi-map of Kamara and Moataz [35]. Similarly to their scheme, DVLH is lossy but we show that under natural assumptions (i.e., updates are Zipf-distributed) the lossiness can be bounded to be a reasonable amount with high probability (Sect. 5.2).[6]

Injection-Secure SSE. An important application of EMMs is to the design of optimal SSE schemes. An SSE scheme encrypts a document collection in such a way that it can support keyword search; that is, given a keyword w, return the encrypted documents that include w. We show how to use FIX to design the first injection-secure SSE scheme. Under the same assumptions and parameterization of FIX mentioned above, the SSE scheme has $O(\log \#\mathbb{L})$ query complexity and $O(\theta \cdot \log^2 \#\mathbb{L})$ add and delete complexity, where θ is a public parameter.

Efficiency. Note that we do not claim that FIX is a practical construction ready for deployment. Rather, it demonstrates how to achieve the non-trivial security notion of injection security. Its cost is mainly due to its use of a dynamic volume hiding scheme as a building block which introduces high communication complexity. However, as highlighted above, there are cases where FIX can perform well at a loss in correctness. Specifically, if the multi-map has a power-law shape then the query, communication, erase and add complexities can be sublinear in the size of the multi-map.

1.2 Related Work

Structured encryption was introduced by Chase and Kamara [16] as a generalization of index-based searchable symmetric encryption (SSE) [17, 46]. The most common and important type of STE schemes are multi-map encryption schemes which are a basic building block in the design of optimal SSE schemes [12, 17, 38], expressive SSE schemes [13, 25, 33, 34, 42] and encrypted databases [14, 32]. STE and encrypted multi-maps have been studied along several dimensions including dynamism [12, 30, 37, 38, 42] and I/O efficiency [4, 5, 12, 15, 20, 22, 41].

Forward and Backward Privacy. The notion of forward privacy was introduced by Stefanov, Papamanthou and Shi [47] and formally defined by Bost [8], who also proposed the first forward-private construction that does not leverage oblivious RAM techniques. Kamara and Moataz pointed out in [34] that the definition of [8] does not necessarily capture the intuitive security guarantee of

---

[6] Recent work by Amjad et al. [3] can also be used to instantiate the underlying dynamic volume-hiding EMM.

forward-privacy and suggested that it be formalized as requiring that updates be leakage-free. Backward privacy was introduced by Bost, Minaud and Ohrimenko [10]. Several follow up works showed how to improve on the constructions of [10], sometimes achieving both forward and backward privacy [1,18,24,27,40,45].

SWiSSSE [29]. Gui, Paterson, Patranabis and Warinschi describe a dynamic SSE scheme called SWiSSSE [29] that prevents file-injection attacks. The main techniques used in the construction are *bucketization* and *randomized write-backs*. The former is used to partially hide the volume pattern whereas the latter is used to disturb the query equality pattern. Both techniques have been used in the past. In particular, bucketization was leveraged by Bost and Fouque [9] as well as by Demertzis, Papadopoulos, Papamanthou and Shintre [21] to partially hide the volume pattern and to disturb the co-occurrence pattern, respectively. Randomized write-backs, on the other hand, can be viewed as a leaky amortized rebuild process, where the encrypted structure is periodically shuffled in order to hide the query equality. Leakage-free (amortized) rebuilds were introduced in the context of ORAM [28] but have also been used to suppress leakage in STE [26,36]. The authors show that their SWiSSSE construction provides some security against a specific injection attack. In this work, we approach the problem differently and provide a formal security definition of injection security and show that our FIX encrypted multi-map and our FIX-based SSE scheme achieves it. FIX's delayed updates share some similarities with the randomized write-backs in [29], but are technically different and lead to different leakage profiles. In particular, FIX's update operation is leakage-free whereas SWiSSSE's is not.

2   Preliminaries

Notation. The set of all binary strings of length n is denoted as $\{0,1\}^n$, and the set of all finite binary strings as $\{0,1\}^*$. $[n]$ is the set of integers $\{1,\ldots,n\}$, and $2^{[n]}$ is the corresponding power set. We write $x \leftarrow \chi$ to represent an element x being sampled from a distribution χ, and $x \xleftarrow{\$} X$ to represent an element x being sampled uniformly at random from a set X. The output x of an algorithm $\mathcal{A}$ is denoted by $x \leftarrow \mathcal{A}$. Given a sequence O of n elements, we refer to its ith element as O_i or $\mathsf{O}[i]$. If T is a set then $\#T$ refers to its cardinality. Given strings x and y, we refer to their concatenation as either $\langle x, y \rangle$ or $x\|y$.

Multi-maps. A static multi-map MM with capacity n is a collection of n label/tuple pairs $\{(\ell_i, \mathbf{v}_i)_i\}_{i \leq n}$ that supports Get operations. We denote the label space of a multi-map by $\mathbb{L}$ and the set of labels stored in a multi-map MM by $\mathbb{L}_{\mathsf{MM}}$. We write $\mathbf{v}_i = \mathsf{MM}[\ell_i]$ to denote getting the tuple associated with label ℓ_i. A multi-map is semi-dynamic if it also supports an insertion operation and it is fully-dynamic if it supports both insertions and deletions. Note that one can define various kinds of insertions and deletions. In this work we focus on additions, appends, erasures and deletions. An addition operation adds a label/tuple pair $(\ell, \mathbf{v})$ to the multi-map and is denoted as $\mathsf{MM}[\ell] := \mathbf{v}$. An append operation appends a tuple to the pre-existing tuple of a label. For example, if the label/tuple pair $(\ell, \mathbf{v})$ is already in the multi-map, then appending $\mathbf{v}'$ to ℓ results in ℓ being associated with the tuple $\mathbf{v}\|\mathbf{v}'$. We sometimes write this as $\mathsf{MM}[\ell]\|\mathbf{v}'$. An erase operation removes a set of values $\mathbf{v}'$ from the tuple $\mathbf{v}$ of a given label ℓ. We sometimes write this $\mathsf{MM}[\ell] - \mathbf{v}'$. A delete operation removes the entire label/tuple pair of a given label.

Document Collections. A document collection is a set of documents $\mathbb{D} = (\mathsf{D}_1, \ldots, \mathsf{D}_n)$, each document consisting of a set of keywords from some universe $\mathbb{W}$. We assume the universe of keywords is totally ordered (e.g., using lexicographic order) and denote by $\mathbb{W}[i]$ the ith keyword in $\mathbb{W}$. We assume every document has an identifier that is independent of its contents and denote it $\mathsf{id}(\mathsf{D}_i)$. We assume the existence of an efficient indexing algorithm that takes as input a data collection $\mathbb{D}$ and outputs a multi-map that maps every keyword w in $\mathbb{W}$ to the identifiers of the documents that contain w. In previous work, this multi-map is referred to as an inverted index or as a database. For consistency, we refer to any multi-map derived in this way from a document collection as a database and denote it DB. Given a keyword w, we denote by $\mathbb{D}(w) \subseteq \mathbb{D}$, the set of all documents that contains w. We refer to the word-length of a document $|\mathsf{D}|$ as its volume. We denote by $\mathsf{co}_{\mathsf{DB}}(w) \subseteq \mathbb{W}$ the set of keywords in $\mathbb{W}$ that co-occur with w; that is, the keywords that are contained in documents that contain w. When DB is clear from the context we omit DB and write only $\mathsf{co}(w)$.

Basic Cryptographic Primitives. A private-key encryption scheme is a set of three polynomial-time algorithms $\mathsf{SKE} = (\mathsf{Gen}, \mathsf{Enc}, \mathsf{Dec})$ such that Gen is a probabilistic algorithm that takes a security parameter k and returns a secret key K; Enc is a probabilistic algorithm takes a key K and a message m and returns a ciphertext c; Dec is a deterministic algorithm that takes a key K and a ciphertext c and returns m if K was the key under which c was produced. Informally, a private-key encryption scheme is secure against chosen-plaintext attacks (CPA) if the ciphertexts it outputs do not reveal any partial information about the plaintext even to an adversary that can adaptively query an encryption oracle. We say a scheme is random-ciphertext-secure against chosen-plaintext attacks (RCPA) if the ciphertexts it outputs are computationally indistinguishable from random even to an adversary that can adaptively query an encryption oracle.[7] In addition to encryption schemes, we also make use of pseudo-random functions (PRF) and permutations (PRP), which are polynomial-time computable functions that cannot be distinguished from random functions by any probabilistic polynomial-time adversary. We refer the reader to [39] for notation and security definitions for these objects.

2.1 Structured Encryption

Structured encryption (STE) schemes encrypt data structures in such a way that they can be privately queried. The first definitions of structured encryption were

---

[7] RCPA-secure encryption can be instantiated practically using either the standard PRF-based private-key encryption scheme or, e.g., AES in counter mode.

presented by Chase and Kamara [16]. STE schemes can be interactive or non-interactive. Interactive schemes produce encrypted structures that are queried or updated through an interactive two-party protocol between a client and a server, whereas non-interactive schemes produce structures that can be queried or updated by sending a single token. These schemes can also be response-hiding or response-revealing where the former reveal the response to queries to the server whereas the latter do not. We recall here the syntax of an interactive response-hiding dynamic structured encryption scheme.

Definition 1 (Interactive response-hiding dynamic structured encryption). *An interactive response-hiding dynamic structured encryption scheme* Σ_{DS} = (Setup, Query, Insert, Delete, Res) *for data type* DS *consists of the following polynomial time algorithms:*

1. $(K, st) \leftarrow$ Setup$_C(1^k, DS)$ *is an algorithm that takes as input the security parameter k and a data structure* DS *and outputs a secret key K and an (optional) state st.*

2. $((r, st'), EDS') \leftarrow$ Query$_{C,S}((K, q, st), EDS)$ *is an interactive protocol executed between a client* **C** *and server* **S**. **C** *inputs the secret key K, a query q and state st.* **S** *inputs the encrypted data structure* EDS. *The protocol outputs a response r and an updated state st' to the client and an updated encrypted structure* EDS' *to the server.*

3. $(st', EDS') \leftarrow$ Insert$_{C,S}((K, st, a), EDS)$ *is an interactive protocol executed between a client* **C** *and server* **S**. *The client inputs a secret key K, a state st and an add operation a. The server inputs an encrypted structure* EDS. *The protocol outputs an updated state st' to the client and an updated encrypted structure* EDS' *to the server.*

4. $(st', EDS') \leftarrow$ Delete$_{C,S}((K, st, d), EDS)$ *is an interactive protocol executed between a client* **C** *and server* **S**. *The client inputs a secret key K, a state st and a delete operation d. The server inputs an encrypted structure* EDS. *The protocol outputs an updated state st' to the client and an updated encrypted structure* EDS' *to the server.*

5. $r \leftarrow$ Res$_C(K, ct)$ *is a deterministic algorithm that takes as input a secret key K and an encrypted query result ct. It outputs a response r.*

The syntax of a response-revealing scheme can be recovered by having Query output the response directly and omitting the Res algorithm.

Adaptive Security. The standard notion of security for STE guarantees that: (1) an encrypted structure reveals no information about its underlying structure beyond the setup leakage $\mathcal{L}_S$; and (2) the various operations that are supported (e.g., query, add, delete) reveal no information about the structure and the operations beyond some stateful operation leakage $\mathcal{L}_O$. If this holds for non-adaptively chosen operations then the scheme is said to be non-adaptively secure. If, on the other hand, the operations can be chosen adaptively, the scheme is said to be adaptively-secure [16,17]. Note that the operation leakage is usually broken down into separate leakage functions—one for each supported operation—but here we consider a single leakage function $\mathcal{L}_O$ for all operations. The advantage of this formulation is that it allows us to more easily capture leakage that is a function of different operations.

Definition 2 (Adaptive Security of dynamic interactive STE). *Let* Σ = (Setup, Query, Insert, Delete, Res) *be an interactive dynamic STE scheme and consider the following probabilistic experiments where* $\mathcal{A}$ *is a stateful adversary,* $\mathcal{S}$ *is a stateful simulator,* $\Lambda = (\mathcal{L}_S, \mathcal{L}_O)$ *is a leakage profile and* $z \in \{0,1\}^*$:

Real$_{\Sigma,\mathcal{A}}(k)$: *given* z, $\mathcal{A}$ *chooses a data structure* DS *and receives an encrypted structure* EDS *from the challenger, where* $(K, st; \mathsf{EDS}) \leftarrow \mathsf{Setup}(1^k, \mathsf{DS})$. $\mathcal{A}$ *then adaptively chooses a polynomial number of operations* $\mathsf{op}_1, \ldots, \mathsf{op}_m$ *and, for each one, the adversary and challenger execute the appropriate protocol with* $\mathcal{A}$ *playing the role of the server and the challenger playing the role of the client. Finally, the adversary outputs a bit* $b \in \{0,1\}$.

Ideal$_{\Sigma,\mathcal{A},\mathcal{S}}(k)$: *given* z, $\mathcal{A}$ *chooses a data structure* DS. *Given* z *and* $\mathcal{L}_S(\mathsf{DS})$ *the simulator* $\mathcal{S}$ *sends an encrypted data structure* EDS *to* $\mathcal{A}$. *The adversary adaptively picks a polynomial number of operations* $\mathsf{op}_1, \ldots, \mathsf{op}_m$ *and, for each one,* $\mathcal{A}$ *and* $\mathcal{S}$ *execute the appropriate protocol with* $\mathcal{A}$ *playing the role of the server and* $\mathcal{S}$ *playing the role of the client. During these executions, the simulator* $\mathcal{S}$ *only receives* $\mathcal{L}_O(\mathsf{DS}, \mathsf{op}_i)$. *Finally, the adversary outputs a bit* $b \in \{0,1\}$.

We say that Σ *is adaptively* $(\mathcal{L}_S, \mathcal{L}_O)$-*secure if there exists a PPT simulator* $\mathcal{S}$ *such that for all PPT adversaries* $\mathcal{A}$, *for all* $z \in \{0,1\}^*$:

$$| \Pr[\mathbf{Real}_{\Sigma,\mathcal{A}}(k) = 1] - \Pr[\mathbf{Ideal}_{\Sigma,\mathcal{A},\mathcal{S}}(k) = 1]| \leq \mathsf{negl}(k).$$

Modeling Leakage. The leakage of an STE scheme Σ is characterized by a leakage profile $\Lambda_\Sigma = (\mathcal{L}_S, \mathcal{L}_O)$ composed of a setup leakage $\mathcal{L}_S$ and an operation leakage $\mathcal{L}_O$. Each of these leakage functions can themselves be functions of various leakage patterns. In this work, all leakage functions and leakage patterns are *stateful*. We recall some leakage patterns that will appear throughout this work:

- the *query equality* qeq takes as input a data structure and a query and reveals if and when the query was repeated
- the *operation equality* oeq takes as input a data structure and an operation and reveals if and when the query associated with the operation appeared in the past.
- the *response length* rlen takes as input a data structure and an query and reveals the length of the query's response.

3   Defining Correlation Security

In this work we focus on security against correlation attacks which are a generalization of injection attacks. We describe our framework in the context of EMMs for concreteness but note that it can be applied to any encrypted data structure. A correlation attack is a query-recovery attack that works in two phases. First, the adversary learns the labels of a subset of operations, e.g., by injecting files or executing an inference attack. Then, it uses leakage to link unknown operations to known operations. We describe a framework that formally captures correlations revealed by various leakage patterns and allows us to formalize security against correlation attacks.

Equality Patterns and Correlation Graphs. An equality pattern reveals if and when two values are the same. Examples include the query equality pattern which reveals if and when two queries are the same and the operation equality pattern which reveals if and when two operations are for the same label. Equality patterns can be defined in different ways (e.g., as binary vectors or binary matrices) but, effectively, they can all be represented as graphs with operations as vertices and edges between two operations if they are for the same label. We call such graphs *correlation graphs*. For example, the query equality and the operation equality of the sequence

$$\mathbf{op} = (\mathsf{op}_1, \mathsf{op}_2, \mathsf{op}_3, \mathsf{op}_4) = \big((\mathsf{qry}, \ell_5), (\mathsf{qry}, \ell_2), (\mathsf{app}, \ell_5, \mathbf{v}), (\mathsf{qry}, \ell_5)\big)$$

can be represented with the graphs $\mathcal{G}_{\mathsf{qeq}}$ and $\mathcal{G}_{\mathsf{oeq}}$ illustrated below:

Leakage patterns reveal information incrementally, per operation, so it will be useful for us to have notation to describe this. Given a leakage profile $\Lambda = (\mathcal{L}_{\mathsf{S}}, \mathcal{L}_{\mathsf{O}})$ and a sequence of operation $(\mathsf{op}_1, \ldots, \mathsf{op}_i)$ we write $\mathcal{G}_i = \mathcal{G}_{i-1} + \mathcal{L}_{\mathsf{O}}(\mathsf{DS}, \mathsf{op}_i)$ to refer to the correlation graph that results from adding $\mathcal{L}_{\mathsf{O}}(\mathsf{DS}, \mathsf{op}_i)$ to $\mathcal{G}_{i-1}$.

Composition of Equality Patterns. Encrypted search schemes often reveal more than a single pattern so when evaluating their security one needs to consider the composition of the patterns. For equality patterns this can be done by taking the union of their correlation graphs. For example, consider a scheme with leakage profile

$$\Lambda = (\mathcal{L}_{\mathsf{S}}, \mathcal{L}_{\mathsf{O}}) = \big(\star, (\mathsf{qeq}, \mathsf{patt})\big)$$

where patt reveals if a query was on the same label of a previous append. The correlation graphs of qeq and patt on the sequence $\mathbf{op}$ above are $\mathcal{G}_{\mathsf{qeq}}$ and $\mathcal{G}_{\mathsf{patt}}$ illustrated below,

and the correlation graph of $\mathcal{L}_{O}$ is

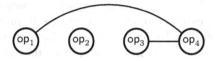

Correlation Security. Intuitively, our notion of correlation security guarantees that a leakage profile hides certain correlations between operations. We formalize this using a game-based definition that guarantees that an adversary cannot distinguish between operations even when given the correlation graph of adversarially-chosen operations.[8] By setting constraints on how exactly the adversary is allowed to choose its operations, one can define security against specific correlation attacks. More formally, let $\mathcal{L}_{O}$ be an operation leakage and let π_1, π_2, π_3 be predicates over sequences of operations. Consider the following probabilistic experiment between a stateful adversary $\mathcal{A}$ and a challenger:

$\mathbf{Corr}_{\mathcal{L}_{O},\mathcal{A}}^{\pi_1,\pi_2,\pi_3}(k)$:

1. $\mathcal{A}$ chooses a data structure DS and receives $\perp$ from the challenger $\mathcal{C}$;
2. Let $\mathcal{G}_0$ be an empty graph;
3. $\mathcal{A}$ adaptively chooses polynomially-many operations $\mathbf{op} = (\mathsf{op}_1, \ldots, \mathsf{op}_m)$ as follows. For all $1 \leq i \leq m$,
   (a) $\mathcal{A}$ chooses and sends an operation op_i such that $\pi_1(\mathsf{op}_1, \ldots, \mathsf{op}_i) = 1$ to the challenger;
   (b) the challenger returns $\mathcal{G}_i = \mathcal{G}_{i-1} + \mathcal{L}_O(\mathsf{DS}, \mathsf{op}_i)$ to $\mathcal{A}$;
4. $\mathcal{A}$ chooses two sequences of operations $\mathbf{op}_0^\star$ and $\mathbf{op}_1^\star$ of polynomial length λ such that $\pi_2(\mathbf{op}, \mathbf{op}_0^\star, \mathbf{op}_1^\star) = 1$ and sends them to the challenger;
5. the challenger samples $b \xleftarrow{\$} \{0,1\}$;
6. for all $1 \leq i \leq \lambda$, let $\mathcal{G}_{m+i} = \mathcal{G}_{m+i-1} + \mathcal{L}_O(\mathsf{DS}, \mathsf{op}_{b,i}^\star)$ to $\mathcal{A}$;
7. $\mathcal{A}$ adaptively chooses polynomially-many operations $\mathbf{op}' = (\mathsf{op}_1', \ldots, \mathsf{op}_{m'}')$ operations as follows. For all $1 \leq i \leq m'$,
   (a) $\mathcal{A}$ chooses and sends an operation op_i' such that $\pi_3(\mathbf{op}, \mathbf{op}_0^\star, \mathbf{op}_1^\star, \mathsf{op}_1', \ldots, \mathsf{op}_i') = 1$ to the challenger;
   (b) the challenger returns $\mathcal{G}_{m+\lambda+i} = \mathcal{G}_{m+\lambda+i-1} + \mathcal{L}_O(\mathsf{DS}, \mathsf{op}_i')$ to $\mathcal{A}$;
8. $\mathcal{A}$ outputs a bit b';
9. The experiment outputs 1 if $b' = b$ and 0 otherwise.

Definition 3 (Correlation security). *We say that a leakage profile $\Lambda = (\mathcal{L}_S, \mathcal{L}_O)$ is (π_1, π_2, π_3)-correlation secure if for all* PPT *adversaries $\mathcal{A}$,*

$$\Pr\left[\mathbf{Corr}_{\mathcal{L}_O,\mathcal{A}}^{\pi_1,\pi_2,\pi_3}(k) = 1\right] \leq \frac{1}{2} + \mathsf{negl}(k).$$

---

[8] Note that correlation-security is a security notion that is defined for leakage profiles not for STE schemes.

Injection Security. As discussed in Sect. 1, injection attacks work by causing updates with known labels and then using leakage to correlate the updates to queries with unknown labels. And while forward privacy prevents direct collections between updates and pre-injection queries it provides no guarantees for post-injection queries and does not prevent indirect correlations between updates and pre-injection queries. In fact, all practical forward-private constructions [1,8,10,24,47] have these limitations. To address these limitations, a leakage profile must prevent correlations between updates and all queries not just pre-injection queries. This can be captured using our definitional framework by imposing the following conditions on the adversary's choice of operations: in step 3. the adversary is free to choose any operation; in step 4. the challenge operations have to be queries and must be different than any query chosen in step 3.; and in step 7. the adversary can choose any update but only queries that are different than the challenge queries. In the definition below, we formalize this intuition.

Definition 4 (Security against injection attacks). *Let* $\mathsf{inj} = (\pi_1, \pi_2, \pi_3)$, *where*

- $\pi_1(\mathbf{op}) = 1$ *for all poly-size sequences of operations* $\mathbf{op}$;
- $\pi_2(\mathbf{op}, \mathbf{op}_0^\star, \mathbf{op}_1^\star)$ *outputs 1 if* $\mathbf{op}_0^\star$ *and* $\mathbf{op}_1^\star$ *are query-only sequences with the same query equality leakage and if none of the queries in* $\mathbf{op}_0^\star$ *and* $\mathbf{op}_1^\star$ *are in* $\mathbf{op}$; *otherwise it outputs 0;*
- $\pi_3(\mathbf{op}, \mathbf{op}_0^\star, \mathbf{op}_1^\star, \mathbf{op}')$ *outputs 1 if none of the queries in* $\mathbf{op}_0^\star$ *and* $\mathbf{op}_1^\star$ *are in* $\mathbf{op}'$; *otherwise it outputs 0.*

We say that a leakage profile $\Lambda = (\mathcal{L}_{\mathsf{S}}, \mathcal{L}_{\mathsf{O}})$ *is secure against file injections if for all* PPT *adversaries* $\mathcal{A}$,

$$\Pr\left[\mathbf{Corr}_{\mathcal{L}_{\mathsf{O}}, \mathcal{A}}^{\mathsf{inj}}(k) = 1 \right] \leq \frac{1}{2} + \mathsf{negl}(k).$$

Notice that Definition 4 allows a leakage profile to reveal correlations between queries but not between updates and queries. This is because the definition: (1) allows the challenge queries to have the same labels as previous and future updates; but (2) prohibits the challenge queries from having the same label as previous or future queries; and (3) prohibits the sequences of challenge queries from having different query equality. In the following Theorem, we show that this is enough to guarantee security against injection attacks in the sense that correlations to both pre- and post-injection queries are prevented.

Theorem 1. *The leakage profile* $\Lambda = (\mathcal{L}_{\mathsf{S}}, \mathcal{L}_{\mathsf{O}}) = (\star, \mathsf{qeq})$ *is injection-secure.*

Proof. Consider the correlation graph $\mathcal{G}$ produced in a $\mathbf{Corr}_{\mathcal{L}_{\mathsf{O}}, \mathcal{A}}^{\mathsf{inj}}$ experiment. By definition of (π_1, π_2, π_3), the queries in the challenge sequence $\mathbf{op}_b^\star = (q_{b,1}, \ldots, q_{b,\lambda})$ are not connected to any other query nodes. Furthermore, since there is no add or delete leakage by the definition of Λ, there are no edges incident to the add and delete nodes. It follows then that there is no path in $\mathcal{G}$ from any adversarially-chosen operation to the challenge queries. Therefore, the best the adversary can do is to guess b, from which the Theorem follows. ∎

4   An Injection-Secure Encrypted Multi-Map

Designing practical injection-secure EMMs (and SSE schemes) is challenging mainly for two reasons. First, it seems unlikely that one can design an injection-secure scheme that leaks the volume pattern which would suggest that any injection-secure scheme would have at least the query complexity of a dynamic volume-hiding scheme which tend to have high query complexity. Second, injection-secure schemes need to break correlations between queries and updates but doing so can be costly. Currently, we are only aware of two ways to do this: either using ORAM techniques or, as we propose, deterministically scheduling update operations.

Our construction $\mathsf{FIX} = (\mathsf{Setup}, \mathsf{Get}, \mathsf{Append}, \mathsf{Erase}, \mathsf{Res})$ makes black-box use of a static volume-hiding multi-map encryption scheme $\Sigma = (\mathsf{Setup}, \mathsf{Get}, \mathsf{Res})$ and a dynamic volume-hiding multi-map encryption scheme $\Delta = (\mathsf{Setup}, \mathsf{Get}, \mathsf{Insert}, \mathsf{Delete}, \mathsf{Res})$. The details of the scheme are in Figures (1) and (2). At a high-level, it works as follows.

Setup. The setup algorithm takes as input a security parameter k and a multi-map MM. It first picks a permutation π from $\{0, \cdots, \#\mathbb{L}_{\mathsf{MM}} - 1\}$ to $\mathbb{L}_{\mathsf{MM}}$ uniformly at random. It then instantiates two multi-maps: (1) a new multi-map MM_n with label space $\mathbb{L}_{\mathsf{MM}}$ and sets, for all $\ell \in \mathbb{L}_{\mathsf{MM}}$, $\mathsf{MM}_n[\ell] := \bot$ (an empty tuple); and (2) a multi-map $\mathsf{MM}_{\mathsf{stash}}$. It also initializes a counter count to 0. The multi-map $\mathsf{MM}_{\mathsf{stash}}$ will be used as a queue to purposely delay updates, while the counter will be used to determine which labels to update at a given time. The setup algorithm then encrypts MM by executing $(K_o, st_o, \mathsf{EMM}_o) \leftarrow \Sigma.\mathsf{Setup}(1^k, \mathsf{MM})$ and MM_n by computing $(K_n, st_n, \mathsf{EMM}_n) \leftarrow \Delta.\mathsf{Setup}(1^k, \mathsf{MM}_n)$. The old encrypted multi-map EMM_o will be queried but never updated whereas the new encrypted multi-map EMM_n will be both queried and updated. Finally, the algorithm outputs a key $K = (K_o, K_n)$, a state $st = (st_o, st_n, \mathsf{MM}_{\mathsf{stash}}, \pi, \mathsf{count})$, and an encrypted multi-map $\mathsf{EMM} = (\mathsf{EMM}_o, \mathsf{EMM}_n)$.

Append and Erase. The append and erase operations of FIX are based on the same core operation we call Push. Given an append operation $\mathsf{op} = (\mathsf{app}, \ell, \mathbf{v})$, the client updates its stash by appending $v\|\mathsf{add}$ to $\mathsf{MM}_{\mathsf{stash}}[\ell]$, for all $v \in \mathbf{v}$. It then "pushes" the changes as explained below. We sometimes refer to $\mathbf{v}$ as ℓ's update tuple.

Given an erase operation $\mathsf{op} = (\mathsf{del}, \ell, \mathbf{v})$ the client does the following. For all values $v \in \mathbf{v}$, if $v\|\mathsf{add}$ already exists in $\mathsf{MM}_{\mathsf{stash}}[\ell]$, it removes it from the stash. Otherwise it adds $v\|\mathsf{del}$ to $\mathsf{MM}_{\mathsf{stash}}[\ell]$. It then "pushes" the changes as described below.

To push its updates, the client retrieves and updates μ label/tuple pairs chosen using the random permutation π. More precisely, for all $0 \leq i \leq \mu - 1$, the client queries EMM_o and EMM_n on $\ell_{\pi(j)}$, where $j = \mathsf{count} + i$, resulting in responses $\mathbf{r}_o$ and $\mathbf{r}_n$, respectively. It then uses $\mathbf{r}_o$, $\mathbf{r}_n$ and its stash to generate a new tuple $\mathbf{v}_n$. $\mathbf{v}_n$ will contain the contents of $\mathbf{r}_n$ and the values in $\mathsf{MM}_{\mathsf{stash}}[\ell_{\pi(j)}]$ of the form $v\|\mathsf{add}$. If any value v in $\mathbf{r}_n$ is also in $\mathsf{MM}_{\mathsf{stash}}[\ell_{\pi(j)}]$ in the form

$v\|\mathtt{del}$, it is removed from $\mathbf{r}_n$. Because EMM_o is a static structure, all the values from $\mathbf{r}_o$ that need to be erased are added to $\mathbf{v}_n$ using a *lazy delete* approach. Specifically, for every value v in $\mathbf{r}_o$ that is in $\mathsf{MM}[\ell_{\pi(j)}]$ in the form $v\|\mathtt{del}$, the client adds $v\|\mathtt{del}\|o$ to $\mathbf{v}_n$. The client then uses $\varDelta$'s delete operation to remove the label/tuple pair for $\ell_{\pi(j)}$ from EMM_n, and inserts the new pair $(\ell_{\pi(j)}, \mathbf{v}_n)$. It also removes $\ell_{\pi(j)}$ from the stash. Finally, it increments the counter by μ and outputs the updated state while the server outputs the updated EMM_n.

Get. This is a two-party protocol between the client and the server. Given a label ℓ, the client queries both EMM_o and EMM_n on ℓ using $\varSigma.\mathsf{Get}$ and $\varDelta.\mathsf{Get}$, respectively. It then computes the union of the results, and removes all the values in $\mathsf{MM}_{\mathsf{stash}}[\ell]$ tagged with $\mathtt{del}$. It also removes all the values in the result set from EMM_o, if they are tagged with $\mathtt{del}\|o$ in the result set from EMM_n. The client then outputs the final result along with the updated state, while the server outputs nothing.

Efficiency. The communication complexity of $\mathsf{FIX.Get}$ is

$$O\big(\mathsf{comm}_{\mathsf{Get}}^{\varSigma}(\ell) + \mathsf{comm}_{\mathsf{Get}}^{\varDelta}(\ell)\big)$$

where $\mathsf{comm}_{\mathsf{Get}}^{\varSigma}, \mathsf{comm}_{\mathsf{Get}}^{\varDelta}$ are the communication complexities of $\varSigma.\mathsf{Get}$ and $\varDelta.\mathsf{Get}$ respectively. The query complexity of FIX is

$$O\big(\mathsf{time}_{\mathsf{Get}}^{\varSigma}(\ell) + \mathsf{time}_{\mathsf{Get}}^{\varDelta}(\ell) + \mathsf{dels}_o(\ell) + \#\mathsf{MM}_{\mathsf{stash}}[\ell]\big)$$

where $\mathsf{time}_{\mathsf{Get}}^{\varSigma}, \mathsf{time}_{\mathsf{Get}}^{\varDelta}$ are the computational complexities of $\varSigma.\mathsf{Get}$ and $\varDelta.\mathsf{Get}$ respectively, $\mathsf{dels}_o(\ell)$ is the number of erasure operations issued for values of ℓ in $\varSigma$, and $\#\mathsf{MM}_{\mathsf{stash}}[\ell]$ is equal to the number of values in the last $\#\mathbb{L}_{\mathsf{MM}}/\mu - 1$ updates associated with ℓ.

Storage complexity is the sum of the storage complexities induced by $\varSigma$ and $\varDelta$. The communication complexities of $\mathsf{FIX.Append}$ and $\mathsf{FIX.Erase}$ are

$$O\big(\mu \cdot (\mathsf{comm}_{\mathsf{Get}}^{\mathsf{FIX}}(\ell) + \mathsf{comm}_{\mathsf{Delete}}^{\varDelta}(\ell) + \mathsf{comm}_{\mathsf{Insert}}^{\varDelta}(\ell))\big)$$

where $\mathsf{comm}_{\mathsf{Get}}^{\mathsf{FIX}}, \mathsf{comm}_{\mathsf{Insert}}^{\varDelta}$ and $\mathsf{comm}_{\mathsf{Delete}}^{\varDelta}$ are the communication complexities of $\mathsf{FIX.Get}$, $\varDelta.\mathsf{Insert}$ and $\varDelta.\mathsf{Delete}$, respectively.

The update complexity of FIX is

$$O\big(\#\mathbf{v} + \mu \cdot (\mathsf{time}_{\mathsf{Get}}^{\mathsf{FIX}}(\ell) + \mathsf{time}_{\mathsf{Delete}}^{\varDelta}(\ell) + \mathsf{time}_{\mathsf{Insert}}^{\varDelta}(\ell))\big)$$

where $\mathsf{time}_{\mathsf{Get}}^{\mathsf{FIX}}$ is the get complexity of FIX and $\mathsf{time}_{\mathsf{Delete}}^{\varDelta}(\ell), \mathsf{time}_{\mathsf{Insert}}^{\varDelta}(\ell)$ are the computational complexities of $\varDelta.\mathsf{Delete}, \varDelta.\mathsf{Insert}$ respectively.

The size of the client state is analyzed in Sect. 4.1. Note that it is independent of the underlying schemes $\varDelta$ and $\varSigma$.

Concrete Efficiency. We now provide a concrete efficiency analysis assuming $\varSigma$ is instantiated with the static volume-hiding scheme VLH [35][9] and that $\varDelta$

---

[9] If truncations in the static encrypted multi-map are not desirable, $\varSigma$ can be instantiated with AVLH from [35].

Let $\Sigma = (\mathsf{Setup}, \mathsf{Get}_{\mathsf{C},\mathsf{S}})$ be a static response-hiding multi-map encryption scheme, $\Delta = (\mathsf{Setup}, \mathsf{Get}_{\mathsf{C},\mathsf{S}}, \mathsf{Insert}_{\mathsf{C},\mathsf{S}}, \mathsf{Delete}_{\mathsf{C},\mathsf{S}})$ be a dynamic response-hiding multi-map encryption scheme. Consider the scheme $\mathsf{FIX} = (\mathsf{Setup}, \mathsf{Get}_{\mathsf{C},\mathsf{S}}, \mathsf{Append}_{\mathsf{C},\mathsf{S}}, \mathsf{Erase}_{\mathsf{C},\mathsf{S}})$ defined as follows:

- $\mathsf{Setup}(1^k, \mathsf{MM})$:
    1. sample a permutation $\pi \xleftarrow{\$} \{\{0, \cdots, \#\mathbb{L}_{\mathsf{MM}} - 1\} \to \mathbb{L}_{\mathsf{MM}}\}$;
    2. initialize a multi-map MM_n with label space $\mathbb{L}_{\mathsf{MM}}$, an empty multi-map $\mathsf{MM}_{\mathsf{stash}}$, and a counter count initialized to 0;
    3. compute
    $$(K_o, st_o, \mathsf{EMM}_o) \leftarrow \Sigma.\mathsf{Setup}(1^k, \mathsf{MM});$$
    4. compute
    $$(K_n, st_n, \mathsf{EMM}_n) \leftarrow \Delta.\mathsf{Setup}(1^k, \mathsf{MM}_n);$$
    5. output (K, st, EMM) where $K := (K_o, K_n)$, $st := (st_o, st_n, \mathsf{MM}_{\mathsf{stash}}, \pi, \mathsf{count})$ and $\mathsf{EMM} := (\mathsf{EMM}_o, \mathsf{EMM}_n)$.
- $\mathsf{Get}_{\mathsf{C},\mathsf{S}}\big((K, st, \ell), \mathsf{EMM}\big)$:
    1. $\mathbf{C}$ parses K as (K_o, K_n), st as $(st_o, st_n, \mathsf{MM}_{\mathsf{stash}}, \pi, \mathsf{count})$;
    2. $\mathbf{S}$ parses EMM as $(\mathsf{EMM}_o, \mathsf{EMM}_n)$;
    3. $\mathbf{C}$ initializes an empty set $\mathbf{v}$;
    4. $\mathbf{C}$ and $\mathbf{S}$ execute
    $$(\mathbf{r}_o, \perp) \leftarrow \Sigma.\mathsf{Get}_{\mathsf{C},\mathsf{S}}\big((K_o, st_o, \ell), \mathsf{EMM}_o\big);$$
    and,
    $$(\mathbf{r}_n, \perp) \leftarrow \Delta.\mathsf{Get}_{\mathsf{C},\mathsf{S}}\big((K_n, st_n, \ell), \mathsf{EMM}_n\big);$$
    5. $\mathbf{C}$ computes $\mathbf{r}_{\mathsf{local}}^+$ and $\mathbf{r}_{\mathsf{local}}^-$ from $\mathsf{MM}_{\mathsf{stash}}[\ell]$ such that
    $$\mathbf{r}_{\mathsf{local}}^+ = \{v : v\|\mathsf{add} \in \mathsf{MM}_{\mathsf{stash}}[\ell]\} \quad \text{and} \quad \mathbf{r}_{\mathsf{local}}^- = \{v : v\|\mathsf{del} \in \mathsf{MM}_{\mathsf{stash}}[\ell]\};$$
    6. $\mathbf{C}$ sets $\mathbf{r}_o^- := \{v : v\|\mathsf{del}\|\mathsf{old} \in \mathbf{r}_n\}$;
    7. $\mathbf{C}$ sets $\mathbf{v} := \big(\mathbf{r}_o \cup \mathbf{r}_n \cup \mathbf{r}_{\mathsf{local}}^+\big) \setminus \big(\mathbf{r}_{\mathsf{local}}^- \cup \mathbf{r}_o^-\big)$;
    8. $\mathbf{C}$ outputs $\mathbf{v}$, while $\mathbf{S}$ outputs $\perp$.

Fig. 1. FIX (Part 1).

is instantiated with our DVLH construction detailed in Sect. 5. We assume that both VLH and DVLH are instantiated with an optimal-time multi-map encryption scheme. The communication complexity of FIX.Get is then equal to

$$O\big(\lambda_o + 2^{s_o} + \lambda_n + 2^{s_n}\big)$$

where λ_o (resp., λ_n) is the parameter of the dynamic pseudo-random transform used in Σ (resp., Δ) and 2^{s_o} (resp., 2^{s_n}) is the largest value outputted by the PRF used by the transform in Σ (resp., Δ).

The query complexity is

$$O\big(\lambda_o + 2^{s_o} + \lambda_n + 2^{s_n} + \mathsf{dels}_o(\ell) + \#\mathsf{MM}_{\mathsf{stash}}[\ell]\big),$$

- $\mathsf{Append}_{\mathbf{C},\mathbf{S}}\big((K,\mu,st,(\ell,\mathbf{v})),\mathsf{EMM}\big)$:
  1. for all $v \in \mathbf{v}$, $\mathbf{C}$ sets $\mathsf{MM}_{\mathsf{stash}}[\ell] := \mathsf{MM}_{\mathsf{stash}}[\ell] \cup \{v\|\mathsf{add}\}$;
  2. $\mathbf{C}$ and $\mathbf{S}$ execute $\mathsf{Push}_{\mathbf{C},\mathbf{S}}\big((K,\mu,st),\mathsf{EMM}\big)$;
- $\mathsf{Erase}_{\mathbf{C},\mathbf{S}}\big((K,\mu,st,(\ell,\mathbf{v})),\mathsf{EMM}\big)$:
  1. for all $v \in \mathbf{v}$,
     (a) if $v\|\mathsf{add} \notin \mathsf{MM}_{\mathsf{stash}}[\ell]$, $\mathbf{C}$ sets $\mathsf{MM}_{\mathsf{stash}}[\ell] := \mathsf{MM}_{\mathsf{stash}}[\ell] \cup \{v\|\mathsf{del}\}$
     (b) else it sets $\mathsf{MM}_{\mathsf{stash}}[\ell] := \mathsf{MM}_{\mathsf{stash}}[\ell] \setminus \{v\|\mathsf{add}\}$
  2. $\mathbf{C}$ and $\mathbf{S}$ execute $\mathsf{Push}_{\mathbf{C},\mathbf{S}}\big((K,\mu,st),\mathsf{EMM}\big)$;
- $\mathsf{Push}_{\mathbf{C},\mathbf{S}}\big((K,\mu,st),\mathsf{EMM}\big)$:
  1. $\mathbf{C}$ parses K as (K_o, K_n) and st as $(st_o, st_n, \mathsf{MM}_{\mathsf{stash}}, \pi, \mathsf{count})$
  2. $\mathbf{S}$ parses EMM as $(\mathsf{EMM}_o, \mathsf{EMM}_n)$;
  3. for all $0 \le i \le \mu - 1$,
     (a) set $j := \mathsf{count} + i \mod \#\mathbb{L}_{\mathsf{MM}}$;
     (b) $\mathbf{C}$ and $\mathbf{S}$ execute

$$(\mathbf{r}_o, \perp) \leftarrow \Sigma.\mathsf{Get}_{\mathbf{C},\mathbf{S}}\big((K_o, st_o, \ell_\pi(j)), \mathsf{EMM}_o\big);$$

and

$$(\mathbf{r}_n, \perp) \leftarrow \Delta.\mathsf{Get}_{\mathbf{C},\mathbf{S}}\big((K_n, st_n, \ell_\pi(j)), \mathsf{EMM}_n\big);$$

     (c) for all $v\|\mathbf{x} \in \mathsf{MM}_{\mathsf{stash}}[\pi(j)]$,
         i. if $\mathbf{x} = \mathsf{add}$, $\mathbf{C}$ sets $\mathbf{r}^+_{\mathsf{local}} := \mathbf{r}^+_{\mathsf{local}} \cup \{v\}$;
         ii. if $\mathbf{x} = \mathsf{del}$,
             A. if $v \notin \mathbf{r}_o$, $\mathbf{C}$ sets $\mathbf{r}^-_{\mathsf{local}} := \mathbf{r}^-_{\mathsf{local}} \cup \{v\}$
             B. else $\mathbf{C}$ sets $\mathbf{r}^+_{\mathsf{local}} := \mathbf{r}^+_{\mathsf{local}} \cup \{v\|\mathsf{del}\|\mathsf{old}\}$;
     (d) $\mathbf{C}$ removes $\ell_{\pi(j)}$'s tuple from $\mathsf{MM}_{\mathsf{stash}}[\ell_{\pi(j)}]$;
     (e) $\mathbf{C}$ computes $\mathbf{v}_n = (\mathbf{r}_n \cup \mathbf{r}^+_{\mathsf{local}}) \setminus \mathbf{r}^-_{\mathsf{local}}$;
     (f) $\mathbf{C}$ and $\mathbf{S}$ execute

$$(\mathbf{r}, \perp) \leftarrow \Delta.\mathsf{Delete}_{\mathbf{C},\mathbf{S}}\left(\left(K_n, st_n, \ell_{\pi(j)}\right), \mathsf{EMM}_n\right);$$

     (g) $\mathbf{C}$ and $\mathbf{S}$ execute

$$(st'_n, \mathsf{EMM}'_n) \leftarrow \Delta.\mathsf{Insert}_{\mathbf{C},\mathbf{S}}\left(\left(K_n, st_n, (\ell_{\pi(j)}, \mathbf{v}_n)\right), \mathsf{EMM}_n\right);$$

  4. $\mathbf{C}$ increments the counter $\mathsf{count} := \mathsf{count} + \mu$;
  5. $\mathbf{C}$ outputs an updated state $st' = (st_o, st'_n, \mathsf{MM}_{\mathsf{stash}}, \pi, \mathsf{count})$, while $\mathbf{S}$ outputs an updated structure $\mathsf{EMM}' = (\mathsf{EMM}_o, \mathsf{EMM}'_n)$.

Fig. 2. FIX (Part 2).

the add and erase communication complexities are

$$O\big(\mu \cdot (\lambda_o + 2^{s_o} + \lambda_n + 2^{s_n})\big)$$

and the add and erase computational complexities are

$$O\big(\#\mathbf{v} + \mu \cdot (\lambda_o + 2^{s_o} + \lambda_n + 2^{s_n} + \mathsf{dels}_o(\ell) + \#\mathsf{MM}_{\mathsf{stash}}[\ell])\big).$$

To get a better sense of the concrete efficiency of our scheme we set the parameters as follows. If μ is set to $O(\log \#\mathbb{L})$, λ_n is set to $O(\lambda_o) = O(\log \#\mathbb{L})$. and s_n to $s_o + \log\log \#\mathbb{L}$ then the query communication and computational complexities are

$$O\left(\log(\#\mathbb{L}) \cdot 2^{s_o}\right),$$

and the append and erase communication and computational complexities are

$$O\left(\log^2(\#\mathbb{L}) \cdot 2^{s_o}\right),$$

where $s_o \approx 10$ for a multi-map with $50,000$ labels, 2^{22} total values and with response-lengths that are Zipf-distributed.

Comparison to Generic Approaches. We now consider how FIX compares to solutions based on ORAM simulation. Specifically, consider a multi-map MM with label space $\mathbb{L}$ that is stored and accessed (in a black-box manner) using an ORAM. Every value of a tuple is stored in a separate block in memory and every get operation is mapped to t ORAM read operations, where t denotes the maximum possible response length of a tuple. To account for future puts, t needs to be set to the maximum response length that will ever be supported and not to s_{max}, the maximum response length in the current multi-map. It is easy to observe that the get operations will be leakage-free. If the ORAM is instantiated with Path ORAM [48], then the computation and communication complexity of a get operation are

$$O(t \cdot \log^2\left(\#\mathbb{L}_{\mathsf{MM}}\right)),$$

which is worse than FIX's complexity when $t = \Omega(2^{s_o})$ and under the same parametrization described above.

Correctness. Notice that FIX, when instantiated with VLH and DVLH, will result in a lossy multi-map encryption scheme. As shown in [35], one way to measure lossyness is to calculate the number of truncated labels in the encrypted multi-map. In particular, one can observe that for FIX the number of truncated labels is at most equal to the sum of the number of truncated labels in both VLH and DVLH. We refer the reader to [35] and Sect. 5.2 for more details on the number of truncations in VLH and DVLH, respectively.

4.1   Client Stash Size

We now analyze the size of the client stash. Since append and erase operations both affect the stash, we use the term *update* to refer to both operations. We consider two settings: (1) the *worst-case* setting where we analyze the stash size independently of the update and tuple length distributions; and (2) an *average-case* setting where updates are chosen uniformly at random and where the update tuple lengths are Zipf distributed.

Worst Case. In this setting, we assume that each update tuple has maximum tuple length s_{max}, i.e., for all updates op $= (\omega, \ell, \mathbf{v})$, where $\omega \in \{\mathsf{app}, \mathsf{del}\}$, $\#\mathbf{v} = s_{max}$. Recall that FIX has $\#\mathbb{L}_{\mathsf{MM}}/\mu$ update cycles where for each cycle the tuples of μ labels get pushed to the encrypted structure. Note that the mapping π that ties a label to its cycle is fixed at setup and never changes. Note that the worst case occurs if every update is mapped to the update cycle that precedes the current one because, in this case, the updates remain in the stash for $\#\mathbb{L}/\mu - 1$ cycles before being evicted and this is the maximum number of cycles possible. Therefore, the size of the stash is at most $\#\mathbb{L}_{\mathsf{MM}} \cdot s_{max}/\mu$, which means it is $O(\#\mathbb{L}^2_{\mathsf{MM}})$ if s_{max} is $O(\#\mathbb{L}_{\mathsf{MM}})$. Interestingly, if we set μ to be $O(s_{max})$, the stash size is $O(\#\mathbb{L}_{\mathsf{MM}})$ which is the size of the state for most state-of-the-art dynamic EMMs. For the rest of this subsection we set $m \stackrel{\circ}{=} \#\mathbb{L}_{\mathsf{MM}}$.

Average Case. The above bound on the stash size helps us understand the limitations of FIX in the worst case but it does not tell us much about how the stash size behaves in practice since clients are very unlikely to generate updates as described above and that all have size s_{max}. This motivates us to study a setting where the update lengths are sampled from some known distribution. More precisely, we assume that the labels to be updated are selected uniformly at random and that the size of their updates is picked uniformly at random from the set

$$U = \left\{ \frac{s_0}{1^s \cdot H_{m,s}}, \frac{s_0}{2^s \cdot H_{m,s}}, \dots, \frac{s_0}{m^s \cdot H_{m,s}} \right\},$$

where $s_0 = s_{\max} \cdot H_{m,s}$. In the Theorem below, we analyze the expected stash size in this average case setting.

Theorem 2. *If the update labels are sampled uniformly at random and if their update lengths are sampled uniformly at random from U, then the expected stash size of* FIX *is at most $H_m \cdot s_{\max}/2\mu$.*

The proof of this Theorem is in the full version [2].

The key takeaway from this Theorem is that if we set μ to be $O(\log m)$, the expected stash size is in the order of $s_{\max}$ (which is at least equal to m) since H_m is upper bounded by $\log m + 1$.

Concentration Bound. For a more robust analysis, we give a high-probability bound on the stash in the following Theorem.

Theorem 3. *If the update labels sampled uniformly at random and if their tuple lengths are sampled from a $\mathcal{Z}_{m,1}$ distribution, then, with probability greater than $1 - \epsilon$ the stash size X is at most*

$$\frac{H_m \cdot s_{\max}}{2\mu} + s_{\max} \cdot \sqrt{\frac{(m - 2\mu) \cdot \ln(1/\epsilon)}{2\mu}}.$$

The proof of this Theorem is in the full version [2].

4.2 Security

We describe and prove the leakage profile of FIX. We first give a black-box description based on the leakage profiles of Σ and Δ and then describe a concrete profile when Σ and Δ are instantiated with state-of-the-art constructions.

Black-box leakage. Let Σ be a static multi-map encryption scheme with leakage profile $\Lambda_\Sigma = (\mathcal{L}_S^\Sigma, \mathcal{L}_Q^\Sigma)$ and Δ be a dynamic multi-map encryption scheme with leakage profile $\Lambda_\Delta = (\mathcal{L}_S^\Delta, \mathcal{L}_O^\Delta)$. The setup leakage of FIX is

$$\mathcal{L}_S(\mathsf{MM}) = \left(\mathcal{L}_S^\Sigma(\mathsf{MM}_o), \mathcal{L}_S^\Delta(\mathsf{MM}_\perp) \right),$$

where MM_o is the original multi-map and $\mathsf{MM}_\perp$ is the multi-map with label space $\mathbb{L}_{\mathsf{MM}}$ and $\mathsf{MM}_\perp[\ell] = \perp$ for all $\ell \in \mathbb{L}_{\mathsf{MM}}$. The operation leakage of FIX is

- $\mathcal{L}_O(\mathsf{MM}, \mathsf{op})$
    1. if op is a query, parse op as ℓ and output $\mathcal{L}_Q^\Sigma(\mathsf{MM}_o, \ell)$ and $\mathcal{L}_O^\Delta(\mathsf{MM}_n, \ell)$;
    2. if op is an append or delete operation then, for all $0 \le i \le \mu - 1$,
        (a) let $j = \mathsf{count} + i \mod m$
        (b) output
            i. $\mathcal{L}_Q^\Sigma(\mathsf{MM}_o, \ell_{\pi(j)})$,
            ii. $\mathcal{L}_O^\Delta(\mathsf{MM}_n, (\mathsf{qry}, \ell_{\pi(j)}))$,
            iii. $\mathcal{L}_O^\Delta(\mathsf{MM}_n, (\mathsf{del}, \ell_{\pi(j)}))$,
            iv. $\mathcal{L}_O^\Delta(\mathsf{MM}_n, (\mathsf{add}, \ell_{\pi(j)}, \mathbf{v}_n))$
        (c) set $\mathsf{count} = \mathsf{count} + \mu$;

where count is a stateful variable initialized to 1.

Theorem 4. *Let* $\Lambda_{\mathsf{FIX}} = (\mathcal{L}_S, \mathcal{L}_O)$ *where* $\mathcal{L}_S$ *and* $\mathcal{L}_O$ *are as above. If* Σ *is* Λ_Σ-*secure and* Δ *is* Λ_Δ-*secure, then* FIX *is* Λ_{FIX}-*secure.*

The proof of this Theorem is in the full version [2].

Concrete Leakage. We now analyze the leakage profile of FIX when its underlying EMMs are instantiated with concrete schemes. Specifically, we assume Σ is a static volume-hiding multi-map encryption scheme with leakage profile

$$\Lambda_\Sigma = (\mathcal{L}_S, \mathcal{L}_Q) = (\mathsf{dsize}(\mathsf{MM}_o), \mathsf{qeq}),$$

where dsize is the data size pattern $\mathsf{dsize}(\mathsf{MM}) = m_{\mathsf{MM}}$. This leakage is acheived by the static volume-hiding scheme VLH [35]. We also assume that Δ has leakage profile

$$\Lambda_\Delta = (\mathcal{L}_S, \mathcal{L}_O) = (\mathsf{dsize}(\mathsf{MM}_n), \mathsf{oeq}).$$

Note that the above leakage profile can be achieved when Δ is instantiated with our DVLH construction from Sect. 5.1.

Theorem 5. *If* Σ *is* (dsize, qeq)-*secure and if* Δ *is* (dsize, oeq)-*secure, then* FIX *is injection-secure.*

The proof of this Theorem is in the full version [2].

5   A Dynamic Volume-Hiding Multi-Map Encryption Scheme

In this section, we introduce our new fully-dynamic volume-hiding multi-map encryption scheme we call DVLH. Our scheme is built on top of a dynamic variant of the pseudo-random transform PRT [35]. We first describe the dynamic version of the PRT, called DPRT, in Fig. 3 and provide a high level description in the following.

Overview. DPRT is a data structure transformation that takes as input a security parameter k, a public parameter λ and a multi-map MM, and outputs a transformed multi-map MM'. Both the multi-map transformation and Get algorithms of DPRT are the same as the ones of PRT. The only difference is that DPRT now has an Insert, Append and an Erase algorithm that can add label/values tuple to the multi-map or append/erase values to/from a tuple in the multi-map. More precisely, all these algorithms take as input a security parameter k, a public parameter λ, a label/values tuple $(\ell, \mathbf{v})$ and a multi-map MM. The Insert algorithm executes DPRT on a multi-map composed of a single label/tuple pair $(\ell, \mathbf{v})$, and then adds the transformed tuple to the input multi-map. Both Append and Erase algorithms initialize an empty multi-map MM*. Then, Append (resp., Erase) removes the dummy entries (if any) from MM[ℓ] and adds the tuple $(\ell, \text{MM}[\ell] \| \mathbf{v})$ (resp., $(\ell, \text{MM}[\ell] \setminus \mathbf{v})$) to MM*. It then executes MM' $\leftarrow$ DPRT$(1^k, \lambda, \text{MM}^\star)$ and replaces MM[ℓ] with the transformed tuple MM'[ℓ].[10]

5.1   Our Construction

Our dynamic volume-hiding scheme DVLH $=$ (Setup, Get$_{\text{C,S}}$, Insert$_{\text{C,S}}$, Delete$_{\text{C,S}}$, Append$_{\text{C,S}}$, Erase$_{\text{C,S}}$) makes use of DPRT—the dynamic version of the pseudo-random transform PRT and black-box use of a dynamic response-hiding multi-map encryption scheme STE$_{\text{MM}}^{\text{RH}}$ that supports both Put and Delete operations, where Delete takes as input a label ℓ and removes its tuple from the multi-map. For our purposes, we would also like STE$_{\text{MM}}^{\text{RH}}$ to be optimal-time and to have update leakage at most $\mathcal{L}_\text{U} = \#\mathbf{v}$. These last two properties are achieved by the constructions given in [1,8] but these constructions do not support Delete; instead, they only support edit$^-$ which takes as input a label ℓ and a value $1 \le i \le \#\text{MM}[\ell]$ and removes the ith element of ℓ's tuple. Note, however, that these schemes also support edit$^+$ which takes as input a label ℓ and a value v and adds v to ℓ's tuple and that this is enough to support Delete with leakage $\mathcal{L}_\text{O}(\text{Delete}, \ell) = \bot$ as follows. Given a label ℓ, it suffices to call the underlying scheme' s edit$^+$ operation on the pair $(\ell, \star)$, where $\star$ is a special symbol outside

---

[10] In this description, we made the implicit assumption that the client knows whether a label ℓ already exists in the multi-map when it performs an Insert or an Append. In general, this is not the case and there would be a need for the client to keep a local state that stores such information.

Let $F : \{0,1\}^k \times \{0,1\}^* \to \{0,1\}^s$ be a pseudo-random function, rank: $\mathbb{R}^n \to \mathbb{R}^n$ be ranking function and $\lambda \in \mathbb{N}$ be a public parameter. Consider the dynamic transform DPRT defined as follows:

- DPRT($1^k, \lambda$, MM):
  1. sample a key $K \xleftarrow{\$} \{0,1\}^k$;
  2. instantiate an empty multi-map MM$'$;
  3. for all $\ell \in \mathbb{L}_{\mathsf{MM}}$,
     (a) let $r := \mathsf{MM}[\ell]$ and $n_\ell = \#r$;
     (b) compute $r' := \mathrm{rank}(r)$;
     (c) let $n'_\ell = \lambda + F_K(\ell \| n_\ell)$;
     (d) if $n'_\ell > n_\ell$, set $\mathsf{MM}'[\ell] := (r', \perp_1, \ldots, \perp_{n'_\ell - n_\ell})$;
     (e) otherwise, set $\mathsf{MM}'[\ell] := (r'_1, \ldots, r'_{n'_\ell})$;
  4. output MM$'$.
- Get(ℓ, MM): output $\mathsf{MM}[\ell]$.
- Insert($1^k, \lambda, (\ell, \mathbf{v})$, MM):
  1. execute $\mathsf{MM}' \leftarrow \mathsf{DPRT}(1^k, \lambda, \{(\ell, \mathbf{v})\})$;
  2. set $\mathsf{MM}[\ell] := \mathsf{MM}'[\ell]$ and output the updated multi-map MM.
- Append($1^k, \lambda, (\ell, \mathbf{v})$, MM):
  1. instantiate an empty multi-map MM*;
  2. remove all dummy entries from $\mathsf{MM}[\ell]$;
  3. set $\mathsf{MM}^\star[\ell] := \mathsf{MM}[\ell] \cup \mathbf{v}$;
  4. execute $\mathsf{MM}' \leftarrow \mathsf{DPRT}(1^k, \lambda, \mathsf{MM}^\star)$;
  5. set $\mathsf{MM}[\ell] := \mathsf{MM}'[\ell]$ and output the updated multi-map MM.
- Erase($1^k, \lambda, (\ell, \mathbf{v})$, MM):
  1. execute DPRT.Append($1^k, \lambda, (\ell, \mathbf{v})$, MM) but replace step 3 with the following:
     - set $\mathsf{MM}^\star[\ell] := \mathsf{MM}[\ell] \setminus \mathbf{v}$;

Fig. 3. DPRT.

of the label space. Then, during a get operation, if the client retrieves a tuple that includes $\star$, it outputs $\perp$.

The details of DVLH are provided in Fig. 4. At a high level it works as follows.

Overview. Unlike VLH^d in [35], DVLH is fully dynamic in the sense that it handles editing existing tuples. Recall that the dynamism of VLH^d is restricted to removing a label/tuple pair, adding a new label/tuple pair, and editing an existing tuple while not modifying its size. The Setup and Get protocols are the same as the ones of VLH^d. So we only describe how all the Update protocols work. The Delete algorithm removes the corresponding $(\ell, \mathbf{v})$ pair from the encrypted multimap. The Append and Erase algorithms execute $r \leftarrow \mathsf{STE}_{\mathsf{MM}}^{\mathsf{RH}}.\mathsf{Get}$ and then remove ℓ from the encrypted multi-map. The Append (resp., Erase) algorithm then executes DPRT.Append (resp., DPRT.Erase) on $(\ell, \mathbf{v})$ and a multi-map consisting of just one tuple $\{(\ell, r)\}$. This outputs a transformed multi-map MM$'$ containing just the updated tuple; ℓ and its corresponding values. Finally, the client and the server execute the $\mathsf{STE}_{\mathsf{MM}}^{\mathsf{RH}}.\mathsf{Put}$ protocol to put the new pair $(\ell, \mathsf{MM}'[\ell])$ into

Let DPRT be the dynamic pseudo-random transform described in Figure 3 and let $\mathsf{STE}_{\mathsf{MM}}^{\mathsf{RH}} = (\mathsf{Setup}, \mathsf{Get}_{\mathbf{C},\mathbf{S}}, \mathsf{Put}_{\mathbf{C},\mathbf{S}}, \mathsf{Delete}_{\mathbf{C},\mathbf{S}})$ be a dynamic response-hiding multi-map encryption scheme. Consider the scheme $\mathsf{DVLH} = (\mathsf{Setup}, \mathsf{Get}_{\mathbf{C},\mathbf{S}}, \mathsf{Insert}_{\mathbf{C},\mathbf{S}}, \mathsf{Append}_{\mathbf{C},\mathbf{S}}, \mathsf{Delete}_{\mathbf{C},\mathbf{S}}, \mathsf{Erase}_{\mathbf{C},\mathbf{S}})$ defined as follows:

- $\mathsf{Setup}(1^k, \lambda, \mathsf{MM})$:
  1. compute $\mathsf{MM}' \leftarrow \mathsf{DPRT}(1^k, \lambda, \mathsf{MM})$ and execute
  $$(K, st, \mathsf{EMM}) \leftarrow \mathsf{STE}_{\mathsf{MM}}^{\mathsf{RH}}.\mathsf{Setup}(1^k, \mathsf{MM}');$$
  2. output (K, st, EMM).
- $\mathsf{Get}_{\mathbf{C},\mathbf{S}}\big((K, st, \ell), \mathsf{EMM}\big)$:
  1. $\mathbf{C}$ and $\mathbf{S}$ execute
  $$(r, \perp) \leftarrow \mathsf{STE}_{\mathsf{MM}}^{\mathsf{RH}}.\mathsf{Get}_{\mathbf{C},\mathbf{S}}\big((K, st, \ell), \mathsf{EMM}\big);$$
  2. $\mathbf{C}$ outputs r and $\mathbf{S}$ outputs $\perp$.
- $\mathsf{Insert}_{\mathbf{C},\mathbf{S}}\big((K, \lambda, st, (\ell, \mathbf{v})), \mathsf{EMM}\big)$:
  1. $\mathbf{C}$ executes $\mathsf{MM}' \leftarrow \mathsf{DPRT}.\mathsf{Insert}\big(1^k, \lambda, (\ell, \mathbf{v}), \mathsf{MM}\big)$ where MM is an empty multi-map;
  2. $\mathbf{C}$ and $\mathbf{S}$ execute
  $$(st', \mathsf{EMM}') \leftarrow \mathsf{STE}_{\mathsf{MM}}^{\mathsf{RH}}.\mathsf{Put}_{\mathbf{C},\mathbf{S}}\bigg((K, st, (\ell, \mathsf{MM}'[\ell])), \mathsf{EMM}\bigg);$$
  3. $\mathbf{C}$ outputs an updated state st' and $\mathbf{S}$ outputs EMM'.
- $\mathsf{Delete}_{\mathbf{C},\mathbf{S}}\big((K, \lambda, st, \ell), \mathsf{EMM}\big)$:
  1. $\mathbf{C}$ and $\mathbf{S}$ execute
  $$(st', \mathsf{EMM}') \leftarrow \mathsf{STE}_{\mathsf{MM}}^{\mathsf{RH}}.\mathsf{Delete}_{\mathbf{C},\mathbf{S}}\big((K, st, \ell), \mathsf{EMM}\big);$$
  2. $\mathbf{C}$ outputs an updated state st' and $\mathbf{S}$ outputs EMM'.
- $\mathsf{Append}_{\mathbf{C},\mathbf{S}}\big((K, \lambda, st, (\ell, \mathbf{v})), \mathsf{EMM}\big)$:
  1. $\mathbf{C}$ and $\mathbf{S}$ execute
  $$(r, \perp) \leftarrow \mathsf{STE}_{\mathsf{MM}}^{\mathsf{RH}}.\mathsf{Get}_{\mathbf{C},\mathbf{S}}\big((K, st, \ell), \mathsf{EMM}\big)$$
  and,
  $$(st^\star, \mathsf{EMM}^\star) \leftarrow \mathsf{STE}_{\mathsf{MM}}^{\mathsf{RH}}.\mathsf{Delete}_{\mathbf{C},\mathbf{S}}\big((K, st, \ell), \mathsf{EMM}\big);$$
  2. $\mathbf{C}$ executes $\mathsf{MM}' \leftarrow \mathsf{DPRT}.\mathsf{Append}\big(1^k, \lambda, (\ell, \mathbf{v}), \{(\ell, r)\}\big)$;
  3. $\mathbf{C}$ and $\mathbf{S}$ execute
  $$(st', \mathsf{EMM}') \leftarrow \mathsf{STE}_{\mathsf{MM}}^{\mathsf{RH}}.\mathsf{Put}_{\mathbf{C},\mathbf{S}}\bigg((K, st^\star, (\ell, \mathsf{MM}'[\ell])), \mathsf{EMM}^\star\bigg);$$
  4. $\mathbf{C}$ outputs an updated state st' and $\mathbf{S}$ outputs EMM'.
- $\mathsf{Erase}_{\mathbf{C},\mathbf{S}}\big((K, \lambda, st, (\ell, \mathbf{v})), \mathsf{EMM}\big)$:
  1. execute $\mathsf{DVLH}.\mathsf{Append}(1^k, \lambda, st, (\ell, \mathbf{v}), \mathsf{EMM})$ but replace step 2 with the following:
     - $\mathbf{C}$ executes $\mathsf{MM}' \leftarrow \mathsf{DPRT}.\mathsf{Erase}\big(1^k, \lambda, (\ell, \mathbf{v}), \{(\ell, r)\}\big)$;

Fig. 4. DVLH.

the encrypted multi-map. Lastly, the Insert algorithm first executes DPRT.Insert on $(\ell, \mathbf{v})$ and an empty multi-map. This outputs a transformed multi-map MM' containing the transformed tuple; ℓ and its corresponding values. The client and the server execute the $\mathsf{STE}_{\mathsf{MM}}^{\mathsf{RH}}$.Put protocol to put the new pair $(\ell, \mathsf{MM}'[\ell])$ into the encrypted multi-map.

Efficiency. If $\mathsf{STE}_{\mathsf{MM}}^{\mathsf{RH}}$ has optimal query complexity, the best and worst case communication complexity for DVLH.Get is the same as VLH.Get which is $O(\lambda)$ and $O(\lambda + \nu)$, where $\nu = 2^s$ is the largest value that can be taken by the pseudo-random function used by the transform. The average case communication complexity is $O(\lambda + 2^{s-1})$. As for storage, it is the same as VLH. A label/tuple deletion has asymptotically the same cost as the $\mathsf{STE}_{\mathsf{MM}}^{\mathsf{RH}}$.Delete protocol. As for Insert, it incurs the same communication cost as $\mathsf{STE}_{\mathsf{MM}}^{\mathsf{RH}}$.Put operation asymptotically, as it executes a Put operation within it.[11] The communication cost of the Append and Erase operations is equal to the sum of the communication costs of the $\mathsf{STE}_{\mathsf{MM}}^{\mathsf{RH}}$.Get, $\mathsf{STE}_{\mathsf{MM}}^{\mathsf{RH}}$.Delete and $\mathsf{STE}_{\mathsf{MM}}^{\mathsf{RH}}$.Put operations asymptotically, as it executes a Get, Delete and Put operations within it.

Correctness. Similarly to $\mathsf{VLH}^{\mathsf{d}}$, the correctness of DVLH is also affected by possible truncations. The difference is that tuples can now be subjected to many truncations. A bound on the number of labels effected by truncations is derived in Sect. 5.2.

Security. We now describe the leakage profile of DVLH assuming $\mathsf{STE}_{\mathsf{MM}}^{\mathsf{RH}}$ is instantiated with one of the standard dynamic multi-map encryption schemes [1,8] all of which have leakage profile $\Lambda_{\mathsf{MM}} = (\mathcal{L}_{\mathsf{S}}, \mathcal{L}_{\mathsf{Q}}, \mathcal{L}_{\mathsf{U}}) = (\mathsf{trlen}, (\mathsf{qeq}, \mathsf{bopeq}, \mathsf{rlen}), \mathsf{ulen})$ where trlen is the total response length ($\mathsf{trlen}(\mathsf{MM}) = \sum_{\ell \in \mathbb{L}} \#\mathsf{MM}[\ell]$), qeq is the query equality pattern that reveals if and when the label has been queried in the past, bopeq is the backward operation equality pattern that reveals whether a query and another operation are over the same label only in the case when the operation occurred before the query, rlen is the response length of a query, and ulen is the number of values in an update. In the following theorem, dsize is the data size pattern which is defined as $\mathsf{dsize}(\mathsf{MM}) = \#\mathbb{L}_{\mathsf{MM}}$ and oeq is the operation equality pattern that captures which operations were over the same label.

Theorem 6. *If* $\mathsf{STE}_{\mathsf{MM}}^{\mathsf{RH}}$ *is a* $(\mathsf{trlen}, (\mathsf{qeq}, \mathsf{bopeq}, \mathsf{rlen}), \mathsf{ulen})$*-secure dynamic multi-map encryption scheme and* F *is a pseudo-random function, then* DVLH *is a* $(\mathsf{dsize}, \mathsf{oeq}, \mathsf{oeq})$*-secure dynamic multi-map encryption scheme.*

The proof of this Theorem is in the full version [2].

Comparison with Existing Work. DVLH is lossy but has a better leakage profile than 2ch and S^4 [3,49]. Zhao, Lam and Wang [51] propose a lossy construction that has the same leakage profile as DVLH with better query complexity but higher update complexity.

---

[11] Note however that, under the assumption of $\mathsf{STE}_{\mathsf{MM}}^{\mathsf{RH}}$ having an optimal query and put complexity, the cost of the Put operation is proportional to the length of the tuple which is in this case equal to $O(\lambda + \nu)$ in the worst case.

5.2   Correctness

To analyze correctness, we need an upper bound on the number of truncations after $t \in \mathbb{N}$ append operations. Here, we use the term "append" interchangeably with "update" since it represents the main non-trivial update. We assume that the updated labels are picked uniformly at random and that only a single value is appended to their tuple.

We focus on multi-maps with Zipf-distributed tuple lengths. More precisely, for a given multi-map size N (i.e., the sum of the tuple lengths) and label space $\mathbb{L}$, we consider multi-maps with tuple lenghts in

$$L = \left\{ \frac{N}{H_{m,1}}, \frac{N}{2 \cdot H_{m,1}}, \dots, \frac{N}{m \cdot H_{m,1}} \right\},$$

where $m \overset{\circ}{=} \#\mathbb{L}$. Before stating our theorem we recall some useful Lemmas related to *negative association*.

Lemma 1 (Independence implies negative association [23]). *If $X_1, \dots, X_n$ are independent random variables, then they are negatively associated.*

Lemma 2 (Zero-one principle [23]). *If $X_1, \dots, X_n$ are zero-one random variables such that $\sum_{i=1}^{n} X_i \leq 1$, then they are negatively associated.*

Lemma 3 (Closure [23]). *Negatively associated random variables satisfy the following closure properties:*

- *if $X_1, \dots, X_n$ are negatively associated, if $Y_1, \dots, Y_m$ are negatively associated, and if $\{X_i\}_i$ and $\{Y_j\}_j$ are mutually independent, then $X_1, \dots, X_n, Y_1, \dots, Y_m$ are negatively associated.*
- *let $X_1, \dots, X_n$ be negatively associated random variables and let $I_1, \dots, I_k \subseteq [n]$ be disjoint index sets for $k \geq 1$. Furthermore, let $\{h_j : \mathbb{R}^{\#I_j} \to \mathbb{R}\}_{j \in [k]}$ be a set of functions that are all either non-decreasing or all non-increasing and define $Y_j := h_j(X_i, i \in I_j)$. Then $Y_1, \cdots, Y_k$ are negatively associated. In other words, non-decreasing or non-increasing functions of disjoint subsets of negatively associated variables are also negatively associated.*

Theorem 7. *If the tuple lengths of a multi-map are assigned to labels uniformly at random from L (without replacement) and if the update labels are sampled independently and uniformly at random from $\mathbb{L}$, then after t updates the number of truncations is at most*

$$\mu + \sqrt{\frac{m \cdot (t+1) \ln(1/\epsilon)}{2}}$$

with probability at least $1 - \epsilon$, where

$$\mu \leq \frac{1}{\nu} \left(\frac{N \cdot H_{\rho,1}}{H_{m,1}} - \lambda \cdot \rho + \frac{\lambda \cdot N \cdot H_{\rho,1}}{m \cdot H_{m,1}} + \frac{(t-\lambda)}{m} \left(N + (t-\lambda)m \right) \right)$$

for all $m, \lambda \in \mathbb{N}$, $t \geq \lambda$ and $\rho = \lfloor N/(\lambda \cdot H_{m,1}) \rfloor$.

The proof of this Theorem is in the full version [2].

6   An Injection-Secure SSE Scheme

We now present the first searchable symmetric encryption scheme that is secure against injection attacks; i.e., that protects pre- and post-injection queries. The construction can be viewed as a variant of the OPQ scheme of [6] with the underlying multi-map encryption scheme instantiated with FIX and with a simple but important modification. Before describing this change, however, it is useful to consider what happens if we were to use OPQ as-is.

The OPQ Scheme. At a high level, the OPQ searchable symmetric encryption scheme is based on an encrypted multi-map but uses it differently than the traditional index-based approach to designing SSE. In other words, instead of encrypting the documents in the collection with a standard encryption scheme and using an EMM to map keywords to document identifiers, OPQ maps the keywords to tuples that consist of the *documents* that contain the keyword. This of course comes at a price in storage but as observed in [6] it suppresses co-occurrence leakage. So one (flawed) attempt at constructing an SSE scheme secure against injection attacks would be to use the OPQ scheme with FIX as its underlying EMM. The problem with this approach is that the insert and delete operations of OPQ reveal the size of the added/deleted document *independently* of the underlying EMM's add/delete leakage profile. This, in turn, means that using OPQ even with FIX as its underlying EMM would not result in an SSE scheme with the appropriate leakage profile.

Overview. To address the limitation discussed above, we modify OPQ so that whenever a document is added or deleted, FIX's insert and delete operations are only invoked a fixed number of times θ which is a public parameter. The scheme, SSE = (Setup, Search, Insert, Delete), is detailed in Fig. 5 and works as follows.

Setup. The Setup algorithm takes as input a security parameter 1^k and a document collection $\mathbb{D} = (D_1, \ldots, D_n)$, where each document D_i is composed of keywords from some space $\mathbb{W}$. It first builds a multi-map MM that maps each keyword $w \in \mathbb{W}$ to a tuple $\mathbf{t} = (t_1, \ldots, t_m)$ constructed as follows. First, it finds the set of documents that contain the keyword w which we denote $\mathbb{D}(w) = \{D \in \mathbb{D} : w \in D\}$. It then concatenates all the documents in $\mathbb{D}(w) = (D_{z_1}, \ldots, D_{z_m})$ resulting in a document $\mathcal{D}^\star = D_{z_1} \| \cdots \| D_{z_m}$. The tuple element t_i of $\mathbf{t}$ is then the ith B-sized block of $\mathcal{D}^\star$, where $B \in \mathbb{N}_{\geq 1}$. For simplicity we assume that, for all $D \in \mathbb{D}$, $|D|$ is a multiple of B but if this isn't the case we just pad the last block to be of size B. It then runs FIX.Setup on MM and outputs a key K, a state st and an encrypted multi-map EMM. Finally, the client outputs the key K, the state st and the encrypted document collection EDB = EMM.

Search. This is a two-party protocol between the client and the server. The client and server execute the FIX.Get protocol where the client's input consists of the key K, the state st and a keyword $w \in \mathbb{W}$, whereas the server's input consists

Let $\theta, B \in \mathbb{N}$ and $\mathsf{FIX} = (\mathsf{Setup}, \mathsf{Get}_{\mathbf{C},\mathbf{S}}, \mathsf{Append}_{\mathbf{C},\mathbf{S}}, \mathsf{Erase}_{\mathbf{C},\mathbf{S}})$ be the dynamic multi-map encryption scheme as defined in Figures (1) and (2). Consider a searchable symmetric encryption scheme $\mathsf{SSE} = (\mathsf{Setup}, \mathsf{Search}_{\mathbf{C},\mathbf{S}}, \mathsf{Insert}_{\mathbf{C},\mathbf{S}}, \mathsf{Delete}_{\mathbf{C},\mathbf{S}})$ as follows:

- $\mathsf{Setup}(1^k, \mathsf{DC})$:
  1. initialize an empty multi-map MM;
  2. For each $w \in \mathbb{W}$,
     (a) compute $(D_1, \ldots, D_n) := \mathsf{DC}(w)$;
     (b) set $D^* := D_1 \| D_2 \| \ldots \| D_n$;
     (c) set $\mathbf{t} := (t_1, \ldots, t_m)$, where $m = |D^*|/B$ and t_i is the ith B-sized block of D^*;
     (d) set $\mathsf{MM}[w] := \mathbf{t}$;
  3. compute $(K, st, \mathsf{EMM}) \leftarrow \mathsf{FIX.Setup}(1^k, \mathsf{MM})$;
  4. output K, st, and $\mathsf{EDC} := \mathsf{EMM}$.
- $\mathsf{Search}_{\mathbf{C},\mathbf{S}}((K, st, w), \mathsf{EDC})$:
  1. $\mathbf{C}$ and $\mathbf{S}$ execute
  $$(\mathbf{v}, \perp) \leftarrow \mathsf{FIX.Get}_{\mathbf{C},\mathbf{S}}((K, st, w), \mathsf{EDC});$$
  2. $\mathbf{C}$ outputs $\mathbf{v}$ and $\mathbf{S}$ outputs $\perp$.
- $\mathsf{Insert}_{\mathbf{C},\mathbf{S}}((K, st, D), \mathsf{EDC})$:
  1. set $\mathbf{t} := (t_1, \ldots, t_m)$, where $m = |D|/B$ and t_i is the ith B-sized block of D;
  2. for each $w \in \mathbb{W}_D$, $\mathbf{C}$ and $\mathbf{S}$ execute
  $$(st', \mathsf{EDC}') \leftarrow \mathsf{FIX.Append}_{\mathbf{C},\mathbf{S}}((K, st, (w, \mathbf{t})), \mathsf{EDC});$$
  3. for all $i \in [\theta - \#\mathbb{W}_D]$, $\mathbf{C}$ and $\mathbf{S}$ execute
  $$(st'', \mathsf{EDC}'') \leftarrow \mathsf{FIX.Append}_{\mathbf{C},\mathbf{S}}((K, st, (\perp, \{\perp\})), \mathsf{EDC}');$$
  4. $\mathbf{C}$ outputs $st = st''$ whereas $\mathbf{S}$ outputs $\mathsf{EDC} = \mathsf{EDC}''$.
- $\mathsf{Delete}_{\mathbf{C},\mathbf{S}}((K, st, D), \mathsf{EDC})$:
  1. set $\mathbf{t} := (t_1, \ldots, t_m)$, where $m = |D|/B$ and t_i is the ith B-sized block of D;
  2. for each $w \in D$, $\mathbf{C}$ and $\mathbf{S}$ execute
  $$(st', \mathsf{EDC}') \leftarrow \mathsf{FIX.Erase}_{\mathbf{C},\mathbf{S}}((K, st, (w, t)), \mathsf{EDC});$$
  3. for all $i \in [\theta - \#\mathbb{W}_D]$, $\mathbf{C}$ and $\mathbf{S}$ execute
  $$(st', \mathsf{EDC}'') \leftarrow \mathsf{FIX.Erase}_{\mathbf{C},\mathbf{S}}((K, st, (\perp, \{\perp\})), \mathsf{EDC}');$$
  4. $\mathbf{C}$ outputs $st = st''$ and $\mathbf{S}$ outputs $\mathsf{EDC} = \mathsf{EDC}''$.

Fig. 5. The SSE searchable symmetric encryption scheme.

of the encrypted document collection EDB. The client outputs the subset of documents $\mathbb{D}(w)$ and the server outputs $\bot$.[12]

Insert. This is a two-party protocol between the client and the server. Given a document D, the client builds a tuple $\mathbf{t} = (t_1, \ldots, t_m)$ composed of B-sized blocks, where $m = |\mathsf{D}|/B$. The client extracts all keywords $\mathbb{W}_\mathsf{D}$ in document D. Then, for each $w \in \mathbb{W}_\mathsf{D}$, the client and server execute FIX.Append where the client's input is K, st and an update $u = (\mathsf{app}, w, \mathbf{t})$ and the server's input is the encrypted document collection EDB. Then, for all $i \in [\theta - \#\mathbb{W}_\mathsf{D}]$, the client and the server execute FIX.Append where the client's input is K, st and an update $u = (\mathsf{app}, \bot, \{\bot\})$ and the server's input is the encrypted document collection EDB. Finally, the client outputs an updated state st' whereas the server outputs an updated encrypted document collection EDB′.

Delete. The Delete protocol is the same as the Insert protocol except that instead of executing FIX.Append, the client and server execute FIX.Erase.

Efficiency. The communication and computational complexities of SSE.Search are the same as the communication and computational complexities of FIX.Get since the former just executes the latter. Once executing the setup protocol and before any update operation, the expected storage complexity is equal to $O((\lambda + \nu) \cdot \#\mathbb{W} \cdot B)$ where B is the block size and ν is the output size of the pseudorandom function in both VLH and DVLH. The size of the stash in the worst-case is at most $\#\mathbb{W}/\mu \cdot |D^\star|$ where $D^\star$ is the largest document stored by SSE.[13] The communication and computational complexities of SSE.Insert and SSE.Delete are θ times the complexities of FIX.Append and FIX.Erase, respectively. Using the same parameters we used to analyze the concrete efficiency of FIX and under the same assumptions, the complexity of SSE.Insert and SSE.Delete is $O(\theta \cdot \log^2(\#\mathbb{L}))$.

Security. The leakage profile of SSE is the same as FIX since all of the former's operations just execute the latter's operations. The only difference is that during Insert and Delete operations θ Append and Erase operations occur but since θ is a public parameter there is no additional leakage. It follows then by Theorem 1 that SSE is secure against file injection attacks.

References

1. Amjad, G., Kamara, S., Moataz, T.: Breach-resistant structured encryption. Proc. Privacy Enhanc. Technol. **245–265**(01), 2019 (2019)
2. Amjad, G., Kamara, S., Moataz, T.: Injection-secure structured and searchable symmetric encryption. Cryptology ePrint Archive (2023)

---

[12] Note that FIX is a black-box construction that, itself, makes use of static and dynamic multi-map encryption schemes. Depending on the correctness guarantees provided by the underlying concrete instantiations, the final output of FIX.Get will vary. For simplicity, we assume here that FIX is instantiated with perfectly correct EMMs.

[13] As shown in Sect. 4, a more realistic bound can also be derived under the assumption that the documents are sampled from some specific distribution such as the Zipf distribution.

3. Amjad, G., Patel, S., Persiano, G., Yeo, K., Yung, M.: Dynamic volume-hiding encrypted multi-maps with applications to searchable encryption. Cryptology ePrint Archive (2021)
4. Asharov, G., Naor, M., Segev, G., Shahaf, I.: Searchable symmetric encryption: Optimal locality in linear space via two-dimensional balanced allocations. In: ACM Symposium on Theory of Computing (STOC '16), STOC '16, pp. 1101–1114, New York, NY, USA, ACM (2016)
5. Asharov, G., Segev, G., Shahaf, I.: Tight tradeoffs in searchable symmetric encryption. J. Cryptol. **34**(2), 1–37 (2021). https://doi.org/10.1007/s00145-020-09370-z
6. Blackstone, L., Kamara, S., Moataz, T.: Revisiting leakage abuse attacks. IACR Cryptol. ePrint Arch. **2019**, 1175 (2019)
7. Blackstone, L., Kamara, S., Moataz, T.: Revisiting leakage abuse attacks. In: 27th Annual Network and Distributed System Security Symposium, NDSS 2020, San Diego, California, USA, February 23–26, 2020. The Internet Society (2020)
8. Bost, R.: Sophos - forward secure searchable encryption. In: ACM Conference on Computer and Communications Security (CCS '16) (2016)
9. Bost, R., Fouque, P.-A.: Thwarting leakage abuse attacks against searchable encryption-a formal approach and applications to database padding. Cryptology ePrint Archive (2017)
10. Bost, R., Minaud, B., Ohrimenko, O.: Forward and backward private searchable encryption from constrained cryptographic primitives. In: ACM Conference on Computer and Communications Security (CCS '17) (2017)
11. Cash, D., Grubbs, P., Perry, J., Ristenpart, T.: Leakage-abuse attacks against searchable encryption. In: ACM Conference on Communications and Computer Security (CCS '15), pp. 668–679. ACM (2015)
12. Cash, D.: Dynamic searchable encryption in very-large databases: data structures and implementation. In: Network and Distributed System Security Symposium (NDSS '14) (2014)
13. Cash, D., Jarecki, S., Jutla, C., Krawczyk, H., Roşu, M.-C., Steiner, M.: Highly-scalable searchable symmetric encryption with support for boolean queries. In: Canetti, R., Garay, J.A. (eds.) CRYPTO 2013. LNCS, vol. 8042, pp. 353–373. Springer, Heidelberg (2013). https://doi.org/10.1007/978-3-642-40041-4_20
14. Cash, D., Ng, R., Rivkin, A.: Improved Structured Encryption for SQL Databases via Hybrid Indexing. In: Sako, K., Tippenhauer, N.O. (eds.) ACNS 2021. LNCS, vol. 12727, pp. 480–510. Springer, Cham (2021). https://doi.org/10.1007/978-3-030-78375-4_19
15. Cash, D., Tessaro, S.: The locality of searchable symmetric encryption. In: Nguyen, P.Q., Oswald, E. (eds.) EUROCRYPT 2014. LNCS, vol. 8441, pp. 351–368. Springer, Heidelberg (2014). https://doi.org/10.1007/978-3-642-55220-5_20
16. Chase, M., Kamara, S.: Structured encryption and controlled disclosure. In: Abe, M. (ed.) ASIACRYPT 2010. LNCS, vol. 6477, pp. 577–594. Springer, Heidelberg (2010). https://doi.org/10.1007/978-3-642-17373-8_33
17. Curtmola, R., Garay, J., Kamara, S., Ostrovsky, R.: Searchable symmetric encryption: improved definitions and efficient constructions. In: ACM Conference on Computer and Communications Security (CCS '06), pp. 79–88. ACM, (2006)
18. Demertzis, I., Chamani, J.G., Papadopoulos, D., Papamanthou, C.: Dynamic searchable encryption with small client storage. IACR Cryptol. ePrint Arch. **2019**, 1227 (2019)
19. Demertzis, I., Papadopoulos, D., Papamanthou, C.: Searchable encryption with optimal locality: achieving sublogarithmic read efficiency. IACR Cryptology ePrint Archive **2017**, 749 (2017)

20. Demertzis, I., Papadopoulos, D., Papamanthou, C.: Searchable encryption with optimal locality: achieving sublogarithmic read efficiency. In: Shacham, H., Boldyreva, A. (eds.) CRYPTO 2018. LNCS, vol. 10991, pp. 371–406. Springer, Cham (2018). https://doi.org/10.1007/978-3-319-96884-1_13

21. Demertzis, I., Papadopoulos, D., Papamanthou, C., Shintre, S.: {SEAL}: Attack mitigation for encrypted databases via adjustable leakage. In: 29th USENIX Security Symposium (USENIX Security 20), pp. 2433–2450 (2020)

22. Demertzis, I., Papamanthou, C.: Fast searchable encryption with tunable locality. In: ACM International Conference on Management of Data (SIGMOD '17), SIGMOD '17, pp. 1053–1067, New York, NY, USA, (2017)

23. Dubhashi, D.P., Ranjan, D.: Balls and bins: a study in negative dependence. BRICS Report Series, **3**(25) (1996)

24. Etemad, M., Küpçü, A., Papamanthou, C., Evans, D.: Efficient dynamic searchable encryption with forward privacy. PoPETs '**18**(1) (2018)

25. Faber, S., Jarecki, S., Krawczyk, H., Nguyen, Q., Rosu, M., Steiner, M.: Rich queries on encrypted data: beyond exact matches. In: Pernul, G., Ryan, P.Y.A., Weippl, E. (eds.) ESORICS 2015. LNCS, vol. 9327, pp. 123–145. Springer, Cham (2015). https://doi.org/10.1007/978-3-319-24177-7_7

26. George, M., Kamara, S., Moataz, T.: Structured encryption and dynamic leakage suppression. In: Canteaut, A., Standaert, F.-X. (eds.) EUROCRYPT 2021. LNCS, vol. 12698, pp. 370–396. Springer, Cham (2021). https://doi.org/10.1007/978-3-030-77883-5_13

27. Ghareh Chamani, J., Papadopoulos, D., Papamanthou, C., Jalili, R.: New constructions for forward and backward private symmetric searchable encryption. In: Proceedings of the 2018 ACM SIGSAC Conference on Computer and Communications Security, CCS '18, ACM, pp. 1038–1055, New York, NY, USA (2018)

28. Goldreich, O., Ostrovsky, R.: Software protection and simulation on oblivious RAMs. J. ACM **43**(3), 431–473 (1996)

29. Gui, Z., Paterson, K.G., Patranabis, S., Warinschi, B.: Swissse: system-wide security for searchable symmetric encryption. Cryptology ePrint Archive, Paper 2020/1328 (2020). https://eprint.iacr.org/2020/1328

30. Hahn, F., Kerschbaum, F.: Searchable encryption with secure and efficient updates. In: ACM Conference on Computer and Communications Security (CCS '14), CCS '14, ACM, pp. 310–320, New York, NY, USA, (2014)

31. Islam, M.S., Kuzu, M., Kantarcioglu, M.: Access pattern disclosure on searchable encryption: Ramification, attack and mitigation. In: Network and Distributed System Security Symposium (NDSS '12) (2012)

32. Kamara, S., Moataz, T.: SQL on structurally-encrypted databases. In: Peyrin, T., Galbraith, S. (eds.) ASIACRYPT 2018. LNCS, vol. 11272, pp. 149–180. Springer, Cham (2018). https://doi.org/10.1007/978-3-030-03326-2_6

33. Kamara, S., Moataz, T.: SQL on structurally-encrypted databases. IACR Cryptol. ePrint Archive **2016**, 453 (2016)

34. Kamara, S., Moataz, T.: Boolean Searchable Symmetric Encryption with Worst-Case Sub-linear Complexity. In: Coron, J.-S., Nielsen, J.B. (eds.) EUROCRYPT 2017. LNCS, vol. 10212, pp. 94–124. Springer, Cham (2017). https://doi.org/10.1007/978-3-319-56617-7_4

35. Kamara, S., Moataz, T.: Computationally Volume-Hiding Structured Encryption. In: Ishai, Y., Rijmen, V. (eds.) EUROCRYPT 2019. LNCS, vol. 11477, pp. 183–213. Springer, Cham (2019). https://doi.org/10.1007/978-3-030-17656-3_7

36. Kamara, S., Moataz, T., Ohrimenko, O.: Structured encryption and leakage suppression. In: Shacham, H., Boldyreva, A. (eds.) CRYPTO 2018. LNCS, vol. 10991, pp. 339–370. Springer, Cham (2018). https://doi.org/10.1007/978-3-319-96884-1_12

37. Kamara, S., Papamanthou, C.: Parallel and dynamic searchable symmetric encryption. In: Sadeghi, A.-R. (ed.) FC 2013. LNCS, vol. 7859, pp. 258–274. Springer, Heidelberg (2013). https://doi.org/10.1007/978-3-642-39884-1_22

38. Kamara, S., Papamanthou, C., Roeder, T.: Dynamic searchable symmetric encryption. In: ACM Conference on Computer and Communications Security (CCS '12). ACM Press (2012)

39. Katz, J., Lindell, Y.: Lindell. Introduction to Modern Cryptography. Chapman & Hall/CRC (2008)

40. Kim, K.S., Kim, M., Lee, D., Park, J.H., Kim, W.H.: Forward secure dynamic searchable symmetric encryption with efficient updates. In: Proceedings of the 2017 ACM SIGSAC Conference on Computer and Communications Security, pp. 1449–1463 (2017)

41. Miers, I., Mohassel, P.: Io-dsse: Scaling dynamic searchable encryption to millions of indexes by improving locality. Cryptology ePrint Archive, Report 2016/830 (2016). http://eprint.iacr.org/2016/830

42. Pappas, V.: Blind seer: A scalable private DBMS. In: Security and Privacy (SP). In: 2014 IEEE Symposium on, pp. 359–374. IEEE (2014)

43. Patel, S., Persiano, G., Yeo, K.: Leakage cell probe model: Lower bounds for key-equality mitigation in encrypted multi-maps. Cryptology ePrint Archive, Report 2019/1132, 2019. https://eprint.iacr.org/2019/1132

44. Patel, S., Persiano, G., Yeo, K., Yung, M.: Mitigating leakage in secure cloud-hosted data structures: Volume-hiding for multi-maps via hashing. In: Proceedings of the 2019 ACM SIGSAC Conference on Computer and Communications Security, CCS '19, pp. 79–93, New York, NY, USA, 2019. Association for Computing Machinery

45. Patranabis, S., Mukhopadhyay, D.: Forward and backward private conjunctive searchable symmetric encryption. In: NDSS Symposium 2021 (virtual) (2021)

46. Song, D., Wagner, D., Perrig, A.: Practical techniques for searching on encrypted data. In: IEEE Symposium on Research in Security and Privacy, pages 44–55. IEEE Computer Society (2000)

47. Stefanov, E., Papamanthou, C., Shi, E.: Practical dynamic searchable encryption with small leakage. In: Network and Distributed System Security Symposium (NDSS '14) (2014)

48. Stefanov, E., et al.: Path oram: An extremely simple oblivious ram protocol. In: ACM Conference on Computer and Communications Security (CCS '13) (2013)

49. Wang, J., Chow, S.S.M.: Simple storage-saving structure for volume-hiding encrypted multi-maps. In: Barker, K., Ghazinour, K. (eds.) DBSec 2021. LNCS, vol. 12840, pp. 63–83. Springer, Cham (2021). https://doi.org/10.1007/978-3-030-81242-3_4

50. Zhang, Y., Katz, J., Papamanthou, C.: All your queries are belong to us: the power of file-injection attacks on searchable encryption. In: USENIX Security Symposium (2016)

51. Zhao, Y., Wang, H., Lam, K.Y.: Volume-hiding dynamic searchable symmetric encryption with forward and backward privacy. Cryptology ePrint Archive (2021)

Hermes: I/O-Efficient Forward-Secure Searchable Symmetric Encryption

Brice Minaud[1] and Michael Reichle[2(✉)]

[1] École Normale Supérieure, PSL University, CNRS, Inria, Paris, France
[2] ETH Zürich, Zurich, Switzerland
`michael.reichle@ens.fr`

Abstract. Dynamic Symmetric Searchable Encryption (SSE) enables a user to outsource the storage of an encrypted database to an untrusted server, while retaining the ability to privately search and update the outsourced database. The performance bottleneck of SSE schemes typically comes from their I/O efficiency. Over the last decade, a line of work has substantially improved that bottleneck. However, all existing I/O-efficient SSE schemes have a common limitation: they are not forward-secure. Since the seminal work of Bost at CCS 2016, forward security has become a de facto standard in SSE. In the same article, Bost conjectures that forward security and I/O efficiency are incompatible. This explains the current status quo, where users are forced to make a difficult choice between security and efficiency.

The central contribution of this paper it to show that, contrary to what the status quo suggests, forward security and I/O efficiency can be realized simultaneously. This result is enabled by two new key techniques. First, we make use of a controlled amount of client buffering, combined with a deterministic update schedule. Second, we introduce the notion of SSE supporting *dummy updates*. In combination, those two techniques offer a new path to realizing forward security, which is compatible with I/O efficiency. Our new SSE scheme, Hermes, achieves sublogarithmic I/O efficiency $\widetilde{\mathcal{O}}\left(\log\log\frac{N}{p}\right)$, storage efficiency $\mathcal{O}(1)$, with standard leakage, as well as backward and forward security. Practical experiments confirm that Hermes achieves excellent performance.

1 Introduction

Encrypted databases are an attractive proposition. A business or hospital may want to outsource its customer database for higher availability, scalability, or persistence, without entrusting plaintext data to an external service. An end-to-end encrypted messaging service may want to store and search user messages, without decrypting them. In a different direction, even if a sensitive database is stored locally, a company may want to keep it encrypted to provide a layer of protection against security breaches and data theft. The adoption by MongoDB

M. Reichle—This work was carried out while the second author was employed by Inria, Paris.

© International Association for Cryptologic Research 2023
J. Guo and R. Steinfeld (Eds.): ASIACRYPT 2023, LNCS 14443, pp. 263–294, 2023.
https://doi.org/10.1007/978-981-99-8736-8_9

of searchable encryption techniques is another recent illustration of the growing demand for encrypted databases [22].

When outsourcing the storage of an encrypted database, a minimal desirable functionality is the ability to search the data. Powerful techniques such as Fully Homomorphic Encryption and Multi-Party Computation allow arbitrary computation on encrypted data, but those approaches incur large overheads, and become prohibitive at scale. At the other end of the spectrum, efficient historical approaches based on structure-preserving or order-preserving encryption are subject to severe attacks, due to the large amount of information leaked to the server [17,23]. In view of this situation, modern research on searchable encryption seeks to offer workable trade-offs between performance, functionality, and security, suited for real-world deployment.

Searchable Symmetric Encryption (SSE). The promise of SSE is to allow a client to outsource an encrypted database to an untrusted server, while retaining the ability to search the data [25]. At minimum, the client is able to issue a search query to retrieve all document identifiers that match a given keyword. In the case of *Dynamic* SSE, the client is also able to modify the contents of the database by issuing update queries, for example to insert or remove entries. The server must be able to correctly process the queries, while learning as little information as possible about the client's data and queries. The security proof accompanying an SSE scheme provides formal guarantees regarding what information is leaked to the server during searches and updates. Typically, this information includes the total size of the database, the repetition of queries, and an identifier (such as the memory address) of the documents that match a query.

Forward Security. In short, forward security asks that updates should leak no information to the server [26]. The first efficient forward-secure SSE was proposed by Bost at CCS 2016 [6]. Since then, forward security has become a de facto standard in SSE [8,13,16,18,24]. One motivation for forward security cited in [6] is that it mitigates certain attacks: the more severe attacks from [27] exploit update leakage, and fail on forward-secure schemes. Forward security is also attractive in update-heavy workloads, for instance a private messaging app. In that setting, the encrypted database is initially empty, and its entire contents are added online through updates. Forward security guarantees that building the database online leaks no information.

I/O Efficiency. Another important design goal for SSE that has emerged in recent years is I/O efficiency [11]. For performance reasons, most SSE designs rely exclusively on symmetric cryptographic primitives. The overhead of symmetric encryption is very small on modern hardware. As a result, the main performance bottleneck is instead determined by how quickly the data can be accessed on disk [5,6,10]. In a nutshell, I/O efficiency asks that lists of identifiers matching the same query should be stored close together in memory, at least at the page level. This is because reading many disjoint locations on disk is much more expensive in latency and throughput than contiguous reads.

The need to store related data in close proximity is not at all innocuous for security. Asking that related data items should be stored in close proximity creates a correlation between the *location* of an encrypted data item in memory, and its *contents*. Since the server can observe the location of data it is asked to retrieve, and we do not want the server to infer information about the contents of that data, this creates a tension between security and efficiency. That is, security asks that there is no correlation between the location of data and its content, while I/O efficiency asks for the opposite.

This tension was captured in an impossibility result by Cash and Tessaro at Eurocrypt 2014 [11]. To measure I/O efficiency, [11] introduces notions of *locality* (number of non-adjacent memory locations accessed per query) and *read efficiency* (ratio between the total amount of memory read by the server to process a query, and the size of the plaintext answer). In brief, Cash and Tessaro show that a secure SSE scheme with linear server storage cannot have both constant locality, and constant read efficiency. This holds true even for static SSE. In another seminal work, at STOC 2016, Asharov *et al.* build an SSE with constant locality and $\widetilde{\mathcal{O}}(\log N)$ read efficiency—even $\widetilde{\mathcal{O}}(\log \log N)$ with a mild restriction on the input database [1].

A different measure of I/O efficiency, called page efficiency, was introduced by Bossuat *et al.* at Crypto 2021 [5] (the same metric was implicit in prior work [20]). Page efficiency is the ratio of memory pages read by the server to process a query, divided by the number of pages necessary to hold the plaintext answer. From a practical standpoint, page efficiency is a very good predictor of performance on modern Solid State Drives (SSDs), whereas locality is mainly relevant for older Hard Disk Drives [5]. From a theoretical standpoint, constant page efficiency is a weaker requirement than the combination and constant locality and constant read efficiency. Interestingly, this weaker requirement sidesteps the impossibility result of Cash and Tessaro: Bossuat *et al.* build a scheme with linear server storage and constant page efficiency [5].

Since the work of Cash and Tessaro [11], many I/O-efficient schemes have been proposed. Of these, the vast majority hold in the *static* setting [1,2,5,11,14,15], where the database is fixed at setup, and does not support updates. To our knowledge, only two constructions have been proposed in the *dynamic* setting, where the database can be updated. The first was presented by Miers and Mohassel at NDSS 2017 under the name IO-DSSE [20]. The second is a recent result presented by Minaud and Reichle at Crypto 2022 [21]. IO-DSSE has non-standard leakage, and incurs a significant performance overhead due to its reliance on an ORAM approach. Further, the security proof is flawed and we give a concrete attack in this work. On the other hand, the main construction of Minaud and Reichle is a theoretical feasibility result, with no instantiation. Neither scheme is forward-secure.

1.1   Our Contributions

Both SSE design goals, I/O efficiency and forward security, date back to 2014 [11,26]. Almost a decade later, there is no satisfactory solution to achieving both at once. This is not a coincidence: the two goals seem to be fundamentally at odds with each other, and it was even conjectured in [6] that both notions are incompatible. While [6] argues only about locality for SSE (page efficiency did not exist at the time), the same argument directly translates to page efficiency. To sum up the argument: a correlation between the identifiers $\mathsf{DB}(w)$ matching keyword w and a newly inserted identifier also matching w breaks forward security. On the other hand, identifiers matching the same keyword w need to be stored in close proximity to satisfy page efficiency. Note that accessing correlated pages still breaks forward security. Consequently, an identifier cannot be written to the server, unless $\mathsf{DB}(w)$ is partially rewritten for each access, in an ORAM-like manner.

This state of affairs raises some troubling questions for SSE. Since I/O efficiency is the main performance bottleneck, if it is mutually exclusive with forward security, then forward security comes at a heavy performance price—hinting at a stronger form of Cash and Tessaro's impossibility result when forward security comes into play. It would also imply that the rich literature on I/O-efficient SSE will have to remain confined to static SSE, or at least non-forward-secure SSE. So far, the conjecture is supported by current work: [6] conjectures that I/O efficiency and forward security are "irreconcilable notions", except via expensive constructions such as ORAM; [20] builds the only dynamic I/O-efficient SSE scheme to date with low update leakage (although still not quite forward-secure), but relies on ORAM; and the only other dynamic I/O-efficient SSE in [21] justifies its high update leakage by stating that forward security is likely expensive for I/O-efficient SSE.

As a first contribution, we give an explicit attack that contradicts the security claim of IO-DSSE [20] in the full version. Our attack leverages a subtle update leakage in IO-DSSE, which was introduced through an optimization of the underlying ORAM. This would seem to further support the conjecture of [6].

As our main contribution, we go against the prevailing wisdom, and show that the previous conjecture is incorrect. We build the first *forward-secure* SSE scheme, Hermes, with linear server storage and sublogarithmic page efficiency $\tilde{\mathcal{O}}\left(\log\log(N/p)\right)$. Notably, Hermes is the first I/O-efficient SSE scheme with forward security. We note that this holds with regard to page efficiency: the question of building a similar scheme with respect to locality remains an intriguing open question. A brief comparison with existing schemes is given in Table 1. Hermes does not rely on ORAM, or any ORAM-like structure. Instead, it makes use of two new technical ideas.

First, we introduce the notion of SSE schemes supporting *dummy updates*. A dummy update can be triggered by the client at any time, and must look indistinguishable from a real update in the server's view. On the other hand, we require that server storage should only grow with an upper bound N on the number of *real* entries in the database: dummy updates create no storage overhead. We present a simple framework to build an SSE scheme $\mathsf{Dummy}(\Sigma)$ supporting dummy updates, based on an underlying suitable SSE scheme Σ. The framework is based on an application of the two-choice allocation process.

Table 1. An overview of relevant dynamic SSE schemes. N is an upper bound on database size, W is an upper bound on the number of keywords, p is the page size.

SSE	Page Efficiency	Storage Efficiency	Client Storage	Forward Sec.
$\Sigma o\phi o\varsigma$, Diana [6,8]	$\mathcal{O}(p)$	$\mathcal{O}(1)$	$\mathcal{O}(W)$	✓
Π_{pack}, Π_{2lev} [9]	$\mathcal{O}(1)$	$\mathcal{O}(p)$	$\mathcal{O}(W)$	✗
IO-DSSE [20]	$\mathcal{O}(\log W)$	$\mathcal{O}\left(1 + \frac{p \cdot W}{N}\right)$	$\mathcal{O}(W)$	✗
LayeredSSE [21]	$\widetilde{\mathcal{O}}\left(\log\log \frac{N}{p}\right)$	$\mathcal{O}(1)$	$\mathcal{O}(1)$	✗
Hermes	$\widetilde{\mathcal{O}}\left(\log\log \frac{N}{p}\right)$	$\mathcal{O}(1)$	$\mathcal{O}(W)$	✓

The second main technical idea is a form of "deamortized" trivial ORAM. An explanation of this technique is deferred to the technical overview below. For now, we note that it involves buffering $\mathcal{O}(W)$ updates on the client side before pushing them to the server, where W is an upper bound on the number of searchable keywords. It was proved in [7] that single-round forward-secure SSE requires $\Omega(W)$ client storage. As a consequence, the new buffer does not increase client storage beyond a constant factor[1]. Interestingly, it is the use of client storage that circumvents the proof sketched in [6] for the incompatibility of forward security and I/O efficiency.

In Sect. 7, we run experiments to choose concrete parameters for Hermes. Although our main contribution is qualitative (showing that forward security and I/O efficiency are compatible), practical experiments show that Hermes performs very well in practice, being outpaced only by purely static schemes.

1.2 Related Work

Several research directions are active within Searchable Encryption. Here, we focus on I/O efficiency. A brief overview of other directions is given in the full version.

The importance of I/O efficiency, and the relevant literature, were presented in the introduction. We do not repeat them here. We simply recall that most prior work on I/O-efficient SSE is limited to *static* SSE [1,2,5,11,14,15], where the database is known in advance and immutable. We are interested in *dynamic* I/O-efficient SSE, which allows for updates to the database. Despite the obvious practical importance of mutable databases, there is still very little work in that area—likely owing to both recency and technical difficulty. We are aware of only two constructions of dynamic I/O-efficient SSE. Since they are directly comparable with this work, they deserve special attention.

The first construction of I/O-efficient Dynamic SSE was presented by Miers and Mohassel at NDSS 2017, under the name IO-DSSE [20]. IO-DSSE opened the

---

[1] Although $\mathcal{O}(W)$ client storage is inherent to sublogarithmic forward-secure SSE as just noted, in practice, this cost may be too high for some applications. Practical tradeoffs to reduce client storage are discussed in the full version.

way in a new area, but suffers from significant limitations. Intuitively, I/O efficiency requires that document identifiers that match the same keyword should be stored in close proximity. For that purpose, IO-DSSE groups identifiers matching the same keyword into *blocks* of a fixed size p. Since the number of documents matching a given keyword need not be a multiple of p, it is usually the case that one of the blocks is *incomplete*, *i.e.* it contains less than p identifiers. As in other works on I/O-efficient SSE, the main technical issue is how to efficiently handle incomplete blocks. Especially, when a new document matching a given keyword is added to the database, the document identifier needs to be appended to the incomplete block associated with the keyword. In that process, it is unclear how to hide to the server which incomplete block is being modified.

The solution proposed by IO-DSSE is to store incomplete blocks in an optimized Oblivious RAM (ORAM) construction. ORAM is a generic solution to hide memory access patterns, but is notoriously expensive in practice. In IO-DSSE, this approach is viable, because IO-DSSE focuses on use cases with few searchable keywords: they target a messaging app scenario, and assume in their experiments that no more than 350 keywords are searchable. Because the number of keywords is small, and there can be at most one incomplete block per keyword, the ORAM overhead remains manageable. By contrast, if we were to run IO-DSSE on the English Wikipedia database (a classic target in SSE literature), which contains millions of keywords, IO-DSSE blows up the size of the database by a factor more than 100 (Sect. 7). A second limitation of IO-DSSE is that its security claim is incorrect. It does not appear that the issue can be fixed without a significant penalty in performance (cf. full version). A third limitation of IO-DSSE is that, independently of the previous security issue, IO-DSSE is not forward-secure. This puts it at odds with most of the rest of modern (non-I/O-efficient) SSE literature, where forward security has become a standard requirement [6,8,13,16,18,24].

A recent work by Minaud and Reichle from Crypto 2022 also targets dynamic I/O-efficient SSE [21]. Like IO-DSSE, [21] introduces useful techniques to build I/O-efficient SSE. However, it is a theoretical work, which only considers asymptotic performance. No practical evaluation is offered. Moreover, none of the constructions is forward-secure. In practice, all the constructions of [21] directly leak which keyword is being updated, which is the worst case with regard to certain file-injection attacks [27]. In contrast, Hermes is efficient in practice, and achieves forward security in the strongest sense: updates leak no information to the server.

Before closing the section, we note that dynamic I/O-efficient SSE could in principle be built using a folklore hierarchical construction, which generically builds dynamic SSE from a static SSE scheme. That construction was sketched in [15,26], and studied in more detail in [13]. Following that approach, one could theoretically build dynamic I/O-efficient SSE by using a static I/O-efficient SSE as underlying static scheme. However, this quickly proves impractical. First, the approach inherently incurs a logarithmic factor in both locality and page efficiency, on top of the I/O cost of the underlying static SSE. As a result, it cannot hope to match the page efficiency of Hermes, which is sublogarithmic. The most natural candidate for the underlying static SSE is the Tethys scheme from [5]: it is the only one to achieve constant page efficiency, hence the only one that would not further deteriorate page efficiency beyond the log factor inherent to the approach. However, Tethys has a quadratic $\mathcal{O}\left(N^2\right)$ setup time. This is problematic, because every N insertions, the generic construction requires building a fresh static SSE instance of size N. This implies that the average computational cost of *one* update would be $\mathcal{O}\left(N^2/N\right) = \mathcal{O}(N)$. Last but not least, the hierarchical approach requires periodically rebuilding a static SSE scheme of size N. Generically, this implies storing the *entire* database on the client side during the rebuilding phase.

1.3   Technical Overview

I/O efficiency and forward security are two important goals of SSE research, but seemingly incompatible. On an intuitive level, this is because I/O efficiency requires that identifiers matching the same keyword should be stored close to each other, so that they can be read together efficiently when the keyword is queried. Forward security requires that when a *new* identifier matching some keyword is added, it cannot be stored close to previous identifiers for the same keyword, since that would leak information about the new identifier to the server. One way to resolve this apparent contradiction is to use ORAM, as was suggested in [6], and later realized in [20]. We start by sketching the ORAM approach, which will serve to explain what Hermes does differently.

A natural way to build page-efficient SSE is to maintain an array of bins of capacity one page each, one bin for each keyword. When the client wishes to insert a new document identifier matching some keyword w, the new document identifier is added to the bin associated with w. Once the bin for keyword w is full, *i.e.* it contains a full page of identifiers matching w, the page of identifiers is inserted into a separate SSE scheme Σ that only contains full pages, and the bin is emptied. Because Σ only contains *full* pages, each page can be stored in an arbitrary location, and the scheme remains page-efficient; hence page efficiency is easy to realize. In order to search for the list of document identifiers that match keyword w, the client needs only to fetch the bin associated with w, and query Σ on w.

The problem with this naive approach is that it is not forward-secure: during an update, the server can see which bin is accessed, hence which keyword is being updated. A generic way to circumvent this leakage is to store the bins in an ORAM, which completely hides access patterns. (Roughly speaking, this approach is the one of IO-DSSE.) Despite the use of ORAM, the approach still has two issues. First, it is *still* not forward-secure: when a page becomes full, the server can observe that a new element is inserted into Σ, hence updates are not leakage-free (this leakage suffices to break the security game of forward-secure SSE). Second, ORAM incurs an $\Omega(\log W)$ overhead, where W is the number of searchable keywords, and is costly in practice.

Challenge 1: achieving forward security. To avoid leaking when a bin becomes full, we could insert a new item in Σ for every client update, regardless of whether the bin is actually full. A bin becomes full after it receives p client updates, where p is the page size (counted in number of memory words, identified here with the size of a document identifier). Asymptotically, we would have storage efficiency $\mathcal{O}(p)$ instead of the desired $\mathcal{O}(1)$. In practice, for 64-bit identifiers and 4kB memory pages, $p = 512$: blowing the size of Σ by a factor p is not acceptable. Instead, we introduce the idea of SSE supporting dummy updates. When a bin is full, the full page is inserted into Σ; when it is not full, the client issues a dummy update to Σ. The promise of dummy updates is that they should be indistinguishable from real updates in the server's view. At the same time, we arrange that they cost nothing in storage: in our actual construction dummy updates do not alter the contents of the encrypted database.

Challenge 2: realizing dummy updates. At a high level, building SSE with dummy updates comes down to building a key-value store that is amenable to fake key queries. For that purpose, we use the two-choice allocation process. In a two-choice process, n values are stored in m bins of fixed capacity c. Each value for key k is stored in the bin $H_1(k)$ or $H_2(k)$, where H_1, H_2 are hash functions mapping into $[1, m]$. We pad the bins to their full capacity c, and encrypt them with an IND-CPA scheme. Intuitively, simulating a dummy query is simple: the client fetches two uniformly random bins, re-encrypts them, and re-uploads them to the server. Setting $c = \widetilde{\mathcal{O}}(\log \log n)$, $m = \widetilde{\mathcal{O}}(n/\log \log n)$ suffices to ensure a negligible probability of overflow, with constant storage efficiency. This idea can be adapted to the SSE setting. We realize it as a framework that builds a scheme $\mathsf{Dummy}(\Sigma)$ supporting dummy updates, based on an underlying suitable forward-secure scheme Σ.

Challenge 3: dispensing with ORAM. Recall that our scheme uses W bins, each of capacity one page. As noted in the introduction, single-round forward-secure SSE requires $\Omega(W)$ client storage [7]. If we buffer W updates on the client before pushing them to the server, we can afford to scan all W bins. This costs W page accesses per W updates, hence $\mathcal{O}(1)$ *amortized* page efficiency. Another way to view this process is that we are performing a trivial ORAM (*i.e.* reading the entire array of bins), amortized over W updates. This basic idea can be deamortized, in such a way that each client update generates $\mathcal{O}(1)$ page accesses in the worst case. The deamortization is somewhat subtle, and proceeds differently depending on the regime of global parameters N, W and p. For that reason, we introduce two schemes, $\mathsf{BigHermes}$ and $\mathsf{SmallHermes}$, respectively for the case $N \geq pW$ and $N \leq pW$. Hermes is the combination of those two schemes, one for each regime.

In the end, the storage and page efficiency of Hermes reduce to those of the underlying scheme supporting dummy updates. Because that scheme relies on the two-choice process, this works out to $\widetilde{\mathcal{O}}(\log \log(N/p))$ page efficiency, and constant storage efficiency. While the ideas of buffering and deamortization, as well as dummy updates, may be natural in hindsight, we view them as the key contributions of this work: to our knowledge, they realize forward security in a way that is fundamentally different from how it was realized in prior works—and one that happens to be compatible with I/O efficiency. We note that both new techniques (the use of dummy updates, for forward security; and the replacement of standard ORAM with "deamortized" trivial ORAM, for efficiency), are modular: we could have introduced intermediate schemes that realize one without the other, although we did not see a compelling reason for it.

2 Preliminaries

2.1 Notation

Let $\lambda \in \mathbb{N}$ be the security parameter. If X is a probability distribution, $x \leftarrow X$ means that x is sampled from X. If $\mathcal{X}$ is a set, $x \leftarrow \mathcal{X}$ means that x is sampled uniformly at random from $\mathcal{X}$. A function $f(\lambda)$ is *negligible* in λ if it is $\mathcal{O}(\lambda^{-c})$ for every $c \in \mathbb{N}$. We write $f = \mathsf{negl}(\lambda)$ for short.

Protocols. Let $\mathsf{prot} = (\mathsf{prot}_A, \mathsf{prot}_B)$ be a protocol between two parties A and B. We denote an execution of protocol prot between A and B with input in_A and in_B respectively by $\mathsf{prot_A}(\mathsf{in}_A) \longleftrightarrow \mathsf{prot_B}(\mathsf{in}_B)$. We may write $\mathsf{prot}(\mathsf{in}_A; \mathsf{in}_B)$ for short, if both executing parties can be inferred from the context.

Data Structures. For concision, in algorithmic descriptions, tables and arrays are implicitly assumed to be initialized with 0's (if they contain integers) or $\perp$'s, unless stated otherwise. Our algorithms will frequently make use of *bins*, which can be thought of as disjoint memory segments of some fixed size $s = f(p, \lambda)$. Bins can contain arbitrary data up to their capacity s. Bins are always implicitly assumed to be padded with 0's up to their full capacity, so that their size remains fixed. In particular, the encryption of a bin reveals no information about the amount of real data contained in the bin.

Cryptographic Primitives. Throughout the article, we use the following cryptographic primitives: (1) Enc is an IND-CPA secure symmetric encryption scheme (assimilated with its encryption algorithm in the notation); (2) PRF is a secure pseudo-random function; (3) H is a collision-resistant hash function (which will be modeled as a random oracle in most security statements).

2.2 Searchable Symmetric Encryption

We recall the notion of searchable symmetric encryption (SSE). A *database* $\mathsf{DB} = \{(w_i, (\mathsf{id}_1, ..., \mathsf{id}_{\ell_i}))\}_{i=1}^{K}$ is a set of K pairs $(w_i, (\mathsf{id}_1, ..., \mathsf{id}_{\ell_i}))$, where w_i is a *keyword*, and $(\mathsf{id}_1, ..., \mathsf{id}_{\ell_i})$ is a tuple of ℓ_i document identifiers matching keyword w_i. The number of distinct keywords is K. We write $\mathsf{DB}(w_i) = (\mathsf{id}_1, ..., \mathsf{id}_{\ell_i})$ for the list of identifiers matching keyword w_i. The *size* of the database DB is the number of distinct keyword-identifier pairs (w_i, id_j), with $\mathsf{id}_j \in \mathsf{DB}(w_i)$. It is equal to $\sum_{i=1}^{K} \ell_i$.

We will usually assume that there is an upper bound W on the total number of keywords: $K \leq W$; and an upper bound N on the size of the database: $\sum_{i=1}^{k} \ell_i \leq N$. Throughout the article, the integer p denotes the page size. We treat p as a variable independent of the size of the database N, in line with previous work. Our complexity analysis holds in the RAM model of computation, where accessing a random memory word costs unit time. Memory is counted in number of memory words, which are assumed to be of size $\mathcal{O}(\lambda)$ bits, as is common in the literature.

Before giving the formal definition, let us sketch how a dynamic SSE scheme operates. The client stores a small state st, while the server stores the encrypted database EDB. The client calls Σ.Setup to initialize both states, on input an initial plaintext database DB. To search the database on keyword w, the client initiates the protocol Σ.Search on input w, and eventually obtains the list of matching identifiers DB(w). As a side effect, Σ.Search may also update the client and server states. Similarly, to add a new keyword-identifier pair (w, id) to the encrypted database, the client initiates Σ.Update on the corresponding input. The following formal definition follows [5, 21], with minor tweaks.

A *dynamic searchable symmetric encryption* scheme Σ is a 4-tuple of PPT algorithms (KeyGen, Setup, Search, Update):

- Σ.KeyGen(1^λ): Takes as input the security parameter λ and outputs client secret key K.
- Σ.Setup(K, N, W, DB): Takes as input the client secret key K, upper bounds N on the database size and W on the number of keywords, and a database DB. Outputs an encrypted database EDB and client state st.
- Σ.Search(K, w, st; EDB): The client receives as input the secret key K, keyword w and state st. The server receives as input the encrypted database EDB. Outputs some data d, an updated state st$'$ for the client, and an updated encrypted database EDB$'$ for the server.
- Σ.Update(K, w, id, op, st; EDB): The client receives as input the secret key K, a keyword-identifier pair (w, id), an operation op $\in \{\text{del}, \text{add}\}$, and state st. The server receives the encrypted database EDB. Outputs an updated state st$'$ for the client, and an updated encrypted database EDB$'$ for the server.

We denote by Search$_C$ (resp. Update$_C$) the client side of the protocol Search (resp. Update), and by Search$_S$ (resp. Update$_S$) its server counterpart. We may omit W in the input of Setup if it is not used.

For concision, in the remainder, the client state st will be omitted in the notation. As is standard in SSE literature, we assume that keywords are preprocessed via a PRF by the client. That is, $w = \text{PRF}_K(\text{H}(k))$ where k is the actual keyword, for some PRF key K known only to the client.

Epochs. To facilitate the description of our schemes, it is convenient to conceptually partition update queries issued by the client into sequences of W consecutive updates. The time frame corresponding to one such sequence of W updates is called an *epoch*. More precisely, the k-th epoch comprises all updates and searches that are performed between the $((k-1) \cdot W + 1)$-th and $(k \cdot W)$-th update. Looking ahead, update queries belonging to the current epoch will typically be preprocessed together on the client side, then progressively pushed to the server during the next epoch.

Correctness. Informally, correctness asks that at the outcome of a Search protocol on keyword w, the client should obtain exactly the identifiers of documents matching w. The following definition asks for perfect correctness. In some cases, we may allow correctness to fail as long as the probability of failure is negligible.

Definition 1 (Correctness). *An* SSE *scheme* Σ *is* correct *if for all sufficiently large* $W, N \in \mathbb{N}$, *for all databases* DB, *and all sequences of search and update operations, provided at most K keywords are used, and the size of the database remains at most N at all times, letting* $K \leftarrow \Sigma.\mathsf{KeyGen}(1^\lambda)$ *and* $EDB \leftarrow \Sigma.\mathsf{Setup}(K, N, W, DB)$, *at the outcome of a search query on keyword w, the client obtains exactly the identifiers of documents matching keyword w at query time. (That is, documents matching w in the initial database* DB *or added by an update query matching w, and not subsequently deleted.)*

Security. We use the standard semantic security notion from [12]. The server is modeled as a honest-but-curious adversary. Intuitively, security asks that the information learned by the server in the course of the scheme's execution is no more than a specified leakage. The allowed leakage is expressed by a *leakage function*, composed of setup leakage $\mathcal{L}_{\mathsf{Stp}}$, search leakage $\mathcal{L}_{\mathsf{Srch}}$, and update leakage $\mathcal{L}_{\mathsf{Updt}}$. The intent is that, when executing Setup on input x, the server should learn no more than $\mathcal{L}_{\mathsf{Stp}}(x)$. To formally capture that requirement, the security definition asks that there exists a PPT simulator that can simulate the view of the server, taking as input only $\mathcal{L}_{\mathsf{Stp}}(x)$. The same goes for Search and Update.

Formally, we define two games, SSEREAL and SSEIDEAL. In both games, the adversary first chooses a database DB. In SSEREAL, the encrypted database EDB is then generated by Setup(K, N, DB). In SSEIDEAL, EDB is instead generated by a stateful PPT algorithm Sim called the *simulator*, on input $\mathcal{L}_{\mathsf{Stp}}(DB, N)$. After receiving EDB, the adversary adaptively issues search and update queries. In SSEREAL, all queries are answered honestly. In SSEIDEAL, search queries on keyword w are simulated by Sim on input $\mathcal{L}_{\mathsf{Srch}}(w)$, and update queries for operation op, keyword w, and identifier id are simulated by Sim on input $\mathcal{L}_{\mathsf{Updt}}(\mathsf{op}, w, \mathsf{id})$. At the end of the game, the adversary outputs a bit b.

Definition 2 (Semantic Security). *Let Σ be an* SSE *scheme and let $\mathcal{L} = (\mathcal{L}_{\mathsf{Stp}}, \mathcal{L}_{\mathsf{Srch}}, \mathcal{L}_{\mathsf{Updt}})$ be a leakage function. The scheme Σ is $\mathcal{L}$-adaptively secure if for all PPT adversaries $\mathcal{A}$, there exists a PPT simulator Sim such that:*

$$|\Pr[\mathrm{SSEREAL}_{\Sigma,\mathcal{A}}(\lambda) = 1] - \Pr[\mathrm{SSEIDEAL}_{\Sigma,\mathsf{Sim},\mathcal{L},\mathcal{A}}(\lambda) = 1]| = \mathsf{negl}(\lambda).$$

Leakage Patterns. To facilitate the description of leakage functions, we make use of the following standard notions from the literature [6]. The *search pattern* $\mathsf{sp}(w)$ for keyword w is the sequence of identifiers of previous search queries on w. The *update pattern* $\mathsf{up}(w)$ for keyword w is the sequence of identifiers of previous update queries on w. The *query pattern* $\mathsf{qp}(w) = (\mathsf{sp}(w), \mathsf{up}(w))$ is the combination of search and update patterns.

Throughout the article, our schemes will be secure with regard to the following leakage function: $\mathcal{L}^{\mathsf{fs}} = (\mathcal{L}^{\mathsf{fs}}_{\mathsf{Stp}}, \mathcal{L}^{\mathsf{fs}}_{\mathsf{Srch}}, \mathcal{L}^{\mathsf{fs}}_{\mathsf{Updt}})$, with $\mathcal{L}^{\mathsf{fs}}_{\mathsf{Stp}}(\mathsf{DB}, W, N) = (W, N)$, $\mathcal{L}^{\mathsf{fs}}_{\mathsf{Srch}}(w_i) = (\mathsf{qp}, a_i, d_i)$ where a_i (resp d_i) is the number of additions (resp deletions) for w_i, and $\mathcal{L}^{\mathsf{fs}}_{\mathsf{Updt}}(\mathsf{op}, w, \mathsf{id}) = \bot$. In words, Setup leaks an upper bound on the size of the database and on the number of keywords; Search reveals the query pattern, and the number of additions and deletions for the searched keyword; and updates leak nothing.

Forward Security and Backward Security. Forward security was introduced and formalized in [6,26], respectively. In this work, we consider a strictly stronger notion of forward security where updates leak no information.

Definition 3 (Forward Security). *An SSE scheme with leakage* $\mathcal{L} = (\mathcal{L}_{\mathsf{Stp}}, \mathcal{L}_{\mathsf{Srch}}, \mathcal{L}_{\mathsf{Updt}})$ *is* forward-secure *if* $\mathcal{L}_{\mathsf{Updt}}(\mathsf{op}, w, \mathsf{id}) = \bot$.

The notion of backward security was formalized in [8], and restricts the leakage incurred by deletions. Since backward security is not the main focus of this work, we refer the reader to [8] for the formal definition. In this work we consider type-II backwards security, which requires that search queries leak the documents currently matching w, when they were inserted, and when all the updates on w happened (but not their content). Note that schemes with leakage $\mathcal{L}^{\mathsf{fs}}$ are forward-secure, and type-II backward-secure.

Remark on Deletions. The concrete SSE constructions presented in this article are involved. Thus, we present them without deletions to improve readability. This however does not reduce their functionality, as all schemes can be extended to support deletions with the generic framework of [6]. Intuitively, given an SSE scheme Σ_{add} that supports additions, it allows to construct a scheme Σ that supports additions and deletions with the same leakage. For this, two instantiations of Σ_{add} are used, Σ_0 for additions and Σ_1 for deletions. Added identifiers are inserted into Σ_0 while deleted keyword-identifier pairs are inserted into Σ_1. Each search request, the client queries Σ_0 and Σ_1 and retrieves identifier lists L_0 and L_1 respectively. The result of the search request then is $L_0 \setminus L_1$. Clearly, if Σ_{add} has leakage $\mathcal{L}^{\mathsf{fs}}$, then Σ also has leakage $\mathcal{L}^{\mathsf{fs}}$.

Efficiency Measures. We recall the notions of storage efficiency [11], and page efficiency [5]. To reduce clutter, the following notation is common to all definitions. Let $\mathsf{K} \leftarrow \mathsf{KeyGen}(1^\lambda)$. Given a database DB, an upper bound W on the number of keywords, and an upper bound N on the size of the database, let EDB $\leftarrow$ Setup(K, N, DB). Let $S = (\text{op}_i, \text{in}_i)_{i=1}^{s}$ be a sequence of search and update queries, where $\text{op}_i \in \{\text{add}, \text{del}, \text{srch}\}$ is an operation and $\text{in}_i = (\text{op}_i, w_i, \text{id}_i, \text{st}_i; \text{EDB}_i)$ its input. (If $\text{op}_i = \text{srch}$, the query is a search query, and id_i is not provided.) After executing all operations op_j in S up to $j \leq i$, let DB_i denote the state of the database, st_i the client state, and EDB_i the encrypted database. The following definitions are borrowed from [21].

Definition 4 (Storage Efficiency). *An SSE scheme has storage efficiency E if for any λ, DB, N, sequence S, and any i, $|\text{EDB}_i| \leq E \cdot |DB_i|$.*

Definition 5 (Page Pattern). *Regard server-side storage as an array of pages, containing the encrypted database EDB. When processing search query Search(in_i) or update query Update(in_i), the server accesses a number of pages $p_1, ..., p_{h'}$. We call these pages the* page pattern, *denoted by PgPat(op_i, in_i).*

Definition 6 (Page Efficiency). *An SSE scheme has page efficiency P if for any λ, DB, N, sequence S, and any i, $|\text{PgPat}(\text{op}_i, \text{in}_i)| \leq P \cdot X$, where X is the number of pages needed to store the document identifiers $\text{DB}_i(w_i)$ matching keyword w_i in plaintext.*

2.3 Allocation Schemes

Two-Choice. Insert n balls into m bins according to the standard two-choice (2C) process [4]. That is, to insert each ball, pick two bins B_α, B_β uniformly at random, and insert the ball into the least loaded bin $B_\gamma \in \{B_\alpha, B_\beta\}$.

Lemma 1 *(2C [21]). Let $\delta(m) = \log\log\log m$ and $m \geq \lambda^{1/\log\log\lambda}$. At the outcome of a sequence of n insertions, the most loaded bin contains $\mathcal{O}(n/m + \delta(m)\log\log m)$ balls, except with negligible probability.*

Layered Two-Choice. Layered two-choice (L2C) is a weighted variant of the two-choice process, introduced in [21]. We sketch a simplified version that suffices for our purpose. Let $p \in \mathbb{N}$. Consider a sequence of insertions of *weighted* balls into m bins. Each weight is an integer in $[1, p]$ and each bin is split into $1 + \log\log m$ independent layers, numbered from 0 to $\log\log m$. (For simplicity, assume $\log\log m$ is an integer.) A ball of weight w is stored in layer 0 if $w \in [0, p/\log m]$, and in layer $i \geq 1$ if $w \in (p2^{i-1}/\log m, p2^i/\log m]$. An insertion of a ball of weight w is similar to a two-choice insertion: pick two bins B_α, B_β uniformly at random, and insert the ball into the bin $B_\gamma \in \{B_\alpha, B_\beta\}$ that contains the fewest balls at layer i. In other words, the difference with the standard two-choice process is that when determining the "least loaded bin", we only look at the number of balls in the same layer as the newly inserted ball, rather than looking at the total number.

The weight of balls can be increased after insertion. Assume the weight w of a ball is increased by v, *i.e.* the ball has weight $w + v$ after the update. The layer of the ball after the update may increase as a result. Let i be the old layer and j be the new layer after the update. If $i \neq j$, the ball of weight $w + v$ is reinserted into layer j. The old ball of weight w at layer i is marked as *residual*, and is still considered for the load computation of its bin.

Define the *load* of a bin to be the sum of the weights of the balls it contains (including residual balls, as noted above). Define the *total weight* to be the sum of the weights of all balls inserted so far, using their current weights if it has been updated. We require that the total weight remains upper-bounded by $w_{\mathsf{max}} = \mathsf{poly}\,(\lambda)$.

Lemma 2 ([21]). *Let* $\delta(\lambda) = \log\log\log\lambda$, $m = \left\lceil \frac{w_{\mathsf{max}}}{\delta(\lambda)\log\log w_{\mathsf{max}}} \right\rceil$, *and assume* $m = \Omega(\lambda^{\frac{1}{\log\log\lambda}})$. *After a sequence of insertions and updates, the load of the most loaded bin is* $\mathcal{O}(p\delta(\lambda)\log\log w_{\mathsf{max}})$, *except with negligible probability.*

In this article, the role of balls will be played by lists of (at most p) identifiers. The weight of a list L is its number of identifiers. When some identifiers I are added to L, if the new weight $|L \cup I|$ is in the same layer as $|L|$, then the new identifiers I are simply added to L, in the same bin. Otherwise, I is inserted in one of the two chosen bins, as if it was a list of weight $|L \cup I|$. (In that case, the list $L \cup I$ is split between both bins.)

3   SSE with Dummy Updates

A first key technique for our results is the introduction of the notion of *dummy updates*. An SSE schemes supports dummy updates if its interface is equipped with a new operation DummyUpdate, taking as input only the client's master key K. For technical reasons, we also require that Setup receives an additional parameter D, an upper bound on the total number of dummy updates.

3.1   Security Definition

Informally, an SSE scheme supporting dummy updates is said to be secure if it is secure in the same sense as a normal SSE scheme, with the added requirement that dummy updates should be indistinguishable from real updates from the server's perspective. (A subtle but important point is that later constructions will ensure that server storage does not depend on D: dummy updates will look indistinguishable from real updates, without actually affecting server storage.)

The security definition for SSE supporting dummy updates is given in Definition 7, with the associated security game in Algorithm 1. Note that this definition naturally extends the standard definition (Definition 2).

Definition 7 (Adaptive Semantic Security with Dummy Updates). *Let* Σ *be an SSE scheme supporting dummy updates,* $\mathcal{A}$ *a stateful PPT adversary, and* Sim *a stateful PPT simulator. Let* $q \in \mathbb{N}$, *and let* $\mathcal{L} = (\mathcal{L}_{\mathsf{Stp}}, \mathcal{L}_{\mathsf{Srch}}, \mathcal{L}_{\mathsf{Updt}})$ *be a leakage function. The games* $\mathrm{SSEREAL}_{\Sigma,\mathcal{A}}^{\mathsf{dum}}$ *and* $\mathrm{SSEIDEAL}_{\Sigma,\mathcal{A},\mathcal{L},\mathcal{A}}^{\mathsf{dum}}$ *are defined in Algorithm 1.* Σ *is* $\mathcal{L}$-*adaptively secure with support for dummy updates if*

$\mathcal{L}_{\mathsf{Updt}}$ *does not depend on its first input* op, *and if for all PPT adversaries* $\mathcal{A}$, *there exists a PPT simulator* Sim *such that:*

$$| \Pr[\mathrm{SSEReal}^{\mathsf{dum}}_{\Sigma,\mathcal{A}}(\lambda) = 1] - \Pr[\mathrm{SSEIdeal}^{\mathsf{dum}}_{\Sigma,\mathsf{Sim},\mathcal{L},\mathcal{A}}(\lambda) = 1]| = \mathsf{negl}\,(\lambda)\,.$$

Algorithm 1. Security games for SSE supporting dummy updates.

$\mathrm{SSEReal}^{\mathsf{dum}}_{\Sigma,\mathcal{A}}$	$\mathrm{SSEIdeal}^{\mathsf{dum}}_{\Sigma,\mathsf{Sim},\mathcal{L},\mathcal{A}}$
1: $\mathsf{K} \leftarrow \Sigma.\mathsf{KeyGen}(1^\lambda)$	1: $(\mathsf{DB}, N, D, W, \mathsf{st}_{\mathcal{A}}) \leftarrow \mathcal{A}(1^\lambda)$
2: $(\mathsf{DB}, N, D, W, \mathsf{st}_{\mathcal{A}}) \leftarrow \mathcal{A}(1^\lambda)$	2: $\mathsf{EDB} \leftarrow \mathsf{Sim}(\mathcal{L}_{\mathsf{Stp}}(\mathsf{DB}, N, D, W))$
3: $\mathsf{EDB} \leftarrow \Sigma.\mathsf{Setup}(\mathsf{K}, N, D, W, \mathsf{DB})$	3: send EDB to $\mathcal{A}$
4: send EDB to $\mathcal{A}$	4: **for all** $1 \le i \le q$ **do**
5: **for all** $1 \le i \le q$ **do**	5: $(\mathsf{op}_i, \mathsf{in}_i, \mathsf{st}_{\mathcal{A}}) \leftarrow \mathcal{A}(\mathsf{st}_{\mathcal{A}})$
6: $(\mathsf{op}_i, \mathsf{in}_i, \mathsf{st}_{\mathcal{A}}) \leftarrow \mathcal{A}(\mathsf{st}_{\mathcal{A}})$	6: **if** $\mathsf{op}_i = \mathsf{srch}$ **then**
7: **if** $\mathsf{op}_i = \mathsf{srch}$ **then**	7: $\mathsf{Sim}(\mathcal{L}_{\mathsf{Srch}}(\mathsf{in}_i)) \leftrightarrow \mathcal{A}(\mathsf{st}_{\mathcal{A}})$
8: Parse $\mathsf{in}_i = w_i$	8: **else**
9: $\Sigma.\mathsf{Search}_C(\mathsf{K}, w_i) \leftrightarrow \mathcal{A}(\mathsf{st}_{\mathcal{A}})$	9: $\mathsf{Sim}(\mathcal{L}_{\mathsf{Updt}}(\mathsf{op}_i, \mathsf{in}_i)) \leftrightarrow \mathcal{A}(\mathsf{st}_{\mathcal{A}})$
10: **else if** $\mathsf{op}_i \in \{\mathsf{add}, \mathsf{del}\}$ **then**	10: output bit $b \leftarrow \mathcal{A}(\mathsf{st}_{\mathcal{A}})$
11: Parse $\mathsf{in}_i = (w_i, \mathsf{id}_i)$	
12: $\Sigma.\mathsf{Update}_C(\mathsf{K}, w_i, \mathsf{id}_i, \mathsf{op}_i) \quad \leftrightarrow$ $\mathcal{A}(\mathsf{st}_{\mathcal{A}})$	
13: **else**	
14: $\Sigma.\mathsf{DummyUpdate}_C(\mathsf{K}) \leftrightarrow \mathcal{A}(\mathsf{st}_{\mathcal{A}})$	
15: output bit $b \leftarrow \mathcal{A}(\mathsf{st}_{\mathcal{A}})$	

3.2   A Framework to Build SSE with Dummy Updates

We now describe a framework that constructs an SSE scheme $\mathsf{Dummy}(\Sigma)$ supporting dummy updates, based on an underlying SSE scheme Σ. Provided Σ is *suitable* in a sense that will be defined shortly, the resulting scheme $\mathsf{Dummy}(\Sigma)$ achieves the following features:

- It is a secure SSE scheme supporting dummy updates (cf. Definition 7).
- Server storage grows only with the number of *real* updates; in particular, it does not depend on the upper bound D on the number of dummy updates.
- Relative to the base scheme Σ, $\mathsf{Dummy}(\Sigma)$ only incurs a $\tilde{\mathcal{O}}\,(\log\log N)$ overhead in communication.

The definition of a *suitable* SSE is given next. Essentially, it requires that server storage should behave like a key-value store. This is how most forward-secure SSE schemes operate. It also requires that running Setup on a non-empty initial database DB is equivalent to running Setup on an empty database, then performing updates to add the contents of DB. Here, "equivalent" means that the client and server states at the outcome of either process are distributed identically. This condition can be fulfilled trivially by any SSE scheme. It is not strictly necessary, but makes the description of the framework, and its security proof, more concise.

278 B. Minaud and M. Reichle

Definition 8 (Suitable SSE). *We say that an SSE scheme Σ is suitable if there exist a key space $\mathcal{K}$, a token space $\mathcal{T}$, and a map keys : $\mathcal{T} \mapsto \mathcal{K}$ such that: (1) Σ.Setup(K, N, W, DB) outputs an encrypted database EDB in the form of an encrypted key-value store that maps a key to encrypted identifiers. (2) Σ.Search(K, w; EDB) is a two-step protocol in which the client first sends a token $\tau \in \mathcal{T}$ and the server responds with EDB$[k_1]$, ..., EDB$[k_q]$ for $k_1, ..., k_q \leftarrow$ keys(τ). (3) Σ.Update($K, (w, \text{id}), \text{op}$; EDB) is a one-step protocol in which the client sends a key $k \in \mathcal{K}$ and value $v = \text{Enc}_{K_{\text{Enc}}}(\text{id})$ and the server stores v in EDB at position k, i.e. sets EDB$[k] = v$. (4) Running the setup routine Setup(K, N, W, DB) is equivalent to running the setup Setup(K, N, W, $\emptyset$) with an empty database and subsequently performing an update operation for each keyword-identifier pair $(w, \text{id}) \in$ DB locally. (5) Σ is forward-secure.*

Construction. A detailed description is given in Algorithm 2. Let us explain it here in text. Let Σ be a suitable SSE scheme. First, observe that it is easy to add dummy updates to Σ if we are willing to let server storage grow linearly with the number of dummy updates: we could simply let DummyUpdate perform a real update with a fresh keyword-identifier pair. Because Σ is forward-secure, the leakage of either type of update would be $\perp$. The problem is that the server would have to store the keyword-identifier pairs arising from dummy updates, potentially blowing up storage overhead. This is what we wish to avoid.

Instead, the idea is to wrap Σ inside an encrypted two-choice allocation scheme (cf. Sect. 2.3). First, Dummy(Σ) initializes a two-choice scheme with $m = N/\widetilde{\mathcal{O}}(\log \log N)$ bins $B_1, ..., B_m$, each of capacity $\widetilde{\mathcal{O}}(\log \log N)$ (where one unit corresponds to the storage cost of one identifier in Σ). Because Σ is suitable, we know server storage in Σ behaves like a key-value store: for each update with token τ, the server stores the corresponding data items under the keys keys(τ). Let H : $\mathcal{K} \to \{1, ..., m\}^2$ map keys to pairs of bins. In Dummy(Σ), whenever Σ would store a data item under a key k, the same item is instead stored in one of the two bins B_α, B_β, where $(\alpha, \beta) \leftarrow$ H(k). The destination bin is chosen among B_α, B_β according to the two-choice process: the item is inserted into whichever bin currently contains fewer items.

In Dummy(Σ), the client always downloads and sends back full bins, padded to their maximal capacity $\widetilde{\mathcal{O}}(\log \log N)$, and encrypted under a key K_{Enc} known only to the client. This is where the $\widetilde{\mathcal{O}}(\log \log N)$ overhead in communication comes from. On the other hand, thanks to the properties of the two-choice process, dummy updates can be realized easily: the client simply asks to access two bins $(\alpha, \beta) \leftarrow$ H(k) for a fresh key k, re-encrypts them, and re-uploads them. This matches the behavior of real updates (up to the IND-CPA security of Enc, and the pseudo-randomness of H, modeled as a random oracle). In more detail, the key k for dummy updates is generated by Σ.Update using a reserved dummy keyword w_{dum}, and a fresh identifier id chosen by the client.

Remark. Although the outline given above is natural, the detailed construction in Algorithm 2 involves some subtlety. During setup, Σ receives as upper bound for the size of the database $N + D$, rather than just N. This is useful for the security proof. It also means that the encrypted database *generated by* Σ may scale with D. However, that database is not needed to run Dummy(Σ), so this has no impact on storage efficiency. To see that the database generated by Σ is not needed by Dummy(Σ), observe in Algorithm 2 that Dummy(Σ) crucially only makes use of the *client-side* part of the protocols of Σ; the only relevant aspect of the server-side part of those protocols is the keys map. This is made possible by the suitability assumption on Σ, which is used very strongly.

Algorithm 2. Dummy(Σ)

Dummy(Σ).Setup(K, N, W, D, DB)

1: Pick dummy keyword w_{dum}
2: $\mathsf{EDB}_\Sigma \leftarrow \Sigma.\mathsf{Setup}(K_\Sigma, N{+}D, W{+}1, \emptyset)$
3: Initialize $m = N/\widetilde{\mathcal{O}}(\log\log N)$ empty bins $B_1, ..., B_m$ of capacity $\widetilde{\mathcal{O}}(\log\log N)$.
4: **for all** $(w, \mathsf{id}) \in \mathsf{DB}$ **do**
5:     $(k, v) \leftarrow \Sigma.\mathsf{Update}_C(K, (w, \mathsf{id}), \mathsf{add})$
6:     $(\alpha, \beta) \leftarrow H(k)$
7:     Insert id into the bin B_γ with fewest items among B_α, B_β
8: **return** $\mathsf{EDB} = (\mathsf{Enc}_{K_{\mathsf{Enc}}}(B_i))_{i=1}^m$

Dummy(Σ).Update($K, (w, \mathsf{id}), \mathsf{op}; \mathsf{EDB}$)

Client:

1: $(k, v) \leftarrow \Sigma.\mathsf{Update}_C(K_\Sigma, (w, \mathsf{id}), \mathsf{add})$
2: **send** k

Server:

1: $(\alpha, \beta) \leftarrow H(k)$
2: **send** $B_\alpha^{\mathsf{enc}}, B_\beta^{\mathsf{enc}}$

Client:

1: Decrypt $B_\alpha^{\mathsf{enc}}, B_\beta^{\mathsf{enc}}$ to B_α, B_β
2: Insert id into the bin B_γ with fewest identifiers among B_α, B_β
3: **send** re-encrypted B_α, B_β

Server:

1: Replace $B_\alpha^{\mathsf{enc}}, B_\beta^{\mathsf{enc}}$ with received bins

Dummy(Σ).KeyGen(1^λ)

1: Sample $K_\Sigma \leftarrow \Sigma.\mathsf{KeyGen}(1^\lambda)$ and encryption key K_{Enc}
2: **return** $K = (K_\Sigma, K_{\mathsf{Enc}})$

Dummy(Σ).Search($K, w; \mathsf{EDB}$)

Client:

1: $\tau \leftarrow \Sigma.\mathsf{Search}_C(K_\Sigma, w)$
2: **send** τ

Server:

1: $k_1, ..., k_q \leftarrow \mathsf{keys}(\tau)$
2: $(\alpha_i, \beta_i) \leftarrow H(k_i)$ for $i \in [1, q]$
3: **send** $\{B_{\alpha_i}^{\mathsf{enc}}, B_{\beta_i}^{\mathsf{enc}}\}_{i=1}^q$

Dummy(Σ).DummyUpdate($K; \mathsf{EDB}$)

Client:

1: Pick fresh identifier id
2: $(k, v) \leftarrow \Sigma.\mathsf{Update}_C(K_\Sigma, (w_{\mathsf{dum}}, \mathsf{id}), \mathsf{add})$
3: **send** k

Server:

1: $(\alpha, \beta) \leftarrow H(k)$
2: **send** $B_\alpha^{\mathsf{enc}}, B_\beta^{\mathsf{enc}}$

Client:

1: **send** re-encrypted B_α, B_β

Server:

1: Replace $B_\alpha^{\mathsf{enc}}, B_\beta^{\mathsf{enc}}$ with received bins

---

Security. The security of Dummy(Σ) follows naturally from that of Σ. Indeed, Dummy(Σ) essentially amounts to running Σ inside encrypted bins, with the difference that Σ is scaled for size $N + D$. As a result, Dummy(Σ) intuitively has at most the same leakage as Σ for Setup, Search and Update, except that D is additionally leaked. Regarding DummyUpdate, the only difference between real and dummy updates is that a new identifier is inserted in the bin with the former, while the bins are re-encrypted without modifying their content with the latter. Since Enc is IND-CCA-secure, and bins are always padded to their full size (cf. Sect. 2.1), the two behaviors are indistinguishable.

Theorem 1. *Let Σ be a suitable, $\mathcal{L}^{\text{fs}}$-adaptively secure SSE scheme. Let* Enc *be an IND-CPA secure encryption scheme. Let* H *be a random oracle. Let $N \geq \lambda$, and $D = \text{poly}(N)$.* Dummy(Σ) *is a correct and secure SSE scheme supporting dummy updates with respect to leakage* $\mathcal{L}_{\text{dum}} = (\mathcal{L}_{\text{Stp}}, \mathcal{L}_{\text{Srch}}, \mathcal{L}_{\text{Updt}})$, *where* $\mathcal{L}_{\text{Stp}}(\text{DB}, N, D, W) = (N, D, W), \mathcal{L}_{\text{Srch}}(w) = (\text{qp}, \ell),$ *and* $\mathcal{L}_{\text{Updt}}(\text{op}, w, \text{id}) = \bot$.

The full proof is postponed to the full version. We sketch it here. Because 2C guarantees a maximum load of $\widetilde{\mathcal{O}}(\log \log N)$ with overwhelming probability if $N \geq \lambda$ (Lemma 1), correctness follows from the correctness of Σ. We turn to security. Let Sim$_\Sigma$ be a simulator for Σ. During setup, the client initializes the encrypted database EDB$_\Sigma$ of Σ and outputs $m = N/\widetilde{\mathcal{O}}(\log \log N)$ encrypted bins. The output leaks nothing but N, since the bins are encrypted. Note that for subsequent updates and searches, the state of Sim$_\Sigma$ still needs to be initialized by simulating EDB$_\Sigma$. (Here, we use the fourth property of Definition 8.) This potentially leaks N, D and W. For search queries, the search token can be sampled via Sim$_\Sigma$. This requires the query pattern qp$_\Sigma$ of Σ and the length ℓ of the identifier list matching the searched keyword. Note that each search and update query induces a corresponding query on Σ. Thus, the query pattern of Dummy(Σ) and Σ are equivalent. Consequently, ℓ and qp are leaked. Similarly, all updates (including dummy updates) can be simulated via Sim$_\Sigma$. As updates leak nothing in Σ, neither dummy nor real updates have any leakage.

3.3 Efficient Instantiations

Definition 9. *A suitable SSE scheme Σ is said to be* efficient *if:*

- *Σ has $\mathcal{O}(1)$ storage efficiency;*
- *If* EDB *contains ℓ values matching keyword w, then for $\tau \leftarrow \Sigma.\text{Search}_C(\text{K}, w)$, $|\text{keys}(\tau)| = \ell$.*

Later, we will only use Σ to store full pages. That is, the atomic items stored in Σ will be identifier lists of size p, rather than single identifiers. Each key will map to one list of size p. Each access to the encrypted database EDB then translates to one page access, and retrieves p identifiers. On the other hand, if Σ is efficient in the sense above, the number of accesses is minimal, hence Σ with full-page items has page efficiency $\mathcal{O}(1)$. Dummy(Σ) then has page efficiency $\widetilde{\mathcal{O}}(\log \log N)$. Moreover, if Σ has $\mathcal{O}(1)$ storage efficiency, so does Dummy(Σ).

Putting both remarks together, we see that if Σ is efficient per Definition 9, then Dummy(Σ) has storage efficiency $\mathcal{O}(1)$, and when used to store full-page items as outlined above, it has page efficiency $\widetilde{\mathcal{O}}(\log \log N)$. To instantiate this idea, the $\Sigma o \phi o \varsigma$ [6] and Diana [8] schemes are good choices: they are both suitable, efficient, and $\mathcal{L}^{\mathsf{fs}}$-adaptively secure (assuming identifiers are encrypted before being stored on the server).

Remark. The Dummy(Σ) framework technically does not exclude the possibility that the sizes of individual search tokens and keys could scale with D, insofar as they are produced by Σ, and $N + D$ is an input of Σ.Setup. In practice, the overhead is at most constant for $\Sigma o\phi o\varsigma$ and Diana, and can be eliminated entirely with a careful instantiation. To simplify the presentation, we have not added formal requirements for that purpose at the framework level.

4 BigHermes: The Big Database Regime

We are now ready to present our main construction, Hermes. The construction differs depending on whether $N \geq pW$ or $N < pW$. This section presents BigHermes, which deals with the case $N \geq pW$. Throughout the section, we assume $N \geq pW$, and let Σ_{dum} be an efficient forward-secure SSE supporting dummy queries, in the sense of Sect. 3.

The final BigHermes construction is rather involved. To simplify the explanation, we build BigHermes progressively. We introduce three variants: $\mathsf{BigHermes}_0$, $\mathsf{BigHermes}_1$, $\mathsf{BigHermes}_2$. The three variants are gradually more complex, but achieve gradually stronger properties. The difference lies in the efficiency guarantees. $\mathsf{BigHermes}_0$ uses the idea of dummy updates from Sect. 3 to achieve sublogarithmic page efficiency, communication and time complexity overheads; but only in an amortized sense. $\mathsf{BigHermes}_1$ shows how $\mathsf{BigHermes}_0$ can be deamortized in page efficiency and communication, notably without the use of ORAM found in prior work [20]. Finally, $\mathsf{BigHermes}_2$ builds on $\mathsf{BigHermes}_1$ to deamortize time complexity, and completes the construction.

4.1 $\mathsf{BigHermes}_0$: Amortized BigHermes

If a list of identifiers matching the same keyword contains exactly p identifiers, let us say that the list is *full.* If it contains less than p identifiers, it is *underfull.* In $\mathsf{BigHermes}_0$, for each keyword w, the server stores exactly one underfull list of identifiers matching w. For that purpose, the server stores W bins $(B_{w_i})_{i=1}^{W}$ of capacity p, one for each keyword. Full lists are stored separately in an instance of Σ_{dum}. When searching for keyword w, the client will retrieve the corresponding bin, and call Σ_{dum}.Search to fetch full lists matching w (if any).

Naively, to perform an update on keyword w, the client could simply fetch the corresponding bin and add the new identifier, emptying the bin into Σ_{dum} if it is full. However, this would trivially break forward security, because the server would learn information about which keyword is being updated. Instead, the scheme proceeds in epochs (cf. Section 2). Each epoch corresponds to W consecutive updates. The client buffers all updates arising during the current epoch, until the buffer contains W updates, and the epoch ends. At the end of the epoch, the client downloads all bins $(B_{w_i})_{i=1}^{W}$ from the server, updates them with the W new identifiers from its buffer, and pushes the updated bins back to the server.

If one of the bins becomes full during this end-of-epoch update, it would be tempting to immediately insert the full list into Σ_{dum}. However, this would again break forward security, as the server would learn how many bins became full during the epoch. To hide that information, $\mathsf{BigHermes}_0$ takes advantage of dummy updates. Observe that during an end-of-epoch update, at most W lists can become full. To hide how many bins become full, $\mathsf{BigHermes}_0$ always performs exactly W updates on Σ_{dum} at the end of the epoch, padding real updates with dummy updates as necessary. From a security standpoint, this approach works because real updates and dummy updates are indistinguishable. From an efficiency standpoint, dummy updates have no impact on the efficiency of Σ_{dum}, as discussed in Sect. 3 (in short, while dummy updates are indistinguishable from real ones for the server, they effectively do nothing). The only cost of dummy updates is in communication complexity, and page efficiency. For both quantities, note that W updates to Σ_{dum} are performed per epoch of W client updates, thus at most one dummy update per client update. Hence, we can instantiate Σ_{dum} for at most $D_{\text{dum}} = N$ dummy updates, and $\mathsf{BigHermes}_0$ directly inherits the same page efficiency and communication overhead as Σ_{dum}.

It remains to discuss the order of (real and dummy) updates on Σ_{dum} at the end of an epoch. This order has an impact on the security of the scheme. To see this, suppose that the following process is used: at the end of an epoch, push full lists to Σ_{dum} for each keyword where this is needed, taking keywords in a fixed order $w_1, w_2, \ldots$; then pad with dummy updates. Now imagine that during an epoch, the client fills a list for keyword w_2, but not for w_1. When the client subsequently performs a search on w_2, the server can see that the locations accessed in Σ_{dum} during the search (partially) match the locations accessed during the first update on Σ_{dum} at the end of the previous epoch (since the first update was for w_2). Since it was the first update, this implies that no update was needed for w_1. The server deduces that no list for w_1 was full at the end of the previous epoch. This breaks security. To avoid that issue, at the end of an epoch, $\mathsf{BigHermes}_0$ first computes all W updates that will need to be issued to Σ_{dum}, then permutes them uniformly at random, before sending the updates to the server. As the security proof will show, this is enough to obtain security.

In the end, $\mathsf{BigHermes}_0$ achieves storage efficiency $\mathcal{O}(1)$, inherited from the same property of Σ_{dum}, and because of the assumption $N \geq pW$, the storage cost of the W bins is $\mathcal{O}(N)$. As noted earlier, $\mathsf{BigHermes}_0$ also inherits the page efficiency and communication overhead of Σ_{dum}. Because the number of entries in the database of Σ_{dum} is at most N/p, it follows that $\mathsf{BigHermes}_0$ has page efficiency and communication overhead $\widetilde{\mathcal{O}}(\log\log(N/p))$. However, this is only in an amortized sense, since batches of W updates are performed together at the end of each epoch.

4.2 BigHermes$_1$: BigHermes with Deamortized Communication

The reason BigHermes$_0$ successfully hides which underfull list requires an update when the client wishes to insert a new keyword-document pair is simple: all underfull lists (bins) are updated at the same time, at the end of an epoch. This approach may be interpreted as hiding the access pattern to bins using a trivial ORAM: the entire set of bins is downloaded, updated locally, and uploaded back to the server. Dummy updates are then used to hide how many full bins are pushed to Σ_{dum}. This approach is possible due to amortization: a trivial ORAM access only occurs once every W client updates, and updates all P bins simultaneously.

In short, BigHermes$_1$ deamortizes BigHermes$_0$ by no longer updating bins all at once at the end of an epoch, and instead updating them one by one over the course of the next epoch. Thus, BigHermes$_1$ may be understood as a "deamortized" trivial ORAM, which turns out to be much more efficient in our setting than directly using a standard ORAM, as in prior work [20]. Among other benefits, this is what allows Hermes to achieve sublogarithmic efficiency, avoiding the logarithmic overhead inherent in ORAM [19]. Let us now explain the algorithm. Pseudo-code is available in Algorithm 3. A visual representation of the update procedure is also given in Fig. 1.

At a high level, at the end of an epoch, the client pre-computes where the W new identifiers from the epoch should be stored on the server, without actually pushing them to the server. To that end, the client maintains a (client-side) table T_{len}, that maps each keyword to the number of matching identifiers currently in the server-side database. Using T_{len}, at the end of an epoch, for each keyword w, the client splits the list of new identifiers matching the keyword into three (possibly empty) sublists: (1) a sublist that completes the content of B_w to a full list (if possible); (2) full sublists of size p; and (3) an underfull sublist of remaining identifiers (if any). Let $\mathsf{CB_{out}}$ be a (client-side) buffer that maps each keyword to sublists (1) and (3). All sublists of type (2) are stored in another buffer CFP that maps an integer in $[1, W/p]$ to either a full list or $\bot$. (Note that there are at most W/p such sublists in total.) Once all keywords are processed in that manner, the content of CFP is shuffled randomly.

Over the course of the next epoch, the contents of CFP and $\mathsf{CB_{out}}$ are pushed to the server according to a fixed schedule. In more detail, during the k-th update operation of the next epoch, the client inserts the new keyword-identifier pair into $\mathsf{CB_{new}}$. This new keyword-identifier pair will not be processed until the end of the current epoch. The client then moves on to pushing updates that were buffered from the end of the previous epoch, proceeding as follows. She downloads the bin B_{w_k} for the k-th keyword from the server. The client then retrieves from $\mathsf{CB_{out}}[w_k]$ the list L_1 that completes the content of B_{w_k} to a list of size p, and the new underfull list L_x. If there are enough new identifiers in L_1 to complete the content of B_{w_k} to a full list, the new full list is written to Σ_{dum}, and the contents of B_{w_k} is replaced with L_x. Otherwise, the client performs a dummy update to Σ_{dum}, and adds the identifiers of L_1 to B_{w_k}. In either case, B_{w_k} is then re-encrypted and uploaded to the server. Finally, if $k \leq W/p$, the client also retrieves $L_S \leftarrow \mathsf{CFP}[k]$. Recall that L_S is either a full list buffered from the previous epoch, or $\bot$. If $L_S = \bot$ the client performs a dummy update, otherwise she writes L_S to Σ_{dum}. In total, from the point of view of the server, during the k-th client update in a given epoch, the bin B_{w_k} is accessed, and if $k \leq W/p$ (resp. $k > W/p$), two (resp. one) updates are performed in Σ_{dum}. Thus, the access pattern during a client update is fully predictable, and reveals no information to the server. Also note that during each epoch, at most $2W$ dummy updates are performed. Hence, a number of at most $D_{\mathsf{dum}} = 2N$ dummy updates are performed on Σ_{dum}.

4.3 BigHermes$_2$: Fully Deamortized BigHermes

Observe that in BigHermes$_1$, the client performs most computation at the end of each epoch. We now sketch how we deamortize even the client computation, and refer to the full version for details.

Recall that the client needs to assign each identifier to a sublist of type (1), (2) or (3). Given this assignment, the sublists can be moved to $\mathsf{CB_{out}}$ and CFP. Observe that after an identifier is assigned to a sublist, it is easy to deamortize the process of moving it into $\mathsf{CB_{out}}$ or CFP. It is less straightforward to assign a fresh identifier id to the correct sublist "on-the-fly" when it is added. Note that when (w, id) is added, it is not possible to look at the list L of all buffered identifiers matching w, as this list might be of size $\mathcal{O}(W)$. We show that a pipeline pre-computation can resolve this problem, with a constant overhead of additional data structures. These are either copies of existing data structures, or tables to store intermediate information, all of size $\mathcal{O}(W)$.

4.4 Security

BigHermes is forward-secure with standard leakage $\mathcal{L}^{\mathsf{fs}}$, as stated next.

Theorem 2. *Let N be an upper bound on the size of the database, let p be the page size, and let W be an upper bound on the number of keywords. Let $N \geq pW$, and assume $N/p \geq \lambda$. Let Σ_{dum} be a forward-secure SSE supporting dummy updates, let Enc be an IND-CPA secure encryption scheme, and let PRF be a secure pseudorandom function (for the preprocessing of keywords). Then BigHermes is correct and $\mathcal{L}^{\mathsf{fs}}$-adaptively semantically secure.*

We now sketch the security proof, and refer to the full version for the full proof. BigHermes stores all full identifier lists of size p in Σ_{dum}, and one underfull sublist per keyword w in the bin B_w. Each search, the corresponding bin is accessed, and the client searches for all full lists on the server in Σ_{dum}. All identifiers that are not retrieved are contained in a buffer on the client. Thus, correctness follows immediately from the correctness of Σ_{dum}.

The setup only leaks W and N to the server, as the bins are encrypted, and the security of Σ_{dum} guarantees that $\mathsf{EDB}_{\Sigma_{\mathsf{dum}}}$ leaks no other information. Further, updates leak no information which follows from two facts: (1) exactly

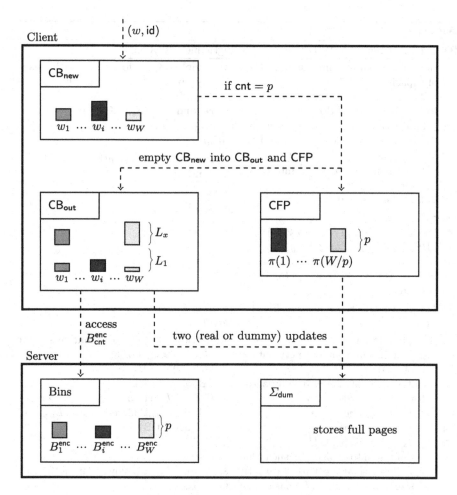

Fig. 1. Sketch of the update schedule of $\mathsf{BigHermes}_1$. (The data structure T_{len} are omitted for clarity.) Each update, the variable cnt is incremented and the dotted lines are executed. See Algorithm 3 for pseudo-code.

Algorithm 3. BigHermes$_1$

BigHermes$_1$.Setup(K, N, W, DB)

1: Initialize W empty bins $B_{w_1}, \ldots, B_{w_W}$ of capacity p
2: Initialize empty database DB$_{\mathsf{dum}}$
3: **for all** keywords w **do**
4:     Split DB(w) into x lists L_i such that L_x has size at most $p-1$, and the remaining lists have size p
5:     Insert pairs $\{(w, L_i)\}_{i=1}^{x-1}$ into DB$_{\mathsf{dum}}$
6:     Insert list L_x into B_w
7:     $T_{\mathsf{len}}[w] \leftarrow |\mathsf{DB}(w)|$
8: cnt $\leftarrow 0$
9: $(N_{\mathsf{dum}}, D_{\mathsf{dum}}, W_{\mathsf{dum}}) = (N/p, 2N, W)$
10: $\mathsf{EDB}_{\Sigma_{\mathsf{dum}}} \leftarrow \Sigma_{\mathsf{dum}}.\mathsf{Setup}(\mathsf{K}_{\Sigma_{\mathsf{dum}}}, N_{\mathsf{dum}}, D_{\mathsf{dum}}, W_{\mathsf{dum}}, \mathsf{DB}_{\mathsf{dum}})$
11: $\mathsf{EDB} \leftarrow (\mathsf{EDB}_{\Sigma_{\mathsf{dum}}}, \{\mathsf{Enc}_{\mathsf{K}_{\mathsf{Enc}}}(B_{w_i})\}_{i=1}^{W})$
    return EDB

BigHermes$_1$.KeyGen(1^λ)

1: Sample $\mathsf{K}_{\mathsf{Enc}}$ for Enc with security parameter λ and $\mathsf{K}_{\Sigma_{\mathsf{dum}}} \leftarrow \Sigma_{\mathsf{dum}}.\mathsf{KeyGen}(1^\lambda)$
2: **return** K = $(\mathsf{K}_{\mathsf{Enc}}, \mathsf{K}_{\Sigma_{\mathsf{dum}}})$

BigHermes$_1$.Search(K, w; EDB)

Client:

1: Perform $\Sigma_{\mathsf{dum}}.\mathsf{Search}(\mathsf{K}_{\Sigma_{\mathsf{dum}}}, w; \mathsf{EDB})$
2: **send** w

Server:

1: **send** B_w^{enc}

BigHermes$_1$.Update(K, (w, id), add; EDB)

Client:

1: **if** cnt $= p$ **then**
2:     $\pi \leftarrow$ uniformly random permuation of $[1, W/p]$
3:     Initialize empty set S of full pages
4:     **for all** keywords w **do**
5:         $L \leftarrow \mathsf{CB}_{\mathsf{new}}[w]$
6:         $r \leftarrow T_{\mathsf{len}}[w] \bmod p$
7:         $T_{\mathsf{len}}[w] = T_{\mathsf{len}}[w] + |L|$
8:         Split L into x lists L_i such that L_1 has size at most $p-r$ (exactly size $p-r$ if $x > 1$), L_x has size at most p, and the remaining lists all have size p
9:         $\mathsf{CB}_{\mathsf{out}}[w] \leftarrow \mathsf{CB}_{\mathsf{out}}[w] \cup \{(L_1, L_x)\}$
10:       $S \leftarrow S \cup \{(w, L_2), \ldots, (w, L_{x-1})\}$
11:     $\mathsf{CFP}[\pi(i)] \leftarrow S[i]$ for $1 \le i \le |S|$
12:     Empty $\mathsf{CB}_{\mathsf{new}}$ and set cnt $= 0$
13: $\mathsf{CB}_{\mathsf{new}}[w] \leftarrow \mathsf{CB}_{\mathsf{new}}[w] \cup \{\mathsf{id}\}$
14: cnt $\leftarrow$ cnt $+ 1$
15: **send** cnt

Server:

1: **send** $B_{\mathsf{cnt}}^{\mathsf{enc}}$

(continue description of update)

Client:

1: Retrieve list L of identifiers from $B_{\mathsf{cnt}} = \mathsf{Dec}_{\mathsf{K}_{\mathsf{Enc}}}(B_{\mathsf{cnt}}^{\mathsf{enc}})$
2: $(L_1, L_x) \leftarrow \mathsf{CB}_{\mathsf{out}}[w_{\mathsf{cnt}}]$
3: $\mathsf{CB}_{\mathsf{out}}[w_{\mathsf{cnt}}] \leftarrow \perp$
4: **if** $L_1 \neq L_x$ **then**   ▷ $x > 1$
5:     Run $\Sigma_{\mathsf{dum}}.\mathsf{Update}(\mathsf{K}, (w_{\mathsf{cnt}}, L_1 \cup L),$ add; EDB)
6:     $B_{\mathsf{cnt}} \leftarrow L_x$
7: **else**   ▷ $x = 1$
8:     Run $\Sigma_{\mathsf{dum}}.\mathsf{DummyUpdate}(\mathsf{K}; \mathsf{EDB})$
9:     $B_{\mathsf{cnt}} \leftarrow L \cup L_1$
10: **if** cnt $\le W/p$ **then**
11:     **if** $\mathsf{CFP}[\mathsf{cnt}] \neq \perp$ **then**
12:         $(w, L_S) \leftarrow \mathsf{CFP}[\mathsf{cnt}]$
13:         Run $\Sigma_{\mathsf{dum}}.\mathsf{Update}(\mathsf{K}, (w, L_S), \mathsf{add};$ EDB)
14:         $\mathsf{CFP}[\mathsf{cnt}] \leftarrow \perp$
15:     **else**
16:         Run $\Sigma_{\mathsf{dum}}.\mathsf{DummyUpdate}(\mathsf{K}; \mathsf{EDB})$
17: **send** $B_{\mathsf{cnt}}^{\mathsf{enc}} \leftarrow \mathsf{Enc}_{\mathsf{K}_{\mathsf{Enc}}}(B_{\mathsf{cnt}})$

Server:

1: Update $B_{\mathsf{cnt}}^{\mathsf{enc}}$

one bin is accessed each update via a fixed schedule known in advance; (2) dummy updates and real updates leak no information, and are indistinguishable in the view of the server, owing to the security of Σ_{dum}.

It remains to consider searches. Each search on keyword w only leaks the query pattern qp, and the length ℓ of the identifier list for w. (Recall from Sect. 2.2 that the query pattern qp is equal to the search pattern sp and update pattern up.) To establish this, we need to show that the view of the server can be simulated using only qp and ℓ. Based on the search pattern and the fact that bins are encrypted with IND-CPA encryption, simulating access to the bin B_w is straightforward. Thus, security reduces to the simulation of Σ_{dum}. Because Σ_{dum} is secure, we know that its behavior can be simulated as long as we can compute the query pattern $\mathsf{qp}_{\Sigma_{\mathsf{dum}}}$ and answer length $\ell_{\Sigma_{\mathsf{dum}}}$ for Σ_{dum}. To see that this is the case, first observe that the number of Σ_{dum}-updates on w and the load of B_w per epoch can be recomputed given only up and ℓ. From there, the simulator can compute the number ℓ_i of full lists for keyword w that were pushed to Σ_{dum} during a given epoch i. Clearly, $\sum_i \ell_i = \ell_{\Sigma_{\mathsf{dum}}}$. To deduce the update pattern $\mathsf{up}_{\Sigma_{\mathsf{dum}}}$ for Σ_{dum}, it remains to determine when each update was performed during the epoch. Intuitively, because updates to Σ_{dum} occurring in a given epoch are permuted uniformly at random, it suffices to choose x updates to Σ_{dum} uniformly at random among updates issued during the epoch (excluding updates already chosen for the same purpose on a different keyword). This yields $\mathsf{up}_{\Sigma_{\mathsf{dum}}}$. On the other hand, each search query to BigHermes triggers exactly one search query to Σ_{dum}: the search pattern of Σ_{dum} matches the search pattern of BigHermes. Thus, the simulator can compute $\mathsf{qp}_{\Sigma_{\mathsf{dum}}}$, and we are done.

4.5 Efficiency

We now analyze the efficiency of BigHermes, when Σ_{dum} is efficient (in the sense of Sect. 3.3). Each client-side data structure, including identifier buffers and tables, has size $\mathcal{O}(W)$. Since there is a constant number of such structures, overall client storage is $\mathcal{O}(W)$. On the server side, Σ_{dum} has storage efficiency $\mathcal{O}(1)$, and the bins require $pW = \mathcal{O}(N)$ storage, hence overall storage efficiency is $\mathcal{O}(1)$. We turn to page efficiency. During each update, one bin of size p is read, and two updates on Σ_{dum} are performed. Since Σ_{dum} only stores full pages, of which there can be at most N/p, Σ_{dum}.Update has page efficiency $\widetilde{\mathcal{O}}(\log\log(N/p))$. Similarly, a search on a keyword w with ℓ matching identifiers induces one bin access and (at most) $\lfloor \ell/p \rfloor$ accesses of $\widetilde{\mathcal{O}}(\log\log(N/p))$ pages each. We conclude that BigHermes has page efficiency $\widetilde{\mathcal{O}}(\log\log(N/p))$.

5 SmallHermes: Overview

In Sect. 4, we have built BigHermes, under the assumption $N \geq pW$. We now build a scheme SmallHermes with the same efficiency and security properties as BigHermes, but in the regime $N \leq pW$. SmallHermes uses some of the same ideas as BigHermes, and combines them with techniques from the recent LayeredSSE scheme [21]. Similar to BigHermes, we present SmallHermes in three steps, each building on the previous one. To provide a concise overview, we only sketch the construction here. The full description can be found in the full version.

SmallHermes$_0$: *Amortized* SmallHermes. SmallHermes stores identifiers in $m = o(N)$ encrypted bins according to L2C (Sect. 2.3). Recall that each bin has capacity $\widetilde{\mathcal{O}}\,(p \log \log(N/p))$, and is conceptually divided into $\log \log(N/p)$ layers. Each list L of (at most p) identifiers matching keyword w is mapped to two bins B_α, B_β. The list L is stored in either B_α or B_β, depending on which bin has fewer items at layer κ, where κ is determined by the size of L. For a search on keyword w, the bins B_α and B_β are retrieved from the server. The client can read the matching identifiers from the bins after decryption. When a list has more than p identifiers, it is split into sublists of size p, which are treated independently.

So far, SmallHermes behaves like LayeredSSE [21]. The main difficulty is how to achieve forward security, that is, how to perform updates with *no* leakage. Here, SmallHermes borrows from BigHermes. Client updates are buffered over the course of an epoch in a client-side buffer CB$_{new}$ of capacity W. At the end of an epoch, the client downloads the entire encrypted database EDB from the server, and performs updates locally. Because we are in the "small database" regime $N \leq pW$, this process has amortized $\mathcal{O}\,(1)$ page efficiency. Of course, it is desirable to deamortize the algorithms, so that the client does not need to download the entire database at the end of an epoch. This is presented next.

SmallHermes$_1$: SmallHermes *with Deamortized Communication.* The communication of SmallHermes$_0$ can be deamortized via client-side pre-computation (similar to Sect. 4.2), yielding a scheme SmallHermes$_1$ with $\widetilde{\mathcal{O}}\,(\log \log(N/p))$ page efficiency and $\mathcal{O}\,(1)$ storage efficiency. To that end, the client stores an additional table T_{load}, which records the load information of each bin on all $\log \log m$ layers. (This requires $\mathcal{O}\,(W \cdot \log \log m)$ client storage but can be improved to $\mathcal{O}\,(W)$ with a more complex pre-computation.) Whenever the client decides to store an identifier in a bin, she updates T_{load} accordingly. Using T_{load}, the client can pre-compute locally in which bin a new identifier should be added. Each epoch, she accesses every bin on a fixed schedule, and inserts identifiers according to the local pre-computation.

In the end, a fresh identifier is written to the server after at most $2W$ client updates. During a client update, at most one bin of size $p\mathcal{O}\,(\log \log(N/p))$ is downloaded. During a search matching ℓ identifiers, exactly $2\lceil \ell/p \rceil$ bins are downloaded. Thus, SmallHermes has $\mathcal{O}\,(\log \log(N/p))$ page efficiency. It also inherits $\mathcal{O}\,(1)$ storage efficiency from L2C. Note that a figure visualizing the update schedule of SmallHermes is given in the full version.

SmallHermes$_2$: *Fully Deamortized* SmallHermes. With a complex but efficient pipeline pre-computation, we can remove the additional $\log \log m$ factor in client storage and deamortize both the communication and computation of SmallHermes. The optimization is based on the observation that for inserting the $\mathcal{O}\,(W)$ new identifiers of CB$_{new}$, we do not require the entire load information of L2C, only the load of relevant bin-layer pairs. For W updates, even if each new identifier requires the load of some bin B_γ at some layer κ, there are at most $2W$ such pairs (γ, κ). The load information of these pairs can be precomputed in a pipeline with three steps, where each step is performed in one epoch. The client can then decide where to insert each of the new identifiers based on the load information, and subsequently push the identifiers to the server. This approach yields an update operation with at most $\mathcal{O}\left(p \log \log(N/p)\right)$ communication *and* computation. In the end, SmallHermes$_2$ achieves the same worst-case sublogarithmic performance in page efficient, communication and computation, as BigHermes$_2$.

It is interesting to note that SmallHermes can be simplified if we are willing to make a natural conjecture about the behavior of the weighted two-choice process. This point is discussed in the full version. The relevant conjecture seems to be a long-standing open problem. If true, a simpler and more elegant variant of SmallHermes can be built, although asymptotic performance remains the same.

5.1   Security and Efficiency

Theorem 3 (Sketch). *If* $N \leq pW$, *then* SmallHermes *is correct and* $\mathcal{L}^{\mathsf{fs}}$*- adaptively semantically secure.*

The full formal statement and proof are deferred to the full version. Let us outline the proof here. Semantic security follows from the following facts. (1) The bins are encrypted, hence only the upper bound N is leaked during setup. (2) During search, $2 \cdot \lceil \ell/p \rceil$ bins are accessed, where ℓ is the number of identifiers matching the searched keyword w. These bins are re-accessed if w is searched again, but look random to the server during the initial search. Thus, a search leaks the search pattern, and the number of sublists. (3) Updates are performed by accessing each bin via a fixed schedule (which solely depends on the number of updates). Hence, updates leak no information.

Each data structure on the client requires $\mathcal{O}(W)$ storage. As there are only a constant number of data structures and pipeline steps, total client storage is $\mathcal{O}(W)$. At most one bin is downloaded each update; and each search on keyword w, exactly $2 \lceil \ell/p \rceil$ bins are retrieved, where ℓ is the length of the list of identifiers matching w. Because each bin is of size $\widetilde{\mathcal{O}}\left(p \log \log(N/p)\right)$, page efficiency is $\widetilde{\mathcal{O}}\left(\log \log(N/p)\right)$, and storage efficiency is $\mathcal{O}(1)$.

6   The Hermes Scheme: Putting Everything Together

We have constructed BigHermes (Sect. 4), an I/O-efficient SSE scheme with forward security in the big database regime, *i.e.* $N \geq pW$. Similarly, we built SmallHermes (Sect. 5) in the regime $N \leq pW$. We combine them to construct Hermes.

Hermes. The Hermes scheme simply uses either BigHermes or SmallHermes, depending on which regime the global parameters N, W and p are in. That is,

Setup, Search, and Update for Hermes behave exactly as in BigHermes, if $N \geq pW$, and as in SmallHermes otherwise. Clearly, Hermes has $\tilde{\mathcal{O}}\left(\log\log(N/p)\right)$ page efficiency and $\mathcal{O}\left(1\right)$ storage efficiency. Further, because both sub-schemes are forward-secure with leakage $\mathcal{L}^{\mathsf{fs}}$ (Theorems 2 and 3), the same holds for Hermes. This is formalized in Theorem 4.

Theorem 4. *Let N be an upper bound on the size of the database, and let W be an upper bound on the number of keywords. Let p be the page size. Assume $p \leq N^{1-1/\log\log\lambda}$, and $N/p \geq \lambda$. Let Enc be an IND-CPA-secure encryption scheme, and let PRF be a secure pseudo-random function. The Hermes is correct and $\mathcal{L}^{\mathsf{fs}}$-adaptively semantically secure.*

The scheme Hermes has $\mathcal{O}\left(W\right)$ client storage, $\mathcal{O}\left(1\right)$ storage efficiency (i.e., $\mathcal{O}\left(N\right)$ server storage) and $\tilde{\mathcal{O}}\left(\log\log(N/p)\right)$ page efficiency. Note that storage is given in memory words (of size $\mathcal{O}\left(\lambda\right)$ bits) and that a document identifier can be stored in a single memory word[2].

7   Experimental Evaluation

All evaluations and benchmarks have been carried out on a computer with an Intel Core i7 8550U 1.80 GHz CPU with 8 cores and an 512 GiB PCIe SSD, running Ubuntu 20.04. The SSD page size is 4 KiB. We chose the setting where document identifiers are encoded on 8 bytes. This allows us to support databases with up to 2^{64} documents, where each page fits $p = 512$ entries. We set $\lambda = 128$.

7.1   Evaluation of 2C and L2C

Hermes uses both the 2C and L2C allocation schemes (Sect. 2.3). We first empirically evaluate the constant c in the page-efficiency bound $c \cdot p \log\log\log(\lambda)$ $\log\log(N/p)$ of those schemes. This is a necessary preliminary step to any concrete instantiation of Hermes, since the constant determines the bin size.

To evaluate the constant, we run experiments allocating balls with total weight $N \in [2^{12}, 2^{22}]$ using L2C and 2C. For each scheme and each parameter set, we perform 10000 trial runs. Each run, we insert balls into $m = \frac{2N}{p\log\log\log(\lambda)\log\log(N/p)}$ bins, adding new balls until a total weight of N is reached. For L2C, ball weights are sampled uniformly at random in $[1, p]$. For 2C, ball weights are set to p. Once all balls are inserted, we measure the load of the most loaded bin, and output the highest number among the 10000 trials. The results are presented in Fig. 2. For $c = 2$, we see that the bound holds with a comfortable margin for all variants. This shows that 2C and L2C behave quite well in practice. The constant $c = 2$ is used for Hermes in the experiments below.

---

[2] Our scheme Hermes can be interpreted as an encrypted multi-map and allows to store other items than just document identifiers. In that case, the client storage becomes $\mathcal{O}\left(n \cdot W\right)$ bits, where n is the bit-length of the items to be stored.

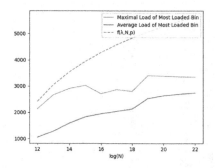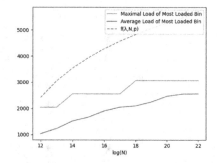

Fig. 2. The loads of L2C (left) and 2C (right) for 10000 runs with balls of total weight N. The function $f(\lambda, N, p) = c \log \log \log(\lambda) \log \log(N/p)$ is the theoretical upper bound for the most loaded bin with constant $c = 2$ and $\lambda = 128$. For L2C, the weights $\{w_i\}$ are chosen at random in $[1, 512]$, and $w_i = 512$ for 2C.

7.2   Evaluation of Hermes

We now analyze the I/O performance of Hermes. Because Hermes is the first forward-secure I/O-efficient scheme, two properties that were thought to be at odds until now, there is no direct point of comparison in the literature. Nevertheless, to provide some means of comparison, we include in the evaluation schemes that are forward-secure but not I/O-efficient, and I/O-efficient but not forward-secure. To represent forward-secure but not I/O-efficient schemes, we include the Diana scheme, which offers state-of-the-art performance [8]. In the category of schemes that are I/O-efficient but not forward-secure, while there are many *static* constructions, the only practical *dynamic* construction we are aware of is IO-DSSE [20]. (As discussed in Sect. 1.2, another dynamic I/O-efficient construction can be found in [21], but it is a theoretical feasibility result, with no concrete instantiation.) To round out the comparison, we also include the *static* scheme Tethys, which attains the best page efficiency.

For each scheme in the comparison, we analyzed its memory access pattern to deduce its I/O workload for search and update queries. We then simulated that workload using the optimized Flexible I/O benchmark tool fio (version 3.19) [3]. The tool measures the throughput of disk accesses under that workload, on an SSD. The same technique was shown in [5] to provide accurate performance estimates. Network latency is not part of the experiment, but we note that it mainly depends on the number of round-trips. For Hermes, this can be reduced to a single roundtrip for both Search and Update (we refer to the full version for a discussion).

For concreteness, we run our experiments on the English Wikipedia database, containing about 140 million entries, and 4.6 million keywords. We assumed that on average, each keyword matches at least p documents. Note that the exact keyword distribution has little impact on the overheads (relative to a plaintext database) of either throughput or server storage by construction: this is a consequence of the page-efficient approach. These parameters fall under the

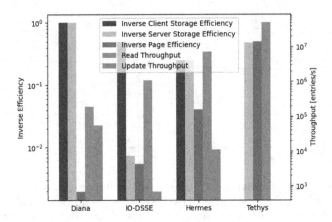

Fig. 3. Read and update I/O throughput, inverse page efficiency, and inverse storage efficiency for various SSE schemes, in logarithmic scale. Higher is better. Note that *inverse client storage efficiency* is W divided by client storage.

regime of SmallHermes, and we used the variant based on weighted 2C from the full version. Due to space limitations, we omit the analysis of Hermes in the other parameter regime. We expect the practical performance of BigHermes$_1$ to be almost the same as SmallHermes$_1$.

Results are presented on Fig. 3. The throughput of Hermes outperforms other dynamic schemes Diana [8] and IO-DSSE [20]. While Diana has slightly better storage and update efficiency, only one identifier is retrieved during each memory access in search, which heavily impacts page efficiency, and hence, throughput. This is typical of schemes that do not target I/O efficiency, and is indeed the main motivation for I/O-efficient SSE. Concretely, the I/O throughput of Hermes improves over Diana by a factor of 37 (resp. 49) for reads (resp. updates) in this setting.

IO-DSSE suffers from poor server storage efficiency when the database contains many keywords, here requiring 150 GB of encrypted data to store a plaintext index of 1.2 GB (compared to only 4.5 GB for Hermes). Hermes also improves over the I/O throughput of IO-DSSE[3] by a factor 6.

In both cases, this is because IO-DSSE relies on ORAM. The gap is expected to increase for larger databases, since Hermes scales sublogarithmically, while IO-DSSE does not.

Note that while Hermes requires about twice the client storage of IO-DSSE, we present tradeoffs between client storage and page efficiency in the full version. Given the right tradeoff, Hermes outperforms IO-DSSE in all metrics.

Tethys [5] outperforms Hermes in throughput and storage. However, Tethys does not support updates, and is only included for reference.

---

[3] When measuring throughput, Fig. 3 uses the repaired version of IO-DSSE, since the original version is insecure (see full version).

In conclusion, Hermes vastly outperforms non-I/O-efficient schemes in throughput, as expected. It is perhaps less expected that it also outperforms IO-DSSE, insofar as it adds forward security. But this is not so surprising when considering that the only known approach to "reasonably secure" dynamic I/O-efficient SSE prior to this work was to use ORAM.

References

1. Asharov, G., Naor, M., Segev, G., Shahaf, I.: Searchable symmetric encryption: optimal locality in linear space via two-dimensional balanced allocations. In: Wichs, D., Mansour, Y. (eds.) 48th ACM STOC, pp. 1101–1114. ACM Press, June 2016. https://doi.org/10.1145/2897518.2897562
2. Asharov, G., Segev, G., Shahaf, I.: Tight tradeoffs in searchable symmetric encryption. J. Cryptol. **34**(2), 9 (2021). https://doi.org/10.1007/s00145-020-09370-z
3. Axboe, J.: Flexible I/O Tester (2020). https://github.com/axboe/fio
4. Azar, Y., Broder, A.Z., Karlin, A.R., Upfal, E.: Balanced allocations. In: Proceedings of the Twenty-sixth Annual ACM Symposium on Theory of Computing, pp. 593–602 (1994)
5. Bossuat, A., Bost, R., Fouque, P.-A., Minaud, B., Reichle, M.: SSE and SSD: page-efficient searchable symmetric encryption. In: Malkin, T., Peikert, C. (eds.) CRYPTO 2021, Part III. LNCS, vol. 12827, pp. 157–184. Springer, Cham (2021). https://doi.org/10.1007/978-3-030-84252-9_6
6. Bost, R.: Σοφος: Forward secure searchable encryption. In: Weippl, E.R., Katzenbeisser, S., Kruegel, C., Myers, A.C., Halevi, S. (eds.) ACM CCS 2016, pp. 1143–1154. ACM Press, October 2016. https://doi.org/10.1145/2976749.2978303
7. Bost, R., Fouque, P.A.: Security-efficiency tradeoffs in searchable encryption. PoPETs **2019**(4), 132–151 (2019). https://doi.org/10.2478/popets-2019-0062
8. Bost, R., Minaud, B., Ohrimenko, O.: Forward and backward private searchable encryption from constrained cryptographic primitives. In: Thuraisingham, B.M., Evans, D., Malkin, T., Xu, D. (eds.) ACM CCS 2017, pp. 1465–1482. ACM Press, October/November 2017. https://doi.org/10.1145/3133956.3133980
9. Cash, D., et al.: Dynamic searchable encryption in very-large databases: data structures and implementation. In: NDSS 2014. The Internet Society, February 2014
10. Cash, D., Jarecki, S., Jutla, C., Krawczyk, H., Roşu, M.-C., Steiner, M.: Highly-scalable searchable symmetric encryption with support for Boolean queries. In: Canetti, R., Garay, J.A. (eds.) CRYPTO 2013, Part I. LNCS, vol. 8042, pp. 353–373. Springer, Heidelberg (2013). https://doi.org/10.1007/978-3-642-40041-4_20
11. Cash, D., Tessaro, S.: The locality of searchable symmetric encryption. In: Nguyen, P.Q., Oswald, E. (eds.) EUROCRYPT 2014. LNCS, vol. 8441, pp. 351–368. Springer, Heidelberg (2014). https://doi.org/10.1007/978-3-642-55220-5_20
12. Curtmola, R., Garay, J.A., Kamara, S., Ostrovsky, R.: Searchable symmetric encryption: improved definitions and efficient constructions. In: Juels, A., Wright, R.N., De Capitani di Vimercati, S. (eds.) ACM CCS 2006, pp. 79–88. ACM Press, October/November 2006. https://doi.org/10.1145/1180405.1180417
13. Demertzis, I., Chamani, J.G., Papadopoulos, D., Papamanthou, C.: Dynamic searchable encryption with small client storage. In: ISOC Network and Distributed System Security - NDSS 2022 (2022)

14. Demertzis, I., Papadopoulos, D., Papamanthou, C.: Searchable encryption with optimal locality: achieving sublogarithmic read efficiency. In: Shacham, H., Boldyreva, A. (eds.) CRYPTO 2018, Part I. LNCS, vol. 10991, pp. 371–406. Springer, Cham (2018). https://doi.org/10.1007/978-3-319-96884-1_13

15. Demertzis, I., Papamanthou, C.: Fast searchable encryption with tunable locality. In: Proceedings of the 2017 ACM International Conference on Management of Data, pp. 1053–1067 (2017)

16. Etemad, M., Küpçü, A., Papamanthou, C., Evans, D.: Efficient dynamic searchable encryption with forward privacy. In: Proceedings on Privacy Enhancing Technologie - PoPETS 2018 (2018)

17. Grubbs, P., Lacharité, M.S., Minaud, B., Paterson, K.G.: Learning to reconstruct: statistical learning theory and encrypted database attacks. In: 2019 IEEE Symposium on Security and Privacy, pp. 1067–1083. IEEE Computer Society Press, May 2019. https://doi.org/10.1109/SP.2019.00030

18. Kamara, S., Moataz, T., Park, A., Qin, L.: A decentralized and encrypted national gun registry. In: 2021 IEEE Symposium on Security and Privacy (SP), pp. 1520–1537. IEEE (2021)

19. Larsen, K.G., Nielsen, J.B.: Yes, there is an oblivious RAM lower bound! In: Shacham, H., Boldyreva, A. (eds.) CRYPTO 2018, Part III. LNCS, vol. 10992, pp. 523–542. Springer, Cham (2018). https://doi.org/10.1007/978-3-319-96881-0_18

20. Miers, I., Mohassel, P.: IO-DSSE: scaling dynamic searchable encryption to millions of indexes by improving locality. In: NDSS 2017. The Internet Society, February/March 2017

21. Minaud, B., Reichle, M.: Dynamic local searchable symmetric encryption. In: Dodis, Y., Shrimpton, T. (eds.) CRYPTO 2022. LNCS, vol. 13510, pp. 91–120. Springer, Lecture Notes in Computer Science (2022). https://doi.org/10.1007/978-3-031-15985-5_4

22. MongoDB: Queryable encryption (2022). https://www.mongodb.com/products/queryable-encryption

23. Naveed, M., Kamara, S., Wright, C.V.: Inference attacks on property-preserving encrypted databases. In: Ray, I., Li, N., Kruegel, C. (eds.) ACM CCS 2015, pp. 644–655. ACM Press, October 2015. https://doi.org/10.1145/2810103.2813651

24. Patranabis, S., Mukhopadhyay, D.: Forward and backward private conjunctive searchable symmetric encryption. In: ISOC Network and Distributed System Security - NDSS 2021 (2021)

25. Song, D.X., Wagner, D., Perrig, A.: Practical techniques for searches on encrypted data. In: 2000 IEEE Symposium on Security and Privacy, pp. 44–55. IEEE Computer Society Press, May 2000. https://doi.org/10.1109/SECPRI.2000.848445

26. Stefanov, E., Papamanthou, C., Shi, E.: Practical dynamic searchable encryption with small leakage. In: NDSS 2014. The Internet Society, February 2014

27. Zhang, Y., Katz, J., Papamanthou, C.: All your queries are belong to us: the power of file-injection attacks on searchable encryption. In: Holz, T., Savage, S. (eds.) USENIX Security 2016, pp. 707–720. USENIX Association, August 2016

Security Proofs and Security Models

To Attest or Not to Attest, This is the Question – Provable Attestation in FIDO2

Nina Bindel[1]($^{(\boxtimes)}$)(iD), Nicolas Gama[1](iD), Sandra Guasch[1], and Eyal Ronen[2](iD)

[1] SandboxAQ, Palo Alto, CA, USA
{nina.bindel,nicolas.gama,sandra.guasch}@sandboxaq.com
[2] Tel Aviv University, Tel Aviv, Israel
eyal.ronen@cs.tau.ac.il

Abstract. FIDO2 is currently the main initiative for passwordless authentication in web servers. It mandates the use of secure hardware authenticators to protect the authentication protocol's secrets from compromise. However, to ensure that only secure authenticators are being used, web servers need a method to attest their properties. The FIDO2 specifications allow for authenticators and web servers to choose between different attestation modes to prove the characteristics of an authenticator, however the properties of most these modes have not been analysed in the context of FIDO2. In this work, we analyse the security and privacy properties of FIDO2 when different attestation modes included in the standard are used, and show that they lack good balance between security, privacy and revocation of corrupted devices. For example, the basic attestation mode prevents remote servers from tracing user's actions across different services while requiring reduced trust assumptions. However in case one device is compromised, all the devices from the same batch (e.g., of the same brand or model) need to be recalled, which can be quite complex (and arguably impractical) in consumer scenarios. As a consequence we suggest a new attestation mode based on the recently proposed TokenWeaver, which provides more convenient mechanisms for revoking a single token while maintaining user privacy.

Keywords: FIDO2 · WebAuthn · attestation · post- compromise security · post-quantum security

1 Introduction

For many years, using passwords as a single authentication mechanism has been one of the biggest cause of security problems in the Internet. Weak passwords, phishing, credential stuffing, and many other attack vectors can have devastating results such as full compromise of accounts and sensitive data. To help prevent such attacks, the Fast Identity Online (FIDO) Alliance proposes their FIDO protocol for passwordless authentication [2].

J. Guo and R. Steinfeld (Eds.): ASIACRYPT 2023, LNCS 14443, pp. 297–328, 2023.
https://doi.org/10.1007/978-981-99-8736-8_10

The protocol uses a secure hardware device called an authenticator (e.g., security keys or certain smart phones) for authentication to a server. The authenticators are able to securely generate and store secret credentials. The FIDO protocol consists of two phases: a registration phase in which the authenticator generates a credential key pair, and the public key is stored at the server, also called Relying Party (RP) (see (3) in Fig. 1); and authentication of the authenticator on the RP using the registered credentials (see (4) in Fig. 1). In both phases the user verifies registration/authentication by entering a gesture (e.g., entering a PIN or pressing a button).

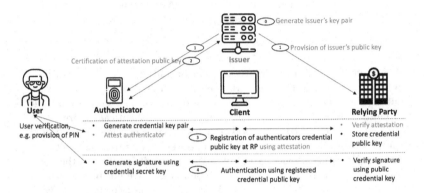

Fig. 1. Message of flow of FIDO2 with attestation (in teal).

The FIDO2 protocol is implemented using two sub-protocols: WebAuthn—a protocol between authenticator, client (e.g., a browser), and RP in which the RP sends a challenge, the authenticator responds with a signature, and the client acts as an intermediary, and CTAP—a protocol between authenticator and client that binds the client to the authenticator to restrict access to the authenticator. FIDO2, and in particular WebAuthn, offers a plethora of different modes such as enterprise mode (which allows identifying information), key storage modes (on the authenticator, encrypted on the server, shared between different devices or not, etc.), or different attestation modes.

1.1 Attestation in FIDO2

FIDO2 supports several attestation modes, that can enforce the use of approved (or of 'different levels certified') secure authenticators. The goal of attestation is to prevent users from using weak or uncertified authenticators that might put the user, the user's company, or the RP at risk.

At the same time, attestation should preserve the privacy of the user. More concretely, a coalition of web servers should not be able to trace FIDO2 actions to a particular authenticator, or to guess if the same authenticator is used for two different accounts (except in enterprise mode). The different attestation modes present in the standard achieve different notions of security and privacy that imply a variety of nuances in the trust assumptions.

For instance, in the *attestation CA* (attCA) mode, the protocol relies on a certificate authority (CA) that issues certificates for different attestation credentials (ideally one per registered credential key per RP) in a way that the attestation keys cannot be linked to each other or the authenticator identifier. However, we need to trust the CA to not reveal the link between the attestation credential and authenticator, to not issue certificates for rogue authenticators, and to be online and available whenever needed.

Another example is the attestation mode basic, where the issuer/manufacturer hardcodes the same attestation key in a batch of at least 100,000 devices (i.e., from the same model or brand). As long as the private attestation key is not leaked and accepted in the trust store of client and servers, this mode provides security against impersonation and unlinkability of user actions among all the devices from the same batch. However, even secure authenticators may be compromised. For example, [13] presents an attack on FIDO2 authenticator implemented inside Samsung's TrustZone Trusted Execution Enviroment (TEE). In basic mode, once one of the keys is leaked, security for all keys in the same batch is lost. Which means that the attestation certificate would need to be revoked on all the servers that trust it, and hardware authenticators would need to be physically replaced. In summary, in this work, we ask the following questions:

Can we provide a unified model that captures the security and privacy properties of all attestation modes? Are there significant limitations to the current FIDO2 attestation modes and can they be overcome?

1.2 Contributions

We can answer the questions above in the affirmative:

- We define a new class of *Extended Passwordless Authentication Protocols with Attestation* (ePlAA) that allows to unify and prove the security and privacy properties for all FIDO2 attestation modes.
- Based on our analysis of current modes, we suggest a new mode called smpTW that improves upon the current basic mode by allowing it to recover security even after an authenticator was compromised.

We analyse the publicly available FIDO2 attestation modes present in the specification. To this end we unify and extend the models from [3,4,10] with the new class ePlAA. We then continue to formally define and prove the different security and privacy definitions for each attestation mode and compare them. We summarize the different properties and considered modes in our and previous work in Table 1 and provide more details in Sect. 2.1.

In our unified analysis, we find that only WebAuthn with attestation mode basic satisfies our desired definitions for authentication security and unlinkability (none and self only satisfy weaker authentication security and attCA only weaker unlinkability). Since basic attestation poses the risk of batch corruptions that might lead to the replacement of the entire authenticator batch, we propose a new attestation mode smpTW based on the (simple) TokenWeaver general attestation scheme proposed in [8]. smpTW is very similar to basic mode and satisfies our desired definitions. However, in constrast to basic mode, it allows to recover security even after an authenticator in the same batch was compromised.

Table 1. WebAuthn properties and considered attestation modes analysed in the literature and this work.

	BBCW [3]	HLW [10]	BCZ [4]	This work
Properties				
Authentication Security	✓	✓	✓	✓
Unlinkability	✗	✓	✗	✓
PQ-readiness	✗	✗	✓	✓
Post-compromise Security	✗	✗	✗	(✓)
Attestation modes				
none	✗	✗	✓	✓
self	✗	✓	✗	✓
basic	(✓)	✗	✗	✓
attCA	✗	✗	✗	✓
smpTW	✗	✗	✗	✓
Adversary type during the protocol phases				
Certification	-	-	-	Active
Registration	Active	Active	Passive	Active
Authentication	Active	Active	Active	Active

Since we are considering potential future improvements to the FIDO2 standard, we analyse the existing schemes from a quantum-resistant perspective: our security reductions between the authentication security and unlinkability of WebAuthn and the collision resistance of hash functions, forgery resistance of signatures, or semantic security of encryption primitives are valid against classical (PPT) and quantum (QPT) polynomial-time adversaries, so that any instantiation of the protocol using post-quantum primitive yields a post-quantum secure passwordless authentication protocol. As efficient instantiations of PQ blind signatures are not yet standardised, we opted for an attestation mode based on *simple TokenWeaver* instead of the full *TokenWeaver*. Together with the work in [4], our work contributes to a full-fledged post-quantum solution including privacy-preserving secure attestation modes.

1.3 Overview of the Paper

We first present background on WebAuthn with attestation, TokenWeaver, and PCS in Sect. 2. In Sect. 3, we define *extended Passwordless Authentication Proto-*

cols with Attestation (ePlAA) which is based on BCZ's [4] ePlA class— we add an
initiation and certification phase to the existing registration and authentication.
We continue with the detailed definition of authentication security and unlinkability in Sect. 4. Section 5 presents the analysis of existing FIDO2 attestation
modes. We present our new attestation mode smpTW in Sect. 6 and conclude in
Sect. 7.

2 Background

We introduce needed background on WebAuthn, such as on its key and attestation modes, and prior security models, as well as on the attestation framework
TokenWeaver and post-compromis security.

Notation. We write $x \leftarrow_\$ X$ for x being the returned value of a probabilistic
algorithm X; we write $x \leftarrow X$ if X is deterministic. Moreover, we denote the
security parameter by λ and the number of oracle queries to oracle $\mathcal{O}$ by $q_\mathcal{O}$.

In addition, we denote the signature scheme used for assertion signatures
(during the authentication phase) by $\Sigma = (\Sigma.\mathsf{KG}, \Sigma.\mathsf{Sign}, \Sigma.\mathsf{Vfy})$ and use
$\Sigma_A = (\Sigma_A.\mathsf{KG}, \Sigma_A.\mathsf{Sign}, \Sigma_A.\mathsf{Vfy})$ to denote the attestation signature scheme.
In addition, symmetric and asymmetric encryption schemes are denoted as
$\mathcal{E}_s = (\mathcal{E}_s.\mathsf{KG}, \mathcal{E}_s.\mathsf{Encrypt}, \mathcal{E}_s.\mathsf{Decrypt})$ and $\mathcal{E}_a = (\mathcal{E}_a.\mathsf{KG}, \mathcal{E}_a.\mathsf{Encrypt}, \mathcal{E}_a.\mathsf{Decrypt})$,
respectively. We denote $\Lambda = (\mathsf{CG}, \mathsf{CVfy})$ the scheme for generating and verifying
digital certificates from issuer's public keys. In addition to signature genera-
tion and verification, these operations also consist of other operations such as
adding/checking an expiration time or revocation mechanisms. We make use
of the standard definitions for existential unforgability under chosen-message
attack (euf-cma), indistinguishably under chosen-plaintext attack (ind-cpa), and
collision resistance (coll-res).

2.1 WebAuthn

The FIDO2 protocol aims at passwordless authentication of users and is run
between a Relying Party (RP), a client, and an authenticator owned by a user.
In addition, an issuer of attestation certificates might be involved, depending on
the attestation type used. A high-level message flow is depicted in Fig. 1. FIDO2
specifies two subprotocols: WebAuthn and CTAP. As this paper is concerned
with attestation, we only focus on the WebAuthn protocol and omit the CTAP
protocol. The current stable version is WebAuthn 2 [14] with an editor's draft
available for WebAuthn 3 [15]. Our results apply for both versions and as such
we will refer to WebAuthn for the remainder of the paper.

Key Modes. WebAuthn offers two key modes: resident and non-resident keys,
where the latter means that the keys are stored (symmetrically encrypted) at
the server as analysed in [10]. Resident keys, in contrast, are stored either locally
or as an encrypted list at a trusted third party to enable key sharing between
different devices such as different phones that can be used as authenticators.

Recently, passkeys [1] have emerged as a new concept of key management. They are resident keys, which can be used from multiple devices as they can be synchronised across devices registered by the same user in a given platform, such as Google, Apple or Microsoft, or they can be used from a nearby device (e.g., using Bluetooth). Passkeys that are migrated across devices are encrypted end-to-end. To cover this new concept, this work focuses on resident keys.

Attestation Modes. During registration, the server sends a preferred attestation conveyance mode (called attestation preferences) together with its challenge. This preference indicates whether the server is in fact not interested in getting an attestation from the authenticator (preference none); if the client is allowed to alter the authenticator's attestation statement, e.g. to remove uniquely identifying information (preference indirect); if the client should forward the authenticator attestation without any changes (preference direct); or if the server is allowed to request uniquely identifying information from authenticators (preference enterprise).

We rule out none because we want to analyse different attestation modes, indirect because we want to be able to consider a malicious client, and enterprise because this work is concerned with the unlinkability of authenticators that is clearly not given when uniquely identifying information is provided. Therefore, we consider only the direct mode (without making this explicit in our abstraction in Fig. 7) in this work, including the analysis from Sect. 5. In mode direct, WebAuthn allows the following attestations modes:

None: The default mode in the specifications is to use no attestation, i.e., no signature is included in the authenticator's response during registration.

Self: The authenticator's response is signed using the secret credential key during registration (and authentication).

Basic: Attestation key pairs are shared by "batches" of at least 100,000 authenticators for privacy reasons.

AttCA: An authenticator can generate multiple Attestation Identity Keys (AIKs) and request certificates for each from one or more attestation CAs. For our analysis we assume authenticators use a fresh AIK when registering to a server in order to prevent trivial privacy attacks.

AnonCA: This mode is similar to AttCA with the difference that certificates are dynamically generated per-credential by a cloud-operated CA owned by the (trusted) manufacturer. We do not consider this mode in this work as for the little public information available it is the same setup as AttCA with the assumption of a fresh AIK per server registration.

In the previous Webauthn 1, another attestation mode using (Elliptic Curve) Direct Anonymous Attestation (DAA), based on [6], was allowed which seemed to offer an interesting compromise between security, privacy, and availability of the CA. It has been deprecated in WebAuthn 2 though.

WebAuthn as Passwordless Authentication Protocol. Recently, several works have been set up to model security and privacy properties of WebAuthn (also of CTAP and of the combination of the two protocols in FIDO2) and to reduce them provably to the security of the involved cryptographic primitives. Barbosa, Boldyreva, Chen, and Warinschi (BBCW) [3] started this line of research, defining the cryptographic class of *Passwordless Authentication (PlA)* and *authentication security* consisting of two subprotocols Register = (rChall, rCom, rRsp, rVrfy) and Authenticate = (aChall, aCom, aRsp, aVrfy).

Authenticator T	Client C	RP S
Registration:		$\xleftarrow{m_{rch}}$ $m_{rch} \leftarrow_\$ $ rChall(S, tb, UV)
	$(m_{rcom}, m_{rcl}) \leftarrow_\$ $ rCom$(\text{id}_S, m_{rch}, \text{tb})$	
	$\xleftarrow{m_{rcom}}$	
$(m, m_{att}, \text{att}, rc_T) \leftarrow_\$ $ rRsp(T, m_{rcom})		
$m_{rrsp} \leftarrow (m, m_{att}, \text{att})$	$\xrightarrow{m_{rrsp}}$	(m_{rrsp}, m_{rcl})
		$\xrightarrow{}$ $(rc_S, d) \leftarrow$ rVrfy(S, m_{rcl}, m_{rrsp})
Authentication:		$\xleftarrow{m_{ach}}$ $m_{ach} \leftarrow_\$ $ aChall(S, tb, UV)
	$(m_{acom}, m_{acl}) \leftarrow_\$ $ aCom$(\text{id}_S, m_{ach}, \text{tb})$	
	$\xleftarrow{m_{acom}}$	
$m_{arsp} \leftarrow_\$ $ aRsp(T, m_{acom})	$\xrightarrow{m_{arsp}}$	(m_{arsp}, m_{acl})
		$\xrightarrow{}$ $(rc_S, d) \leftarrow$ aVrfy(S, m_{acl}, m_{arsp})

Fig. 2. WebAuthn flow [4]; attestation values are highlighted in teal.

BBCW proved WebAuthn with attestation mode basic to be secure against active adversaries during Register and Authenticate. However, they assume each authenticator has a different attestation key (batch size equals 1). Hence, no privacy is preserved. Bindel, Cremers, and Zhao (BCZ) [4] extended BBCW's framework modeling various additional properties of FIDO2 (calling the resulting class extended PlA (ePlA)) with attestation mode none and analysed the protocol's readiness for the post-quantum transition. In parallel, Hanzlik, Loss, and Wagner (HLW) [10] extended BBCW's framework in a different way, adding non-resident keys under attestation mode self to the analysis. Moreover, they are the first to define privacy formally (i.e., *unlinkability* of authenticators) for FIDO2.

Returning to the details of WebAuthn as ePlA, during registration, the RP first samples a challenge (in rChall) and sends it together with other information (as m_{rch}) to the client. The client then computes a command and a client message (m_{rcom} and m_{rcl}, respectively, in rCom) and sends m_{rcom} to the authenticator. The authenticator samples a credential key pair and chooses the attestation mode (states in att) and generates the attestation statement m_{att} (potentially including an attestation signature) depending on the attestation mode, packs the information in m_{rrsp} and sends it to the client. The client forwards it, together with m_{rcl} to the RP. The RP verifies the attestation statement (after checking that att is in the set of its accepted attestation modes) and makes a decision d whether it accepts the registration. We depict the flow of the WebAuthn protocol between the authenticator, the client, and the relying party (RP) (i.e. without the issuer) in Fig. 2.

The authentication message flow is very similar to the registration one, the biggest difference being the assertion signature is generated using the credential secret key. We recall the formal abstraction of Authenticate as given in [4] in Fig. 3; we define Register *including attestation* in Fig. 7, Sect. 5.

---

aChall(π_S^i, tb, UV): // 1. Server

1 π_S^i.ch ←$ \{0,1\}^{\geq \lambda}$
2 π_S^i.tb ← tb, $\pi_S^i.UV$ ← UV
3 m_{ach} ← (id$_S$, π_S^i.ch, $\pi_S^i.UP$, $\pi_S^i.UV$)
4 π_S^i.st$_{exe}$ ← running
5 **return** m_{ach}

aRsp(π_T^j, rc$_T$, m_{acom}): // 3. Authenticator

6 (id, h, UP, UV) ← m_{acom}
7 **if** rc$_T$[id] = ⊥: **return** (⊥, rc$_T$)
8 **if** π_T^j.suppUV = false **and** UV = true: **return** (⊥, rc$_T$)
9 rc$_T$[id].n ← rc$_T$[id].n + 1
10 ad ← (H(id), rc$_T$[id].n, UP, UV)
11 σ ←$ rc$_T$[id].Σ.Sign(rc$_T$[id].sk, (ad, h))
12 m_{arsp} ← (rc$_T$[id].cid, ad, σ, rc$_T$[id].uid)
13 π_T^j.agCon ← (id, h, rc$_T$[id].n, UV, UP)
14 π_T^j.sid ← (H(id), rc$_T$[id].cid, h, n)
15 π_T^j.st$_{exe}$ ← accepted
16 **return** (m_{arsp}, rc$_T$)

aCom(id$_S$, m_{ach}, tb): // 2. Client

17 (id, ch, UV) ← m_{ach}
18 **if** id $\neq$ id$_S$: **return** ⊥
19 m_{acl} ← (ch, tb)
20 UP ← true, h ← H(m_{acl})
21 m_{acom} ← (id, h, UP, UV)
22 **return** (m_{acom}, m_{acl})

aVrfy(π_S^i, rc$_S$, m_{acl}, m_{arsp}): // 4. Server

23 (ch, tb) ← m_{acl}, (cid, ad, σ, uid) ← m_{arsp}
24 (h, n, UP, UV) ← ad
25 **if** rc$_S$[cid] = ⊥: **return** (rc$_S$, 0)
26 **if** π_S^i.ch $\neq$ ch **or** π_S^i.tb $\neq$ tb **or** $h \neq$ H(id$_S$) **or** $UP \neq$ true **or** $UV \neq \pi_S^i.UV$ **or** rc$_S$[cid].Σ.Vfy(rc$_S$[cid].pk, (ad, H(m_{acl})), σ) = 0 **or** $n \leq$ rc$_S$[cid].n: **return** (rc$_S$, 0)
27 rc$_S$[cid].n ← n
28 π_S^i.agCon ← (id$_S$, H(m_{acl}), n, UV, UP)
29 π_S^i.sid ← (h, cid, H(m_{acl}), n)
30 π_S^i.st$_{exe}$ ← accepted
31 **return** (rc$_S$, 1)

Fig. 3. Authentication of WebAuthn as described in [4] as instantiation of ePIA = (Register, Authenticate).

2.2 TokenWeaver and Post-Compromise Security

TokenWeaver [8] is an attestation framework that is able to provide Post-Compromise Security (PCS) [7] for Trusted Execution Environments (TEEs) while still preserving the users' privacy. The goal of PCS [7] is to recover from a compromise of an honest party and regain lost security. If the honest party performs a "healing" step, the attacker is "locked out" and the compromised secrets are replaced with new ones unknown to the attacker.

In the context of FIDO2, the TEE is the authenticator. For example, in basic mode, if an authenticator is compromised, we lose all security claims that rely on the compromised attestation secret key. In TokenWeaver's "healing" step, the authenticator can be provisioned with a new attestation key. Upon such a provision request, the authenticator either recovers or detects a compromise, thus achieving PCS.

The full TokenWeaver solution is based on using ephemeral attestation signing keys, provisioned in a privacy preserving protocol based on blind signatures. The authors also discussed a simplified *Global Attestation Key* variant. In the

FIDO2 context, this smpTW mode, is very similar to the basic mode, but periodically rotates a short-lived "batch" attestation key. PCS is achieved by the provisioning protocol that is used by the device to get the next epoch's attestation key. smpTW allows the system to recover from or detect a compromise when the previous global attestation key expires.

3   Definition of Extended Passwordless Authentication Protocols with Attestation

To analyse the security (i.e., passwordless authentication and PCS) and privacy (i.e., unlinkability) properties of WebAuthn with different attestation modes, we follow the line of work started with [3]. Namely, they defined the cryptographic primitive *Passwordless Authentication* (PlA) protocols and view WebAuthn as an instantiation of PlA. [4] defined *extended* PlA (ePlA) to give a more fine-grained analysis. In this section we present our new class of ePlA *with Attestation* (ePlAA) that 1) unifies the classes used in [4,10] to the extend possible and 2) extends it by allowing different attestations modes.

We define ePlAA for four entities — authenticators T, clients C, servers S, and issuers I each having a state to store information — by four phases, Initiate, Certification, Register and Authenticate described as follows.

We assume that if an algorithm gets a specific entity as input (e.g., an authenticator T) it also gets its state (e.g., st_T) as input and potentially updates it during the algorithm without making this explicit. The initial state of a server for attestation type basic, for example, is empty and later updated (e.g., with the initialisation context that includes the issuers public key pk_I to verify the authenticator's attestation signature, see Fig. 7).

Moreover, we associate every party with an ID, e.g., id_T of authenticator T that uniquely identifies the authenticator.

Initiate: is the initialisation of authenticators, servers, and issuers, resulting in initialisation contexts ic_T, ic_S, and ic_I. In addition, the authenticators' attestation material att_m is defined (see Sect. 4.3 for more details).

Certification: is the certification of an authenticator's attestation key run between an authenticator T, a client C, and an issuer I and after a successful run of Initiate. At the end, both T and I hold certification contexts, which are relevant for subsequent registrations and authentications. Certification can be decomposed into the following algorithms

   $m_{cgen} \leftarrow_\$ cGen(T)$: The *attestation key generation* takes as input an authenticator T, and outputs a generation[1] message m_{cgen}.

   $(m_{crsp}, cc_I) \leftarrow_\$ cRsp(I, id_T, m_{cgen})$: The *certification response* takes as input an issuer I, a authenticator ID id_T, and a generation message m_{cgen}, and outputs a response message m_{crsp} and an issuer's certification context cc_I.

---

[1] The name is chosen since during many of the attestation modes, the attestation key is generated on the authenticator during this step.

$(cc_T, d) \leftarrow \mathsf{cVrfy}(T, \mathsf{id}_I, m_{\mathsf{crsp}})$: The *certification verification* takes as input an authenticator T, a server identity id_S, and a response message m_{crsp}, and outputs a authenticator-associated certification context cc_T and a decision bit $d \in \{0, 1\}$.

Register: is a two-pass challenge-response protocol run between an authenticator T, a client C, and a server S, and at most once per tuple (T, S) (i.e., not for additional clients) and after a successful run of Certification between T and an issuer. At the end, both T and S hold registration contexts, which are relevant for subsequent authentications. Register can be decomposed as follows:

$m_{\mathsf{rch}} \leftarrow_{\$} \mathsf{rChall}(S, \mathsf{tb}, UV)$: The *challenge generation* takes as input a server S, an authenticator binding state tb^2, and a user verification condition $UV \in \{\mathsf{true}, \mathsf{false}\}$ (which indicates whether user verification is required), and outputs a challenge message m_{rch}.

$(m_{\mathsf{rcom}}, m_{\mathsf{rcl}}) \leftarrow \mathsf{rCom}(\mathsf{id}_S, m_{\mathsf{rch}}, \mathsf{tb})$: The *client command algorithm* takes as input the intended server identity id_S, a challenge message m_{rch}, and an authenticator binding state tb, and outputs a client message m_{rcl} and a command message m_{rcom}.

$(m_{\mathsf{rrsp}}, rc_T, \mathsf{sid}, \mathsf{agCon}) \leftarrow_{\$} \mathsf{rRsp}(T, m_{\mathsf{rcom}})$: The *registration response* takes as inputs an authenticator T (and implicitly its initialisation and certification context ic_T and cc_t that are included in st_T) and a command message m_{rcom}, and outputs a response message m_{rrsp}, an authenticator-associated registration context rc_T, a session id sid, and the agreed content from the authenticators's perspective agCon.

$(rc_S, d, \mathsf{sid}, \mathsf{agCon}) \leftarrow \mathsf{rVrfy}(S, m_{\mathsf{rcl}}, m_{\mathsf{rrsp}})$: The *registration verification* takes as inputs a server S, a client message m_{rcl}, and a response message m_{rrsp}, and outputs a server-associated registration context rc_S, a decision bit d, a session id sid, and the agreed content from the server's perspective to indicate whether the registration request was accepted.

Authenticate: is a two-pass challenge-response protocol run between an authenticator T, a client C, and a server S after a successful run of Register, in which both T and S generated their registration contexts. S either accepts or rejects the authentication attempt. Authenticate can be decomposed as follows:

$m_{\mathsf{ach}} \leftarrow_{\$} \mathsf{aChall}(S, \mathsf{tb}, UV)$: The *challenge generation* takes as input a server S, an authenticator binding state tb, and a user verification condition $UV \in \{\mathsf{true}, \mathsf{false}\}$, and outputs a challenge message m_{ach}.

$(m_{\mathsf{acl}}, m_{\mathsf{acom}}) \leftarrow \mathsf{aCom}(\mathsf{id}_S, m_{\mathsf{ach}}, \mathsf{tb})$: the *client command algorithm* inputs the intended server identity id_S, a challenge message m_{ach}, and a binding state tb, and outputs a client message m_{acl} and a command message m_{acom}.

$(m_{\mathsf{arsp}}, rc_T) \leftarrow_{\$} \mathsf{aRsp}(T, m_{\mathsf{acom}})$: The *authentication response* takes as inputs an authenticator T (implicitly along with its associated contexts ic_T, cc_T, and rc_T stored in the state st_T) and a command message m_{acom}, and

---

^{2} WebAuthn [14, Sec 5.8] optionally uses token binding [12] to cryptographically bind the information provided by the authenticator to the TLS layer, as modelled in [4].

outputs a response message m_{arsp} and the updated registration context rc_T.

$(\mathsf{rc}_S, d) \leftarrow \mathsf{aVrfy}(S, m_{\mathsf{acl}}, m_{\mathsf{arsp}})$: The *authentication verification* takes as inputs a server S (implicitly along with its associated registration contexts ic_S and rc_S stored st_S), a client message m_{acl}, and a response message m_{arsp}, and outputs the updated registration context rc_S and a decision bit d indicating whether the authentication request was accepted.

We assume all initialisation, certification, and registration contexts to be initialised with the empty set without making this explicit in the pseudo-codes.

Similar to [3,4], we model concurrent or sequential sessions of a server S or issuer I, and sequential sessions of an authenticator T, using the following notation. π_S^i is the i-th instance of server sessions, i.e., $S = \{\pi_S^i\}_i$; π_I^k is the k-th instance of issuer sessions, i.e., $I = \{\pi_I^k\}_k$; and π_T^j is the j-th instance of either server-authenticator or issuer-authenticator sessions, i.e., $T = \{\pi_T^j\}_j$.

Extending the session variables defined in [4], the following variables are used by our ePIAA protocol.

$\pi_I^k, \pi_T^j, \pi_S^i$: k-th issuer, j-th authenticator, i-th server session.

$\pi_I^k.\mathsf{sid}$, $\pi_T^j.\mathsf{sid}$, $\pi_S^i.\mathsf{sid}$: Issuer, authenticator, and server session identifiers. The session identifiers of two distinct sessions (between server/issuer and authenticator) are expected to be the same.

$\pi_S^i.\mathsf{ch}$: Registration/authentication challenge, generated in rChall/aChall.

$\pi_T^j.\mathsf{st_{exe}}$, $\pi_S^i.\mathsf{st_{exe}}$, $\pi_I^k.\mathsf{st_{exe}}$: Execution statuses being either $\{\bot, \text{running}, \text{accepted}\}$ and updated in respective algorithms.

$\pi_S^i.\mathsf{pkCP}$: List of accepted assertion signature schemes by S.

$\pi_S^i.\mathsf{attPol}$: Attestation policy of the server, e.g., which attestation modes and algorithms are accepted.

$\pi_T^j.\mathsf{att}$: Attestation mode chosen by the authenticator. Implicitly, this includes also the algorithm that is used for the attestation signature (if attestation signatures are generated).

$\pi_T^j.\mathsf{suppUV}$: Variable indicating whether T supports user verification.

$\pi_I^k.\mathsf{agCon}$, $\pi_S^i.\mathsf{agCon}$, $\pi_T^j.\mathsf{agCon}$: The contents that are expected to be agreed in session with the same session ID.

4 Security and Privacy Definition of ePIAA

We continue refining the security and privacy properties from [4,10] definitions to cover attestation for our new class ePIAA defined in the previous section. We first describe our threat model(s) for the passwordless authentication and unlinkability of ePIAA. Next we define the oracles that are allowed to be accessed during the two experiments, authenticator groups, and session partnering, before we then formally define passwordless authentication security (PAuth) and unlinkability (UnI) of ePIAA.

4.1 Threat Model

First of all, as common in this line of research, we do not model the user. Following [4], we assume that the users always provide the user presence or user verification confirmation when it is required and leave the users implicit in the authentication and unlinkability experiments. In addition, we assume that there is only one set of credentials per server to be active at a time, as otherwise the user needs to make a choice which credential to use, as implicitly assumed in [4].

Table 2. Assumptions for the passwordless authentication and unlinkability experiments in each phase, with adversary types in the channels between the different participants. Entities which can be controlled by the adversary are highlighted in teal. (*) denotes some natural restrictions on the challenge entities that decide on a win in the security and privacy experiments, which are further specified in this section.

Phase	Passwordless Authentication		Unlinkability	
	$\mathcal{A}$ type	Entities	$\mathcal{A}$ type	Entities
Initialisation $I\text{-}T$	None	I, T	Active	I, T
Initialisation $I\text{-}S$	Passive	I, S	Active	I, S
Certification	Active	I, T^*, C	Active	I, T^*, C^*
Registration	Active	T^*, C, S^*	Active	T^*, C^*, S
Authentication	Active	T^*, C, S^*	Active	T^*, C^*, S

We continue describing assumptions on the four entities: authenticators, servers, clients, and issuers. First, we assume the identifier id_S of each server S is unique and we consider that some selected *authenticators* can be corrupted both in the authentication and unlinkability experiment. This is defined in more detail in the experiments and in the different instantiations. In particular, we do not assume authenticators to be "tamper-proof", i.e., the adversary is allowed to read locally stored contexts of authenticators, which means that they will have access to the private keys corresponding to the credentials used to register into a specific service, and to the attestation private key. Moreover, we assume *servers* to be malicious in both experiments (with the exception of the winning server during the authentication security). In addition, we allow malicious *clients* for both experiments (with the exception of the two clients interacting with the target authenticators in the unlinkability experiment). These exceptions correspond to the asterisks in Table 2 which summarizes our assumptions modeled. Regarding issuers, for the authentication experiment we assume the issuer behaves properly, meaning it initializes authenticators honestly and certifies them according to their attestation material. For unlinkability we assume malicious issuers and that existing issuers can be corrupted by an adversary. This includes an issuer revealing information about the certificates issued to the different authenticators in order to break their unlinkability.

After describing the threat model of the different involved entities, we turn now to additional assumptions during the respective phases. The *initialisation* phase does not need to be trusted during the unlinkability experiment. Therefore, we allow the adversary to initialise authenticators and servers with any issuer. In the case of the authentication experiment, we assume the communication channel between issuer and authenticator to be authenticated and confidential. Hence, it is considered trusted and we do not allow active or passive adversaries between these two entities. Such a direct connection could be possible during manufacturing time. We do allow, however, the adversary to access the issuer's public key—denoted by giving access to ic_S. We assume further, an active adversary in the *certification phase* (for both unlinkability and authentication experiments). We make no security assumptions on the communication channels between authenticator, client, and server in the *authentication* or *registration phases* for both authentication and unlinkability.

$\text{NEWT}(T, \text{suppUV}, (I, k))$:

32 **if** $\text{suppUV}_T \neq \perp$: **return** $\perp$
33 **if** $I \notin \mathcal{L}_I$: **return** $\perp$ // only if in $\text{Expt}_{\text{ePIAA}}^{\text{PAuth}}()$
34 Initiate (T, π_T^k)
35 $\text{suppUV}_T \leftarrow \text{suppUV}$
36 **return**

$\text{NEWS}(S, \text{pkCP}, \text{attPol}, (I, k))$:

37 **if** $\text{pkCP}_S \neq \perp$ **and** $\text{attPol} \neq \perp$: **return** $\perp$
38 **if** $I \notin \mathcal{L}_I$: **return** $\perp$ // only if in $\text{Expt}_{\text{ePIAA}}^{\text{PAuth}}()$
39 Initiate (S, π_I^k)
40 $\text{pkCP}_S \leftarrow \text{pkCP}, \text{attPol}_S \leftarrow \text{attPol}$
41 **return**

$\text{CORRUPT}(T, G)$:

42 **if** $T \in G$: **return** $\perp$
43 $\forall i: \mathcal{L}_{\text{frsh}} \leftarrow \mathcal{L}_{\text{frsh}} \setminus \{(S_i, T)\}$
44 **return** $\{rc_T[S_i]\}_i, ic_T, cc_T$

$\text{CORRUPTI}(I)$:

45 **return** ic_I, cc_I

$\text{CGEN}(T, h)$:

46 **if** $\pi_I^k \neq \perp$ **or** $\pi_T^h \neq \perp$ **or** $ic_T = \perp$: **return** $\perp$
47 $m_{\text{cgen}} \leftarrow_\$ \text{cGen}(\pi_T^h)$
48 **return** m_{cgen}

$\text{CRESP}((I, k), m_{\text{cgen}}, \text{id}_T)$:

49 **if** $\pi_I^k.\text{st}_{\text{exe}} \neq \text{running}$: **return** $\perp$
50 $(m_{\text{crsp}}, cc_I) \leftarrow_\$ \text{cRsp}(\pi_I^k, \text{id}_T, m_{\text{cgen}})$
51 **return** m_{crsp}

$\text{CCOMPL}((T, h), m_{\text{rrsp}})$:

52 $\pi_T^h.\text{st}_{\text{exe}} \neq \text{running}$: **return** $\perp$
53 $(cc_T, d) \leftarrow \text{cVrfy}(T, \text{id}_I, m_{\text{crsp}})$
54 **return** d

$\text{RCHALL}((S, i), \text{tb}, UV)$:

55 **if** $\text{pkCP}_S = \perp$ **or** $\text{attInfo}_S = \perp$ **or** $\pi_S^i \neq \perp$:
    return $\perp$
56 $\pi_S^i.\text{pkCP} \leftarrow \text{pkCP}_S, \pi_S^i.\text{attInfo} \leftarrow \text{attInfo}_S$
57 $m_{\text{rch}} \leftarrow_\$ \text{rChall}(\pi_S^i, \text{tb}, UV)$
58 **return** m_{rch}

$\text{RRESP}((T, j), m_{\text{rcom}})$:

59 **if** $\text{suppUV}_T = \perp$ **or** $\pi_T^j \neq \perp$ **or** $ic_T = \perp$ **or**
    $cc_T = \perp$:
60   **return** $\perp$
61 $(m_{\text{rrsp}}, rc_T, \text{sid}, \text{agCon}) \leftarrow_\$ \text{rRsp}(\pi_T^j, m_{\text{rcom}})$
62 // set $\pi_T^j.\text{sid} \leftarrow \text{sid}, \pi_T^j.\text{agCon} \leftarrow \text{agCon}$ in
    rRsp
63 **if** $\pi_T^j.\text{sid} \in \{S_L, S_R\}$: $\mathcal{L}_{\text{ch}}^r \leftarrow \mathcal{L}_{\text{ch}}^r \cup (T)$ // only
    if in $\text{Expt}_{\text{ePIAA}}^{\text{PAuth}}()$
64 $\text{Ar}_c[\pi_T^j.\text{sid}] \leftarrow T$
65 **return** m_{rrsp}

$\text{RCOMPL}((S, i), m_{\text{rcl}}, m_{\text{rrsp}})$:

66 **if** $\text{pkCP}_S = \perp$ **or** $\text{attInfo}_S = \perp$ **or** $\pi_S^i.\text{st}_{\text{exe}} \neq$
    running: **return** $\perp$
67 $(rc_S, d, \text{sid}, \text{agCon}) \leftarrow_\$ \text{rVrfy}(\pi_S^i, m_{\text{rcl}}, m_{\text{rrsp}})$
68 # $\pi_S^i.\text{sid} \leftarrow \text{sid}, \pi_S^i.\text{agCon} \leftarrow \text{agCon}$ in rVrfy
69 **if** $d = 1$ **and** $\text{Ar}_c[\pi_S^i.\text{sid}] \neq \perp$:
70     $\mathcal{L}_{\text{frsh}} \leftarrow \mathcal{L}_{\text{frsh}} \cup \{(S, \text{Ar}_c[\pi_S^i.\text{sid}])\}$
71 $\text{Ar}_c[\pi_S^i.\text{sid}] \leftarrow \perp$
72 **return** d

$\text{ACHALL}((S, i), \text{tb}, UV)$:

73 **if** $\text{pkCP}_S = \perp$ **or** $\text{attInfo}_S = \perp$ **or** $\pi_S^i \neq \perp$:
    return $\perp$
74 $\pi_S^i.\text{pkCP} \leftarrow \text{pkCP}_S, \pi_S^i.\text{attInfo} \leftarrow \text{attInfo}_S$
75 $m_{\text{ach}} \leftarrow_\$ \text{aChall}(\pi_S^i, \text{tb}, UV)$
76 **return** m_{ach}

$\text{ARESP}((T, j), m_{\text{acom}})$:

77 **if** $\text{suppUV}_T = \perp$ **or** $\pi_T^j \neq \perp$: **return** $\perp$
78 $\pi_T^j.\text{suppUV} \leftarrow \text{suppUV}_T$
79 $(m_{\text{arsp}}, rc_T) \leftarrow_\$ \text{aRsp}(\pi_T^j, m_{\text{acom}})$
80 **if** $\pi_T^j.\text{sid} \in \{S_L, S_R\}$: $\mathcal{L}_{\text{ch}}^a \leftarrow \mathcal{L}_{\text{ch}}^a \cup (T)$ // only
    if in $\text{Expt}_{\text{ePIAA}}^{\text{PAuth}}()$
81 **return** m_{arsp}

$\text{ACOMPL}((S, i), m_{\text{acl}}, m_{\text{arsp}})$:

82 **if** $\pi_S^i = \perp$ **or** $\pi_S^i.\text{st}_{\text{exe}} \neq \text{running}$: **return** $\perp$
83 $(rc_S, d) \leftarrow \text{aVrfy}(\pi_S^i, m_{\text{acl}}, m_{\text{arsp}})$
84 **if** $d = 1$ **and** $\text{inGroup}(G, m_{\text{arsp}}, rc_S) = 1$ **and**
    win-auth = 0:
85   win-auth $\leftarrow \text{Win-auth}(S, i)$
86 **return** d

Fig. 4. Oracles for experiments defined in Fig. 5 and 6; differences to the definitions of [4,10] are highlighted in teal.

4.2   Oracles

We describe all oracles (except RLEFT, RRIGHT, ALEFT, ARIGHT) used in the unlinkability and authentication experiments in Fig. 4.

During the game executions the adversary can create new servers and (initialised) authenticators through the oracles NEWS and NEWT, respectively. In these two oracles, initiate functions Initiate(S) and Initiate(T) are called, respectively. These functions run the respective initialisation operations for servers and authenticators that we define in the instantiations in Sect. 5. By invoking the oracles rCHALL, rRESP, and rCOMPL the adversary is able to actively interfere during the registration of authenticators. Moreover, via the oracles aCHALL, aRESP and aCOMPL, it can actively interfere during authentication. It is important to note that we do not allow the adversary to initialize tokens and servers with information from an issuer created by the adversary itself during the authentication experiment as we assume the channel between issuer and authenticator to be secure as described above. However, the adversary is allowed to initialise authenticators and servers in the unlinkability experiment with information from an issuer created by such an adversary. Furthermore, the adversary can also query the CORRUPT oracle to reveal an authenticator's registration, certification, and initialisation contexts. It is important to emphasize that our CORRUPT definition differs from [4] in three aspects: 1) it is independent of the sever and as such it reveals *all* registration contexts of the authenticator, 2) it also reveals the initialisation and certification context of the authenticator as a natural extension to cover attestation modes, 3) and additionally it receives an authenticator group G which defines a set of authenticators that cannot be corrupted. The definition of the group is defined per instantiation. More information about authenticator groups is provided in Sect. 4.3. We additionally give the adversary access to the CORRUPTI oracle to reveal the internal state of an issuer contained in the initialization and certification contexts. Although the adversary can already read and modify the information exchanged between authenticator and issuer during the certification phase through the individual certification oracles, with this corrupt issuer oracle the adversary will also get access to any private keys or private configuration information an issuer may keep. This oracle will only be available in the unlinkability experiment since, as we mentioned in the previous section, we consider the issuer to be trusted in the authentication experiment.

In addition, in a particular stage of the unlinkability experiment, $\mathcal{A}$ will be given access to RLEFT, RRIGHT, ALEFT, ARIGHT oracles (defined in Fig. 6), which will run the algorithms in the registration and authentication phases with two randomly assigned authenticators.

4.3   Authenticator Groups

We introduce a group of authenticators G as some set of authenticators that share the same attestation material att_m which is defined in Initiate and shared by the authenticators with the server during Register. For example, a group may describe a set of authenticators which have attestation keys that have been issued by the same issuer, with the same validity period, or even the same attestation keys. For a meaningful definition of unlinkability, we assume that there are at least two authenticators per group.

We use a static group definition in the authentication security and unlinkability experiments, meaning that the adversary chooses the group of the target authenticator(s) in advance. However, this group could be defined dynamically given the actions of the adversary during the execution of the experiment. We claim that given that the execution of the protocol is independent of the group chosen by the adversary, the security results are the same.

We additionally define a method $inGroup(G, m_{arsp}, rc_S)$, which receives as input a group G, an authentication message response m_{arsp} and a server registration context rc_S. It outputs 1 if and only if m_{arsp} was created by an authenticator that is in G.

In the next two subsections, we give the notions of secure passwordless authentication and unlinkability in connection with a group of authenticators G. More concretely, when proving the property of passwordless authentication, the adversary is able to corrupt any authenticator but those in the same group as the authenticator that is impersonated. In the unlinkability experiment, the adversary tries to distinguish two authenticators which are in the same group.

Intuitively, our definitions of different groups correspond to the following real-world scenarios. For example, an adversary may be restricted to corrupt authenticators of different brand/different models than the one it tries to impersonate. This corresponds to authenticators of different certification levels, of which some may be easier or harder to compromise. The different certification levels can be proven using attestation and as such, this oracle allows us to be more fine-grained regarding the adversary ability to corrupt entities for different attestation modes.

Section 5 includes a description of att_m, and therefore of G, for each instantiation using a different attestation mode.

4.4 Session Partnering

Partnering identifies authenticator, issuer, and server sessions that are successfully communicating with each other as expected, and is encoded through matching session identifiers. More precisely, we say a server (resp., issuer) session π_S^i (resp., π_I^k) *partners with an authenticator session* π_T^j if and only if $\pi_S^i.sid = \pi_T^j.sid \neq \bot$ (resp., $\pi_I^k.sid = \pi_T^j.sid \neq \bot$). We say a server (resp., issuer) session π_S^i (resp., π_I^k) *partners with an authenticator* T if it partners with one of T's sessions. We say an authenticator T is the *registration (resp., initialisation) partner* of a server S (resp., issuer I), if the registration context of T at S (resp., the initialisation or certification context at I) has been set, i.e., $rc_T[id_S] \neq \bot$ (resp., $ic_T[id_I] \neq \bot$ or $cc_T[id_I] \neq \bot$).

4.5 Passwordless Authentication Experiment for ePIAA

Aiming at similar security properties as [4], we say an ePIAA provides *password-less authentication* (PAuth) if servers accept authentication responses if and only if they were generated by a unique honest partnered authentication session. The winning conditions are the same as in [4] except that we add that the adversary can also win by exploiting the certification (i.e., the attestation). Moreover, our definition depends on the choice of an authenticator group G. The resulting experiment is given in Fig. 5.

We call a server session a *test session* if it accepts a response message coming from an authenticator in G. An ePIAA is secure if for every test session π_S^i (i.e., with $\pi_S^i.\text{st}_{\text{exe}} = \text{accepted}$ and with $\text{inGroup}(G, m_{\text{arsp}}, rc_S) = 1$), such that none of the following four winning conditions hold:

1. the non-$\perp$ session identifiers of two authenticator sessions collide.
2. the non-$\perp$ session identifiers of two server sessions collide.
3. All the tokens that registered to the server S are fresh (not corrupted), yet, none of them has a partnering session[3]
4. the agreed contents of a pair of partnered server session $\pi_{S'}^{i'}$ and authenticator session $\pi_{T'}^{j'}$ are distinct and $\text{CORRUPT}(T', G)$ has not been queried.

$\text{Expt}_{\text{ePIAA}}^{\text{PAuth}}(\mathcal{A}, G)$:

1 $\mathcal{L}_{\text{frsh}} \leftarrow \emptyset$, win-auth $\leftarrow 0$, $\text{Ar}_c \leftarrow \emptyset$
2 $N > 0$, for $k = 1..N$: $I_k \leftarrow \text{Initiate}(I)$, $\mathcal{L}_I \leftarrow \{I_1..I_k\}$
3 $() \leftarrow_\$ \mathcal{A}^{\mathcal{O}, I_1..I_k}(1^\lambda)$ //$\mathcal{A}$ can use different issuers to initialize authenticators and servers
4 **return** win-auth

Win-auth(S, i):

5 **if** $\exists(T_1, j_1), (T_2, j_2)$ such that $(T_1, j_1) \neq (T_2, j_2)$ and $\pi_{T_1}^{j_1}.\text{sid} = \pi_{T_2}^{j_2}.\text{sid} \neq \perp$: **return** 1
6 **if** $\exists(S_1, i_1), (S_2, i_2)$ such that $(S_1, i_1) \neq (S_2, i_2)$ and $\pi_{S_1}^{i_1}.\text{sid} = \pi_{S_2}^{i_2}.\text{sid} \neq \perp$: **return** 1
7 **if** $\forall T$ such that $rc_T[\text{id}_S] \neq \perp$, ($\neg\exists j$ such that $\pi_S^i.\text{sid} = \pi_T^j.\text{sid}$, and $(S, T) \in \mathcal{L}_{\text{frsh}}$) : **return** 1
8 **if** $\exists(S', i'), (T', j')$ such that $\pi_{S'}^{i'}.\text{sid} = \pi_{T'}^{j'}.\text{sid} \neq \perp$ and $(S', T') \in \mathcal{L}_{\text{frsh}}$ and $\pi_{S'}^{i'}.\text{agCon} \neq$ $\pi_{T'}^{j'}.\text{agCon}$ and (if $G \neq \{\}$ then $T' \in G$): **return** 1
9 **return** 0

Fig. 5. Security experiment for ePIAA Protocols ePIAA = (Initiate, Certification, Register, Authenticate), with oracles $\mathcal{O}$ defined in Fig. 4; differences to [4] are highlighted in teal.

Finally, we define authentication security for ePIAA.

Definition 1 (PAuth for ePIAA). *Let* Compl $\in \{\text{PPT}, \text{QPT}\}$. *Let* ePIAA = (Initiate, Certification, Register, Authenticate) *be an Extended Passwordless Authentication Protocol with Attestation. We say that for any group* G *of authenticators sharing the same attestation material* att_m, *ePIAA provides secure passwordless authentication, or PAuth for short, if for all* Compl *adversaries* $\mathcal{A}$ *the advantage*

---

[3] We have rephrased the respective condition in [4] which said "any registration partner of S" to avoid ambiguities. The meaning, however, has been maintained.

$$\mathsf{Adv}_{\mathsf{ePIAA}}^{\mathsf{PAuth}}(\mathcal{A}, \mathsf{G}) := \Pr\left[\mathsf{Expt}_{\mathsf{ePIAA}}^{\mathsf{PAuth}}(\mathcal{A}, \mathsf{G}) = 1\right]$$

in winning the game $\mathsf{Expt}_{\mathsf{ePIAA}}^{\mathsf{PAuth}}$ *defined in Fig. 5 is negligible in the security parameter* λ. *During the game* $\mathsf{Expt}_{\mathsf{ePIAA}}^{\mathsf{PAuth}}$, $\mathcal{A}$ *has access to the following oracles:* cGEN, cRESP, cCOMPL, rCHALL, rRESP, rCOMPL, aCHALL, aRESP, aCOMPL, NEWT, NEWS, *and* CORRUPT *(see Fig. 4).*

4.6   Unlinkability Experiment for ePIAA

The first formal definition of privacy in FIDO2, together with an analysis of attestation mode self has been given in [10]. Privacy (or more precisely *unlinkability*) essentially means that different registrations of the same authenticator can not be linked, either in one server or across several servers. On the other hand, a server may be able to link several authentication sessions to the same authenticator in terms of being related to the same registration event, however different servers may not be able to link different authentication sessions to the same device. Data that is exchanged outside of the protocol is out of the scope of the definition (e.g., metadata that could be used to link interactions of the authenticator(s)). [10] defines three types of unlinkability: strong, medium, and weak. We adapt their definition to the case of residential credentials, mostly to rule out trivial attacks and to focus on the unlinkability properties of different attestation modes, and resulting in a definition closest to the *medium unlinkability* in [10].

We additionally use the notion of *group unlinkability*, meaning that a protocol provides unlinkability as long as the adversary is restricted to try to link authenticators of the same group G (see Sect. 4.3). Similarly to the authentication experiment where we use the CORRUPT oracle that receives a group G as input, the definition of *group* may change for each one of the attestation modes.

In [8], the authors propose a new attestation protocol named TokenWeaver that promises higher privacy guarantees and as such is interesting as an additional attestation mode in FIDO2. Therefore, our extension of the unlinkability definition from [10] to cover different attestation modes, is designed to also apply to TokenWeaver.

We define in Fig. 6 the unlinkability experiment consisting of three phases:

Phase 1. The Adversary $\mathcal{A}_1$ gets as input the group G and a set of issuers initialised by the experiment, and is allowed to interact with the oracles defined in Fig. 4. Its output is stored in st_1.

Phase 2. The Adversary $\mathcal{A}_2$ gets as input st_1 and group G and chooses two target authenticators $T_0, T_1 \in \mathsf{G}$ and two target servers S_L, S_R. The challenger runs InitRL, initialising the oracles RLEFT, ALEFT, RRIGHT, ARIGHT, where S_L, S_R have been assigned to R/ALEFT and R/ARIGHT respectively and T_0 and T_1 have been randomly assigned to either R/ALEFT or R/ARIGHT using a bit b. Additionally, $\mathcal{A}_2$ provides an output st_2.

Phase 3. The Adversary $\mathcal{A}_3$ receives the output st_2 of the previous adversary and is allowed to interact with all the oracles defined so far, except creating new authenticators with NEWT or certify/re-certify the chosen authenticators T_0 and T_1 through oracles CGEN, CRESP, and CCOMPL (see Fig. 6). This is to ensure that 1) when we define unlinkability with respect to a group G, both authenticators remain in this group through the next phases of the experiment, and 2) that the whole set of authenticators participating in the experiment is stable. Oracles R/ALEFT and R/ARIGHT are oracles through which the adversary can query either authenticator T_0 or T_1 to run the algorithms meant to be run by the authenticator in the registration (RLEFT, RRIGHT) and authentication (ALEFT, ARIGHT) phases of the ePlAA protocol. Finally, $\mathcal{A}_3$ outputs a bit $\hat{b}$.

Following [10], we define a number of lists using our notation to rule out trivial attacks in the experiments:

$\mathcal{L}_{ch}^r$: all authenticators for which the RRESP oracle was called to register with servers S_L or S_R.

$\mathcal{L}_{ch}^a$: all authenticators for which the ARESP oracle was called to authenticate with servers S_L or S_R.

$\mathcal{L}_{lr}^r$: authenticators $\in \{T_0, T_1\}$ for which the RLEFT or RRIGHT oracles were called to register with servers S_L or S_R.

$\mathcal{L}_{lr}^a$: authenticators $\in \{T_0, T_1\}$ for which the ALEFT or ARIGHT oracles were called to authenticate with servers S_L or S_R.

The experiment outputs 1 if

1. $\hat{b} = b$ and $S_{unl^*} = (\mathcal{L}_{ch}^r \cap \mathcal{L}_{lr}^a) \cup (\mathcal{L}_{lr}^r \cap \mathcal{L}_{ch}^a)$ is empty,
2. $\mathcal{A}$ has not corrupted the authenticators T_0 and T_1 (therefore, $\mathcal{A}$ has not gotten access to any credentials stored in such authenticators as part of the registration with servers S_L or S_R), and
3. T_0 and T_1 belong to the same group G of authenticators sharing the same attestation information.

The main differences between this experiment, depicted in Fig. 6, and the one in [10] are highlighted in teal. Essentially, the changes arise since we consider attestation modes and residential (instead of non-residential) keys. More concretely, 1) we allow the adversary $\mathcal{A}_1$ to create and corrupt authenticators (with restrictions reflected through $\mathcal{L}_{frsh}$); 2) we add initialization and certification phases involving an issuer; 3) we consider authenticator groups G defined through shared attestation information; 4) as mentioned above, we consider the medium unlinkability notion from [10], as our experiment conditions imply that the set $\mathcal{L}_{lr}^a \cup \mathcal{L}_{ch}^a$ is empty. Still the experiment allows us to analyse unlinkability in terms of servers not being able to link different registrations to the same authenticator.

Definition 2 (Group unlinkability for ePlAA). *Let* Compl $\in$ {PPT, QPT}. *Let* ePlAA = (Initiate, Certification, Register, Authenticate) *be an Extended Passwordless Authentication Protocol with Attestation. We say that for any group*

$\mathsf{Expt}^{\mathsf{Unl}}_{\mathsf{ePIAA}}(\mathcal{A}, \mathsf{G}) \ \#\mathcal{A} = (\mathcal{A}_1, \mathcal{A}_2, \mathcal{A}_3):$

10 $\mathcal{L}_{\mathsf{frsh}} \leftarrow \emptyset, \mathcal{L}^r_{\mathsf{ch}} \leftarrow \emptyset, \mathcal{L}^a_{\mathsf{ch}} \leftarrow \emptyset, \mathcal{L}^r_{\mathsf{lr}} \leftarrow \emptyset, \mathcal{L}^a_{\mathsf{lr}} \leftarrow \emptyset, \mathsf{Win\text{-}priv} \leftarrow 0,$
11 $N > 0,$ for $k = 1..N$: $T_k \leftarrow \mathsf{Initiate}(I)$
12 $st_1 \leftarrow_\$ \mathcal{A}_1^{\mathcal{O}, I_1 \cdots I_k}(1^\lambda, \mathsf{G})$ # Phase 1
13 $(T_0, T_1, S_L, S_R, st_2) \leftarrow_\$ \mathcal{A}_2(st_1, \mathsf{G})$ # Phase 2
14 $\mathsf{InitRL}(T_0, T_1, S_L, S_R)$
15 $\mathcal{O}' \leftarrow (\mathcal{O} \setminus \{\mathrm{NEWT}, \mathrm{cGen}(T_{0/1}, \cdot), \mathrm{cRESP}(\cdot, \mathrm{id}_{T_{0/1}}), \mathrm{cCompl}(T_{0/1}, \cdot)\})$

16 $\hat{b} \leftarrow_\$ \mathcal{A}_3^{\mathcal{O}', \mathrm{LEFT}, \mathrm{RIGHT}, I_1 \cdots I_k}(st_2, \mathsf{G})$ # Phase 3
17 return $\mathsf{Win\text{-}priv}(b, \hat{b})$

$\mathsf{Win\text{-}priv}(b, \hat{b}):$

18 $S_{\mathsf{unl}*} = (\mathcal{L}^r_{\mathsf{ch}} \cap \mathcal{L}^a_{\mathsf{lr}}) \cup (\mathcal{L}^r_{\mathsf{lr}} \cap \mathcal{L}^a_{\mathsf{ch}})$
19 if $b = \hat{b}$ and $S_{\mathsf{unl}*} = \emptyset$ and $(S_L, T_b), (S_R, T_{b-1}), (S_R, T_b), (S_L, T_{b-1}) \in \mathcal{L}_{\mathsf{frsh}}$ and $T_b, T_{b-1} \in \mathsf{G}$
    : return 1
20 return 0

$\mathsf{InitRL}(T_0, T_1, S_L, S_R):$

21 if $\mathsf{suppUV}_{T_0} = \bot$ or $\mathsf{suppUV}_{T_1} = \bot$ or $\mathsf{cc}_{T_0} = \bot$ or $\mathsf{cc}_{T_1} = \bot$: return $\bot$ # We let $\mathcal{A}$ create
    and certify new authenticators in Phase 1
22 $b \leftarrow_\$ \{0,1\}$
23 Initialise oracles $\mathrm{R/ALEFT}_{T_b, S_L}$ and $\mathrm{R/ARIGHT}_{T_{b-1}, S_R}$
24 $\mathcal{L}_{\mathsf{frsh}} \leftarrow \mathcal{L}_{\mathsf{frsh}} \cup \{(S_L, T_0), (S_L, T_1), (S_R, T_0), (S_R, T_1)\}$ # for privacy add all four combinations
25 return

$\mathrm{R/ALEFT}_{T_b, S_L}(m):$

26 $S \leftarrow \mathrm{Extract}(m)$ # Obtains from m the server it is intended for
27 if $S \neq S_L$: return $\bot$
28 $j \leftarrow_\$ 0$, while $\pi^j_{T_b} \neq \bot$:
    $j \leftarrow j + 1$ # find next new token session
29 return $\mathrm{rRESP}'((T_b, j), m)$ # in RLEFT
30 return $\mathrm{aRESP}'((T_b, j), m)$ # in ALEFT

$\mathrm{rRESP}'((T, j), m_{\mathsf{rcom}}):$

36 if $\pi^j_T \neq \bot$: return $\bot$
37 $(m_{\mathsf{rrsp}}, \mathsf{rc}_T) \leftarrow_\$ \mathsf{rRsp}(\pi^j_T, m_{\mathsf{rcom}})$
38 $\mathcal{L}^r_{\mathsf{lr}} \leftarrow \mathcal{L}^r_{\mathsf{lr}} \cup T$
39 return m_{rrsp}

$\mathrm{R/ARIGHT}_{T_{b-1}, S_R}(m):$

31 $S \leftarrow \mathrm{Extract}(m)$ # Obtains from m the server it is intended for
32 if $S \neq S_R$: return $\bot$
33 $j \leftarrow_\$ 0$, while $\pi^j_{T_{b-1}} \neq \bot$:
    $j \leftarrow j + 1$ # find next new token session
34 return $\mathrm{rRESP}'((T_{b-1}, j), m)$ # in RLEFT
35 return $\mathrm{aRESP}'((T_{b-1}, j), m)$ # in ALEFT

$\mathrm{aRESP}'((T, j), m_{\mathsf{acom}}):$

40 if $\pi^j_T \neq \bot$: return $\bot$
41 $\pi^j_T.\mathsf{suppUV} \leftarrow \mathsf{suppUV}_T$
42 $(m_{\mathsf{arsp}}, \mathsf{rc}_T) \leftarrow_\$ \mathsf{aRsp}(\pi^j_T, m_{\mathsf{acom}})$
43 $\mathcal{L}^a_{\mathsf{lr}} \leftarrow \mathcal{L}^a_{\mathsf{lr}} \cup T$
44 return m_{arsp}

Fig. 6. Group unlinkability experiment for ePIAA Protocols ePIAA = (Initiate, Certification, Register, Authenticate), with oracles $\mathcal{O}$ defined in Fig. 4 and Compl $\in$ {PPT, QPT}. Differences to [10] are highlighted in teal.

G *of authenticators sharing the same attestation material* att_m, *ePIAA provides group unlinkability (Unl), if for all* Compl *adversaries* $\mathcal{A}$ *the advantage*

$$\mathsf{Adv}^{\mathsf{Unl}}_{\mathsf{ePIAA}}(\mathcal{A}, \mathsf{G}) := \Pr\left[\mathsf{Expt}^{\mathsf{Unl}}_{\mathsf{ePIAA}}(\mathcal{A}, \mathsf{G}) = 1\right]$$

in winning the game $\mathsf{Expt}^{\mathsf{Unl}}_{\mathsf{ePIAA}}$ *defined in Fig. 6 by trying to distinguish authenticators in the same group* G *is negligible in the security parameter* λ. *During* $\mathsf{Expt}^{\mathsf{Unl}}_{\mathsf{ePIAA}}$, $\mathcal{A}$ *has access to the following oracles:* cGEN, cRESP, cCOMPL, rCHALL, rRESP, rCOMPL, aCHALL, aRESP, aCOMPL, NEWT, NEWS, CORRUPT, *and* CORRUPTI *(see Fig. 4).*

5   WebAuthn and Different Attestations Modes as Instantiations of ePlAA

In this section we explain how we abstract WebAuthn with different attestation modes as ePlAA, and provide the different attestation modes and their analysis regarding their unlinkability and passwordless authentication.

5.1   WebAuthn with Attestation as ePlAA

It is important to recall that we do not consider the RP's preference enterprise (which would signal to the authenticator to include uniquely identifying information), and we (only) consider mode direct (i.e., the RP is interested in attestation directly from the authenticator and unaltered by the client, see Sect. 2.1). Therefore, when adding attestation to the abstraction of [4], only the authenticator's response (rRsp) and the RP's verification (rVrfy) change during Register = (rChall, rCom, rRsp, rVrfy), see Fig. 7. In addition, Initiate and

---

$\mathsf{rChall}(\pi_S^i, \mathsf{tb}, UV)$: // 1. Server

45 $\pi_S^i.\mathsf{ch} \leftarrow_\$ \{0,1\}^{\geq\lambda}$, $\pi_S^i.\mathsf{tb} \leftarrow \mathsf{tb}$
46 $\pi_S^i.UV \leftarrow UV$, $\pi_S^i.\mathsf{uid} \leftarrow_\$ \{0,1\}^{\leq 4\lambda}$
47 $m_{\mathsf{rch}} \leftarrow (\mathsf{id}_S, \pi_S^i.\mathsf{ch}, \pi_S^i.\mathsf{uid}, \pi_S^i.\mathsf{pkCP}, \pi_S^i.UV)$
48 $\pi_S^i.\mathsf{st_{exe}} \leftarrow \mathsf{running}$
49 **return** m_{rch}

$\mathsf{rRsp}(\pi_T^j, m_{\mathsf{rcom}})$: // 3. Authenticator

50 $(\mathsf{id}, \mathsf{uid}, h, \mathsf{pkCP}, UP, UV) \leftarrow m_{\mathsf{rcom}}$
51 **if** at least one algorithm in pkCP is supported
52      $\Sigma \leftarrow \mathsf{pkCP}[i]$ with smallest i possible
53 **else return** $(\perp, \perp)$
54 **if** $\pi_T^j.\mathsf{suppUV} = \mathsf{false}$ **and** $UV = \mathsf{true}$: **return** $(\perp, \perp)$
55 $(pk, sk) \leftarrow_\$ \Sigma.\mathsf{KG}()$, $\mathsf{cid} \leftarrow_\$ \{0,1\}^{\geq\lambda}$, $n \leftarrow 0$
56 $m \leftarrow (\mathsf{H}(\mathsf{id}), n, \mathsf{cid}, pk, \Sigma, UP, UV)$
57 $\mathsf{att} \leftarrow \mathsf{att}_T$
58 **if** $\mathsf{att} = \mathsf{none}$:
59      $m_{\mathsf{att}} \leftarrow \{\}$
60 **elseif** $\mathsf{att} = \mathsf{self}$:
61      $s_A \leftarrow \Sigma.\mathsf{Sign}(sk, (m, h))$
62      $m_{\mathsf{att}} \leftarrow (\Sigma, s_A)$
63 **elseif** $\mathsf{att} = \mathsf{basic}$ or $\mathsf{att} = \mathsf{attCA}$ or $\mathsf{att} = \mathsf{smpTW}$:
64      $(ak, \mathsf{cert}_{vk}) \leftarrow \mathsf{cc}_T$
65      $s_A \leftarrow_\$ \Sigma_A.\mathsf{Sign}(ak, (m, h))$
66      $m_{\mathsf{att}} \leftarrow (\Sigma_A, s_A, \mathsf{cert}_{vk})$
67 **else**
68   **return** $(\perp, \perp)$
69 $m_{\mathsf{rrsp}} \leftarrow (m, m_{\mathsf{att}}, \mathsf{att})$
70 $\mathsf{rc}_T[\mathsf{id}] \leftarrow (\mathsf{uid}, \mathsf{cid}, sk, n, \Sigma)$
71 $\pi_T^j.\mathsf{agCon} \leftarrow (\mathsf{id}, h, \mathsf{cid}, n, \mathsf{pkCP}, pk, \Sigma, UV, UP, \Sigma_A, \mathsf{att})$
72 $\pi_T^j.\mathsf{sid} \leftarrow (\mathsf{H}(\mathsf{id}), \mathsf{cid}, n)$
73 $\pi_T^j.\mathsf{st_{exe}} \leftarrow \mathsf{accepted}$
74 **return** $(m_{\mathsf{rrsp}}, \mathsf{rc}_T)$

$\mathsf{rCom}(\mathsf{id}_S, m_{\mathsf{rch}}, \mathsf{tb})$: // 2. Client

75 $(\mathsf{id}, \mathsf{ch}, \mathsf{uid}, \mathsf{pkCP}, UV) \leftarrow m_{\mathsf{rch}}$
76 **if** $\mathsf{id} \neq \mathsf{id}_S$: **return** $\perp$
77 $m_{\mathsf{rcl}} \leftarrow (\mathsf{ch}, \mathsf{tb})$
78 $UP \leftarrow \mathsf{true}$, $h \leftarrow \mathsf{H}(m_{\mathsf{rcl}})$
79 $m_{\mathsf{rcom}} \leftarrow (\mathsf{id}, \mathsf{uid}, h, \mathsf{pkCP}, UP, UV)$
80 **return** $(m_{\mathsf{rcom}}, m_{\mathsf{rcl}})$

$\mathsf{rVrfy}(\pi_S^i, m_{\mathsf{rcl}}, m_{\mathsf{rrsp}})$: // 4. Server

81 $pk_I \leftarrow \mathsf{ic}_S$
82 $(\mathsf{ch}, \mathsf{tb}) \leftarrow m_{\mathsf{rcl}}$, $(m, m_{\mathsf{att}}, \mathsf{att}) \leftarrow m_{\mathsf{rrsp}}$, $b \leftarrow 0$
83 **if** $\mathsf{att} \notin \pi_S^i.\mathsf{attPol}$:
84   **return** $(\perp, 0)$
85 $(h, n, \mathsf{cid}, pk, \Sigma, UP, UV) \leftarrow m$
86 **if** $\mathsf{att} = \mathsf{none}$:
87      $b \leftarrow 1$
88 **elseif** $\mathsf{att} = \mathsf{self}$:
89      $(\Sigma, s_A) \leftarrow m_{\mathsf{att}}$
90      $b \leftarrow \Sigma.\mathsf{Vfy}(vk, (m, \mathsf{H}(\mathsf{id}_S)))$
91 **elseif** $\mathsf{att} = \mathsf{basic}$ or $\mathsf{att} = \mathsf{attCA}$ or $\mathsf{att} = \mathsf{smpTW}$:
92      $(\Sigma_A, s_A, \mathsf{cert}_{vk}) \leftarrow m_{\mathsf{att}}$
93      $b \leftarrow [\Sigma_A.\mathsf{Vfy}(vk, (m, \mathsf{H}(\mathsf{id}_S)))$ and $\Lambda.\mathsf{CVfy}(\mathsf{cert}_{vk}, pk_I)]$
94 **else**
95   **return** $(\perp, 0)$
96 **if** $h \neq \mathsf{H}(\mathsf{id}_S)$ or $n \neq 0$ or $\mathsf{ch} \neq \pi_S^i.\mathsf{ch}$ or $\mathsf{tb} \neq \pi_S^i.\mathsf{tb}$ or $\Sigma \notin \pi_S^i.\mathsf{pkCP}$ or $UP \neq \mathsf{true}$ or $UV \neq \pi_S^i.UV$ or $b \neq 1$: **return** $(\perp, 0)$
97 $\mathsf{rc}_S[\mathsf{cid}] \leftarrow (\pi_S^i.\mathsf{uid}, pk, n, \Sigma)$
98 $\pi_S^i.\mathsf{agCon} \leftarrow (\mathsf{id}_S, \mathsf{H}(m_{\mathsf{rcl}}), \mathsf{cid}, n, \pi_S^i.\mathsf{pkCP}, pk, \Sigma, UV, UP, \Sigma_A, \mathsf{att})$
99 $\pi_S^i.\mathsf{sid} \leftarrow (\mathsf{H}(\mathsf{id}), \mathsf{cid}, n)$
100 $\pi_S^i.\mathsf{st_{exe}} \leftarrow \mathsf{accepted}$
101 **return** $(\mathsf{rc}_S, 1)$

Fig. 7. Registration of authenticators using different attestation modes of WebAuthn as ePlAA = (Initiate, Certification, Register, Authenticate), with Initiate and Certification as described in the figures of the respective attestation modes and Authenticate as in Fig. 3 ; operations needed for attestation are in teal.

Certification change when instantiating WebAuthn with different attestation modes and is therefore described in the following subsections. Authenticate, however, stays the same for all attestation modes and is depicted in Fig. 3.

We denote the attestation certificate generated (using CG) by the issuer over the public attestation key vk with cert_{vk}. Certification verification is denoted by CVfy using the issuer's public key pk_I.

According to the specifications, during the authenticator's response, it proceeds to create the credential key pair and decides which attestation mode to use. Depending on the attestation, the authenticator proceeds differently as outlined in Fig. 7. In all cases it generates an attestation statement m_{att}, which is included in m_{rrsp} together with the chosen attestation mode att.

From the specifications, it is however, not clear how the attestation mode is chosen. To analyse the unlinkability and authentication properties, we assume that during Initiate, the manufacturer defines the attestation mode $\mathsf{att}_T \in$ {none, self, basic, attCA, smpTW} on each authenticator, depending on its soft- and hardware capabilities. It is important to emphasize that this does not necessarily reflect *all* the attestation modes that an authenticator *can* support. For example, all authenticators can support attestation modes none and self, even if $\mathsf{att}_T = $ basic. It is still reasonable to assume that the authenticator always tries the most advanced attestation, as the authenticator only gets the RP's attestation preference direct, but no further instructions. This is different for RP preference none, as specifications define that in this case the authenticator uses only self or none. Since in our analysis self and none do not have different properties regarding Definition 1 and Definition 2, we decided to refrain from modelling this detail to keep it simpler.

It is interesting to note that while all authenticators should be able to use self attestation, it might be desirable not to. More concretely, while the advantage of self is that the authenticator 'proves' the ownership of the secret credential key, the gain of an adversary registering a public credential key without knowledge of the secret key is rather low. Therefore, the advantage of this extra guarantee is unclear. In addition, the attestation signature (in particular, when considering the potential larger PQ signatures) poses an overhead. Therefore, manufacturers might choose none over self. Indeed, none is the default attestation mode.

Moving on with the description of Fig. 7, in rVrfy the RP checks whether att is allowed under its policies (attPol). If yes, it proceeds depending on the attestation mode. Otherwise, it rejects the registration attempt, updates rc_S, outputs $d = 0$, and notifies the user (out-of-band) that the authenticator does not meet the RPs requirements.

5.2 Attestation Mode none and self

For the attestation modes none and self, there is essentially no attestation. As such there is no attestation key pair, and therefore essentially no certification. This is shown in Fig. 8.

Initiate

Initiate(I): // 1. Issuer

102 $\mathsf{ic}_I \leftarrow \{\}$
103 **return**

Initiate(S, π_I^k): // 2. Server

104 $\mathsf{ic}_S \leftarrow \{\}$
105 **return**

Initiate(T, π_I^k): // 3. Authenticator

106 $\mathsf{att}_T \leftarrow$ none or self
107 $\mathsf{att}_m \leftarrow \{\}$
108 $\mathsf{ic}_T \leftarrow \mathsf{ic}_T \cup \{\mathsf{att}_T, \mathsf{att}_m\}$
109 **return**

Certification

cGen(π_T^j): // 1. Token

110 **return** $m_{\mathsf{cgen}} \leftarrow \{\}$

cRsp($\pi_I^k, \mathsf{id}_T, m_{\mathsf{cgen}}$): // 2. Issuer

111 **return** $(m_{\mathsf{crsp}}, \mathsf{cc}_I) \leftarrow (\{\}, \{\})$

cVrfy($\pi_T^j, \mathsf{id}_I, m_{\mathsf{crsp}}$): // 3. Authenticator

112 **return** $(\mathsf{cc}_T, d) \leftarrow (\mathsf{ic}_T, 1)$

Fig. 8. Initialisation and certification of WebAuthn with attestation none and self as an ePIAA = (Initiate, Certification, Register, Authenticate); Register and Authenticate as in Fig. 7 and 3, respectively.

REG((S, i), (T, j), tb, UV):

113 **if** $\mathsf{pkCP}_S = \bot$ **or** $\mathsf{attInfo}_S = \bot$ **or** $\mathsf{suppUV}_T = \bot$ **or** $\pi_S^i \neq \bot$ **or** $\pi_T^j \neq \bot$ **or** $\mathsf{rc}_T[S] \neq \bot$ **or**
      $\mathsf{ic}_T = \bot$ **or** $\mathsf{cc}_T = \bot$: **return** $\bot$
114 $\pi_S^i.\mathsf{pkCP} \leftarrow \mathsf{pkCP}_S$, $\pi_S^i.\mathsf{attInfo} \leftarrow \mathsf{attInfo}_S$, $\pi_T^j.\mathsf{suppUV} \leftarrow \mathsf{suppUV}_T$
115 $m_{\mathsf{rch}} \leftarrow_\$ \mathsf{rChall}(\pi_S^i, \mathsf{tb}, UV)$
116 $(m_{\mathsf{rcom}}, m_{\mathsf{rcl}}) \leftarrow \mathsf{rCom}(\mathsf{id}_S, m_{\mathsf{rch}}, \mathsf{tb})$
117 $(m_{\mathsf{rrsp}}, \mathsf{rc}_T, \mathsf{sid}, \mathsf{agCon}) \leftarrow_\$ \mathsf{rRsp}(\pi_T^j, m_{\mathsf{rcom}})$
118 $(\mathsf{rc}_S, d, \mathsf{sid}, \mathsf{agCon}) \leftarrow_\$ \mathsf{rVrfy}(\pi_S^i, m_{\mathsf{rcl}}, m_{\mathsf{rrsp}})$
119 $\mathcal{L}_{\mathsf{frsh}} \leftarrow \mathcal{L}_{\mathsf{frsh}} \cup \{(S, T)\}$
120 **if** $S \in \{S_L, S_R\}$: $\mathcal{L}_{\mathsf{ch}}^r \leftarrow \mathcal{L}_{\mathsf{ch}}^r \cup (T)$ // only if in $\mathsf{Expt}_{\mathsf{ePIAA}}^{\mathsf{Unl}}()$
121 **return** $(m_{\mathsf{rch}}, m_{\mathsf{rcl}}, m_{\mathsf{rcom}}, m_{\mathsf{rrsp}}, d)$

Fig. 9. Oracle description of REG; differences to [4] are highlighted in teal.

Instead, an 'empty' attestation signature (in case of none) or a signature generated using the secret credential key (in case of self) is sent. As such, self attestation proves the knowledge of the credential secret key.

Given that the attestation material att_m is empty for these attestation modes, the group G is empty too. For the passwordless authentication experiment, this means that the adversary can corrupt *any* authenticator (however test sessions that originate from a call to this oracle are excluded from the winning conditions). During the unlinkability experiment the adversary can choose any two authenticators.

Since attestation modes none and self do not give any security assurance during Register, trust on first use has been assumed in [4]. In Definition 1 of PAuth, we, however, allow an active adversary. This definition can not be satisfied by WebAuthn with attestation mode none or self. Therefore, we define a weaker variant of PAuth (called PAuth-w), assuming a passive adversary as in [4].

The difference between PAuth and PAuth-w is that instead of accessing the oracles RCHALL, RRESP, and RCOMPL, the adversary is only allowed access to an oracle REG given in Fig. 9. By invoking the REG oracle, $\mathcal{A}$ is able to eavesdrop on honest registrations between servers and authenticators of its choice. From the definition of PAuth and PAuth-w it is clear that protocols providing PAuth, also provide PAuth-w.

We can prove WebAuthn with attestation types none or self to be PAuth-w secure and provide the theorem and proof in the full version of this paper [5]. This theorem is essentially the same as [4, Theorem 1] adapted to our ePIAA class definition.

Likewise, we prove in [5] that WebAuthn with none or self is unlinkable. The proof idea is simply that since there is no attestation, there is also no information provided that can be used to link the tokens.

5.3   Attestation Mode basic

In the basic attestation mode, the authenticator's attestation key pair is shared with at least 99,999 other authenticators [14, Sec 14.4.1], forming a *batch* (e.g., all devices from a specific model). The secret attestation key is embedded in the authenticator, together with a certificate for the public attestation key. Therefore, essentially there is no Certification and most operations are done during Initiate as shown in Fig. 10, e.g., the attestation key is generated and put on all hardware authenticators of a batch during Initiate.

Initiate

Initiate(I): // 1. Issuer
122 $(sk_I, vk_I) \leftarrow_\$ \Lambda.\mathsf{KG}()$
     //Issuer's key pair
123 Define batches of at least 100 000
     authenticators each
124 $D = [\cdot]$ // Batch data
125 For every batch B:
126    $(ak_B, vk_B) \leftarrow_\$ \Sigma_A.\mathsf{KG}()$
       // Batch key pair
127    $\mathsf{cert}_B \leftarrow \Lambda.\mathsf{CG}(sk_I, vk_B)$
       // Certificate of vk_B
128    $D[B] \leftarrow \{ak_B, \mathsf{cert}_{vk_B}, vk_I\}$
129 $ic_I \leftarrow \{sk_I, vk_I, D\}$
130 **return**

Initiate(S, π_I^k): // 2. Server
131 $ic_S \leftarrow ic_S \cup \{vk_I\}$
132 **return**

Initiate(T, π_I^k): // 3. Authenticator
133 $\mathsf{att}_T \leftarrow$ basic
134 Find batch B with $id_T \in B$:
135    $\{ak_B, \mathsf{cert}_{vk_B}, vk_I\} \leftarrow D[B]$
136    $\mathsf{att}_m \leftarrow \{\mathsf{cert}_B, vk_I\}$
       // Attestation material
137 $ic_T \leftarrow ic_T \cup \{\mathsf{att}_T, ak_B, \mathsf{att}_m\}$
138 **return**

Certification

cGen(π_T^j): // 1. Authenticator
139 **return** $m_{cgen} \leftarrow \{\}$

cRsp(π_I^k, id_T, m_{cgen}): // 2. Issuer
140 **return** $(m_{crsp}, cc_I) \leftarrow (\{\}, \{\})$

cVrfy(π_T^j, id_I, m_{crsp}): // 3. Authenticator
141 $\{\mathsf{att}_T, ak_B, \mathsf{att}_m\} \leftarrow ic_T$
142 $\{\mathsf{cert}_B, vk_I\} \leftarrow \mathsf{att}_m$
143 **if** $\Sigma_A.\mathsf{KVfy}(\mathsf{cert}_B, ak_B) = 1$: // Verification of attestation certificate
144   **return** $(cc_T, d) \leftarrow (ic_T, 1)$
145 **else** : **return** $(cc_T, d) \leftarrow (\bot, 0)$

Fig. 10. Initialisation and certification of WebAuthn with attestation mode basic as ePIAA = (Initiate, Certification, Register, Authenticate); Register and Authenticate as in Fig. 7 and 3, respectively.

We define the attestation material att_m as consisting of the certificate of the respective batch attestation public key cert_B, and the issuer's public key vk_I. This means that in the passwordless authentication experiment the adversary won't be able to corrupt authenticators from the same batch as the one for which a successful authentication needs to happen according to the winning conditions. In the unlinkability experiment, the adversary will try to distinguish between two authenticators from the same batch.

During rRsp (see Fig. 7), data is signed using the secret attestation key ak and sent together with m_{rrsp} and the certificate $cert_{vk}$. During rVrfy, the server will check that the attestation type matches those supported by the server, and verify the attestation signature and the attestation certificate. We assume (see Fig. 10), the issuer public key is shared out of band with the server in advance.

Passwordless Authentication. An adversary making a CORRUPT query for an authenticator of the same batch as the winning authenticator, would be able to generate attestation signatures. To exclude this attack, we allow the adversary to corrupt only authenticators of other batches than the test session. More concretely, we define the authenticator group G as the batch of the winning authenticator. This enables us to allow malicious adversaries also during registration, formalised in the next theorem. It is important to emphasize that while restricting authenticator corruptions to the group limits the adversary's power, the statement is still a significant improvement over previous analysis that needed to assume an honest registration.

Theorem 1 (PAuth of WebAuthn with basic). *Let WebAuthn with attestation mode* basic *be an instantiation of an ePIAA* ePIAA = (Initiate, Certification, Register, Authenticate) *as in Fig. 10, 7, and 3 . Let* 2^{λ_1} *and* 2^{λ_2} *be the sizes of the value spaces for credential id* cid *and the challenge nonce sampled during authentication respectively. Moreover, Let* G *be a group of authenticators sharing the same attestation materials* att_m, *i.e., the same batch. Assume that the underlying function* H *is* $\epsilon_H^{coll\text{-}res}$*-collision resistant, and the signature schemes* Σ, Σ_A *are* $\epsilon_\Sigma^{euf\text{-}cma}$*-euf-cma and* $\epsilon_{\Sigma_A}^{euf\text{-}cma}$*-euf-cma secure against PPT/QPT adversaries. For any PPT/QPT adversary* $\mathcal{A}$ *against* PAuth *of ePIAA for a test session* π, *it holds that*

$$\mathsf{Adv}^{auth}_{\mathsf{WebAuthn\text{-}basic}}(\mathcal{A}, \mathsf{G}) \leq \binom{q_{\mathrm{RRESP}}}{2} 2^{-\lambda_1} + \binom{q_{\mathrm{ACHALL}}}{2} 2^{-\lambda_2}$$
$$+ \epsilon_H^{coll\text{-}res} + 2q_{\mathrm{RRESP}} \cdot (\epsilon_\Sigma^{euf\text{-}cma} + \epsilon_{\Sigma_A}^{euf\text{-}cma}).$$

Proof sketch. The main part of the proof is very similar to that for the mode none (cf. the full version of this paper [5]), which is based on the analysis in [4]. Namely, we first assume that credential ids cid and random challenges ch are unique, and that hash functions with different inputs produce different outputs. Assuming unique identifiers and collision-resistant hash functions, we can rule out an adversary winning via conditions 1 and 2. $\mathcal{A}$ needs to forge a valid authentication message m_{arsp} without the collaboration of an authenticator in order to win with condition 3. For that, either $\mathcal{A}$ forges the assertion signature (i.e., it needs to be able to break the euf-cma security of the assertion signature scheme), or it registers a different credential during the registration phase (i.e., it needs to forge a valid registration message m_{rrsp}). Given that $\mathcal{A}$ is not allowed to corrupt authenticators of the same group, which share the same attestation key that signs such message, $\mathcal{A}$ would need to break the euf-cma security of the attestation signature scheme. Similarly, $\mathcal{A}$ may win by forging the attestation signature via condition 4.

Unlinkability. Analysing the unlinkability of WebAuthn with attestation mode basic is similar to the mode none (cf. the full version of this paper [5]) as well, except that for basic the adversary is restricted to choose authenticators T_0 and T_1 from the group G (i.e., the same batch B containing at least two authenticators). We provide the formal statement next.

Theorem 2 (Unl of WebAuthn with basic). *Let WebAuthn with attestation mode* basic *be an instantiation of an ePlAA ePlAA = (Initiate, Certification, Register, Authenticate) as in Fig. 10, 7, and 3 . Let* G *be the group of authenticators in the same batch B. Then for a* PPT/QPT *adversary* $\mathcal{A}$ *it holds*

$$\mathsf{Adv}^{\mathsf{Unl}}_{\mathsf{WebAuthn\text{-}basic}}(\mathcal{A}, \mathsf{G}) = 0.$$

Initiate

Initiate(I): // 1. Issuer

146 $(sk_I, vk_I) \leftarrow_\$ \mathsf{KG}()$
     // Issuer's signing/verification key pair
147 $(dk_I, ek_I) \leftarrow_\$ \mathsf{KG}()$
     // Issuer's decryption/encryption key pair
148 $\mathsf{ic}_I \leftarrow \{(sk_I, vk_I), (dk_I, ek_I)\}$
149 **return**

Initiate(T, π_I^k): // 2. Authenticator

150 $(dk_T, ek_T) \leftarrow_\$ \mathsf{KG}()$ // Endorsement key
151 $\mathsf{cert}_T \leftarrow \mathsf{CG}(sk_I, ek_T)$
     // Endorsement certificate
152 $\mathsf{att}_m \leftarrow \{vk_I\}$ // Attestation material
153 $\mathsf{ic}_T \leftarrow \mathsf{ic}_T \cup \{dk_T, ek_T, \mathsf{cert}_T, ek_I\}$
154 **return**

Initiate(S, π_I^k): // 2. Server

155 $\mathsf{ic}_S \leftarrow \mathsf{ic}_S \cup \{vk_I\}$
156 **return**

Certification

cGen(π_T^j): // 1. Authenticator

157 $(ak, vk) \leftarrow_\$ \Sigma.\mathsf{KG}()$ // Attestation key/AIK
158 $\sigma_{vk} \leftarrow_\$ \Sigma.\mathsf{Sign}(ak, vk)$
159 $k_1 \leftarrow_\$ \mathcal{E}_s.\mathsf{KG}$ // Symmetric Key
160 $c \leftarrow \mathcal{E}_s.\mathsf{Encrypt}(k_1, (vk, \sigma_{vk}, \mathsf{cert}_T))$
161 $k \leftarrow \mathcal{E}_a.\mathsf{Encrypt}(ek_I, k_1)$
162 $m_{\mathsf{cgen}} \leftarrow \{c, k\}$
163 **return** m_{cgen}

cRsp($\pi_I^k, \mathsf{id}_T, m_{\mathsf{cgen}}$): // 2. Issuer

164 $k_1 \leftarrow \mathcal{E}_a.\mathsf{Decrypt}(dk_I, k)$
165 $(vk, \sigma_{vk}, \mathsf{cert}_T) \leftarrow \mathcal{E}_s.\mathsf{Decrypt}(k_1, c)$
166 **if** $\Sigma.\mathsf{Vfy}(vk, vk, \sigma_{vk}) = 0$ **or**
         $\Lambda.\mathsf{CVfy}(vk_I, \mathsf{cert}_T) = 0$: **return** $\perp$
167 $\mathsf{cert}_{vk} \leftarrow \mathsf{CG}(sk_I, vk)$
168 $k_2 \leftarrow_\$ \mathcal{E}_s.\mathsf{KG}()$ // Symmetric Key
169 $c \leftarrow \mathcal{E}_s.\mathsf{Encrypt}(k_2, (\mathsf{cert}_{vk}, \mathsf{H}(vk)))$
170 $k \leftarrow \mathcal{E}_a.\mathsf{Encrypt}(ek_T, k_2)$
     // with ek_T from cert_T
171 **return** $(m_{\mathsf{crsp}}, \mathsf{cc}_I) \leftarrow (\{c, k\}, \{(T, \mathsf{cert}_{vk})\})$

cVrfy($\pi_T^j, \mathsf{id}_I, m_{\mathsf{crsp}}$): // 3. Authenticator

172 $k_2 \leftarrow \mathcal{E}_a.\mathsf{Decrypt}(dk_T, k)$
173 $(\mathsf{cert}_{vk}, h) \leftarrow \mathcal{E}_s.\mathsf{Decrypt}(k_2, c)$
174 **if** $h \neq \mathsf{H}(vk)$: **return** $\perp$
175 $\mathsf{cc}_T \leftarrow \mathsf{cc}_T \cup (ak, \mathsf{cert}_{vk})$
176 **return** $(\mathsf{cc}_T, 1)$

Fig. 11. Initialisation and certification of WebAuthn with attestation attCA as an ePlAA = (Initiate, Certification, Register, Authenticate); Register and Authenticate as in Fig. 7 and 3, respectively.

Proof sketch. Given that $\mathcal{A}$ is restricted to select two authenticators of the same batch, the attestation key used to sign the registration message and the certificate created by the issuer will be the same for both authenticators. Therefore, no information is provided to the adversary that can be used to distinguish T_0 and T_1. This is true even if the adversary corrupts issuers or if it provides invalid information to the authenticators or servers during initialization as the registration will fail.

5.4 Attestation Mode attCA

For attestation mode attCA, it is assumed that the authenticator is based on
a trusted platform module (TPM) that holds a specific endorsement key (EK)
[9,14]. This key is used to authenticate subsequent communications with the
attestation CA. A TPM may create multiple attestation identity key (AIK) pairs
and asks the issuer for a certificate for each AIK. The Initiate and Certification
phases of this attestation mode are depicted in Fig. 11.

The attestation material att_m is defined as the issuer's public key vk_I. In the
passwordless authentication experiment, the adversary is not allowed to corrupt
authenticators with AIKs certified by the same issuer; in the unlinkability experiment, the adversary will have to try to distinguish between two authenticators
with AIKs certified by the same issuer.

Passwordless Authentication. The authentication security analysis of
Webauthn with attCA given formally in the next theorem is very similar to
using attestation mode basic. The main difference is that the adversary can also
try to win the experiment by forging the certificate of the endorsement key.

Theorem 3 (PAuthof WebAuthn with attCA). *Let WebAuthn with attestation mode* attCA *be an instantiation of an ePIAA* ePIAA = (Initiate, Certification,
Register, Authenticate) *as in Fig. 11, 7, and 3. Let 2^{λ_1} and 2^{λ_2} be the sizes of
the value spaces for credential id* cid *and the challenge nonce sampled during
authentication, respectively. Moreover, Let* G *be a group of authenticators sharing the same attestation materials* att_m *(i.e., authenticators with attestation and
endorsement keys certified by the same issuer signing keypair). Assume that the
underlying function* H *is $\epsilon_H^{coll\text{-}res}$-collision resistant, the signature schemes* Σ, Σ_A
*are $\epsilon_\Sigma^{euf\text{-}cma}$-euf-cma and $\epsilon_{\Sigma_A}^{euf\text{-}cma}$-euf-cma secure, and the certificate generation
scheme* Λ *is also $\epsilon_{\Sigma_\Lambda}^{euf\text{-}cma}$-euf-cma secure against* PPT/QPT *adversaries. For any*
PPT/QPT *adversary* $\mathcal{A}$ *against* PAuth *of* ePIAA *for a test session* π, *it holds that*

$$\mathsf{Adv}^{\mathsf{PAuth\text{-}w}}_{\mathsf{WebAuthn\text{-}attCA}}(\mathcal{A}, \mathsf{G}) \leq \binom{q_{\mathrm{RRESP}}}{2} 2^{-\lambda_1} + \binom{q_{\mathrm{ACHALL}}}{2} 2^{-\lambda_2}$$

$$+\epsilon_H^{coll\text{-}res} + 2q_{\mathrm{RRESP}} \cdot (\epsilon_\Sigma^{euf\text{-}cma} + \epsilon_{\Sigma_A}^{euf\text{-}cma}) + 2q_{\mathrm{cGEN}} \cdot \epsilon_{\Sigma_\Lambda}^{euf\text{-}cma}.$$

Proof sketch. The proof is very similar to the proof of Theorem 1 with the addition that the adversary can also win via conditions 3 and 4 as follows. The
adversary could forge a valid certificate $cert_T$ (i.e., it breaks the euf-cma security
of the certificate generation scheme) for an endorsement key pair by its own
choice. Moreover, it generates an AIK and asks the issuer to certify the AIK.
The issuer will generate the certificate for the public AIK, and encrypts it under
the adversary-chosen endorsement key.

Unlinkability. Different from the other attestation modes, during WebAuthn
with attCA the issuer is trusted. In particular, issuers keep track of authenticators

and their attestation certificates. As such, an adversary corrupting an issuer via CORRUPTI can trivially win the Unl experiment. Therefore, we do not give access to CORRUPTI, defining a weaker unlinkability notion (called Unl-w). From the definition of Unl and Unl-w it is clear that protocols providing Unl, also provide Unl-w.

Under the assumptions defined for Unl-w, analysing the unlinkability of WebAuthn with attestation mode attCA is the same as in the previous modes. The authenticator group G essentially corresponds to all authenticators with attestation certificates generated by the same issuer. As such $\mathcal{A}$ has to choose two authenticators with attestation keys certified with the same issuer key pair (i.e., $\forall T \in$ G, $(ak_T, \mathsf{cert}_{vk^T})$ are such that $\Lambda.\mathsf{CVfy}(vk_I, \mathsf{cert}_{vk^T}) = 1$). When calling to the registration oracles, these authenticators provide attestation signatures generated with different attestation keys. They can, however, be verified with the same issuer public key vk_I. This way, there is no additional information provided to $\mathcal{A}$ that provides an advantage for winning the game.

Theorem 4 (Unl-w of WebAuthn with attCA). *Let WebAuthn with attestation mode* attCA *be an instantiation of an ePlAA* ePlAA = (Initiate, Certification, Register, Authenticate) *as in Fig. 11, 7, and 3. Let* G *be the group of authenticators where* $\forall T \in$ G, $(ak_T, \mathsf{cert}_{vk^T})$ *are such that* $\Lambda.\mathsf{CVfy}(vk_I, \mathsf{cert}_{vk^T}) = 1$. *Then for a* PPT/QPT *adversary* $\mathcal{A}$ *it holds*

$$\mathsf{Adv}^{\mathsf{Unl-w}}_{\mathsf{WebAuthn-attCA}}(\mathcal{A}, \mathsf{G}) = 0.$$

Proof sketch. The proof follows the proof for the attestation mode none which is given in the full version of the paper [5] with the change that no access is given to CORRUPTI.

6 Simple TokenWeaver as a New Attestation Mode for WebAuthn

WebAuthn with attestation mode basic is currently the only mode that provides both PAuth and Unl. One limitation is that Unl is limited for authenticators in the same (large) batch. The requirement for large batch size leads to a more significant limitation—PAuth is preserved as long asno other authenticator in the batch has been corrupted. Compromising a single authenticator means that we lose PAuth for any server that supports the batch's attestation key. The only way to recover security is to revoke the entire batch of at least 100,000 authenticators! In this section, we propose a new attestation mode called smpTW that is able to overcome this limitation.

6.1 The smpTW att Mode

WebAuthn with smpTW is very similar to WebAuthn with attestation mode basic, but with an added mechanism that allows for periodic provisioning of new attestation keys to achieve PCS. smpTW is described in Fig. 12.

Initiate

Initiate(I): // 1. Issuer

177 $(dk_I, ek_I) \leftarrow_\$ \mathcal{E}_a.\mathsf{KG}()$
    // Issuer's decryption/encryption key pair
178 $ic_I \leftarrow (dk_I, ek_I)$
179 $ic_I.\mathcal{L}_T[\mathsf{id}_T] \leftarrow \{\}$
180 **return**

Initiate(S, π_I^k): // 2. Server

181 $ic_S, cc_S \leftarrow \{\}, \{\}$
182 **return**

Initiate(T, π_I^k): // 3. Authenticator

183 $\mathsf{att}_T \leftarrow \mathsf{SmpTW}$
184 $t_T \leftarrow_\$ \{0,1\}^{\geq \lambda}$
    //Token sampled by the authenticator
185 $ic_I.\mathcal{L}_T[\mathsf{id}_T] \leftarrow t_T$
186 $ic_T \leftarrow \{\mathsf{att}_T, t_T, ic_I.ek_I\}$
187 **return**

Update

Update(π_I^k, P): // 1. Issuer for Period P

188 $(sk_{I,P}, vk_{I,P}) \leftarrow_\$ \Lambda.\mathsf{KG}$
    //Issuer's period key pair
189 Define batches of at least 100 000 tokens each
190 $D_P = [\cdot]$ //Batch data for Period P
191 For every batch B:
192     $(ak_{B,P}, vk_{B,P}) \leftarrow_\$ \Sigma_A.\mathsf{KG}()$
    //Batch key pair
193     $\mathsf{cert}_{B,P} \leftarrow \Lambda.\mathsf{CG}(sk_{I,P}, vk_{B,P})$
    // Certificate of $vk_{B,P}$
194     $D_P[B] \leftarrow \{ak_{B,P}, \mathsf{cert}_{vk_{B,P}}, vk_{I,P}\}$
195 $cc_I \leftarrow \{sk_{I,P}, vk_{I,P}, D_P\}$
196 **return**

Update(π_S^i, P, π_I^k): // 2. Server for Period P

197 $cc_{S,P} \leftarrow cc_{S,P} \cup \{cc_I.vk_{I,P}\}$
198 **return**

Update(π_T^j, P, π_I^k): // 3. Authenticator for P

199 **return**

Certification

cGen(π_T^j): // 1. Authenticator

200 $t_T, ek_I \leftarrow ic_T$
201 $k_1 \leftarrow_\$ \mathcal{E}_s.\mathsf{KG}$ // Symmetric Key
202 $cc_T.k_2 \leftarrow_\$ \mathcal{E}_s.\mathsf{KG}$ // Symmetric Key
203 $c \leftarrow \mathcal{E}_s.\mathsf{Encrypt}(k_1, (t_T, k_2, \mathsf{id}_T))$
204 $k \leftarrow \mathcal{E}_a.\mathsf{Encrypt}(ek_I, k_1)$
205 **return** $m_{\mathsf{cgen}} \leftarrow (c, k)$

cRsp($\pi_I^k, \mathsf{id}_T, m_{\mathsf{cgen}}$): // 2. Issuer

206 $dk_I, \mathcal{L}_T \leftarrow ic_I, D_P \leftarrow cc_I$
207 $k_1 \leftarrow \mathcal{E}_a.\mathsf{Decrypt}(dk_I, k)$
208 $(t_{\mathsf{recv}}, k_2, \mathsf{id}_T') \leftarrow \mathcal{E}_s.\mathsf{Decrypt}(k_1, c)$
209 $t_T \leftarrow \mathcal{L}_T[\mathsf{id}_T']$
210 **if** $t_T = \perp$ **or** $t_{\mathsf{recv}} \neq t_T$: **return** $\perp$
211 Find batch B with $\mathsf{id}_T \in B$:
212     $\{ak_{B,P}, \mathsf{cert}_{vk_{B,P}}, vk_{I,P}\} \leftarrow D_P[B]$
213 $\mathsf{att}_m \leftarrow \{\mathsf{cert}_{B,P}, vk_{I,P}\}$ //attestation
    material
214 $t_T \leftarrow_\$ \{0,1\}^{\geq \lambda}$
    //New token sampled by the issuer
215 $ic_I.\mathcal{L}_T[\mathsf{id}_T'] \leftarrow t_T$
216 $c \leftarrow \mathcal{E}_s.\mathsf{Encrypt}(k_2, (ak_{B,P}, \mathsf{att}_m, t_T))$
217 $m_{\mathsf{crsp}} \leftarrow (c)$
218 **return** $(m_{\mathsf{crsp}}, cc_I)$

cVrfy($T, \mathsf{id}_T, m_{\mathsf{crsp}}$): // 3. Authenticator

219 $c \leftarrow m_{\mathsf{crsp}}, k_2 \leftarrow cc_T$
220 $(ak_{B,P}, \mathsf{att}_m, t_T) \leftarrow \mathcal{E}_s.\mathsf{Decrypt}(k_2, c)$
221 $\{\mathsf{cert}_{B,P}, vk_{I,P}\} \leftarrow \mathsf{att}_m$
222 **if** $\Sigma_A.\mathsf{KVfy}(\mathsf{cert}_{B,P}, ak_{B,P}) = 1$ **and**
    $\Lambda.\mathsf{CVfy}(\mathsf{cert}_{B,P}, pk_I)$:// Verify keypair
223     $cc_T \leftarrow (ak_{B,P}, \mathsf{att}_m, t_T)$
224   **return** $(cc_T, 1)$
225 **else** : **return** $(cc_T, 0)$

Fig. 12. Initialisation and certification of WebAuthn with the new attestation type smpTW.

As in basic, the same attestation keys and certificates are provided to a batch of authenticators, who will use them to sign the messages during registration in a remote web server. However, unlike basic, in smpTW the attestation keys are only valid for a limited time period. During Initiate, the authenticator is provisioned only with a secret one-time token, and the issuer's public encryption key.

For each period, the Update algorithms are called to generate the new period's attestation keys for all batches, and provision the servers with the new public keys. The new attestation keys are provisioned to the authenticators during Certification. Communication during Certification is protected using symmetric keys generated by the authenticator and sent to the issuer encrypted under its

---

OUpdateI(I, P):

226 **if** $ic_I = \perp$: **return** $\perp$
227 Update(I, P)

OUpdateS(S, I, P):

228 **if** $cc_I = \perp$ **or** $ic_I = \perp$: **return** $\perp$
229 Update(S, P)

Fig. 13. Description of new oracles to run Update for issuers and servers.

public key. During Certification, the authenticator "spends" its one-time token in exchange for a new valid token and the next period's attestation keys.

This periodic certification protocol allows for the security of the entire batch to "heal" after an authenticator from the batch and its attestation keys were compromised. If a compromised authenticator runs the Certification algorithms before the adversary it will "lock" the adversary out (as the token can only be used once) and security will be recovered. If the adversary runs Certification first, the user will learn that it was compromised as they are "locked out". The user can then ask the issuer to revoke the compromised authenticator and security will be recovered after the next period's Update. We combine this new mode, with a requirement for periodic re-registration of authenticators by the remote servers to fully "heal" and achieve PCS for the authentication process. For a full discussing of the PCS property we refer to [8].

smpTW is based on the TokenWeaver general attestation scheme proposed in [8]. While the original scheme allows for instant revocation of attestation keys of specific users and might allow for faster detection or recovery from compromises, smpTW is simpler to implement and—contrary to TokenWeaver—it is based on cryptographic primitives with post-quantum variants that are currently being standardized.

For the security and privacy analysis of this attestation mode, we introduce in Fig. 13 two new oracles to support the new Update algorithms. In the full version of this paper [5], we provide the full analysis of the PAuth and Unl properties of smpTW and we prove the following theorems:

Theorem 5 (PAuth Security of WebAuthn with smpTW). *Let* Compl $\in$ {PPT, QPT}. *Let WebAuthn with attestation mode* smpTW *be an instantiation of an ePlAA* ePlAA = (Initiate, Update*, Certification, Register, Authenticate) *as in Fig. 12, 7, and 3. Let* 2^{λ_1}, 2^{λ_2} *and* 2^{λ_3} *be the sizes of the value spaces for credential id* cid, *the challenge nonce sampled during authentication, and tokens* t_T *used during certification, respectively. Moreover, let* G *be a group of authenticators sharing the same attestation materials* att_m *(i.e., the same batch). Assume that the underlying function* H *is* $\epsilon_H^{\text{coll-res}}$-*collision resistant, and the signature schemes* Σ *and* Σ_A *and the encryption schemes* $\mathcal{E}_a$ *and* $\mathcal{E}_s$ *are* $\epsilon_\Sigma^{\text{euf-cma}}$- *and* $\epsilon_{\Sigma_A}^{\text{euf-cma}}$-*euf-cma secure, and* $\epsilon_{\mathcal{E}_a}^{\text{ind-cpa}}$- *and* $\epsilon_{\mathcal{E}_s}^{\text{ind-cpa}}$-*ind-cpa secure, respectively, against* Compl *adversaries. For any* Compl *adversary* $\mathcal{A}$ *against* PAuth *of* ePlAA *for a test session* π, *it holds that*

$$\text{Adv}_{\text{WebAuthn-simpleTW}}^{\text{PAuth}}(\mathcal{A}, G) \leq \binom{q_{\text{RRESP}}}{2} 2^{-\lambda_1} + \binom{q_{\text{ACHALL}}}{2} 2^{-\lambda_2} + \epsilon_H^{\text{coll-res}}$$
$$+ 2q_{\text{RRESP}} \cdot (\epsilon_\Sigma^{\text{euf-cma}} + \epsilon_{\Sigma_A}^{\text{euf-cma}}) + 2q_{\text{cRESP}} \cdot (\epsilon_{\mathcal{E}_a}^{\text{ind-cpa}} + 2^{-\lambda_3})$$
$$+ 2q_{\text{cGEN}} \cdot (\epsilon_{\mathcal{E}_a}^{\text{ind-cpa}} + \epsilon_{\mathcal{E}_s}^{\text{ind-cpa}}).$$

Proof sketch. The proof is based on the one for the mode basic (cf. the full version of this paper [5]), which is based on the analysis in [4]. The main idea is that for winning via conditions 3 or 4, $\mathcal{A}$ needs to be able to register a new public key, for which it will need to break either the euf-cma security of the assertion signature scheme or of the attestation signature scheme. Alternatively, $\mathcal{A}$ may try to get a valid attestation key pair to register the public key. In the proof, we restrict $\mathcal{A}$ to not being able to corrupt authenticators from the batch B which form the group G, and for it being able to either impersonate an authenticator from that group in front of an issuer, or learn the attestation key pair the issuer sends to an honest authenticator from that group during the Update phase, $\mathcal{A}$ needs to break the security of the encryption schemes used for securing the communications between issuer and authenticators. $\mathcal{A}$ winning via conditions 1 and 2 is ruled out by initial assumptions regarding unique identifiers and collision-resistant hash functions.

Theorem 6 (Unl of WebAuthn with smpTW). *Let* $\mathsf{Compl} \in \{\mathsf{PPT}, \mathsf{QPT}\}$. *Let WebAuthn with attestation mode* smpTW *be an instantiation of an ePlAA* $\mathsf{ePlAA} = (\mathsf{Initiate}, \mathsf{Update}, \mathsf{Certification}, \mathsf{Register}, \mathsf{Authenticate})$ *as in Fig. 12, 7, and 3. Let* G *be the group of authenticators in the same batch* B. *Then,*

$$\mathsf{Adv}^{\mathsf{Unl}}_{\mathsf{WebAuthn\text{-}smpTW}}(\mathcal{A}, \mathsf{G}) = 0.$$

Proof sketch. Note that in the unlinkability experiment the adversary is restricted to choose two authenticators from the same group G, and after that the adversary is not allowed to query any certification oracles (at least for such authenticators). Then, unless we reach the next epoch and the attestation/issuer public key certificates expire before the target tokens are registered in the target servers, the behaviour of the experiment is exactly the same as in basic mode. Otherwise, in case these certificates expired, the registration in the target servers would fail equally for the target authenticators, and therefore there isn't any additional advantage for $\mathcal{A}$. In case $\mathcal{A}$ runs the OUPDATEI and OUPDATES oracles from Fig. 13 in phase 3, registration in the target servers would fail as well for both target authenticators and $\mathcal{A}$ wouldn't get an additional advantage.

7   Conclusion

As summarised in Table 3, the four different attestation modes provide different (group) security and privacy guarantees. It turns out that none and self are the most privacy preserving attestation modes as they satisfy Unl under no

Table 3. Summary of authentication security and unlinkability proven.

Attestation mode	PAuth-w	PAuth	Unl-w	Unl	att_m
none	✓	✗	✓	✓	$\{\}$
self	✓	✗	✓	✓	$\{\}$
basic	✓	✓	✓	✓	cert_B
attCA	✓	✓	✓	✗	vk_I
smpTW	✓	✓	✓	✓	$\mathsf{cert}_{B,P}, vk_{I,P}$

restrictions to the authenticator group (as att_m is empty). However, Webauthn with attestation modes none or self is not PAuth secure. It can provide the weaker notion PAuth-w where there is no active adversary during Register.

attCA on the other hand, provides passwordless authentication security PAuth (if no authenticator certified by the same issuer as the winning authenticator has been corrupted) but relies strongly on the trust of the issuer and as such only satisfies the weaker notion Unl-w where issuers are not allowed to be corrupted.

Lastly, basic is the only current WebAuthn attestation mode that provides both PAuth and Unl. However, PAuth is preserved only if no other authenticator in the batch has been corrupted. Given the large batch size of 100,000 or more, this poses both a security risk and an inconvenience in case one authenticator is compromised and the entire batch has to be replaced. Our proposal for a new attestation mode smpTW, which also satisfies both PAuth and Unl, overcomes this limitation by providing a healing mechanism.

All the modes analysed rely on cryptographic primitives that already have PQ standardization candidates selected by NIST [11] and are thus "PQ ready". However, future work is required to design efficient instantiations with PQ secure primitives that take into account the increase in size and computational cost required by these new primitives.

Acknowledgments. Icons in Fig. 1 from flaticon with premium account. The fourth author is partly supported by ISF grant no. 1807/23 and the Len Blavatnik and the Blavatnik Family Foundation.

References

1. Alliance, F.: Passkeys FAQ (2023). https://fidoalliance.org/passkeys/#faq
2. Alliance, F.: What is FIDO?. https://fidoalliance.org/what-is-fido/ (2023)
3. Barbosa, M., Boldyreva, A., Chen, S., Warinschi, B.: Provable security analysis of FIDO2. In: Malkin, T., Peikert, C. (eds.) CRYPTO 2021. LNCS, vol. 12827, pp. 125–156. Springer, Cham (2021). https://doi.org/10.1007/978-3-030-84252-9_5
4. Bindel, N., Cremers, C., Zhao, M.: FIDO2, CTAP 2.1, and WebAuthn 2: provable security and post-quantum instantiation. In: 44th IEEE Symposium on Security and Privacy, SP 2023, San Francisco, CA, USA, May 21-25, 2023, pp. 1471–1490. IEEE (2023). https://doi.org/10.1109/SP46215.2023.10179454
5. Bindel, N., Gama, N., Guasch, S., Ronen, E.: To attest or not to attest, this is the question – Provable attestation in FIDO2 (full version). IACR Cryptol. ePrint Arch., 2023/1398 (2023). https://eprint.iacr.org/2023/1398
6. Camenisch, J., Drijvers, M., Lehmann, A.: Universally composable direct anonymous attestation. In: Cheng, C.-M., Chung, K.-M., Persiano, G., Yang, B.-Y. (eds.) PKC 2016. LNCS, vol. 9615, pp. 234–264. Springer, Heidelberg (2016). https://doi.org/10.1007/978-3-662-49387-8_10
7. Cohn-Gordon, K., Cremers, C., Garratt, L.: On post-compromise security. In: 2016 IEEE 29th Computer Security Foundations Symposium (CSF), pp. 164–178. IEEE (2016)
8. Cremers, C., Jacomme, C., Ronen, E.: TokenWeaver: privacy preserving and post-compromise secure attestation. IACR Cryptol. ePrint Arch., 1691 (2022). https://eprint.iacr.org/2022/1691

9. Group, T.I.W.: A CMC profile for AIK certificate enrollment, version 1.0, revision 7 (2011). https://trustedcomputinggroup.org/wp-content/uploads/IWG_CMC_Profile_Cert_Enrollment_v1_r7.pdf
10. Hanzlik, L., Loss, J., Wagner, B.: Token meets wallet: formalizing privacy and revocation for FIDO2. In: 44th IEEE Symposium on Security and Privacy, SP 2023, San Francisco, CA, USA, May 21-25, 2023, pp. 1491–1508. IEEE (2023). https://doi.org/10.1109/DSP46215.2023.10179373
11. NIST: Selected algorithms 2022. https://csrc.nist.gov/Projects/post-quantum-cryptography/selected-algorithms-2022 (2023)
12. Popov, A., Nystroem, M., Balfanz, D., Hodges, J.: The token binding protocol version 1.0 (2018). https://www.rfc-editor.org/rfc/rfc8471#section-1
13. Shakevsky, A., Ronen, E., Wool, A.: Trust Dies in Darkness: shedding light on Samsung's TrustZone Keymaster design. In: 31st USENIX Security Symposium (USENIX Security 22), pp. 251–268. USENIX Association, Boston, MA (2022). https://www.usenix.org/conference/usenixsecurity22/presentation/shakevsky
14. W3C: Web authentication: an API for accessing public key credentials level 2 (2021). https://www.w3.org/TR/webauthn-2/
15. W3C: Web authentication: an API for accessing public key credentials level 3 (2023). https://w3c.github.io/webauthn/

The Pre-Shared Key Modes of HPKE

Joël Alwen[1]($^{(\boxtimes)}$), Jonas Janneck[2], Eike Kiltz[2], and Benjamin Lipp[3]

[1] AWS-Wickr, Seattle, USA
alwenjo@amazon.com
[2] Ruhr-Universität Bochum, Bochum, Germany
{jonas.janneck,eike.kiltz}@rub.de
[3] Max Planck Institute for Security and Privacy, Bochum, Germany
benjamin.lipp@mpi-sp.org

Abstract. The Hybrid Public Key Encryption (HPKE) standard was recently published as RFC 9180 by the Crypto Forum Research Group (CFRG) of the Internet Research Task Force (IRTF). The RFC specifies an efficient public key encryption scheme, combining asymmetric and symmetric cryptographic building blocks.

Out of HPKE's four modes, two have already been formally analyzed by Alwen et al. (EUROCRYPT 2021). This work considers the remaining two modes: $\mathsf{HPKE_{PSK}}$ and $\mathsf{HPKE_{AuthPSK}}$. Both of them are "pre-shared key" modes that assume the sender and receiver hold a symmetric pre-shared key. We capture the schemes with two new primitives which we call pre-shared key public-key encryption (pskPKE) and pre-shared key authenticated public-key encryption (pskAPKE). We provide formal security models for pskPKE and pskAPKE and prove (via general composition theorems) that the two modes $\mathsf{HPKE_{PSK}}$ and $\mathsf{HPKE_{AuthPSK}}$ offer active security (in the sense of insider privacy and outsider authenticity) under the Gap Diffie-Hellman assumption.

We furthermore explore possible post-quantum secure instantiations of the HPKE standard and propose new solutions based on lattices and isogenies. Moreover, we show how HPKE's basic $\mathsf{HPKE_{PSK}}$ and $\mathsf{HPKE_{AuthPSK}}$ modes can be used black-box in a simple way to build actively secure post-quantum/classic-hybrid (authenticated) encryption schemes. Our hybrid constructions provide a cheap and easy path towards a practical post-quantum secure drop-in replacement for the basic HPKE modes $\mathsf{HPKE_{Base}}$ and $\mathsf{HPKE_{Auth}}$.

Keywords: Authenticated Public Key Encryption · Post-Quantum Hybrid · Open Standards · HPKE

1 Introduction

The Hybrid Public Key Encryption (HPKE) standard was published as RFC 9180 [4] by the Crypto Forum Research Group (CFRG) of the Internet Research Task Force (IRTF)[1] in February 2022. The RFC specifies an efficient public key

---

[1] https://irtf.org/cfrg.

© International Association for Cryptologic Research 2023
J. Guo and R. Steinfeld (Eds.): ASIACRYPT 2023, LNCS 14443, pp. 329–360, 2023.
https://doi.org/10.1007/978-981-99-8736-8_11

encryption scheme, combining asymmetric and symmetric cryptographic building blocks. While this an old and relatively well understood paradigm, the new standard was developed in an effort to address issues in previous standardizations of hybrid public key encryption. For example, HPKE relies on modern cryptographic building blocks, provides test vectors to ease development of interoperable implementations, and already received some cryptographic analysis during its development, inspired by the "analysis-prior-to-deployment" design philosophy adopted for the development of the TLS 1.3 protocol [20]. At the time of development of HPKE, two IETF standardization efforts already started building upon it: the Messaging Layer Security (MLS) protocol [3], and the Encrypted Client Hello privacy extension of TLS 1.3 [21]. Since its publication, HPKE has also been adopted by other higher-level protocols, like the published RFC 9230 Oblivious DNS over HTTPS [16], and the Distributed Aggregation Protocol for Privacy Preserving Measurement [15], and thus, has become an important building block of today's and the future Internet.

The HPKE standard may appear to resemble a "public key encryption" approach, aligning with the KEM/DEM paradigm [9]. Indeed, it incorporates a Key Encapsulation Mechanism (KEM) and an Authenticated Encryption with Associated Data (AEAD), functioning as a Data Encapsulation Mechanism (DEM) based on the KEM/DEM paradigm. However, upon closer inspection HPKE turns out to be more complex than this perfunctory description implies. First, HPKE actually consists of 2 different KEM/DEM constructions. Moreover, each construction can also be instantiated with a pre-shared key (psk) known to both sender and receiver, which is used in the key schedule KS to derive the DEM key. In total this gives rise to 4 different *modes* for HPKE.

The *basic* mode $\mathsf{HPKE_{Base}}$ makes use of a standard KEM to obtain a "message privacy and integrity" only mode. This mode can be extended to $\mathsf{HPKE_{PSK}}$ to support authentication of the sender via a psk. The remaining 2 HPKE modes make use of a different KEM/DEM construction built from a rather nonstandard KEM variant called *Authenticated KEM* (AKEM) [1]. An AKEM can be thought of the KEM analogue of signcryption [22]. In particular, sender and receiver both have their own public/private keys. Each party requires their own private and the other party's public key to perform en/decryption. The AKEM-based HPKE modes also intend to authenticate the sender to the receiver. Just as in the KEM-based case, the AKEM/DEM construction can be instantiated in modes either without psk ($\mathsf{HPKE_{Auth}}$) or with a psk ($\mathsf{HPKE_{AuthPSK}}$). The HPKE RFC constructs a KEM and an AKEM based on specific Diffie-Hellman groups (such as P-256, P-384, P-521 NIST curves [19], Curve25519, or Curve448 [17]). Alwen, Blanchet, Hauck, Kiltz, Lipp, and Riepel [1] have analyzed the security of the Diffie-Hellman AKEM and showed that it can be securely combined with a key schedule KS and an AEAD to obtain concrete security bounds for the $\mathsf{HPKE_{Auth}}$ modes, as defined in the HPKE standard, see Table 1. Their work explicitly leaves analyzing the remaining two HPKE modes $\mathsf{HPKE_{PSK}}$ and $\mathsf{HPKE_{AuthPSK}}$ for future work.

Table 1. HPKE modes and their security.

HPKE mode	Authenticated?	PSK?	Primitive	Security
HPKE$_{Base}$	–	–	PKE	CCA$_{PKE}$ (folklore)
HPKE$_{Auth}$	√	–	APKE [1]	Insider-CCA & Outsider-Auth [1]
HPKE$_{PSK}$	–	√	pskPKE (Sect. 3)	CCA & Auth (Sect. 4)
HPKE$_{AuthPSK}$	√	√	pskAPKE (Sect. 3)	Insider-CCA & Outsider-Auth (Sect. 4)

APPLICATIONS OF HPKE'S PSK MODES. One class of use cases for HPKE's PSKs is a sender to transferring security guarantees from external cryptographic applications to an HPKE ciphertext. More concretely, a sender might want to transfer the post-quantum security guarantees provided by a particular PSK source to a (maybe even only otherwise classically secure) HPKE ciphertext. One such source might be PSKs distributed via an include out-of-band method (e.g., in person) or PSKs agreed upon using a post-quantum secure KEM (as demonstrated in Sect. 5).

In another example, HPKE's PSKs can be used to transfer the strong authenticity guarantees of an ongoing Messaging Layer Security (MLS) group containing both sender and receiver to 1-on-1 messages between the two. MLS sessions include an HPKE (and signature) public key for each party in the group known to all other group members. A party's signature public key is authenticated via an associated credential binding it to its owner (e.g. an X.509 certificate issued by a CA). Each user also signs their own HPKE public key to assert their ownership to rest of the group. To provide authenticity even over many years, MLS must account for signatures and HPKE keys being corrupted mid session. Rather than assuming the credentials for a corrupt signing key will be revoked, MLS instead gives users the ability to update their keys periodically (or at will). To ensure the old keys are no longer of any use, MLS also equips the group with a sequence of shared symmetric group keys. Whenever a user updates their signature or HPKE key, a new group key is produced in a way that ensures knowing the updating client's old state (including their signature and HPKE private keys) is insufficient to learn the new group key. An MLS group including both parties A and B can now be used to provide strong sender authentication for HPKE$_{AuthPSK}$ ciphertexts (e.g. beyond the authenticity provided by static credentials). Say, A wants to send a private message to B. On the one hand A use their HPKE keys from the MLS session to encrypt and authenticate the message, thereby inheriting the authenticity guarantees of the credentials in the MLS session. On the other hand, A can also derive a *psk* off of the current MLS group key (e.g. using MLS's "exporter" functionality) for use with HPKE$_{AuthPSK}$. Intuitively, this provides the added guarantee to B that the sender is also *currently* in the MLS session. The same method using HPKE$_{PSK}$ in place of HPKE$_{AuthPSK}$ gives B the guarantee that the sender is a current member of the group.

1.1 Our Contributions

So far, there has only been a formal analysis of the basic mode $HPKE_{Base}$ and the authenticated mode $HPKE_{Auth}$. In this work we focus on the HPKE standard in its pre-shared key mode, both in its basic form $HPKE_{PSK}$ and in its authenticated mode $HPKE_{AuthPSK}$. Furthermore, we explore possible future post-quantum instantiations of the HPKE standard. To this end we make the following contributions.

PRE-SHARED KEY (AUTHENTICATED) PUBLIC KEY ENCRYPTION. We begin, in Sect. 3, by introducing pre-shared key public key encryption (pskPKE) and pre-shared key authenticated public key encryption (pskAPKE) schemes, where the syntax of pskPKE matches that of the single-shot basic pre-shared mode $HPKE_{PSK}$, and the syntax of pskAPKE matches that of the single-shot authenticated pre-shared mode $HPKE_{AuthPSK}$. Compared to their respective non pre-shared modes PKE and APKE, encryption and decryption additionally input *psk*, a uniform symmetric key shared between the sender and the receiver. In terms of security, we define (active, multi-user) security notions capturing both authenticity (Auth) and privacy (CCA) for pskPKE and pskAPKE.

For pskPKE, privacy is essentially standard CCA security for PKE with the difference that the adversary additionally has access to an encryption oracle (which requires the secret pre-shared key to compute the ciphertext) and it is allowed to adaptively corrupt pre-shared (symmetric) keys and long-term (asymmetric) keys. Security holds as long as at least one of the pre-shared and long-term keys used in the challenge ciphertext/forgery has not been corrupted. Authenticity for pskPKE schemes provides the adversary with the same oracles, and the adversary's goal is to non-trivially forge a fresh ciphertext, i.e., one that does not come from the encryption oracle.

Similar to APKE [1], for pskAPKE we consider so called weaker outsider and stronger insider security variants for privacy, and only outsider security for authenticity. Intuitively, outsider notions model settings where the adversary is an outside observer. Conversely, insider notions model settings where the adversary is somehow directly involved; in particular, even selecting some of the long-term asymmetric secrets used to produce target ciphertexts. A bit more formally, we call an honestly generated asymmetric key pair secure if the secret key was not (explicitly) leaked to the adversary and leaked if it was. An asymmetric key pair is called corrupted if it was sampled arbitrarily by the adversary. A scheme is outsider-secure if target ciphertexts are secure when produced using secure key pairs. Meanwhile, insider security holds even if one secure and one corrupted key pair are used. For example, insider privacy (Insider-CCA) for pskAPKE requires that an encapsulated key remains indistinguishable from random despite the encapsulating ciphertext being produced using corrupted sender keys (but secure receiver keys). Note that insider authenticity implies (but is stronger than) Key Compromise Impersonation (KCI) security as KCI security only requires authenticity for leaked (but not corrupt) receiver keys.

We remark that, for simplicity, our modeling assumes the pre-shared key *psk* to be uniformly random from some sufficiently large key-space. Indeed, The

HPKE RFC mandates the PSK have at least 32 bytes of entropy to counter Partitioning Oracle Attacks [18] to which HPKE is vulnerable because it is currently only specified for AEAD schemes that are not key-committing. Thus in practice, say, hashing such a PSK to a 32 byte string prior to use with HPKE would, at least in the random oracle model, result in a near uniform distribution.

pskKEM/DEM CONSTRUCTION. In Sect. 4, we consider the pskKEM/DEM constructions that combine a KEM (AKEM) together with an AEAD (acting as a DEM) to obtain pskPKE (pskAPKE). First, we construct pskPKE[KEM, KS, AEAD] from a KEM, a key schedule KS, and an AEAD. To encrypt a message, a KEM ciphertext/key pair (c, K) is generated. Next, the KEM key K is fed together with the pre-shared key psk into KS to obtain the DEM key which in turn is used to AEAD-encrypt the message. At an intuitive level, the DEM key remains uniform as long as one of K or psk is uniform, meaning one of the receiver's asymmetric key or the pre-shared key has not been corrupted. We will present two concrete security theorems bootstrapping privacy and authenticity of our pskPKE construction from standard security properties of the underlying KEM, KS, and AEAD. Similarly, we can construct pskAPKE[AKEM, KS, AEAD] by replacing the KEM with an AKEM in the first step of the construction above. We will again present two concrete security theorems bootstrapping privacy and authenticity of our pskAPKE construction from standard security properties of the underlying AKEM, KS, and AEAD. See also Table 2.

Table 2. Security properties needed to prove Outsider-Auth and Insider-CCA security of pskAPKE obtained by the pskAKEM/DEM construction.

	AKEM			AEAD	
	Outsider-Auth	Outsider-CCA	Insider-CCA	INT-CTXT	IND-CPA
Outsider-Auth$_{pskAPKE}$	X	X		X	
Insider-CCA$_{pskAPKE}$			X	X	X

AN ANALYSIS OF THE HPKE$_{PSK}$ AND HPKE$_{AuthPSK}$ MODES. Using the above mentioned transformations, the two modes HPKE$_{PSK}$ and HPKE$_{AuthPSK}$ of the HPKE standard can be obtained as pskPKE[DH-KEM, KS, AEAD] and pskAPKE[DH-AKEM, KS, AEAD]. Here DH-KEM is the well known Diffie-Hellman based KEM, DH-AKEM is the Diffie-Hellman based AKEM from [1], key schedule KS is constructed via the functions Extract and Expand both instantiated with HMAC, and AEAD is instantiated using AES-GCM or ChaCha20-Poly1305. Hence, our theorems from Sect. 4 provide concrete bounds for CCA and Auth security of HPKE$_{PSK}$, and Insider-CCA and Outsider-Auth security of HPKE$_{AuthPSK}$.

334 J. Alwen et al.

HYBRID APKE. In Sect. 5, we analyze a natural black-box construction of a hybrid APKE from an AKEM and from HPKE$_{\mathsf{AuthPSK}}$. Intuitively, the resulting scheme's security depends on either one of two AKEM schemes being secure. (We remark that essentially same construction and analogous proof also construct hybrid PKE from a KEM and HPKE$_{\mathsf{PSK}}$.) One interesting application of this construction is building a PQ/classic-hybrid APKE which can be done by combining a PQ secure AKEM with a classically secure one (in HPKE$_{\mathsf{AuthPSK}}$). In comparison with the CPA secure PQ/classic-hybrid variant of HPKE in [2] our construction enjoys CCA security. Moreover, unlike [2], our construction uses both the PQ AKEM and HPKE as black-boxes meaning it can be easily implemented using only the standard interfaces to the two schemes. For these reasons our hybrid construction provides a cheap and easy path towards a practical PQ-secure (A)PKE drop-in replacement for plain HPKE.

POST-QUANTUM AKEM. As we have seen, AKEM schemes are the fundamental primitive underlying natural APKE and pskAPKE schemes. The HPKE standard in its HPKE$_{\mathsf{Auth}}$ and HPKE$_{\mathsf{AuthPSK}}$ modes relies on the Diffie-Hellman based DH-APKE instantiation. Unfortunately, none of them offers security against attackers equipped with a quantum computer. In Sect. 6 we propose two generic constructions of AKEM from basic primitives that can be instantiated in a post-quantum secure way.

A well-known approach for constructing a post-quantum AKEM is to combine a post-quantum KEM with a post-quantum signature [10]. Unfortunately, the Encrypt-then-Sign (EtS) approach turns out not to be Insider-CCA secure [10]. The Sign-then-Encrypt (StE) approach is in fact Insider-CCA and Outsider-Auth secure but extending it to Sign-then-KEM in a natural way would add unnecessary overhead through the required detour over the KEM/DEM framework. Our first construction extends EtS approach to the new "Encrypt-then-Sign-then-Hash" (EtStH) approach. It combines a KEM, a digital signature SIG, and a hash function to obtain AKEM. Concretely, AKEM encryption produces a KEM ciphertext/key pair (c, K') and then uses the sender's secret key to sign ciphertext c and the sender's public and verification key. Finally, the DEM key is derived from K', the signature and all the public keys using a hash function. Security in the sense of Insider-CCA and Outsider-Auth is proved under the assumption that the hash function is a PRF. Our scheme can be instantiated, for example, with any post-quantum secure KEM and signature scheme, for example Kyber [8] and Dilithium [11].

Our second AKEM construction relies on a non-interactive key-exchange scheme NIKE. Key encapsulation first computes an ephemeral NIKE key pair and defines the ephemeral public key as the ciphertext. Next, it derives the DEM key from the following two NIKE keys: The first (authentication) key between sender's secret key and the receiver's public key. The second (privacy) key between the ephemeral secret key and the receiver's public key. Note that the knowledge of the receiver's secret key allows to recover both NIKE keys and hence the DEM key. Security in the sense of Insider-CCA and Outsider-Auth is proved assuming the NIKE to be actively secure [13]. Instantiating it with

the (actively secure) Diffie-Hellman NIKE [13], we obtain (a variant of) the
DH-AKEM from the HPKE standard. But it can also be instantiated with the
post-quantum secure NIKE from lattices [14] and from isogenies [12]. We remark
that our NIKE approach provides deniability, whereas our more efficient EtStH
construction does not.

2 Preliminaries

2.1 Notations

SETS AND ALGORITHMS. We write $h \xleftarrow{\$} S$ to denote that the variable h is
uniformly sampled from the finite set S. For an integer n, we define $[n] :=
\{1, \dots, n\}$. The notation $[\![b]\!]$, where b is a boolean statement, evaluates to 1 if
the statement is true and 0 otherwise.

We use uppercase letters $\mathcal{A}, \mathcal{B}$ to denote algorithms. Unless otherwise stated,
algorithms are probabilistic, and we write $(y_1, \dots) \xleftarrow{\$} \mathcal{A}(x_1, \dots)$ to denote that
$\mathcal{A}$ returns $(y_1, \dots)$ when run on input $(x_1, \dots)$. We write $\mathcal{A}^\mathcal{B}$ to denote that $\mathcal{A}$
has oracle access to $\mathcal{B}$ during its execution. For a randomised algorithm $\mathcal{A}$, we
use the notation $y \in \mathcal{A}(x)$ to denote that y is a possible output of $\mathcal{A}$ on input x.
SECURITY GAMES. We use standard code-based security games [6]. A *game* G
is a probability experiment in which an adversary $\mathcal{A}$ interacts with an implicit
challenger that answers oracle queries issued by $\mathcal{A}$. The game G has one *main
procedure* and an arbitrary amount of additional *oracle procedures* which describe
how these oracle queries are answered. We denote the (binary) output b of game
G between a challenger and an adversary $\mathcal{A}$ as $G^\mathcal{A} \Rightarrow b$. $\mathcal{A}$ is said to *win* G
if $G^\mathcal{A} \Rightarrow 1$, or shortly $G \Rightarrow 1$. Unless otherwise stated, the randomness in the
probability term $\Pr[G^\mathcal{A} \Rightarrow 1]$ is over all the random coins in game G.

We now recall definitions for (authenticated) KEMs (Sect. 2.2), authenticated
PKE schemes (Sect. 2.3), and digital signatures (Sect. 2.6). Standard definitions
of pseudo-random functions (Sect. 2.4), Authenticated Encryption with Associated Data (Sect. 2.5), and non-interactive key exchange (Sect. 2.7) are postponed
to the appendix.

2.2 (Authenticated) Key Encapsulation Mechanisms

We first recall syntax and security of a KEM.

Definition 1 (KEM). *A key encapsulation mechanism* KEM *consists of three
algorithms:*

- Gen *outputs a key pair* (sk, pk), *where* pk *defines a key space* $\mathcal{K}$.
- Encaps *takes as input a (receiver) public key* pk, *and outputs an encapsulation
  c and a shared secret* $K \in \mathcal{K}$ *(or* $\bot$*).*
- *Deterministic* Decaps *takes as input a (receiver) secret key* sk *and an encapsulation* c, *and outputs a shared key* $K \in \mathcal{K}$ *(or* $\bot$*).*

We require that for all $(sk, pk) \in \mathsf{Gen}$,

$$\Pr_{(c,K) \xleftarrow{\$} \mathsf{Encaps}(pk)} [\mathsf{Decaps}(sk, c) = K] = 1 \ .$$

To KEM we associate the two sets $\mathcal{SK} := \{sk \mid (sk, pk) \in \mathsf{Gen}\}$ and $\mathcal{PK} := \{pk \mid (sk, pk) \in \mathsf{Gen}\}$. We assume (w.l.o.g.) that there is a function $\mu : \mathcal{SK} \to \mathcal{PK}$ such that for all $(sk, pk) \in \mathsf{Gen}$ it holds $\mu(sk) = pk$. We further define $\mathcal{PK}'$ to be the set of all efficiently recognizable public keys (by Encaps), i.e., $\mathcal{PK}' := \{pk \in \{0,1\}^* \mid \bot \notin \mathsf{Encaps}(pk)\}$. Note that $\mathcal{PK} \subseteq \mathcal{PK}'$ by correctness, but $\mathcal{PK}'$ could potentially contain "benign looking" public keys outside of $\mathcal{PK}$. We will also require a property of the KEM called η-key spreadness:

$$\forall pk \in \mathcal{PK}' : H_\infty(K \mid (c, K) \xleftarrow{\$} \mathsf{Encaps}(pk)) \geq \eta,$$

where H_∞ denotes the min-entropy. This property will assure that an honestly generated key K has sufficient min-entropy, even if it was generated using a pk outside $\mathcal{PK}$.

Listing 1: Game (n, q_d, q_c)-CCA for KEM. Adversary $\mathcal{A}$ makes at most q_d queries to DECAP, and at most q_c queries to CHALL.

(n, q_d, q_c)-CCA	Oracle $\mathrm{DECAP}(j \in [n], c)$
01 **for** $i \in [n]$	07 **if** $\exists K : (pk_j, c, K) \in \mathcal{E}$
02 $(sk_i, pk_i) \xleftarrow{\$} \mathsf{Gen}$	08 **return** K
03 $\mathcal{E} \leftarrow \emptyset$	09 $K \leftarrow \mathsf{Decaps}(sk_j, c)$
04 $b \xleftarrow{\$} \{0, 1\}$	10 **return** K
05 $b' \xleftarrow{\$} \mathcal{A}^{\mathrm{DECAP},\mathrm{CHALL}}(pk_1, \dots, pk_n)$	
06 **return** $[\![b = b']\!]$	Oracle $\mathrm{CHALL}(j \in [n])$
	11 $(c, K) \xleftarrow{\$} \mathsf{Encaps}(pk_j)$
	12 **if** $b = 1$
	13 $K \xleftarrow{\$} \mathcal{K}$
	14 $\mathcal{E} \leftarrow \mathcal{E} \cup \{(pk_j, c, K)\}$
	15 **return** (c, K)

Privacy in the sense of multi-user chosen-ciphertext security is defined via the game in Listing 1. The advantage of an adversary $\mathcal{A}$ is defined as

$$\mathsf{Adv}_{\mathcal{A},\mathsf{KEM}}^{(n,q_d,q_c)\text{-CCA}} := \left| \Pr[(n, q_d, q_c)\text{-CCA}(\mathcal{A}) \Rightarrow 1] - \frac{1}{2} \right| \ .$$

Next, we recall syntax and security of an authenticated KEM (AKEM) [1].

Definition 2 (AKEM). *An authenticated key encapsulation mechanism* AKEM *consists of three algorithms:*

- Gen *outputs a key pair* (sk, pk), *where* pk *defines a key space* $\mathcal{K}$.
- $\mathsf{AuthEncap}$ *takes as input a (sender) secret key* sk *and a (receiver) public key* pk, *and outputs an encapsulation* c *and a shared secret* $K \in \mathcal{K}$ (or $\bot$).

- *Deterministic* AuthDecap *takes as input a (sender) public key pk, a (receiver) secret key sk, and an encapsulation c, and outputs a shared key $K \in \mathcal{K}$ (or $\perp$).*

We require that for all $(sk_1, pk_1) \in$ Gen, $(sk_2, pk_2) \in$ Gen,

$$\Pr_{(c,K) \xleftarrow{\$} \mathsf{AuthEncap}(sk_1, pk_2)} [\mathsf{AuthDecap}(pk_1, sk_2, c) = K] = 1 \ .$$

Sets $\mathcal{SK}$, $\mathcal{PK}$, $\mathcal{PK}'$, function μ, and η-key spreadness are defined as in the the KEM case.

Privacy (in the sense of insider and outsider CCA security) is defined via game Listing 2. Oracles AENCAP and ADECAP can be called with arbitrary public keys $pk \in \mathcal{PK}' \supseteq \mathcal{PK}$, i.e., arbitrary strings that pass AKEM's internal verification check. The insider setting is modeled using the REPSK oracle which can be used by the adversary to corrupt a sender's secret key sk. (Here we can assume $sk \in \mathcal{SK}$ since secret keys are usually seeds and can be efficiently verified.)

Note that this security notion is equivalent to the one from [1]. In the outsider case, the adversary cannot corrupt secret keys, i.e., $r_{sk} = 0$. The advantage is defined as

$$\mathsf{Adv}_{\mathcal{A},\mathsf{AKEM}}^{(n,q_e,q_d,q_c,r_{sk})\text{-Insider-CCA}} := \left| \Pr[(n, q_e, q_d, q_c, r_{sk})\text{-Insider-CCA}(\mathcal{A}) \Rightarrow 1] - \frac{1}{2} \right| ,$$

$$\mathsf{Adv}_{\mathcal{A},\mathsf{AKEM}}^{(n,q_e,q_d,q_c)\text{-Outsider-CCA}} := \mathsf{Adv}_{\mathcal{A},\mathsf{AKEM}}^{(n,q_e,q_d,q_c,0)\text{-Insider-CCA}} .$$

Authenticity is defined via the game in Listing 3.

$$\mathsf{Adv}_{\mathcal{A},\mathsf{AKEM}}^{(n,q_e,q_d)\text{-Outsider-Auth}} := \left| \Pr[(n, q_e, q_d)\text{-Outsider-Auth}(\mathcal{A}) \Rightarrow 1] - \frac{1}{2} \right| .$$

2.3 Authenticated Public Key Encryption

We recall syntax and security of an authenticated PKE (APKE) [1].

Definition 3 (APKE). *An authenticated public key encryption scheme* APKE *consists of the following three algorithms:*

- Gen *outputs a key pair (sk, pk).*
- AuthEnc *takes as input a (sender) secret key sk, a (receiver) public key pk, a message m, associated data aad, a bitstring info, and outputs a ciphertext c.*
- *Deterministic* AuthDec *takes as input a (receiver) secret key sk, a (sender) public key pk, a ciphertext c, associated data aad and a bitstring info, and outputs a message m.*

Listing 2: Game $(n, q_e, q_d, q_c, r_{sk})$-Insider-CCA for AKEM. Adversary $\mathcal{A}$ makes at most q_e queries to AENCAP, at most q_d queries to ADECAP, at most q_c queries to CHALL, and at most r_{sk} queries to REPSK.

$(n, q_e, q_d, q_c, r_{sk})$-Insider-CCA	Oracle $\text{CHALL}(i \in [n], j \in [n])$
01 **for** $i \in [n]$	13 **if** $j \in \Gamma_{pk}$
02 $\quad (sk_i, pk_i) \overset{\$}{\leftarrow}$ Gen	14 $\quad$ **return** $\bot$
03 $\mathcal{E}, \Gamma_{pk} \leftarrow \emptyset$	15 $(c, K) \overset{\$}{\leftarrow}$ AuthEncap(sk_i, pk_j)
04 $b \overset{\$}{\leftarrow} \{0,1\}$	16 **if** $b = 1$
05 $b' \overset{\$}{\leftarrow} \mathcal{A}^{\text{AENCAP},\text{ADECAP},\text{CHALL},\text{REPSK}}(pk_1, \ldots, pk_n)$	17 $\quad K \overset{\$}{\leftarrow} \mathcal{K}$
06 **return** $[\![b = b']\!]$	18 $\quad \mathcal{E} \leftarrow \mathcal{E} \cup \{(pk_i, pk_j, c, K)\}$
	19 **return** (c, K)
Oracle $\text{AENCAP}(i \in [n], pk \in \mathcal{PK}')$	
07 $(c, K) \overset{\$}{\leftarrow}$ AuthEncap(sk_i, pk)	Oracle $\text{REPSK}(i \in [n], sk \in \mathcal{SK})$
08 **return** (c, K)	20 $(pk_i, sk_i) \leftarrow (\mu(sk), sk)$
	21 $\Gamma_{pk} \leftarrow \Gamma_{pk} \cup \{i\}$
Oracle $\text{ADECAP}(pk \in \mathcal{PK}', j \in [n], c)$	
09 **if** $\exists K : (pk, pk_j, c, K) \in \mathcal{E}$	
10 $\quad$ **return** K	
11 $K \leftarrow$ AuthDecap(pk, sk_j, c)	
12 **return** K	

We require that for all messages $m \in \{0,1\}^*$, $aad \in \{0,1\}^*$, $info \in \{0,1\}^*$,

$$\Pr_{\substack{(sk_S, pk_S) \overset{\$}{\leftarrow} \text{Gen} \\ (sk_R, pk_R) \overset{\$}{\leftarrow} \text{Gen}}} \left[\begin{array}{l} c \leftarrow \text{AuthEnc}(sk_S, pk_R, m, aad, info), \\ \text{AuthDec}(sk_R, pk_S, c, aad, info) = m \end{array} \right] = 1 .$$

Sets $\mathcal{SK}$, $\mathcal{PK}$, $\mathcal{PK}'$, function μ, and η-key spreadness are defined as in the the KEM case.

PRIVACY. We define the game (n, q_e, q_d, q_c)-Insider-CCA in Listing 4, which is the strongest privacy notion for APKE defined in [1].

The advantage of $\mathcal{A}$ is

$$\text{Adv}_{\mathcal{A},\text{APKE}}^{(n, q_e, q_d, q_c)\text{-Insider-CCA}} := \left| \Pr[(n, q_e, q_d, q_c)\text{-Insider-CCA}(\mathcal{A}) \Rightarrow 1] - \frac{1}{2} \right| .$$

AUTHENTICITY. Furthermore, in Listing 5 we recall the (n, q_e, q_d)-Outsider-Auth game from [1]. The advantage of $\mathcal{A}$ is defined as

$$\text{Adv}_{\mathcal{A},\text{APKE}}^{(n, q_e, q_d)\text{-Outsider-Auth}} := \Pr[(n, q_e, q_d)\text{-Outsider-Auth} \Rightarrow 1].$$

Note that in contrast to the privacy case we use the weaker outsider notion instead of the insider notion for authenticity. This is because [1] show that the HPKE$_{\text{Auth}}$ construction cannot fulfill insider authenticity for any possible instantiation. Since the same attack can be run against HPKE$_{\text{PSK}}$, we omit the definition here.

Listing 3: Game (n, q_e, q_d)-Outsider-Auth for AKEM. Adversary $\mathcal{A}$ makes at most q_e queries to AENCAP, and at most q_d queries to ADECAP.

(n, q_e, q_d)-Outsider-Auth	Oracle AENCAP$(i \in [n], pk \in \mathcal{PK}')$
01 **for** $i \in [n]$	07 $(c, K) \xleftarrow{\$} \mathsf{AuthEncap}(sk_i, pk)$
02 $(sk_i, pk_i) \xleftarrow{\$} \mathsf{Gen}$	08 $\mathcal{E} \leftarrow \mathcal{E} \cup \{(pk_i, pk, c, K)\}$
03 $\mathcal{E} \leftarrow \emptyset$	09 **return** (c, K)
04 $b \xleftarrow{\$} \{0, 1\}$	
05 $b' \xleftarrow{\$} \mathcal{A}^{\mathrm{AENCAP}, \mathrm{ADECAP}}(pk_1, \ldots, pk_n)$	Oracle ADECAP$(pk \in \mathcal{PK}', j \in [n], c)$
06 **return** $[\![b = b']\!]$	10 **if** $\exists K : (pk, pk_j, c, K) \in \mathcal{E}$
	11 **return** K
	12 $K \leftarrow \mathsf{AuthDecap}(pk, sk_j, c)$
	13 **if** $b = 1 \wedge pk \in \{pk_1, \ldots, pk_n\} \wedge K \neq \perp$
	14 $K \xleftarrow{\$} \mathcal{K}$
	15 $\mathcal{E} \leftarrow \mathcal{E} \cup \{(pk, pk_j, c, K)\}$
	16 **return** K

2.4 Pseudorandom Functions

A keyed function F with a finite key space $\mathcal{K}$, input length n, and a finite output range $\mathcal{R}$ is a function $F : \mathcal{K} \times \{0, 1\}^* \to \mathcal{R}$.

Definition 4 (Multi-Instance Pseudorandom Function). *The* (n_k, q_{PRF}) *-PRF advantage of an adversary* $\mathcal{A}$ *against a keyed function* F *with finite key space* $\mathcal{K}$, *and finite range* $\mathcal{R}$ *is defined as*

$$\mathsf{Adv}_{\mathcal{A}, F}^{(n_k, q_{\mathsf{PRF}})\text{-PRF}} := \left| \Pr_{K_1, \ldots, K_{n_k} \xleftarrow{\$} \mathcal{K}} [\mathcal{A}^{F(K_1, \cdot), \ldots, F(K_{n_k}, \cdot)}] - \Pr[\mathcal{A}^{f_1(\cdot), \ldots, f_{n_k}(\cdot)}] \right|,$$

where $f_i : \{0, 1\}^* \to \mathcal{R}$ *for* $i \in [n_k]$ *are chosen uniformly at random from the set of functions mapping to* $\mathcal{R}$ *and* $\mathcal{A}$ *makes at most* q_{PRF} *queries in total to the oracles* $F(K_i, \cdot)$, f_i *resp.*

Definition 5 (2-Keyed Function). *A 2-keyed function* F *with finite key spaces* $\mathcal{K}_1$ *and* $\mathcal{K}_2$, *and finite range* $\mathcal{R}$ *is a function*

$$F : \mathcal{K}_1 \times \mathcal{K}_2 \times \{0, 1\}^* \to \mathcal{R}.$$

2.5 Authenticated Encryption with Associated Data

We recall standard syntax and security for AEAD schemes.

Definition 6 (AEAD). *A nonce-based authenticated encryption scheme with associated data and key space* $\mathcal{K}'$ *consists of the following two algorithms:*

- *Deterministic algorithm* AEAD.Enc *takes as input a key* $k \in \mathcal{K}'$, *a message* m, *associated data* aad, *and a nonce and outputs a ciphertext* c.
- *Deterministic algorithm* AEAD.Dec *takes as input a key* $k \in \mathcal{K}'$, *a ciphertext* c, *associated data* aad *and a nonce* nonce *and outputs a message* m *or the failure symbol* $\perp$.

Listing 4: Game (n, q_e, q_d, q_c)-Insider-CCA for APKE in which adversary $\mathcal{A}$ makes at most q_e queries to AENC, at most q_d queries to ADEC and at most q_c queries to CHALL.

(n, q_e, q_d, q_c)-Insider-CCA	Oracle $\text{ADEC}(pk \in \mathcal{PK}', j \in [n], c, aad, info)$
01 **for** $i \in [n]$	09 **if** $(pk, pk_j, c, aad, info) \in \mathcal{E}$
02 $\quad (sk_i, pk_i) \xleftarrow{\$} \mathsf{Gen}$	10 $\quad$ **return** $\bot$
03 $\mathcal{E} \leftarrow \emptyset$	11 $m \leftarrow \mathsf{AuthDec}(pk, sk_j, c, aad, info)$
04 $b \xleftarrow{\$} \{0, 1\}$	12 **return** m
05 $b' \xleftarrow{\$} \mathcal{A}^{\text{AENC},\text{ADEC},\text{CHALL}}(pk_1, \dots, pk_n)$	
06 **return** $[\![b = b']\!]$	Oracle $\text{CHALL}(sk \in \mathcal{SK}, j \in [n], m_0, m_1, aad, info)$
	13 **if** $|m_0| \neq |m_1|$ **return** $\bot$
Oracle $\text{AENC}(i \in [n], pk \in \mathcal{PK}', m, aad, info)$	14 $c \xleftarrow{\$} \mathsf{AuthEnc}(sk, pk_j, m_b, aad, info)$
07 $c \xleftarrow{\$} \mathsf{AuthEnc}(sk_i, pk, m, aad, info)$	15 $\mathcal{E} \leftarrow \mathcal{E} \cup \{(\mu(sk), pk_j, c, aad, info)\}$
08 **return** c	16 **return** c

Listing 5: Game (n, q_e, q_d)-Outsider-Auth for APKE in which adversary $\mathcal{A}$ makes at most q_e queries to AENC and at most q_d queries to ADEC.

(n, q_e, q_d)-Outsider-Auth	Oracle $\text{AENC}(i \in [n], pk \in \mathcal{PK}', m, aad, info)$
01 **for** $i \in [n]$	06 $c \xleftarrow{\$} \mathsf{AuthEnc}(sk_i, pk, m, aad, info)$
02 $\quad (sk_i, pk_i) \xleftarrow{\$} \mathsf{Gen}$	07 $\mathcal{E} \leftarrow \mathcal{E} \cup \{(pk_i, pk, c, aad, info)\}$
03 $\mathcal{E} \leftarrow \emptyset$	08 **return** c
04 $(i^*, j^*, c^*, aad^*, info^*) \xleftarrow{\$} \mathcal{A}^{\text{AENC},\text{ADEC}}(pk_1, \dots, pk_n)$	
05 **return** $[\![(pk_{i^*}, pk_{j^*}, c^*, aad^*, info^*) \notin \mathcal{E}$	Oracle $\text{ADEC}(pk \in \mathcal{PK}', j \in [n], c, aad, info)$
$\quad \wedge \mathsf{AuthDec}(pk_{i^*}, sk_{j^*}, c^*, aad^*, info^*) \neq \bot]\!]$	09 $m \leftarrow \mathsf{AuthDec}(pk, sk_j, c, aad, info)$
	10 **return** m

We require that for all $aad \in \{0, 1\}^*, m \in \{0, 1\}^*, nonce \in \{0, 1\}^{N_{nonce}}$

$$\Pr_{k \xleftarrow{\$} \mathcal{K}'} [\mathsf{AEAD.Dec}(k, \mathsf{AEAD.Enc}(k, m, aad, nonce), aad, nonce) = m] = 1 ,$$

where N_{nonce} is the length of the nonce in bits.

We define the multi-instance security game (n, q_d)-INT-CTXT in Listing 6 and (n, q_d)-CCA in Listing 7. Note that an AEAD scheme which is IND-CPA and INT-CTXT secure is also CCA secure [5]. The advantage of an adversary $\mathcal{A}$ is

$$\mathsf{Adv}_{\mathcal{A},\mathsf{AEAD}}^{(n, q_d)\text{-INT-CTXT}} := \left| \Pr[(n, q_d)\text{-INT-CTXT}(\mathcal{A}) \Rightarrow 1] - \frac{1}{2} \right|$$

$$\mathsf{Adv}_{\mathcal{A},\mathsf{AEAD}}^{(n, q_d)\text{-CCA}} := \left| \Pr[(n, q_d)\text{-CCA}(\mathcal{A}) \Rightarrow 1] - \frac{1}{2} \right| .$$

2.6   Digital Signatures

Definition 7 (Signature Scheme). *A signature scheme* $\mathsf{SIG} = (\mathsf{Gen}, \mathsf{Sign}, \mathsf{Vfy})$ *consists of three algorithm:*

Listing 6: Game (n, q_d)-INT-CTXT for AEAD. Adversary $\mathcal{A}$ makes at most one query per index i to ENC and at most q_d queries in total to DEC.

(n, q_d)-INT-CTXT	Oracle $\text{ENC}(i \in [n], m, aad)$
01 **for** $i \in [n]$	08 $c \leftarrow \text{AEAD.Enc}(k_i, m, aad, nonce_i)$
02 $\quad k_i \overset{\$}{\leftarrow} \mathcal{K}'$	09 $\mathcal{E} \leftarrow \mathcal{E} \cup \{i, m, c, aad\}$
03 $\quad nonce_i \overset{\$}{\leftarrow} \{0,1\}^{Nnonce}$	10 **return** $(c, nonce_i)$
04 $\mathcal{E} \leftarrow \emptyset$	
05 $b \overset{\$}{\leftarrow} \{0,1\}$	Oracle $\text{DEC}(i \in [n], c, aad)$
06 $b' \overset{\$}{\leftarrow} \mathcal{A}^{\text{ENC,DEC}}$	11 **if** $b = 0$
07 **return** $[\![b = b']\!]$	12 $\quad m \leftarrow \text{AEAD.Dec}(k_i, c, aad, nonce_i)$
	13 **else if** $\exists m' : (i, m', c, aad) \in \mathcal{E}$
	14 $\quad m \leftarrow m'$
	15 **else**
	16 $\quad m \leftarrow \bot$
	17 **return** m

Listing 7: Game (n, q_d)-CCA for AEAD. Adversary $\mathcal{A}$ makes at most one query per index i to ENC and at most q_d queries in total to DEC.

(n, q_d)-CCA	Oracle $\text{ENC}(i \in [n], m_0, m_1, aad)$
01 **for** $i \in [n]$	08 $c \leftarrow \text{AEAD.Enc}(k_i, m_b, aad, nonce_i)$
02 $\quad k_i \overset{\$}{\leftarrow} \mathcal{K}'$	09 $\mathcal{E} \leftarrow \mathcal{E} \cup \{i, c, aad\}$
03 $\quad nonce_i \overset{\$}{\leftarrow} \{0,1\}^{Nnonce}$	10 **return** $(c, nonce_i)$
04 $\mathcal{E} \leftarrow \emptyset$	
05 $b \overset{\$}{\leftarrow} \{0,1\}$	Oracle $\text{DEC}(i \in [n], c, aad)$
06 $b' \overset{\$}{\leftarrow} \mathcal{A}^{\text{ENC,DEC}}$	11 **if** $(i, c, aad) \in \mathcal{E}$
07 **return** $[\![b = b']\!]$	12 $\quad$ **return** $\bot$
	13 $m \leftarrow \text{AEAD.Dec}(k_i, c, aad, nonce_i)$
	14 **return** m

- *Key generation* Gen *generates a secret signing key sigk and a verification key vk.*
- *Signing* Sign*: On input a signing key sigk and a message m, outputs a signature σ.*
- *Verification* Vfy*: On input a verification key vk, a message m, and a signature σ, deterministically outputs a bit b.*

The signature scheme fulfills correctness if for all $(sigk, vk) \overset{\$}{\leftarrow}$ Gen *it holds*

$$\Pr_{\sigma \overset{\$}{\leftarrow} \text{Sign}(sk, m)} [\text{Vfy}(vk, m, \sigma) = 1] = 1.$$

To SIG we associate the two sets $\mathcal{SK} := \{sigk \mid (sigk, vk) \in \text{Gen}\}$ and $\mathcal{VK} := \{vk \mid (sigk, vk) \in \text{Gen}\}$. We assume (w.l.o.g.) that there is a function $\mu' : \mathcal{SK} \to \mathcal{VK}$ such that for all $(sigk, vk) \in$ Gen it holds $\mu'(sigk) = vk$.

Definition 8 (Strong Unforgeability). *Let* SIG $=$ (Gen, Sign, Vfy) *be a signature scheme. We define multi-user strong unforgeability against a chosen message attack (*SUF-CMA*) via the* (n, q_s)-SUF-CMA *game in Listing 8. The advantage of an adversary $\mathcal{A}$ is* $\text{Adv}_{\mathcal{A}, \text{SIG}}^{(n, q_s)\text{-SUF-CMA}} = \Pr[(n, q_s)\text{-SUF-CMA}(\mathcal{A}) \Rightarrow 1].$

Listing 8: Game (n, q_s)-SUF-CMA for SIG. Adversary $\mathcal{A}$ makes at most q_s queries to SIGN.

(n, q_s)-SUF-CMA	Oracle SIGN($i \in [n], m$)
01 **for** $i \in [n]$	06 $\sigma \xleftarrow{\$} \mathsf{Sign}(sigk_i, m)$
02 $(sigk_i, vk_i) \xleftarrow{\$} \mathsf{Gen}$	07 $Q \leftarrow Q \cup \{(i, m, \sigma)\}$
03 $Q \leftarrow \emptyset$	08 **return** σ
04 $(i^*, m^*, \sigma^*) \xleftarrow{\$} \mathcal{A}^{\text{SIGN}}(vk_1, \ldots, vk_n)$	
05 **return** $[\![\mathsf{Vfy}(vk_{i^*}, m^*, \sigma^*) = 1$	
$\wedge\ (i^*, m^*, \sigma^*) \notin Q]\!]$	

2.7 Non-Interactive Key Exchange

Definition 9 (Non-Interactive Key Exchange). *A* NIKE *scheme consists of a setup, two algorithms* NIKE.KeyGen, NIKE.SharedKey *and a shared key space* $\mathcal{SHK}$. *The algorithms are defined as follows:*

- NIKE.KeyGen *outputs a pair of public and secret key* (sk, pk).
- NIKE.SharedKey *takes a secret key sk and a public key pk and outputs either a shared key in* $\mathcal{SHK}$ *or the failure symbol* $\perp$.

The NIKE *fulfills correctness if for all* $(sk_1, pk_1) \xleftarrow{\$}$ NIKE.KeyGen, $(sk_2, pk_2) \xleftarrow{\$}$ NIKE.KeyGen, *it holds*

$$\mathsf{NIKE.SharedKey}(sk_1, pk_2) = \mathsf{NIKE.SharedKey}(sk_2, pk_1).$$

The security definition for actively secure NIKE can be found in the full version.

3 Pre-Shared Key (Authenticated) Encryption

In this section, we define syntax and security of pre-shared key public key encryption (pskPKE) and pre-shared key authenticated public key encryption (pskAPKE). The former is an extension of common public key encryption with an additional pre-shared symmetric key that has already been shared between the parties. The latter is an analogue extension of authenticated public key encryption (APKE). The pre-shared key (*psk*) has two functionalities. First, it provides an additional layer of privacy since the security does not have to rely on the asymmetric key only. Second, it also provides authenticity. The intuition behind security is that even if one of the two keys, either the asymmetric key or the (symmetric) pre-shared key, is corrupted or in any other way insecure, the scheme should still guarantee security.

We start with defining the syntax of pskPKE and pskAPKE in Sect. 3.1 and then define the security model for privacy (Sect. 3.2) and authenticity (Sect. 3.3).

3.1 Syntax

Definition 10 (pskPKE). *A pre-shared key public key encryption scheme* pskPKE *consists of the following four algorithms:*

- GenSK *outputs a key pair* (sk, pk).
- GenPSK *outputs a pre-shared key* psk.
- pskEnc *takes as input a (receiver) public key* pk, *a pre-shared key* psk, *a message* m, *associated data* aad, *a bitstring* $info$, *and outputs a ciphertext* c.
- *Deterministic* pskDec *takes as input a (receiver) secret key* sk, *a pre-shared key* psk, *a ciphertext* c, *associated data* aad *and a bitstring* $info$, *and outputs a message* m.

We require that for all messages $m \in \{0,1\}^*, aad \in \{0,1\}^*, info \in \{0,1\}^*,$

$$\Pr_{\substack{(sk,pk) \xleftarrow{\$} \mathsf{GenSK} \\ psk \xleftarrow{\$} \mathsf{GenPSK}}} \begin{bmatrix} c \leftarrow \mathsf{pskEnc}(pk, psk, m, aad, info), \\ \mathsf{pskDec}(sk, psk, c, aad, info) = m \end{bmatrix} = 1 \ .$$

Definition 11 (pskAPKE). *A pre-shared key Authenticated public key encryption scheme* pskAPKE *consists of the following four algorithms:*

- GenSK *outputs a key pair* (sk, pk).
- GenPSK *outputs a pre-shared key* psk.
- pskAEnc *takes as input a (sender) secret key* sk, *a (receiver) public key* pk, *a pre-shared key* psk, *a message* m, *associated data* aad, *a bitstring* $info$, *and outputs a ciphertext* c.
- *Deterministic* pskADec *takes as input a (sender) public key* pk, *a (receiver) secret key* sk, *a pre-shared key* psk, *a ciphertext* c, *associated data* aad *and a bitstring* $info$, *and outputs a message* m.

We require that for all messages $m \in \{0,1\}^*, aad \in \{0,1\}^*, info \in \{0,1\}^*,$

$$\Pr_{\substack{(sk_S,pk_S) \xleftarrow{\$} \mathsf{GenSK} \\ (sk_R,pk_R) \xleftarrow{\$} \mathsf{GenSK} \\ psk \xleftarrow{\$} \mathsf{GenPSK}}} \begin{bmatrix} c \leftarrow \mathsf{pskAEnc}(sk_S, pk_R, psk, m, aad, info), \\ \mathsf{pskADec}(pk_S, sk_R, psk, c, aad, info) = m \end{bmatrix} = 1 \ .$$

Sets $\mathcal{SK}, \mathcal{PK}, \mathcal{PK}'$, and function μ are defined as in the the KEM case.

3.2 Privacy

Privacy is defined via the games in Listing 9 (pskPKE) and Listing 10 (pskAPKE). The idea is based on the standard CCA definition for PKE with the following modifications.

For the game in Listing 9, the adversary is provided with an encryption oracle ENC since, in contrast to standard PKE, encryption requires the knowledge of

Listing 9: Game $(n, q_e, q_d, q_c, r_{pk}, r_{psk})$-CCA for pskPKE. Adversary $\mathcal{A}$ makes at most q_e queries to ENC, at most q_d queries to DEC, at most q_c queries to CHALL, at most r_{pk} queries to REPPK, and at most r_{psk} queries to REPPSK.

$(n, q_e, q_d, q_c, r_{pk}, r_{psk})$-CCA	Oracle CHALL$(i \in [n], j \in [n], m_0, m_1, aad, info)$
01 **for** $i \in [n]$	16 **if** $\|m_0\| \neq \|m_1\| \vee (j \in \Gamma_{pk} \wedge (i,j) \in \Gamma_{psk})$
02 $\quad (sk_i, pk_i) \xleftarrow{\$} $ Gen	17 $\quad$ **return** $\perp$
03 $\quad$ **for** $j \in [i]$	18 $c \xleftarrow{\$} $ pskEnc$(pk_j, psk_{ij}, m_b, aad, info)$
04 $\qquad psk_{ij} \xleftarrow{\$} $ GenPSK	19 $\mathcal{E} \leftarrow \mathcal{E} \cup \{(pk_j, psk_{ij}, c, aad, info)\}$
05 $\qquad psk_{ji} \leftarrow psk_{ij}$	20 **return** c
06 $\mathcal{E}, \Gamma_{pk}, \Gamma_{psk} \leftarrow \emptyset$	
07 $b \xleftarrow{\$} \{0,1\}$	Oracle REPPK$(j \in [n], pk \in \mathcal{PK}')$
08 $b' \xleftarrow{\$} \mathcal{A}^{\text{ENC,DEC,CHALL,REPPK,REPPSK}}(pk_1, \dots, pk_n)$	21 $(sk_j, pk_j) \leftarrow (\perp, pk)$
09 **return** $[\![b = b']\!]$	22 $\Gamma_{pk} \leftarrow \Gamma_{pk} \cup \{j\}$
Oracle ENC$(i \in [n], j \in [n], m, aad, info)$	Oracle REPPSK$(i \in [n], j \in [n], psk)$
10 $c \xleftarrow{\$} $ pskEnc$(pk_j, psk_{ij}, m, aad, info)$	23 $psk_{ij} \leftarrow psk$
11 **return** c	24 $psk_{ji} \leftarrow psk$
	25 $\Gamma_{psk} \leftarrow \Gamma_{psk} \cup \{(i,j), (j,i)\}$
Oracle DEC$(i \in [n], j \in [n], c, aad, info)$	
12 **if** $sk_j = \perp \vee (pk_j, psk_{ij}, c, aad, info) \in \mathcal{E}$	
13 $\quad$ **return** $\perp$	
14 $m \leftarrow $ pskDec$(sk_j, psk_{ij}, c, aad, info)$	
15 **return** m	

Listing 10: Game $(n, q_e, q_d, q_c, r_{pk}, r_{sk}, r_{psk})$-Insider-CCA for pskAPKE. Adversary $\mathcal{A}$ makes at most q_e queries to ENC at most q_d queries to DEC, at most q_c queries to CHALL, at most r_{pk} queries to REPPK, at most r_{sk} queries to REPSK, and at most r_{psk} queries to REPPSK.

$(n, q_e, q_d, q_c, r_{pk}, r_{sk}, r_{psk})$-Insider-CCA	Oracle CHALL$(i \in [n], j \in [n], m_0, m_1, aad, info)$
01 **for** $i \in [n]$	18 **if** $\|m_0\| \neq \|m_1\| \vee sk_i = \perp \vee (j \in \Gamma_{pk} \wedge (i,j) \in \Gamma_{psk})$
02 $\quad (sk_i, pk_i) \xleftarrow{\$} $ Gen	19 $\quad$ **return** $\perp$
03 $\quad$ **for** $j \in [i]$	20 $c \xleftarrow{\$} $ pskAEnc$(sk_i, pk_j, psk_{ij}, m_b, aad, info)$
04 $\qquad psk_{ij} \xleftarrow{\$} $ GenPSK	21 $\mathcal{E} \leftarrow \mathcal{E} \cup \{(pk_i, pk_j, psk_{ij}, c, aad, info)\}$
05 $\qquad psk_{ji} \leftarrow psk_{ij}$	22 **return** c
06 $\mathcal{E}, \Gamma_c, \Gamma_{pk}, \Gamma_{psk} \leftarrow \emptyset$	
07 $b \xleftarrow{\$} \{0,1\}$	Oracle REPPK$(j \in [n], pk \in \mathcal{PK}')$
08 $b' \xleftarrow{\$} \mathcal{A}^{\text{ENC,DEC,CHALL,REPPK,REPSK,REPPSK}}(pk_1, \dots, pk_n)$	23 $(sk_j, pk_j) \leftarrow (\perp, pk)$
09 **return** $[\![b = b']\!]$	24 $\Gamma_{pk} \leftarrow \Gamma_{pk} \cup \{j\}$
Oracle ENC$(i \in [n], j \in [n], m, aad, info)$	Oracle REPSK$(j \in [n], sk \in \mathcal{SK})$
10 **if** $sk_i = \perp$	25 $(sk_j, pk_j) \leftarrow (sk, \mu(sk))$
11 $\quad$ **return** $\perp$	26 $\Gamma_{pk} \leftarrow \Gamma_{pk} \cup \{j\}$
12 $c \xleftarrow{\$} $ pskAEnc$(sk_i, pk_j, psk_{ij}, m, aad, info)$	
13 **return** c	Oracle REPPSK$(i \in [n], j \in [\ell], psk)$
	27 $psk_{ij} \leftarrow psk$
Oracle DEC$(i \in [n], j \in [n], c, aad, info)$	28 $psk_{ji} \leftarrow psk$
14 **if** $sk_j = \perp \vee (pk_j, psk_{ij}, c, aad, info) \in \mathcal{E}$	29 $\Gamma_{psk} \leftarrow \Gamma_{psk} \cup \{(i,j), (j,i)\}$
15 $\quad$ **return** $\perp$	
16 $m \leftarrow $ pskADec$(pk_i, sk_j, psk_{ij}, c, aad, info)$	
17 **return** m	

the corresponding pre-shared key. We further strengthen the security model by allowing corrupted keys. This is modeled by two oracles, REPPK and REPPSK. Oracle REPPK models the corruption of an asymmetric key pair, where the

Listing 11: Game $(n, q_e, q_d, r_{pk}, r_{psk})$-Auth for pskPKE. Adversary $\mathcal{A}$ makes at at most q_e queries to ENC, at most q_d queries to DEC, at most r_{pk} queries to REPPK, and at most r_{psk} queries to REPPSK.

$(n, q_e, q_d, r_{pk}, r_{psk})$-Auth	Oracle DEC$(i \in [n], j \in [n], c, aad, info)$
01 **for** $i \in [n]$	12 **if** $sk_j = \bot$
02 $\quad (sk_i, pk_i) \xleftarrow{\$} $ Gen	13 $\quad$ **return** $\bot$
03 $\quad$ **for** $j \in [i]$	14 $m \leftarrow$ pskDec$(sk_j, psk_{ij}, c, aad, info)$
04 $\quad\quad psk_{ij} \xleftarrow{\$} $ GenPSK	15 **return** m
05 $\quad\quad psk_{ji} \leftarrow psk_{ij}$	
06 $\mathcal{E}, \Gamma_{psk} \leftarrow \emptyset$	Oracle REPPK$(j \in [n], pk \in \mathcal{PK}')$
07 $(i^*, j^*, c^*, aad^*, info^*) \xleftarrow{\$} \mathcal{A}^{\text{ENC,DEC,REPPK,REPPSK}}(pk_1, \ldots, pk_n)$	16 $(sk_j, pk_j) \leftarrow (\bot, pk)$
08 **return** $[\![(i^*, j^*) \notin \Gamma_{psk} \wedge sk_{j^*} \neq \bot$	
$\quad \wedge (pk_{j^*}, psk_{i^* j^*}, c^*, aad^*, info^*) \notin \mathcal{E}$	Oracle REPPSK$(i \in [n], j \in [n], psk)$
$\quad \wedge$ pskDec$(sk_{j^*}, psk_{i^* j^*}, c^*, aad^*, info^*) \neq \bot]\!]$	17 $psk_{ij} \leftarrow psk$
	18 $psk_{ji} \leftarrow psk$
Oracle ENC$(i \in [n], j \in [n], m, aad, info)$	19 $\Gamma_{psk} \leftarrow \Gamma_{psk} \cup \{(i,j), (j,i)\}$
09 $c \xleftarrow{\$} $ pskEnc$(pk_j, psk_{ij}, m, aad, info)$	
10 $\mathcal{E} \leftarrow \mathcal{E} \cup \{(pk_j, psk_{ij}, c, aad, info)\}$	
11 **return** c	

Listing 12: Game $(n, q_e, q_d, r_{pk}, r_{psk})$-Outsider-Auth for pskAPKE. Adversary $\mathcal{A}$ makes at most q_e queries to ENC, at most q_d queries to DEC, at most r_{pk} queries to REPPK, and at most r_{psk} queries to REPPSK.

$(n, q_e, q_d, r_{pk}, r_{psk})$-Outsider-Auth	Oracle DEC$(i \in [n], j \in [n], c, aad, info)$
01 **for** $i \in [n]$	14 **if** $sk_j = \bot$
02 $\quad (sk_i, pk_i) \xleftarrow{\$} $ Gen	15 $\quad$ **return** $\bot$
03 $\quad$ **for** $j \in [i]$	16 $m \leftarrow$ pskADec$(pk_i, sk_j, psk_{ij}, c, aad, info)$
04 $\quad\quad psk_{ij} \xleftarrow{\$} $ GenPSK	17 **return** m
05 $\quad\quad psk_{ji} \leftarrow psk_{ij}$	
06 $\mathcal{E}, \Gamma_{pk}, \Gamma_{psk} \leftarrow \emptyset$	Oracle REPPK$(i \in [n], pk \in \mathcal{PK}')$
07 $(i^*, j^*, c^*, aad^*, info^*) \xleftarrow{\$} \mathcal{A}^{\text{ENC,DEC,REPPK,REPPSK}}(pk_1, \ldots, pk_n)$	18 $(sk_i, pk_i) \leftarrow (\bot, pk)$
08 **return** $[\![(i^* \notin \Gamma_{pk} \vee (i^*, j^*) \notin \Gamma_{psk}) \wedge sk_{j^*} \neq \bot$	19 $\Gamma_{pk} \leftarrow \Gamma_{pk} \cup \{i\}$
$\quad \wedge (pk_{i^*}, pk_{j^*}, psk_{i^* j^*}, c^*, aad^*, info^*) \notin \mathcal{E}$	
$\quad \wedge$ pskADec$(pk_{i^*}, sk_{j^*}, psk_{i^* j^*}, c^*, aad^*, info^*) \neq \bot]\!]$	Oracle REPPSK$(i \in [n], j \in [n], psk)$
	20 $psk_{ij} \leftarrow psk$
Oracle ENC$(i \in [n], j \in [n], m, aad, info)$	21 $psk_{ji} \leftarrow psk$
09 **if** $sk_i = \bot$	22 $\Gamma_{psk} \leftarrow \Gamma_{psk} \cup \{(i,j), (j,i)\}$
10 $\quad$ **return** $\bot$	
11 $c \xleftarrow{\$} $ pskAEnc$(sk_i, pk_j, psk_{ij}, m, aad, info)$	
12 $\mathcal{E} \leftarrow \mathcal{E} \cup \{(pk_i, pk_j, psk_{ij}, c, aad, info)\}$	
13 **return** c	

adversary is allowed to replace the public key of a user with $pk \in \mathcal{PK}'$ (with or without knowing the matching private key). Since the game is not able to decrypt queries to a corrupted receiver's key anymore, we return $\bot$ on such queries. To keep track of corrupted keys, the game maintains a set Γ_{pk} containing all corrupted indices j. Similarly, oracle REPPSK models the corruption of a pre-shared key between two chosen users. Set Γ_{psk} keeps track of sender and receiver pairs for which the corresponding psk was corrupted. Provided with the additional oracles, it should still be hard to guess the challenge bit, i.e., which of the two messages given to the challenge oracle was encrypted. To avoid trivial wins, we disallow the challenge oracle to be queried on pairs of users for which both the receiver's key as well as the pre-shared key were corrupted.

However, the challenge query is allowed if at most one of them is corrupted. (Note that in particular the adversary is still allowed to issue challenge queries for a corrupted psk.) In that sense we model an "insider setting". An insider notion for pskPKE cannot be formulated stronger because it does not make any sense to allow corrupted senders in the sense of a corrupted sk since it is not used for encryption.[2] The advantage of adversary $\mathcal{A}$ is

$$\mathsf{Adv}^{(n,q_e,q_d,q_c,r_{pk},r_{psk})\text{-CCA}}_{\mathcal{A},\mathsf{pskPKE}} := \left| \Pr[(n, q_e, q_d, q_c, r_{pk}, r_{psk})\text{-CCA}(\mathcal{A}) \Rightarrow 1] - \frac{1}{2} \right|.$$

The definition of CCA security for pskAPKE (Listing 10) works similar with the following changes. The main difference compared to pskPKE is that the asymmetric part of the encryption is authenticated which means that the sender's secret key is also involved. To take attacks into account which could make use of corrupted senders, we make the following modification. The game provides another oracle REPSK which allows the adversary to replace an asymmetric secret key directly, which means they are also allowed to query all the other oracles on corrupted sender keys. This is exactly what is called the "Insider" setting in [1] and signcryption [10]. This means in particular that the encryption of two different messages is indistinguishable even if the sender's asymmetric key was adversarially chosen. As in the case of pskPKE, the psk can also be corrupted in the sense of an insider attack, i.e., the sender is corrupted. However, due to the symmetric nature of the pre-shared key, this implies a security loss for the receiver as well and we have to exclude trivial wins in the same way as for pskPKE. Therefore, the same security requirement as for pskPKE holds, i.e., in addition to the corruption of a sender's secret key either a receiver's key or the pre-shared key can be corrupted and security still holds. We also define outsider security as the simplified setting, where the adversary does not have access to the REPSK oracle, i.e., $r_{pk} = 0$. The advantage of adversary $\mathcal{A}$ is

$$\mathsf{Adv}^{(n,q_e,q_d,q_c,r_{pk},r_{sk},r_{psk})\text{-Insider-CCA}}_{\mathcal{A},\mathsf{pskAPKE}}$$

$$:= \left| \Pr[(n, q_e, q_d, q_c, r_{pk}, r_{sk}, r_{psk})\text{-Insider-CCA}(\mathcal{A}) \Rightarrow 1] - \frac{1}{2} \right|,$$

$$\mathsf{Adv}^{(n,q_e,q_d,q_c,r_{pk},r_{psk})\text{-Outsider-CCA}}_{\mathcal{A},\mathsf{pskAPKE}} := \mathsf{Adv}^{(n,q_e,q_d,q_c,r_{pk},0,r_{psk})\text{-Insider-CCA}}_{\mathcal{A},\mathsf{pskAPKE}}.$$

3.3 Authenticity

Authenticity is defined via the games in Listing 11 (pskPKE) and Listing 12 (pskAPKE). For the game in Listing 11, the goal is to forge a fresh ciphertext, i.e., one that was not output by the encryption oracle and that does not decrypt to $\bot$. Further, we do not allow corrupted receiver keys for the challenge, i.e. $sk_{j^*} \neq \bot$, since the decryption would not be possible anymore. As in the privacy

---

[2] To prevent confusion we do explicitly call this notion insider secure and only use the term "insider" if it is possible to the (asymmetric) secret key of a sender. See also the security definition of the pskAPKE.

case, we model corrupted keys via oracle REPPK which allows the adversary to replace an asymmetric key and oracle REPPSK which allows to replace a pre-shared key. Due to the structure of a pskPKE, authenticity cannot rely on the asymmetric keys since the sender needs no secret material for the encryption. Hence, authenticity can only be achieved via the pre-shared key. To avoid trivial wins, the game excludes forgeries for which the corresponding pre-shared key was corrupted, i.e., replaced via oracle REPPSK. This means, an adversary wins if they can forge a new valid ciphertext for which the pre-shared key was not corrupted given encryption and decryption oracles as well corruption oracles for both the keys. The advantage of adversary $\mathcal{A}$ is

$$\mathsf{Adv}_{\mathcal{A},\mathsf{pskPKE}}^{(n,q_e,q_d,r_{pk},r_{psk})\text{-}\mathsf{Auth}} := \Pr[(n,q_e,q_d,r_{pk},r_{psk})\text{-}\mathsf{Auth}(\mathcal{A}) \Rightarrow 1].$$

For the Auth security of a pskAPKE (Listing 12) there is only a slight modification. Encryption pskAEnc also inputs the asymmetric sender's secret key, which is why the authenticity can now also rely on the sender's asymmetric key and not only on the pre-shared key. In the game, this is used for a stronger notion which considers corruptions of the sender's key and corruptions of the pre-shared key. The adversary's forgery is accepted if at most one of the keys was corrupted. This means, it should be hard to forge a fresh ciphertext even if the sender's key or the pre-shared key were corrupted but not both. The advantage of adversary $\mathcal{A}$ is

$$\mathsf{Adv}_{\mathcal{A},\mathsf{pskAPKE}}^{(n,q_e,q_d,r_{pk},r_{psk})\text{-}\mathsf{Outsider\text{-}Auth}} := \Pr[(n,q_e,q_d,r_{pk},r_{psk})\text{-}\mathsf{Outsider\text{-}Auth}(\mathcal{A}) \Rightarrow 1].$$

One could also define Insider-Auth security for pskAPKE by allowing the adversary to choose the secret key of the receiver of a forgery (and adjust the non-triviality condition accordingly). Since we do not use Insider-Auth for pskAPKE in the following, we omit the formal definition.

4 HPKE's Constructions of a PskPKE and PskAPKE

4.1 Generic Constructions

We construct a pskPKE and a pskAPKE from an (authenticated) key encapsulation mechanism KEM (AKEM), a 2-keyed function KS (where KS_1 denotes KS keyed in the first input and KS_2 keyed in the second input), and a nonce-based authenticated encryption with additional data scheme AEAD. More concretely, that is pskPKE[KEM, KS, AEAD] where pskPKE.GenSK = KEM.Gen, and the pre-shared key generation pskPKE.GenPSK samples a uniformly random element from the appropriate key space. Encryption and decryption are defined in Listing 13 and Listing 14, respectively.

4.2 Security of pskPKE and pskAPKE

The following Theorems 1–4 state privacy and authenticity of our constructions pskPKE[KEM, KS, AEAD] and pskAPKE[AKEM, KS, AEAD].

Listing 13: Encryption and decryption functions of the pre-shared-key PKE scheme pskPKE[KEM, KS, AEAD], built from KEM, KS, and AEAD.

pskEnc($pk, psk, m, aad, info$)	pskDec($sk, psk, (c_1, c_2), aad, info$)
01 $(c_1, K) \xleftarrow{\$} \mathsf{Encaps}(pk)$	05 $K \leftarrow \mathsf{Decaps}(sk, c_1)$
02 $(k, nonce) \leftarrow \mathsf{KS}(K, psk, info)$	06 $(k, nonce) \leftarrow \mathsf{KS}(K, psk, info)$
03 $c_2 \leftarrow \mathsf{AEAD.Enc}(k, m, aad, nonce)$	07 $m \leftarrow \mathsf{AEAD.Dec}(k, c_2, aad, nonce)$
04 **return** (c_1, c_2)	08 **return** m

Listing 14: Encryption and decryption function of the pre-shared-key APKE scheme pskAPKE[AKEM, KS, AEAD], built from AKEM, KS, and AEAD.

pskAEnc($sk, pk, psk, m, aad, info$)	pskADec($pk, sk, psk, (c_1, c_2), aad, info$)
01 $(c_1, K) \xleftarrow{\$} \mathsf{AuthEncap}(sk, pk)$	05 $K \leftarrow \mathsf{AuthDecap}(pk, sk, c_1)$
02 $(k, nonce) \leftarrow \mathsf{KS}(K, psk, info)$	06 $(k, nonce) \leftarrow \mathsf{KS}(K, psk, info)$
03 $c_2 \leftarrow \mathsf{AEAD.Enc}(k, m, aad, nonce)$	07 $m \leftarrow \mathsf{AEAD.Dec}(k, c_2, aad, nonce)$
04 **return** (c_1, c_2)	08 **return** m

Theorem 1 (KEM CCA + KS_1 PRF + KS_2 PRF + AEAD CCA $\Rightarrow$ pskPKE CCA). *For any $(n, q_e, q_d, q_c, r_{pk}, r_{psk})$-CCA adversary $\mathcal{A}$ against pskPKE[KEM, KS, AEAD], there exists an (n, q_d, q_c)-CCA adversary $\mathcal{B}$ against KEM, a $(q_c, q_d + q_c)$-PRF adversay $\mathcal{C}_1$ against KS_1, a $(q_e + q_d + q_c, q_e + q_d + q_c)$-PRF adversary $\mathcal{C}_2$ against KS_2, and a $(q_e + q_c, q_d)$-CCA adversary $\mathcal{D}$ against AEAD such that*

$$
\mathsf{Adv}^{(n, q_e, q_d, q_c, r_{pk}, r_{psk})\text{-CCA}}_{\mathcal{A}, \mathsf{pskPKE[KEM,KS,AEAD]}} \leq \mathsf{Adv}^{(n, q_d, q_c)\text{-CCA}}_{\mathcal{B}, \mathsf{KEM}} + \mathsf{Adv}^{(q_c, q_d + q_c)\text{-PRF}}_{\mathcal{C}_1, KS_1}
$$
$$
+ \mathsf{Adv}^{(q_e + q_d + q_c, q_e + q_d + q_c)\text{-PRF}}_{\mathcal{C}_2, KS_2} + \mathsf{Adv}^{(q_e + q_c, q_d)\text{-CCA}}_{\mathcal{D}, \mathsf{AEAD}}
$$
$$
+ \frac{q_e^2 + q_c^2 + q_e q_c}{2^\eta}.
$$

Proof (Sketch). To prove CCA security for the pskPKE, we use CCA security of the underlying KEM to replace the KEM keys with uniformly random values. Together with a uniformly random psk, they can be used as PRF keys. Depending on the challenge query and which keys were corrupted, we can use either the PRF property when keyed on the first (KS_1) or the second input (KS_2). For the second input we also need the KEM key to have enough entropy to avoid collisions. This yields random symmetric keys and the theorem follows by the CCA of AEAD. The full proof can be found in the full version. □

Theorem 2 (AKEM Insider-CCA + KS_1 PRF + KS_2 PRF + AEAD CCA $\Rightarrow$ pskAPKE Insider-CCA). *For any $(n, q_e, q_d, q_c, r_{pk}, r_{sk}, r_{psk})$-Insider-CCA adversary $\mathcal{A}$ against the scheme pskAPKE[AKEM, KS, AEAD], there exists an $(n, q_e, q_d, q_c, r_{sk})$-Insider-CCA adversary $\mathcal{B}$ against AKEM, a $(q_c, q_d + q_c)$-PRF adversary $\mathcal{C}_1$ against KS_1, a $(q_e + q_d + q_c, q_e + q_d + q_c)$-PRF adversary $\mathcal{C}_2$ against*

KS_2, and a $(q_e + q_c, q_d)$-CCA *adversary* $\mathcal{D}$ *against* AEAD *such that*

$$\mathsf{Adv}^{(n,q_e,q_d,q_c,r_{pk},r_{sk},r_{psk})\text{-Insider-CCA}}_{\mathcal{A},\mathsf{pskAPKE[AKEM,KS,AEAD]}} \leq \mathsf{Adv}^{(n,q_e,q_d,q_c,r_{sk})\text{-Insider-CCA}}_{\mathcal{B},\mathsf{AKEM}} + \mathsf{Adv}^{(q_c,q_d+q_c)\text{-PRF}}_{\mathcal{C}_1,\mathsf{KS}_1}$$

$$+ \mathsf{Adv}^{(q_e+q_d+q_c,q_e+q_d+q_c)\text{-PRF}}_{\mathcal{C}_2,\mathsf{KS}_2}$$

$$+ \mathsf{Adv}^{(q_e+q_c,q_d)\text{-CCA}}_{\mathcal{D},\mathsf{AEAD}} + \frac{q_e^2 + q_c^2 + q_e q_c}{2^n}.$$

Proof (Sketch). Since we want to achieve Insider-CCA security for the pskAPKE, we have to simulate the REPSK oracle which can be done by reducing to an Insider-CCA secure AKEM. The remaining part of the proof is essentially the same as for Theorem 1. The full proof can be found in the full version. □

Theorem 3 (KEM CCA + KS_1 PRF + KS_2 PRF + AEAD INT-CTXT $\Rightarrow$ pskPKE Auth). *For any* $(n, q_e, q_d, r_{pk}, r_{psk})$-Auth *adversary* $\mathcal{A}$ *against the scheme* pskPKE[KEM, KS, AEAD], *there exists a* (n, q_d, q_e)-CCA *adversary* $\mathcal{B}$ *against* KEM, *a* (q_e, q_e)-PRF *adversary* $\mathcal{C}_1$ *against* KS_1, *a* (q_d, q_d)-PRF *adversary* $\mathcal{C}_2$ *against* KS_2, *and a* $(2q_e + q_d + 1, q_d + 1)$-INT-CTXT *adversary* $\mathcal{D}$ *against* AEAD *such that*

$$\mathsf{Adv}^{(n,q_e,q_d,r_{pk},r_{psk})\text{-Auth}}_{\mathcal{A},\mathsf{pskPKE[KEM,KS,AEAD]}} \leq \mathsf{Adv}^{(n,q_d,q_e)\text{-CCA}}_{\mathcal{B},\mathsf{KEM}} + \mathsf{Adv}^{(q_e,q_e)\text{-PRF}}_{\mathcal{C}_1,\mathsf{KS}_1} + \mathsf{Adv}^{(q_d,q_d)\text{-PRF}}_{\mathcal{C}_2,\mathsf{KS}_2}$$

$$+ \mathsf{Adv}^{(2q_e+q_d+1,q_d+1)\text{-INT-CTXT}}_{\mathcal{D},\mathsf{AEAD}} + \frac{q_e(q_e + q_d - 1)}{|\mathcal{K}|}.$$

Proof (Sketch). We use the CCA security of KEM to ensure that the key K fed into KS_2 is uniform random such that, with high probability, there are no key collisions. Together with the pre-shared key, at least one of the inputs is uniformly random and the PRF property of KS yields a random output. Then, this output can be used for the AEAD such that decryption queries (with respect to an honest *psk*) can be rejected. The full proof can be found in the full version. □

Theorem 4 (AKEM Outsider-CCA + AKEM Outsider-Auth + KS_1 PRF + KS_2 PRF + AEAD INT-CTXT $\Rightarrow$ pskAPKE Outsider-Auth). *For any* $(n, q_e, q_d, r_{pk}, r_{psk})$-Outsider-Auth *adversary* $\mathcal{A}$ *against the scheme* pskAPKE[AKEM, KS, AEAD], *there exists an* $(n, 0, q_d, q_c)$-CCA *adversary* $\mathcal{B}$ *against* AKEM, *a* $(q_e + q_d, q_e + q_d)$-PRF *adversay* $\mathcal{C}_1$ *against* KS_1, *a* $(q_e + q_d, q_e + q_d)$-PRF *adversary* $\mathcal{C}_2$ *against* KS_2, *and a* $(2q_e + q_d + 1, q_d + 1)$-INT-CTXT *adversary* $\mathcal{D}$ *against* AEAD *such that*

$$\mathsf{Adv}^{(n,q_e,q_d,r_{pk},r_{psk})\text{-Outsider-Auth}}_{\mathcal{A},\mathsf{pskAPKE[AKEM,KS,AEAD]}} \leq \mathsf{Adv}^{(n,q_e,q_d,q_e)\text{-Outsider-CCA}}_{\mathcal{B}_1,\mathsf{AKEM}}$$

$$+ \mathsf{Adv}^{(n,q_e,q_d)\text{-Outsider-Auth}}_{\mathcal{B}_2,\mathsf{AKEM}}$$

$$+ \mathsf{Adv}^{(q_e+q_d,q_e+q_d)\text{-PRF}}_{\mathcal{C}_1,\mathsf{KS}_1} + \mathsf{Adv}^{(q_d,q_d)\text{-PRF}}_{\mathcal{C}_2,\mathsf{KS}_2}$$

$$+ \mathsf{Adv}^{(2q_e+q_d+1,q_d+1)\text{-INT-CTXT}}_{\mathcal{D},\mathsf{AEAD}} + \frac{q_e(q_e + q_d - 1)}{|\mathcal{K}|}.$$

Proof (Sketch). To achieve Outsider-Auth security for pskAPKE, we need to first use Outsider-CCA security and Outsider-Auth security of AKEM to replace the KEM secret in encryption and decryption by random values. Together with the pre-shared keys they can be used as inputs to KS where, depending on the query, either the KEM shared secret or the *psk* act as the PRF key. Next, the PRF output can be used to construct an adversary against INT-CTXT security of AEAD. The full proof can be found in Sect. 4.4.   □

4.3   The Security of HPKE's PSK Modes

The HPKE standard's specification of the $HPKE_{PSK}$ mode corresponds to the construction pskPKE[KEM, KS, AEAD] (Listing 13), and the one of the $HPKE_{AuthPSK}$ mode to the construction pskAPKE[AKEM, KS, AEAD] (Listing 14) with one exception. The HPKE standard explicitly defines an identifier for each *psk*, the *psk_id*, and the actual key schedule function takes it as an additional parameter alongside the KEM key K, the *psk*, and the *info* bitstring that we consider in our model. For simplicity, we abstract away the *psk_id* and consider it to be encoded as part of *info*, as both are simply hashed into the context of the key derivation. HPKE uses the following specific components:

- KEM is the standard Diffie-Hellman DH-KEM which fulfills CCA security assuming the Gap Diffie-Hellman assumption.
- AKEM is the Diffie-Hellman DH-AKEM from [1] which is proved Insider-CCA and Outsider-Auth-secure assuming the Gap Diffie-Hellman assumption.
- The key schedule KS is constructed via the functions Extract and Expand both instantiated with HMAC [1, Section 6.2]. If we assume HMAC to be a PRF when keyed on either of the inputs, the assumptions for KS hold as well.
- AEAD is instantiated using AES-GCM or ChaCha20-Poly1305, which are shown to fulfill IND-CPA and INT-CTXT security [7] and thus also IND-CCA security.

Thus, applying the composition theorems from the last section, we achieve CCA and Auth security for $HPKE_{PSK}$, and Insider-CCA and Outsider-Auth security for $HPKE_{AuthPSK}$.

4.4   Proof of Theorem 4

Proof. We describe several games depicted in Listing 15.

Game G_0. This is the $(n, q_e, q_d, r_{pk}, r_{psk})$-Outsider-Auth game for pskAPKE[AKEM, KS, AEAD], thus we have

$$\Pr[G_0 \Rightarrow 1] = \Pr[(n, q_e, q_d, r_{pk}, r_{psk})\text{-Outsider-Auth}(\mathcal{A}) \Rightarrow 1].$$

Game G_1. We insert a set Λ to log the outputs of KS to use the stored outputs if KS is queried on the same parameters again. This is only done for encryption oracle queries for which the receiver's key was not replaced, i.e. $j \notin \Gamma_{pk}$ (checked

Listing 15: Games $G_0 - G_8$ for the proof of Theorem 4.

$G_0 - G_8$	
01 **for** $i \in [n]$	Oracle $\text{DEC}(i \in [n], j \in [n], (c_1, c_2), aad, info)$
02 $\quad (sk_i, pk_i) \xleftarrow{\$} \text{GenSK}$	26 **if** $sk_j = \bot$
03 $\quad$ **for** $j \in [i]$	27 $\quad$ **return** $\bot$
04 $\quad\quad psk_{ij} \xleftarrow{\$} \mathcal{K}_{psk}$	28 $K \leftarrow \text{AuthDecap}(pk_i, sk_j, c_1)$
05 $\quad\quad psk_{ji} \leftarrow psk_{ij}$	29 **if** $\exists K' : (pk_i, pk_j, c_1, K') \in \hat{\mathcal{E}}$ // $G_2 - G_8$
06 $\mathcal{E}, \mathcal{E}', \Gamma_{pk}, \Gamma_{psk}, \Lambda \leftarrow \emptyset$	30 $\quad K \leftarrow K'$ // $G_2 - G_8$
07 $(i^*, j^*, (c_1^*, c_2^*), aad^*, info^*) \xleftarrow{\$} \mathcal{A}^{\text{ENC},\text{DEC},\text{REPPK},\text{REPPSK}}(pk_1, \ldots, pk_n)$	31 $\quad (k, nonce) \leftarrow \text{KS}(K, psk_{ij}, info)$ // $G_0 - G_8$
08 **return** $[\![(i^* \notin \Gamma_{pk} \vee (i^*, j^*) \notin \Gamma_{psk}) \wedge sk_{j^*} \neq \bot$	32 **else if** $i \notin \Gamma_{pk} \wedge K \neq \bot$ // $G_5 - G_8$
$\quad\quad \wedge (pk_{i^*}, pk_{j^*}, psk_{i^* \cdot j^*}, (c_1^*, c_2^*), aad^*, info^*) \notin \mathcal{E}$	33 $\quad K \xleftarrow{\$} \mathcal{K}$ // $G_5 - G_8$
$\quad\quad \wedge \text{pskADec}(pk_{i^*}, sk_{j^*}, psk_{i^* \cdot j^*}, (c_1^*, c_2^*), aad^*, info^*) \neq \bot]\!]$	34 $\quad \hat{\mathcal{E}} \leftarrow \hat{\mathcal{E}} \cup \{(pk_i, pk_j, c_1, K)\}$ // $G_5 - G_8$
	35 $\quad (k, nonce) \xleftarrow{\$} \mathcal{K}' \times \{0,1\}^{N_{nonce}}$ // $G_6 - G_8$
	36 **else** // $G_6 - G_8$
Oracle $\text{ENC}(i \in [n], j \in [n], m, aad, info)$	37 $\quad (k, nonce) \leftarrow \text{KS}(K, psk_{ij}, info)$ // $G_6 - G_8$
09 **if** $sk_i = \bot$	38 $(k, nonce) \leftarrow \text{KS}(K, psk_{ij}, info)$ // $G_0 - G_5$
10 $\quad$ **return** $\bot$	39 **if** $i \notin \Gamma_{pk} \vee (i, j) \notin \Gamma_{psk}$ // $G_1 - G_8$
11 $(c_1, K) \xleftarrow{\$} \text{AuthEncap}(sk_i, pk_j)$	40 $\quad$ **if** $\exists k', nonce' : (k', nonce', i, j, K, psk_{ij}, info) \in \Lambda$ // $G_1 - G_8$
12 $(k, nonce) \leftarrow \text{KS}(K, psk_{ij}, info)$	41 $\quad\quad (k, nonce) \leftarrow (k', nonce')$ // $G_1 - G_8$
13 **if** $j \in \Gamma_{pk}$ // $G_2 - G_8$	42 $\quad$ **else if** $i \in \Gamma_{pk}$ // $G_7 - G_8$
14 $\quad K \xleftarrow{\$} \mathcal{K}$ // $G_2 - G_8$	43 $\quad\quad (k, nonce) \xleftarrow{\$} \mathcal{K}' \times \{0,1\}^{N_{nonce}}$ // $G_7 - G_8$
15 $\quad \hat{\mathcal{E}} \leftarrow \hat{\mathcal{E}} \cup \{(pk_i, pk_j, c_1, K)\}$ // $G_2 - G_8$	44 $m \leftarrow \text{AEAD.Dec}(k, c_2, aad, nonce)$ // $G_1 - G_8$
16 $\quad (k, nonce) \leftarrow \text{KS}(K, psk_{ij}, info)$ // $G_2 - G_8$	45 $m \leftarrow \bot$ // G_8
17 **if** $\exists k', nonce' : (k', nonce', i, j, K, psk_{ij}, info) \in \Lambda$ // $G_1 - G_8$	46 **if** $\exists m' : (k, nonce, m', (c_1, c_2), aad) \in \mathcal{E}'$ // G_8
18 $\quad$ **abort** // $G_3 - G_8$	47 $\quad m \leftarrow m'$ // G_8
19 $\quad (k, nonce) \leftarrow (k', nonce')$ // $G_1 - G_8$	48 **else**
20 $(k, nonce) \xleftarrow{\$} \mathcal{K}' \times \{0,1\}^{N_{nonce}}$ // $G_4 - G_8$	49 $\quad m \leftarrow \text{AEAD.Dec}(k, c_2, aad, nonce)$ // $G_1 - G_8$
21 $\Lambda \leftarrow \Lambda \cup \{(k, nonce, i, j, K, psk_{ij}, info)\}$ // $G_1 - G_8$	50 $m \leftarrow \text{AEAD.Dec}(k, c_2, aad, nonce)$ // $G_0 - G_1$
22 $c_2 \leftarrow \text{AEAD.Enc}(k, m, aad, nonce)$	51 $\Lambda \leftarrow \Lambda \cup \{(k, nonce, i, j, K, psk_{ij}, info)\}$ // $G_1 - G_8$
23 $\mathcal{E} \leftarrow \mathcal{E} \cup \{(pk_i, pk_j, psk_{ij}, (c_1, c_2), aad, info)\}$	52 **return** m
24 $\mathcal{E}' \leftarrow \mathcal{E}' \cup \{(k, nonce, m, (c_1, c_2), aad)\}$ // G_8	
25 **return** (c_1, c_2)	Oracle $\text{REPPK}(i \in [n], pk)$
	53 $(sk_i, pk_i) \leftarrow (\bot, pk)$
	54 $\Gamma_{pk} \leftarrow \Gamma_{pk} \cup \{i\}$
	Oracle $\text{REPPSK}(i \in [n], j \in [n], psk)$
	55 $psk_{ij} \leftarrow psk$
	56 $psk_{ji} \leftarrow psk$
	57 $\Gamma_{psk} \leftarrow \Gamma_{psk} \cup \{(i,j), (j,i)\}$

in Line 13), as well as for decryption queries for which not both the sender's key and the *psk* were replaced, i.e. for queries on indices $i \notin \Gamma_{pk} \vee (i,j) \notin \Gamma_{psk}$ (checked in Line 39). Since the change is only conceptual, we have

$$\Pr[G_0 \Rightarrow 1] = \Pr[G_1 \Rightarrow 1].$$

Game G_2. If the corresponding receiver key has not been corrupted via REPPK, i.e. $j \notin \Gamma_{pk}$, we replace the KEM secret in oracle ENC by a uniformly random value (Line 14) and store the output to return consistent queries to oracle DEC. The difference is the advantage of a CCA adversary $\mathcal{B}_1$ against AKEM:

$$|\Pr[G_1 \Rightarrow 1] - \Pr[G_2 \Rightarrow 1]| \leq \text{Adv}^{(n,q_e,q_d,q_e)\text{-CCA}}_{\mathcal{B}_1,\text{AKEM}}.$$

Adversary $\mathcal{B}_1$ against CCA security of an AKEM can simulate G_1/G_2 by issuing a challenge query to the CCA experiment for any ENC query with $j \notin \Gamma_{pk}$ and a decryption query for any DEC query. Any other query, i.e. ENC queries with $j \in \Gamma_{pk}$, can be answered by using the AKEM adversary's own encapsulation oracle.

Game G_3. In G_3, the game aborts in the encryption oracle if the corresponding receiver's key was not replaced and there already exists an entry in Λ with the queried parameters (Line 18). The difference is negligible in the size of the key space of KEM. Since K was randomly chosen in the previous game, the probability of having such an entry is at most $\frac{|A|}{|\mathcal{K}|}$. Note that A is filled with another element at most once per ENC/DEC query. This yields the following advantage:

$$|\Pr[\mathsf{G}_2 \Rightarrow 1] - \Pr[\mathsf{G}_3 \Rightarrow 1]| \leq \frac{q_e(q_e + q_d - 1)}{|\mathcal{K}|}.$$

Game G_4. If the receiver's key was not replaced and we do not abort, we replace the output of KS in the encryption oracle with uniformly random values of the respective domain (Line 19). The game difference is the advantage of a PRF adversary $\mathcal{C}_1$ against KS_1:

$$|\Pr[\mathsf{G}_4 \Rightarrow 1] - \Pr[\mathsf{G}_5 \Rightarrow 1]| \leq \mathsf{Adv}_{\mathcal{C}_1,\mathsf{KS}_1}^{(q_e,q_e)\text{-PRF}}.$$

The changes in Game G_1 ensure consistent outputs of KS, i.e. queries on ENC or DEC with the same parameters lead to the same output of KS (or the game aborts in the for pskEnc). Hence, games G_3 and G_4 can only be distinguished by distinguishing the real output of KS from a uniformly random one. This can be turned into an adversary against PRF security of KS_1, i.e. keyed on the first input. Note that K is chosen uniformly at random due to the changes in Game G_2. There are at most q_e different instances for the PRF and at most the same number of queries.

Game G_5. In Game G_5, the decryption oracle is modified. If there KEM parameter set was not queried before, i.e. the parameters do not occur in $\hat{\mathcal{E}}$, the sender was not corrupted and the shared KEM secret K is not $\perp$ (Line 32), K is replaced by a uniformly random value and the result is stored in $\hat{\mathcal{E}}$. Due to these conditions, the setup matches with oracles of an Auth adversary against AKEM and such an adversary can simulate the games. This results in the following advantage:

$$|\Pr[\mathsf{G}_4 \Rightarrow 1] - \Pr[\mathsf{G}_5 \Rightarrow 1]| \leq \mathsf{Adv}_{\mathcal{B}_2,\mathsf{AKEM}}^{(n,q_e,q_d)\text{-Outsider-Auth}}.$$

Game G_6. The game is modified by choosing uniformly random values instead of the real output of KS in the same case as for the previous game (Line 32). This can be turned into an adversary against PRF security of KS_1, i.e. keyed in the first input. There are at most q_d different instances and at most q_d different queries resulting in

$$|\Pr[\mathsf{G}_5 \Rightarrow 1] - \Pr[\mathsf{G}_6 \Rightarrow 1]| \leq \mathsf{Adv}_{\mathcal{C}_1,\mathsf{KS}_1}^{(q_d,q_d)\text{-PRF}}.$$

Game G_7. We modify the game by replacing the output of KS by uniformly random values similar to the last game modification but in the following case while querying the decryption oracle: not both the sender's key and the *psk* were corrupted ($i \notin \Gamma_{\mathsf{pk}} \vee (i,j) \notin \Gamma_{\mathsf{psk}}$, Line 39), there is no corresponding element in

Λ (Line 42), and the sender's key was corrupted, i.e. $i \in \Gamma_{\text{pk}}$ (Line 42). This can be turned into a PRF adversary $\mathcal{C}_2$ against KS_2, i.e. keyed in the second input:

$$|\Pr[\text{G}_7 \Rightarrow 1] - \Pr[\text{G}_8 \Rightarrow 1]| \le \text{Adv}_{\mathcal{C}_2,\text{KS}_2}^{(q_d,q_d)\text{-PRF}}.$$

The two conditions $i \notin \Gamma_{\text{pk}} \vee (i,j) \notin \Gamma_{\text{psk}}$ and $i \in \Gamma_{\text{pk}}$ imply that $(i,j) \notin \Gamma_{\text{psk}}$ which means that the *psk* was not replaced and was therefore chosen uniformly at random in the beginning of the game. Thus, the two games can be simulated by adversary $\mathcal{C}_2$ via their own evaluation oracle. We have at most q_d different indices for the PRF game and at most the same number of queries.

Game G_8. In this game, we replace the actual decryption in an honest decryption oracle query with $\bot$ (Line 45). Distinguishing the game difference can be turned into an INT-CTXT adversary $\mathcal{D}_1$ against AEAD:

$$|\Pr[\text{G}_7 \Rightarrow 1] - \Pr[\text{G}_8 \Rightarrow 1]| \le \text{Adv}_{\mathcal{D}_1,\text{AEAD}}^{(q_e+q_d,q_d)\text{-INT-CTXT}}.$$

Adversary $\mathcal{D}_1$ is formally constructed in Listing 16. Note that k and *nonce* are uniformly random such that the adversary can use their own decryption oracle either on a new index or on a previous index in case the same parameters were queried before and the element is in Λ. Further, encryption queries can also be simulated in each case. If there is an encryption query with a corrupted receiver's key, the adversary can compute the encryption on their own. Otherwise, they can use their own encryption oracle. The abort in cases of a parameter set being queried before (Line 18) prevents the need of querying the encryption oracle twice which is not possible for the INT-CTXT game for an AEAD. There are at most $q_e + q_d$ different keys and adversary $\mathcal{D}_1$ makes at most q_d queries to their decryption oracle DEC_{AEAD}.

Reduction to Game G_8. Winning Game G_8 can be reduced to an INT-CTXT adversary $\mathcal{D}_2$ against AEAD:

$$\Pr[\text{G}_8 \Rightarrow 1] \le \text{Adv}_{\mathcal{D}_2,\text{AEAD}}^{(q_e+1,1)\text{-INT-CTXT}}.$$

The adversary can simulate the decryption oracle since in cases $i \notin \Gamma_{\text{pk}} \vee (i,j) \notin \Gamma_{\text{psk}}$, they can output $\bot$ (or the original encryption if it was produced during the experiment). In cases $(i,j) \in \Gamma_{\text{psk}}$, they can compute the output by their own. For the encryption oracle, the adversary can use their own encryption oracle or compute the output on their own similar to the adversary from the last game hop. The output of the adversary against game G_8 can then be used to issue a decryption query in the INT-CTXT experiment on either a new key or a previous key if the output parameters $i^*, j^*, c_1^*, info^*$ match with that key. Matching parameters can be identified by computing $K^* \leftarrow \text{Decaps}(sk_{j^*}, c_1^*)$ and comparing $(i^*, j^*, K^*, psk_{i^*j^*}, info^*)$ to set Λ similar to Line 16 or Line 39 in Listing 16. If the adversary against G_8 wins, the adversary against the INT-CTXT experiment has a valid ciphertext which does not decrypt to $\bot$ due to the winning condition of G_8. That means they can distinguish between the real or random case since the result of the decryption query must be unequal to $\bot$ in the real case.

Putting everything together, we obtain the stated bound. □

Listing 16: Adversary $\mathcal{D}_1$ against INT-CTXT security for AEAD having access to oracles $\text{ENC}_{textscAEAD}$ and DEC_{AEAD}.

```
D₁^{ENC_{textscAEAD},DEC_AEAD}

01  for i ∈ [n]
02      (sk_i, pk_i) ⟵$ GenSK
03      for j ∈ [i]
04          psk_{ij} ⟵$ K_{psk}
05          psk_{ji} ← psk_{ij}
06  ε, ε', Γ_pk, Γ_psk, Λ ← ∅
07  (i*, j*, (c₁*, c₂*)), aad*, info*) ⟵$ A^{ENC,DEC,REPPK,REPPSK}(pk₁, ..., pk_n)
08  return [(i* ∈ Γ_pk ∨ (i*, j*) ∉ Γ_psk) ∧ sk_{j*} ≠ ⊥
            ∧ (pk_{i*}, pk_{j*}, psk_{i*j*}, (c₁*, c₂*), aad*, info*) ∉ ε
            ∧ pskADec(pk_{i*}, sk_{j*}, psk_{i*j*}, (c₁*, c₂*), aad*, info*) ≠ ⊥]

Oracle ENC(i ∈ [n], j ∈ [n], m, aad, info)

09  if sk_i = ⊥
10      return ⊥
11  (c₁, K) ⟵$ AuthEncap(sk_i, pk_j)
12  (k, nonce) ← KS(K, psk_{ij}, info)
13  if j ∉ Γ_pk
14      K ⟵$ K
15      ε̂ ← ε̂ ∪ {(pk_i, pk_j, c₁, K)}
16      if ∃ℓ' : (ℓ', i, j, psk_{ij}, info) ∈ Λ
17          abort
18      ℓ ← ℓ + 1                              //new key
19      c₂ ← ENC_{textscAEAD}(ℓ, m, aad)        //enc query
20      Λ ← Λ ∪ {(ℓ, i, j, K, psk_{ij}, info)}
21  else
22      c₂ ← AEAD.Enc(k, m, aad, nonce)
23  ε ← ε ∪ {(pk_i, pk_j, psk_{ij}, (c₁, c₂), aad, info)}
24  ε' ← ε' ∪ {(k, nonce, m, (c₁, c₂), aad)}
25  return (c₁, c₂)

Oracle DEC(i ∈ [n], j ∈ [n], (c₁, c₂), aad, info)

26  if sk_j = ⊥
27      return ⊥
28  K ← AuthDecap(pk_i, sk_j, c₁)
29  if ∃K' : (pk_i, pk_j, c₁, K') ∈ ε̂
30      K ← K'
31      (k, nonce) ← KS(K, psk_{ij}, info)
32  else if i ∉ Γ_pk ∧ K ≠ ⊥
33      K ⟵$ K
34      ε̂ ← ε̂ ∪ {(pk_i, pk_j, c₁, K)}
35      (k, nonce) ⟵$ K' × {0,1}^{N_{nonce}}
36  else
37      (k, nonce) ← KS(K, psk_{ij}, info)
38  if i ∉ Γ_pk ∨ (i, j) ∈ Γ_psk
39      if ∃ℓ' : (ℓ', i, j, K, psk_{ij}, info) ∈ Λ
40          m ← DEC_{AEAD}(ℓ', c₂, aad)          //dec query on old key
41      else if i ∈ Γ_pk
42          ℓ ← ℓ + 1                           //new key
43          m ← DEC_{AEAD}(ℓ, c₂, aad)           //dec query on new key
44          Λ ← Λ ∪ {(ℓ, i, j, K, psk_{ij}, info)}
45  else
46      m ← AEAD.Dec(k, c₂, aad, nonce)
47  return m

Oracle REPPK(i ∈ [n], pk)

48  (sk_i, pk_i) ← (⊥, pk)
49  Γ_pk ← Γ_pk ∪ {i}

Oracle REPPSK(i ∈ [n], j ∈ [n], psk)

50  psk_{ij} ← psk
51  psk_{ji} ← psk
52  Γ_psk ← Γ_psk ∪ {(i, j), (j, i)}
```

5   Hybrid Post-Quantum APKE

We want to build an HPKE scheme which is secure against classical as well as quantum adversaries. To not rely solely on relatively new post-quantum primitives, a common way is to use combiners which combine well studied classical primitives and post-quantum primitives at the same time. This hybrid approach allows for security against future quantum adversaries but is still secure in a classical setting if current post-quantum primitives are broken. To this end, we use the pre-shared key mode of HPKE to build a combiner from which we can instantiate a hybrid post-quantum construction.

Let pskAPKE[AKEM_1, KS, AEAD] be a pre-shared key PKE based on an authenticated KEM $\text{AKEM}_1 = (\text{Gen}_1, \text{AuthEncap}_1, \text{AuthDecap}_1)$, a two-keyed function KS, and an authenticated encryption with associated data AEAD as in Listing 14. Further, let $\text{AKEM}_2 = (\text{Gen}_2, \text{AuthEncap}_2, \text{AuthDecap}_2)$ be a second authenticated KEM. From these components, we can construct an APKE using the shared secret of the second KEM as the pre-shared key of the pskAPKE. We remark that the same construction also works for non-authenticated primitives, i.e., we can construct a PKE PKE[KEM_1, KEM_2, KS, AEAD] built from pskPKE[KEM_1, KS, AEAD] and a KEM_2.

The following two theorems state that the APKE is secure (in the sense of Insider-CCA and Outsider-Auth) if at least one of the underlying AKEMs, AKEM_1 or AKEM_2, is secure.

Listing 17: Authenticated PKE $\mathsf{APKE}[\mathsf{AKEM}_1, \mathsf{AKEM}_2, \mathsf{KS}, \mathsf{AEAD}]$ built from $\mathsf{pskAPKE}[\mathsf{AKEM}_1, \mathsf{KS}, \mathsf{AEAD}]$ and AKEM_2

$\underline{\mathsf{Gen}}$	$\underline{\mathsf{Enc}((sk_1, sk_2), (pk_1, pk_2), m, aad, info)}$
01 $(sk_1, pk_1) \xleftarrow{\$} \mathsf{Gen}_1$	06 $(c', K') \xleftarrow{\$} \mathsf{AuthEncap}_2(sk_2, pk_2)$
02 $(sk_2, pk_2) \xleftarrow{\$} \mathsf{Gen}_2$	07 $(c_1, c_2) \xleftarrow{\$} \mathsf{pskAEnc}(sk_1, pk_1, K', m, aad, c'\|info)$
03 $sk \leftarrow (sk_1, sk_2)$	08 **return** $((c_1, c_2), c')$
04 $pk \leftarrow (pk_1, pk_2)$	
05 **return** (sk, pk)	$\underline{\mathsf{Dec}((pk_1, pk_2), (sk_1, sk_2), ((c_1, c_2), c'), aad, info)}$
	09 $K' \leftarrow \mathsf{AuthDecap}_2(sk_2, c')$
	10 $m \leftarrow \mathsf{pskADec}(pk_1, sk_1, K', (c_1, c_2), aad, c'\|info)$
	11 **return** m

Theorem 5. *Let* AKEM_1 *and* AKEM_2 *be two AKEMs,* KS *a two-keyed function, and* AEAD *an AEAD. If* KS *is a PRF in both keys,* AEAD *is IND-CCA secure, and* AKEM_1 *or* AKEM_2 *is CCA secure, then the construction in Listing 17 is a CCA secure APKE. In particular, for any* (n, q_e, q_d, q_c)-*Insider-CCA adversary* $\mathcal{A}$ *against* $\mathsf{APKE}[\mathsf{AKEM}_1, \mathsf{AKEM}_2, \mathsf{KS}, \mathsf{AEAD}]$ *there exists a* $(n + 1, q_e, q_d, q_c)$-*Insider-CCA adversary* $\mathcal{B}_1$ *against* AKEM_1, *a* (n, q_e, q_d, q_c, q_c)-*Insider-CCA adversary* $\mathcal{B}_2$ *against* AKEM_2, *a* $(q_c, q_d + q_c)$-*PRF adversary* $\mathcal{C}_1$ *against* KS_1, *a* $(q_c, q_d + q_c)$-*PRF adversary* $\mathcal{C}_2$ *against* KS_2, *and a* (q_c, q_d)-*CCA adversary* $\mathcal{D}$ *against* AEAD *such that*

$$\mathsf{Adv}_{\mathcal{A}, \mathsf{APKE}[\mathsf{AKEM}_1, \mathsf{AKEM}_2, \mathsf{KS}, \mathsf{AEAD}]}^{(n, q_e, q_d, q_c)\text{-Insider-CCA}} \leq$$
$$\min\{\mathsf{Adv}_{\mathcal{B}_1, \mathsf{AKEM}_1}^{(n+1, q_e, q_d, q_c)\text{-Insider-CCA}} + \mathsf{Adv}_{\mathcal{C}_1, \mathsf{KS}_1}^{(q_c, q_d + q_c)\text{-PRF}},$$
$$\mathsf{Adv}_{\mathcal{B}_2, \mathsf{AKEM}_2}^{(n, q_e, q_d, q_c, q_c)\text{-Insider-CCA}} + \mathsf{Adv}_{\mathcal{C}_2, \mathsf{KS}_2}^{(q_c, q_d + q_c)\text{-PRF}}\} + \mathsf{Adv}_{\mathcal{D}, \mathsf{AEAD}}^{(q_c, q_d)\text{-CCA}}$$

Proof (Sketch). The first part of the proof is very similar to Theorem 2 except that the queries to KS_2 can be saved. The second part transforms the KEM secret of AKEM_2 into a uniformly random value using its Insider-CCA security which can then be used as input to KS_2 as a regular *psk*. These outputs are uniformly random values and the remaining transformations are as for the first part. The full proof can be found in the full version. ☐

Theorem 6. *Let* AKEM_1 *and* AKEM_2 *be two AKEMs,* KS *a two-keyed function, and* AEAD *an AEAD. If* KS *is a PRF in both keys,* AEAD *is INT-CTXT and IND-CPA secure, and* AKEM_1 *or* AKEM_2 *is Outsider-Auth secure, then the construction in Listing 17 is a Outsider-Auth secure APKE. In particular, for any* (n, q_e, q_d)-*Outsider-Auth adversary* $\mathcal{A}$ *against* $\mathsf{APKE}[\mathsf{AKEM}_1, \mathsf{AKEM}_2, \mathsf{KS}, \mathsf{AEAD}]$, *there exists a* $(n + 1, 0, q_d, q_c)$-*Outsider-CCA adversary* $\mathcal{B}_1$ *against* AKEM_1, *a* $(n + 1, q_e, q_d)$-*Outsider-Auth adversary* $\mathcal{B}_2$ *against* AKEM_1, *a* $(n, 0, q_d, q_e)$-*Outsider-CCA adversary* $\mathcal{B}'_1$ *against* AKEM_2, *a* (n, q_e, q_d)-*Outsider-Auth adversary* $\mathcal{B}'_2$ *against* AKEM_2, *a* $(q_e + q_d, q_e +$

q_d)-PRF *adversary* C_1 *against* KS_1, *a* (q_d, q_d)-PRF *adversary* C_2 *against* KS_2, *a* $(2q_e + q_d + 1, q_d + 1)$-INT-CTXT *adversary* $\mathcal{D}$ *against* AEAD *such that*

$$\mathsf{Adv}^{(n,q_e,q_d)\text{-Outsider-Auth}}_{\mathcal{A},\mathsf{APKE}[\mathsf{AKEM}_1,\mathsf{AKEM}_2,\mathsf{KS},\mathsf{AEAD}]} \leq$$
$$\min\{\mathsf{Adv}^{(n+1,q_e,q_d,q_e)\text{-Outsider-CCA}}_{\mathcal{B}_1,\mathsf{AKEM}_1} + \mathsf{Adv}^{(n+1,q_e,q_d)\text{-Outsider-Auth}}_{\mathcal{B}_2,\mathsf{AKEM}_1}$$
$$+ \mathsf{Adv}^{(q_e+q_d,q_e+q_d)\text{-PRF}}_{\mathcal{C}_1,\mathsf{KS}_1},$$
$$\mathsf{Adv}^{(n,0,q_d,q_e)\text{-Outsider-CCA}}_{\mathcal{B}'_1,\mathsf{AKEM}_2} + \mathsf{Adv}^{(n,q_e,q_d)\text{-Outsider-Auth}}_{\mathcal{B}'_2,\mathsf{AKEM}_2}$$
$$+ \mathsf{Adv}^{(q_d,q_d)\text{-PRF}}_{\mathcal{C}_2,\mathsf{KS}_2}\}$$
$$+ \mathsf{Adv}^{(2q_e+q_d+1,q_d+1)\text{-INT-CTXT}}_{\mathcal{D},\mathsf{AEAD}} + \frac{q_e(q_e + q_d - 1)}{|\mathcal{K}|}.$$

Proof (Sketch). The first part of the proof is very similar to Theorem 4 except that the queries to KS_2 can be saved. The second part transforms the KEM secret of AKEM_2 into a uniformly random value using its Insider-CCA and Outsider-Auth security which can then be used as input to KS_2 as a regular *psk* in encryption and decryption oracle. These outputs are uniformly random values and the remaining transformations are as for the first part. The full proof can be found in the full version. □

POST-QUANTUM INSTANTIATION. Consequently, one can combine $\mathsf{HPKE}_{\mathsf{AuthPSK}}$ with a post-quantum secure AKEM to obtain an APKE scheme with hybrid security. Analogously, one can combine $\mathsf{HPKE}_{\mathsf{PSK}}$ with a post-quantum secure KEM (such as Kyber) to obtain a PKE with hybrid security. In the next section, we discuss how to construct post-quantum secure AKEM schemes.

6 Post-Quantum AKEM Constructions

6.1 KEM-then-Sign-then-Hash

A well-known approach for constructing a post-quantum AKEM is to combine a post-quantum KEM with a post-quantum signature [10]. This could obviously applied to the classical setting as well but with much worse performance than the NIKE-based construction of HPKE which achieves authentication almost for free.

Our new construction extends the (insecure) Encrypt-then-Sign (EtS) paradigm to Encrypt-then-Sign-then-Hash (EtStH). Let $\mathsf{KEM} = (\mathsf{KEM.Gen}, \mathsf{Encaps}, \mathsf{Decaps})$ be a KEM and $\mathsf{SIG} = (\mathsf{Gen}, \mathsf{Sign}, \mathsf{Vfy})$ be a signature scheme. We construct $\mathsf{AKEM}^{\mathsf{EtStH}}[\mathsf{KEM}, \mathsf{SIG}, \mathsf{H}]$ as shown in Listing 18. The key generation outputs a public key tuple and a private key tuple. The first component of both tuples is the receiver's public/private key and the second component is the sender's public/private key.

Listing 18: $\mathsf{AKEM}^{\mathsf{EtStH}}[\mathsf{KEM}, \mathsf{SIG}, \mathsf{H}]$ from a KEM $\mathsf{KEM} = (\mathsf{KEM.Gen}, \mathsf{Encaps},$ $\mathsf{Decaps})$, a signature scheme $\mathsf{SIG} = (\mathsf{SIG.Gen}, \mathsf{Sign}, \mathsf{Vfy})$, and a random oracle H.

Gen	AuthDecap$((pk_1, vk_1), (sk_2, sigk_2), (c, \sigma))$
01 $(sk, pk) \xleftarrow{\$} \mathsf{KEM.Gen}$	08 **if** $\mathsf{Vfy}(vk_1, c\|pk_1\|\mu(sk_2)\|\mu'(sigk_2), \sigma) \neq 1$
02 $(sigk, vk) \xleftarrow{\$} \mathsf{SIG.Gen}$	09 $\quad K \leftarrow \perp$
03 **return** $((sk, sigk), (pk, vk))$	10 **else**
	11 $\quad K' \leftarrow \mathsf{Decaps}(sk_2, c)$
AuthEncap$((sk_1, sigk_1), (pk_2, vk_2))$	12 $\quad K \leftarrow \mathsf{H}(K', \sigma\|pk_1\|vk_1\|\mu(sk_2)\|\mu'(sigk_2))$
04 $(c, K') \xleftarrow{\$} \mathsf{Encaps}(pk_2)$	13 **return** K
05 $\sigma \xleftarrow{\$} \mathsf{Sign}(sigk_1, c\|\mu(sk_1)\|pk_2\|vk_2)$	
06 $K \leftarrow \mathsf{H}(K', \sigma\|\mu(sk_1)\|\mu'(sigk_1)\|pk_2\|vk_2)$	
07 **return** $((c, \sigma), K)$	

Theorem 7 (KEM CCA + H PRF $\Rightarrow$ AKEM Insider-CCA). *If KEM is a CCA secure key encapsulation mechanism and H is a PRF, then* $\mathsf{AKEM}^{\mathsf{EtStH}}[\mathsf{KEM}, \mathsf{SIG}, \mathsf{H}]$ *is an Insider-CCA secure AKEM. In particular, for every* $(n, q_e, q_d, q_c, r_{sk})$-*Insider-CCA adversary* $\mathcal{A}$ *against* $\mathsf{AKEM}^{\mathsf{EtStH}}[\mathsf{KEM}, \mathsf{SIG}, \mathsf{H}]$ *there exists a* (n, q_d, q_c)-*CCA adversary* $\mathcal{B}$ *against KEM and a* $(q_c, q_d + q_c)$-*PRF adversary* $\mathcal{C}$ *against H such that*

$$\mathsf{Adv}^{(n, q_e, q_d, q_c, r_{sk})\text{-Insider-CCA}}_{\mathcal{A}, \mathsf{AKEM}^{\mathsf{EtStH}}[\mathsf{KEM}, \mathsf{SIG}, \mathsf{H}]} \leq \mathsf{Adv}^{(n, q_d, q_c)\text{-CCA}}_{\mathcal{B}, \mathsf{KEM}} + \mathsf{Adv}^{(q_c, q_d + q_c)\text{-PRF}}_{\mathcal{C}, \mathsf{H}}.$$

Proof (Sketch). We use the CCA security of KEM to make the KEM keys random, such that the key to H is uniformly random. Using the PRF property of H gives a uniformly random value for the final key. The full proof can be found in the full version. $\quad\square$

Theorem 8 (SIG SUF-CMA $\Rightarrow$ AKEM Outsider-Auth). *If SIG is an SUF-CMA secure signature scheme, then* $\mathsf{AKEM}^{\mathsf{EtStH}}[\mathsf{KEM}, \mathsf{SIG}, \mathsf{H}]$ *is an Outsider-Auth secure AKEM. In particular, for every* (n, q_e, q_d)-*Outsider-Auth adversary* $\mathcal{A}$ *there exists a* (n, q_e)-*SUF-CMA adversary* $\mathcal{B}$ *against SIG such that*

$$\mathsf{Adv}^{\text{Outsider-Auth}}_{\mathcal{A}, \mathsf{AKEM}^{\mathsf{EtStH}}[\mathsf{KEM}, \mathsf{SIG}, \mathsf{H}]} \leq \mathsf{Adv}^{(n, q_e)\text{-SUF-CMA}}_{\mathcal{B}, \mathsf{SIG}}.$$

Proof (Sketch). Queries to the decapsulation oracle containing invalid signatures cannot be distinguished by an adversary due to the definition of the scheme. Valid queries can be used against the SUF-CMA security of SIG. The full proof can be found in the full version. $\quad\square$

6.2 AKEM from NIKE

We can build an AKEM from a NIKE. Let $\mathsf{NIKE} = (\mathsf{Setup}, \mathsf{NIKE.KeyGen}, \mathsf{NIKE.SharedKey})$ be a NIKE and H a 2-keyed function, then we can construct an AKEM $\mathsf{AKEM}^{\mathsf{NIKE}}[\mathsf{NIKE}, \mathsf{H}]$ as defined in Listing 19. By H_1, we denote function H keyed in the first component and by H_2 function H keyed in the second component.

Listing 19: $\mathsf{AKEM}^{\mathsf{NIKE}}[\mathsf{NIKE},\mathsf{H}]$ from $\mathsf{NIKE} = (\mathsf{NIKE.KeyGen}, \mathsf{NIKE.SharedKey})$ where the setup parameters are known to every user.

Gen	$\mathrm{AuthDecap}(sk_2, pk_1, pk^*)$
01 $(sk, pk) \xleftarrow{\$} \mathsf{NIKE.KeyGen}$	08 $K_1 \leftarrow \mathsf{NIKE.SharedKey}(sk_2, pk_1)$
02 **return** (sk, pk)	09 $K_2 \leftarrow \mathsf{NIKE.SharedKey}(sk_2, pk^*)$
	10 $K \leftarrow \mathsf{H}(K_1, K_2)$
$\mathrm{AuthEncap}(sk_1, pk_2)$	11 **return** K
03 $(sk^*, pk^*) \xleftarrow{\$} \mathsf{NIKE.KeyGen}$	
04 $K_1 \leftarrow \mathsf{NIKE.SharedKey}(sk_1, pk_2)$	
05 $K_2 \leftarrow \mathsf{NIKE.SharedKey}(sk^*, pk_2)$	
06 $K \leftarrow \mathsf{H}(K_1, K_2)$	
07 **return** (pk^*, K)	

Theorem 9 (NIKE Active + H_2 PRF $\Rightarrow$ AKEM Insider-CCA). *Let* NIKE *be a NIKE and* H *a 2-keyed function. If* NIKE *is* Active *secure and* H_2 *a* PRF, *then* $\mathsf{AKEM}^{\mathsf{NIKE}}[\mathsf{NIKE},\mathsf{H}]$ *is* Insider-CCA *secure. In particular for any adversary* $\mathcal{A}$ *against* $(n, q_e, q_d, q_c, r_{sk})$-Insider-CCA *security of* $\mathsf{AKEM}^{\mathsf{NIKE}}[\mathsf{NIKE},\mathsf{H}]$ *there exists an* $(n + q_c, q_e + 2q_d, 0, q_e + q_d + q_c, q_e + 2q_d, q_c)$-Active *adversary against* NIKE *and a* (q_c, q_c)-PRF *adversary* $\mathcal{C}$ *against* H_2 *such that*

$$\mathsf{Adv}^{(n,q_e,q_d,q_c,r_{sk})\text{-Insider-CCA}}_{\mathcal{A},\mathsf{AKEM}^{\mathsf{NIKE}}[\mathsf{NIKE},\mathsf{H}]} \leq \mathsf{Adv}^{(n+q_c,q_e+2q_d,0,q_e+q_d+q_c,q_e+2q_d,q_c)\text{-Active}}_{\mathcal{B},\mathsf{NIKE}} + \mathsf{Adv}^{(q_c,q_c)\text{-PRF}}_{\mathcal{C},\mathsf{H}_2}.$$

Proof (Sketch). Assuming an active secure NIKE, the second shared key, K_2 is indistinguishable from random. We show that by constructing an adversary against an Active secure NIKE using an Insider-CCA adversary against $\mathsf{AKEM}^{\mathsf{NIKE}}[\mathsf{NIKE},\mathsf{H}]$ by simulating the corruptions from REPSK by registering corrupt users in the NIKE game. Then, every other query can be answered by registering a new key (if the query was made with a chosen public key) or computed by the simulator themselves. The test query of the adversary against NIKE is then directly embedded int the challenge query of the Insider-CCA game. With H_2 being a PRF, we can further show that the resulting key is also uniformly random. The full proof can be found in the full version. □

Theorem 10 (NIKE Active + H_1 PRF $\Rightarrow$ AKEM Outsider-Auth). *Let* $\mathsf{NIKE} = (\mathsf{Setup}, \mathsf{NIKE.KeyGen}, \mathsf{NIKE.SharedKey})$ *be a NIKE and* H *a 2-keyed function. If* NIKE *is* Active *secure and* H_1 *a* PRF, *then* $\mathsf{AKEM}^{\mathsf{NIKE}}[\mathsf{NIKE},\mathsf{H}]$ *is* Outsider-Auth *secure. In particular, for every* (n, q_e, q_d)-Outsider-Auth *adversary against* $\mathsf{AKEM}^{\mathsf{NIKE}}[\mathsf{NIKE},\mathsf{H}]$ *there exists an* $(n, q_e + 2q_d, 0, q_e, 2q_e + 2q_d, q_d)$-Active *adversary against* NIKE *and a* (q_d, q_d)-PRF *adversary* $\mathcal{C}$ *against* H_1 *such that*

$$\mathsf{Adv}^{(n,q_e,q_d)\text{-Outsider-Auth}}_{\mathcal{A},\mathsf{AKEM}^{\mathsf{NIKE}}[\mathsf{NIKE},\mathsf{H}]} \leq \mathsf{Adv}^{(n,q_e+2q_d,0,q_e,2q_e+2q_d,q_d)\text{-Active}}_{\mathcal{B},\mathsf{NIKE}} + \mathsf{Adv}^{(q_d,q_d)\text{-PRF}}_{\mathcal{C},\mathsf{H}_1}.$$

Proof (Sketch). The structure is similar to the proof of Theorem 9 except that the test query is embedded in the decapsulation oracle instead of the challenge oracle and that it is only embedded for queries with honest public keys. The full proof can be found in the full version. □

Acknowledgements. The authors thank the anonymous reviewers to point out an error in our NIKE construction and an error in one of our proofs. They also thank Doreen Riepel for very helpful feedback and discussions. Jonas Janneck was supported by the European Union (ERC AdG REWORC - 101054911). Eike Kiltz was supported by the Deutsche Forschungsgemeinschaft (DFG, German Research Foundation) under Germany's Excellence Strategy – EXC 2092 CASA - 390781972, and by the European Union (ERC AdG REWORC - 101054911).

References

1. Alwen, J., Blanchet, B., Hauck, E., Kiltz, E., Lipp, B., Riepel, D.: Analysing the HPKE standard. In: Canteaut, A., Standaert, F.-X. (eds.) EUROCRYPT 2021, Part I. LNCS, vol. 12696, pp. 87–116. Springer, Cham (2021). https://doi.org/10.1007/978-3-030-77870-5_4
2. Anastasova, M., Kampanakis, P., Massimo, J.: PQ-HPKE: post-quantum hybrid public key encryption. IACR Cryptology ePrint Archive, p. 414 (2022). https://eprint.iacr.org/2022/414
3. Barnes, R., Beurdouche, B., Robert, R., Millican, J., Omara, E., Cohn-Gordon, K.: The Messaging Layer Security (MLS) Protocol. Internet-Draft draft-ietf-mls-protocol-20, Internet Engineering Task Force (2023, work in Progress). https://datatracker.ietf.org/doc/draft-ietf-mls-protocol/20/
4. Barnes, R.L., Bhargavan, K., Lipp, B., Wood, C.A.: Hybrid public key encryption. RFC 9180, RFC Editor (2022). https://www.rfc-editor.org/rfc/rfc9180.html
5. Bellare, M., Namprempre, C.: Authenticated encryption: relations among notions and analysis of the generic composition paradigm. In: Okamoto, T. (ed.) ASIACRYPT 2000. LNCS, vol. 1976, pp. 531–545. Springer, Heidelberg (2000). https://doi.org/10.1007/3-540-44448-3_41
6. Bellare, M., Rogaway, P.: Code-based game-playing proofs and the security of triple encryption. Cryptology ePrint Archive, Report 2004/331 (2004). https://eprint.iacr.org/2004/331
7. Bellare, M., Tackmann, B.: The multi-user security of authenticated encryption: AES-GCM in TLS 1.3. In: Robshaw, M., Katz, J. (eds.) CRYPTO 2016, Part I. LNCS, vol. 9814, pp. 247–276. Springer, Heidelberg (2016). https://doi.org/10.1007/978-3-662-53018-4_10
8. Bos, J., et al.: Crystals-kyber: a CCA-secure module-lattice-based KEM. In: 2018 IEEE European Symposium on Security and Privacy (EuroS&P), pp. 353–367. IEEE (2018)
9. Cramer, R., Shoup, V.: SIAM Journal on Computing
10. Dent, A.W., Zheng, Y. (eds.): Practical Signcryption. Information Security and Cryptography. Springer, Heidelberg (2010). https://doi.org/10.1007/978-3-540-89411-7
11. Ducas, L., et al.: CRYSTALS-Dilithium: a lattice-based digital signature scheme. IACR TCHES **2018**(1), 238–268 (2018). https://doi.org/10.13154/tches.v2018.i1.238-268. https://tches.iacr.org/index.php/TCHES/article/view/839
12. Duman, J., Hartmann, D., Kiltz, E., Kunzweiler, S., Lehmann, J., Riepel, D.: Group action key encapsulation and non-interactive key exchange in the qrom.

In: Agrawal, S., Lin, D. (eds.) ASIACRYPT 2022, Part II. LNCS, vol. 13792, pp. 36–66. Springer, Cham (2023). https://doi.org/10.1007/978-3-031-22966-4_2

13. Freire, E.S.V., Hofheinz, D., Kiltz, E., Paterson, K.G.: Non-interactive key exchange. In: Kurosawa, K., Hanaoka, G. (eds.) PKC 2013. LNCS, vol. 7778, pp. 254–271. Springer, Heidelberg (2013). https://doi.org/10.1007/978-3-642-36362-7_17

14. Gajland, P., de Kock, B., Quaresma, M., Malavolta, G., Schwabe, P.: Swoosh: practical lattice-based non-interactive key exchange. Cryptology ePrint Archive (2023)

15. Geoghegan, T., Patton, C., Rescorla, E., Wood, C.A.: Distributed Aggregation Protocol for Privacy Preserving Measurement. Internet-Draft draft-ietf-ppm-dap-04, Internet Engineering Task Force (2023, work in Progress). https://datatracker.ietf.org/doc/draft-ietf-ppm-dap/04/

16. Kinnear, E., McManus, P., Pauly, T., Verma, T., Wood, C.A.: Oblivious DNS over HTTPS. Technical report 9230 (2022). https://doi.org/10.17487/RFC9230. https://www.rfc-editor.org/info/rfc9230

17. Langley, A., Hamburg, M., Turner, S.: Elliptic curves for security. RFC 7748, RFC Editor (2016). https://www.rfc-editor.org/rfc/rfc7748.html

18. Len, J., Grubbs, P., Ristenpart, T.: Partitioning oracle attacks. In: Bailey, M., Greenstadt, R. (eds.) USENIX Security 2021, pp. 195–212. USENIX Association (2021)

19. National Institute of Standards and Technology: Digital Signature Standard (DSS). FIPS Publication 186-4 (2013). https://doi.org/10.6028/nist.fips.186-4

20. Paterson, K.G., van der Merwe, T.: Reactive and proactive standardisation of TLS. In: Chen, L., McGrew, D., Mitchell, C. (eds.) SSR 2016. LNCS, vol. 10074, pp. 160–186. Springer, Cham (2016). https://doi.org/10.1007/978-3-319-49100-4_7

21. Rescorla, E., Oku, K., Sullivan, N., Wood, C.A.: TLS Encrypted Client Hello. Internet-Draft draft-ietf-tls-esni-16, Internet Engineering Task Force (2023, work in Progress). https://datatracker.ietf.org/doc/draft-ietf-tls-esni/16/

22. Zheng, Y.: Digital signcryption or how to achieve cost(signature & encryption) ≪ cost(signature) + cost(encryption). In: Kaliski Jr., B.S. (ed.) CRYPTO 1997. LNCS, vol. 1294, pp. 165–179. Springer, Heidelberg (1997). https://doi.org/10.1007/BFb0052234

Unified View for Notions of Bit Security

Shun Watanabe[1] and Kenji Yasunaga[2]

[1] Tokyo University of Agriculture and Technology, Tokyo, Japan
shunwata@cc.tuat.ac.jp
[2] Tokyo Institute of Technology, Tokyo, Japan
yasunaga@c.titech.ac.jp

Abstract. A theoretical framework of the bit security of cryptographic primitives/games was first introduced in a pioneering work by Micciancio and Walter (Eurocrypt 2018), and an alternative framework was introduced by the authors (Asiacrypt 2021). First, we observe that quantitative results in the latter framework are preserved even if adversaries are allowed to output the failure symbol. With this slight modification, we show that the notion of bit security in the latter framework is equivalent to that in the former framework up to constant bits. Also, we demonstrate that several existing notions of advantages can be captured in a unified way. Based on this equivalence, we show that the reduction algorithm of Hast (J. Cryptology, 2004) gives a tight reduction of the Goldreich-Levin hard-core predicate to the hardness of one-way functions. These two results resolved open problems that remained.

Furthermore, in the latter framework, we show that all games we need to care about are decision games. Namely, for every search game G, there is the corresponding decision game G' such that G has λ-bit security if and only if G' has λ-bit security. The game G' consists of the real and the ideal games, where attacks in the ideal game are never approved. Such games often appear in game-hopping security proofs. The result justifies such security proofs because they lose no security. Finally, we provide a distribution replacement theorem. Suppose a game using distribution Q in a black-box manner is λ-bit secure, and two distributions P and Q are computationally λ-bit secure indistinguishable. In that case, the game where Q is replaced by P is also λ-bit secure.

Keywords: Bit security · operational approach · Goldreich-Levin theorem

1 Introduction

Quantifying the security levels of cryptographic primitives is a significant task both for theoreticians and practitioners around information security and cryptography. The evaluations directly affect using cryptographic primitives in our daily lives. We usually say that primitive P has λ-bit security (or security level λ) if we need 2^λ operations to break P. Although the statement is simple, we encounter difficulties formalizing such security levels exactly. In particular, the

J. Guo and R. Steinfeld (Eds.): ASIACRYPT 2023, LNCS 14443, pp. 361–389, 2023.
https://doi.org/10.1007/978-981-99-8736-8_12

difficulty is defining bit security for *decision games*, such as pseudorandom generators and encryption schemes. For search games, such as the security games of one-way functions and signature schemes, the well-known expression of $\log_2(T/\varepsilon)$ can be justified for attacker A with computational cost T and winning probability ε; If we run A in total N times, the probability that some adversary wins the game is amplified to εN. Thus it is sufficient to choose $N = 1/\varepsilon$ for winning the game with a probability of almost one. Hence, the total cost is $TN = 2^{\log_2(T/\varepsilon)}$.

In decision games, the attacker tries to distinguish two possible cases ($u = 0$ and $u = 1$). Even the random-guessing attacker can correctly predict the secret value u with probability $1/2$. Thus, we usually define the advantage of the attacker A as $\mathsf{Adv}_A = 2|p - 1/2|$, where p is the winning probability of A. We need to evaluate the security level of the primitive by assuming the existence of attacker A with advantage Adv_A.

In order to clarify the subtlety, let us consider the following decision game to distinguish between the pseudorandom number generator (PRG) and the true random number generator (TRG): the outcome (y, z) of PRG consists of the image $y = f(x)$ of a one-way permutation f over $\{0,1\}^n$ and its hard-core predicate $z = h(x)$; the outcome (y, z) of TRG consists of $y = f(x)$ and a random bit $z = \sigma$ that is independent of the seed x. For this game, we can consider the following two possible attacks:

1. *Linear test attack:* For a prescribed binary vector v of length $n + 1$, the adversary computes the inner product of v and (y, z); if the outcome is 0, the adversary outputs 0 (PRG); and outputs 1 (TRG) otherwise. For such an attack, the output distribution A_u of the adversary A given $u \in \{0,1\}$ ($u = 0$ for PRG and $u = 1$ for TRG) are $A_0 = (1/2+\varepsilon_1, 1/2-\varepsilon_1)$ and $A_1 = (1/2, 1/2)$ for some bias ε_1, where $A_u = (p_0, p_1)$ means that $\Pr[A = 0 \mid u] = p_0$ and $\Pr[A = 1 \mid u] = p_1$. The (standard) advantage of this attack is $\mathsf{Adv}_A = \varepsilon_1$.

2. *Inversion attack:* First, the adversary tries to invert the one-way permutation, which will succeed with probability ε_2. If the inversion is successful and $h(x)$ coincides with z, the adversary outputs 0 (PRG); otherwise (if the inversion is unsuccessful or $h(x) \neq z$), the adversary outputs 1 (TRG). For such an attack, the output distribution of the adversary A given $u \in \{0,1\}$ consists of $A_0 = (\varepsilon_2, 1 - \varepsilon_2)$ and $A_1 = (\varepsilon_2/2, 1 - \varepsilon_2/2)$. The (standard) advantage of this attack is $\mathsf{Adv}_A = \varepsilon_2/2$.

It is known that, for an appropriately chosen vector v, the advantage of the linear test can be $\varepsilon_1 \geq 2^{-n/2}$ (cf. [1,8]). When we use a random-guessing inversion attack, where A chooses a random value x', the inversion succeeds with probability $\varepsilon_2 = 2^{-n}$. Does this imply that the linear test attack is exponentially more sophisticated than the inversion attack? Or is this inner-product attack a basic one, as is the inversion attack?

In order to circumvent the subtlety mentioned above in defining bit security for decision games, Micciancio and Walter [16] introduced an alternative definition of advantage; when the random secret is U and the adversary's output is A, their advantage is defined as the ratio $\mathsf{Adv}^{\mathrm{MW}} = \frac{I(U \wedge A)}{H(U)}$ between the mutual information and the Shannon entropy. They showed that, under a certain assumption, their advantage could be approximated by the *conditional squared (CS) advantage* $\mathsf{Adv}^{\mathrm{CS}}$ to be explained later (see (8)). In fact, $\mathsf{Adv}^{\mathrm{MW}}$ was only used to justify the CS advantage, and the bit security of specific results in [16] is evaluated with respect to the CS advantage. They used $\min_A\{\log_2(T_A/\mathsf{Adv}_A^{\mathrm{CS}})\}$ as the definition of bit security, where T_A is the computational cost of A. Even though the results obtained by their definition match our intuition, the definition lacks an *operational meaning*. The quantity of $\log_2(T_A/\mathsf{Adv}_A^{\mathrm{CS}})$ is just a combination of the two values T_A and $\mathsf{Adv}_A^{\mathrm{CS}}$. We cannot explain the meaning of this quantity from its definition. A good example of the quantity with operational meaning is the Shannon entropy $H(X)$ of the information source X. When we define the minimum average length of lossless compression functions f for X as $\mathrm{MinLen}(X) := \min_f\{\mathbb{E}[\|f(X)\|]\}$, we can show that the Shannon entropy approximates it as $H(X) \leq \mathrm{MinLen}(X) < H(X) + 1$. Hence, we say that $H(X)$ is the length limit of lossless compression of X.

In [20], Watanabe and Yasunaga introduced a framework for evaluating the security level of primitives with operational meanings. In their framework, there are two types of adversaries attacking a security game G. The *inner* adversary A plays a usual security game G. The *outer* adversary B invokes A sufficiently many times to achieve a winning probability close to one. If the total computational cost needed to achieve this task is 2^λ, game G is said to be λ-bit secure. Notably, they *characterized* their notion by advantages. They showed that the bit security of game G is approximated by $\min_A\{\log_2(T_A/\mathsf{Adv}_A)\}$,[1] where Adv_A is equal to the winning probability of A in G for search games and is the *Rényi advantage* of A for decision games. The Rényi advantage was introduced in [20] and is defined as the Rényi divergence of order $1/2$ between the output distributions of two cases in the decision game.

Several problems remained open in [20]. Regarding the Goldreich-Levin theorem [9,10], they proved that a λ-bit secure one-way function gives a λ-bit secure hard-core predicate against *balanced* adversaries. The balanced adversaries are restricted such that the probability of outputting each value (0 or 1) must be at least constant. An example is a linear test attack described above; when $u = 1$ (TRG), the test (adversary) outputs 0 and 1 with probability $1/2$, a constant. Such adversaries, however, may not be typical in security proofs. The inversion attack described above is typical in many security proofs. Since the success probability of inversion is usually small and close to zero, the attack is not balanced. Removing the balanced-adversary condition in the Goldreich-Levin theorem has been an open problem. The result was in contrast to the framework of Micciancio and Walter [16], where they showed that the Goldreich-Levin reduction [9,10] was indeed optimal.

Another open problem was the relationship between the two frameworks [16, 20]. Although finding similar features in the two definitions seems complicated, they mostly share the same quantitative results. The exception was the

---

[1] More precisely, it should be expressed by $\min_A\{\log_2 T_A + \log_2\lceil 1/\mathsf{Adv}_A\rceil\}$ as Adv_A may take values greater than 1 for decision games.

Goldreich-Levin theorem, as described above. Clarifying the relation is helpful for researchers analyzing and evaluating concrete cryptographic primitives.

1.1   Our Results

In this work, we further study the framework of [20] and resolve open problems. First, we observe that the results of [20] preserve even if inner adversaries for decision games are allowed to output the failure symbol $\perp$ as well as $\{0, 1\}$. See Sect. 3 for the details. This slight modification reveals a relation between the bit security notions of [20] and [16]. We show that the CS advantage of [16] for decision games is bounded above by the Rényi advantage. In other words, the Rényi advantage evaluates adversaries more pessimistically than the CS advantage. As an extreme case, there is an attack that achieves $\Theta(\delta)$ in the Rényi advantage but has 0 in the CS advantage (see Table 1). The above relation implies that if decision primitive P has λ-bit security in [20], P also has λ-bit security in [16]. Even though the converse is not necessarily true (see Sect. 1.3), we show that the CS advantage can be increased to the same level as the Rényi advantage if we appropriately modify the attack; essentially, the modified adversary relabels the output of the original adversary. Thus, we can transform an adversary so that the CS advantage is almost the same as the Rényi advantage. These two directions of bounds imply that the two notions of bit security in [16,20] are equivalent within constant bits. We compare the three advantages (standard (TV), CS, and Rényi) for several attacks in Sect. 1.3.

Furthermore, we demonstrate that several existing notions of advantages [13, 15,16] can be captured in a unified way. Specifically, the three quantities in [13,15,16] are the same except for a constant factor. Based on this equivalence, we show that the reduction algorithm of Hast [13] gives a tight[2] reduction of the Goldreich-Levin hard-core predicate [10] to the hardness of one-way functions. Namely, we resolved another open problem that remained in [20]. Although we can derive a similar result from our general transformation described above together with the tightness result of the Goldreich-Levin theorem in [16], we give proof through the reduction of Hast [13]. An advantage of this route is that we can obtain an explainable algorithm (namely, Hast's algorithm) for improving the Goldreich-Levin algorithm. Although the transformation enables the adversary to have the Rényi advantage at the same level as the CS advantage, it may not be easy to understand the factor for improvement. We believe Hast's improved algorithm can be a hint for designing algorithms/reductions that attain high Rényi advantages.

In addition to the above, we give several results regarding the framework of [20]. We show that every search game can be replaced by a specific decision game, named a *canonical* game. Specifically, we show that a search game has λ-bit security if and only if the corresponding canonical game has λ-bit security. In canonical games, while the adversary plays as usual in the real game, attacks

---

[2] We say a reduction is tight if it can be used to show that λ-bit security implies $(\lambda - o(\lambda))$-bit security.

by the adversary will never be approved in the ideal game. This treatment of adversaries often appears in game-hopping security proofs [4,18]; e.g., the adversary may play a game where every forgery of the signature cannot be approved. Our result may justify such a treatment in security proofs because such game-hopping loses no security. We also provide a distribution replacement theorem. Suppose that game G^Q using black-box access to distribution Q is λ-bit secure and two distributions P and Q are λ-bit secure indistinguishable. The theorem asserts that game G^P, where distribution Q is replaced by P, is also λ-bit secure. This result is a generalization of [20, Theorem 9], where the sufficient condition is that distributions P and Q are information-theoretically close enough in the Hellinger distance. Our result relaxed the requirement into the computational one. It guarantees that λ-bit secure indistinguishability is sufficient for preserving the λ-bit security of games. As an instance, we apply the theorem to the leftover hash lemma (LHL) [6,14] and show that the seed of a λ-bit secure randomness extractor using universal hash functions can be safely replaced by the output of a λ-bit secure PRG. As a side result (and maybe implicit from [20]), we show that the entropy loss in the LHL to preserve λ-bit security in the framework of [20] is λ.

1.2   Related Work

Micciancio and Walter [16] initiated the theoretical study of quantifying the security level of cryptographic primitives. They proposed a framework for evaluating the bit security based on the Shannon entropy and the mutual information. A key novelty of their framework was allowing the adversary to output the failure symbol $\perp$ in security games. They showed that their notion of bit security could be characterized by the advantage introduced by Levin [15]. Levin's notion appeared in evaluating the security of the hard-core predicate of Goldreich and Levin [10]. Hast [13] studied efficient reduction algorithms for improving the Goldreich-Levin theorem against nearly one-sided adversaries.

Watanabe and Yasunaga [20] introduced another framework for quantifying the bit security of games with an operational meaning. One of their contributions was characterizing the bit security using the Rényi advantage.[3] The standard advantage of $2|p - 1/2|$ for the winning probability p in decision games may behave differently from the Rényi advantage, according to the discussion in [20].

---

[3] In the classic result of the Bayesian hypothesis testing [7], the error probability is characterized by the Chernoff information asymptotically; the asymptotic characterization has been used in the context of cryptography [2]. In the derivation of Chernoff's characterization, while the upper bound on the error probability is non-asymptotic, the lower bound involves a cumbersome reminder term. For this reason, instead of using Chernoff's characterization, the authors of [20] used a slightly weaker (but non-asymptotic) lower bound on the error probability in terms of the Rényi divergence of order $1/2$; it is weaker in the sense that the coefficient in the exponent is twice as large as that of the upper bound. Such a weaker lower bound is rarely used in the context of statistics, but it is useful in the context of cryptography since it only affects 1 bit in the bit security.

Our study mainly relies on their framework to evaluate bit security. A small but crucial difference is that we allow the adversary to output the failure symbol in the game. The modification enables us to unify several existing notions of advantages [13,15,16], reveal the relation to the framework of [16], and give an optimal reduction algorithm for the Goldreich-Levin theorem.

The entropy loss of randomness extractors is inevitable [17]. The LHL-based extractors achieve an optimal entropy loss of $2 \log(1/\varepsilon)$ for closeness ε to the uniform distribution in the total variation distance. Barak et al. [3] studied the possibilities of reducing the loss to $\log(1/\varepsilon)$ for several primitives. It is shown in [21] that the same reduction of the entropy loss can be achieved for all primitives when using the bit security framework of [16]. In other words, a λ-bit entropy loss in LHL is sufficient to preserve λ-bit security in bit security of [16]. In this work, we explicitly state that the same thing also holds in the framework of [20].

1.3   Comparing Two Frameworks of Bit Security

Sensitivity to Attacks. We show the equivalence of the two notions of bit security in [16] and [20] up to a constant. The first one is given by $\min_A \{\log_2 (T_A / \mathsf{Adv}_A^{\mathrm{CS}})\}$, and the second one is characterized by $\min_A \{\log_2 T_A + \log_2 \lceil 1/\mathsf{Adv}_A^{\mathrm{Renyi}} \rceil\}$, where $\mathsf{Adv}_A^{\mathrm{CS}}$ and $\mathsf{Adv}_A^{\mathrm{Renyi}}$ are the CS and the Rényi advantages of adversary A, respectively. We stress that the two quantities coincide only when we optimize over adversaries. In fact, $\mathsf{Adv}_A^{\mathrm{Renyi}}$ is always bounded below by $\mathsf{Adv}_A^{\mathrm{CS}}$ for any adversary A, but $\mathsf{Adv}_A^{\mathrm{CS}}$ can be significantly smaller than $\mathsf{Adv}_A^{\mathrm{Renyi}}$. In this sense, there may be a risk of underestimating the potential impact of attacks when evaluating the bit security with $\mathsf{Adv}_A^{\mathrm{CS}}$. This is caused by the fact that $\mathsf{Adv}_A^{\mathrm{CS}}$ is *sensitive* to the labeling of the output of the adversary. While the failure symbol has a special role in $\mathsf{Adv}_A^{\mathrm{CS}}$, it is just one of the symbols in $\mathsf{Adv}_A^{\mathrm{Renyi}}$, and thus relabeling of symbols has no impact on $\mathsf{Adv}_A^{\mathrm{Renyi}}$.

The above concern can be illustrated by comparing the advantages of the following four types of attacks, summarized in Table 1. The first one, a balanced attack without $\perp$, is a type of attack such as the linear test attack mentioned above. The second one, an unbalanced attack with $\perp$, is an attack such as the inversion attack for PRG mentioned above. The third one, an unbalanced attack without $\perp$, is a type of attack that may occur in an attack against a decisional Diffie-Hellman (DDH) problem using an oracle for a computational Diffie-Hellman (CDH) problem. The CDH is a typical example of the so-called *privately-verifiable* search problem [11]. This type of attack naturally occurs when the privately-verifiable search oracle is available. The final attack, a balanced 0/1-unbalanced $\perp$ attack, is introduced for comparison. This attack can be realized by modifying the second attack for PRG; the adversary outputs $\perp$ when the inversion attack succeeded; otherwise, it outputs a random bit.

For the first two attacks, the advantages of $\mathsf{Adv}^{\mathrm{CS}}$ and $\mathsf{Adv}^{\mathrm{Renyi}}$ do not make a difference. However, while $\mathsf{Adv}^{\mathrm{Renyi}} = \Theta(\delta)$ for the third and the fourth attacks,

Table 1. Comparison of advantages for four types of attacks

Attacks	$\mathsf{Adv}^{\mathrm{TV}}$	$\mathsf{Adv}^{\mathrm{CS}}$	$\mathsf{Adv}^{\mathrm{Renyi}}$
Balanced attack without $\perp$ $\quad A_0 = (1/2 + \delta, 1/2 - \delta)$ $\quad A_1 = (1/2, 1/2)$ e.g.) Linear test attack for PRG	δ	δ^2	$\Theta(\delta^2)$
Unbalanced attack with $\perp$ $\quad A_0 = (\delta, 0, 1 - \delta)$ $\quad A_1 = (\delta/2, \delta/2, 1 - \delta)$ e.g.) Inversion attack for PRG	$\delta/2$	$\delta/2$	$\Theta(\delta)$
Unbalanced attack without $\perp$ $\quad A_0 = (\delta, 1 - \delta)$ $\quad A_1 = (\delta/p, 1 - \delta/p)$ e.g.) CDH oracle attack for DDH	$(1 - 1/p)\delta$	$(1 - 1/p)^2\delta^2$	$\Theta(\delta)$
Balanced 0/1-unbalanced $\perp$ attack $\quad A_0 = (1/2 - \delta/2, 1/2 - \delta/2, \delta)$ $\quad A_1 = (1/2 - \delta/4, 1/2 - \delta/4, \delta/2)$ e.g.) Inversion attack using $\perp$	$\delta/2$	0	$\Theta(\delta)$

$\mathsf{Adv}^{\mathrm{CS}}$ varies much for these cases. Namely, the CS advantage is inherently sensitive to attacks. For more detail on the comparison, see Sect. 4.2.

Flexible Use of Two Advantages. By comparing the two notions of bit security in [16,20], although these two quantities almost match when optimizing attacks, they have different benefits. Thus, we can flexibly use the two notions depending on the situation. First, the CS advantage is useful for developing and analyzing algorithms/reductions that effectively use the failure symbol (or erasure in the context of decoding). This usefulness has been exploited in past work [15,16] and this work (Sect. 5 and [13]). Second, when we want to avoid underestimating the adversary's ability, it is safer to use the Rényi advantage for evaluation since the CS advantage may have sensitivity to attacks, as discussed above. Finally, the CS advantage has an advantage for the ease of computation; the Rényi advantage may need a complicated calculus. Several inequalities ((2), Lemma 1, Lemma 2, and Theorem 1) in this paper may help it.

1.4   Paper Organization

We review the framework of [20] in Sect. 3. In Sect. 4, we compare the two notions of advantages, the CS advantage of [16] and the Rényi advantage of [20], where the former can be seen as a unified notion as it is equivalent to other notions in the literature [13,15]. As a result, we show that two notions of bit security in [16,20] are equivalent within constant bits. We show a tight reduction of the Goldreich-Levin theorem in Sect. 5. In Sect. 6, we show a canonical decision game such that every search game preserves its bit security in the corresponding canonical game. We prove the distribution replacement theorem in Sect. 7. We conclude the paper in Sect. 8.

2   Preliminaries

In this section, we present several basic notions and their properties to be used in proofs of the main results.

Let P and Q be probability distributions over a finite set Ω. For a distribution P over Ω and $A \subseteq \Omega$, we denote by $P(A)$ the probability of event A, which is equal to $\sum_{x \in A} P(x)$.

The *total variation distance* between P and Q is

$$d_{\mathsf{TV}}(P, Q) = \max_{A \subseteq \Omega} |P(A) - Q(A)| = \frac{1}{2} \sum_{x \in \Omega} |P(x) - Q(x)|.$$

The *Hellinger distance* between P and Q is

$$d_{\mathsf{HD}}(P, Q) = \sqrt{\frac{1}{2} \sum_{x \in \Omega} \left(\sqrt{P(x)} - \sqrt{Q(x)} \right)^2} = \sqrt{1 - \sum_{x \in \Omega} \sqrt{P(x) \cdot Q(x)}},$$

which takes values in $[0, 1]$. The *Rényi divergence of order* $1/2$ is defined by[4]

$$D_{1/2}(P\|Q) = -2 \ln \sum_{x \in \Omega} \sqrt{P(x)Q(x)}.$$

The Hellinger distance and the total variation distance can be related as follows:

$$d_{\mathsf{HD}}(P, Q)^2 \leq d_{\mathsf{TV}}(P, Q) \leq \sqrt{2} \cdot d_{\mathsf{HD}}(P, Q). \tag{1}$$

On the other hand, by noting $1 - 1/t \leq \ln t \leq t - 1$ for $t > 0$, the Hellinger distance and the Rényi divergence of order $1/2$ can be related as follows:[5]

$$d_{\mathsf{HD}}(P, Q)^2 \leq \frac{1}{2} \cdot D_{1/2}(P\|Q) \leq \frac{d_{\mathsf{HD}}(P, Q)^2}{1 - d_{\mathsf{HD}}(P, Q)^2} \leq 2 \cdot d_{\mathsf{HD}}(P, Q)^2, \tag{2}$$

where the last inequality holds if $d_{\mathsf{HD}}(P, Q)^2 \leq 1/2$.

We present a few technical lemmas used in the paper.

---

[4] When P and Q have disjoint support, we set $D_{1/2}(P\|Q) = \infty$.
[5] The second inequality holds as long as $D_{1/2}(P\|Q) < \infty$.

Lemma 1. *For given distributions P and Q with $P \ll Q$,[6] we have*

$$D_{1/2}(P\|Q) \leq D(P\|Q) \leq \sum_{x \in \mathcal{X}^+} \frac{(P(x) - Q(x))^2}{Q(x)} \leq 2\beta_Q^{-1} d_{\mathsf{TV}}(P, Q)^2,$$

where $\beta_Q = \min_{x \in \mathcal{X}^+} Q(x)$, $\mathcal{X}^+ = \{x : Q(x) > 0\}$, *and* $D(P\|Q) = \sum_{x \in \Sigma} P(x) \log(P(x)/Q(x))$ *is the* Kullback-Leibler (KL) *divergence.*

Proof. The first inequality follows from the fact that the Rényi divergence is monotonically non-decreasing with respect to α and $D(P\|Q) = \lim_{\alpha \to 1} D_\alpha(P\|Q)$. For the last inequality, see [12, Lemma 4.1]; the second inequality appears in the middle of the proof of [12, Lemma 4.1]. $\qquad\square$

Lemma 2. *Let A_0 and A_1 be distributions over $\{0, 1, \bot\}$ such that $A_0 = (\delta, 1 - \delta, 0)$ and $A_1 = (q\delta, 1 - q\delta, 0)$, where $0 \leq \delta \leq 1/32$ and $0 \leq q\delta \leq 1$. Then,*

$$D_{1/2}(A_0\|A_1) \geq \phi(q) \cdot \delta$$

for $\phi(q) = (1 - \sqrt{q})^2 - q/16$. The same conclusion holds when $A_0 = (1/2 - \delta/2, 1/2 - \delta/2, \delta)$ and $A_1 = (1/2 - q\delta/2, 1/2 - q\delta/2, q\delta)$. In particular, $\phi(q) > 1/2$ for $q \leq 1/16$.

Proof. The first claim is the same as [20, Lemma 8]. The second one follows from the fact that the value $\sum_{x \in \{0, 1, \bot\}} \sqrt{A_0(x) A_1(x)}$ is the same as the first case. $\square$

3   Bit Security Framework of [20]

An n-bit game $G = (X, R, \{O_\theta\}_\theta)$, played by an inner adversary A and an outer adversary B, consists of an algorithm X, a Boolean function R, and oracles $\{O_\theta\}_\theta$. The success probability of A is

$$\varepsilon_A = \Pr\left[u \xleftarrow{R} \{0, 1\}^n; x \leftarrow X(u); a \leftarrow A^{\{O_\theta(\cdot)\}_\theta}(x) : R(u, x, a) = 1\right].$$

We consider two types of games: decision games ($n = 1$) and search games ($n \gg 1$). The success probability of the pair (A, B) is defined depending on the game type. For decision games, the success probability of (A, B) is

$$\varepsilon_{A,B}^{\mathsf{decn}} = \Pr\left[u \xleftarrow{R} \{0, 1\}; b \leftarrow B^{O_A^{\mathsf{decn}}} : b = u\right], \tag{3}$$

where O_A^{decn} is the oracle that, given the ith query, computes $x_i \leftarrow X(u)$ and replies with $a_i \leftarrow A_i^{\{O_\theta(\cdot)\}_\theta}(x_i)$. For search games, the success probability of (A, B) is

$$\varepsilon_{A,B}^{\mathsf{srch}} = \Pr\left[\{(j, a_j)\}_j \leftarrow B^{O_A^{\mathsf{srch}}} : \exists i, (i, a_i) \in b \land R(u_i, x_i, a_i) = 1\right], \tag{4}$$

---

[6] Here, $P \ll Q$ indicates that $\{x : P(x) > 0\} \subseteq \{x : Q(x) > 0\}$.

where O_A^{srch} is the oracle that, given the ith query, chooses $u_i \in \{0,1\}^n$ uniformly at random, computes $x_i \leftarrow X(u_i)$, and replies with $a_i \leftarrow A_i^{\{O_\theta(\cdot)\}_\theta}(x_i)$.

Let T_A denote the computational complexity for running the experiment

$$\left[u \xleftarrow{R} \{0,1\}^n; x \leftarrow X(u); a \leftarrow A^{\{O_\theta(\cdot)\}_\theta}(x) \right].$$

For simplicity, we call T_A the computational complexity (or cost) of A. We can employ various computational complexity measures, such as time complexity and circuit complexity, as T_A. The only restriction is that an N-times use of the same algorithm of cost T can be done with cost NT. The bit security of an n-bit game $G = (X, R, \{O_\theta\}_\theta)$ for error probability μ is defined to be

$$\text{BS}_G^\mu := \min_{A,B} \left\{ \log_2(N_{A,B} \cdot T_A) : \varepsilon_{A,B} \geq 1 - \mu \right\}$$

$$= \min_A \left\{ \log_2 T_A + \log_2 \min_B \{ N_{A,B} : \varepsilon_{A,B} \geq 1 - \mu \} \right\},$$

where $N_{A,B}$ is the number of invocations to A made by the outer adversary B and $\varepsilon_{A,B}$ is $\varepsilon_{A,B}^{\text{decn}}$ for $n = 1$, and is $\varepsilon_{A,B}^{\text{srch}}$ for $n \gg 1$. We say G has λ-bit security if $\text{BS}_G^\mu \geq \lambda$.

Roughly speaking, the bit security of the game is at least λ if the computational complexity of the adversary for achieving the success probability $1 - \mu$ is at least 2^λ. The bit security is defined without taking into account the computational complexity of B. The reason is that the complexity of B can be relatively small compared to the total computational complexity; See [20] for details.

In [20], the authors showed that the bit security of decision games could be characterized as[7]

$$\text{BS}_G^\mu = \min_A \left\{ \log_2 T_A + \log_2 \left\lceil \frac{1}{\text{Adv}_{G,A}^{\text{Renyi}}} \right\rceil \right\} + \mathcal{O}(1). \tag{5}$$

where the *Rényi advantage* is defined as

$$\text{Adv}_{G,A}^{\text{Renyi}} := D_{1/2}(A_0 \| A_1),$$

where A_u is the output distribution of A in the game G under the condition that $u \in \{0,1\}$ is chosen in the game. For the case of search games, the bit security is characterized by the winning probability of A as usual. See Appendix A for the detailed statements. When we want to emphasize that A_u is the conditional distribution of the output of A given secret value $U = u$, we denote $P_{A|U}(\cdot|u)$. We use A_u and $P_{A|U}(\cdot|u)$ interchangeably in the rest of the paper. For simplicity, we may write $\text{Adv}_A^{\text{Renyi}}$ for $\text{Adv}_{G,A}^{\text{Renyi}}$.

In [20], the bit security was defined based on a game in which an inner adversary outputs $a \in \{0,1\}^n$. However, the general results in [20, Section 3], where (5) and the theorems in Appendix A were derived, do not depend on

---

[7] The ceiling function appears since the inner adversary must be invoked at least once even if the Rényi advantage is larger than 1.

the fact that $a \in \{0,1\}^n$. Thus, for the convenience of relating the bit security defined in [20] with another one in [16], we allow an inner adversary to output the failure symbol $\perp$.

For an adversary A for a decision game, we write $A_u = (A_u(0), A_u(1), A_u(\perp))$ for $u \in \{0,1\}$. We may simply write $A_u = (A_u(0), A_u(1))$ if A never outputs $\perp$.

4 Rényi Advantage and Conditional Squared Advantage

This section discusses the connection between the Rényi advantage and the advantage used in [16], which we term the conditional squared (CS) advantage. The former was used in [20] to characterize their notion of bit security for decision games; on the other hand, the latter was used in [16] to characterize their notion of bit security for decision games.

Let $\psi : \{0, 1, \perp\} \to \{1, 0, -1\}$ be the function given by $\psi(0) = 1$, $\psi(1) = -1$, and $\psi(\perp) = 0$. Then, we define (see also Appendix B)

$$\mathsf{Adv}_A^{\mathrm{CS}} := \mathbb{E}\left[\frac{\psi(A)}{\sqrt{\mathbb{E}[\psi(A)^2]}}\psi(U)\right]^2 \tag{6}$$

$$= \frac{4\left(\Pr(A = U) - \frac{1}{2}\Pr(A \neq \perp)\right)^2}{\Pr(A \neq \perp)} \tag{7}$$

$$= \Pr(A \neq \perp)\left(2\Pr(A = U | A \neq \perp) - 1\right)^2. \tag{8}$$

It can be verified that $0 \leq \mathsf{Adv}_A^{\mathrm{CS}} \leq 1$. Historically speaking, the expression (6) was introduced by Levin in [15]; the expression (7) was introduced (up to the constant factor of 4) by Hast in [13, Theorem 3] to characterize the success probability of the modified Goldreich-Levin algorithm; Micciancio and Walter introduced the expression (8) in [16, Theorem 1, Definition 10], and they initiated the use of this quantity as an advantage to characterize their notion of bit security.

Although the two notions of advantages $\mathsf{Adv}_A^{\mathrm{Renyi}}$ and $\mathsf{Adv}_A^{\mathrm{CS}}$ appear to be different quantities, in fact, they are closely related quantitatively. We first show that $\mathsf{Adv}_A^{\mathrm{CS}}$ can be upper bounded by $\mathsf{Adv}_A^{\mathrm{Renyi}}$ up to a constant.

Theorem 1. *For an arbitrary adversary A for decision games, it holds that*

$$\mathsf{Adv}_A^{\mathrm{CS}} \leq 4\mathsf{Adv}_A^{\mathrm{Renyi}}. \tag{9}$$

Proof. First, by noting that

$$\Pr(A \neq \perp) = \frac{1}{2}\left(A_0(0) + A_1(0) + A_0(1) + A_1(1)\right)$$

and

$$2\Pr(A = U) - \Pr(A \neq \perp) = \frac{1}{2}\left(A_0(0) - A_1(0) + A_1(1) - A_0(1)\right),$$

we can bound $\mathsf{Adv}_A^{\mathsf{CS}}$ as

$$
\begin{aligned}
\mathsf{Adv}_A^{\mathsf{CS}} &= \frac{(A_0(0) - A_1(0) + A_1(1) - A_0(1))^2}{2(A_0(0) + A_1(0) + A_0(1) + A_1(1))} \\
&\leq \frac{(|A_0(0) - A_1(0)| + |A_1(1) - A_0(1)|)^2}{2(A_0(0) + A_1(0) + A_0(1) + A_1(1))} \\
&\leq \max_{a \in \{0,1\}} \frac{4(A_0(a) - A_1(a))^2}{2(A_0(0) + A_1(0) + A_0(1) + A_1(1))} \\
&\leq \max_{a \in \{0,1\}} \frac{2(A_0(a) - A_1(a))^2}{A_0(a) + A_1(a)}.
\end{aligned}
\tag{10}
$$

Next, by noting that the inequality

$$
(s - t)^2 = ((\sqrt{s} - \sqrt{t})(\sqrt{s} + \sqrt{t}))^2 \leq 2(\sqrt{s} - \sqrt{t})^2
$$

holds for any $0 \leq s, t \leq 1$ satisfying $s + t = 1$, we have

$$
\begin{aligned}
\frac{2(A_0(a) - A_1(a))^2}{A_0(a) + A_1(a)} &= 2(A_0(a) + A_1(a)) \left(\frac{A_0(a)}{A_0(a) + A_1(a)} - \frac{A_1(a)}{A_0(a) + A_1(a)} \right)^2 \\
&\leq 4(A_0(a) + A_1(a)) \left(\sqrt{\frac{A_0(a)}{A_0(a) + A_1(a)}} - \sqrt{\frac{A_1(a)}{A_0(a) + A_1(a)}} \right)^2 \\
&= 4 \left(\sqrt{A_0(a)} - \sqrt{A_1(a)} \right)^2 \\
&\leq 4 \sum_{a' \in \{0,1,\perp\}} \left(\sqrt{A_0(a')} - \sqrt{A_1(a')} \right)^2 \\
&= 8 d_{\mathsf{HD}}(A_0, A_1)^2
\end{aligned}
\tag{11}
$$

for every $a \in \{0,1\}$. Thus, by combining (10) and (11), and by using the left inequality of (2), we have (9).   □

Theorem 1 implies that, up to constant bits, if a decision game is λ bit secure in [20], then it is also λ bit secure in the sense of [16].

In general, it is not possible to derive an upper bound on $\mathsf{Adv}_A^{\mathsf{Renyi}}$ in terms of $\mathsf{Adv}_A^{\mathsf{CS}}$. For instance, for the inversion attack mentioned in Sect. 1, $\mathsf{Adv}_A^{\mathsf{Renyi}} = \Theta(\varepsilon)$ while $\mathsf{Adv}_A^{\mathsf{CS}} = \varepsilon^2$. However, for a given adversary A, we can always construct an adversary $\tilde{A}$ having the same cost and $\mathsf{Adv}_{\tilde{A}}^{\mathsf{CS}}$ is as large as $\mathsf{Adv}_A^{\mathsf{Renyi}}$.

Theorem 2. *For an adversary A of a decision game satisfying $\mathsf{Adv}_A^{\mathsf{Renyi}} \leq 1$, there exists an adversary $\tilde{A}$ having the same cost as A, and it satisfies*

$$
\mathsf{Adv}_A^{\mathsf{Renyi}} \leq 12 \mathsf{Adv}_{\tilde{A}}^{\mathsf{CS}}.
$$

Proof. To prove Theorem 2, we use the following lemma from [16, Lemma 1]. Since the proof was absent in [16], we also give a proof for completeness.

Lemma 3 ([16]). *For a given adversary A of a decision game and for each symbol $z \in \{0, 1, \perp\}$, let $\tilde{A}^z$ be an adversary defined as follows: first $\tilde{A}^z$ run A; if the output a of A satisfies $a = z$ and $A_0(z) \geq A_1(z)$, then $\tilde{A}^z$ outputs 0; if the output a of A satisfies $a = z$ and $A_0(z) < A_1(z)$, then $\tilde{A}^z$ outputs 1; otherwise (i.e., $a \neq z$), $\tilde{A}^z$ outputs $\perp$.[8] Then, $\tilde{A}^z$ has the same cost as A and satisfies*

$$\mathsf{Adv}_{\tilde{A}^z}^{\mathsf{CS}} = \frac{1}{2} \frac{(A_0(z) - A_1(z))^2}{(A_0(z) + A_1(z))}. \tag{12}$$

Proof. The probability that $\tilde{A}^z$ does not output $\perp$ is $\Pr(\tilde{A}^z \neq \perp) = \frac{A_0(z) + A_1(z)}{2}$, and the probability that $\tilde{A}^z$ outputs the correct value is $\Pr(\tilde{A}_z = U) = \frac{A_0(z)}{2}$ if $A_0(z) \geq A_1(z)$ and $\Pr(\tilde{A}_z = U) = \frac{A_1(z)}{2}$ if $A_0(z) < A_1(z)$. Thus, by substituting these probabilities into (7), we have (12). $\qquad\square$

Now, we are ready to prove Theorem 2. Under the assumption $\mathsf{Adv}_A^{\mathsf{Renyi}} \leq 1$, (2) implies

$$
\begin{aligned}
\mathsf{Adv}_A^{\mathsf{Renyi}} &= D_{1/2}(A_0 \| A_1) \\
&\leq 4 d_{\mathsf{HD}}(A_0, A_1)^2 \\
&= 2 \sum_{a \in \{0,1,\perp\}} (\sqrt{A_0(a)} - \sqrt{A_1(a)})^2 \\
&\leq 6 \max_{a \in \{0,1,\perp\}} (\sqrt{A_0(a)} - \sqrt{A_1(a)})^2 \\
&= 6 \max_{a \in \{0,1,\perp\}} \frac{(A_0(a) - A_1(a))^2}{(\sqrt{A_0(a)} + \sqrt{A_1(a)})^2} \\
&\leq 6 \max_{a \in \{0,1,\perp\}} \frac{(A_0(a) - A_1(a))^2}{(A_0(a) + A_1(a))}.
\end{aligned}
$$

Thus, by Lemma 3, we can construct an adversary $\tilde{A}$ satisfying the claim of the theorem. $\qquad\square$

Since $\mathsf{Adv}_A^{\mathsf{Renyi}}$ can be unbounded while $\mathsf{Adv}_{\tilde{A}}^{\mathsf{CS}} \leq 1$, the assumption $\mathsf{Adv}_A^{\mathsf{Renyi}} \leq 1$ in Theorem 2 is crucial. Even though $\mathsf{Adv}_A^{\mathsf{Renyi}}$ can be larger than 1 in general, by using Theorem 2 together with an additional argument, we can show that λ bit security in the sense of [16] implies λ bit security in the sense of [20] up to constant bits as follows. To prove the contraposition, suppose that there exists an adversary A such that $\log T_A + \log\lceil 1/\mathsf{Adv}_A^{\mathsf{Renyi}}\rceil$ is smaller than λ (i.e., not λ bit secure in the sense of [20]). If $\mathsf{Adv}_A^{\mathsf{Renyi}} \leq 1$, we can directly apply Theorem 2 and conclude that the game is not λ bit secure in the sense of [16] as well. When $\mathsf{Adv}_A^{\mathsf{Renyi}} > 1$, for a parameter $0 \leq \theta \leq 1$, let us consider the following adversary A^θ. First, A^θ flips a coin C that takes 1 with probability θ and 0 with probability $1 - \theta$; when $C = 1$, A^θ runs A and outputs A's outcome; when $C = 0$,

---

[8] Note that $\tilde{A}^z$ outputs only one of 0 or 1 and $\perp$ with positive probability.

A^θ always outputs $\perp$. Then, the cost of this adversary is $T_{A^\theta} = T_A + \mathcal{O}(1),$[9] and the distributions of outcomes can be written as $A_u^\theta = \theta A_u + (1 - \theta)A_{\texttt{triv}}$, where $A_{\texttt{triv}}(\perp) = 1$. By the joint convexity of the Rényi divergence of order $1/2$ [19, Theorem 11], we can verify that the Rényi advantage of A^θ given by

$$\mathsf{Adv}_{A^\theta}^{\mathrm{Renyi}} = D_{1/2}(\theta A_0 + (1 - \theta)A_{\texttt{triv}} \| \theta A_1 + (1 - \theta)A_{\texttt{triv}})$$

is a convex (and thus continuous) function of $0 \leq \theta \leq 1$, and $\mathsf{Adv}_{A^0}^{\mathrm{Renyi}} = 0$ and $\mathsf{Adv}_{A^1}^{\mathrm{Renyi}} = \mathsf{Adv}_A^{\mathrm{Renyi}}$. Thus, there exists θ' such that $\mathsf{Adv}_{A^{\theta'}}^{\mathrm{Renyi}} = 1$. Since $\log T_{A^{\theta'}}$ is smaller than $\lambda + \mathcal{O}(1)$, by applying Theorem 2, we can show the existence of an adversary $\tilde{A}^{\theta'}$ such that $\log T_{\tilde{A}^{\theta'}} + \log(1/\mathsf{Adv}_{\tilde{A}^{\theta'}}^{\mathrm{CS}})$ is smaller than λ up to a constant, which implies that the game is not λ bit secure in the sense of [16].

4.1   A Sufficient Condition that $\mathsf{Adv}_A^{\mathrm{Renyi}} \leq 1$

We observe that the Rényi advantage must be at most 1 for some class of decision games, although it is generally unbounded by definition. Intuitively, the class consists of games such that the game for $u = 0$ is identical to the game for $u = 1$ with some probability.

Let G be a decision game. We write $G = (G_0, G_1)$, where G_u is the game when the secret is $u \in \{0,1\}$. We say game G is *identical to game G' with probability p* if G is equal to G' with probability p and is equal to some game G'' with probability $1 - p$.

Proposition 1. *Let $G = (G_0, G_1)$ be a decision game. If G_u is identical to G_{1-u} with probability at least $1/e$ for some $u \in \{0,1\}$, then $\mathsf{Adv}_A^{\mathrm{Renyi}} \leq 1$ for any adversary A.*

Proof. Without loss of generality, we assume that G_0 is identical to G_1 with probability $\gamma \geq 1/e$. For an adversary A for game G, suppose that the output distribution when $u = 0$ is $A_0 = (p_0, p_1, p_\perp)$, where $p_0 + p_1 + p_\perp = 1$. Let $A_1 = (p_0', p_1', p_\perp')$ be the output distribution when $u = 1$. By assumption, we have $p_a' \geq \gamma \cdot p_a$ for every $a \in \{0, 1, \perp\}$. Thus,

$$\sum_{a \in \{0,1,\perp\}} \sqrt{A_0(a)A_1(a)} = \sum_{a \in \{0,1,\perp\}} \sqrt{p_a \cdot p_a'} \geq \sqrt{\gamma} \geq \sqrt{1/e}.$$

Hence, we have

$$\mathsf{Adv}_A^{\mathrm{Renyi}} = -2\ln \sum_{a \in \{0,1,\perp\}} \sqrt{A_0(a)A_1(a)} \leq -2\ln(\sqrt{1/e}) = 1.$$

$\square$

---

[9] We assume that the cost is evaluated with respect to the worst case, such as the circuit size. If the cost is evaluated on average, T_{A^θ} is as small as $\theta T_A + \mathcal{O}(1)$. However, we only use the fact that T_{A^θ} is smaller than $T_A + \mathcal{O}(1)$ in the following argument.

The hard-core predicate *distinguishing* game described in Sect. 5.1 satisfies the condition in the proposition. In this game, the adversary receives $(f(x), h(x))$ for random input x when $u = 0$, and $(f(x), \sigma)$ for random bit σ when $u = 1$, where f is a one-way function and h is its hard-core predicate. Since the probability distribution of $(f(x), \sigma)$ is equal to the distribution $\frac{1}{2}(f(x), h(x)) + \frac{1}{2}(f(x), 1 - h(x))$, the game for $u = 1$ is identical to the game for $u = 0$ with probability $1/2$, which is at least $1/e$.

Note also that the Rényi advantage of an adversary cannot be larger than the Rényi advantage achieved by computationally unbounded adversaries. In the case of the above-mentioned hard-core predicate, we can verify that the Rényi divergence between the distributions of $(f(x), h(x))$ and $(f(x), \sigma)$ is bounded by 1.

4.2 Comparison

Even though Theorem 1 and Theorem 2 imply that the two notions of bit security in [16,20] are equivalent within a constant, we stress that two quantities coincide only when we optimize over adversaries. In this section, we illustrate the difference between the two notions of bit security for a typical attack that may occur in the privately-verifiable primitives.

Difference in Privately-Verifiable Primitives. Let us consider an attack against a decision Diffie-Hellman (DDH) problem using an oracle for a computational Diffie-Hellman (CDH) problem. Let G be a polynomial-time group-generation algorithm that outputs a description of a cyclic group $\mathbb{G}$ of prime order p and a generator $g \in \mathbb{G}$. The CDH problem is to compute g^{xy} from (g^x, g^y) for random $x, y \in \mathbb{Z}_p$. The success probability of an adversary A' for the CDH game of G is defined by

$$\varepsilon_{A'}^{\mathrm{cdh}} = \Pr\left[(\mathbb{G}, p, g) \leftarrow G; x, y \xleftarrow{R} \mathbb{Z}_p; a \leftarrow A(\mathbb{G}, p, g, g^x, g^y) : a = g^{xy}\right]$$

The DDH problem is to distinguish (g^x, g^y, g^z) from (g^x, g^y, g^{xy}) for random $x, y, z \in \mathbb{Z}_p$. The success probability of A for the DDH game of G is defined by

$$\varepsilon_A^{\mathrm{ddh}} = \Pr\left[\begin{array}{l} u \xleftarrow{R} \{0,1\}; (\mathbb{G}, p, g) \leftarrow G; \\ x, y, z \xleftarrow{R} \mathbb{Z}_p; (g_0, g_1) = (g^{xy}, g^z) \end{array} : u \leftarrow A(\mathbb{G}, p, g, g^x, g^y, g_u)\right].$$

Let us consider the following adversary A for DDH invoking A' as an oracle for CDH. Given (g^x, g^y, g_u), the adversary A invokes A' with input (g^x, g^y) to obtain a candidate w of g^{xy}. Then, if $w = g_u$, A outputs $a = 0$; otherwise, A outputs $a = 1$. For this adversary, the output distribution A_u of A given u is $A_0 = (\varepsilon_{A'}^{\mathrm{cdh}}, 1 - \varepsilon_{A'}^{\mathrm{cdh}})$ and $A_1 = (\varepsilon_{A'}^{\mathrm{cdh}}/p, 1 - \varepsilon_{A'}^{\mathrm{cdh}}/p)$. Note that, for adversary A that does not output $\perp$, the CS advantage coincides with the square of the standard advantage (total variation distance). Thus, we have $\mathsf{Adv}_A^{\mathrm{CS}} = (1 - 1/p)^2 (\varepsilon_{A'}^{\mathrm{cdh}})^2$. On the other hand, using Lemma 2, we can verify that the Rényi advantage is $\mathsf{Adv}_A^{\mathrm{Renyi}} = \Omega(\varepsilon_{A'}^{\mathrm{cdh}})$. When $\varepsilon_{A'}^{\mathrm{cdh}} \simeq 2^{-\lambda}$, this attack implies that the bit security of [16] must be at most 2λ, while that of [20] is reduced to λ.

Comparing Three Advantages. In Table 1 of Sect. 1.3, the standard advantage using the total variation distance $\mathsf{Adv}^{\mathrm{TV}}$, the CS advantage $\mathsf{Adv}^{\mathrm{CS}}$, and the Rényi advantage $\mathsf{Adv}^{\mathrm{Renyi}}$ are compared for four types of attacks: (1) balanced attack without $\perp$; (2) unbalanced attack with $\perp$; (3) unbalanced attack without $\perp$; and (4) balanced 0/1-unbalanced $\perp$ attack.

The first two attacks already appeared in Sect. 1 as the linear test attack and the inversion attack for PRG. The third attack appeared just above as the DDH attack using the CDH oracle. For comparison, we introduce another *unusual* attack for PRG as the fourth attack. Recall the situation in Sect. 1 where the adversary A, given $(f(x), z)$, tries to distinguish whether $z = h(x)$ or z is a random bit, where f is a one-way permutation, x is a random input, and h is a hard-core predicate. We consider adversary A such that A tries to invert $f(x)$ and outputs $\perp$ if the inversion succeeded and $h(x) = z$. Otherwise, A outputs a random bit. The output distribution of A consists of $A_0 = (1/2-\delta/2, 1/2-\delta/2, \delta)$ and $A_1 = (1/2 - \delta/4, 1/2 - \delta/4, \delta/2)$, where δ is the success probability of the inversion attack. Note that the CS advantage of this adversary is 0 since it outputs 0 and 1 with the same probabilities in either case of $u \in \{0, 1\}$.

For all types of attacks, the standard advantage is roughly δ. The values of $\mathsf{Adv}^{\mathrm{TV}}$ and $\mathsf{Adv}^{\mathrm{CS}}$ are computed by a straightforward calculation; the values of $\mathsf{Adv}^{\mathrm{Renyi}}$ can be derived by Lemma 1, Lemma 2, and Theorem 1. Note that the bit security of [16] is roughly $\log \frac{1}{\mathsf{Adv}^{\mathrm{CS}}}$ and that of [20] is roughly $\log \frac{1}{\mathsf{Adv}^{\mathrm{Renyi}}}$.

From the table, we can find that the two notions of bit security coincide for the first two attacks; however, there are discrepancies for the last two attacks. As discussed above, the CS advantage can be a square of the Rényi advantage for the privately-verifiable problems. Furthermore, the fourth attack demonstrates the CS advantage may take 0 even if the other advantages take $\Theta(\delta)$. Although $\mathsf{Adv}^{\mathrm{CS}}$ can be increased to the same level as $\mathsf{Adv}^{\mathrm{Renyi}}$ by using the transformation of Theorem 2, it is possible to underestimate the adversary's ability when using $\mathsf{Adv}^{\mathrm{CS}}$ as evaluation. In this sense, it seems that $\mathsf{Adv}^{\mathrm{Renyi}}$ is preferable to $\mathsf{Adv}^{\mathrm{CS}}$ when evaluating the impact of attacks.

5   Hard-Core Predicate Game

5.1   Distinguisher and Predictor

For a one-way function $f : \{0, 1\}^n \to \{0, 1\}^m$, a function $h : \{0, 1\}^n \to \{0, 1\}$ is termed a hard-core predicate if the value of $h(x)$ cannot be predicted from the function output $f(x)$. When we discuss the security of the hard-core predicate, there are two types of formulations: the prediction game and the distinguishing game. Even though it is more common to define the security of the hard-core predicate in terms of the prediction game, since the distinguishing game is more suitable for the formulation of bit security in [20], we first introduce the distinguishing game and later discuss the connection between the two formulations.

In the distinguishing game of hard-core predicate, when $u = 0$, an inner adversary A observes $(f(x), h(x))$ for random $x \in \{0, 1\}^n$; when $u = 1$, the inner adversary A observes $(f(x), \sigma)$, where σ is a random bit that is independent of

x. Based on the observation, the inner adversary A outputs an estimate a of u or $\perp$. Then, the outer adversary B invokes the inner adversary $N_{A,B}$ times so that the success probability $\varepsilon_{A,B}$ of estimating u is at least $1 - \mu$. The bit security of the hard-core predicate is defined as the minimum of $\log_2(N_{A,B} \cdot T_A)$ under the constraint $\varepsilon_{A,B} \geq 1 - \mu$, where T_A is the cost of the inner adversary.

On the other hand, in the prediction game of hard-core predicate, a predictor $\mathcal{P}$ observes $f(x)$, and outputs an estimate of $h(x)$ or $\perp$. Following the terminology in [13], a predictor $\mathcal{P}$ is said to be an (ε, δ)-*predictor* if the *rate* is

$$\delta = \Pr(\mathcal{P}(f(x)) \neq \perp)$$

and the *advantage* is

$$\varepsilon = \Pr(\mathcal{P}(f(x)) = h(x)) - \frac{1}{2}\Pr(\mathcal{P}(f(x)) \neq \perp).$$

In other words, (ε, δ)-predictor $\mathcal{P}$ has CS advantage $\mathsf{Adv}_{\mathcal{P}}^{\mathsf{CS}} = \frac{4\varepsilon^2}{\delta}$.

The following theorem connects the Rényi advantage of the distinguishing game and the CS advantage of the prediction game.

Theorem 3. *For a given one-way function f with hard-core predicate h, let A be an inner adversary for the hard-core predicate distinguishing game. Then, there exists a predictor $\mathcal{P}$ of the hard-core predicate that invokes A once and*[10]

$$\mathsf{Adv}_{\mathcal{P}}^{\mathsf{CS}} \geq \frac{1}{3}\mathsf{Adv}_{A}^{\mathsf{Renyi}}. \tag{13}$$

Proof. Using adversary A, similarly to [13, Section 6], we construct a predictor as follows. Let $P_{A|U}(\cdot|u)$ be the distribution of the output of A given u, i.e.,

$$P_{A|U}(a|0) = \Pr(A(f(x), h(x)) = a),$$
$$P_{A|U}(a|1) = \Pr(A(f(x), \sigma) = a).$$

Note the support of $(f(x), h(x))$ is included in the support of $(f(x), \sigma)$.[11] Thus, if the adversary A outputs a symbol a with positive probability under $u = 0$, then A must output a with positive probability under $u = 1$ as well, i.e., $P_{A|U}(\cdot|0) \ll P_{A|U}(\cdot|1)$.

Let $a^\star \in \{0, 1, \perp\}$ be such that $P_{A|U}(a^\star|1) > 0$ and

$$\max_{\substack{a \in \{0,1,\perp\}: \\ P_{A|U}(a|1)>0}} \frac{(P_{A|U}(a|0) - P_{A|U}(a|1))^2}{P_{A|U}(a|1)} = \frac{(P_{A|U}(a^\star|0) - P_{A|U}(a^\star|1))^2}{P_{A|U}(a^\star|1)}.$$

Then, by Lemma 1, we have

$$D_{1/2}(P_{A|U}(\cdot|0)\|P_{A|U}(\cdot|1)) \leq 3\frac{(P_{A|U}(a^\star|0) - P_{A|U}(a^\star|1))^2}{P_{A|U}(a^\star|1)}. \tag{14}$$

---

[10] As we can find from the proof, the output alphabet of A being $\{0, 1, \perp\}$ is not crucial; the same argument goes through for any output alphabet $\mathcal{A}$ if replace the factor of $\frac{1}{3}$ by $\frac{1}{|\mathcal{A}|}$ in (13).

[11] Here, the support is the set of realizations that occur with positive probability.

We consider two cases separately.

When $P_{A|U}(a^\star|0) \geq P_{A|U}(a^\star|1)$: In this case, we consider the following predictor $\mathcal{P}$. First, we sample the uniform random bit σ. Second,

- If $A(f(x), \sigma) = a^\star$, then $\mathcal{P}$ outputs σ;
- If $A(f(x), \sigma) \neq a^\star$, then $\mathcal{P}$ outputs $\bot$.

The rate of this predictor is

$$
\begin{aligned}
\delta &= \Pr(\mathcal{P}(f(x)) \neq \bot) \\
&= \Pr(A(f(x), \sigma) = a^\star) \\
&= P_{A|U}(a^\star|1).
\end{aligned}
$$

On the other hand, the success probability of the predictor is

$$
\begin{aligned}
\Pr(\mathcal{P}(f(x)) = h(x)) &= \Pr(\sigma = h(x))\Pr(A(f(x), \sigma) = a^\star|\sigma = h(x)) \\
&= \Pr(\sigma = h(x))\Pr(A(f(x), h(x)) = a^\star) \\
&= \frac{P_{A|U}(a^\star|0)}{2}.
\end{aligned}
$$

Thus, the advantage of this predictor is

$$
\begin{aligned}
\varepsilon &= \Pr(\mathcal{P}(f(x)) = h(x)) - \frac{1}{2}\Pr(\mathcal{P}(f(x)) \neq \bot) \\
&= \frac{P_{A|U}(a^\star|0) - P_{A|U}(a^\star|1)}{2}.
\end{aligned}
$$

Then, by using (14), we have

$$
\begin{aligned}
\frac{\varepsilon^2}{\delta} &= \frac{(P_{A|U}(a^\star|0) - P_{A|U}(a^\star|1))^2}{4P_{A|U}(a^\star|1)} \\
&\geq \frac{1}{12}D_{1/2}(P_{A|U}(\cdot|0)\|P_{A|U}(\cdot|1)),
\end{aligned}
$$

which implies (13).

When $P_{A|U}(a^\star|0) < P_{A|U}(a^\star|1)$: In this case, we consider the following predictor. First, we sample the uniform random bit σ. Second,

- If $A(f(x), \sigma) = a^\star$, then $\mathcal{P}$ outputs $\sigma \oplus 1$;
- If $A(f(x), \sigma) \neq a^\star$, then $\mathcal{P}$ outputs $\bot$.

The rate of this predictor is

$$
\begin{aligned}
\delta &= \Pr(\mathcal{P}(f(x)) \neq \bot) \\
&= \Pr(A(f(x), \sigma) = a^\star) \\
&= P_{A|U}(a^\star|1).
\end{aligned}
$$

On the other hand, the success probability of this predictor is

$$
\begin{aligned}
\Pr(\mathcal{P}(f(x)) = h(x)) &= \Pr(\sigma = h(x) \oplus 1, A(f(x), \sigma) = a^\star) \\
&= \Pr(A(f(x), \sigma) = a^\star) - \Pr(\sigma = h(x), A(f(x), \sigma) = a^\star) \\
&= P_{A|U}(a^\star|1) - \Pr(\sigma = h(x)) \Pr(A(f(x), \sigma) = a^\star | \sigma = h(x)) \\
&= P_{A|U}(a^\star|1) - \Pr(\sigma = h(x)) \Pr(A(f(x), h(x)) = a^\star) \\
&= P_{A|U}(a^\star|1) - \frac{P_{A|U}(a^\star|0)}{2}.
\end{aligned}
$$

Thus, the advantage of this predictor is

$$
\begin{aligned}
\varepsilon &= \Pr(\mathcal{P}(f(x)) = h(x)) - \frac{1}{2}\Pr(\mathcal{P}(f(x)) \neq \perp) \\
&= \frac{P_{A|U}(a^\star|1) - P_{A|U}(a^\star|0)}{2}.
\end{aligned}
$$

Then, by using (14), we have

$$
\begin{aligned}
\frac{\varepsilon^2}{\delta} &= \frac{(P_{A|U}(a^\star|1) - P_{A|U}(a^\star|0))^2}{4P_{A|U}(a^\star|1)} \\
&\geq \frac{1}{12} D_{1/2}(P_{A|U}(\cdot|0) \| P_{A|U}(\cdot|1)),
\end{aligned}
$$

which implies (13).   □

As a corollary of Theorem 3, we show that the CS advantage of the adversary for the hard-core predicate (distinguishing) game can be bounded below by the Rényi advantage (divided by twelve).

Corollary 1. *For a given one-way function f with hard-core predicate h, let A be an inner adversary for the distinguishing game. Then, there exists an adversary A' of the hard-core predicate distinguishing game that invokes A once and*

$$
\mathsf{Adv}_{A'}^{\mathrm{CS}} \geq \frac{1}{12}\mathsf{Adv}_A^{\mathrm{Renyi}}.
$$

Proof. By Theorem 3, there exists an (ε, δ)-predictor $\mathcal{P}$ that invokes A once and $\frac{\varepsilon^2}{\delta} \geq \frac{1}{12}\mathsf{Adv}_A^{\mathrm{Renyi}}$. Let A' be an adversary defined as follows for given input $(f(x), z)$:

- If $\mathcal{P}(f(x)) = z$, then A' outputs 0;
- If $\mathcal{P}(f(x)) = z \oplus 1$, then A' outputs 1;
- If $\mathcal{P}(f(x)) = \perp$, then A' outputs $\perp$.

Obviously, the rate of this adversary is

$$
\Pr(A'(f(x), z)) \neq \perp) = \Pr(\mathcal{P}(f(x)) \neq \perp) = \delta.
$$

Furthermore, the advantage of this adversary is

$$\Pr(A'(f(x), z) = U) - \frac{1}{2}\Pr(A'(f(x), z) \neq \bot)$$

$$= \frac{1}{2}\Pr(\mathcal{P}(f(x)) = h(x)) + \frac{1}{2}\Pr(\mathcal{P}(f(x)) = \sigma \oplus 1) - \frac{1}{2}\Pr(A'(f(x), z) \neq \bot)$$

$$= \frac{1}{2}\Pr(\mathcal{P}(f(x)) = h(x)) + \frac{1}{2}\Pr(\mathcal{P}(f(x)) \neq \bot) \cdot \frac{1}{2} - \frac{1}{2}\Pr(A'(f(x), z) \neq \bot)$$

$$= \frac{1}{2}\varepsilon.$$

Thus, the CS advantage of this adversary is $\mathsf{Adv}_{A'}^{\mathsf{CS}} = \frac{\varepsilon^2}{\delta} \geq \frac{1}{12}\mathsf{Adv}_A^{\mathsf{Renyi}}$. $\qquad\square$

5.2   Reduction by Goldreich-Levin Algorithm

For a given one-way function $f(x)$, let $g(x, r) = (f(x), r)$ be a function from $\{0, 1\}^n \times \{0, 1\}^n$ to $\{0, 1\}^m \times \{0, 1\}^n$. Then, it is known that $h(x, r) = x \cdot r$ plays a role in the hard-core predicate. This section aims to connect the bit security of $g(x, r)$ and the bit security of the hard-core predicate $h(x, r)$. To that end, we consider the reduction algorithm, the so-called Goldreich-Levin algorithm. In order to evaluate the efficiency of the Goldreich-Levin algorithm, we use the following result by Hast [13].

Theorem 4 ([13])**.**   *Let $\mathcal{P}$ be a predictor of the hard-core $h(x, r) = x \cdot r$ with cost $T_{\mathcal{P}}$. Define $t = \log(4/\mathsf{Adv}_{\mathcal{P}}^{\mathsf{CS}})$. Then, there exists an algorithm Inv that runs in cost (expected time) $(T_{\mathcal{P}} + t \log n) \cdot t \cdot \mathcal{O}(n^2)$ and satisfies*

$$\Pr_{x \in_R \{0,1\}^n} \left(f(\mathsf{Inv}(f(x))) = f(x) \right) = \Omega\left(\mathsf{Adv}_{\mathcal{P}}^{\mathsf{CS}} \right).$$

By combining Theorem 4 and Theorem 3, we have the following estimate of the efficiency of the Goldreich-Levin algorithm in terms of the bit security, which is a generalization of [20, Theorem 4] for adversaries without β-balanced assumption.

Theorem 5. *Let $f : \{0, 1\}^n \to \{0, 1\}^m$ be a λ-bit secure one-way function. Then, for a function $g(x, r) = (f(x), r)$, the function $h(x, r) = x \cdot r$ is a $(\lambda - \alpha)$-bit secure hard-core predicate for g, where $\alpha = \log\left(((\lambda + 2)\log n) \cdot (\lambda + 2) \cdot \mathcal{O}(n^2) \right) + \log \ln(1/\mu) + \mathcal{O}(1)$.*

Proof. Assume for contradiction that h is not $(\lambda - \alpha)$-bit secure hard-core for g. Then, by Theorem 9, there exists an inner adversary A (for the distinguishing game of the hard-core predicate) such that the cost is T_A and the Rényi advantage is

$$\mathsf{Adv}_A^{\mathsf{Renyi}} > \frac{T_A}{2^{(\lambda - \alpha)}} \cdot \ln(1/4\mu).$$

By Theorem 3, there exists a predictor $\mathcal{P}$ of the hard-core predicate h with cost T_A such that

$$\mathsf{Adv}_{\mathcal{P}}^{\mathrm{CS}} > \frac{T_A}{2^{(\lambda-\alpha)+1}} \ln(1/4\mu).$$

Then, by Theorem 4, there exists an inner adversary A' of the OWF game that run in cost $T_{A'} = (T_A + t \log n) \cdot t \cdot \mathcal{O}(n^2)$ with success probability $\varepsilon_{A'} = \Omega(T_A \cdot 2^{-(\lambda-\alpha)})$, where $t = \log(4/\mathsf{Adv}_{\mathcal{P}}^{\mathrm{CS}}) \leq \lambda+2$. It follows from Theorem 8 that the bit security of OWF game is bounded above by $\log T_{A'} + \log(1/\varepsilon_{A'}) + \log\ln(1/\mu) + 1$, which is at most[12]

$$\lambda - \alpha + \log\left(((\lambda+2)\log n) \cdot (\lambda+2) \cdot \mathcal{O}(n^2)\right) + \log\ln(1/\mu) + \mathcal{O}(1).$$

By choosing $\alpha = \log\left(((\lambda+2)\log n) \cdot (\lambda+2) \cdot \mathcal{O}(n^2)\right) + \log\ln(1/\mu) + \mathcal{O}(1)$, f is not a λ bit secure one-way function, a contradiction. Hence, the statement follows.

$\square$

6   Search Games as Decision Games

We show that every λ-bit secure search game can be formalized as a decision game with (almost) λ-bit security. The search game is usually defined such that the adversary's success probability is small enough. Hence, it seems natural to define the decision game where the adversary tries to distinguish the following two cases of *real* and *ideal* games. While the real game is almost the same as the original search game, the ideal game is an idealized one where the adversary's solution will never be approved. For example, the unforgeability game of the signature scheme is usually defined as a search game. We may define the corresponding ideal game such that the adversary cannot forge the signature. Such games often appear in game-hopping security proofs. When a party generates a secure signature of a message in a security game, we usually consider another game in which the forgery of the message is never approved. We realize the approval of the solution of the search game by adding an oracle in a decision game.

For an n-bit search game $G = (X, R, \{O_\theta\}_\theta)$, we define the *canonical decision game* G' of G such that $G' = (X, R', O')$ is a 1-bit game where the success probability of an inner adversary A is

$$\varepsilon_A = \Pr\left[\begin{array}{l} u' \xleftarrow{R} \{0,1\}; u \xleftarrow{R} \{0,1\}^n; \\ x \leftarrow X(u); a' \leftarrow A^{O'}(x) \end{array} : a' = u'\right],$$

where $O' = \{O_\theta\}_\theta \cup O_{\mathrm{aprv}}$ and O_{aprv} is an oracle that can be accessed only once and is defined as

$$O_{\mathrm{aprv}}(a) = \begin{cases} 1 & (R(u,x,a) = 1) \wedge (u' = 0) \\ 0 & \text{otherwise} \end{cases}.$$

---

[12] We assume $T_A \geq 1$.

The additional oracle O_{aprv} answers whether the given value a satisfies the relation R only when $u' = 0$. In the ideal game, where $u = 1$, the oracle always answers 0, meaning that every valid solution a is never approved.

We show that the canonical game preserves the bit security of the underlying search game. The result implies no bit-security loss in transforming original games into such idealized games. It also justifies that every search game can be defined as a decision game.

Theorem 6. *If a search game G satisfies*

$$\mathrm{BS}_G^\mu \geq \lambda + \log_2 \frac{\ln(1/\mu)}{\ln(1/4\mu)} + 2,$$

then the corresponding canonical decision game G' satisfies $\mathrm{BS}_{G'}^\mu \geq \lambda$. Conversely, if G' satisfies

$$\mathrm{BS}_{G'}^\mu \geq \lambda + \log_2 \frac{\ln(1/2\mu)}{1 - \mu} + 2,$$

then G satisfies $\mathrm{BS}_G^\mu \geq \lambda$.

Proof. Suppose that $\mathrm{BS}_{G'}^\mu < \lambda$. It follows from Theorem 9 that there is an inner adversary A with computational complexity T_A for game G' that satisfies

$$d_{\mathsf{HD}}(A_0, A_1)^2 > \frac{T_A \cdot \ln(1/4\mu)}{2^{\lambda+1}}$$

for $\lambda \geq \log_2 \ln(1/4\mu)$. By (1), we have

$$d_{\mathsf{TV}}(A_0, A_1) > \frac{T_A \cdot \ln(1/4\mu)}{2^{\lambda+1}}.$$

Since the only way that A obtains the information on u' is to make queries to O_{aprv}, the above inequality implies that A queries a value a to O_{aprv} satisfying $R(u, x, a) = 1$ with probability more than $T_A \cdot \ln(1/4\mu)/2^{\lambda+1}$. Hence, A can be used as an inner adversary of the search game G. Namely, the inner adversary simulates A and monitors the oracle queries of A. If A queries a to the oracle O_{aprv}, the adversary outputs a. It follows from Theorem 8 that

$$\mathrm{BS}_G^\mu < \log_2 T_A + \lambda + 1 - \log_2(T_A \cdot \ln(1/4\mu)) + \log_2 \ln(1/\mu) + 1$$
$$= \lambda + \log_2 \frac{\ln(1/\mu)}{\ln(1/4\mu)} + 2,$$

a contradiction.

For the other direction, suppose that $\mathrm{BS}_G^\mu < \lambda$. Theorem 2 of [20] implies that there is an inner adversary A with computational complexity T_A for game G that satisfies the success probability

$$\varepsilon_A > \frac{T_A(1 - \mu)}{2^\lambda}.$$

Consider an inner adversary A' of game G' that simulates $a \leftarrow A$ and queries a to O_{aprv}. Finally, A' outputs 0 if the answer from O_{aprv} is 1, and 1 otherwise. The computational complexity of A' is T_A. Let $A'_{u'}$ be the output distribution of A' when $u' \in \{0,1\}$ is chosen as a secret. Then, $\Pr[A'_0 = 0] > T_A(1-\mu)/2^\lambda$ and $\Pr[A'_1 = 0] = 0$. By using [20, Lemma 8] with $q = 0$, we have

$$D_{1/2}(A'_0 \| A'_1) > \frac{T_A(1-\mu)}{2^\lambda}.$$

Theorem 1 of [20] implies that

$$\mathrm{BS}^\mu_{G'} < \log_2 T_A + \lambda - \log_2(T_A(1-\mu)) + \log_2 \ln(1/2\mu) + 2$$
$$= \lambda + \log_2 \frac{\ln(1/2\mu)}{1-\mu} + 2,$$

a contradiction. □

Theorem 6 implies that all the security games we need to consider are decision games if a constant difference of bit security can be ignored.

7   Distribution Replacement Theorem

Let $G = (X, R, \{O_i\}_i)$ be an n-bit security game. Suppose that G uses a probability distribution Q in a black-box manner. Namely, whenever some player makes a query to Q, the player will receive a sample according to Q. We denote the game by G^Q for clarity. Let P be another distribution that is supposed to be (computationally) close to Q. The question is, when G^Q is λ-bit secure, to what extent does Q need to be indistinguishable from P to preserve that G^P is λ-bit secure? We prove a natural reduction showing that λ-bit secure indistinguishability is sufficient to replace the ideal distribution Q.

Before proving the theorem, we formally define the distribution indistinguishability game. For two distributions P and Q, let $G^{\mathrm{ind}}_{P,Q} = (X, R, O)$ be a 1-bit security game such that X is empty, the oracle O outputs a sample from P when $u = 0$, and Q otherwise, and $R(u, x, a) = 1 \Leftrightarrow u = a$. Namely, the game is to discriminate between P and Q by oracle queries. For example, if $D_{1/2}(P\|Q) \leq 2^{-\lambda}$, the number of samples needed to distinguish P from Q must be $\Omega(2^\lambda)$, which is a standard result of the Bayesian hypothesis testing. Since the number of samples is a lower bound of the computational complexity for the discrimination with high probability, the bit security must be at least $\lambda - \mathcal{O}(1)$.

Due to Theorem 6, it is sufficient to prove the theorem for decision games.

Theorem 7. *Let G^Q be a 1-bit security game with black-box access to distribution Q. Let P be a probability distribution such that game $G^{\mathrm{ind}}_{P,Q}$ has λ-bit security. If game G^Q has λ-bit security, then game G^P has $(\lambda - \alpha)$-bit security for $\alpha = 3 + \log_2(\ln(1/2\mu)/\ln(1/4\mu))$.*

Proof. Suppose that G^P is not $(\lambda - \alpha)$-bit secure. By Theorem 9, there is an inner adversary A for game G^P with computational complexity T_A such that

$$d_{\mathsf{HD}}(A_0^P, A_1^P) > \sqrt{\frac{T_A \cdot \ln(1/4\mu)}{2^{\lambda-\alpha+1}}} \qquad (15)$$

for $\lambda \geq \log_2 \ln(1/4\mu)$, where A_u^P is the output distribution of A when $u \in \{0,1\}$ is chosen in G^P. We define A_0^Q and A_1^Q for the game G^Q similarly.

For a 1-bit game G, we write $G := (G_0, G_1)$, where G_u is the game G in which the secret bit $u \in \{0,1\}$ is chosen. In other words, G is the game where a secret bit $u \in \{0,1\}$ is randomly chosen and plays game G_u.

By following the above notation, we write $G^D = (G_0^D, G_1^D)$ for $D \in \{P, Q\}$. Also, we define a new game $G_u^{P,Q} := (G_u^P, G_u^Q)$. Consider an inner adversary A for the game G^D. For $u \in \{0,1\}$ and $D \in \{P, Q\}$, let A_u^D be the output distribution of A in G^D when u is chosen as the secret bit. Then, by definition, we have

$$\mathsf{Adv}_{G^D,A}^{\mathrm{Renyi}} = D_{1/2}(A_0^D \| A_1^D) \quad \text{and} \quad \mathsf{Adv}_{G_u^{P,Q},A}^{\mathrm{Renyi}} = D_{1/2}(A_u^P \| A_u^Q)$$

for $u \in \{0,1\}$ and $D \in \{P, Q\}$.

We show that the Rényi advantage of A in game $G_u^{P,Q}$ is bounded by that in $G_{P,Q}^{\mathrm{ind}}$. We construct an inner adversary $\tilde{A}$ for the game $G_{P,Q}^{\mathrm{ind}}$ by using A. The adversary $\tilde{A}$ runs the game $G_u^{P,Q}$ in which A plays. Whenever the game makes an oracle query, $\tilde{A}$ replies with an answer obtained by querying to the oracle O. By definition of $G_{P,Q}^{\mathrm{ind}}$, each answer from O is an independent sample according to P if the secret bit $\tilde{u}$ of $G_{P,Q}^{\mathrm{ind}}$ is 0, and Q otherwise. Thus, $\tilde{A}$ correctly simulates A in the game G_u^P when $\tilde{u} = 0$, and G_u^Q otherwise. Finally, $\tilde{A}$ outputs the same value as those of A in $G_u^{P,Q}$. Note that $\tilde{A}$ is an inner adversary of $G_{P,Q}^{\mathrm{ind}}$ and its computational complexity is T_A. Since $G_{P,Q}^{\mathrm{ind}}$ has λ-bit security, it follows from Theorem 8 that

$$\lambda \leq \mathsf{BS}_{G_{P,Q}^{\mathrm{ind}}}^{\mu} \leq \log_2\left(\frac{T_A \cdot \ln(1/2\mu)}{\mathsf{Adv}_{G_{P,Q}^{\mathrm{ind}},\tilde{A}}^{\mathrm{Renyi}}}\right), \qquad (16)$$

where $\mathsf{Adv}_{G_{P,Q}^{\mathrm{ind}},\tilde{A}}^{\mathrm{Renyi}} = D_{1/2}(\tilde{A}^P \| \tilde{A}^Q)$, and $\tilde{A}^D$ is the output distribution of $\tilde{A}$ in game $G_{P,Q}^{\mathrm{ind}}$ when the oracle outputs a sample according to D. Since $\tilde{A}$ correctly simulates A in the game $G_u^{P,Q}$, we have

$$\mathsf{Adv}_{G_{P,Q}^{\mathrm{ind}},\tilde{A}}^{\mathrm{Renyi}} = \mathsf{Adv}_{G_u^{P,Q},A}^{\mathrm{Renyi}} = D_{1/2}(A_u^P \| A_u^Q). \qquad (17)$$

Thus, by (2), (16), and (17),

$$d_{\mathsf{HD}}(A_u^P, A_u^Q) \leq \sqrt{\frac{1}{2} \cdot D_{1/2}(A_u^P \| A_u^Q)} \leq \sqrt{\frac{T_A \cdot \ln(1/2\mu)}{2^{\lambda+1}}} \qquad (18)$$

for $u \in \{0, 1\}$.

The triangle inequality of d_{HD} and (18) implies that

$$d_{\mathsf{HD}}(A_0^P, A_1^P) \leq d_{\mathsf{HD}}(A_0^P, A_0^Q) + d_{\mathsf{HD}}(A_0^Q, A_1^Q) + d_{\mathsf{HD}}(A_1^Q, A_1^P)$$

$$\leq d_{\mathsf{HD}}(A_0^Q, A_1^Q) + \sqrt{\frac{T_A \cdot \ln(1/2\mu)}{2^{\lambda-1}}}. \tag{19}$$

It follows from (15) and (19) that

$$d_{\mathsf{HD}}(A_0^Q, A_1^Q) > \sqrt{\frac{T_A \cdot \ln(1/4\mu)}{2^{\lambda-\alpha+1}}} - \sqrt{\frac{T_A \cdot \ln(1/2\mu)}{2^{\lambda-1}}}$$

$$\geq \sqrt{\frac{2T_A \cdot \ln(1/2\mu)}{2^{\lambda}}}$$

by assumption on α. Then, we have

$$\mathsf{Adv}_{A,G^Q}^{\mathrm{Renyi}} = D_{1/2}(A_0^Q \| A_1^Q) \geq 2d_{\mathsf{HD}}(A_0^Q, A_1^Q)^2 > \frac{4T_A \cdot \ln(1/2\mu)}{2^{\lambda}}.$$

By Theorem 8, the bit security of G^Q is at most

$$\log_2 T_A + \log_2 \left(\frac{1}{\mathsf{Adv}_{A,G^Q}^{\mathrm{Renyi}}} \right) + \log_2 \ln(1/2\mu) + 2 < \lambda,$$

a contradiction. Therefore, we have shown that G^P is $(\lambda - \alpha)$-bit secure. $\quad\square$

Theorem 7 is a generalization of [20, Theorem 9], where the condition is that $d_{\mathsf{HD}}(P, Q) \leq 2^{-\lambda/2}$. The above theorem only requires a computational condition that $G_{P,Q}^{\mathrm{ind}}$ has λ-bit security.

7.1   Application to Randomness Extraction

A randomness extractor is a procedure that converts a min-entropy source to an almost uniform distribution. The *min-entropy* of distribution X over $\{0, 1\}^n$ is defined as $H_{\mathsf{min}}(X) = -\log_2 \max_{x \in \{0,1\}^n} P_X(x)$. Here, we define a seeded extractor through a 1-bit security game.

Definition 1. *A function* $\mathsf{Ext} : \{0,1\}^n \times \{0,1\}^d \to \{0,1\}^m$ *is said to be a* (k, λ)-*extractor if for every distribution* X *over* $\{0,1\}^n$ *with* $H_{\mathsf{min}}(X) \geq k$, *a 1-bit security game* $G_{\mathsf{Ext},X}^{\mathrm{ext}} := G_{P,Q}^{\mathrm{ind}}$ *has* λ-*bit security for* $P = (\mathsf{Ext}(X, S), S)$ *and* $Q = U_{m+d}$, *where* $S = U_d$.

The above is a definition of a *computational* extractor. We can define an *information-theoretic* extractor as usual. Although the total variation distance is usually used for the definition, the Rényi divergence of order $1/2$ is a natural choice for cryptographic purposes, as we have seen so far. We say Ext is a (k, ε)-*it-extractor* if for every distribution X with $H_{\mathsf{min}}(X) \geq k$,

$$D_{1/2}((\mathsf{Ext}(X, S), S) \| U_{m+d}) \leq \varepsilon.$$

We can see that if Ext is a $(k, 2^{-\lambda})$-it-extractor, then Ext is a (k, λ)-extractor.

It is well-known that a family of universal hash functions gives an information-theoretic extractor. The claim is also known as *the leftover hash lemma (LHL)* [6,14]. Although the lemma usually says that the extractor's output is close to the uniform distribution in the total variation distance, we need the closeness in the Rényi divergence of order $1/2$. We have the following strengthened version of the leftover hash lemma.

Lemma 4 (LHL for Rényi Divergence). *Let* $\mathcal{H} = \{H : \{0,1\}^n \to \{0,1\}^m\}$ *be a* universal *family of hash functions; Namely, for any distinct* $x, x' \in \{0,1\}^n$, $\Pr_{H \sim \mathcal{H}}(H(x) = H(x')) \leq 2^{-m}$. *Suppose that* $|\mathcal{H}| = 2^d$ *and* $m = k - \lambda - 1$. *Then, function* Ext $: \{0,1\}^n \times \{0,1\}^d \to \{0,1\}^m$ *defined by* Ext$(x, H) = H(x)$ *is a* $(k, 2^{-\lambda})$-*it-extractor.*

Proof. It is shown in [21, Theorem 3] that the construction of Ext gives an extractor for the Hellinger distance[13]. Namely, for the defined parameters, we have that
$$d_{\mathsf{HD}}((\mathsf{Ext}(X, S), S), U_{m+d}) \leq 2^{-(\lambda+2)/2}.$$
By (2), it holds that
$$D_{1/2}((\mathsf{Ext}(X, S), S)\|U_{m+d}) \leq 4 \cdot d_{\mathsf{HD}}((\mathsf{Ext}(X, S), S), U_{m+d})^2 \leq 2^{-\lambda}.$$
Hence, the statement follows.   □

We apply Theorem 7 to the LHL. We consider replacing the seed of the extractor with the output of a pseudorandom generator (PRG). Suppose that $g : \{0,1\}^{d'} \to \{0,1\}^d$ is a λ-bit secure PRG. In other words, the game $G^{\mathsf{ind}}_{g(U_{d'}),U_d}$ has λ-bit security. Since the extractor of Lemma 4 is a (k, λ)-extractor, Theorem 7 guarantees that the seed of the LHL can be replaced by the output of g. Namely, the distribution $(H(X), g(S'))$ is λ-bit secure indistinguishable from the uniform distribution U_{m+d}, where X is a source with $H_{\min}(X) \geq k$, $S' = U_{d'}$, and H is randomly chosen from a family of universal hash functions using the seed $g(S')$.[14]

Entropy Loss in LHL. The *entropy loss* of (k, ε)-it-extractors Ext $: \{0,1\}^n \times \{0,1\}^d \to \{0,1\}^m$ is defined as $k - m$, which is the amount of entropy lost for extracting randomness from entropy sources. It is proved in [17] that the entropy loss of $2\log(1/\varepsilon)$ is necessary for constructing a (k, ε)-it-extractor where the closeness ε is measured in the total variation distance. Large entropy loss is critical for applications where the amount of entropy is limited, such as biometric

---

[13] The claim can also be recovered by combining the leftover hash lemma of [5] for the KL divergence D and the relation that $d_{\mathsf{HD}}(P, Q)^2 \leq D_{1/2}(P\|Q) \leq D(P\|Q)$.

[14] Barak et al. [3] studied a similar but different problem. In [3, Section 4], they considered the problem trying to achieve that $(\mathsf{Ext}(X, g(S')), S')$ is close to the uniform distribution. Namely, the seed S' of the PRG g is revealed. In our case, $g(S')$ is revealed but not S'.

information. Barak et al. [3] showed that the loss could be reduced to $\log(1/\varepsilon)$ for some applications, including several decision primitives and all search primitives. It is shown in [21] that the same entropy loss can be achieved in the framework of [16]. The entropy loss for preserving λ-bit security in the above lemma is $\lambda+1$. Thus, the framework of [20] could reduce the entropy loss in LHL by half, as similarly shown in [3,21].

8   Future Perspective

This paper has shown that the two notions of bit security in [16,20] are equivalent by proving that the CS and the Rényi advantages can be related. Thus, in future research on bit security, we can flexibly use these two advantages depending on the situation. For instance, as seen in Sect. 5, the CS advantage might be useful in the context of reduction via decoding with erasure (cf. [13]). On the other hand, we might use nice properties of the Rényi divergence, such as the convexity, to evaluate the Rényi advantage for certain types of randomized adversaries.

Acknowledgements. This work was supported in part by JSPS KAKENHI Grant Numbers 23H00468, 23K17455, and 20H02144.

A   Characterization of Bit Security of [20]

The following theorems are the characterization proved in [20].

Theorem 8. *[20, Theorem 1] Let G be an n-bit security game, and A be its inner adversary with success probability $\varepsilon_A > 0$, computational complexity T_A, and Rényi advantage $\mathsf{Adv}_A^{\mathrm{Renyi}} > 0$. Then, we have*

$$
\mathrm{BS}_G^\mu \leq \begin{cases} \log_2 T_A + \log_2\left(\frac{1}{\varepsilon_A}\right) + \log_2 \ln(1/\mu) + 1 & n > 1 \\ \log_2 T_A + 2\log_2\left(\frac{1}{2(\varepsilon_A - 1/2)}\right) + \log_2 \ln(1/2\mu) + 2 & n = 1 \\ \log_2 T_A + \log_2\left(\frac{1}{\mathsf{Adv}_A^{\mathrm{Renyi}}}\right) + \log_2 \ln(1/2\mu) + 2 & n = 1 \end{cases}.
$$

Theorem 9. *[20, Theorem 2] If an n-bit game G is not λ-bit secure, i.e., $\mathrm{BS}_G^\mu < \lambda$, then there exists an inner adversary A for the game such that A has computational complexity T_A and satisfies*

$$
\varepsilon_A > \frac{T_A}{2^\lambda}(1 - \mu)
$$

for the search-type game $n > 1$; and

$$
\mathsf{Adv}_A^{\mathrm{Renyi}} = D_{1/2}(P_{A|U}(\cdot|0)\|P_{A|U}(\cdot|1)) > \frac{T_A}{2^\lambda} \cdot \ln(1/4\mu)
$$

and

$$
d_{\mathsf{HD}}(P_{A|U}(\cdot|0), P_{A|U}(\cdot|1)) > \min\left\{\frac{1}{\sqrt{2}}, \sqrt{\frac{T_A}{2^{\lambda+1}} \cdot \ln(1/4\mu)}\right\}.
$$

for the decision-type game $n = 1$.

B   Equivalence of (6)–(8)

Note that

$$\mathbb{E}[\psi(A)^2] = \Pr(A \neq \perp) \qquad (20)$$

and

$$\begin{aligned}
\mathbb{E}[\psi(A)\psi(U)] &= \Pr(A = U) - \Pr(A \neq \perp, A \neq U) \\
&= \Pr(A = U) - \big(\Pr(A \neq \perp) - \Pr(A \neq \perp, A = U)\big) \\
&= 2\Pr(A = U) - \Pr(A \neq \perp),
\end{aligned} \qquad (21)$$

where we used

$$\Pr(A = U) = \Pr(A \neq \perp, A = U) \qquad (22)$$

in the third equality. By substituting (20) and (21) into (6), we have (7). By noting (22), (8) follows from (7).

References

1. Alon, N., Goldreich, O., Hastad, J., Peralta, R.: Simple construction of almost k-wise independent random variables. Random Struct. Algor. **3**(3), 289–304 (1992)
2. Baignères, T., Sepehrdad, P., Vaudenay, S.: Distinguishing distributions using Chernoff information. In: Heng, S.-H., Kurosawa, K. (eds.) ProvSec 2010. LNCS, vol. 6402, pp. 144–165. Springer, Heidelberg (2010). https://doi.org/10.1007/978-3-642-16280-0_10
3. Barak, B., et al.: Leftover hash lemma, revisited. In: Rogaway, P. (ed.) CRYPTO 2011. LNCS, vol. 6841, pp. 1–20. Springer, Heidelberg (2011). https://doi.org/10.1007/978-3-642-22792-9_1
4. Bellare, M., Rogaway, P.: The security of triple encryption and a framework for code-based game-playing proofs. In: Vaudenay, S. (ed.) EUROCRYPT 2006. LNCS, vol. 4004, pp. 409–426. Springer, Heidelberg (2006). https://doi.org/10.1007/11761679_25
5. Bennett, C.H., Brassard, G., Crépeau, C., Maurer, U.M.: Generalized privacy amplification. IEEE Trans. Inf. Theory **41**(6), 1915–1923 (1995). https://doi.org/10.1109/18.476316
6. Bennett, C.H., Brassard, G., Robert, J.-M.: How to reduce your enemy's information (extended abstract). In: Williams, H.C. (ed.) CRYPTO 1985. LNCS, vol. 218, pp. 468–476. Springer, Heidelberg (1986). https://doi.org/10.1007/3-540-39799-X_37
7. Chernoff, H.: A measure of asymptotic efficiency for tests of a hypothesis based on the sum of observations. Ann. Math. Stat. **23**(4), 493–507 (1952)
8. Dodis, Y., Steinberger, J.: Message authentication codes from unpredictable block ciphers. In: Halevi, S. (ed.) CRYPTO 2009. LNCS, vol. 5677, pp. 267–285. Springer, Heidelberg (2009). https://doi.org/10.1007/978-3-642-03356-8_16
9. Goldreich, O.: The foundations of cryptography - volume 1: basic techniques. Cambridge University Press (2001). http://www.wisdom.weizmann.ac.il/%7Eoded/foc-vol1.html. https://doi.org/10.1017/CBO9780511546891

10. Goldreich, O., Levin, L.A.: A hard-core predicate for all one-way functions. In: Johnson, D.S. (ed.) Proceedings of the 21st Annual ACM Symposium on Theory of Computing, pp. 25–32, 14-17 May 1989, Seattle, Washington, USA. ACM (1989). https://doi.org/10.1145/73007.73010

11. Goldwasser, S., Tauman Kalai, Y.: Cryptographic assumptions: a position paper. In: Kushilevitz, E., Malkin, T. (eds.) TCC 2016. LNCS, vol. 9562, pp. 505–522. Springer, Heidelberg (2016). https://doi.org/10.1007/978-3-662-49096-9_21

12. Götze, F., Sambale, H., Sinulis, A.: Higher order concentration for functions of weakly dependent random variables. Electron. J. Probab. **24**(85), 1–19 (2019)

13. Hast, G.: Nearly one-sided tests and the Goldreich-Levin predicate. J. Cryptol. **17**, 209–229 (2004)

14. Impagliazzo, R., Levin, L.A., Luby, M.: Pseudo-random generation from one-way functions (extended abstracts). In: Johnson, D.S. (ed.) Proceedings of the 21st Annual ACM Symposium on Theory of Computing, 14-17 May 1989, Seattle, Washington, USA, pp. 12–24. ACM (1989). https://doi.org/10.1145/73007.73009

15. Levin, L.A.: Randomness and non-determinism. J. Symbolic Logic **58**(3), 1102–1103 (1993). https://doi.org/10.1137/S0895480197329508

16. Micciancio, D., Walter, M.: On the bit security of cryptographic primitives. In: Nielsen, J.B., Rijmen, V. (eds.) EUROCRYPT 2018. LNCS, vol. 10820, pp. 3–28. Springer, Cham (2018). https://doi.org/10.1007/978-3-319-78381-9_1

17. Radhakrishnan, J., Ta-Shma, A.: Bounds for dispersers, extractors, and depth-two superconcentrators. SIAM J. Discrete Math. **13**(1), 2–24 (2000). https://doi.org/10.1137/S0895480197329508

18. Shoup, V.: Sequences of games: a tool for taming complexity in security proofs. IACR Cryptology ePrint Archive, p. 332 (2004). http://eprint.iacr.org/2004/332

19. van Erven, T., Harremoës, P.: Rényi divergence and Kullback-Leibler divergence. IEEE Trans. Inform. Theory **60**(7), 3797–3820 (2014)

20. Watanabe, S., Yasunaga, K.: Bit security as computational cost for winning games with high probability. In: Tibouchi, M., Wang, H. (eds.) ASIACRYPT 2021. LNCS, vol. 13092, pp. 161–188. Springer, Cham (2021). https://doi.org/10.1007/978-3-030-92078-4_6

21. Yasunaga, K.: Replacing probability distributions in security games via Hellinger distance. In: Tessaro, S., (ed.) 2nd Conference on Information-Theoretic Cryptography (ITC 2021), volume 199 of Leibniz International Proceedings in Informatics (LIPIcs), pp. 1–15, Dagstuhl, Germany (2021). Schloss Dagstuhl – Leibniz-Zentrum für Informatik. https://drops.dagstuhl.de/opus/volltexte/2021/14336. https://doi.org/10.4230/LIPIcs.ITC.2021.17

The Relationship Between Idealized Models Under Computationally Bounded Adversaries

Cong Zhang[1,3(✉)] and Mark Zhandry[2]

[1] Zhejiang University, Hangzhou, China
congresearch@zju.edu.cn
[2] NTT Research, Sunnyvale, CA, USA
[3] ZJU-Hangzhou Global Scientific and Technological Innovation Center, Hangzhou, China

Abstract. The random oracle, generic group, and generic bilinear map models (ROM, GGM, GBM, respectively) are fundamental heuristics used to justify new computational assumptions and prove the security of efficient cryptosystems. While known to be invalid in some contrived settings, the heuristics generally seem reasonable for real-world applications.

In this work, we ask: *which heuristics are closer to reality?* Or conversely, which heuristics are a larger leap? We answer this question through the framework of computational indifferentiability, showing that the ROM is a strictly "milder" heuristic than the GGM, which in turn is strictly milder than the GBM. While this may seem like the expected outcome, we explain why it does not follow from prior works, and is not the a priori obvious conclusion. In order to prove our results, we develop new ideas for proving computational indifferentiable separations.

1 Introduction

In this work, we ask:

What is the relationship between the random oracle,
generic group, and generic bilinear map models?

Using known black-box separations, the answer may seem obvious: groups yield public key encryption (PKE) [DH76], while Impagliazzo and Rudich [IR89] show that random oracles cannot. Likewise, bilinear maps give identity-based encryption [BF01], while Papakonstantinou, Rackoff, and Vahlis [PRV12] show that generic groups cannot. In the other direction, bilinear maps seem to imply everything that can be constructed from groups, which in turn seem to imply everything that can be constructed from random oracles. Thus, one may be tempted to conclude that ROM<GGM<GBM.

The authorship order is randomized, and all authors contributed equally.
Work supported in Part by Zhejiang University Education Foundation Qizhen Scholar Foundation.

J. Guo and R. Steinfeld (Eds.): ASIACRYPT 2023, LNCS 14443, pp. 390–419, 2023.
https://doi.org/10.1007/978-981-99-8736-8_13

We argue, however, that the above is far from the complete picture. The random oracle model is almost always used in conjunction with standard-model computational assumptions. For example, the famous examples of Full Domain Hash signatures [BR96], Fujisaki-Okamoto CCA-secure encryption [FO99], and Fiat-Shamir [FS87, PS96] all use computational tools, namely trapdoor permutations, weak PKE, and public coin arguments, respectively.

In such settings, it no longer suffices to just consider the implied cryptosystems of a particular model in isolation. Take Full Domain Hash: here one assumes an object that implies PKE. In this world, Impagliazzo and Rudich does not apply, since they explicitly construct a world where PKE does *not* exist. If both the Full Domain Hash world and generic group model imply PKE, how do we now compare the two models?

Looking deeper, the aforementioned separations assume a computationally *unbounded* adversary. This is more or less inherent, and one of the key insights of [IR89]: since in the real world we believe PKE exists, you can always build PKE "from random oracles" by ignoring the random oracle and just using the assumed PKE scheme. To avoid such trivialities, black box separations like [IR89, PRV12] generally allow for computationally unbounded adversaries, but only count query complexity. Thus, any cryptosystem that does not use the provided oracles will be trivially insecure.

On the other hand, when actually applying the random oracle model to cryptosystems, one almost always must consider computationally *bounded* adversaries, lest the standard-model building blocks like trapdoor permutations, etc., cannot exist. But this is exactly antithetical to the usual paradigm of black box separations.

So in a world where computational assumptions exist (which is widely believed to be the world we live in!) what does it mean to compare the random oracle, generic group, and generic bilinear map models?

1.1 Motivation

The random oracle model (ROM) of Bellare and Rogaway [BR93] is ubiquitous in modern cryptography. The goal of this model is to justify the security of cryptosystems in cases where it is unknown how to prove the security solely relative to standard, widely accepted computational assumptions on a hash function. Instead, the hash function is modeled as a uniformly random function that can only be accessed by making evaluation queries. ROM protocols tend to be simpler and more efficient than their standard-model counterparts, and sometimes require milder computational assumptions.

Now, there are somewhat contrived examples [CGH98] of schemes that are proven secure in the ROM, but cannot be instantiated by *any* concrete hash function. Because of this, the ROM is sometimes called a *heuristic*. These counterexamples, however, have never been applied to actual deployed cryptosystems. The ROM can therefore be seen as a middle-ground, offering reasonable justification for security while resulting in more efficient protocols. This compromise has lead the ROM to be an important component in practical cryptosystems.

The generic group and generic bilinear map models are two other "idealized" models that are also very important for cryptography. Similar to the random oracle model, the generic group model (GGM) of Shoup [Sho97] treats a cryptographic (cyclic) *group* as having uniformly random labels for the group elements. The generic bilinear map model (GBM), as defined by Boneh and Boyen [BB04], extends the model to cryptographic pairings.

Like the ROM, impossibilities exist for generic groups [Den02], leading them to be considered heuristics. Nevertheless, the generic group and bilinear models have been particularly useful for justifying the hardness of the many computational assumptions made on cryptographic groups and bilinear maps. For example, the discrete logarithm, decisional (bilinear) Diffie-Hellman, Diffie-Hellman inversion, Diffie-Hellman exponent, and decision linear assumptions can all be proven hard in the respective generic model. The generic bilinear map model has also been used to directly prove the security of cryptosystems, such as recent constructions of broadcast encryption [AY20] and traitor tracing [Zha20] from pairings. The generic group models are also useful tools for showing the limits of group-based cryptosystems through black box separations, such as [PRV12, RSS20, ZZ18].

Can Generic Groups Be Built from Random Oracles? While generic groups and bilinear maps have found many uses in cryptography, they are generally considered a worse heuristic than random oracles. After all, known groups have significant algebraic structure that may help distinguish them from their generic counterparts. For elliptic curve groups, an element and its inverse have the same x coordinate, and pairings can give rise to attacks if parameters are not chosen properly [MVO91]. For finite fields, index calculus methods lead to subexponential time attacks.

Consider, therefore, the following possibility: under a suitable computational assumption, say decisional Diffie-Hellman (DDH) in elliptic curve groups, a random oracle H can be used to "build" a generic group G or even a bilinear map. Such a G would be of tremendous use to cryptography. All the computational assumptions made on groups could be simultaneously justified under the much more widely accepted ROM heuristic. Likewise, designing group and pairing-based cryptosystems would become easier, as they can be proven directly in the generic models as opposed to a reduction to a computational assumption. Such a possibility would show that, in the regime of computational assumptions, generic groups and random oracles collapse into equivalent objects, and the deviation from the real world is identical.

The above possibility may initially sound far-fetched, but it is not contradicted by prior impossibilities. Moreover, the recent work of Zhandry and Zhang [ZZ20] gives some hope: they use random oracles to "upgrade" certain *standard-model* key agreement schemes (which exist under standard computational assumptions) into an "idealized" model for public key agreement. Could it be that similar ideas could lead to a method for upgrading a sufficiently good standard-model cryptographic group/bilinear map into a generic group/bilinear map, relying only on the ROM heuristic?

1.2   Our Results

Our main result is to refute the above possibility, showing that

$$\text{ROM} \lhd \text{GGM} \lhd \text{GBM}$$

Here, $A \lhd B$ means that B implies A *without* additional computational assumptions, but A cannot be used to build B even *with* computational assumptions. Our conceptual contribution is to formalize $\lhd$ using the indifferentiability framework of Maurer, Renner, and Holenstein [MRH04], where we specifically must consider *computationally bounded* adversaries[1] in order to account for the existence of computational assumptions.

At a technical level, we must design efficient adversaries for any supposed generic group built from a random oracle, and for any supposed generic bilinear map built from a generic group. This is challenging and requires novel approach, as black box separations typically crucially rely on unbounded attacks.

1.3   Interpretation

Results relative to random oracles or other idealized models must be interpreted. This is especially important when deciding if a proposed scheme improves on the existing state-of-the-art: is a random oracle scheme actually better than a generic group scheme, and if so, how much are we willing to "pay" for it in terms of additional computational assumptions?

Towards answering these kinds of questions, we can view an idealized model as roughly consisting of two parts. The first, which has received the most attention, is a "standard-model" part, which tells us which types of standard-model cryptosystems are implied by the model without any additional building blocks. Understanding this part of an idealized model is the usual goal of black box constructions and separations. In the decades of research on constructions and impossibilities, the community has developed a decent picture about this part of random oracles, generic groups, and generic bilinear maps.

By considering indifferentiability under computationally bounded adversaries, we incorporate *all* cryptosystems which exist in the standard model. Along the implied cryptosystems axis, the models therefore all become identical. But our results show that there is still another axis in which the models are different. This is the part of the model that is not realizable in the standard model under computational assumptions, the part that makes the model "heuristic." This heuristic part has been largely unexplored, and there is no reason to expect any correlation between the standard-model and heuristic parts. For example, [ZZ20] can be interpreted as showing the heuristic parts of random oracles and ideal public key encryption are the same. Understanding the heuristic parts of idealized models is therefore important for understanding the relative security of cryptosystems based on idealized models. Our results show that the heuristic parts of generic bilinear maps are stronger (or worse than)

---

[1] [MRH04] uses the terminology of "computational reducibility" for this concept.

than that of generic groups, which is stronger than that of random oracles, thus giving the first ever separations along this axis.

In the following, we will give an overview of our approach to comparing the various models and our solutions for separating them.

1.4   Formalizing Our Goal Using Indifferentiability

As mentioned above, a random oracle is just a random function H. A generic group [Sho97] is slightly more complicated: we imagine fixing a generator g of the group, and letting $L(x) = g^x$, which we will call the labeling function. In a generic group, the labeling function L is modelled as a random injection $L : \mathbb{Z}_p \rightarrow \{0,1\}^n$, together with an oracle A computing the group operation: $A(x, y, b) \mapsto L(\ L^{-1}(x) + (-1)^b L^{-1}(y)\ )$. The generic bilinear map model is defined similarly.

Remark 1. Note that we do not consider the Maurer's model [Mau05], which has no labels and instead supplies entropy-less handles for group elements. This model has numerous limitations relative to Shoup's model [Zha22]. It is even incomparable to random oracles: random oracles imply signatures, but Maurer's generic group model does not [DHH+21].

Consider a construction G of a cryptographic group from a random oracle H, which we will denote as G^H. G^H contains a labeling function L^H, and an addition function A^H. We would like to define what it means for G^H to be a generic group. A first attempt would require that oracle access to L^H, A^H (but *not* H) be *indistinguishable* from the oracles of a generic group interface. Such an indistinguishable group is actually very easy to construct. Simply set L to be, say, a Feistel network with the random oracle as the round function and A the function that applies the appropriate operations to achieve the group operation. By Luby and Rackoff [LR88], a 4-round Feistel network with a random hidden round function is a strong PRP, which is enough to justify security.

The problem with the above is that a real-world attacker would be able to make queries to H as well, since H represents a concrete hash function known to everyone. But once we allow the attacker to query H, clearly, L^H, A^H, H is trivially distinguishable from a generic group: the attacker can run L^H for himself by making queries to H, and then compare that to what the L oracle outputs. In the L^H, A^H, H case, the outputs would match, while in the generic group case, they clearly would not.

The solution, as demonstrated by Maurer, Renner, and Holenstein [MRH04], is to use the notion of *indifferentiability*. Here, we define the "real world" as the setting where the adversary has oracle access to L^H, A^H and H. In the "ideal world", the adversary has access to a true generic group, and a "simulated" random oracle H. In the ideal world, a simulator S answers random oracle queries, potentially by keeping state and also by making queries to the generic group. In doing so, the simulator hopes to simulate a random oracle that is "consistent," so that the attacker cannot distinguish the two worlds. If such a simulator exists, we say that (L, A) is indifferentiable from a generic group.

Where do computational assumptions fit in? Suppose a construction of a generic group from a random oracle relied on a computational assumption. This would imply that indifferentiability only holds against computationally bounded distinguishers, since any computational assumption would be meaningless for an unbounded distinguisher. Therefore, we will say that $\mathcal{A}$ *computationally implies* $\mathcal{B}$ if there is a construction that is indifferentiable with respect to all computationally bounded distinguishers. If indifferentiability holds also against computationally *unbounded* distinguishers, we say that $\mathcal{A}$ *statistically implies* $\mathcal{B}$.

Our ultimate goal will be to demonstrate that one idealized model $\mathcal{A}$ is "strictly milder" than another model $\mathcal{B}$, meaning that $\mathcal{B}$ can be used to construct $\mathcal{A}$, while $\mathcal{A}$ *cannot* be used to construct $\mathcal{B}$. Importantly, we want this to hold regardless of the computational assumptions one may assume. Thus we say that $\mathcal{A}$ is *strictly milder* than that of $\mathcal{B}$ if (1) $\mathcal{B}$ statistically implies $\mathcal{A}$ (so $\mathcal{B}$ implies $\mathcal{A}$ even if no computational assumptions hold), while (2) $\mathcal{A}$ does not even *computationally* imply $\mathcal{B}$ (so that $\mathcal{A}$ does not imply $\mathcal{B}$ even under the strongest plausible assumptions). In this case, we write $\mathcal{A} \lhd \mathcal{B}$.

As explained above, our notion of comparison between idealized models is largely orthogonal to what is implied by black box separations, which typically look only at computationally unbounded adversaries.

1.5   Technical Overview

Warm-Up: Generic Groups Statistically Imply Random Oracles. We first explain how generic groups imply random oracles. This result is not entirely trivial. The natural choice would be to set the labeling function of the generic group as the random oracle. However, this function has homomorphisms that the random oracle does not. In particular, given $L(x)$ and $L(y)$, it is possible to compute $L(x+y)$. This is not possible for a random oracle.

Our solution is simple: we just truncate the labeling function, setting $H(x)$ to be the first, say, half the bits of $L(x)^2$. The intuition is that, given only half the bits of $L(x)$, it is impossible to meaningfully query the addition oracle. As a result, since $L(x)$ on its own is a random oracle we obtain a random oracle[3].

To turn this into an indifferentiability proof, we have to explain how to simulate L and A, given a true random oracle H. The idea is that, for any query to $L(x)$, the simulator will query $H(x)$, set the first half of $L(x)$ to be $H(x)$, and then choose a random string for the second half. The addition oracle A is simulated by looking at the L queries made so far; if one of the input labels is not amongst the L queries, A rejects. The reason this simulator works, roughly, is that the distinguisher cannot make a query to A unless it knows the entire label. Since obtaining the second half of the label required querying L, this means the simulator will know the value for every label queried to A. This allows the simulator to answer queries to A correctly.

---

[2] Deleting any super-logarithmic number of bits will do.

[3] Technically $L(x)$ is a random injection. But a truncated random injection is indistinguishable from a random oracle.

Random Oracles do not (Computationally) Imply Generic Groups. Suppose we have a purported construction $G^H = (L^H, A^H)$ of a cryptographic group from a random oracle H. How do we show that G^H can be differentiated from a generic group, using a computationally efficient distinguisher?

Intuitively, we should find some property P that holds for a generic group, but does not hold for *any* G^H. At this point it should be obvious that any standard group assumption, such as hardness of discrete logarithms, cannot serve as the property P — because there exists some groups in which this computational assumption is believed to be hard. Therefore, if we let G^H be such a group (where H is not used at all), then any efficient adversary for the security property is then impossible. This is exactly why [IR89] and most subsequent black box separations move to computationally unbounded settings, but this is not an option for us. This means we cannot actually use security properties that are true of standard-model cryptographic groups, and different ideas are needed.

Our idea is to use a variant of the discrete logarithm problem, which importantly is trivially false on standard model groups but easily proved to hold on generic groups. Our variant is what we call the *discrete log identification* (DLI) problem, informally defined as: given $h = L(x)^4$, construct a (probabilistic, efficient) circuit C such that $C(x)$ accepts with overwhelming probability, but $C(x')$ rejects with overwhelming probability on all $x' \neq x$. The DLI problem is trivially easy on standard-model groups: set $C(x')$ to be 1 if and only if $L(x') = h$, where $L(x') = g^{x'}$ is computed as part of C. On the other hand, the DLI problem is readily shown to be hard on generic groups; importantly, the circuit C is oracle-free, meaning it cannot evaluate $L(x')$ since doing so requires queries to the generic group oracles.

While the DLI problem is easily solvable on standard-model groups, it remains to show that the DLI problem is solvable on any group G^H built from a random oracle H, where the attacker (but not C!) can also make queries to H. The difficulty is that G^H may use the random oracle, but the circuit C cannot; as a result $C(x')$ cannot readily compute $L^H(x')$ for itself, and it is therefore not obvious how to make the attack work. The natural approach, following techniques from the literature on black box separations, is to try to "compile out" the oracle H. That is, an attacker can easily construct an *oracle aided* circuit $C^H(x')$ breaking the DLI problem by computing $L^H(x')$ using the oracle H. Then, the hope is to anticipate the oracle queries C will make to H, have the adversary query on those points for itself. This task is usually accomplished by running C^H for itself on several random inputs, recording all queries that were made. Then the adversary hardcodes the query answers into C to get an oracle-free circuit, which C outputs.

Unfortunately, it is not a priori obvious that such a strategy should work, or even that the DLI problem should be easy on groups built from random oracles. To see why, consider an analogous *pre-image identification* (PI) problem for hash functions, where the goal is, given an image h, to compute a circuit that accepts

---

[4] Remember that for standard-model groups, $L(x)$ denotes the value g^x for a fixed generator g, and here x is the discrete log of h.

only x such that $H(x) = h$. This PI problem is similarly easy for standard-model hash functions, but hard in the random oracle model. One could hope to break the PI problem on any hash function built from a random oracle by similarly compiling out the random oracle queries. But since it is trivial to build a random oracle from a random oracle (even with indifferentiability), and the PI problem is hard for random oracles, we cannot hope to build an attack on the PI problem in our setting.

Therefore, in order to develop our algorithm for the DLI problem, we must exploit the fact that G^H implements a group in order to compile out H from C^H. In particular, along with the labeling function L^H, we must somehow leverage the addition oracle A^H which maps $(L^H(y), L^H(z), b) \mapsto L^H(y + (-1)^b z)$. This addition oracle potentially makes queries to the random oracle H.

Consider computing $L^H(x)$ from x, which in turn makes queries to the random oracle H. Let Q_x be the set of query/answer pairs made during this process. Consider running the addition oracle $A^H(L^H(y), L^H(z), b = 0)$, where y, z are random conditioned on $y + z = x$. The output of this addition is $L^H(y + z) = L^H(x)$. For each query/answer pair $(\mathsf{que}, \mathsf{res}) \in Q_x$, there are roughly three possibilities:

1. With non-negligible probability over the choice of y, z, $A^H(L^H(y), L^H(z), b = 0)$ makes a query to H on que.
2. The label $L^H(x)$ does not "depend" on the answer res at all.
3. The label $L^H(x)$ depends on res, but $A^H(L^H(y), L^H(z), b = 0)$ queries que with negligible probability.

Now consider running C^H on input x. We claim that we can hardcode query answers into C, by collecting queries into a list, denoted as $S_{\mathsf{que\text{-}res}}$, to guarantee that it will reconstruct $L^H(x)$ without making any queries at all:

- In Case 1, consider the following procedure: choose a random y, compute $h_y = L^H(y)$, and then compute $h_z = A^H(h, h_y, 1) = L^H(x - y) = L^H(z)$, where we implicitly define $z = x - y$ (we do not know it). Note that y, z are random conditioned on $y + z = x$. Then, run $A^H(h_y, h_z, 0)$, collecting all oracle queries made during this process into $S_{\mathsf{que\text{-}res}}$. For Case 1, we know that with non-negligible probability $(\mathsf{que}, \mathsf{res})$ will be amongst the queries in $S_{\mathsf{que\text{-}res}}$. By repeating several times, we obtain that $S_{\mathsf{que\text{-}res}}$ contains $(\mathsf{que}, \mathsf{res})$ with high probability. We then include $S_{\mathsf{que\text{-}res}}$ in the description of C, using $S_{\mathsf{que\text{-}res}}$ to answer any query.
- In Case 2, since $L^H(x)$ does not depend on res, when evaluating $L^H(x)$ we can change the response H yields on que to a random value independent of H, without affecting the ultimate labeling. Therefore, for any query not in $S_{\mathsf{que\text{-}res}}$, we will just have C respond with a uniformly random string.
- In Case 3, it must be that $A^H(h_y, h_z, 0)$ must have, in some sense, been able to figure out res from the inputs h_y, h_z. But this in particular means that $L^H(y)$ or $L^H(z)$ must query H on que, in order for the labels to have information about res. We notice that y and z are both uniform, and in particular distributed identically, and so the probability that $L^H(y)$ resulted

in query que is at least $1/2$. But then we can collect (que, res) by additionally recording in $S_{\text{que-res}}$ all queries made when computing $h_y = L^H(y)$ above. By repeating the process several times, we obtain (que, res) with high probability.

Now consider evaluating $C(x')$ for $x' \neq x$. In this case, if we got lucky and correctly anticipated all queries C would make to H, we correctly compute the right label for x', which will be unequal to h; hence $C(x')$ rejects as desired. On the other hand, if we did not anticipate all the queries, we just replace the query answers with random values; while this means we compute an incorrect label for x', intuitively the random response to the oracle query should only serve to inject further randomness into the label, and it should still be the case that our incorrect label is different from $L^H(x)$. The result is a procedure for compiling out the H queries made by C, resulting in an oracle-free C which accepts exactly the discrete log x.

The above sketch is imprecise and ignores numerous low-level details, which we work through in Sect. 3.

Generic Bilinear Maps are Stronger than Generic Groups. We next turn to extend our techniques to separate generic bilinear maps from generic groups. This setting is far more challenging than the separation above, owing to the fact that generic groups have a lot more structure to exploit.

Since generic groups imply generic groups, we cannot rely solely on the group structure (addition operation) of a bilinear map in order to achieve a separation from generic groups. We instead must factor in the pairing (multiplication operation). The difficulty is that the pairing is also in some sense a restricted group operation (in the multiplicative group $\mathbb{Z}_p^*$), and it could be the case that the generic group structure can be used to implement the pairing. Essentially what we must do is show that a single cryptographic group cannot simultaneously be used to implement both the group operation and pairing operation. This is a very different problem from our separation above, which showed that the group structure could not be obtained from random oracle in the first place.

In terms of the proof strategy, it is possible in the generic group model (denoted by $\mathcal{G} = (\mathcal{G}^{\text{label}}, \mathcal{G}^{\text{add}})$) to learn information about a label on a point x (i.e., $\mathcal{G}^{\text{label}}(x)$) through the addition oracle, in which case one does not necessarily have to even know x. More concretely, given two labels on points y and z such that $y + z = x$, one can call the addition oracle to the underlying generic group model to obtain the label on x. Therefore, if we try to adapt our proof technique from above, this means our procedure for collecting query/response pairs will no longer work: when running $L^{\mathcal{G}}(x)$[5], the algorithm might make labeling queries on points $(x_1, \ldots, x_q)$, whereas our procedure for generating a database $S_{\text{que-res}}$ may only store query/response pairs with form of addition $(\mathcal{G}^{\text{label}}(y_i), \mathcal{G}^{\text{label}}(z_i), \mathcal{G}^{\text{label}}(y_i + z_i))$, without explicitly knowing either y_i or z_i. As a result, the oracle-free C would fail the simulation: when C runs $L^{S_{\text{que-res}}}(x)$ and needs the label on x_i (i.e., $\mathcal{G}^{\text{label}}(x_i)$), although C knows that $\mathcal{G}^{\text{label}}(x_i)$ exists

---

[5] Here we abuse the notation of L as the labeling function of the bilinear map group.

in the database $S_{\text{que-res}}$ (say, in a tuple $(\mathcal{G}^{\text{label}}(y_i), \mathcal{G}^{\text{label}}(z_i), \mathcal{G}^{\text{label}}(x_i))$ such that $x_i = y_i + z_i$), it does not know which tuple corresponds to $\mathcal{G}^{\text{label}}(x_i)$.

Our core technique to solve this difficulty is to extract the explicit values x_i from those addition queries. Note that, although the tuple above does not specifically give the value x_i, y_i or z_i, it indeed leaks some side information: a linear constraint that $y_i + z_i = x_i$. Our strategy is to collect as many linear-independent constraints, form a linear system and extract x_i by solving the linear system. The following is the sketch of our strategy. Let $\mathcal{G}^{\text{label}}$ be the labeling oracle for underlying generic group, and $L^{\mathcal{G}}, L_T^{\mathcal{G}}$ the supposed labeling function for the source and target groups of an indifferentiable bilinear map construction. When running $L^{\mathcal{G}}(x)$, let Q_x^{sou} denote the vector of queries made to $\mathcal{G}^{\text{label}6}$, and Q_x^{tar} the vector of queries made when computing $L_T^{\mathcal{G}}(x)$.

Now imagine having a label $L^{\mathcal{G}}(x)$ for a random unknown x, and a scalar u, and "raising" $L^{\mathcal{G}}(x)$ to the u power, computing $L^{\mathcal{G}}(ux)$ using repeated doubling. By tracking the queries made to the generic group, we can compute an explicit matrix $N_{ux,x}$ such that[7]

$$Q_{ux}^{\text{sou}} = N_{ux,x} \cdot Q_x^{\text{sou}}. \tag{1}$$

The vectors $Q_x^{\text{sou}}, Q_{ux}^{\text{sou}}$ remain unknown, but the matrix $N_{ux,x}$ is computed in the clear. The intuition for the linearity of Eq. 1 is due the linear structure of the underlying generic group.

If we additionally had a second label $L^{\mathcal{G}}(y)$ for a random unknown y, we can imagine computing $L_T^{\mathcal{G}}(z)$ for $z = xy$ using the pairing. By tracking the queries this pairing operation makes to the underlying generic group, we can compute explicit matrices $M_{z,x}, M_{z,y}$ such that

$$Q_z^{\text{tar}} = M_{z,x} \cdot Q_x^{\text{sou}} + M_{z,y} \cdot Q_y^{\text{sou}}. \tag{2}$$

Again, the linearity of Eq. 2 is due to the linear structure of the underlying generic group. By raising $L^{\mathcal{G}}(y)$ and $L_T^{\mathcal{G}}(z)$ to the u, and also pairing $L^{\mathcal{G}}(ux)$ with $L^{\mathcal{G}}(y)$ and $L^{\mathcal{G}}(x)$ with $L^{\mathcal{G}}(uy)$, we can similarly compute the explicit matrices $N_{uy,y}, N_{uz,z}^{\text{tar}}, M_{uz,ux}, M_{uz,y}, M_{uz,x}, M_{uz,uy}$ such that

$$\begin{aligned} Q_{uy}^{\text{sou}} &= N_{uy,y} \cdot Q_y^{\text{sou}} \\ Q_{uz}^{\text{tar}} &= N_{uz,z}^{\text{tar}} \cdot Q_z^{\text{tar}} \\ &= (N_{uz,z}^{\text{tar}} \cdot M_{z,x}) \cdot Q_x^{\text{sou}} + (N_{uz,z}^{\text{tar}} \cdot M_{z,y}) \cdot Q_y^{\text{sou}} \end{aligned} \tag{3}$$

$$\begin{aligned} Q_{uz}^{\text{tar}} &= M_{uz,ux} \cdot Q_{ux}^{\text{sou}} + M_{uz,y} \cdot Q_y^{\text{sou}} \\ &= (M_{uz,ux} \cdot N_{ux,x}) \cdot Q_x^{\text{sou}} + (M_{uz,y}) \cdot Q_y^{\text{sou}} \end{aligned} \tag{4}$$

---

[6] Technically, $L(x)$ may make queries to the generic group addition oracle. However, we can replace such queries with queries to L_0, since L can trace the origin of all labels to L_0 queries.

[7] Technically there should be a constant term as well. But we can assume Q_x^{sou} contains 1, in which case this constant term can be absorbed into $N_{ux,x}$.

$$Q_{uz}^{\mathsf{tar}} = M_{uz,x} \cdot Q_x^{\mathsf{sou}} + M_{uz,uy} \cdot Q_{uy}^{\mathsf{sou}}$$
$$= (M_{uz,x}) \cdot Q_x^{\mathsf{sou}} + (M_{uz,uy} \cdot N_{uy,y}) \cdot Q_y^{\mathsf{sou}} . \qquad (5)$$

One way the above equations can hold is if:

$$N_{uz,z}^{\mathsf{tar}} \cdot M_{z,x} = M_{uz,ux} \cdot N_{ux,x} = M_{uz,x} \qquad (6)$$
$$N_{uz,z}^{\mathsf{tar}} \cdot M_{z,y} = M_{uz,y} = M_{uz,uy} \cdot N_{uy,y} \qquad (7)$$

Suppose additionally that the various M matrices were full row rank. Equations 6 and 7 then allow us to compute the various N matrices from the M matrices. Fortunately, computing those M matrices only requires knowing the labels $L^{\mathcal{G}}(x), L^{\mathcal{G}}(y), L^{\mathcal{G}}(ux)$, and $L^{\mathcal{G}}(uy)$, but does not require knowing the actual scalar u.

Now consider having just the labels $L^{\mathcal{G}}(x), L^{\mathcal{G}}(ux)$ for unknown x, u. We can sample a random y', and implicitly set $y = xy'$ by computing $L^{\mathcal{G}}(y) = L^{\mathcal{G}}(xy')$ and $L^{\mathcal{G}}(uy) = L^{\mathcal{G}}(uxy')$. Then using the above, we can compute $N_{ux,x}$.

We note that $N_{ux,x}$ acts as a representation of the discrete log between $L^{\mathcal{G}}(x)$ and $L^{\mathcal{G}}(ux)$, in the sense that it allows us to transform the vector Q_x^{sou} to Q_{ux}^{sou}. In particular, we demonstrate that we can use $N_{ux,x}$, together with "compiling out" techniques analogous to our ROM/GGM separation to create a circuit (that does not make any oracle queries!) which identifies the discrete log u. Thus, in any bilinear map created from a generic group, the discrete log identification problem is easy, meaning the bilinear map cannot be ideal.

The above sketch assumed that Eqs. 6 and 7 hold, and that the M matrices were row full rank. However, we argue that this is, to some degree, without loss of generality:

- If Eqs. 6 or 7 failed to hold, then setting Eqs. 3, 4, and 5 to be equal would give non-trivial linear equations over $Q_x^{\mathsf{sou}}, Q_y^{\mathsf{sou}}$. By choosing u, y at random for ourselves (in which case we know Q_y^{sou}), this gives non-trivial equations over Q_x^{sou}, given just $L^{\mathcal{G}}(x)$. We can repeat this process many times. Either (1) we eventually learn enough equations to completely recover Q_x^{sou}, or (2) we eventually stop obtaining new linearly independent equations. In (1), we can easily break discrete problem. In (2), we can let $\hat{Q}_x^{\mathsf{sou}}$ be a subset of Q_x^{sou} of free variables. Then we show that we can repeat the above process using the $\hat{Q}$ vectors in place of Q, and the analogous Eqs. 6 and 7 will now hold.
- If the matrices M are not row full rank, then this implies that the pairing operation does not actually require the entire Q vectors. Intuitively, this allows us to again project onto subsets $\hat{Q}$ of the Q vectors and carry out the above experiment using these smaller vectors. In this case, the projected matrices will indeed be row full rank.

The above sketch leaves out numerous low-level technical details, which we work through in Sect. 4.

2   Preliminaries

Notation. For a finite set S, we denote a uniformly random sample s from S as $s \xleftarrow{\$} S$. We say a function $\epsilon(\lambda)$ is negligible if $\epsilon \in o(\lambda^{-\omega(1)})$, and is non-negligible otherwise. We let negl denote an arbitrary negligible function. If we say some $q(n)$ is poly, we mean that there is some polynomial $t(n)$ such that for all sufficiently large n, $q(n) \leq t(n)$. We say a function $\rho(n)$ is noticeable if the inverse $1/\rho(n)$ is poly. Throughout, we denote $\lambda \in \mathbb{N}$ as the security parameter, and we use a non-uniform circuit model of computation. An algorithm A is a collection of circuits $\{C_\lambda\}_{\lambda \in \mathbb{N}}$ with domain Dom_λ and range Ran_λ, respectively. When considering interactive algorithms $(A_1, \ldots, A_n)$, algorithms are treated as a sequence of circuits $C_\lambda^{(1)}, C_\lambda^{(2)}, \ldots$, where the domain of $C_\lambda^{(i)}$ is denoted as $\mathsf{Dom}_\lambda^{(i)} = \mathsf{stat}_\lambda^{(i)} \times \mathsf{input}_\lambda^{(i-1)}$, the range of $C_\lambda^{(i)}$ is denoted as $\mathsf{Ran}_\lambda^{(i)} = \mathsf{stat}_\lambda^{(i+1)} \times \mathsf{output}_\lambda^{(i)}$. Here, $\mathsf{stat}_\lambda^{(i)}$ ($\mathsf{input}_\lambda^{(i)}$, $\mathsf{output}_\lambda^{(i)}$) is the space of the state (inputs, outputs) that $C_\lambda^{(i)}$ sends to $C_\lambda^{(i+1)}$, respectively.

Games. A game is initiated by a probabilistic interactive algorithm C, called a challenger, and a predicate function $\mathsf{pf} : \{0,1\}^* \to [0,1]$. The challenger takes the security parameter as input and interacts with k non-communicating parties $(A_1, \ldots, A_k)$, where $(C, A_1, \ldots, A_k)$ forms a complete set. We call $A = (A_1, \ldots, A_k)$ the adversary. In the end of the game, the challenger C outputs a bit b; if $b = 1$ we say the adversary wins the game, otherwise we say the adversary loses. Let $\mathrm{Cl}(A)$ be a class of adversaries. We say a game (C, pf) is hard with respect to $\mathrm{Cl}(A)$, if for any adversary $A \in \mathrm{Cl}(A)$, there exists a negligible ϵ such that $\Pr[A \text{ wins}] \leq \mathsf{pf} + \epsilon$.

Cryptosystems. A cryptosystem Σ is a set of algorithms, which typically are non-interactive. Σ is accessible via two interfaces $\Sigma.hon$ and $\Sigma.adv$, where $\Sigma.hon$ provides an honest interface through which the system can be accessed by all parties in a black-box manner, and $\Sigma.adv$ models the adversarial access to the inner working part of Σ.

Random Oracle Model (ROM) [BR93]. A hash function is a function $H : \{0,1\}^* \to \{0,1\}^n$. The random oracle model is an idealized model proposed by Bellare and Rogaway [BR93, FS87], which assumes the existence of a truly random publicly accessible hash function H. This means $H(x)$ is chosen uniformly at random and independently for each x. H can be queried on any input x; each query has unit cost, so that a PPT algorithm can only make a polynomial number of queries. If the domain is fixed-length, say $\{0,1\}^{2n}$, then this primitive is called ideal compression function.

Generic Group Model (GGM) [Sho97]. For our purposes, a cryptographic group is a set $\mathcal{G}$ of sufficiently large prime size p ($p \geq 2^{\omega(\log \lambda)}$), endowed with an efficiently computable group operation. Equivalently, a cryptographic group is a (not necessarily efficient) embedding of the additive group $\mathbb{Z}_p$ into some set.

The generic group model is an idealized model which assumes the existence of a random embedding from $\mathbb{Z}_p$. Concretely, a generic group is a pair $\mathcal{G} = (\mathcal{G}^{label}, \mathcal{G}^{add})$. Here, $\mathcal{G}^{label}$ is a "labeling" function that is a random injection from $\mathbb{Z}_p$ to S, giving the embedding of $\mathbb{Z}_p$ into S. $\mathcal{G}^{add}$ is the induced group operation: $\mathcal{G}^{add}(\mathcal{G}^{label}(z_1), \mathcal{G}^{label}(z_2), b) = \mathcal{G}^{label}(z_1 + (-1)^b z_2)$. We will write $\mathcal{G}^{add}(h_1, h_2) = \mathcal{G}^{add}(h_1, h_2, 0)$. These functions can be queried on any input at unit cost.

Generic Bilinaer Maps (GBM) [BB04]. For our purposes, a bilinear map consists of three sets $\mathbb{G}_1, \mathbb{G}_2, \mathbb{G}_T$ of prime size p, each endowed with a group structure. Additionally, there is an efficiently computable map $e : \mathbb{G}_1 \times \mathbb{G}_2 \to \mathbb{G}_T$ such that $e(g_1^{z_1}, g_2^{z_2}) = e(g_1, g_2)^{z_1 z_2}$ for some fixed generators $g_1 \in \mathbb{G}_1, g_2 \in \mathbb{G}_2$.

The generic bilinear map model is an idealized model which assumes the existence of random embeddings from $\mathbb{Z}_p$ into the groups $\mathcal{B}_1, \mathcal{B}_2, \mathcal{B}_T$. Concretely, a generic bilinear group is a tuple $\mathcal{BG} = (\mathcal{B}_1^{label}, \mathcal{B}_2^{label}, \mathcal{B}_T^{label}, \mathcal{B}_1^{add}, \mathcal{B}_2^{add}, \mathcal{B}_T^{add}, \mathcal{B}^{multi})$. Here, $\mathcal{B}_i^{label}$ and $\mathcal{B}_i^{add}$ are as in the generic group case, where $i \in \{1, 2, T\}$. $\mathcal{B}^{multi}$ is then defined as

$$\mathcal{B}^{multi}(\, \mathcal{B}_1^{label}(z_1)\, ,\, \mathcal{B}_2^{label}(z_2)\,) = \mathcal{B}_T^{label}(z_1 \times z_2)\ .$$

As before, all queries incur unit cost. We say a GBM is symmetric if $\mathcal{B}_1 = \mathcal{B}_2$.

Indifferentiability [MRH04]. Maurer, Renner and Holenstein (MRH) propose the framework of indifferentiability, and this framework formalizes a set of necessary and sufficient conditions for one cryptosystem to securely be replaced with another one in arbitrary environment. Since then, a number of cryptographic primitives justify the structural soundness via this framework; those primitives include hash functions [CDMP05, DRS09], blockciphers [ABD+13, CHK+16, DSSL16], domain extenders [CDMS10], authenticated encryption with associated data [BF18], and public key cryptosystems [ZZ20]. When it comes to the framework of indifferentiability, we typically consider that a cryptosystem implements either some ideal objects $\mathcal{F}$, or a construction $C^{\mathcal{F}'}$ which applies underlying ideal objects $\mathcal{F}'$.

Definition 1 (Indifferentiability [MRH04]). *Let Σ_1 and Σ_2 be two cryptosystems and $\mathcal{S}$ be a simulator. The indifferentiability advantage of a differentiator $\mathcal{D}$ against (Σ_1, Σ_2) with respect to $\mathcal{S}$ is*

$$Adv_{\Sigma_1, \Sigma_2, \mathcal{S}, \mathcal{D}}^{indif}(1^\lambda) := \Pr[\text{Real}_{\Sigma_1, \mathcal{D}}] - \Pr[\text{Ideal}_{\Sigma_2, \mathcal{S}, \mathcal{D}}],$$

where games $\text{Real}_{\Sigma_1, \mathcal{D}}$ and $\text{Ideal}_{\Sigma_2, \mathcal{S}, \mathcal{D}}$ are defined in Fig. 1. We say Σ_1 is indifferentiable from Σ_2, if there exists an efficient simulator $\mathcal{S}$ such that for any efficient differentiator $\mathcal{D}$, the advantage above is negligible. Moreover, we say Σ_1 is statistically indifferentiable from Σ_2, if there exists an efficient simulator such that, for any unbounded differentiator $\mathcal{D}$, the advantage above is negligible.

Below, we also use the notations in [BF18] and consider the definition above to two systems with interfaces as:

$$(\Sigma_1.\text{hon}(X), \Sigma_1.\text{adv}(x)) := (C^{\mathcal{F}_1}(X), \mathcal{F}_1(x)); (\Sigma_2.\text{hon}(X), \Sigma_2.\text{adv}(x)) := (\mathcal{F}_2(X), \mathcal{F}_2(x)),$$

Real$_{\Sigma_1,\mathcal{D}}$:	HonestR(X)	Ideal$_{\Sigma_2,\mathcal{S},\mathcal{D}}$:	HonestI(X)
$b \leftarrow \mathcal{D}^{\text{HonestR,AdvR}}$	Return Σ_1.hon(X).	$b \leftarrow \mathcal{D}^{\text{HonestI,AdvI}}$	Return Σ_2.hon(X).
Return b.	AdvR(X)	Return b.	AdvI(X)
	Return Σ_1.adv(X).		Return $\mathcal{S}^{\Sigma_2.\text{adv}(\cdot)}(X)$.

Fig. 1. Indifferentiability of Σ_1 and Σ_2, where $\mathcal{S}$ is the simulator and $\mathcal{D}$ is the adversary.

where $\mathcal{F}_1$ and $\mathcal{F}_2$ are two ideal objects sampled from their distributions and $C^{\mathcal{F}_1}$ is a construction of $\mathcal{F}_2$ by calling $\mathcal{F}_1$. MRH prove the composition theorem for the framework of indifferentiability; for simplicity, we give a game-based formalization from [RSS11].

Theorem 1 (Composition Theorem). *Let $\Sigma_1 := (C^{\mathcal{F}_1}, \mathcal{F}_1)$ and $\Sigma_2 := (\mathcal{F}_2, \mathcal{F}_2)$ be two systems that Σ_1 is indifferentiable from Σ_2 with respect to a simulator $\mathcal{S}$, then Σ_1 is as secure as Σ_2 for any single-stage game. More concretely, let G be a single-stage game, then for any adversary $\mathcal{A}$, there is an adversary B and a differentiator $\mathcal{D}$ such that*

$$\Pr[G^{C^{\mathcal{F}_1},\mathcal{A}^{\mathcal{F}_1}}] \leq \Pr[G^{\mathcal{F}_2,\mathcal{A}^{\mathcal{F}_2}}] + \text{Adv}^{\text{indif}}_{\Sigma_1,\Sigma_2,\mathcal{S},\mathcal{D}}.$$

The proof of Theorem 1 is straightforward; due to space limit, we skip it here. Next, we give the formal definition of the separation between two idealized models in the framework of indifferentiability against computational adversaries.

Definition 2 (Computational Indifferentiable Separation [MRH04]). *Let Σ_1, Σ_2 be two idealized models, we say Σ_2 is computational indifferentiably separated from Σ_1 if for any efficient algorithm A and any efficient simulator $\mathcal{S}$, there exists an efficient differentiator $\mathcal{D}_{A,\mathcal{S}}$ and a noticeable function $\rho(n)$ such that*

$$\text{Adv}^{\text{indif}}_{A^{\Sigma_1},\Sigma_2,\mathcal{S},\mathcal{D}_{A,\mathcal{S}}}(1^\lambda) := \left| \Pr[\text{Real}_{\Sigma_1,\mathcal{D}_{A,\mathcal{S}}}] - \Pr[\text{Ideal}_{\Sigma_2,\mathcal{S},\mathcal{D}_{A,\mathcal{S}}}] \right| \geq \rho(n).$$

Observe that, if an idealized model Σ_2 is computational indifferentiably separated from another idealized model Σ_1, it means that, we cannot build a scheme A^{Σ_1} such that A^{Σ_1} is indifferentiable from Σ_2, even under arbitrarily strong computational assumptions.

3   ROM ◁ GGM

In this section, we prove that random oracles are strictly milder than generic groups. Concretely, we establish our theorem as follows: 1) the generic group model is computational indifferentiably separated from the random oracle model; 2) the generic group model statistically implies the random oracle model. For the former case, we first present the formal definition of the discrete log identification (DLI) problems in Sect. 3.1, then prove that ROM does not computationally imply GGM in Sect. 3.2; for the latter case, we build an indifferentiable random oracle model from the generic group model in Sect. 3.3.

3.1   Discrete Log Identification

In this section, we present the formal description of the discrete log identification problems with respect to (w.r.t.) concrete groups, generic groups, and groups in ROM, respectively. Let $(\mathbb{G}, g, p)$ be a concrete group description, where $\mathbb{G}$ is a cyclic group of prime order p generated by g, we define DLI w.r.t. concrete groups as follows.

Definition 3 (DLI w.r.t. the concrete group.) *Given a concrete group description* $(\mathbb{G}, g, p)$, *a group element* $h := g^x$, *where* $x \xleftarrow{\$} \mathbb{Z}_p$, *an efficient algorithm outputs a circuit* C *such that* C *identifies* x *with good probability, concretely,*

- $\Pr[C(x) = 1] \geq 1 - \epsilon;$
- *for any noticeable function* ρ, $\Pr_{x' \neq x}[C(x') = 1] \leq \rho,$

where ϵ *is negligible and the probability is over the sampling of* x' *and* C*'s randomness. We say DLI w.r.t. the concrete group is hard if no efficient adversary outputs such a circuit.*

Trivial to note that, for any concrete group description (i.e., groups in the standard model), DLI is easy; we set $C(x')$ to be 1 if and only if $g^{x'} = h$. Next, we extend DLI to idealized models. Let $\mathcal{G} = (\mathcal{G}^{\mathsf{label}}, \mathcal{G}^{\mathsf{add}})$ be a generic group and $G^H = (L^H, A^H)$ be a group in the random oracle model, we define DLI w.r.t the generic groups and groups in ROM as follows.

Definition 4. (DLI w.r.t. generic groups.) *Given a generic group* $\mathcal{G} = (\mathcal{G}^{\mathsf{label}}, \mathcal{G}^{\mathsf{add}})$, *a group element* $h := \mathcal{G}^{\mathsf{label}}(x)$, *where* $x \xleftarrow{\$} \mathbb{Z}_p$, *an efficient algorithm with access to* $\mathcal{G}$ *outputs a "query-free" circuit* C_{GGM} *such that* C_{GGM} *identifies* x *with good probability, specifically,*

- $\Pr[C_{\mathsf{GGM}}(x) = 1] \geq \frac{1}{2};$
- *for any noticeable function* ρ, $\Pr_{x' \neq x}[C_{\mathsf{GGM}}(x') = 1] \leq \rho,$

where the probability is over the sampling of x' *and* C_{GGM}*'s randomness. We say DLI w.r.t. generic groups is hard if no efficient adversary outputs such a circuit.*

Definition 5. (DLI w.r.t. groups in the ROM.) *Given a group in the ROM* $G^H = (L^H, A^H)$, *a group element* $h := L^H(x)$, *where* $x \xleftarrow{\$} \mathbb{Z}_p$, *an efficient algorithm with access to the random oracle* H *outputs a "query-free" circuit* $C_{\mathsf{G\text{-}ROM}}$ *such that* $C_{\mathsf{G\text{-}ROM}}$ *identifies* x *with good probability, specifically,*

- $\Pr[C_{\mathsf{G\text{-}ROM}}(x) = 1] \geq \frac{3}{4};$
- *for any noticeable function* ρ, $\Pr_{x' = x}[C_{\mathsf{G\text{-}ROM}}(x') = 1] \leq \rho,$

where the probability is over the sampling of x' *and* $C_{\mathsf{G\text{-}ROM}}$*'s randomness. We say DLI w.r.t. groups in the random oracle model is hard if no efficient adversary outputs such a circuit.*

$$\begin{array}{|l|}
\hline
\mathcal{B}^{\mathcal{G}}(\mathcal{G}^{\mathsf{label}}(1), \mathcal{G}^{\mathsf{label}}(x)): \\
S \leftarrow \emptyset;\ C_{\mathsf{GGM}} \leftarrow \mathcal{A}^{\mathcal{G}}(\mathcal{G}^{\mathsf{label}}(1), \mathcal{G}^{\mathsf{label}}(x)); \\
\text{for } i = 0 \text{ to } p - 1, \\
\quad \text{if } C_{\mathsf{GGM}}(i) = 1,\ S \leftarrow S \cup \{i\}; \\
y \xleftarrow{\$} S; \\
\text{return } y. \\
\hline
\end{array}$$

Fig. 2. A query-efficient adversary breaks Discrete Logarithm in the GGM

Remark 2. Careful readers may argue that it would be more clear if we define the second condition to be "$\Pr_{x' \neq x}[C_{\mathsf{GGM}}(x') = 1] \leq \epsilon$, where ϵ is negligible". We stress that we define it as such for purpose. Recall that, we apply the framework of indifferentiability for our separation, which means that we must build an efficient simulator. We prove our result via contraposition and proceed to assume that C_{GGM} accepts x with some noticeable probability, say ρ, then we can choose proper parameters (based on ρ) to build an efficient simulator (more details as shown below). However, if we define the second condition as "$\Pr_{x' \neq x}[C_{\mathsf{GGM}}(x') = 1] \leq \epsilon$", then we need to show that C_{GGM} accepts x with non-negligible probability. Note that every noticeable function is non-negligible, but the converse is not true for general, which means it is not sufficient to prove "C_{GGM} accepts x with noticeable probability". On the other hand, for the first condition that "$\Pr[C_{\mathsf{GGM}}(x) = 1] \geq \frac{1}{2}$" and "$\Pr[C_{\mathsf{G\text{-}ROM}}(x) = 1] \geq \frac{3}{4}$", we stress that we need a noticeable gap between C_{GGM} and $C_{\mathsf{G\text{-}ROM}}$ in our proof, and the value "$\frac{1}{2}$" and "$\frac{3}{4}$" are just chosen for ease.

3.2 GGM Is Computational Indifferentiably Separated from ROM

In this section, we give evidence that the random oracle model is strictly milder heuristic than the generic group model. Formally,

Theorem 2. *GGM is computational indifferentiably separated from ROM.*

Proof. Let $\mathcal{G} = (\mathcal{G}^{\mathsf{label}}, \mathcal{G}^{\mathsf{add}})$ be a generic group and $G^H = (L^H, A^H)$ be any group in the ROM, respectively. The argument goes in three steps:

1. DLI w.r.t. G^H is easy.
2. If G^H is indifferentiable from generic groups and DLI w.r.t. G^H is easy, then DLI w.r.t. generic groups is also easy.
3. DLI w.r.t. generic groups is hard.

The three steps above form a contradiction, so the premise "G^H is indifferentiable from generic groups" cannot hold, completing the proof.

Below we prove the three steps one by one; for readability, we do them in reverse order, starting from step 3.

Lemma 1. *DLI w.r.t. generic groups is hard.*

Proof. Assuming there is an efficient adversary $\mathcal{A}$ making at most q queries to $\mathcal{G}$ which breaks DLI, we can convert $\mathcal{A}$ into a query-efficient adversary $\mathcal{B}$, as shown in Fig. 2, that breaks Discrete Logarithm in the GGM[8].

According to the description of $\mathcal{B}$, we have that $\mathcal{B}$ makes at most q queries to $\mathcal{G}$. We set ρ to be $\frac{1}{q^{12}}$ and mbound to be $1 + \frac{p-1}{q^6}$, respectively; applying Markov's inequality, it is apparent that $\Pr[|S| > \text{mbound}] \leq \frac{1}{q^6}$. Therefore, we have that

$$
\Pr[\mathcal{B} \text{ outputs } x] = \sum_{i=1}^{p} \Pr[|S| = i] \cdot (\frac{1}{i}) \cdot \Pr[x \in S \mid |S| = i]
$$

$$
\geq \Pr[|S| \leq \text{mbound}] \cdot (\frac{1}{\text{mbound}}) \cdot \Pr[x \in S \mid |S| \leq \text{mbound}].
$$

Note that $\Pr[x \in S] \geq 1/2$, which means that $\Pr[x \in S \mid |S| \leq \text{mbound}]$ should be close to $1/2$, because $|S| \leq \text{mbound}$ happens with high probability. Formally, we denote A and B to be the events "$x \in S$" and "$|S| \leq \text{mbound}$", respectively, we have that

$$
\Pr[\mathsf{A}|\mathsf{B}] = \frac{\Pr[\mathsf{A}] - \Pr[\mathsf{A}|\neg\mathsf{B}]\Pr[\neg\mathsf{B}]}{\Pr[\mathsf{B}]} \geq \frac{\Pr[\mathsf{A}] - \Pr[\neg\mathsf{B}]}{\Pr[\mathsf{B}]} = 1 - \frac{1 - \Pr[\mathsf{A}]}{\Pr[\mathsf{B}]}.
$$

Substituting into the inequalities above, we have that,

$$
\Pr[\mathcal{B} \text{ outputs } x] \geq (1 - \frac{1}{q^6}) \cdot (\frac{1}{1 + \frac{p-1}{q^6}}) \cdot (1 - \frac{1}{2} \cdot (1 - \frac{1}{q^6}))
$$

$$
\geq \frac{1}{2} \cdot (1 - \frac{1}{q^6}) \cdot \frac{q^6}{q^6 + p - 1} = \Theta(\frac{q^6}{p}) > O(\frac{q^2}{p}),
$$

which contradicts the hardness of discrete log in the GGM [Sho97].

Lemma 2. *If G^H is indifferentiable from $\mathcal{G}$ and DLI w.r.t. G^H is easy, then DLI w.r.t. $\mathcal{G}$ is easy.*

Proof. Let $\mathcal{A}^H$ be an adversary which breaks DLI with respect to G^H, that is, $\mathcal{A}^H$ takes $(L^H(1), L^H(x))$ as inputs, makes at most q queries to H, outputs a query-free circuit $C_{\text{G-ROM}}$ such that $C_{\text{G-ROM}}$ identifies x with good probability. According to the definition of indifferentiability, we know that there exists a simulator S that makes at most $q^* = \text{poly}(q)$ queries to $\mathcal{G}$ and simulates the random oracle H properly. That is, in the ideal world, given the adversary $\mathcal{A}$ that takes $(\mathcal{G}^{\mathsf{label}}(1), \mathcal{G}^{\mathsf{label}}(x))$ as inputs, $\mathcal{A}^{S^{\mathcal{G}}} = \mathcal{A}^{(S^{\mathcal{G}})}$ outputs a query-free circuit C_{GGM}[9]. By definition, we have that no efficient differentiator $\mathcal{D}$ distinguishes these two

---

[8] Note that $\mathcal{B}$ is time-inefficient if p is super-polynomial, which is not a problem in our setting since the lower bound of discrete log in the GGM [Sho97] only counts the number of oracle queries.

[9] Note that $\mathcal{A}^S$ is the adversary against DLI with respect to $\mathcal{G}$.

circuits, i.e., $C_{\text{G-ROM}}$ and C_{GGM}. Next, we claim that C_{GGM} also identifies x with good probability.

C_{GGM} *Accepts* x *with Good Probability.* In this part, we prove that if $\Pr[C_{\text{GGM}}(x) = 1] < \frac{1}{2}$, then there exists an efficient differentiator which breaks indifferentiability.

Differentiator in real world $\mathcal{D}_{\text{real}}$	Differentiator in ideal world $\mathcal{D}_{\text{ideal}}$
$x \xleftarrow{\$} \mathbb{Z}_p$; $\mathsf{U}_1 \leftarrow L^H(1), \mathsf{U}_2 \leftarrow L^H(x)$; $C_{\text{G-ROM}} \leftarrow \mathcal{A}^H(\mathsf{U}_1, \mathsf{U}_2)$; if $C_{\text{G-ROM}}(x) = 1$, return 1; return 0.	$x \xleftarrow{\$} \mathbb{Z}_p$; $\mathsf{U}_1 \leftarrow \mathcal{G}^{\text{label}}(1), \mathsf{U}_2 \leftarrow \mathcal{G}^{\text{label}}(x)$; $C_{\text{GGM}} \leftarrow \mathcal{A}^{\mathcal{S}^{\mathcal{G}}}(\mathsf{U}_1, \mathsf{U}_2)$; if $C_{\text{GGM}}(x) = 1$, return 1; return 0.

Fig. 3. Differentiator-1 against Indifferentiability.

According to the differentiator in Fig. 3, we have that $\Pr[\mathcal{D}_{\text{real}} = 1] \geq \frac{3}{4}$ but if $\Pr[C_{\text{GGM}}(x) = 1] < \frac{1}{2}$, we have that $\Pr[\mathcal{D}_{\text{ideal}} = 1] < \frac{1}{2}$, which means the advantage of the differentiator in Fig. 3 is at least $\frac{3}{4} - \frac{1}{2} = \frac{1}{4}$.

C_{GGM} *Accepts* x' ($x' \neq x$) *with Small Probability.* In this part, we prove that for any noticeable function ρ, $\Pr_{x' \neq x}[C_{\text{GGM}}(x') = 1] \leq \rho$. By contraposition, we assume that there exists a noticeable function ρ^*, such that $\Pr_{x' \neq x}[C_{\text{GGM}}(x') = 1] > \rho^*$, then we proceed to build an efficient differentiator that breaks indifferentiability. Let n be a polynomial such that $n \geq \frac{1}{\rho^*}$, we build our differentiator in Fig. 4.

Differentiator in real world $\mathcal{D}_{\text{real}}$	Differentiator in ideal world $\mathcal{D}_{\text{ideal}}$
$x \xleftarrow{\$} \mathbb{Z}_p$; $z_1, \ldots, z_n \xleftarrow{\$} \mathbb{Z}_p \setminus \{x\}$; $\mathsf{U}_1 \leftarrow L^H(1), \mathsf{U}_2 \leftarrow L^H(x)$; $C_{\text{G-ROM}} \leftarrow \mathcal{A}^H(\mathsf{U}_1, \mathsf{U}_2)$; for $i = 1$ to n; $\quad$ if $C_{\text{G-ROM}}(z_i) = 1$, then return 0; return 1.	$x \xleftarrow{\$} \mathbb{Z}_p$; $z_1, \ldots, z_n \xleftarrow{\$} \mathbb{Z}_p \setminus \{x\}$; $\mathsf{U}_1 \leftarrow \mathcal{G}^{\text{label}}(1), \mathsf{U}_2 \leftarrow \mathcal{G}^{\text{label}}(x)$; $C_{\text{GGM}} \leftarrow \mathcal{A}^{\mathcal{S}^{\mathcal{G}}}(\mathsf{U}_1, \mathsf{U}_2)$; for $i = 1$ to n; $\quad$ if $C_{\text{GGM}}(z_i) = 1$, then return 0; return 1.

Fig. 4. Differentiator-2 against Indifferentiability.

In the real world, by the statement of Lemma 2, we have that for any noticeable function, say $\frac{0.05}{n}$, $\Pr[C_{\text{GGM}}(z_i) = 1] \leq \frac{0.05}{n}$. According to the differentiator in Fig. 4, immediately observe that $\Pr[\mathcal{D}_{\text{real}} = 1] \leq n \cdot \frac{0.05}{n}$, due to union bound.

On the other hand, in the ideal world, if $\Pr_{x' \neq x}[C_{\text{GGM}}(x') = 1] > \rho^*$, then,

$$\Pr[\mathcal{D}_{\text{ideal}} = 1] \geq \left(1 - (1 - \rho^*)^n\right) \geq \left(1 - (1 - \rho^*)^{\frac{1}{\rho^*}}\right)$$

$$\geq (1 - \frac{1}{e}) \cdot (1 - (1 - \frac{1}{p})^n) > (1 - \frac{1}{e}) \cdot \frac{1}{2} \geq 0.2.$$

For the first inequality above, $\mathcal{D}_{\text{ideal}} = 0$ means that $\forall i, C_{\text{GGM}}(z_i) = 0$, and due to independence of z_i, it is apparent that

$$\Pr[\mathcal{D}_{\text{ideal}} = 1 | (\forall i, z_i \neq x)] \geq 1 - (1 - \rho^*)^n.$$

Therefore, the advantage of the differentiator in Fig. 4 is at least $(0.2 - 0.05) > 0.1$. Therefore, we conclude that if G^H is indifferentiable from $\mathcal{G}$ and DLI w.r.t. G^H is easy, then DLI w.r.t. $\mathcal{G}$ is easy. To complete the proof, it suffices to show that DLI w.r.t. any group in the random oracle model is easy.

Lemma 3. *Discrete log identification with respect to G^H is easy.*

Proof. Let $G^H = (L^H, A^H)$ be a group in the random oracle model. By correctness, it is natural to assume that 1) $\forall x' \neq x, L^H(x') \neq L^H(x)$; 2) $\forall x, x' \in \mathbb{Z}_p, A^H(L^H(x), L^H(x')) = L^H(x + x')$. In this lemma, we strengthen our results by only requiring that:

$$\Pr_{x' \neq x}[L^H(x') = L^H(x)] \leq \epsilon;$$
$$\Pr[A^H(L^H(x), L^H(x')) = L^H(x + x')] \geq 1 - \epsilon, \tag{8}$$

where ϵ is negligible and the probability is over the sampling of x, x' and the random oracle H (we explicitly assume that L^H is deterministic, otherwise L^H can be easily distinguished from $\mathcal{G}^{\text{label}}$). Note that, for a proper group in ROM, these two requirements must hold, otherwise we can easily distinguish G^H from a generic group $\mathcal{G}$; in other words these are minimal requirements. Let q be an integer such that $1 \leq q \leq \text{poly}$, we assume that for a single group operation, the algorithms L^H and A^H makes at most q queries to H. Next, we prove that the discrete log identification problem with respect to G^H is easy by constructing an efficient adversary $\mathcal{A}^H$ and a query-free circuit $C_{\text{G-ROM}}$ in Fig. 5.

We clarify some undefined notations in Fig. 5; n is a sufficient large integer that'll be specified below, and by $\{(\text{que}_1, \text{res}_1), \dots, (\text{que}_q, \text{res}_q)\} \overset{\text{query}}{\Longleftarrow} L^H(r_i)$, we means that when running the algorithm $L^H(r_i)$, L makes queries $(\text{que}_1, \dots, \text{que}_q)$ to H and the oracle H responds with $(\text{res}_1, \dots, \text{res}_q)$. Note that for a single group operation, the algorithms (L^H or A^H) make at most q queries. We next prove that $C_{\text{G-ROM}}$ identifies x with good probability, which indicates that DLI with respect to G^H is easy.

$C_{\text{G-ROM}}$ *Accepts x with Good Probability.* Here we prove that $\Pr[C_{\text{G-ROM}}(x) = 1] \geq \frac{3}{4}$. By definition, we know that $C_{\text{G-ROM}}(x)$ runs algorithm $L^{S_{\text{que-res}}}(x)$, and outputs 1 if and only if $L^{S_{\text{que-res}}}(x) = L^H(x)$. For any $x, y \in \mathbb{Z}_p$, we denote

$$Q_x := \{(\text{que}_1, \text{res}_1), \dots, (\text{que}_q, \text{res}_q)\} \overset{\text{query}}{\Longleftarrow} L^H(x);$$
$$Q_{x,y} := \{(\text{que}_1, \text{res}_1), \dots, (\text{que}_q, \text{res}_q)\} \overset{\text{query}}{\Longleftarrow} A^H(L^H(x), L^H(y)).$$

According to the description of $\mathcal{A}^H$ in Fig. 5, we have that

$$S_{\text{que-res}} = Q_{x-r,r} \cup Q_{r_1} \cup \dots \cup Q_{r_n}.$$

$\mathcal{A}^H(L^H(1), L^H(x))$:

$S_{\text{que-res}} \leftarrow \Phi, r, r_1, \ldots, r_n \xleftarrow{\$} \mathbb{Z}_p$;

computes $L^H(-r)$ and $L^H(x-r) \leftarrow \mathcal{A}^H(L^H(x), L^H(-r))$;

$\{(\text{que}_1, \text{res}_1), \ldots, (\text{que}_q, \text{res}_q)\} \xleftarrow{\text{query}} \mathcal{A}^H(L^H(x-r), L^H(r))$; //Queries in group addition

$S_{\text{que-res}} \leftarrow S_{\text{que-res}} \cup \{(\text{que}_1, \text{res}_1), \ldots, (\text{que}_q, \text{res}_q)\}$; //Collecting queries in group addition

for $i = 1$ to n,

    $\{(\text{que}_1, \text{res}_1), \ldots, (\text{que}_q, \text{res}_q)\} \xleftarrow{\text{query}} L^H(r_i)$; //Queries in group labeling

    $S_{\text{que-res}} \leftarrow S_{\text{que-res}} \cup \{(\text{que}_1, \text{res}_1), \ldots, (\text{que}_q, \text{res}_q)\}$; //Collecting frequent queries

return $C_{\text{G-ROM}}(\,\cdot\,, S_{\text{que-res}}, L^H(x))$.

$C_{\text{G-ROM}}(\cdot, S_{\text{que-res}}, L^H(x))$:

takes $z \in \mathbb{Z}_p$ as inputs; runs $\text{str} \leftarrow L^{S_{\text{que-res}}}(z)^a$;

when L calls $S_{\text{que-res}}$ with a query que,

if $\exists(\text{que}, \text{res}) \in S_{\text{que-res}}$

    then respond with res; //If the query in $S_{\text{que-res}}$, then responds with the corresponding res.

    else respond with a uniformly sampled res; $S_{\text{que-res}} \leftarrow S_{\text{que-res}} \cup \{(\text{que}, \text{res})\}$;

if $\text{str} = L^H(x)$, return 1;

return 0.

---

^{a} Here we abuse the notation $S_{\text{que-res}}$ as both the set of the query-response tuples and the oracle.

Fig. 5. Efficient Adversary $\mathcal{A}^H$ and query-free circuit $C_{\text{G-ROM}}$ with respect to G^H.

We immediately observe that if $Q_x \subseteq S_{\text{que-res}}$, then $L^{S_{\text{que-res}}}(x) = L^H(x)$, which means $C_{\text{G-ROM}}(x) = 1$. Unfortunately, the statement that $Q_x \subseteq S_{\text{que-res}}$ might not hold because some query in Q_x may be completely ignored when running $\mathcal{A}^H(L^H(x-r), L^H(r))$. Observe that there are two kinds of query-free functions to compute the group element $L^H(x)$, that is, $L^H(x) = \text{func}_1(x, Q_x) = \text{func}_2(x - r, r, Q_{x-r} \cup Q_r \cup Q_{x-r,r})$. func_1 corresponds to computing the group element through the group labeling operation $L^H(x)$, and func_2 corresponds to computing the group element $L^H(x)$ through the group addition operation $\mathcal{A}^H(L^H(x - r), L^H(r))^{10}$. We argue that the only queries we care about are actually in $Q_x \cap (Q_{x-r} \cup Q_r \cup Q_{x-r,r})$, denoted as Q_x^*. Concretely, both func_1 and func_2 are query-free and they reach out to the same output with high probability. Note that func_1 will output $L^H(x)$, no matter what the responses of $(Q_{x-r} \cup Q_r \cup Q_{x-r,r}) \setminus Q_x$ are, and func_2 will output $L^H(x)$, no matter what the responses of $Q_x \setminus (Q_{x-r} \cup Q_r \cup Q_{x-r,r})$ are. Therefore, the group representation $L^H(x)$ is in fact independent of the queries in $Q_x \setminus Q_x^{*11}$, meaning that it is sufficient to prove that $Q_x^* \subset S_{\text{que-res}}$ with high probability.

Note that $Q_{x-r,r} \subset S_{\text{que-res}}$, therefore it is enough to show that $Q_x \cap (Q_{x-r} \cup Q_r) \subset S_{\text{que-res}}$. However, the fact is that both Q_{x-r} and Q_r are unknown to

---

^{10} Here we abuse the notation $L^H(x)$ as both the group element and group labeling operation on x.

^{11} We can view those queries as insensitive queries and replacing the responses to random strings would not affect the encoding value $L^H(x)$ with high probability.

$\mathcal{A}^H$. To resolve this barrier, we show that with high probability the queries in $Q_x \cap (Q_{x-r} \cup Q_r)$ are all frequent queries (defined below). Thus, we can draw sufficiently large number of samples, say $r_1, \ldots, r_n$, record all the queries made in $L^H(r_i)$, and capture all the frequent queries. In other words, we show that

$$Q_x \cap (Q_{x-r} \cup Q_r) \subset Q_{r_1} \cup \cdots \cup Q_{r_n} \subset S_{\text{que-res}}.$$

Now we define the frequent query as follows: let $q_{\text{frq}} = 100q$ and $n = q_{\text{frq}}{}^2 \cdot q$, we say a query (que, res) is a frequent query, if

$$\Pr[(\text{que}, \text{res}) \in Q_z : z \xleftarrow{\$} \mathbb{Z}_p] \geq \frac{1}{q_{\text{frq}}}.$$

We first prove that $Q_{r_1} \cup \cdots \cup Q_{r_n}$ captures all the frequent queries with high probability. In fact, there are at most $\text{Num}_{\text{frq}} = q \cdot q_{\text{frq}}$ frequent queries (denoted by $(\text{que}_1, \text{res}_1), \ldots, (\text{que}_{\text{Num}_{\text{frq}}}, \text{res}_{\text{Num}_{\text{frq}}}))$, and for each query (e.g., $(\text{que}_i, \text{res}_i))$, we have that,

$$\Pr[(\text{que}_i, \text{res}_i) \notin Q_{r_1} \cup \cdots \cup Q_{r_n}] \leq \left(1 - \frac{1}{q_{\text{frq}}}\right)^n = \left(1 - \frac{1}{q_{\text{frq}}}\right)^{q_{\text{frq}}(q \cdot q_{\text{frq}})} \leq e^{-q \cdot q_{\text{frq}}}.$$

Thus, by union bound, it's apparent that

$$\Pr[(\text{que}_i, \text{res}_i) \in Q_{r_1} \cup \cdots \cup Q_{r_n} : \forall i \in [\text{Num}_{\text{frq}}]] \geq 1 - (q \cdot q_{\text{frq}})e^{-q \cdot q_{\text{frq}}} \geq 1 - 100e^{-100}.$$

Now, it remains to be shown that, with high probability, the queries in $Q_x \cap (Q_{x-r} \cup Q_r)$ are all frequent queries. Note that, r is uniformly sampled, which means that the distribution of $(x - r)$, even conditioned on x, is uniform. Therefore, for all queries in Q_{x-r} (i.e., $(\text{que}_1, \text{res}_1), \ldots, (\text{que}_q, \text{res}_q))$, if $(\text{que}_i, \text{res}_i)$ is not a frequent query, then,

$$\Pr[(\text{que}_i, \text{res}_i) \in Q_x] \leq \frac{1}{q_{\text{frq}}}.$$

By a union bound, we have that

$$\Pr[(Q_x \cap Q_{x-r}) \text{ contains non-frequent queries}] \leq \frac{q}{q_{\text{frq}}} = \frac{1}{100}.$$

Symmetrically, we conclude that

$$\Pr[(Q_x \cap Q_r) \text{ contains non-frequent queries}] \leq \frac{q}{q_{\text{frq}}} = \frac{1}{100},$$

which means that

$$\Pr[Q_x \cap (Q_{x-r} \cup Q_r) \text{ are all frequent queries}] \geq 1 - \frac{1}{50}.$$

Combining together, we have that

$$\Pr[Q_x^* \in S_{\text{que-res}}] \geq 1 - \frac{1}{50} - 100e^{-100} \geq \frac{3}{4},$$

which means $\Pr[C_{\text{G-ROM}} \text{ accepts } x] \geq \frac{3}{4}$.

$C_{\text{G-ROM}}$ *Accepts* x' $(x' \neq x)$ *with Small Probability.* To strengthen our result, we here prove that $C_{\text{G-ROM}}$ accepts x' $(x' \neq x)$ with negligible probability. By definition, we have that $C_{\text{G-ROM}}(x')$ runs $L^{S_{\text{que-res}}}(x')$ and outputs 1 if and only if $C_{\text{G-ROM}}(x') = L^H(x)$. We denote

$$Q_{x'} := \left\{ (\mathsf{que}_1, \mathsf{res}_1), \ldots, (\mathsf{que}_q, \mathsf{res}_q) \right\} \xleftarrow{\text{query}} L^H(x'),$$

and there are three cases:

- **Case 1:** $Q_{x'} \subset S_{\text{que-res}}$ and $L^H(x') = L^H(x)$;
- **Case 2:** $Q_{x'} \subset S_{\text{que-res}}$ and $L^H(x') \neq L^H(x)$;
- **Case 3:** $Q_{x'} \not\subset S_{\text{que-res}}$.

Immediately observe that if $Q_{x'} \subset S_{\text{que-res}}$, then $C_{\text{G-ROM}}(x') = L^{S_{\text{que-res}}}(x') = L^H(x')$, and thus

$$\Pr[C_{\text{G-ROM}}(x') = 1 | \text{Case } 1] = \Pr_{x' \neq x}[L^H(x') = L^H(x)] \leq \epsilon;$$

$$\Pr[C_{\text{G-ROM}}(x') = 1 | \text{Case } 2] = 0.$$

It suffices to prove that $\Pr[C_{\text{G-ROM}}(x') | \text{Case } 3] \leq \text{negl}$. We observe that, in either case, $S_{\text{que-res}}$ simulates a well-distributed random oracle (via lazy sampling). In fact, $S_{\text{que-res}}$ stores all the query-response tuples that $\mathcal{A}^H$ calls in Fig. 5; for query $\mathsf{que} \in S_{\text{que-res}}$, it responds with the corresponding res and for others it responds with uniformly sampled string. Therefore, by Eq. 8, we have that

$$\Pr_{x' \neq x}[L^{S_{\text{que-res}}}(x') = L^{S_{\text{que-res}}}(x)] \leq \epsilon.$$

However, what we need to prove is that $\Pr[L^{S_{\text{que-res}}}(x') = L^H(x)] \leq \text{negl}$, but it is unnecessary that $L^{S_{\text{que-res}}}(x) = L^H(x)$. To circumvent this gap, we define an event "$S_{\text{que-res}}$ is good", if once the nonce of $S_{\text{que-res}}$ is fixed, $\Pr_{x' \neq x}[L^{S_{\text{que-res}}}(x') = L^{S_{\text{que-res}}}(x)] \leq \sqrt{\epsilon}$ (the distribution now is only over the sampling of x and x'), and otherwise we say $S_{\text{que-res}}$ is bad. When $S_{\text{que-res}}$ is good, we have that, for any string str, $\Pr[L^{S_{\text{que-res}}}(x') = \mathsf{str}] \leq 2\sqrt[4]{\epsilon}$. By applying a simple partitioning argument in good and bad $S_{\text{que-res}}$, it's apparent that $\Pr[S_{\text{que-res}} \text{ is bad}] \leq \sqrt{\epsilon}$. Now we have that,

$$
\begin{aligned}
\Pr[L^{S_{\text{que-res}}}(x') = L^H(x)] &= \Pr[L^{S_{\text{que-res}}}(x') = L^H(x) | S_{\text{que-res}} \text{ is good}] \cdot \Pr[S_{\text{que-res}} \text{ is good}] \\
&\quad + \Pr[L^{S_{\text{que-res}}}(x') = L^H(x) | S_{\text{que-res}} \text{ is bad}] \cdot \Pr[S_{\text{que-res}} \text{ is bad}] \\
&\leq \Pr[L^{S_{\text{que-res}}}(x') = L^H(x) | S_{\text{que-res}} \text{ is good}] + \Pr[S_{\text{que-res}} \text{ is bad}] \\
&\leq 2\sqrt[4]{\epsilon} + \sqrt{\epsilon} \leq \text{negl}.
\end{aligned}
$$

Combining together, we establish the entire proof. $\qquad\square$

3.3   GGM Implies ROM

In this section, we build an indifferentiable ROM from GGM. Although it is simple, the result appears to be previously unknown.

Building Blocks. Our construction consists of two building blocks:

- $\mathcal{G} = (\mathcal{G}^{\mathsf{label}}, \mathcal{G}^{\mathsf{add}})$ is a generic group that maps $\mathbb{Z}_p$ to some set $S := \{0,1\}^s$;
- Trunc_n^s is a truncation function that takes s-bit string as inputs and outputs its first n bits.

Here we require $s \geq 2\log p + \lambda$ and $n := \lfloor \frac{\log p}{2} \rfloor$. Note that Trunc_n^s truncates any $\mathcal{G}^{\mathsf{label}}(x)$ into an n-bit string. Now, we build an indifferentiable compression function $\mathcal{H}$ that maps $\{0,1\}^{2n} \rightarrow \{0,1\}^n$ as follows:

$$\mathcal{H}(x) = \mathsf{Trunc}_n^s(\mathcal{G}^{\mathsf{label}}(x)).$$

We note that every bit of $\mathcal{H}(x)$ is random and independent, meaning that the outputs are well-distributed. Applying the domain extension technique in [CDMP05], it is straightforward to have an indifferentiable random oracle model from ideal compression functions. Besides, the composition theorem indicates that indifferentiability is transitive, thus it is sufficient to prove that the construction above is indifferentiable from ideal compression function.

Theorem 3 (Indifferentiable Ideal Compression Function). $\mathcal{H}$ *is indifferentiable from an ideal compression function $\mathcal{O}$. More precisely, there is a simulator $\mathcal{S}$ such that for all $(q_{\mathcal{G}^{\mathsf{label}}}, q_{\mathcal{G}^{\mathsf{add}}})$-query differentiator $\mathcal{D}$ with $q_{\mathcal{G}^{\mathsf{label}}} + q_{\mathcal{G}^{\mathsf{add}}} \leq q$, we have*

$$\mathrm{Adv}_{\mathcal{H},\mathcal{O},\mathcal{S},\mathcal{D}}^{\mathsf{indif}} \leq \frac{q^2 + q}{2^\lambda}.$$

The simulator makes at most q queries to $\mathcal{O}$.

$\mathcal{S}.\mathcal{G}^{\mathsf{label}}(x)$:	$\mathcal{S}.\mathcal{G}^{\mathsf{add}}(\mathsf{Z}_0, \mathsf{Z}_1)$:
if $\exists (x,y) \in T_{\mathsf{label}}$,	if $\exists ((\mathsf{Z}_0, \mathsf{Z}_1, \mathsf{Z}_2) \vee (\mathsf{Z}_1, \mathsf{Z}_0, \mathsf{Z}_2)) \in T_{\mathsf{add}}$, return Z_2;
$\quad$ return y;	if $\exists ((x_0, \mathsf{Z}_0) \wedge (x_1, \mathsf{Z}_1) \wedge (x_0 + x_1, \mathsf{Z}_2)) \in T_{\mathsf{label}}$, return Z_2;
$r \twoheadleftarrow \{0,1\}^{s-n}$,	if $\exists ((x_0, \mathsf{Z}_0) \wedge (x_1, \mathsf{Z}_1)) \in T_{\mathsf{label}}$ and $(x_0 + x_1, \mathsf{Z}_2) \notin T_{\mathsf{label}}$,
$T_{\mathsf{label}} \leftarrow T_{\mathsf{label}} \cup \{(x, \mathcal{O}(x) \| r)\}$,	$\quad r \twoheadleftarrow \{0,1\}^{s-n}$, $T_{\mathsf{label}} \leftarrow T_{\mathsf{label}} \cup \{(x_0 + x_1, \mathcal{O}(x_0 + x_1) \| r)\}$,
return $\mathcal{O}(x) \| r$.	$\quad$ return $\mathcal{O}(x_0 + x_1) \| r$;
	return $\perp$.

Fig. 6. Simulator for ideal compression function in terms of two sub-simulators associated with oracle $\mathcal{O}$. These two sub-simulators share two tables $(T_{\mathsf{label}}, T_{\mathsf{add}})$ as joint state (which are initialized empty).

Proof Sketch. According to the definition of indifferentiability, the adversary has one honest interface $\mathcal{H}$ and two adversarial interfaces $\mathcal{G}^{\mathsf{label}}$ and $\mathcal{G}^{\mathsf{add}}$[12]. Therefore, we need to build an efficient simulator $\mathcal{S}$ that can simulate $(\mathcal{G}^{\mathsf{label}}, \mathcal{G}^{\mathsf{add}})$ properly, which means, for any (even computationally unbounded) differentiator $\mathcal{D}$, the view of $\mathcal{D}$ in the real game is close to the view in the ideal game. In the following, we illustrate the description of our simulator in Fig. 6 and then we give the high-level intuition of our proof strategy.

We immediately observe that our simulator makes at most q queries to the ideal compression function $\mathcal{O}$, and that it keeps two tables each of size at most q, meaning that $\mathcal{S}$ is efficient. In the following, we present the intuitive idea of why $\mathcal{S}$ works. Note that $\mathcal{G}$ is a generic group model, hence the responses of a proper simulator should follow the following rules:

- Rule 1: The responses of $\mathcal{G}^{\mathsf{label}}$ are statistically uniform in $\{0,1\}^s$;
- Rule 2: There do not exist $x_0 \neq x_1$ such that $\mathcal{G}^{\mathsf{label}}(x_0) = \mathcal{G}^{\mathsf{label}}(x_1)$;
- Rule 3: $\mathcal{H}(x) = \mathsf{Trunc}_n^s(\mathcal{G}^{\mathsf{label}}(x))$;
- Rule 4: $\mathcal{G}^{\mathsf{label}}(x_0 + x_1) = \mathcal{G}^{\mathsf{add}}(\mathcal{G}^{\mathsf{label}}(x_0), \mathcal{G}^{\mathsf{label}}(x_1))$,
- Rule 5: $\forall Z \notin \{\mathcal{G}^{\mathsf{label}}(x)\}_{x \in \mathbb{Z}_p}, \mathcal{G}^{\mathsf{add}}(Z, \cdot) = \bot$.

Next, we show our simulator achieves those five rules. Observe that rule 1 and 3 trivially hold.

Rule 2. The only way to break this rule is if a collision occurs. As r is uniformly sampled, this bad event is trivially bounded by $\frac{q^2}{2^{s-n}} \leq \frac{q^2}{2^\lambda}$.

Rule 4. Note that, when running $\mathcal{G}^{\mathsf{add}}(Z_0, Z_1)$, if Z_0, Z_1 are the known valid encoding (Z_0, Z_1 have already been put into T_{label}), then this equation holds for free. The only bad event that breaks this rule is when $\mathcal{A}$ makes the addition query before the labeling queries (in the real world, the response is $\mathcal{G}^{\mathsf{label}}(x_0 + x_1)$, while in the ideal world, the simulator outputs $\bot$ instead).

However, if this bad event occurs, then it means that the adversary needs to predict a valid encoding $\mathcal{G}^{\mathsf{label}}(x)$. Of course, the adversary could have the first n bits of $\mathcal{G}^{\mathsf{label}}(x)$, but it has to guess the last $s - n$ bits, which in fact is independent of the adversary's view. Thus this bad event is apparently bounded by $\frac{q*p}{2^{s-n}} \leq \frac{q}{2^\lambda}$.

Rule 5. By the description of $\mathcal{S}.\mathcal{G}^{\mathsf{add}}$, we know that, the simulator always responds with $\bot$ except that both Z_0, Z_1 are the known valid encoding, meaning that if Z is an invalid encoding, $\mathcal{S}.\mathcal{G}^{\mathsf{add}}$ always outputs $\bot$.

4   GGM ⊲ GBM

In this section, we extend our technique to separate the generic bilinear map (GBM) from the generic group model (GGM). Concretely, we establish our theorem as follows: (1) GBM is computational indifferentiably separated from GGM;

---

[12] For ease of exposition, we here only illustrate the simulation for the addition procedure, and subtraction can be simulated identically.

(2) GBM statistically implies GGM. For the former case, we first present the formal definition of DLI problems w.r.t. generic bilinear groups and bilinear groups in the GGM in Sect. 4.1 and then prove that GGM cannot computationally imply GBM in Sect. 4.2; for the latter case, we build an indifferentiable GGM from GBM in the full version of this paper [ZZ21].

Comparing to the techniques in Sect. 3, the one separating GBM from GGM is much more challenging, due to the fact that generic groups have more structure to exploit when attempting to build a bilinear group. Here, we denote $\mathcal{BG} := (\mathcal{B}^{\text{label}}, \mathcal{B}^{\text{label}}_T, \mathcal{B}^{\text{add}}, \mathcal{B}^{\text{add}}_T, \mathcal{B}^{\text{multi}})$ as a generic bilinear group and $B^{\mathcal{G}} = (L^{\mathcal{G}}, L^{\mathcal{G}}_T, A^{\mathcal{G}}, A^{\mathcal{G}}_T, M^{\mathcal{G}})$ be a bilinear group in the GGM. Note that, in the GGM, we can learn $\mathcal{G}^{\text{label}}(x)$ through the oracle $\mathcal{G}^{\text{add}}$ even without knowing x. For instance, given $\mathcal{G}^{\text{label}}(y)$ and $\mathcal{G}^{\text{label}}(z)$ such that $y + z = x$, we can obtain $\mathcal{G}^{\text{label}}(x)$ by group addition operation, i.e., $\mathcal{G}^{\text{add}}(\mathcal{G}^{\text{label}}(y), \mathcal{G}^{\text{label}}(z))$. Therefore, if we adapt our technique from Sect. 3, our procedure for collecting query/response pairs will fail. Concretely, when running $L^{\mathcal{G}}(x)$, the algorithm might make labeling queries on points $(x_1, \ldots, x_q)$, whereas our procedure for generating a database $S_{\text{que-res}}$ may only store query/response pairs with form of addition $(\mathcal{G}^{\text{label}}(y_i), \mathcal{G}^{\text{label}}(z_i), \mathcal{G}^{\text{label}}(y_i + z_i))$, without explicitly knowing either y_i or z_i. As a result, the query-free C fails: when C runs $L^{S_{\text{que-res}}}(x)$ and needs $\mathcal{G}^{\text{label}}(x_i)$, although C knows that $\mathcal{G}^{\text{label}}(x_i)$ exists in $S_{\text{que-res}}$, it does not know which tuple corresponds to $\mathcal{G}^{\text{label}}(x_i)$.

To resolve this difficulty, we propose new techniques: given the addition queries in $S_{\text{que-res}}$, we extract the explicit values x_i so that every relevant query is a labeling query, and the query-free circuit C works. Intuitively, although the tuple above does not specifically give the value x_i, y_i or z_i, it indeed leaks some side information: a linear constraint that $y_i + z_i = x_i$. Our strategy is to collect as many linear-independent constraints, form a linear system and extract x_i by solving the corresponding linear system.

4.1 Discrete Log Identification

In this section, we present the formal description of the discrete log identification problems w.r.t. generic bilinear groups and bilinear groups in the GGM. Formally,

Definition 6 (DLI w.r.t. generic bilinear groups.). *Given a generic bilinear group* $\mathcal{BG} := (\mathcal{B}^{\text{label}}, \mathcal{B}^{\text{label}}_T, \mathcal{B}^{\text{add}}, \mathcal{B}^{\text{add}}_T, \mathcal{B}^{\text{multi}})$, *a source group element* $h := \mathcal{B}^{\text{label}}(x)$, *where* $x \xleftarrow{\$} \mathbb{Z}_p$, *a PPT algorithm with access to* $\mathcal{BG}$ *outputs a "query-free" circuit* C_{GBM} *such that* C_{GBM} *identifies* x *with good probability, specifically,*

- $\Pr[C_{\text{GBM}}(x) = 1] \geq \frac{1}{2}$;
- *for any noticeable function* ρ, $\Pr_{x' \neq x}[C_{\text{GBM}}(x') = 1] \leq \rho$,

where the probability is over the sampling of x' *and* C_{GBM}*'s randomness. We say DLI w.r.t. generic bilinear groups is hard if no PPT adversary outputs such a circuit.*

Definition 7 (DLI w.r.t. bilinear groups in the GGM.). *Given a bilinear group in the GGM* $B^{\mathcal{G}} = (L^{\mathcal{G}}, L_T^{\mathcal{G}}, A^{\mathcal{G}}, A_T^{\mathcal{G}}, M^{\mathcal{G}})$, *a group element* $h := L^{\mathcal{G}}(x)$, *where* $x \xleftarrow{\$} \mathbb{Z}_p$, *a PPT algorithm with access to* $\mathcal{G}$ *outputs a "query-free" circuit* $C_{\text{B-GGM}}$ *such that* $C_{\text{B-GGM}}$ *identifies* x *with good probability, specifically,*

- $\Pr[C_{\text{B-GGM}}(x) = 1] \geq \frac{3}{4}$;
- *for any noticeable function* ρ, $\Pr_{x'=x}[C_{\text{B-GGM}}(x') = 1] \leq \rho$,

where the probability is over the sampling of x' *and* $C_{\text{B-GGM}}$*'s randomness. We say DLI w.r.t. bilinear groups in the generic group model is hard if no PPT adversary outputs such a circuit.*

Applying exactly the same analysis as in Sect. 3.1, we note that DLI with respect to generic bilinear groups is hard.

4.2 GBM Is Computational Indifferentiably Separated from GGM

The high-level strategy of our proof is similar to the one in Sect. 3.2:

1. For any $B^{\mathcal{G}}$, we prove that DLI w.r.t $B^{\mathcal{G}}$ is easy;
2. For any $B^{\mathcal{G}}$, we prove that if $B^{\mathcal{G}}$ is indifferentiable from $\mathcal{BG}$ and DLI w.r.t. $B^{\mathcal{G}}$ is easy, then DLI w.r.t. $\mathcal{BG}$ is also easy.

Therefore, if there exists a bilinear group $B^{\mathcal{G}}$ indifferentiable from GBM, then DLI w.r.t. generic bilinear groups is easy.

Theorem 4. *GBM is computational indifferentiably separated from GGM.*

Proof. Let $\mathcal{BG} = (\mathcal{B}^{\text{label}}, \mathcal{B}_T^{\text{label}}, \mathcal{B}^{\text{add}}, \mathcal{B}_T^{\text{add}}, \mathcal{B}^{\text{multi}})$ be a generic bilinear group and $B^{\mathcal{G}} = (L^{\mathcal{G}}, L_T^{\mathcal{G}}, A^{\mathcal{G}}, A_T^{\mathcal{G}}, M^{\mathcal{G}})$ be a bilinear group in the GGM, respectively. Same as in the proof of Theorem 2, we establish our proof by proving the following two lemmas.

Lemma 4. *If* $B^{\mathcal{G}}$ *is indifferentiable from* $\mathcal{BG}$ *and DLI w.r.t.* $B^{\mathcal{G}}$ *is easy, then DLI w.r.t.* $\mathcal{BG}$ *is easy.*

The proof of Lemma 4 is exactly the same as in Lemma 2, and due to space limit, we give the proof in the full version of this paper [ZZ21].

Lemma 5. *Discrete log identification is easy with respect to* $B^{\mathcal{G}}$.

Proof. Let $B^{\mathcal{G}} = (L^{\mathcal{G}}, L_T^{\mathcal{G}}, A^{\mathcal{G}}, A_T^{\mathcal{G}}, M^{\mathcal{G}})$ be a bilinear group in the GGM. By correctness, it is natural to assume that 1) $\forall x \neq y, L^{\mathcal{G}}(x) \neq L^{\mathcal{G}}(y), L_T^{\mathcal{G}}(x) \neq L_T^{\mathcal{G}}(y)$; 2) $\forall x, y \in \mathbb{Z}_p, A^{\mathcal{G}}(L^{\mathcal{G}}(x), L^{\mathcal{G}}(y)) = L^{\mathcal{G}}(x+y), A_T^{\mathcal{G}}(L_T^{\mathcal{G}}(x), L_T^{\mathcal{G}}(y)) = L_T^{\mathcal{G}}(x+y)$; 3) $\forall x, y \in \mathbb{Z}_p, M^{\mathcal{G}}(L^{\mathcal{G}}(x), L^{\mathcal{G}}(y)) = L_T^{\mathcal{G}}(xy)$. Similar as above, we also strengthen our results by only requiring that:

$$\Pr_{x \neq y}[L^{\mathcal{G}}(x) = L^{\mathcal{G}}(y), L_T^{\mathcal{G}}(x) = L_T^{\mathcal{G}}(y)] \leq \epsilon; \Pr[M^{\mathcal{G}}(L^{\mathcal{G}}(x), L^{\mathcal{G}}(y)) = L_T^{\mathcal{G}}(xy)] \geq 1 - \epsilon;$$

$$\Pr[A^{\mathcal{G}}(L^{\mathcal{G}}(x), L^{\mathcal{G}}(y)) = L^{\mathcal{G}}(x+y), A_T^{\mathcal{G}}(L_T^{\mathcal{G}}(x), L_T^{\mathcal{G}}(y)) = L_T^{\mathcal{G}}(x+y)] \geq 1 - \epsilon,$$

$\mathcal{A}^{\mathcal{G}}(L^{\mathcal{G}}(1), L^{\mathcal{G}}(x))$:

$S_{\text{que-res}} \leftarrow \Phi, u, y_1, \ldots, y_n, z_1, \ldots, z_n \xleftarrow{\$} \mathbb{Z}_p$;

Computes $L^{\mathcal{G}}(ux)$ by repeated doubling and $L_T^{\mathcal{G}}(ux) \leftarrow M^{\mathcal{G}}(L^{\mathcal{G}}(1), L^{\mathcal{G}}(ux))$;

$\{(\text{que}_1^{\text{A}}, \text{res}_1^{\text{A}}), \ldots, (\text{que}_{q_1}^{\text{A}}, \text{res}_{q_1}^{\text{A}})\} \xleftarrow{\text{query}^{\text{A}}} M^{\mathcal{G}}(L^{\mathcal{G}}(1), L^{\mathcal{G}}(ux))$; //Addition queries in pairing

$\{(\text{que}_1^{\text{L}}, \text{res}_1^{\text{L}}), \ldots, (\text{que}_{q_2}^{\text{L}}, \text{res}_{q_2}^{\text{L}})\} \xleftarrow{\text{query}^{\text{L}}} M^{\mathcal{G}}(L^{\mathcal{G}}(1), L^{\mathcal{G}}(ux))$; //Labeling queries in pairing

$S_{\text{que-res}} \leftarrow S_{\text{que-res}} \cup \{(\text{que}_1^{\text{L}}, \text{res}_1^{\text{L}}), \ldots, (\text{que}_{q_2}^{\text{L}}, \text{res}_{q_2}^{\text{L}})\}$; //Collecting labeling queries in pairing

> Extract the explicit values from addition queries by solving a linear system;
> Transform addition queries to labeling queries;
> $\{(\text{que}_1^{\text{L-tr}}, \text{res}_1^{\text{A}}), \ldots, (\text{que}_{q_1}^{\text{L-tr}}, \text{res}_{q_2}^{\text{A}})\} \leftarrow \text{Transf}^{\mathcal{G}}((\text{que}_1^{\text{A}}, \text{res}_1^{\text{A}}), \ldots, (\text{que}_{q_1}^{\text{A}}, \text{res}_{q_1}^{\text{A}}))$.

$S_{\text{que-res}} \leftarrow S_{\text{que-res}} \cup \{(\text{que}_1^{\text{L-tr}}, \text{res}_1^{\text{A}}), \ldots, (\text{que}_{q_1}^{\text{L-tr}}, \text{res}_{q_1}^{\text{A}})\}^{a}$; //Collecting transformed queries

for $i = 1$ to n,

$\quad \{(\text{que}_1^{\text{L}}, \text{res}_1^{\text{L}}), \ldots, (\text{que}_q^{\text{L}}, \text{res}_q^{\text{L}})\} \xleftarrow{\text{query}^{\text{L}}} L^{\mathcal{G}}(y_i)$; //Labeling queries in source group

$\quad S_{\text{que-res}} \leftarrow S_{\text{que-res}} \cup \{(\text{que}_1^{\text{L}}, \text{res}_1^{\text{L}}), \ldots, (\text{que}_q^{\text{L}}, \text{res}_q^{\text{L}})\}$; //Collecting frequent labeling queries

for $i = 1$ to n,

$\quad \{(\text{que}_1^{\text{L}}, \text{res}_1^{\text{L}}), \ldots, (\text{que}_q^{\text{L}}, \text{res}_q^{\text{L}})\} \xleftarrow{\text{query}^{\text{L}}} L_T^{\mathcal{G}}(z_i)$; //Labeling queries in target group

$\quad S_{\text{que-res}} \leftarrow S_{\text{que-res}} \cup \{(\text{que}_1^{\text{L}}, \text{res}_1^{\text{L}}), \ldots, (\text{que}_q^{\text{L}}, \text{res}_q^{\text{L}})\}$; //Collecting frequent labeling queries

return $C_{\text{B-GGM}}(\,\cdot\,, S_{\text{que-res}}, u, L_T^{\mathcal{G}}(ux))$.

$C_{\text{B-GGM}}(\cdot, S_{\text{que-res}}, u, L_T^{\mathcal{G}}(ux))$:

takes $y \in \mathbb{Z}_p$ as inputs; computes $z \leftarrow uy$;

runs $\text{str} \leftarrow L_T^{S_{\text{que-res}}}(z)^{b}$;

when L_T calls $S_{\text{que-res}}$ with a labeling query que^{L},

if $\exists (\text{que}^{\text{L}}, \text{res}^{\text{L}}) \in S_{\text{que-res}}$,

$\quad$ then responds with res^{L}; //If the query in $S_{\text{que-res}}$, then responds with the corresponding res^{L}.

$\quad$ else responds with a uniformly sampled res^{L}; $S_{\text{que-res}} \leftarrow S_{\text{que-res}} \cup \{(\text{que}^{\text{L}}, \text{res}^{\text{L}})\}$;

if $\exists (\text{que}^{\text{L-tr}}, \text{res}^{\text{A}}) \in S_{\text{que-res}}$ and $\text{que}^{\text{L}} = \text{que}^{\text{L-tr}}$,

$\quad$ then responds with res^{A}; //If the query in $S_{\text{que-res}}$, then responds with the corresponding res^{A}.

$\quad$ else responds with a uniformly sampled res^{L}; $S_{\text{que-res}} \leftarrow S_{\text{que-res}} \cup \{(\text{que}^{\text{L}}, \text{res}^{\text{L}})\}$;

if $\text{str} = L_T^{\mathcal{G}}(ux)$,

$\quad$ then return 1;

return 0.

---

^{a} $q_1 + q_2 = q$.

^{b} Here we abuse the notation $S_{\text{que-res}}$ as both the set of the query-response tuples and the oracle.

Fig. 7. Efficient Adversary $\mathcal{A}^{\mathcal{G}}$ and Query-free Circuit $C_{\text{B-GGM}}$ with respect to $B^{\mathcal{G}}$.

where the distribution is over the sampling of x, y and the generic group model $\mathcal{G}$ (we explicitly assume that $B^{\mathcal{G}}$ is deterministic, otherwise $B^{\mathcal{G}}$ can be easily distinguished from $B\mathcal{G}$). As in Sect. 3.2, for a proper bilinear group in the GGM, these requirements must hold. Next we prove that, for any bilinear group $B^{\mathcal{G}}$, the DLI problem is easy. Let q be an integer that $1 \leq q \leq \text{poly}$, we assume that for a single group operation, the algorithm makes at most q queries to $\mathcal{G}$ (i.e., $\mathcal{G}^{\text{label}}(\cdot), \mathcal{G}^{\text{add}}(\cdot, \cdot)$). For the group labeling operations, i.e., $L^{\mathcal{G}}$ and $L_T^{\mathcal{G}}$, we assume that without loss of generality that those algorithms only make labeling queries (i.e., $\mathcal{G}^{\mathsf{label}}$). Next, we prove that the discrete log identification problem with respect to $B^{\mathcal{G}}$ is easy by constructing an efficient adversary $\mathcal{A}^{\mathcal{G}}$ and a query-free circuit $C_{\mathsf{B\text{-}GGM}}$ in Fig. 7.

Observe that if we succeed in transforming the addition queries to the labeling queries (code in the red box in Fig. 7), then applying exactly the same analysis in Lemma 3, $C_{\mathsf{B\text{-}GGM}}$ identifies x with good probability and thus we complete our proof. Due to space limit, we elaborate this "Transform" in the full version of this paper [ZZ21].

Acknowledgements. We thank Mohammad Mahmoody, David Wu and Fermi Ma for the insightful discussions and comments on this paper. We thank the anonymous reviewers for the constructive comments on an earlier draft of this paper.

References

[ABD+13] Andreeva, E., Bogdanov, A., Dodis, Y., Mennink, B., Steinberger, J.P.: On the indifferentiability of key-alternating ciphers. In: Canetti, R., Garay, J.A. (eds.) CRYPTO 2013, Part I. LNCS, vol. 8042, pp. 531–550. Springer, Heidelberg (2013). https://doi.org/10.1007/978-3-642-40041-4_29

[AY20] Agrawal, S., Yamada, S.: Optimal broadcast encryption from pairings and LWE. In: Canteaut, A., Ishai, Y. (eds.) EUROCRYPT 2020, Part I. LNCS, vol. 12105, pp. 13–43. Springer, Cham (2020). https://doi.org/10.1007/978-3-030-45721-1_2

[BB04] Boneh, D., Boyen, X.: Short signatures without random oracles. In: Cachin, C., Camenisch, J.L. (eds.) EUROCRYPT 2004. LNCS, vol. 3027, pp. 56–73. Springer, Heidelberg (2004). https://doi.org/10.1007/978-3-540-24676-3_4

[BF01] Boneh, D., Franklin, M.: Identity-based encryption from the weil pairing. In: Kilian, J. (ed.) CRYPTO 2001. LNCS, vol. 2139, pp. 213–229. Springer, Heidelberg (2001). https://doi.org/10.1007/3-540-44647-8_13

[BF18] Barbosa, M., Farshim, P.: Indifferentiable authenticated encryption. In: Shacham, H., Boldyreva, A. (eds.) CRYPTO 2018, Part I. LNCS, vol. 10991, pp. 187–220. Springer, Cham (2018). https://doi.org/10.1007/978-3-319-96884-1_7

[BR93] Bellare, M., Rogaway, P.: Random oracles are practical: a paradigm for designing efficient protocols. In: Denning, D.E., Pyle, R., Ganesan, R., Sandhu, R.S., Ashby, V. (eds.) ACM CCS 93, pp. 62–73. ACM Press, November 1993

[BR96] Bellare, M., Rogaway, P.: The exact security of digital signatures-how to sign with RSA and rabin. In: Maurer, U. (ed.) EUROCRYPT 1996. LNCS, vol. 1070, pp. 399–416. Springer, Heidelberg (1996). https://doi.org/10.1007/3-540-68339-9_34

[CDMP05] Coron, J.-S., Dodis, Y., Malinaud, C., Puniya, P.: Merkle-Damgård revisited: how to construct a hash function. In: Shoup, V. (ed.) CRYPTO 2005. LNCS, vol. 3621, pp. 430–448. Springer, Heidelberg (2005). https://doi.org/10.1007/11535218_26

[CDMS10] Coron, J.-S., Dodis, Y., Mandal, A., Seurin, Y.: A Domain Extender for the Ideal Cipher. In: Micciancio, D. (ed.) TCC 2010. LNCS, vol. 5978, pp. 273–289. Springer, Heidelberg (2010). https://doi.org/10.1007/978-3-642-11799-2_17

[CGH98] Canetti, R., Goldreich, O., Halevi, S.: The random oracle methodology, revisited (preliminary version). In: 30th ACM STOC, pp. 209–218. ACM Press, May 1998

[CHK+16] Coron, J.-S., Holenstein, T., Künzler, R., Patarin, J., Seurin, Y., Tessaro, S.: How to build an ideal cipher: the indifferentiability of the Feistel construction. J. Cryptol. **29**(1), 61–114 (2016)

[Den02] Dent, A.W.: Adapting the weaknesses of the random Oracle model to the generic group model. In: Zheng, Y. (ed.) ASIACRYPT 2002. LNCS, vol. 2501, pp. 100–109. Springer, Heidelberg (2002). https://doi.org/10.1007/3-540-36178-2_6

[DH76] Diffie, W., Hellman, M.E.: New directions in cryptography. IEEE Trans. Inf. Theory **22**(6), 644–654 (1976)

[DHH+21] Döttling, N., Hartmann, D., Hofheinz, D., Kiltz, E., Schäge, S., Ursu, B.: On the impossibility of purely algebraic signatures. In: Nissim, K., Waters, B. (eds.) TCC 2021, Part III. LNCS, vol. 13044, pp. 317–349. Springer, Cham (2021). https://doi.org/10.1007/978-3-030-90456-2_11

[DRS09] Dodis, Y., Ristenpart, T., Shrimpton, T.: Salvaging Merkle-Damgård for practical applications. In: Joux, A. (ed.) EUROCRYPT 2009. LNCS, vol. 5479, pp. 371–388. Springer, Heidelberg (2009)

[DSSL16] Dodis, Y., Stam, M., Steinberger, J.P., Liu, T.: Indifferentiability of confusion-diffusion networks. In: Fischlin, M., Coron, J.-S. (eds.) EUROCRYPT 2016. Part II, volume 9666 of LNCS, pp. 679–704. Springer, Heidelberg (2016)

[FO99] Fujisaki, E., Okamoto, T.: Secure integration of asymmetric and symmetric encryption schemes. In: Wiener, M.J. (ed.) CRYPTO'99. LNCS, vol. 1666, pp. 537–554. Springer, Heidelberg (1999)

[FS87] Fiat, A., Shamir, A.: How to prove yourself: Practical solutions to identification and signature problems. In: Odlyzko, A.M. (ed.) CRYPTO'86. LNCS, vol. 263, pp. 186–194. Springer, Heidelberg (1987)

[IR89] Impagliazzo, R., Rudich, S.: Limits on the provable consequences of one-way permutations. In: 21st ACM STOC, pp. 44–61. ACM Press, May 1989

[LR88] Luby, M., Rackoff, C.: How to construct pseudorandom permutations from pseudorandom functions. SIAM J. Comput. **17**(2) (1988)

[Mau05] Maurer, U.: Abstract models of computation in cryptography. In: Smart, N.P. (ed.) Cryptography and Coding 2005. LNCS, vol. 3796, pp. 1–12. Springer, Heidelberg (2005). https://doi.org/10.1007/11586821_1

[MRH04] Maurer, U., Renner, R., Holenstein, C.: Indifferentiability, impossibility results on reductions, and applications to the random Oracle methodology. In: Naor, M. (ed.) TCC 2004. LNCS, vol. 2951, pp. 21–39. Springer, Heidelberg (2004). https://doi.org/10.1007/978-3-540-24638-1_2

[MVO91] Menezes, A., Vanstone, S.A., Okamoto, T.: Reducing elliptic curve logarithms to logarithms in a finite field. In: 23rd ACM STOC, pp. 80–89. ACM Press, May 1991

[PRV12] Papakonstantinou, P.A., Rackoff, C.W., Vahlis, Y.: How powerful are the DDH hard groups? Cryptology ePrint Archive, Report 2012/653 (2012). https://eprint.iacr.org/2012/653

[PS96] Pointcheval, D., Stern, J.: Security proofs for signature schemes. In: Maurer, U. (ed.) EUROCRYPT 1996. LNCS, vol. 1070, pp. 387–398. Springer, Heidelberg (1996). https://doi.org/10.1007/3-540-68339-9_33

[RSS11] Ristenpart, T., Shacham, H., Shrimpton, T.: Careful with composition: limitations of the indifferentiability framework. In: Paterson, K.G. (ed.) EUROCRYPT 2011. LNCS, vol. 6632, pp. 487–506. Springer, Heidelberg (2011). https://doi.org/10.1007/978-3-642-20465-4_27

[RSS20] Rotem, L., Segev, G., Shahaf, I.: Generic-group delay functions require hidden-order groups. In: Canteaut, A., Ishai, Y. (eds.) EUROCRYPT 2020, Part III. LNCS, vol. 12107, pp. 155–180. Springer, Cham (2020). https://doi.org/10.1007/978-3-030-45727-3_6

[Sho97] Shoup, V.: Lower bounds for discrete logarithms and related problems. In: Fumy, W. (ed.) EUROCRYPT 1997. LNCS, vol. 1233, pp. 256–266. Springer, Heidelberg (1997). https://doi.org/10.1007/3-540-69053-0_18

[Zha20] Zhandry, M.: New techniques for traitor tracing: size $N^{1/3}$ and more from pairings. In: Micciancio, D., Ristenpart, T. (eds.) CRYPTO 2020, Part I. LNCS, vol. 12170, pp. 652–682. Springer, Cham (2020). https://doi.org/10.1007/978-3-030-56784-2_22

[Zha22] Zhandry, M.: To Label, or Not To Label (in Generic Groups). In: Dodis, Y., Shrimpton, T. (eds.) CRYPTO 2022. LNCS, vol. 13509, pp. 66–96. Springer, Cham (2022). https://doi.org/10.1007/978-3-031-15982-4_3

[ZZ18] Zhandry, M., Zhang, C.: Impossibility of order-revealing encryption in idealized models. In: Beimel, A., Dziembowski, S. (eds.) TCC 2018, Part II. LNCS, vol. 11240, pp. 129–158. Springer, Cham (2018). https://doi.org/10.1007/978-3-030-03810-6_5

[ZZ20] Zhandry, M., Zhang, C.: Indifferentiability for public key cryptosystems. In: Micciancio, D., Ristenpart, T. (eds.) CRYPTO 2020, Part I. LNCS, vol. 12170, pp. 63–93. Springer, Cham (2020). https://doi.org/10.1007/978-3-030-56784-2_3

[ZZ21] Zhandry, M., Zhang, C.: The relationship between idealized models under computationally bounded adversaries. Cryptology ePrint Archive (2021)

Just How Fair is an Unreactive World?

Srinivasan Raghuraman[1] and Yibin Yang[2]

[1] Visa Research and MIT, Cambridge, USA
[2] Georgia Institute of Technology, Atlanta, USA
yyang811@gatech.edu

Abstract. Fitzi, Garay, Maurer, and Ostrovsky (J. Cryptology 2005) showed that in the presence of a dishonest majority, no primitive of cardinality $n-1$ is complete for realizing an arbitrary n-party functionality with *guaranteed output delivery*. In this work, we show that in the presence of $n-1$ corrupt parties, no *unreactive* primitive of cardinality $n-1$ is complete for realizing an arbitrary n-party functionality with *fairness*. We show more generally that for $t > \frac{n}{2}$, in the presence of t malicious parties, no *unreactive* primitive of cardinality t is complete for realizing an arbitrary n-party functionality with *fairness*. We complement this result by noting that $(t+1)$-wise fair exchange is complete for realizing an arbitrary n-party functionality with *fairness*. In order to prove our results, we utilize the primitive of fair coin tossing and the notion of *predictability*. While this notion has been considered in some form in past works, we come up with a novel and non-trivial framework to employ it, one that readily generalizes from the setting of two parties to multiple parties, and also to the setting of unreactive functionalities.

Keywords: Secure computation · Unreactive functionalities · Fair coin tossing

1 Introduction

Secure multiparty computation (MPC) [30] allows a set of n mutually mistrusting parties to perform a joint computation on their inputs that reveals only the output of the computation and nothing else. Several definitions of MPC have been considered in the literature. Often, they have a lot to do with the kinds of adversaries we are trying to achieve security against, and in particular, the number of parties t that the adversary is allowed to corrupt. The most commonly used definition is that of *security-with-abort*, where the adversary is allowed to abort or quit after learning its output, even if the honest parties do not learn theirs. In contrast to security-with-abort, one can consider stronger notions of security such as *fairness* and *guaranteed output delivery*. Fairness means that either all parties get the output or none do. Guaranteed output delivery means that all parties get the output. In settings where a majority of the participating parties can be corrupted, that is, $t \geq \frac{n}{2}$, all feasibility results [8,9,15,28,30] that design a protocol for MPC only provide security-with-abort. On the other

© International Association for Cryptologic Research 2023
J. Guo and R. Steinfeld (Eds.): ASIACRYPT 2023, LNCS 14443, pp. 420–450, 2023.
https://doi.org/10.1007/978-981-99-8736-8_14

hand, when only up to $t < \frac{n}{3}$ parties can be corrupted, then there exist MPC protocols with guaranteed output delivery [8,9] (this result can be extended to a setting where up to $t < \frac{n}{2}$ parties can be corrupted assuming the existence of a broadcast channel [15,28]). Cleve [10] showed that dishonest majority fair coin tossing is impossible, inferring that MPC with even fairness is impossible in general for $t \geq \frac{n}{2}$ (although several works [3,4,16,18] showed the existence of non-trivial functions for which MPC with fairness and even guaranteed output delivery is possible in the dishonest majority setting).

Given the above fairly tight characterization of what can be achieved in the realm of MPC, a natural question is whether additional resources, that we call *channels* or *functionalities*[1], help to achieve stronger security for MPC, and if so, by how much. Indeed, as we noted above, a broadcast channel moves the boundary from $t < \frac{n}{3}$ to $t < \frac{n}{2}$ for MPC with guaranteed output delivery. Even the impossibility result of Cleve [10] can be trivially bypassed with access to a fair exchange functionality. One of the seminal works in this line is that of Fitzi, Garay, Maurer, and Ostrovsky [13] who studied functionalities that enable MPC with guaranteed output delivery in the presence of a dishonest majority. They showed that no functionality of cardinality[2] $n - 1$ is complete for n-party MPC. More generally, for $n \geq 3$ and $\beta < n$, they show that no functionality of cardinality β is complete when $t \geq \lceil \frac{\beta-1}{\beta+1} \cdot n \rceil$. Also, when $t \geq n - 2$, no functionality of cardinality $\beta < n$ is complete (they also show a primitive of cardinality n that is complete for n-party MPC when $t \geq n - 2$).

The impossibility results in [13] are derived by showing the *impossibility of broadcast* given a functionality of cardinality β. Cohen and Lindell [12] showed that the presence of a broadcast channel is inconsequential to achieving the goal of fairness, that is, they showed that any protocol for fair computation that uses a broadcast channel can be compiled into one that does not use a broadcast channel assuming one-way functions (they also showed that assuming the existence of a broadcast channel, any protocol for fair secure computation can be compiled into one that provides guaranteed output delivery). Therefore, the impossibility results of [13] does not extend to MPC with fairness, giving rise to the question of whether there exist functionalities of cardinality $\beta < n$ that are complete for MPC with fairness.

Gordon et al. [17] propose primitives that are complete for MPC with fairness[3]. However, these primitives are of cardinality n, and thus do not answer the question of whether a primitive of cardinality less then n can be complete for MPC with fairness. Recently, Kumaresan et al. [23] propose a functionality of cardinality 2 called *synchronizable fair exchange* ($\mathcal{F}_{\mathsf{SyX}}$) that is complete

---

[1] These channels may be implemented via a trusted third party, or hardware or cryptographic assumptions.

[2] Cardinality refers to the number of parties interacting with a single instance of the ideal primitive.

[3] In fact, some of their primitives are also complete for MPC with guaranteed output delivery. The upside of these primitives is that unlike [13], their primitive complexity is independent of the function being computed.

for MPC with fairness in the presence of a dishonest majority, thus answering the question raised above. However, $\mathcal{F}_{\text{SyX}}$ is a *reactive* functionality. Reactive functionalities can be invoked multiple times and potentially maintain states between invocations. Therefore, reactive functionalities clearly have the potency to be far more powerful than *unreactive* functionalities that can only be invoked once. However, in practice, unreactive functionalities are more desirable than reactive ones. Even with the emergence of enclave technologies, it is a known fact that persistent storage is undesirable and exposes a larger attacking surface. Using such technologies to instantiate unreactive functionalities is more secure in practice. For this and other reasons, the assumption of having a reactive functionality is undoubtedly strong one and hard one to justify. Indeed, if one could achieve the same things that $\mathcal{F}_{\text{SyX}}$ does, but with unreactive functionalities, that would be preferable. Given this, we pose the following question that we *completely* address in our work:

> *Just how fair is an unreactive world with only unreactive functionalities?*
> *Is MPC with fairness achievable with unreactive functionalities?*

False Folklore. At first glance, it might seem that reactive functionalities can be emulated by using unreactive functionalities and standard authenticated secret sharing techniques (to share the state after each stage of the reactive functionality). This "folklore" emulation is *not secure when considering fair MPC.* This is because reactive functionalities can provide the honest parties with non-trivial output even if the adversary aborts. However, if one emulates a reactive functionality using an unreactive one and secret sharing, honest parties cannot obtain such outputs after the adversary aborts since the adversary needs to provide its shares for the emulation. This is crucial because in the multiparty setting, invoking reactive functionalities once may be sufficient for the adversary to get the output, but not the honest party, which is what makes our result non-trivial.

Our Contributions. In this work, we show that an unreactive world is not very fair. On the negative side, we show that unreactive functionalities of cardinality β upper bounded by $n-1$ are incomplete for MPC with fairness. More generally, for $t > \frac{n}{2}$ and $\beta \leq t$, no unreactive functionality of cardinality β is complete for MPC with fairness. We establish this result by showing that a specific n-party primitive, *fair coin tossing*, cannot be realized using unreactive functionalities of cardinality t in the presence of t malicious parties for $t > \frac{n}{2}$.

One could view our work as an extension of the result of [10] to the setting of unreactive functionalities. However, the extension is non-trivial as the techniques of [10] face several challenges in the setting of unreactive functionalities. In order to surmount these challenges, we introduce a *novel* protocol-attacking framework based on the notion of *predictability*. This notion has been considered in some form in past works (e.g., [2, 10, 20, 21]), but our framework is the first that readily generalizes from the setting of two parties to multiple parties, and also to the setting of unreactive functionalities.

On the positive side, we show that for $t \geq \frac{n}{2}$[4] and $\beta = t + 1$, the unreactive functionality of β-wise fair exchange is complete for MPC with fairness. For $t = \frac{n}{2}$ and $\beta = 2$, the unreactive functionality of 2-wise fair exchange is complete for MPC with fairness. This *entirely* covers the space of parameters for t and β. We summarize our contributions in Table 1 and in the (informal) theorem below.

Theorem (informal).

- *For $\frac{n}{2} < t < n$, there does not exist a fair coin tossing protocol using unreactive primitives of cardinality upper bounded by t.*
- *For $\frac{n}{2} < t < n$, there exists a protocol for arbitrary MPC with fairness using $(t + 1)$-wise fair exchange.*
- *For $t = \frac{n}{2}$, there exists a protocol for arbitrary MPC with fairness using 2-wise fair exchange.*

Note that our results have very interesting consequences. For instance, our results show that a 2-wise fair coin toss cannot be used to obtain a 3-wise fair coin toss in the presence of 2 malicious parties. Note that this is in contrast to the world of security-with-abort, where oblivious transfer or 2-wise MPC with abort can be used to obtain n-wise MPC with abort for all $n \geq 2$ [22].

Table 1. Our contributions.

t	Insufficient functionalities for fair coin tossing	Sufficient functionalities for fair MPC
$t < \frac{n}{2}$	–	Local computation [14]
$t = \frac{n}{2}$	Local computation [10]	2-wise fair exchange [**ours**]
$t > \frac{n}{2}$	Arbitrary unreactive t-wise [**ours**]	$(t + 1)$-wise fair exchange[a] [**ours**]

[a] Or 2-wise $\mathcal{F}_{\mathsf{SyX}}$ (see [23]).

Full Version. The full version of this paper is [29].

1.1 Related Work on Coin Tossing

To the best of our knowledge, we are the *first* to characterize the feasibility of fair MPC in the presence of unreactive functionalities. Since our lower bounds are based on the primitive of coin tossing, we provide a brief summary of some of the known results on coin tossing. While there are many works in the coin tossing literature, we focus on the ones most relevant to our work. We also note that our lower bounds make use of the notion of predictability, which has been considered in some form in past works (e.g., [2,10,20,21]).

Cleve [10] showed that for any n-party R-round coin tossing protocol where parties are connected with k communication channels, there exists an adversary

---

[4] Note that for $t < \frac{n}{2}$, no functionality is needed for MPC with fairness.

that can bias the honest parties' common output bit by $\Theta(\frac{1}{R})$. Prior to [10]'s lower bound, Awerbuch et al. [5] designed a coin tossing protocol with $\Theta(\frac{1}{\sqrt{R}})$ bias[5]. [5]'s protocol works under *any* hardness assumption and for *any* number of parties. Since then, there have been numerous works that focus on eliminating this gap between $\Theta(\frac{1}{\sqrt{R}})$ for the protocols and $\Theta(\frac{1}{R})$ in the lower bound.

Many works (e.g., [1,7,19,27]) have tried to design new coin tossing protocols to get as close to [10]'s bound as possible, while others (e.g., [6,25]) tried to prove a tighter bound. In the positive direction, the setting is computational and often assumes the existence of *oblivious transfer* (OT).

Other lines of work focus on coin tossing protocols or even general multi-party computations with weaker security guarantees. We refer the reader to the full version for details.

1.2   Technical Overview

Upper Bounds. We note that fair MPC can be reduced to fair reconstruction of a secret [17,23]. We simply demonstrate that a $(t+1)$-wise fair exchange suffices to perform fair reconstruction in the presence of t malicious parties. Intuitively, this follows from the fact that there is always an honest party who is part of the $(t+1)$-wise fair exchange and hence learns the result of the exchange if the adversary does. Our more interesting upper bound is for the case of $t = \frac{n}{2}$ where 2-wise fair exchange suffices. The intuition of the protocol that achieves this is the following. Let s denote the secret to be reconstructed. We secret share s using an $(\frac{n}{2}+1)$-out-of-n secret sharing. Our protocol will require all pairs of parties to exchange their shares using 2-wise fair exchanges. Notice that both the adversary and the honest parties are one share away from the output. Thus, for anyone to learn the output, at least one pair of parties, one of whom is honest and the other malicious, must perform a 2-wise exchange successfully. But on doing so, both sides have enough shares to reconstruct s.

Lower Bounds. A first attempt at proving our lower bounds would be to consider the lower bounds of [10] and somehow generalize them to a model that allows the use unreactive functionalities of cardinality at least 2. We call this model an *unreactive world*, which we formally define in Sect. 3.1. However, this exercise turns out to be a futile one. Right off the bat, for some parameters, fair MPC is not achievable in [10]'s model, but is achievable in ours, as shown by our upper bounds (see Sect. 3.3). Thus, one needs a different approach to prove lower bounds in unreactive worlds.

To this end, we utilize the notions of *predictability* and a *predictor* for coin tossing protocols (see Definitions 4 and 6).[6] At a high level, a predictor is some computation which allows parties to calculate the final output of a coin tossing protocol after executing just a prefix of it. A very intuitive understanding of

---

[5] [10] specified [5]'s protocol for the 2-party case and analyzed the bias.

[6] Our method of employing predictors and predictabilities to attack coin tossing protocols is distinct from other those considered in prior works (e.g. [2,10,20,21]).

predictability is the following. Consider the beginning of the protocol, where parties have access to their local state[7] and nothing else. It is easy to see that the set of all parties can jointly predict the output of the protocol at this stage, while individual parties may not, in fact, should not, be able to. However, at the end of the protocol, each individual party is able to predict the final output. Thus, over the course of protocol, predictability of every subset of parties evolves. Our proof demonstrates and exploits the fact that there are points in the protocol where some subsets of parties can predict the output non-negligibly better than others. In our proof, we call such a non-negligible difference in predictabilities as a *gap*. The crucial step of our proofs will be to locate a gap that will help us construct adversarial strategies that will bias the output of an honest party non-negligibly. We call such a gap an *attackable gap*.

To locate an attackable gap, we introduce the notion of a *predictor graph*. The vertices of this graph are predictors. Two predictors are connected by an edge in the predictor graph if and only if they form what we call an *attackable pair* (see Definitions 5 and 7). It turns out that a non-negligible gap in the predictabilities of an attackable pair is an attackable gap. Thus, it suffices to find an attackable pair with a non-negligible gap. By virtue of the triangle inequality, this reduces to the following problem: find a path of polynomial length in the predictor graph whose endpoints are predictors with a non-negligible gap. Our entire proof technique is demonstrating how to find such paths and thus locate an attackable gap.

As a toy illustration of our technique, we consider the following simple example described in Fig. 1. Consider a 6-party 1-round coin tossing protocol among the 6 parties $\{A, B, C, D, E, F\}$ which only uses the 4-wise unreactive functionalities $\mathcal{F}^{(1)}_{\{C,D,E,F\}}, \mathcal{F}^{(1)}_{\{A,B,E,F\}}, \mathcal{F}^{(1)}_{\{A,B,C,D\}}$ in that order ($\mathcal{F}^{(1)}_{\mathbb{S}}$ denotes the unreactive functionality which is connected to the set of parties $\mathbb{S}$). At the beginning of the protocol (Fig. 1a), no party can predict the output; at the end of the protocol (Fig. 1d), all parties can predict the output. After $\mathcal{F}^{(1)}_{\{C,D,E,F\}}$ is executed (Fig. 1b), if the parties $\{C, D\}$ can predict the output, they will be able to attack the parties $\{A, B\}$ since $\{A, B\}$ *have not received any messages*. Otherwise, the parties $\{C, D\}$ cannot predict the output with one message, and the parties $\{E, F\}$ *will be able to predict* the output with two messages after $\mathcal{F}^{(1)}_{\{A,B,E,F\}}$ is executed (Fig. 1c), and so they can attack the parties $\{C, D\}$.

Let us now translate this intuition into our language of predictor graphs and attackable gaps (see Fig. 2). For $i \in \{0, 1, 2\}$ and $S \in \{\{A, B\}, \{C, D\}, \{E, F\}\}$, let $P^{(i)}_S$ denote the predictability of the parties in the set S after having received i messages through invocations of unreactive functionalities. Note that $P^{(0)} = \frac{1}{2}$ as no party can predict the output at the beginning of the protocol, and $P^{(2)} = 1$ as all parties can predict the output at the end of the protocol. We construct a graph whose nodes are $P^{(i)}_S$ and edges connect attackable pairs. We formally

---

[7] Let us assume that the local state contains all the randomness that the party will ever use through the course of the protocol.

define attackable pairs later, but to get a feel for them, let us explain why $P_{\{A,B\}}^{(0)}$ and $P_{\{C,D\}}^{(1)}$ constitute an attackable pair. After the execution of $\mathcal{F}_{\{C,D,E,F\}}^{(1)}$, $\{C,D\}$ each holds 1 message while $\{A,B\}$ each holds 0 messages. Thus, if the parties $\{C,D\}$ can predict the output with 1 message, they will be able to attack the parties $\{A,B\}$ as noted before. There is more to this story, but it turns out that the attackable pairs correspond to precisely the edges in the predictor graph in Fig. 2. Notice that the predictor graph has a path from $P_{\{A,B\}}^{(0)}$ to $P_{\{E,F\}}^{(2)}$. Recall that $P_{\{A,B\}}^{(0)} = \frac{1}{2}$ and $P_{\{E,F\}}^{(2)} = 1$. By the triangle inequality, at least one of $\left|P_{\{C,D\}}^{(1)} - P_{\{A,B\}}^{(0)}\right|$ and $\left|P_{\{E,F\}}^{(2)} - P_{\{C,D\}}^{(1)}\right|$ must be non-negligible, i.e., at least one of the attackable pairs suffers from an attackable gap.

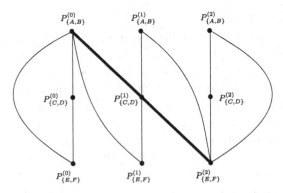

Fig. 1. Toy illustration of our technique.

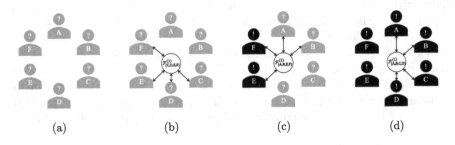

Fig. 2. The *predictor graph* corresponding to the toy illustration from Fig. 1. The dark thicker edges constitute a *path* in the predictor graph that demonstrates the existence of an *attackable gap*.

Our Attack versus Those Based on [10]. One may wonder how our approach of using predictors differs from those in prior works. Indeed, both [10] (and other past works) and our work design adversarial strategies that use "back-up" values of parties in the protocol (captured as the predictor in this work), i.e., the value that a party (or a set of parties) should output in the case that all other parties abort. [10] uses the fact that these values begin as *independent from one another* and *become more and more correlated as the protocol execution progresses*. Our work uses the fact that these values begin as *independent from the final outcome* and *become a better prediction of the final outcome as the protocol execution progresses*. Our approach is not only more intuitive but also generalizes to the multiparty setting and the setting of unreactive functionalities.

2 Preliminaries

2.1 Notation and Definitions

For $n \in \mathbb{N}$, let $[n] = \{1, 2, \ldots, n\}$. Let $\lambda \in \mathbb{N}$ denote the security parameter. Symbols in with an arrow over them such as $\vec{a}$ denote vectors. By a_i we denote the i-th element of the vector $\vec{a}$. By $\mathrm{poly}(\cdot)$, we denote any function which is bounded by a polynomial in its argument. An algorithm $\mathcal{T}$ is said to be PPT if it is modeled as a probabilistic Turing machine that runs in time polynomial in λ. Informally, we say that a function is negligible, denoted by $\delta(\lambda)$, if it vanishes faster than the inverse of any polynomial in λ. Similarly, we denote a function is non-negligible as $\epsilon(\lambda)$.

Let $\mathcal{X}, \mathcal{Y}$ be two probability distributions over some set S. Their *statistical distance* is

$$\mathbf{SD}\,(\mathcal{X}, \mathcal{Y}) \overset{\text{def}}{=} \max_{T \subseteq S} \{|\Pr[\mathcal{X} \in T] - \Pr[\mathcal{Y} \in T]|\}$$

We say that $\mathcal{X}$ and $\mathcal{Y}$ are ν-close if $\mathbf{SD}\,(\mathcal{X}, \mathcal{Y}) \leq \nu$ denoted by $\mathcal{X} \approx_\nu \mathcal{Y}$. We say that $\mathcal{X}$ and $\mathcal{Y}$ are identical if $\mathbf{SD}\,(\mathcal{X}, \mathcal{Y}) = 0$ denoted by $\mathcal{X} \equiv \mathcal{Y}$.

2.2 Secure Computation

We recall most of the definitions regarding secure computation from [12,16]. We present them here for the sake of completeness and self-containedness. Consider the scenario of n parties $P_1, \ldots, P_n$ with private inputs $x_1, \ldots, x_n \in \mathcal{X}$.

Functionalities. A functionality f is a randomized process that maps n-tuples of inputs to n-tuples of outputs, that is, $f : \mathcal{X}^n \to \mathcal{Y}^n$. We write $f = (f^1, \ldots, f^n)$ if we wish to emphasize the n outputs of f, but stress that if $f^1, \ldots, f^n$ are randomized, then the outputs of $f^1, \ldots, f^n$ are correlated random variables. Here, we refer to n as the *cardinality* of the functionality f.

Adversaries. We consider security against *static t-threshold adversaries*, that is, adversaries that corrupt a set of at most t parties, where $0 \leq t < n$[8]. We assume the adversary to be malicious. That is, the corrupted parties may deviate arbitrarily from an assigned protocol.

Model. We assume the parties are connected via a fully connected point-to-point network; we refer to this model as the point-to-point model. We sometimes assume that the parties are given access to a physical broadcast channel (defined in the full version)[9] in addition to the point-to-point network; we refer to this model as the broadcast model. The communication lines between parties are assumed to be ideally authenticated and private (and thus an adversary cannot read or modify messages sent between two honest parties). Furthermore, the delivery of messages between honest parties is guaranteed.

Protocol. An n-party protocol for computing a functionality f is a protocol running in polynomial time and satisfying the following functional requirement: if for every $i \in [n]$, party P_i begins with private input $x_i \in \mathcal{X}$, then the joint distribution of the outputs of the parties is statistically close to $(f^1(\overrightarrow{x}), \ldots, f^n(\overrightarrow{x}))$. We assume that the protocol is executed in a synchronous network, that is, the execution proceeds in rounds: each round consists of a *send phase* (where parties send their message for this round) followed by a *receive* phase (where they receive messages from other parties). The adversary, being malicious, is also *rushing* which means that it can see the messages the honest parties send in a round, before determining the messages that the corrupted parties send in that round.

The security of a protocol is analyzed by comparing what an adversary can do in a real protocol execution to what it can do in an ideal scenario that is secure by definition. This is formalized by considering an *ideal* computation involving an incorruptible *trusted party* to whom the parties send their inputs. The trusted party computes the functionality on the inputs and returns to each party its respective output. Loosely speaking, a protocol is secure if any adversary interacting in the real protocol (where no trusted party exists) can do no more harm than if it were involved in the above-described ideal computation. In the full version we recall formal definitions for the same from [12] and [16].

2.3 Coin Tossing Protocols

In this section, we formally define coin tossing protocols. While we follow prior works, we present the definitions for the sake of completeness.

Definition 1 (Coin Tossing Protocols). *Consider a protocol π among $n \in \mathbb{N}$ parties $P_1, \ldots, P_n$ where each party P_i takes as input the string 1^λ and outputs*

---

[8] Note that when $t = n$, there is nothing to prove.
[9] This can also be viewed as working in the $\mathcal{F}_{bc}$-hybrid model. See Sect. 2.4.

a single bit $res_i \in \{0, 1\}$ after the execution of π. The protocol π is said to be a coin tossing protocol *if and only if when all parties follow the protocol:*

- *[**Uniform Coin**] For all $i \in [n]$,*

$$\left| \Pr[res_i = 0] - \frac{1}{2} \right| \leq \delta_i(\lambda)$$

for some negligible function $\delta_i(\lambda)$.
- *[**Agreement**] For any $i, j \in [n]$,*

$$\Pr[res_i = res_j] = 1$$

Given the above, throughout our work, we will denote the output of a coin tossing protocol by *res*, as opposed to considering res_i for each $P_{i \in [n]}$.

The security property called *t*-resistance of coin tossing protocols is that even if $t \in [n-1]$ parties in the *n*-party coin tossing protocol π are corrupted and deviate arbitrarily from the protocol, the remaining $n - t$ honest parties each agree on and output a uniform bit.

Definition 2 (*t*-resistance). *Consider a coin tossing protocol π among $n \in \mathbb{N}$ parties $P_1, \ldots, P_n$. The protocol π is said to be t-resistant (where $t \in [n-1]$) if and only if when any t parties are corrupt and deviate arbitrarily from π, and the remaining $n - t$ honest parties execute π:*

- *[**Uniform Coin**] For any output $\widetilde{res}_i$ of honest P_i where $i \in [n]$*

$$\left| \Pr[\widetilde{res}_i = 0] - \frac{1}{2} \right| \leq \delta_i(\lambda)$$

for some negligible function $\delta_i(\lambda)$.
- *[**Agreement**] For any $i, j \in [n]$ such that P_i and P_j are honest,*

$$\Pr[\widetilde{res}_i = \widetilde{res}_j] = 1$$

Throughout our work, if an *n*-party coin tossing protocol satisfies *t*-resistance, we call it an *n*-party *t*-fair coin tossing protocol. We may omit *t* and *n* if it is clear from context.

In Definitions 1 and 2, we ask that honest parties make *perfect agreement*, that is, the probability that they agree is 1. This is merely for ease of presentation. All of our results also apply to the setting where honest parties only make statistical agreement, that is, they agree with overwhelming probability in λ. We elaborate on this in Sect. 7.

A critical notion, introduced by [10], is that of *bias*, which is a measure of the non-uniformity (with respect to a uniform coin) of the honest party's coin in the presence of an adversary.

Definition 3 (Bias). *Consider a coin tossing protocol π among $n \in \mathbb{N}$ parties $P_1, \ldots, P_n$. We say an adversary (set of corrupt parties) can bias an honest party P_k (for $k \in [n]$) by $\nu(\lambda)$ if and only if the output $\widetilde{res}_k$ of P_k satisfy*

$$\left| \Pr[\widetilde{res}_k = 0] - \frac{1}{2} \right| \geq \nu(\lambda)$$

2.4   The Hybrid Model

We recall the definition of the hybrid model from [12] and [16]. The hybrid model combines both the real and ideal worlds. Specifically, an execution of a protocol π in the $\mathcal{G}$-hybrid model, for some functionality $\mathcal{G}$, involves parties sending normal messages to each other (as in the real model) and, in addition, having access to a trusted party computing $\mathcal{G}$. The parties communicate with this trusted party in exactly the same way as in the ideal models described above; the question of which ideal model is taken must be specified.

Let $\mathsf{type} \in \{\mathsf{g.d.}, \mathsf{fair}\}$. Let $\mathcal{G}$ be a functionality and let π be an n-party protocol for computing some functionality f, where π includes real messages between the parties as well as calls to $\mathcal{G}$. Let $\mathcal{A}$ be a non-uniform probabilistic polynomial-time machine with auxiliary input z. $\mathcal{A}$ corrupts at most t parties, where $0 \leq t < n$. Denote by $\mathcal{I} \subseteq [n]$ the set of indices of the parties corrupted by $\mathcal{A}$. Let $\mathrm{HYBRID}^{\mathcal{G},\mathsf{type}}_{\pi,\mathcal{I},\mathcal{A}(z)}(\overrightarrow{x}, \lambda)$ be the random variable consisting of the view of the adversary and the output of the honest parties, following an execution of π with ideal calls to a trusted party computing $\mathcal{G}$ according to the ideal model "type" where P_i begins by holding x_i for every $i \in [n]$. Security in the model "type" can be defined in the standard way. We call this the $(\mathcal{G}, \mathsf{type})$-hybrid model. We will suppress type and simply state that we are working in the $\mathcal{G}$-hybrid model. This is because type is implied by the context, $\mathcal{G}$. For instance, unless specified otherwise, when $\mathcal{G} = \mathcal{F}_{\mathsf{bc}}$ (broadcast functionality), $\mathsf{type} = \mathsf{g.d.}$.

2.5   Unreactive Functionalities

Consider a functionality $\mathcal{G}$ with an associated type type. We say that $\mathcal{G}$ is unreactive if and only if the computation performed by $\mathcal{G}$ can be realized by a circuit with access to randomness[10]. An alternative characterization would be that $\mathcal{G}$ only has one phase and hence can be emulated by a one-time[11] trusted third-party with access to randomness. Therefore, an instance of $\mathcal{G}$ will (1) receive the inputs; (2) compute the intended program to obtain the outputs; and (3) deliver the outputs (according to the type). After the delivery process, the instance will be totally obliterated, i.e., it can no longer be accessed. This would mean that different invocations of the same functionality $\mathcal{G}$ can be seen as invocations of multiple "different" functionalities.

3   Bypassing [10]'s Lower Bound in Unreactive Worlds

3.1   Our Model: The Unreactive World

Let $n, \beta \in \mathbb{N}$ and $\beta < n$. Our (n, β)-unreactive world is a hybrid model where n parties $\mathbb{P} \triangleq \{P_1, \ldots, P_n\}$ are equipped with:

---

[10] One way to model this is to consider circuits besides regular computational gates, additionally have "random" gates that simply produce random bits as output.

[11] No internal state is retained between invocations of the functionality.

1. A broadcast channel, in which any of the parties can act as the broadcaster.
2. An arbitrary number of arbitrary unreactive functionalities of type type = g.d. whose cardinality is upper bounded by β.

Protocols in (n, β)-unreactive world adhere to a specific syntax which called the (n, R, β)-*unreactive syntax*. For simplicity, we first consider the case of $\beta = n - 1$. The $(n, R, n-1)$-unreactive syntax describes an R-round protocol that takes the following form:

- Each P_i generates its own local random tape r_i.
- For each round $k \in [R]$, there are n unreactive functionalities of cardinality $n - 1$ being executed *in sequence* denoted by $\mathcal{F}^{(k)}_{\mathbb{P}\backslash\{P_1\}}, \mathcal{F}^{(k)}_{\mathbb{P}\backslash\{P_2\}}, \ldots, \mathcal{F}^{(k)}_{\mathbb{P}\backslash\{P_n\}}$. $\mathcal{F}^{(k)}_{\mathbb{S}}$ denotes the unreactive functionality which is connected to the set of parties $\mathbb{S}$ in the round k.
- After the unreactive functionality phase, each round will also contain a broadcast phase, where each party (from P_1 to P_n) broadcasts in order.
- Finally, each party P_i calculates the output by invoking a procedure Π_i on its random tape r_i and the $2R(n - 1)$ messages it obtained in the protocol.

We describe the $(n, R, n-1)$-unreactive syntax algorithmically in the full version.

We generalize the $(n, R, n - 1)$-unreactive syntax to the (n, R, β)-unreactive syntax arbitrary $\beta < n$ as follows. The main difference lies in the unreactive functionality phase of each round, where there are $\binom{n}{\beta}$ unreactive functionalities of cardinality β being executed in sequence. These $\binom{n}{\beta}$ unreactive functionalities are connected to the $\binom{n}{\beta}$ different β-sized subsets of the n parties. Finally, each party P_i calculates the output by invoking a procedure Π_i on its random tape r_i and the $R(\binom{n-1}{\beta-1} + (n - 1))$ messages it obtained in the protocol.

Formally, let $\mathbb{S}_1, \ldots, \mathbb{S}_{\binom{n}{\beta}}$ be an ordering of the $\binom{n}{\beta}$ β-sized subsets of the n parties. The (n, R, β)-unreactive syntax describes an R-round protocol that takes the following form:

- Each P_i generates its own local random tape r_i.
- For each round $k \in [R]$, there are $\binom{n}{\beta}$ unreactive functionalities of cardinality β being executed *in sequence* denoted by $\mathcal{F}^{(k)}_{\mathbb{S}_1}, \mathcal{F}^{(k)}_{\mathbb{S}_2}, \ldots, \mathcal{F}^{(k)}_{\mathbb{S}_{\binom{n}{\beta}}}$.
- After the unreactive functionality phase, each round will also contain a broadcast phase, where each party (from P_1 to P_n) broadcasts in order.
- Finally, each party P_i calculates the output by invoking a procedure Π_i on its random tape r_i and the $R(\binom{n-1}{\beta-1} + (n - 1))$ messages from the execution.

Note that the (n, R, β)-unreactive syntax supports unreactive functionalities of cardinality below β as well. Indeed, a functionality of cardinality k can be emulated by some functionality of cardinality k' for any $k \leq k'$.

Additionally, the ordering of the unreactive functionalities can be *entirely arbitrary*. This follows from the proof of Lemma 1, which applies to any ordering, particularly because of the step titled *Sequentialization* (see the full version). Looking ahead, the fact that the ordering may be arbitrary is crucial when we prove our lower bound in the presence of general threshold adversaries.

Generality. We present the following lemma which shows that our (n, R, β)-unreactive syntax captures all protocols that can be designed in our model. We provide a sketch and defer the full proof of the lemma to the full version.

Lemma 1. *Let* $n, \beta \in \mathbb{N}$ *and* $\beta < n$. *Given an* R-*round protocol among* n *parties in the* (n, β)-*unreactive world that makes at most* γ *parallel invocations to any of the functionalities in any given step, there exists an* $R \cdot \mathcal{O}(\binom{n}{\beta}\gamma)$-*round protocol among* n *parties that follows our* $(n, R \cdot \mathcal{O}(\binom{n}{\beta}\gamma), \beta)$-*unreactive syntax.*

3.2 Fairness Versus Guaranteed Output Delivery

We recall here some of the results from [12].

Lemma 2. *[12] Consider* n *parties* $P_1, \dots, P_n$ *in a model with a broadcast channel. Then, assuming the existence of one-way functions, for any functionality* $f : \mathcal{X}^n \to \mathcal{Y}^n$, *if there exists a protocol* π *which securely computes* f *with fairness, then there exists a protocol* π' *which securely computes* f *with guaranteed output delivery.*

Lemma 3. *[12] Consider* n *parties* $P_1, \dots, P_n$ *in a model with a broadcast channel. Then, assuming the existence of one-way functions, for any functionality* $f : \mathcal{X}^n \to \mathcal{Y}^n$, *if there exists a protocol* π *which securely computes* f *with fairness, then there exists a protocol* π' *which securely computes* f *with fairness and does not make use of the broadcast channel.*

Preliminaries: $I \subseteq [n]$. The functionality proceeds as follows:

- Sample a uniform bit $b \leftarrow \{0, 1\}$.
- Send b to all parties P_i for $i \in I$.

Fig. 3. The ideal functionality $\mathcal{F}_{\text{coin}}$.

From the above lemmas, it is clear that assuming one-way functions, we can stick to the following conventions:

- While proving lower bounds, we show that there is no n-party t-fair coin tossing protocol (as defined in Sect. 2.3) in an (n, β)-unreactive world for certain values of n, t, β. From Lemma 2, this shows that there is no n-party protocol that realizes the functionality $\mathcal{F}_{\text{coin}}$ (see Fig. 3) with fairness in the presence of t corruptions in a hybrid model where parties have access to unreactive functionalities of cardinality upper bounded by β (that is, an (n, β)-unreactive world without broadcast). In particular, this shows that unreactive functionalities of cardinality β are incomplete for n-party fair MPC in the presence of t corruptions.

– While proving upper bounds, or designing protocols to realize any arbitrary functionality $\mathcal{F}$ in the presence of t corruptions, we will construct protocols that achieve security with fairness against t corruptions in our (n, β)-unreactive world for certain values of n, t, β. From Lemma 3, this shows that there exist protocols that realize $\mathcal{F}$ with fairness in the presence of t corruptions in our (n, β)-unreactive world without broadcast. In particular, this shows that unreactive functionalities of cardinality β are complete for n-party fair MPC in the presence of t corruptions.

3.3 Bypassing [10]'s Lower Bound in Unreactive Worlds

As evidenced by Cleve's lower bound in [10] for fair coin tossing in the presence of a dishonest majority, MPC with fairness is impossible in the presence of a dishonest majority if parties are only equipped with communication channels[12], even when the adversary is only allowed to corrupt $\lceil \frac{n}{2} \rceil$ parties. In this section, we present two simple and elegant MPC protocols with fairness in the presence of a dishonest majority by leveraging unreactive functionalities of cardinality at least 2, which lets us bypass Cleve's lower bound. The existence of these protocols motivates the exploration of lower bounds in unreactive worlds, which is the main focus of this work. Meanwhile, it also shows that Cleve's technique in its vanilla form (and also, many similar techniques [20] based on [10] from past works) is no longer sufficient to tackle the problem of proving lower bounds in the unreactive world. In general, consider n parties out of which t may be malicious ($\frac{n}{2} \leq t < n$) in the (n, β)-unreactive world. Recall that β denotes the cardinality of the unreactive functionalities that are provided.

The Case of $\beta > t$. Unsurprisingly, if parties have access to an unreactive functionality of cardinality $\beta > t$, there is a very straightforward protocol for fair MPC. Let $\mathbb{P} = \{P_1, \ldots, P_n\}$. The MPC protocol proceeds as follows.

1. All parties perform an unfair MPC that computes the result and β-out-of-β shares it to the parties $\{P_1, \ldots, P_\beta\}$.
2. $P_1, \ldots, P_\beta$ perform a β-wise exchange using the available β-wise functionality to reconstruct the result.
3. Each party P_i in $\{P_1, \ldots, P_\beta\}$ broadcasts the result if it obtained it in the previous step.

To see that this protocol is fair, note that an adversary corrupting only t parties cannot learn the output in step 1 since it only has $t < \beta$ shares. To get the result, the adversary needs to let step 2 execute correctly. However, if step 2 executes correctly, all honest parties get the result as well. Some standard authentication techniques need to be used to ensure that the parties submit correct shares, etc. For more details, we refer the reader to [23].

---

[12] More precisely, as long as the channels are *one-directional*, such as *OT channels*, Cleve's lower bound holds.

The Case of $t = \frac{n}{2}$. The case of $t = \frac{n}{2}$ is rather interesting, and not representative of the case of $t \geq \frac{n}{2}$. In fact, 2-wise unreactive functionalities, in particular, 2-wise exchange suffices for fair MPC. Let $\mathbb{P} = \{P_1, \ldots, P_n\}$. The MPC protocol proceeds as follows.

1. All parties perform an unfair MPC that computes the result and $(\frac{n}{2}+1)$-out-of-n shares it to all the parties.
2. For each $i, j \in [n]$ where $i < j$, parties P_i and P_j perform a 2-wise exchange for their shares.
3. For each $k \in [n]$, if a party P_k receives at least $\frac{n}{2}$ shares in the previous step, it broadcast any $(\frac{n}{2}+1)$ shares it has (including its own).
4. For each $k \in [n]$, if a party P_k has at least $\frac{n}{2}+1$ shares, it recovers the result.

To see that this protocol is fair, an adversary corrupting only $\frac{n}{2}$ parties cannot learn the output in step 1 since it only has $\frac{n}{2}$ shares. To learn the output, the adversary needs to at least exchange one share with some honest party in step 2. Note that this honest party will get at least $\frac{n}{2}$ (1 from the adversary, $\frac{n}{2} - 1$ from other honest parties) in step 2 so it already has enough shares to recover the result, and will broadcast the shares to all honest parties in step 3. Some standard authentication techniques need to be used to ensure that the parties submit correct shares, etc. For more details, we refer the reader to [23].

4   Alice and Bob: Same World, Different Proofs

In Sect. 3.3, we showed that for any $\frac{n}{2} \leq t < n$, there exists an n-party MPC protocol with fairness in the (n, β)-unreactive world as long as $\beta > t$. Interestingly, we showed that there exists an n-party MPC protocol with fairness in the presence of $\frac{n}{2}$ corruptions in the $(n, 2)$-unreactive world. We remind the reader that [23] presents an n-party MPC protocol with fairness in the presence of $n-1$ corruptions assuming the existence of 2-wise *reactive* functionalities, namely, in an $(n, 2)$-"*reactive*" *world*. A natural attempt is to construct an n-party MPC protocol with fairness in the presence of $n-1$ corruptions in the $(n, 2)$-unreactive world. Unfortunately, it turns out that for any $\frac{n}{2} < t < n$, there is no n-party MPC protocol with fairness in the (n, t)-unreactive world. This shows that our results are tight *with our matching upper bounds and lower bounds*. We will present these lower bounds by showing that there exists no n-party $(n-1)$-fair coin tossing protocol (see Definition 1) in the $(n, n-1)$-unreactive world in Sect. 5 and later generalize this lower bound to threshold adversaries in Sect. 6 for all $\frac{n}{2} < t < n$. As a warm-up, we show that there is no 2-party 1-fair coin tossing protocol in the $(2, 1)$-unreactive world. This is the most unsurprising case since the $(2, 1)$-unreactive world is identical to the two-party model used by [10].

In the $(2, 1)$-unreactive world, 1-wise functionalities are local computations and the broadcast channel can be viewed as a communication channel between the two parties. Thus, it is identical to the two-party model used by [10]. We emphasize that this is the *only* unreactive world that is not stronger than Cleve's.

Our proof technique in Sect. 5 in the case of two parties can be viewed as a different take on the result of [10]. Crucially, this allows us to generalize the lower bound of the $(2,1)$-unreactive world to other unreactive worlds. We remind the reader that applying [10]'s technique is not sufficient for unreactive worlds in general (and in fact, it only works for the $(2,1)$-unreactive world) since we can easily bypass [10]'s impossibility in some unreactive worlds as shown in Sect. 3.3. Looking ahead, our proof captures "fairness" in a more natural way by introducing a notion we call *predictability*.

A two-party coin tossing protocol has two parties, Alice and Bob, who share a communication channel. A round in the protocol corresponds to each party sending a message to the other. For simplicity, the protocol is assumed to be serialized such that Alice sends the first message and Bob sends the second message. Specifically, the protocol is captured as (1) Alice and Bob generate local randomness r_A and r_B; (2) for the next R rounds, Alice sends message $m_{B,i}$ followed by Bob's message $m_{A,i}$; and (3) Alice outputs $A(r_A, m_{A,1}, \ldots, m_{A,R})$ and Bob outputs $B(r_B, m_{B,1}, \ldots, m_{B,R})$. We assume that the protocol satisfies perfect agreement. That is, $A(r_A, \ldots, m_{A,R}) = B(r_B, \ldots, m_{B,R}) = res$.

Recall that the notion of fairness requires that the adversary cannot learn the output of the protocol without the honest parties learning it too. Naturally, this means that in an *unfair* coin tossing protocol, the adversary should be able to "predict" the output of the coin res at some point while the honest party cannot. Note that res, the honest output of the coin toss, should become "predictable" at the end of the protocol. Consider the following probabilities:

$$\mathsf{Pred}_{A,0} \triangleq \Pr[A(r_A, 0, \ldots) = res]$$

$$\mathsf{Pred}_{B,0} \triangleq \Pr[B(r_B, 0, \ldots) = res]$$

$$\mathsf{Pred}_{A,1} \triangleq \Pr[A(r_A, m_{A,1}, 0, \ldots) = res]$$

$$\mathsf{Pred}_{B,1} \triangleq \Pr[B(r_B, m_{B,1}, 0, \ldots) = res]$$

$$\ldots$$

$$\mathsf{Pred}_{A,R} \triangleq \Pr[A(r_A, m_{A,1}, \ldots, m_{A,R}) = res]$$

$$\mathsf{Pred}_{B,R} \triangleq \Pr[B(r_B, m_{B,1}, \ldots, m_{B,R}) = res]$$

We denote the *predictability* of Alice (resp. Bob) with i messages as $\mathsf{Pred}_{A,i}$ (resp. $\mathsf{Pred}_{B,i}$) where $\mathsf{Pred}_{A,i}$ (resp. $\mathsf{Pred}_{B,i}$) are defined as above. In other words, $\mathsf{Pred}_{A,i}$ can be viewed as Alice's ability to use the partial information she received in the first i rounds to figure out the output. Specifically, Alice uses her partial information and imagines Bob quits at that point. We further name the random variable associated with $\mathsf{Pred}_{A,i}$ (resp. $\mathsf{Pred}_{B,i}$) a *predictor* $\Pi_{A,i}$ (resp. $\Pi_{B,i}$). For example, $\Pi_{A,0} = A(r_A, 0, \ldots)$.

Remark 1. Our predictor is essentially the "back-up" value known in the coin-tossing literature. In particular, it is used in [10] and many subsequent works. Informally, this "back-up" value is the output of the honest party if other parties abort. Naturally, this "back-up" value should "predict" the final result as close as possible to ensure fairness. However, as we will show, the adversary can also use this "back-up" value to "predict" the output to "learn" the output in advance.

From definition of res, $\mathsf{Pred}_{A,R} = \mathsf{Pred}_{B,R} = 1$, capturing that the output of the protocol must be predictable in the end. We now argue that a fair coin tossing protocol must satisfy the following: the predictability of Alice and Bob at the beginning of the protocol should be statistically close to $\frac{1}{2}$. That is, $|\mathsf{Pred}_{A,0} - \frac{1}{2}| \leq \delta_1(\lambda), |\mathsf{Pred}_{B,0} - \frac{1}{2}| \leq \delta_2(\lambda)$ for some negligible functions $\delta_1(\lambda)$ and $\delta_2(\lambda)$.

Consider the following two adversarial strategies for Alice, $\mathcal{A}_b$ where $b \in \{0,1\}$: Alice generates r_A and invokes the predictor $\Pi_{A,0}$; if the value returned by the predictor is b, Alice quits, otherwise plays honestly. If the protocol achieves a fair coin, $\mathcal{A}_b$'s bias on Bob's output must be negligible. That is, we have the following two negligible terms (one each for $b \in \{0,1\}$).

$$\left| \Pr[\Pi_{A,0} = b \wedge \Pi_{B,0} = b] + \Pr[\Pi_{A,0} = 1 - b \wedge res = b] - \frac{1}{2} \right|$$

Therefore, $|\Pr[\Pi_{A,0} = \Pi_{B,0}] - \Pr[\Pi_{A,0} = res]| \leq \delta(\lambda)$ for some negligible function $\delta(\lambda)$. Note that $|\Pr[\Pi_{A,0} = 0] - \frac{1}{2}|$ must be negligible. This can be seen by considering an adversarial strategy for Bob where Bob unconditionally quits at the beginning of the protocol. Similarly, $|\Pr[\Pi_{B,0} = 0] - \frac{1}{2}|$ must also be negligible. Furthermore, since $\Pi_{B,0}$ and $\Pi_{A,0}$ are independent, $|\Pr[\Pi_{A,0} = \Pi_{B,0}] - \frac{1}{2}|$ must be negligible, which implies that $|\frac{1}{2} - \Pr[\Pi_{A,0} = res]|$ is negligible. That is, $|\mathsf{Pred}_{A,0} - \frac{1}{2}| \leq \delta_1(\lambda)$ for some negligible function $\delta_1(\lambda)$. Similarly, $|\mathsf{Pred}_{B,0} - \frac{1}{2}| \leq \delta_2(\lambda)$ for some negligible function $\delta_2(\lambda)$.

We then consider how these predictors are related to each other. Consider the point in the protocol right after the first message $m_{B,1}$ is delivered from Alice to Bob. That is, Bob holds $r_B, m_{B,1}$ while Alice only holds r_A. Crucially, Bob can currently launch an attack to conditionally let Alice output $\Pi_{A,0}$. Similarly, Alice can conditionally let Bob output $\Pi_{B,1}$. Looking ahead, we will show that if $|\mathsf{Pred}_{B,1} - \mathsf{Pred}_{A,0}|$ is non-negligible, there is an adversarial strategy for either Alice or Bob that can bias the other (honest) party's output by this non-negligibly. We now argue the existence of a pair of predictabilities that differ non-negligibly. We say that such a pair induces a non-negligible *gap*. Consider the following triangle inequality:

$$\sum_{i=1}^{R} |\mathsf{Pred}_{B,i} - \mathsf{Pred}_{A,i-1}| + |\mathsf{Pred}_{A,i} - \mathsf{Pred}_{B,i}| \geq |\mathsf{Pred}_{A,R} - \mathsf{Pred}_{A,0}| \quad (1)$$

Note that $|\mathsf{Pred}_{A,R} - \mathsf{Pred}_{A,0}| \geq \frac{1}{2} - \delta(\lambda)$ for some negligible function $\delta(\lambda)$. A straightforward averaging argument indicates that at least one term of the left hand side should be statistically close to $\frac{1}{2R}$. Crucially, every single term on the left hand side reflects some middle point of the entire execution. For example, $|\mathsf{Pred}_{A,i} - \mathsf{Pred}_{B,i}|$ is where both parties finish i rounds.

Without loss of generality, assume that $|\mathsf{Pred}_{B,1} - \mathsf{Pred}_{A,0}| \geq \frac{1}{2R} - \delta(\lambda)$ for some negligible function $\delta(\lambda)$. Consider the following two adversarial strategies for Bob, $\mathcal{A}_{B,b}$ where $b \in \{0,1\}$: (1) Bob gets $m_{B,1}$ from Alice; (2) invokes the predictor $\Pi_{B,1}$; and (3) quits if the result is b, and plays honestly otherwise. The biases induced on Alice's output bias_b^A by $\mathcal{A}_{B,b}$ will be:

$$\text{bias}_b^A = \left| \Pr[\Pi_{B,1} = b \wedge \Pi_{A,0} = b] + \Pr[\Pi_{B,1} = 1 - b \wedge res = b] - \frac{1}{2} \right|$$

Similarly, consider the following two adversarial strategies for Alice, $\mathcal{A}_{A,b}$ where $b \in \{0,1\}$: (1) Alice sends $m_{B,1}$ to Bob; (2) invokes the predictor $A(r_A, 0, \ldots)$; and (3) quits if the result is b, and plays honestly otherwise. The biases induced on Bob's output bias_b^B by $\mathcal{A}_{A,b}$ will be:

$$\text{bias}_b^B = \left| \Pr[\Pi_{A,0} = b \wedge \Pi_{B,1} = b] + \Pr[\Pi_{A,0} = 1 - b \wedge res = b] - \frac{1}{2} \right|$$

Consider the sum of these four biases:

$$\text{bias}_0^A + \text{bias}_1^A + \text{bias}_0^B + \text{bias}_1^B$$

It is:

$$\left| \Pr[\Pi_{B,1} = 0 \wedge \Pi_{A,0} = 0] + \Pr[\Pi_{B,1} = 1 \wedge res = 0] - \frac{1}{2} \right|$$

$$+ \left| \Pr[\Pi_{B,1} = 1 \wedge \Pi_{A,0} = 1] + \Pr[\Pi_{B,1} = 0 \wedge res = 1] - \frac{1}{2} \right|$$

$$+ \left| \Pr[\Pi_{A,0} = 0 \wedge \Pi_{B,1} = 0] + \Pr[\Pi_{A,0} = 1 \wedge res = 0] - \frac{1}{2} \right|$$

$$+ \left| \Pr[\Pi_{A,0} = 1 \wedge \Pi_{B,1} = 1] + \Pr[\Pi_{A,0} = 0 \wedge res = 1] - \frac{1}{2} \right|$$

$$\geq |\Pr[\Pi_{B,1} = res] - \Pr[\Pi_{B,1} = \Pi_{A,0}]| + |\Pr[\Pi_{A,0} = \Pi_{B,1}] - \Pr[\Pi_{A,0} = res]|$$

$$\geq |\Pr[\Pi_{B,1} = res] - \Pr[\Pi_{A,0} = res]|$$

$$= |\text{Pred}_{B,1} - \text{Pred}_{A,0}| \geq \frac{1}{2R} - \delta(\lambda)$$

As a result, at least 1 out of these 4 adversarial strategies can induce a $\Omega(\frac{1}{R})$ bias on the output of the corresponding honest party. We emphasize that the two adversarial strategies we construct for Alice do not use her *latest* predictor. Namely, even though Alice can decide to quit and let Bob output $\Pi_{B,1}$ after receiving $m_{A,1}$, she does not utilize the predictor $\Pi_{A,1}$.

No matter which term on the left-hand side of Eq. (1) induces a non-negligible gap[13], we can mimic the above to construct 4 adversarial strategies where at least 1 of them will induce a non-negligible bias.

We end this section by summarizing how our adversary is constructed and why it works. Our attack in the case of two parties essentially relies on finding

---

[13] Note $|\text{Pred}_{A,R} - \text{Pred}_{B,R}| = 0$, so the gap will *not* be in this term.

a non-negligible gap between the predictabilities of two parties. But we require more. Consider the pair of predictors associated with the predictabilities that differ non-negligibly. Our proof technique relies on the fact that there exists two adversarial strategies, each using one of the predictors and forcing the honest party to output the result of the other predictor. Apart from being intuitive, this is crucial for our technique since it allows us to construct a telescoping sum such as in Eq. (1) *a la* [10]. Doing so reproduces the non-negligible gap which we can then utilize to argue the existence of adversarial strategies that induce non-negligible bias. For example, the pair of predictors $\Pi_{B,2}$ and $\Pi_{A,0}$ is suitable for our technique. This is because an adversarial strategy that uses $\Pi_{B,2}$ cannot force Alice to output the result of $\Pi_{A,0}$ as at this point in the protocol, Alice already has her first message $m_{A,1}$ from Bob. Looking ahead, the ability to find the above suitable gap is the core methodology we use to generalize this proof strategy to the case of n parties in the presence of $n-1$ corruptions in the $(n, n-1)$-unreactive world (see Sect. 5) and threshold corruptions (see Sect. 6).

Finally, we note that our predictors are just subroutines of the honest protocol, and hence our adversarial strategies make use of the same computation power as the honest parties. This is in contrast to the unbounded adversarial strategies in the coin-tossing literature (e.g., [11]).

5   All-But-One Corruptions in Unreactive Worlds

In this section, we show how we can extend our impossibility proof technique from Sect. 4 to the multi-party unreactive worlds in the presence of all-but-one corruptions. We will show that there exists no n-party $(n-1)$-fair coin tossing protocol in the $(n, n-1)$-unreactive world. That is, in the presence of $n-1$ corruptions, $(n-1)$-wise unreactive functionalities are insufficient for fairness. Recall that, without loss of generality, an n-party coin tossing protocol in the $(n, n-1)$-unreactive world can be captured by the $(n, R, n-1)$-unreactive syntax.

An n-party coin tossing protocol following the $(n, R, n-1)$-unreactive syntax is an R-round protocol, where each party will get $2R(n-1)$ messages from functionalities and the broadcast channel. Specifically, in each round, the functionality without P_1 is enabled first, the functionality without P_2 is enabled second, ..., the functionality without P_n is enabled nth and each party (from P_1 to P_n) becomes broadcaster in order. We abstract the description of the protocol as n procedures $\{\Pi_1, \ldots, \Pi_n\}$. Each party i will (1) generate randomness r_i; (2) receive $2R(n-1)$ messages $\{m_{i,1}, \ldots, m_{i,2R(n-1)}\}$ in sequence; and (3) output $\Pi_i(r_i, m_{i,1}, \ldots, m_{i,2R(n-1)})$. Note that some messages are delivered synchronously. For example, after the first functionality connected to $\mathbb{P} \setminus \{P_1\}$ is executed, all parties except P_1 will get their first message simultaneously.

We assume that the protocol achieves perfect agreement. That is, $\Pi_i(r_i, m_{i,1}, \ldots, m_{i,2R(n-1)}) = \Pi_j(r_j, m_{j,1}, \ldots, m_{j,2R(n-1)}) = res$ for any i and j.

5.1 Generalizing Predictors and Predictabilities

Recall that in two-party setting, the predictor with i messages of Alice is defined by the random variable $A(r_a, m_{A,1}, \ldots, m_{A,i}, 0, \ldots)$. That is, it calculates Alice's output when Alice has received her first i messages correctly, and the rest messages from then are 0s caused by Bob having quit at that point. Furthermore, the predictability with i messages is defined by the probability that the output of the corresponding predictor is equal to the honest output res. We can extend predictors and predictabilities as follows.

Definition 4 (Predictor/Predictability, n-party, $(n-1)$-corruptions). *For an n-party coin tossing protocol among parties $\mathbb{P} \triangleq \{P_1, \ldots, P_n\}$, the predictor of party P_i with j messages is the output of an honest party P_i, where P_i is executed with malicious $\mathbb{P} \setminus \{P_i\}$ such that the adversary will follow the protocol honestly to allow P_i to obtain its first j messages correctly and then quits. We denote this predictor by $\Pi_{i,j}$. The predictability of party P_i with j messages is defined as $\mathsf{Pred}_{i,j} \triangleq \Pr[\Pi_{i,j} = res]$ where res is the output of the honest executed protocol (assuming perfect agreement). The probabilities are taken over the randomness of all parties and hybrid functionalities.*

Remark 2. Note that our definition of a predictor and predictability is *independent* of the model. Furthermore, we define predictors for each *individual* party. This choice is guided by the fact that we consider all-but-one corruptions.

Consider the predictors/predictabilities for a coin tossing protocol following the $(n, R, n-1)$-unreactive syntax. For example, $\Pi_{1,1}$ is the output of an honest P_1 executed with malicious $\mathbb{P} \setminus \{P_1\}$ such that the adversary (1) generates correct randomness; (2) participates in two unreactive functionalities correctly where they are connected with $\mathbb{P} \setminus \{P_1\}$ and $\mathbb{P} \setminus \{P_2\}$, which will send the first message to P_1 correctly; and (3) quits by sending zeros to all other functionalities. Note that each party will get $2R(n-1)$ messages in total in an honest execution of this protocol. From the agreement (assuming perfect) requirement of coin tossing protocol, we know $\Pi_{i,2R(n-1)} = res$ for all $i \in [n]$. This implies that the predictability $\mathsf{Pred}_{i,2R(n-1)} = 1$. Similar to the two-party setting, if the n-party coin tossing protocol is $(n-1)$-*fair*, we now argue that the predictability of each party at the beginning of the protocol (i.e., after seeing 0 messages) should be statistically close to $\frac{1}{2}$. For each $i \in [n]$, we call $\Pi_{i,0}$ the initial predictor for P_i and the $\Pi_{i,2R(n-1)}$ the final predictor for P_i.

Lemma 4. *Consider an n-party coin tossing protocol among parties $\mathbb{P} \triangleq \{P_1, \ldots, P_n\}$ and the associated predictors/predictabilities (see Definition 4). If the protocol is $(n-1)$-fair (see Definition 2), then for all $i \in [n]$,*

$$\left| \mathsf{Pred}_{i,0} - \frac{1}{2} \right| \leq \delta^{(i)}(\lambda)$$

for some negligible function $\delta^{(i)}(\lambda)$.

Proof. See the full version.   □

We end this section by noting that if an n-party coin tossing protocol is $(n-1)$-fair, the predictability gap between $\Pi_{1,0}$ and $\Pi_{n,2R(n-1)}$ must be $\Omega(1)$. We next show how this gap implies an attackable gap as in the two-party setting.

5.2   Attackable Non-negligible Gaps

Recall how we constructed adversaries in the two-party setting. Specifically, we construct 4 predict-and-quit adversaries. These 4 adversaries rely on two underlying predictors – one predictor $\Pi_{A,i}$ of Alice and another predictor $\Pi_{B,j}$ of Bob. Crucially, they need to satisfy the following two requirements:

1. These two predictors are interchangeably attackable, and form an attackable pair. That is, when a malicious Alice holds enough information to calculate $\Pi_{A,i}$, she should still be able to let Bob output $\Pi_{B,j}$. A similar requirement holds for a malicious Bob.
2. The predictability of these two predictors has a gap, namely, $|\Pr[\Pi_{A,i} = res] - \Pr[\Pi_{B,j} = res]| \geq \epsilon(\lambda)$ for some non-negligible function $\epsilon(\lambda)$.

Note that in the two-party setting where Alice and Bob send messages in sequence, when Bob has j messages from Alice, Alice should already have received $j-1$ messages. This means that a predict-and-quit Bob based on the predictor $\Pi_{B,j}$ can only conditionally let Alice output $\Pi_{A,k}$ where $k \geq j-1$. Similarly, when Alice has i messages from Bob, Bob should already have received i messages. That means that a predict-and-quit Alice based on the predictor $\Pi_{A,i}$ can only conditionally let Bob output $\Pi_{B,k}$ where $k \geq i$. Thus, in order to satisfy bullet point 1 above, we will have $j \geq i$ and $i \geq j-1$, that is, $j = i$ or $j = i+1$.

To show that there is an attackable predictor pair satisfying bullet point 2, we observe that the predictability gap between $\mathsf{Pred}_{A,0}$ and $\mathsf{Pred}_{B,R}$ must be $\Omega(1)$ in a two-party R-round *fair* coin tossing protocol. Imagine a graph where each vertex represents a predictor and two vertices share an edge if and only if they can form an attackable pair (I.e., bullet point 1). Crucially, there exists a predictor path of length $\mathcal{O}(R)$ in the graph from $\Pi_{A,0}$ to $\Pi_{B,R}$, namely $\Pi_{A,0} \to \Pi_{B,1} \to \Pi_{A,1} \to \cdots \to \Pi_{B,R}$. Therefore, by the triangle inequality, there exists at least one attackable predictor pair (i.e., an edge in the graph) on the path such that their predictability gap is $\Omega(\frac{1}{R})$.

We now transplant the above idea to the n-party setting in the $(n, n-1)$-unreactive world. In fact, using our new predictor/predictability notion, if an n-party coin tossing protocol (following the $(n, R, n-1)$-unreactive syntax) has two predictors such that (1) their predictabilities have a non-negligible gap; and (2) they can attack each other interchangeably, we can mimic the 4 adversaries we constructed in the two-party setting where at least 1 of them will induce a non-negligible bias. For example, assume there is a non-negligible gap between $\mathsf{Pred}_{1,0}$ and $\mathsf{Pred}_{2,1}$. We can construct two adversaries corrupting $\mathbb{P} \setminus \{P_2\}$ (resp.

$\mathbb{P} \setminus \{P_1\}$) that based on the output of $\Pi_{1,0}$ (resp. $\Pi_{2,1}$) conditionally let P_2 (resp. P_1) output $\Pi_{2,1}$ (resp. $\Pi_{1,0}$). We emphasize the underlying reason why an adversary (corrupting $\mathbb{P} \setminus \{P_1\}$) can let P_1 output $\Pi_{1,0}$ based on $\Pi_{2,1}$: the adversary can get the first message of P_2 without letting P_1 get its first message since the first unreactive functionality is among $\mathbb{P} \setminus \{P_1\}$. A predictor may not always be able to "attack" another predictor. For example, $\Pi_{2,1}$ cannot "attack" $\Pi_{3,0}$. Formally, an attackable predictor pair is defined as follows.

Definition 5 (Attackable Pair). *Consider an n-party coin tossing protocol and associated predictors/predictabilities (see Definition 4). Π_{i_1,j_1} and Π_{i_2,j_2} form an attackable predictor pair if they satisfy the following properties:*

- *$i_1 \neq i_2$.*
- *When an adversary corrupting $\mathbb{P} \setminus \{P_{i_1}\}$ (resp. $\mathbb{P} \setminus \{P_{i_2}\}$) obtains sufficient information to calculate Π_{i_2,j_2} (resp. Π_{i_1,j_1}), it can still let P_{i_1} (resp. P_{i_2}) output Π_{i_1,j_1} (resp. Π_{i_2,j_2}) by quitting.*

Remark 3. In any n-party coin tossing protocol, after the invocation of any hybrid functionality (unreactive or broadcast), the *latest* predictors of any two different parties form an attackable pair.

In the previous section, we show that an n-party fair coin tossing protocol must have an $\Omega(\frac{1}{2})$ gap between $\mathsf{Pred}_{1,0}$ and $\mathsf{Pred}_{n,2R(n-1)}$. Again, imagine a graph where each node represents a predictor and two nodes share an edge if and only if they can form an attackable pair (see Definition 5). We call this graph the *predictor graph*. If there is a (polynomial-length) path connecting $\Pi_{1,0}$ and $\Pi_{n,2R(n-1)}$ in the graph, we can argue the existence of an attackable pair whose predictabilities differ non-negligibly. Recall that the n parties are connected via $(n-1)$-wise unreactive functionalities and a broadcast channel. For all $k \in [R]$, round k proceeds as follows: $\mathcal{F}^{(k)}_{\mathbb{P}\setminus\{P_1\}}, \mathcal{F}^{(k)}_{\mathbb{P}\setminus\{P_2\}}, \ldots, \mathcal{F}^{(k)}_{\mathbb{P}\setminus\{P_n\}}$, P_1 broadcasts, P_2 broadcasts, $\ldots$, P_n broadcasts. We have the following lemma.

Lemma 5. *Consider an n-party coin tossing protocol following the $(n, R, n-1)$-unreactive syntax and associated predictors/predictabilities (see Definition 4).*

- *(**right after all unreactive functionalities/broadcast**) For any $1 \leq p \leq 2R$, $(\Pi_{1,p(n-1)}, \Pi_{n,p(n-1)})$ is an attackable pair.*
- *(**right after each unreactive functionality/broadcast**) For any $i \in [n-1]$, any $0 \leq p < 2R$, $(\Pi_{i+1,p(n-1)+i}, \Pi_{i,p(n-1)+i-1})$ is an attackable pair.*

Proof. See the full version. $\qquad\square$

By Lemma 5, there exists a path from $\Pi_{1,0}$ to $\Pi_{n,2R(n-1)}$ in the predictor graph of length $\mathcal{O}(nR)$: $\Pi_{1,0} \to \Pi_{2,1} \to \Pi_{3,2} \to \cdots \to \Pi_{n,n-1} \to \Pi_{1,n-1} \to \Pi_{2,n} \to \cdots \to \Pi_{n,2R(n-1)}$. As a result, there exists at least one attackable predictor pair (i.e., an edge on the path) such that their predictability gap is $\Omega(\frac{1}{2nR})$. Without loss of generality, assume $|\mathsf{Pred}_{2,1} - \mathsf{Pred}_{1,0}|$ is $\Omega(\frac{1}{nR})$. By mimicking the 4 adversaries we constructed in the two-party setting, there exists at least 1 adversary corrupting $\mathbb{P} \setminus \{P_1\}$ (or $\mathbb{P} \setminus \{P_2\}$) that can bias the output of P_1 (or P_2) by $\Omega(\frac{1}{nR})$.

Theorem 1. *For any n-party coin tossing protocol in the $(n, n-1)$-unreactive world, following the $(n, R, n-1)$-unreactive syntax, there exists a predict-and-quit adversarial strategy corrupting $n-1$ parties that can bias the output of the honest party by $\Omega(\frac{1}{nR})$.*

We conclude this section by giving an intuitive reason why the above attackable predictor pairs should be considered. Note that the protocol execution is a sequence of invocations of hybrid functionalities ($(n-1)$-wise unreactive functionalities and the broadcast channel). Since broadcast can be viewed as a primitive delivering useful output to all parties except the broadcaster, each hybrid functionality delivers messages to $n-1$ parties. Consider these hybrid functionalities one by one. After the kth hybrid functionality is invoked, we consider the predictor pair formed by the *latest* predictors of (1) the party A_k who does not connect to this primitive; and (2) the party B_k who does not connect to the next primitive. By Remark 3, they form an attackable pair. Furthermore, all these attackable pairs will form a chain since B_k is precisely A_{k+1} and, importantly, the next primitive will not deliver any message to B_k/A_{k+1}[14], so the latest predictor of B_k/A_{k+1} stays the same. This chain will begin with some initial predictor[15] and end at some final predictor, and we know that the predictabilities corresponding to any initial predictor and any final predictor have a gap of $\Omega(1)$. This exactly reflects the path we have presented above.

Communication Channels v.s. Unreactive $\mathcal{F}$s v.s. Reactive $\mathcal{F}$s. [10] shows that there is no n-party $\lceil \frac{n}{2} \rceil$-fair coin tossing protocol in a model where parties are connected via communication channels. In Sect. 3.3, we show that by leveraging $(n-1)$-wise unreactive functionalities, Cleve's impossibility result can be easily bypassed. In this section, we show that there is no n-party $(n-1)$-fair coin tossing protocol even using $(n-1)$-wise unreactive functionalities. However, our impossibility can also be bypassed by leveraging reactive functionalities as shown in [23]. This might be counter-intuitive since our proof technique is general. Namely, one can apply our predictor/predictability framework to Cleve's model or even the one with reactive functionalities in [23]. What causes the difference in results when we apply our proof techniques in different models? The difference lies in the attackable predictor pairs. Informally, there will be potentially fewer attackable predictor pairs in the reactive model. In the same vein, there will be potentially more attackable predictor pairs in [10]'s model. See the full version for more discussions.

6   Threshold Corruptions in Unreactive Worlds

In this section, we consider any $t > \frac{n}{2}$ in the (n, t)-unreactive world. As it turns out, t-wise unreactive functionalities are insufficient for n-party t-fair coin

---

[14] B_k/A_{k+1} is either not in the next unreactive functionality or it is the next broadcaster.

[15] Note that after the first unreactive functionality is enabled, the predictor of the party being "kicked-out" is still an initial predictor.

tossing for $t > \frac{n}{2}$. We will show this impossibility by further extending the notion of predictors/predictabilities to threshold adversaries. More importantly, we will show the existence of a non-negligible gap of predictability between an (extended) attackable predictor pair.

Note that all protocols in the (n, t)-unreactive world can be viewed as following the (n, R, t)-unreactive syntax. Recall that the main difference between the $(n, R, n-1)$-unreactive syntax and the (n, R, t)-unreactive syntax lies in the unreactive functionality phase in each round. That is, it will be a sequence of $\binom{n}{t}$ different t-wise unreactive functionalities connecting each subset of t parties. As a result, each party will receive $R(\binom{n-1}{t-1} + (n-1))$ in total. We do not specify the order of these t-wise unreactive functionalities in each round. In general, they can be arranged in any fixed order.

Throughout this section, consider an n-party coin tossing protocol following the (n, R, t)-unreactive syntax, where all the parties output res.

6.1 Generalizing Predictor and Predictability

When considering all-but-one corruptions, there will be a unique honest party. Thus, when an honest party is attacked by the other $n - 1$ parties by quitting, its following execution can be viewed as a local computation. However, when we consider t corruptions, even if t parties quit and start to forward zeros, there might still be information exchanged between honest parties. Therefore, we need to augment our predictors/predictabilities to support a set of honest parties.

Definition 6 (Predictor/Predictability, n-party, t-corruption). *For an n-party coin tossing protocol among parties $\mathbb{P} \triangleq \{P_1, \ldots, P_n\}$ in the presence of $t > \frac{n}{2}$ corruptions, the predictor of party P_i with j messages and an honest set H (where $H \subset \mathbb{P}$, $|H| = n - t$ and $P_i \in S$) is the output of the honest party P_i when H is executed honestly with malicious $\mathbb{P} \setminus H$ such that the adversary will follow the protocol honestly to allow P_i to obtain its first j messages correctly and then immediately quit. We denote this predictor by $\Pi_{i,j,H}$. The predictability of party P_i with j messages and an honest set H is defined as $\mathsf{Pred}_{i,j,H} \triangleq \Pr[\Pi_{i,j,H} = res]$ where res is the output of the honest executed protocol (assuming perfect agreement). The probabilities are taken over the randomness of all parties and hybrid functionalities.*

Definition 4 is a special case of Definition 6 (where $t = n - 1$). In particular, $\Pi_{i,j}$ in Definition 4 is the same as $\Pi_{i,j,\{P_i\}}$ in Definition 6 (where $t = n - 1$).

Consider the predictors/predictabilities (Definition 6) of a protocol following the (n, R, t)-unreactive syntax. Obviously, for any i, any party set S where $P_i \in S$ and $|S| = n - t$, we have $\mathsf{Pred}_{i,R(\binom{n-1}{t-1} + (n-1)),S} = 1$. We now argue that if the protocol is t-fair, the initial predictabilities should be statistically close to $\frac{1}{2}$. For each i and compatible S, we call $\Pi_{i,0,S}$ the initial predictor and $\Pi_{i,R(\binom{n-1}{t-1} + (n-1)),S}$ the final predictor.

Lemma 6. *Consider an n-party coin tossing protocol in the presence of $t > \frac{n}{2}$ corruptions among parties $\mathbb{P} \triangleq \{P_1, \ldots, P_n\}$ following the (n, R, t)-unreactive syntax and associated predictors/predictabilities (see Definition 6). If the protocol is t-fair, then for all $i \in [n]$, for all $H \subseteq \mathbb{P}$ where $|H| = n - t$ and $P_i \in H$,*

$$\left| \mathsf{Pred}_{i,0,H} - \frac{1}{2} \right| \leq \delta^{(i,H)}(\lambda)$$

for some negligible function $\delta^{(i,H)}(\lambda)$.

Proof. See the full version. □

6.2   Attackable Non-negligible Gaps

From the above discussion, if an n-party coin tossing protocol following the (n, R, t)-unreactive syntax is t-fair, we know that any initial predictability is statistically close to $\frac{1}{2}$ and any final predictability is 1. As in the case of $t = n-1$, to construct a valid adversary, it suffices to find several (extended) attackable predictor pairs (see Definition 7), which together forms a "chain" connecting an initial predictor and a final predictor.

Definition 7 (Attackable Pair, Extended). Π_{i_1,j_1,H_1} *and* Π_{i_2,j_2,H_2} *form a attackable pair if they satisfy the following properties:*

- $H_1 \cap H_2 = \varnothing$.
- *When an adversary corrupting $\mathbb{P} \setminus H_1$ (resp. $\mathbb{P} \setminus H_2$) obtains sufficient information to calculate Π_{i_2,j_2,H_2} (resp. Π_{i_1,j_1,H_1}), it can still let P_{i_1} (resp. P_{i_2}) output Π_{i_1,j_1,H_1} (resp. Π_{i_2,j_2,H_2}) by quitting.*

As in the case of $t = n - 1$, a natural way to find these pairs is by considering the point right after each hybrid functionality (i.e., t-wise unreactive functionalities and the broadcast channel) is executed in an honest execution. That is, after each hybrid functionality is executed, we append the predictor pair formed by the *latest* predictors of (1) the parties that do not participate in this hybrid functionality; and (2) the parties that do not participate in the next hybrid functionality. In the specific case of $t = n - 1$, this strategy directly induces a valid chain. However, there are following two major challenges in using this methodology when $t \neq n - 1$.

1. Since each unreactive functionality is connected to t parties, the sets of parties *not* participating in two consecutive unreactive functionalities may overlap. For example, consider two consecutive functionalities *not* connecting $\{A, B\}$ and $\{B, C\}$. Clearly, the predictor of $\{A, B\}$ and the predictor of $\{B, C\}$ cannot form an attackable pair. This is not an issue when $t = n - 1$.
2. The broadcast channel can be viewed as an $(n-1)$-wise functionality, namely, a party sending a message to all other parties. That is, only the broadcaster can be viewed as "not participating" in the broadcast channel. When $t \neq n-1$, the broadcaster itself cannot form a predictor.

We present how we resolve these two challenges separately by rearranging unreactive functionalities in the syntax and considering the broadcast channel invocations in a batched manner. That is, we provide methods to construct a valid chain of attackable pairs if the syntax of the protocol only provided either unreactive functionalities or the broadcast channel. In the end, we explain how to solder these two types of chains together to get a valid chain for the protocol following the (n, R, t)-unreactive syntax.

Resolving Challenge 1: Rearrange Unreactive Functionalities. Consider a protocol which only uses unreactive functionalities and no broadcast channel. That is, we only need to resolve challenge 1. Note that, as we mentioned, the syntax of the protocol can place the $\binom{n}{t}$ unreactive functionalities *in any order*. Thus, a straightforward solution is to consider whether we can place these functionalities in some order such that any two consecutive functionalities leave out disjoint sets of parties. We also need to satisfy this property for the first and the last functionality to allow for $R > 1$ rounds. This introduces a well-formed problem on graphs:

Consider an integer n, the set $N = [n]$ and an integer $\frac{n}{2} < t < n$. n and t induce an undirected graph (V, E) as follows: each vertex represents a subset of N of size $(n - t)$ (so $|V| = \binom{n}{n-t} = \binom{n}{t}$); two vertices share an edge if and only if two underlying sets are disjoint. Does (V, E) contain a Hamilton cycle?

Clearly, the introduced graph when $t = n - 1$ contains a Hamilton cycle, which reflects our attackable chain in Sect. 5.2. Incidentally, the above graph is called a *Kneser graph*, introduced by Lovász in [24]. In graph theory, the Kneser graph $K(n, k)$ has as vertices all k-element subsets of an n-element ground set, and an edge between any two disjoint sets [26]. That is, we are trying to find a Hamilton cycle in $K(n, n-t)$. Recently, Merino et al. [26] proved that all Kneser graphs $K(n, k)$, where $n \geq 3$ and $0 < 2k < n$, admit a Hamilton cycle, except the well-known *Petersen graph* $K(5, 2)$.[16]

Therefore, for any $n \geq 3$ and $t > \frac{n}{2}$, except for $n = 5$ and $t = 3$, the Kneser graph $K(n, n-t)$ has a Hamilton cycle. We can order the t-wise functionalities in the order guided by the Hamilton cycle of the Kneser graph $K(n, n - t)$. In this way, after each functionality is executed, consider the predictor pair formed by the latest predictors of (1) the parties do not connect to this functionality; and (2) the parties do not connect to the next functionality. The predictors are of two disjoint sets, so they form an attackable pair. We emphasize that here we consider a Hamilton cycle rather than a *Hamilton path*. This is because with a cycle, this order can be repeated $R > 1$ times. Namely, *assume there is no broadcast*, the last functionality of some round is followed by the first functionality of the next round. We need to ensure this pair is attackable as well.

So far, we have constructed the attackable chain for any protocol that only uses unreactive functionalities, except for the special case of $n = 5, t = 3$, which we will resolve later.

---

[16] This is a conjecture since the 1970s.

Resolving Challenge 2: Batch Broadcast. Consider a protocol which only uses a broadcast and no unreactive functionality. That is, we only need to resolve challenge 2. Consider a sequence of $n - t$ parties, who take turns to invoke the broadcast. As long as these $n - t$ parties are honest and the first broadcast happens correctly, these $n-t$ parties should all get $n-t-1$ new correct messages. On the one hand, an adversary corrupting the other t parties can choose to only deliver either 0 or $n - t - 1$ new correct messages to each honest party for these broadcasts. On the other hand, an adversary corrupting these $n - t$ parties can utilize the predictor based on all $n - t$ broadcast messages to decide whether to reveal all $n - t$ messages to the honest parties. Conceptually, these $n - t$ parties can be viewed as an entity where all broadcasts are batched into one.

Thus, we can view a sequence of broadcasts from P_1 to P_n as a sequence of $(n-t)$-batched broadcasts. That is, it can be viewed as a sequence of t-wise functionalities, where in each functionality, the t parties connecting to it will receive a batched broadcast from the other $(n-t)$ parties (i.e., the broadcasters). Specifically, the first batched broadcast will connect to $\mathbb{P} \setminus \{P_1, \ldots, P_{n-t}\}$, the second batched broadcast will connect to $\mathbb{P} \setminus \{P_{n-t+1}, \ldots, P_{2(n-t)}\}$ and so on. For the last batched broadcast, if $(n - t) \nmid n$, we add parties $P_1, \ldots, P_{(n-t)-(n \mod (n-t))}$ to the last batch as *dummy* broadcasters. They did not provide new messages in the last batched broadcast. Notably, since $t > \frac{n}{2}$, there will be at least three batched broadcasts.

Let us now consider a single round execution of these batched broadcasts. After each batched broadcast is executed, consider the predictor pair formed by the latest predictors of (1) the broadcasters of this batched broadcast; and (2) the broadcasters of the next batched broadcast. This predictor pair is attackable. We emphasize that the latest predictor of the "next" broadcasters can utilize not only the broadcast messages from this batched broadcast but also those they are going to broadcast in the next batched broadcast. For example, after $\{P_1, \ldots, P_{n-t}\}$ broadcast, $\{P_{n-t+1}, \ldots, P_{2(n-t)}\}$ as an entity, before making batched-broadcast, can already utilize the predictor based on the first $2(n-t)$ messages. This is crucial since this means that the latest predictor of the "next" broadcasters stays unchanged after their own broadcasting, which indicates that the above attackable pairs can form a chain.

However, this chain is not a valid one for arguing a non-negligible gap. This is because (1) it does not begin with an initial predictor; (2) it cannot be used directly if we consider $R > 1$ rounds. Unlike an unreactive functionality that leaves out $\{P_1, \ldots, P_{n-t}\}$ where these parties do not get any new messages after the functionality is executed, a batched broadcast from $\{P_1, \ldots, P_{n-t}\}$ will indeed also make these parties each get $n-t-1$ new correct messages[17]. In other words, after the first batched broadcast, the latest predictor of the broadcasters are not an initial predictor. We fix the above issues by adding a *dummy* batched broadcast from party $\{P_{n-t+1}, \ldots, P_{2(n-t)}\}$ at beginning of each round. Note that this is a dummy batched broadcast so the predictor of any parties would be unchanged after broadcasting. Essentially, $\{P_{n-t+1}, \ldots, P_{2(n-t)}\}$ is disjoint

---

[17] Note this is not a problem if $t = n - 1$.

with the first broadcaster set and the last broadcaster set in a round, and so can be used to solder the chains of two consecutive rounds and, more importantly, solder the first chain to some initial predictor.

Resolving Challenges 1&2. Consider a protocol in our (n, R, t)-unreactive syntax which uses both unreactive functionalities and a broadcast channel. Our above fixes imply that we can construct attackable predictor pair chains for the unreactive functionalities phase and the broadcast phase in each round. The remaining thing is to argue that we can glue all these chains. Recap that for the unreactive functionality fix, we rely on a Hamilton cycle in the Kneser graph $K(n, n - t)$. Since it is a cycle, we can use this cycle beginning from the vertex representing $\{P_{n-t+1}, \ldots, P_{2(n-t)}\}$. By doing so, all chains could be soldered together since (1) the set of parties not connecting to the last unreactive functionality in each round is disjoint with $\{P_{n-t+1}, \ldots, P_{2(n-t)}\}$, which is also the first *dummy* batched broadcaster in each round; and (2) the set of the last batched broadcasters is disjoint with $\{P_{n-t+1}, \ldots, P_{2(n-t)}\}$, which is also the set of parties not connecting to the first unreactive functionality in the next round.

Resolving the Special Case of $n = 5, t = 3$. Even though we do not have Hamilton cycle in $K(5, 2)$, we can add dummy unreactive functionalities into our syntax. Crucially, it suffices to find a path that traverses every vertex in the graph (perhaps more than once) from the vertex $\{P_{n-t+1}, \ldots, P_{2(n-t)}\}$ and goes back. It is well-known that on removing any vertex, the Petersen graph or $K(5, 2)$ is *Hamiltonian*. Thus, we can find such a path in $K(5, 2)$ of length 18. To sum up, we have the following theorem.

Theorem 2. *For any n-party coin tossing protocol in the (n, t)-unreactive world, following the (n, R, t)-unreactive syntax, there exists a predict-and-quit adversarial strategy corrupting $\frac{n}{2} < t < n$ parties that can bias the output of some honest party by $\Omega\left(\frac{1}{\binom{n}{t}R}\right)$.*

Remark 4. It might appear that the $\binom{n}{t}$ term in Theorem 2 limits its applicability to a logarithmic number of parties in λ. However, as we will see in Sect. 7.2, this is not the case, and a careful refinement allows us to conclude that the bias from Theorem 2 can be improved to $\Omega(\frac{1}{F})$, where F is the number of *non-dummy* invocations to unreactive functionalities (see Theorem 3).

7   Refinements: Cosmetic and Crucial

In this section, we show how to extend our lower bounds to coin tossing protocols that achieve just statistical agreement (as opposed to perfect like before). Additionally, we provide a general lower bound for coin tossing protocols in unreactive worlds where the bias induced by our adversary depends only on the *actual* number of hybrid functionalities invoked during the protocol, rather than the potentially much larger $\binom{n}{t}R$.

7.1 Ruling Out Statistical Agreement

For ease of presentation, throughout the paper, we focused on coin tossing protocol with perfect agreement. Our proof technique (i.e., Sects. 4 to 6) can be naturally extended to the statistical agreement setting, where the outputs of any two honest parties will differ with probability at most $\delta(\lambda)$ for some negligible function $\delta(\lambda)$. This can be done by applying a "Substitution Lemma" that allows replacement of random variables that are negligibly close. We explain this in more detail in the full version. Thus, all of our analyses can be extended naturally to rule out coin tossing protocols with statistical agreement as well.

7.2 Relaxing the Need to Follow the Unreactive Syntax

Our theorems (see Theorems 1 to 2) consider coin tossing protocols following the unreactive syntax. This is general since we can always compile a protocol in an unreactive world to one that follows the corresponding unreactive syntax (see Lemma 1). However, this compilation will result in a blow-up in the number of rounds, which impacts the bias induced by our predict-and-quit adversaries. Note that the compilation only inserts *dummy* hybrid functionalities. Crucially, in an execution, the values of our predictabilities stay unchanged after a dummy hybrid functionality is invoked. That is, if there exists only F (non-dummy) invocations to hybrid functionalities in a coin tossing protocol, we should only need to include $\mathcal{O}(F)$ terms on the left-hand side of the triangle inequality (e.g., Eq. (1)) which captures the sum of a chain of attackable pairs. This indicates the existence of an attackable predictor pair where their predictabilities have a gap of $\Omega(\frac{1}{F})$. Thus, we have the theorem as follows.

Theorem 3. *For any n-party coin tossing protocol in the (n,t)-unreactive world, with $\frac{n}{2} < t < n$, that involves at most F invocations of hybrid functionalities (unreactive or the broadcast), there exists a predict-and-quit adversarial strategy corrupting t parties that can bias the output of some honest party by $\Omega\left(\frac{1}{F}\right)$.*

References

1. Alon, B., Omri, E.: Almost-optimally fair multiparty coin-tossing with nearly three-quarters malicious. In: Hirt, M., Smith, A. (eds.) TCC 2016, Part I. LNCS, vol. 9985, pp. 307–335. Springer, Heidelberg (2016). https://doi.org/10.1007/978-3-662-53641-4_13

2. Alon, B., Omri, E., Paskin-Cherniavsky, A.: MPC with friends and foes. In: Micciancio, D., Ristenpart, T. (eds.) CRYPTO 2020, Part II. LNCS, vol. 12171, pp. 677–706. Springer, Cham (2020). https://doi.org/10.1007/978-3-030-56880-1_24

3. Asharov, G.: Towards characterizing complete fairness in secure two-party computation. In: Lindell, Y. (ed.) TCC 2014. LNCS, vol. 8349, pp. 291–316. Springer, Heidelberg (2014). https://doi.org/10.1007/978-3-642-54242-8_13

4. Asharov, G., Beimel, A., Makriyannis, N., Omri, E.: Complete characterization of fairness in secure two-party computation of Boolean functions. In: Dodis, Y., Nielsen, J.B. (eds.) TCC 2015, Part I. LNCS, vol. 9014, pp. 199–228. Springer, Heidelberg (2015). https://doi.org/10.1007/978-3-662-46494-6_10

5. Awerbuch, B., Blum, M., Chor, B., Goldwasser, S., Micali, S.: How to implement Bracha's o(log n) byzantine agreement algorithm. Unpublished manuscript **1**(2), 10 (1985)

6. Beimel, A., Haitner, I., Makriyannis, N., Omri, E.: Tighter bounds on multiparty coin flipping via augmented weak martingales and differentially private sampling. SIAM J. Comput. **51**(4), 1126–1171 (2022)

7. Beimel, A., Omri, E., Orlov, I.: Protocols for multiparty coin toss with dishonest majority. In: Rabin, T. (ed.) CRYPTO 2010. LNCS, vol. 6223, pp. 538–557. Springer, Heidelberg (2010). https://doi.org/10.1007/978-3-642-14623-7_29

8. Ben-Or, M., Goldwasser, S., Wigderson, A.: Completeness theorems for non-cryptographic fault-tolerant distributed computation (extended abstract). In: 20th Annual ACM Symposium on Theory of Computing, pp. 1–10. ACM Press, Chicago, IL, USA, 2–4 May 1988. https://doi.org/10.1145/62212.62213

9. Chaum, D., Crépeau, C., Damgård, I.: Multiparty unconditionally secure protocols (extended abstract). In: 20th Annual ACM Symposium on Theory of Computing, pp. 11–19. ACM Press, Chicago, IL, USA, 2–4 May 1988. https://doi.org/10.1145/62212.62214

10. Cleve, R.: Limits on the security of coin flips when half the processors are faulty (extended abstract). In: 18th Annual ACM Symposium on Theory of Computing, pp. 364–369. ACM Press, Berkeley, CA, USA , 28–30 May 1986. https://doi.org/10.1145/12130.12168

11. Cleve, R., Impagliazzo, R.: Martingales, collective coin flipping and discrete control processes. Other Words **1**(5) (1993)

12. Cohen, R., Lindell, Y.: Fairness versus guaranteed output delivery in secure multiparty computation. J. Cryptol. **30**(4), 1157–1186 (2016). https://doi.org/10.1007/s00145-016-9245-5

13. Fitzi, M., Garay, J.A., Maurer, U., Ostrovsky, R.: Minimal complete primitives for secure multi-party computation. J. Cryptol. **18**(1), 37–61 (2004). https://doi.org/10.1007/s00145-004-0150-y

14. Fitzi, M., Gisin, N., Maurer, U., von Rotz, O.: Unconditional byzantine agreement and multi-party computation secure against dishonest minorities from scratch. In: Knudsen, L.R. (ed.) EUROCRYPT 2002. LNCS, vol. 2332, pp. 482–501. Springer, Heidelberg (2002). https://doi.org/10.1007/3-540-46035-7_32

15. Goldreich, O., Micali, S., Wigderson, A.: How to play any mental game or A completeness theorem for protocols with honest majority. In: Aho, A. (ed.) 19th Annual ACM Symposium on Theory of Computing, pp. 218–229. ACM Press, New York City, NY, USA, 25–27 May 1987. https://doi.org/10.1145/28395.28420

16. Gordon, S.D., Hazay, C., Katz, J., Lindell, Y.: Complete fairness in secure two-party computation. J. ACM **58**(6), 24:1–24:37 (2011)

17. Gordon, D., Ishai, Y., Moran, T., Ostrovsky, R., Sahai, A.: On complete primitives for fairness. In: Micciancio, D. (ed.) TCC 2010. LNCS, vol. 5978, pp. 91–108. Springer, Heidelberg (2010). https://doi.org/10.1007/978-3-642-11799-2_7

18. Gordon, S.D., Katz, J.: Complete fairness in multi-party computation without an honest majority. In: Reingold, O. (ed.) TCC 2009. LNCS, vol. 5444, pp. 19–35. Springer, Heidelberg (2009). https://doi.org/10.1007/978-3-642-00457-5_2

19. Haitner, I., Tsfadia, E.: An almost-optimally fair three-party coin-flipping protocol. In: Shmoys, D.B. (ed.) 46th Annual ACM Symposium on Theory of Computing, pp. 408–416. ACM Press, New York, NY, USA, 31 May–3 June 2014. https://doi.org/10.1145/2591796.2591842

20. Halevi, S., Ishai, Y., Kushilevitz, E., Makriyannis, N., Rabin, T.: On fully secure MPC with solitary output. In: Hofheinz, D., Rosen, A. (eds.) TCC 2019, Part I. LNCS, vol. 11891, pp. 312–340. Springer, Cham (2019). https://doi.org/10.1007/978-3-030-36030-6_13

21. Hirt, M., Zikas, V.: Adaptively secure broadcast. In: Gilbert, H. (ed.) EUROCRYPT 2010. LNCS, vol. 6110, pp. 466–485. Springer, Heidelberg (2010). https://doi.org/10.1007/978-3-642-13190-5_24

22. Kilian, J.: Founding cryptography on oblivious transfer. In: 20th Annual ACM Symposium on Theory of Computing, pp. 20–31. ACM Press, Chicago, IL, USA, 2–4 May 1988). https://doi.org/10.1145/62212.62215

23. Kumaresan, R., Raghuraman, S., Sealfon, A.: Synchronizable exchange. Cryptology ePrint Archive, Report 2020/976 (2020). https://eprint.iacr.org/2020/976

24. Lovász, L.: Kneser's conjecture, chromatic number, and homotopy. J. Comb. Theory Ser. A **25**(3), 319–324 (1978)

25. Maji, H.K., Wang, M.: Black-box use of one-way functions is useless for optimal fair coin-tossing. In: Micciancio, D., Ristenpart, T. (eds.) CRYPTO 2020, Part II. LNCS, vol. 12171, pp. 593–617. Springer, Cham (2020). https://doi.org/10.1007/978-3-030-56880-1_21

26. Merino, A., Mütze, T., et al.: Kneser graphs are hamiltonian. arXiv preprint arXiv:2212.03918 (2022)

27. Moran, T., Naor, M., Segev, G.: An optimally fair coin toss. In: Reingold, O. (ed.) TCC 2009. LNCS, vol. 5444, pp. 1–18. Springer, Heidelberg (2009). https://doi.org/10.1007/978-3-642-00457-5_1

28. Rabin, T., Ben-Or, M.: Verifiable secret sharing and multiparty protocols with honest majority (extended abstract). In: 21st Annual ACM Symposium on Theory of Computing, pp. 73–85. ACM Press, Seattle, WA, USA, 15–17 May 1989. https://doi.org/10.1145/73007.73014

29. Raghuraman, S., Yang, Y.: Just how fair is an unreactive world? Cryptology ePrint Archive, Report 2022/1655 (2022). https://eprint.iacr.org/2022/1655

30. Yao, A.C.C.: How to generate and exchange secrets (extended abstract). In: 27th Annual Symposium on Foundations of Computer Science, pp. 162–167. IEEE Computer Society Press, Toronto, Ontario, Canada, 27–29 October 1986. https://doi.org/10.1109/SFCS.1986.25

Author Index

J. Guo and R. Steinfeld (Eds.): ASIACRYPT 2023, LNCS 14443, p. 451, 2023.
https://doi.org/10.1007/978-981-99-8736-8

Printed in the United States
by Baker & Taylor Publisher Services